Sinister Forces

A Grimoire of American Political Witchcraft

Book Three:

The Manson Secret

Peter Levenda

TrineDay
Walterville, Oregon

TrineDay
PO Box 577
Walterville, OR 97489

www.TrineDay.com
support@TrineDay.com

Library of Congress Control Number: 2011929359

Levenda, Peter
Sinister Forces—A Grimoire of American Political Witchcraft: The Manson Secret / Peter Levenda ; with forward by Paul Krassner — 1st ed.
p. cm.
ISBN 13—978-0-9841858-3-2
1. Political Corruption—United States. 2. Central Intelligence Agency (CIA)—MK-ULTRA—Operation BLUEBIRD. 3. Behavior Modicfication—United States. 4. Occultism—United States—History. 5. Crime—Serial Killers—Charles Manson—Son of Sam. 6. Secret Societies—United States.
1. Title
364.1'3230973—

First Edition
10 9 8 7 6 5 4 3 2 1

Printed in the USA

Distribution to the Trade by:
Independent Publishers Group (IPG)
814 North Franklin Street
Chicago, Illinois 60610
312.337.0747
www.ipgbook.com
frontdesk@ipgbook.com

For Judith McNally
1947-2006

The sinister is always the unintelligible, the impressive, the numinous. Wherever something divine appears, we begin to experience fear.

—Adolf Guggenbuhl-Craig

Book Three: The Manson Secret

Table of Contents

DEVIL'S WITCHE
DEVIL'S HOLE
DEATH VALLEY

FOREWORD

CHARLIE'S DEVILS

BY PAUL KRASSNER

The history of civilization is the history of warfare between secret societies.
—Ishmael Reed

In 1971, I began to write an article, "The Rise of Sirhan Sirhan in the Scientology Hierarchy," for my satirical magazine, *The Realist.* Then, in the course of my research, a strange thing happened. I learned of the *actual* involvement of Charles Manson with Scientology. In fact, there had been an E-Meter at the Spahn Ranch where his "family" stayed. Suddenly, I no longer had any reason to use Sirhan Sirhan as my protagonist. Reality will transcend allegory every time. So, although I had announced that I was going to publish that article, I started investigating the Manson case instead. Nevertheless, Scientology sued me for $750,000 for just those nine words—whoops, there goes the whole petty cash account—but I chose to fight them on 1st Amendment grounds, and they eventually dropped the suit.

I corresponded with Manson, visited his female killers in prison and—in a classic example of participatory journalism—took an acid trip with family members Squeaky Fromme and Sandra Good. Ed Sanders' book, *The Family,* mentioned that Los Angeles police had discovered porn flicks in a loft at the crime scene, the home actress Sharon Tate shared with her director husband, Roman Polanski (in London at the time of the murders). And yet, the prosecutor in Manson's trial, Vincent Bugliosi, denied in his book, *Helter Skelter,* that any porn flicks had been found. It was possible that the police had in fact uncovered them but lied to Bugliosi.

I learned why when I consulted San Francisco private investigator Hal Lipset, whose career had been the basis for *The Conversation,* starring Gene Hackman. Lipset informed me that not only did Los Angeles police seize porn movies and videotapes, but also that individual officers were *selling* them. He had talked with one police source who told him exactly which porn flicks were available—a total of seven hours' worth for a quarter-million dollars. Lipset began reciting a litany of those porn videos. The most notorious was Greg Bautzer, an attorney for financier Howard Hughes, together with Jane Wyman, the former wife of then-Governor Ronald Reagan. There was Sharon Tate with Dean Martin. There was Sharon with Steve McQueen. There was Sharon with two black bisexual men.

"The cops weren't too happy about *that* one," Lipset recalled.

There was reportedly a video of Cass Elliot from The Mamas and The Papas in an orgy with Yul Brynner, Peter Sellers and Warren Beatty. Coincidentally, Brynner and Sellers, together with John Phillips of The Mamas and The Papas, had offered a $25,000 reward for the capture of the killers. I always felt these executioners had a prior connection with their victims. I finally tracked down a reporter who had hung around with police and seen a porn video of Susan Atkins with one of her victims, Wojciech Frykowski. When I asked Manson about that, he responded: "You are ill advised and misled. [Victim Jay] Sebring done Susan's hair and I think he sucked one or two of her dicks. I'm not sure who she was walking out from her stars and cages, that girl *loves* dick, you know what I mean, hon. Yul Brynner, Peter Sellers..."

Manson was abandoned by his mother and lived in various institutions after he was 8 years old. He learned early how to survive in captivity. When he was 14, he got arrested for stealing bread and was jailed. He was supposed to go to reform school, but instead went to Boys Town in Nebraska. He ran away from Boys Town and got arrested again, beginning his lifelong career as a prison inmate, and meeting organized crime figures who became his role models—and future contacts. He tossed horseshoes with Frank Costello, hung out with Frankie Carbo, and learned how to play the guitar from Alvin "Creepy" Karpas. Eventually, he was introduced to Scientology by fellow prisoners while he was at McNeil Island Penitentiary. He needed less deconditioning than his cellmates, who had spent more time in the outside world. One of his teachers said that, with Scientology, Charlie's ability to psych people out quickly was intensified so that he could zero in on their weaknesses and fears immediately. Thus, one more method was now stored in his manipulation tool chest.

When Manson was released in 1967, he went to the Scientology Center in San Francisco. Family member "Little Paul" Watkins, who accompanied him there, told me, "Charlie said to them, 'I'm Clear'—what do I do now?' But they expected him to sweep the floor. Shit, he had done *that* in prison." In Los Angeles, he went to the Scientology Celebrity Center. Now this was more like it. Here he could mingle with the elite. I managed to obtain a copy of the original log entry: "7/31/68, new name, Charlie Manson, Devt., No address, In for processing = Ethics = Type III." The receptionist—who, by Type III, meant "psychotic"—sent him to the Ethics office, but he never showed up.

At the Spahn Ranch, Manson eclectically combined his version of Scientology auditing with post-hypnotic techniques he had learned in prison, with geographical isolation and subliminal motivation, with sing-along sessions and encounter games, with LSD and mescaline, with transactional analysis and brainwashing rituals, with verbal probing and the sexual longevity that he had practiced upon himself for all those years in the privacy of his cell. Ultimately, in August 1969, he sent members of his well-programmed family off to slay Sharon Tate and her unborn baby, hairstylist and dealer to the stars Jay Sebring, would-be screenwriter Wojciech Frykowski, and his girlfriend, coffee heiress Abigail Folger. Revenge for a drug deal gone sour.

Ed Sanders wrote, "In the days before his death, Sebring had complained to a receptionist at his hair salon that someone had burned him for $2,000 worth of cocaine and he wanted vengeance." On Friday evening, just a few hours before the massacre took place, Joel Rostau—the boyfriend of Sebring's receptionist and an intermediary in a cocaine ring—visited Sebring and Frykowski at the Tate house to deliver mescaline and coke. During the Manson trial, several associates of Sebring were murdered, including Rostau, whose body was found in the trunk of a car in New York.

The next night, Manson accompanied his followers to kill supermarket mogul Leno LaBianca and his wife. Ostensibly, they were selected at random, but a police report showed that LaBianca was a heavy gambler. He owed $30,000 to Frankie Carbo's organization. I asked Manson about a little black book he was supposed to get from LaBianca. He wrote back, "The black book was what the CIA and a mob of market players had, Hollywood Park [race track] and numbers rackets to move in the Governor's office legally."

* * *

Ed Sanders and I were on a panel at the University of Missouri, where he stated, "In the course of my research in Los Angeles, it became evident that Robert Kennedy was killed by a *group* of people including Sirhan Sirhan." In *The Family*, he had written, in reference to the Process Church, to which Manson had ties, "It is possible that the Process had a baleful influence on Sirhan Sirhan, since Sirhan is known, in the spring of '68, to have frequented clubs in Hollywood in occult pursuits. He has talked several times subsequent to Robert Kennedy's death about an occult group from London which he knew about and which he really wanted to go to London to see."

Since the London-based Process Church had been an offshoot of Scientology, this looked like it could be a case of satirical prophecy. I was tempted to return to my original premise involving Sirhan, but it was too late. I had already become obsessed with my Manson research. I recalled that, in the summer of 1968, while the Yippies were planning for a Festival of Life at the Democratic National Convention in Chicago, some zealots from the Process cult visited me in New

York. They were hyper-anxious to meet Timothy Leary and kept pestering me for his phone number. The Process, founded by Scientology dropouts, first came to the U.S. from London in 1967. Members were called "mind benders" and proclaimed their "dedication to the elimination of the grey forces."

In January 1968, they became the Process Church of the Final Judgment, a New Orleans-based religious corporation. They claimed to be in direct contact with both Jesus and Lucifer, and had wanted to be called the Church of the Process of Unification of Christ and Satan, but local officials presumably objected to their taking the name of Satan in vain. The Process struck me as a group of occult provocateurs, using radical Christianity as a front. They were adamantly interested in Yippie politics. They boasted to me of various rallies which their *vibrations alone* had transformed into riots. They implied that there was some kind of connection between the assassination of Bobby Kennedy and their own mere presence on the scene.

Bernard Fensterwald, head of the Committee to Investigate Assassinations, told me that Sirhan Sirhan had some involvement with the Process. Peter Chang, the district attorney of Santa Cruz, showed me a letter from a Los Angeles police official to the chief of police in San Jose, warning him that the Process had infiltrated biker gangs and hippie communes. And Ed Sanders wrote in *Win* (Workshop in Nonviolence) magazine, "[W]ord came out of Los Angeles of a current FBI investigation of the RFK murder, the investigation growing, as the source put it, out of 'the Manson case.' Word came from another source, this one in the halls of Government itself, that several police and investigatory jurisdictions have information regarding other murders that may have been connected to the Robert Kennedy shooting: murders that occurred after RFK's. A disturbing fact in this regard is that one agency in the Federal Bureaucracy (not the FBI) has stopped a multi-county investigation by its own officers that would have probed into such matters as the social and religious activities of Sirhan Sirhan in early '68, and into the allegations regarding RFK-connected murders."

In 1972, Paulette Cooper, author of *The Scandal of Scientology*, put me in touch with Lee Cole, a former Scientologist who was now working with the Process Church. His role was to provide information on Scientology to the Process. I contacted him and flew to Chicago. We made an appointment to visit the Process headquarters. The Process men were dressed all in black, with large silver crosses hanging from their necks. They called each other "Brother" and they had German shepherds that seemed to be menacing. The Brothers tried to convince me that Scientology, not the Process, was responsible for creating Manson. But what else could I have expected?

* * *

Charles Manson's *real* family consisted of con artists, pimps, drug dealers, thieves, muggers, rapists and murderers. He had known only power relationships within an army of control junkies. Charlie was America's Frankenstein monster, a logical product of the prison system—racist, paranoid and violent—even if hippie astrologers thought that his fate had been predetermined because he was a triple Scorpio. A psychiatrist at San Quentin Prison told me of an incident he observed during Manson's trial. A black inmate said to Manson, "Look, I don't wanna know about your theories on race, I don't wanna hear anything about religion, I just wanna know one thing—how'd you get them girls to obey you like that?" The reply: "I got a knack."

Actually, Manson told me, "I only picked up girls who had already been tossed away by society." And he would fill that void. After having lived behind bars most of his life, he ended up in the Haight-Ashbury area in the Summer of Love. Oh, those luscious runaways. And so he began to explore and exploit countercultural values.

I was gathering piece after piece of a mind-boggling jigsaw puzzle, without having any model to pattern it after. The evidence indicated that members of the Manson family had actually but unknowingly served as a hit-squad for a drug ring. Manson had instructed the girls to do whatever family member Tex Watson told them. When Manson was charged, Watson was also charged, but federal authorities held Watson in a Texas prison with no explanation—not even his own lawyers were allowed to see him—while Bugliosi prosecuted the Manson trial in California. In order to find Manson guilty, the jury had to be convinced that Charlie's devils were zombies who followed his orders without question. In order to find *Watson* guilty, the jury had to be convinced that he was *not* a zombie and knew exactly what he was doing.

Conspiracy researcher Mae Brussell put me in contact with Preston Guillory, a former deputy sheriff, who told me, "We had been briefed for a few weeks prior to the actual raiding of Spahn Ranch. We had a sheaf of memos on Manson, that they had automatic weapons at the ranch, that citizens had complained about hearing machine-guns fired at night, that firemen from the local fire station had been accosted by armed members of Manson's band and told to get out of the area, all sorts of complaints like this. We had been advised to put anything relating to Manson on a memo submitted to the station, because they were supposedly gathering information for the raid we were going to make. Deputies at the station of course started asking, 'Why aren't we going to make the raid sooner?' I mean, Manson's a parole violator, machine-guns have been heard, we know there's narcotics and we know there's booze. He's living at the Spahn Ranch with a bunch of minor girls in complete violation of his parole. Deputies at the station quite frankly became very annoyed that no action was being taken about Manson. My contention is this—the reason Manson was left on the street was because our department thought that he was going to attack the Black Panthers. We were getting intelligence briefings that Manson was anti-black and he had supposedly killed a Black Panther, the body of which could not be found, and the department thought that he was going to launch an attack on the Black Panthers...."

If that's true, then it was racism in the Sheriff's Department which turned law enforcers into unintentional collaborators in a mass murder. But what if there was some other, deeper reason? Guillory told me, "Before the Tate killings, [Manson] had been arrested at Malibu twice for statutory rape. Never got [imprisoned for parole violation]. Manson liked to ball young girls, so he just did his thing and he was released, and they didn't put any parole hold on him. But somebody very high up was controlling everything that was going on and was seeing to it that we didn't bust Manson." And, in this third book of the *Sinister Forces* trilogy, Peter Levenda presents the historical context for an underlying scenario which could well provide that missing link. For a quarter-century, he has diligently researched political witchcraft in the United States, culminating in what he calls the "Manson Secret."

Meanwhile, Charlie has become a cultural symbol. In surfer jargon, a "manson" is a crazy, reckless surfer. For comedians, Manson has become a generic joke reference. I asked him how he felt about that. He wrote back: "I don't know what a generic is, Joke. I think I know what that means. That means you talk bad about Reagan or Bush. I've always ran poker games and whores and crime. I'm a crook. You make the reality in court and press. I just ride and play the cards that were pushed on me to play. Mass killer, it's a job, what can I say."

—Paul Krassner is the author of *One Hand Jerking: Reports From an Investigative Satirist*; he publishes *The Disneyland Memorial Orgy* at paulkrassner.com.

PROLOGUE

February – September 2003
Kuala Lumpur

God is great; there is no God but God, and Mohammad is his prophet. The speaker-amplified cry of the muezzin echoes off the tall buildings around the park. It should be an auspicious ending. Auspicious, not suspicious. But with the subject matter and the time of night and the thrumming nervousness of the streets it is too tempting to be anything but suspicious. Even God is a suspect now. God most of all.

I started this when I was not yet twenty-five years old. I am now fifty-two. It is impossible to communicate what this means in terms of a single project, especially a writing project that takes place in solitude with all the wings of life flapping around me, beating at my windows, noisy and oblivious to my daily anxieties and dreads, my occasional attack of euphoria and self-congratulation over a well-written line or a fortuitous discovery. There is a thin line that separates solitude from loneliness, and I cross it every day and sometimes even in my sleep.

During the years I worked on this book, I also worked in the world, like a Sufi, "in the world but not of it," or so it would seem to most people. Yet, I managed to develop lines of business for American and European companies abroad, lived and worked in Asia for many years, was responsible for expense budgets that exceeded ten million dollars and for sales that nudged one hundred million, spread over five continents and thirty countries. This type of multiple personality disorder is common among Americans, and is endemic among New Yorkers: this shadow life running parallel and sometimes perpendicular to the daily life of mortgages and credit card bills, a child's education and doctor's visits. Yet, through it all, I have not succumbed to drink or drugs or institutionalized madness, and for this I am grateful.

I keep a bottle of Absolut in the freezer, however, and I drink some now, the colored lights of the city outside my window twinkling like acid-dream fireflies in the tropical night. I am alone. The files are stacked on the floor, the dining-room table, the chairs all around me. Outside, incongruously, the sing-song warble of the muezzin calls the Muslim faithful to prayer. Inside the mosque, dozens of barefoot, sarong-clad men kneel, facing Mecca and its ancient lump of meteoric rock, and bow, surrendering themselves to God. God will protect them from evil, from demons, from unclean thoughts, from Western decadence, from American imperialism and currency speculators. From *Ibliss* and *Shaitan* and all the Islamic demons. *Ein feste Burg*, Luther would have said. *A mighty fortress is our God.*

But my demons will not leave me alone. Their traces are everywhere around me, but mostly on paper, in the files. And in my head. I can feel them, whistling through cranial corridors, taunting the prisoners I have chained in there and tried to forget, tormenting me with memories. With dreams. With morgue photographs. Autopsy reports. Lists of dead names. A political *Necronomicon.*

I light a candle, the flame flickers. It glints, winking like an evil eye, off the wavy blade of the kriss I keep near my bedside. I also need protection tonight, from what I do not know and cannot name. Only feel.

Unknown to me and to the world at large, Al Qaeda operatives met not far from my apartment and began the plotting for the September 11 attack. It was a critical moment in history, this meeting; "pivotal," some in the intelligence community have said. And it happened in darkness, in the shadows. Two lives running parallel to each other, one in the daylight of the mosque and the loudspeaker prayers, and the other at night in an apartment full of the mutterings of bombers and saboteurs, like muffled oars.

While I dug and dug, mining data and researching through every type of material in an effort to disinter the sinister forces that lie dead but dreaming beneath the American political landscape, events were in progress to change the world forever. Fundamentalist Islamic militants were preparing to "bring the war home," as we used to say in the 1960s, and launch an attack on the very American landscape I was writing about. And they played right into the hands of their enemies. It was all a Republican administration needed in order to launch the twenty-first century equivalent of an Inquisition at home, and a Crusade abroad.

But I did not know this at the time. All I felt was the foreboding, the sense of impending doom, and I attributed this to my research and my unhealthy concentration on evil, on mental disorders, on murder and assassination and magic.

The files. Thirty years of hunting and searching. Mistakes. Missteps. False starts. Foul matter. I was a thin, nervous, sickly youth when I started. Bespectacled and academic. Solitary and anxious. I was not the type to have guns pointed at me, to have my life threatened by soldiers, spies. Not because I was good, or even innocent. But because I was not a soldier, not an intelligence agency cowboy strapped with an Ingram Mach-10 and a "get out of jail free" card. I was a reader. A writer. The passive-aggressive type. I asked questions. Terrorists don't have questions, only answers.

But in the last thirty years I have been stalked, surveilled, photographed, searched, researched, detained and denounced by a variety of agencies and individuals, in a number of countries, and for various reasons. I guess I have a problem with authority. But in my defense I have to say that pure research—of the academic variety—is bloodless. Worse, it is dishonest. Historians are cheats, like crooked accountants cooking the books. They manipulate data and create fiction in the guise of gospel. To get the taste and smell and feel of history, you have to get your hands dirty.

Or wet.

The vodka is ice-cold and flows like syrup, the way it is supposed to. The way it did in Moscow in 1996, when I visited the Metropole Hotel and Dzherzinsky Square and the Lubyanka with a former member of the former KGB. A pilgrimage of sorts, shrines to espionage and assassination legend. Outside, now, the temperature is mild for this time of year, for this tropical place. Standing in my window, backlit by my apartment lights, I can gaze out to my right and my left and see rain forest in the distance. Jungle. But straight ahead, behind the mosque and the Citibank building, stand the tallest buildings in the world.

I'm wasting time. Procrastinating. The files—like the *grimoires*, the workbooks of the medieval sorcerers—sit patiently inside, full of blood and secrets. Fat toads, fed on flies and their maggoty children.

> *Darwin Scott.* Stabbed nineteen times with a kitchen knife. Charles Manson's uncle, murdered a few months before the Tate and LaBianca slayings.
> *Frank Olson.* Falls ten floors to his death outside a New York City hotel room, his CIA handler standing at the window, looking down, making a phone call.
> *Donna Lauria.* Shot to death in New York City. The Son of Sam saga begins.
> *Sharon Tate.* Pregnant. Stabbed to death.
> *Nancy Warren.* Pregnant. Beaten and strangled to death.
> *Marina Habe.* Abducted, raped and murdered on New Year's Eve.
> *Michael Prokes.* Suicide. Immediately before he takes his life, he holds a press conference claiming the CIA was withholding an audio tape made during the Jonestown massacre.

Michael Carr. Automobile crash on the West Side Highway. A Son of Sam cleanup operation?
Drucilla Carr. Suicide.
Howard Green and Carol Marron. Dead in New Jersey. Their bodies found drained of blood.
Dorothy Blackburn. Murdered. Body found in upstate New York. The Arthur Shawcross murders begin.
Joel Dean Pugh. Both wrists and throat slashed. Death ruled a suicide.
Steve Brandt. Gossip columnist. Close friend of Sharon Tate. Afraid for his life after the Manson killings, he flees to New York City. Suicide. Months later, I begin working for his father.
Charlene Caffritz. Had secret Manson videotapes. Suicide by drug overdose.
Joel Rostau. Murdered in New York City.
Ronald Hughes. Manson defense attorney. Murdered.
Laurence Merrick. Manson filmmaker. Murdered.

The names of the victims go on and on.

From Black Dahlias to Red Dragons. From stabbings, to shootings, to subtle poisonings and suspicious "suicides." The blood of these victims stains the black and white pages, and the black and white American soul. I did not come to Malaysia only to wind up as the caretaker of these hideous memories, these dead and staring eyes, these voiceless corpses. But I can hear the clank of the sliding trays in the morgues back in the States and the dull hiss of the minds gone … awry. This is the hand I fear most, the hand behind these outrages, several and satanic, for it is one hand and not many that I see, a single nightmare, an epistemological singularity, evil in its finest—most finely-woven, most sub-atomic—form.

The Muslims have finished praying. They walk to their cars. The women in veils called *tudung*, the men in those narrow, dark, brimless caps called *songkok*, made famous by news photos of Sukarno back in the 1960s, in the Year of Living Dangerously. The Malaysian Prime Minister, beleaguered on all sides by the Asian economic crisis of 1997-99, blamed his country's decline on international Jewish bankers and other, unnamed, "sinister forces." *Sinister forces.* A blast from the past. Our past.

It's all in the files.

Here, photographs of the mass graves at Auschwitz. Here, photographs of Catholic monks and priests, monsignors and bishops, reviewing the Nazi troops marching through small towns in Croatia.

There, crime scene shots in California, New York, Mexico, Texas … there, declassified documents coyly hinting at monstrous deeds committed by government officials; there, the arrogant testimony of colonels, crusaders, and Company shrinks.

I walk over to the windows, but am afraid to look up, worried that the hand will strike from there as easily as from a cluttered government office cubicle or a slowly cruising Lincoln Continental. MacArthur was afraid to look up. Hillenkoetter was afraid to look up. Who am I to second-guess these men? Generals and admirals, men with the stink of blood on their hands from the defense of America in time of war; men who sent boys off to the jungles of Asia to fight the Japanese, or commanded naval convoys where flames burned the water in some kind of alchemical allegory, to the deranged counterpoint of screams. This is the hard math of life and death, the calculus of survival. War makes us all scientists for a time. And these men—these military commanders with ribbons and medals who saw tens of thousands march into battle or sail into holocaust, who ordered planes and bombs and all our technology into the feverish, frenzied air—feared *space*, and the threat of alien, sinister forces from above.

Daylight is worrying the edges of the Asian night. The files are open, tossed, backs broken, pages marked. The connective tissue to all of this is here. Strong. Unbreakable. Strings of connections that weave fatal chains whose links laugh at canned history, at consensus reality. In the bookstores in Kuala Lumpur and on the newsstands, you can buy copies of our own, red-blooded American hero Henry Ford's anti-Semitic tract, *The International Jew*, published by some white supremacist, no-name press in South Africa.

And so it goes.

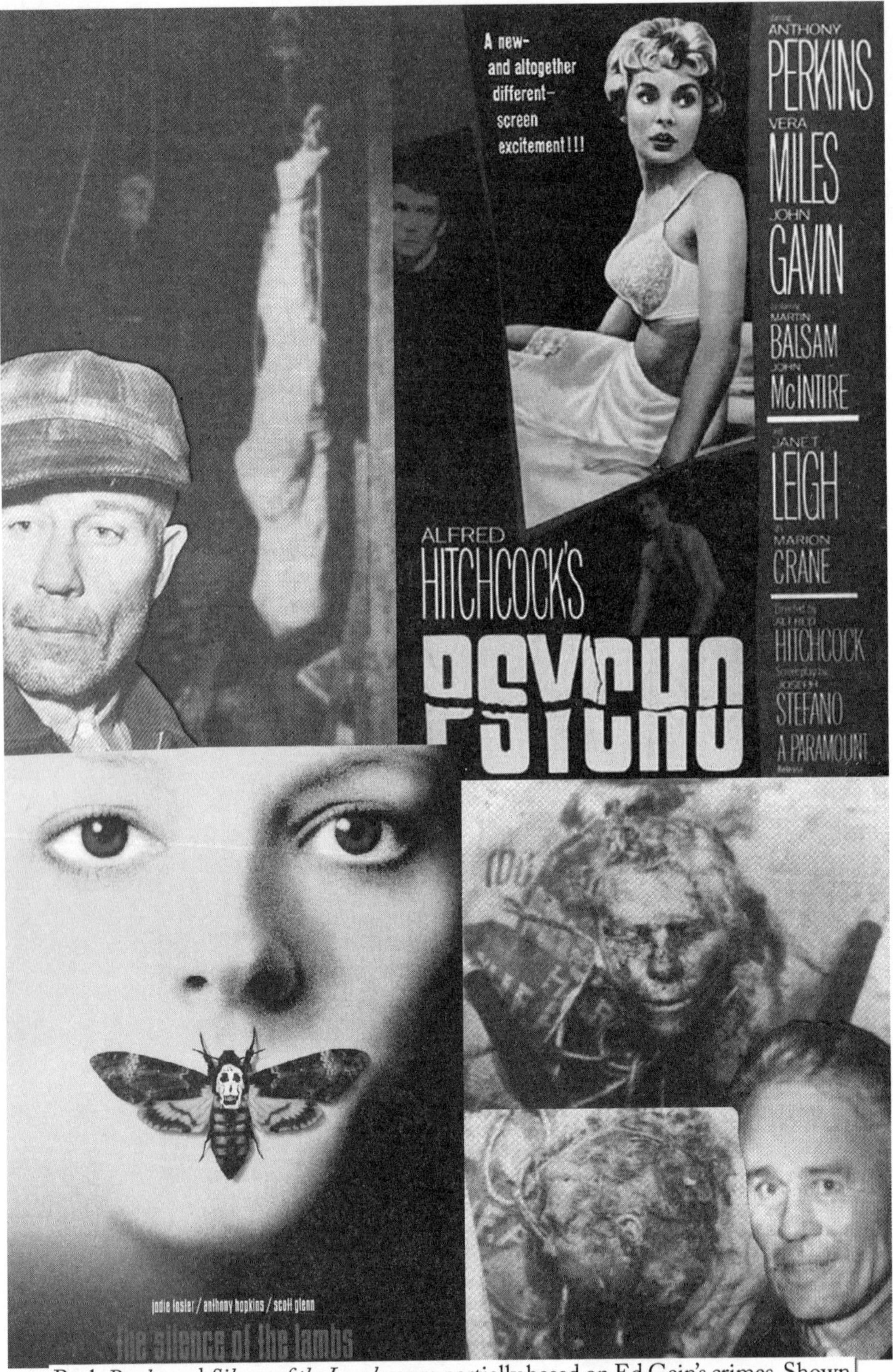

Both *Psycho* and *Silence of the Lambs* were partially based on Ed Gein's crimes. Shown are Ed Gein and headless cadaver, and Gein and his "homemade" shrunken heads.

SECTION FIVE

MAGIC IN THEORY AND PRACTICE

The strange behavior of future shamans has not failed to attract the attention of scholars, and from the middle of the past century several attempts have been made to explain the phenomenon of shamanism as a mental disorder. But the problem was wrongly put. For, on the one hand, it is not true that shamans always are or always have to be neuropathics; on the other hand, those among them who had been ill became shamans precisely because they had succeeded in becoming cured.

—Mircea Eliade[1]

To add confessional uniformity to institutional centralization—to control minds as well as bodies—was an understandable ambition of governments, and the pursuit of spiritual dissidents in the courts could be its practical outcome. Control of political loyalties was, after all, felt to rest on control of denominational ones.

—Stuart Clark[2]

... beneath the open surface of our society lie connections and relationships of long standing, virtually immune to disclosure, and capable of great crimes, including serial murder.... These forces are still with us, and they are not benign.

—Peter Dale Scott[3]

Magick is a faculty of wonderfull vertue, full of most high mysteries, containing the most profound Contemplation of most secret things, together with the nature, power, quality, substance, and vertues thereof, as also the knowledge of whole nature, and it doth instruct us concerning the differing, and agreement of things amongst themselves, whence it produceth its wonderfull effects, by uniting the vertues of things through the application of them one to the other, and to their inferior suitable subjects, joyning and knitting them together thoroughly by the powers, and vertues of the superior Bodies.

—Cornelius Agrippa, *First Book of Occult Philosophy*, Chapter II

Scenes from the 1931 film, *M*, Fritz Lang's first sound presentation, and the first movie ever made about a serial killer. It was based on child-killer and axe-murderer Peter Kuerten, the "Vampire of Duesseldorf," of whom Mr. Lang had read in the newspaper. The Nazis banned the film in 1934.

Chapter Sixteen

Psycho

I was going to show you how a soul with a weak hold on its tenant could be expelled by another; how, indeed, half-a-dozen personalities could take turns to live in one body. That they are real, independent souls is shown by the fact that not only do the contents of the mind differ—which might conceivably be a fake—but their handwritings, their voices, and that in ways which are quite beyond anything we know in the way of conscious simulation, or even possible simulation.

These personalities are constant quantities; they depart and return unchanged. It is then sure that they do not exist merely by manifestation; they need no body for existence.

—Aleister Crowley[4]

Osiris married his sister Isis and succeeded Ra as king of the earth. However, his brother Set hated him. Set killed Osiris, cut him into many pieces, and scattered the fragments over a wide area.

Isis gathered up the fragments, embalmed them, and resurrected Osiris as king of the nether world, king of the land of the dead.… Isis and Osiris had a son, Horus, who defeated Set in battle and became king of the earth. Thus in this myth we see the fragmentation, death, healing, and resurrection of the self in a new form. This is the cycle through which the successfully treated DID (dissociative identity disorder) patient must pass.

—Colin A. Ross[5]

To me, black and white films from the early days of cinema have always seemed somewhat … existential. Something to do with film noir, I suppose. One is forced to concentrate more on the story being told, the characterizations, camera angles, etc., as if searching for a hidden meaning. Since there is no color, the shadings are all done with light and darkness, with strips of shadow and sharp, cutting edges: like some kind of Zoroastrian struggle taking place, frame by frame.

This is especially true, I think, of Fritz Lang's masterpiece, *M.*

This is Lang's first sound film, and it is also the first film ever made about a serial killer. Though released in 1931, its issues are strikingly modern and relevant. The film could have been made yesterday, and it humbles us to realize that people agonized over the same moral and legal issues in Weimar Berlin as they do in twenty-first century New York. Briefly, the story is this:

A series of child abductions and murders is taking place in a city in Germany. Little girls are being seduced by gifts of candy and balloons, their bodies sometimes found, sometimes not, a little while later. Details of the crimes are not given, but we are meant to understand that they are hideous. The killer is sending letters to the police and the newspapers, taunting them. The letters are being analyzed by police graphologists in what is perhaps the first instance on film of "profiling."

We know the identity of the killer from the beginning. It is a man named Beckert who is played to perfection by a young Peter Lorre, a Hungarian actor who at the time was also working on a Brecht piece (and similarities between the Lang film and Brecht's work have been noted before). Lorre would rise to prominence in American films later in his career—notably *Casablanca*, *Passage to Marseilles*, etc.—and his pop eyes and strange, lisping voice would become the mainstay of cartoon villains for decades to come.

Beckert has a nervous habit of whistling a melody from Grieg's *Peer Gynt*, and that is how he is eventually identified, by a group of street criminals who want to stop the intense pressure being put on their illegal businesses by the police who are turning the city—and the underworld—inside out in their search for the murderer. Thus, we have both the police and the criminal organizations looking for the killer, the criminals somewhat more successful in that they do not have to rely on the niceties of search and seizure laws to conduct their sweep of the city. That Beckert is eventually captured is a foregone conclusion; what is fascinating is how the killer describes the uncontrollable compulsion that leads him to murder, the fact that he cannot remember the murders themselves, and the struggle of society over what to do with a man who is an "involuntary" killer, a man who cannot be held responsible for his actions. The discussion of how the murderer—if brought to the police—would probably get off with a "not guilty by reason of insanity" plea and be free to walk the streets and kill more little girls is so contemporary that we are shocked into a realization that this conundrum has been going on, continuously and unresolved, since at least that time.

The term "serial killer" is not used, as that phrase was developed in America fifty years after the release of the film; yet the pattern of murders, amnesia, the killer's taunting letters to the police, etc. are identical to those with which we are now familiar from both real-life instances of serial murder as well as the more fanciful treatments by Hollywood.

Is the serial killer a metaphor for something deeper? The Fritz Lang film stops well short of the type of mythologizing of, say, *The Silence of the Lambs.*

The 1931 film treats the murderer as a human being suffering from a serious sickness—perhaps mental, perhaps spiritual—that renders him unfit for human society and which puts both the police and the criminal organizations into counterpoint against a case of "real" criminality: we are forced to admit that perhaps the common criminal is simply the mirror image of a policeman, whereas the serial killer is beyond all comparison with normal human activity, legal or illegal.

Modern writers like Thomas Harris (who created the unforgettable Hannibal Lecter) have taken this idea one step further: if the serial killer is indeed outside the normal realm of human behavior, then—on an existential level—what does he represent? By comparing the bizarre actions and beliefs of a serial killer to those of cannibals, primitive shamans, etc., we are drawn to the conclusion that these extreme cases of human behavior—eating human flesh, becoming possessed by spiritual forces—point the way to a different view of society, and of reality itself. Thomas Harris' killers are seeking transformation: either spiritual or psychological transformation or actual physical change. They use murder, torture, and pain as means to this end. In this they are no different from organized killing societies such as the SS, for Hitler himself believed he was using the Nazi Party to create a "new man."

This almost visceral urge to evolve into something different, something other, may indeed be the manifestation of a genetic impulse. Transformation is a theme of many ancient spiritual practices, from the Siberian shaman changing himself into an animal to the dead Egyptian Pharoah becoming a god, to the transformative rites of the Catholic Mass, to the intense ecstatic rituals of Haitian voudon in which the devotee is temporarily possessed by a god and behaves accordingly. Ancient religion and primitive religion are obsessed by the idea of personal transformation; it is only in the richer and more developed countries that this concept is forgotten as people desperately try to hold on to the status quo. They suddenly have a lot to lose if they become something … other.

Thus, the mythology of the serial killer is a warning, perhaps, that this urge is not to be ignored because otherwise it will manifest in very dangerous, very unhealthy ways. And should the reader believe that this "mythology" is a fabrication of novelists and Hollywood scriptwriters, let us examine the myths of some of America's most famous serial murderers to see how deeply religious concepts and iconography adorned their chambers of horrors.

DSM-IV

Before we delve directly into the shamanistic and initiatory aspects of some celebrated serial murderers, let us define our terms. We will discuss the religio-occult terms as we come across them, but for now we should focus on what mainstream psychiatry thinks about such things as multiple personality disorder (MPD), dissociative identity disorder (DID), post-traumatic stress disorder (PTSD), and the whole field of acute mental illness in general. In order to do this, we must consult that bible of the psychiatric profession, the *Diagnostic and Statistical Manual: Mental Disorders*, more commonly referred to as *DSM*.

The first edition of the *DSM* was not published until 1951, following a period of confusion and disorganization in the profession that began in the 1920s, when efforts were undertaken to create an international "Standard Nomenclature of Disease." Various attempts at codifying mental illness by adopting a specific vocabulary were attempted—with varying degrees of success—throughout the 1930s. All of this changed with the onset of World War II.

Many readers may be surprised to learn that the celebrated *DSM* is actually the result of an American *military* mission to provide a comprehensive classification system of mental disease. As the war broke out, psychiatrists realized, "There was a need to account accurately for all causes of morbidity, hence the need for a suitable diagnosis for every case seen by the psychiatrist, a situation not faced in civilian life. Only about 10% of the total cases seen fell into any of the categories ordinarily seen in public mental hospitals. Military psychiatrists, induction station psychiatrists, and Veterans Administration psychiatrists, found themselves operating within the limits of a nomenclature specifically not designed for 90% of the cases handled."[6] In other words, *ninety percent* of the mental illness cases encountered by the military fell outside the normal run of what was experienced in a civilian setting. As an example:

> Relatively minor personality disturbances, which became of importance only in the military setting, had to be classified as, "Psychopathic Personality."[7]

(We may be forgiven if we suggest, therefore, that perhaps some of what we have come to know as mental illnesses are in actuality mental states or conditions not conducive to following orders, marching in lockstep, and blowing someone's brains out.)

The Navy then began to develop its own classification system in 1944, and the Army came up with its own version in 1945, a version that eventually became the one used by the Veterans Administration in 1946. However, by 1948 there were "at least three nomenclatures (Standard, Armed Forces, and Veterans Administration)" in general use, none of which agreed completely with the new International Statistical Classification.[8] What happened next seems dull and unexceptional, except perhaps to a Burgess (*A Clockwork Orange*) or maybe a Blatty (*Twinkle, Twinkle Killer Kane*). To quote once again from the very first edition of the *DSM*:

> Following the adoption of new nomenclatures by the Army and Veterans Administration, the Committee on Nomenclature and Statistics of the

> American Psychiatric Association postponed change in its recommended official nomenclature pending some evidence as to the usability of the new systems. In 1948, the Committee undertook to learn from the Army and Veterans Administration how successful the changes had been ...[9]

In other words, the American military was guiding the American Psychiatric Association in the creation of what would become the *Diagnostic and Statistical Manual: Mental Disorders.*

Many Americans know—or are dimly aware—that the excellent interstate highway system in the United States is the result of a Defense Department initiative, designed to enable motorized armor to move swiftly from one area of the country to another in the event of an attack or evacuation. What many Americans do not know is the extent to which the Army and the Navy contributed to other aspects of American life that we take for granted, such as for example the classification of mental disease.

> There were many other details to arrange; the consideration of a proper place for the operation gave rise to much mental labour. It is, generally speaking, desirable to choose the locality of a recent battle; and the greater the number of slain the better. (There should be some very desirable spots in the vicinity of Verdun for black magicians who happen to flourish after the vulgar year 1917).
>
> —Aleister Crowley, *Moonchild*[10]

"Shell shock" was a common concept among the medical profession during World War I. Some of our more famous psychiatrists—such as William Sargant, mentioned in Books I and II in the context of his relationship to Dr. Frank Olson—cut their eye teeth on treating shell shock in World War I veterans. They used everything from drugs to hypnosis to analysis in an effort to ease the suffering of these mentally-wounded soldiers. In fact, Andre Breton—the celebrated *eminence gris* of the Surrealist movement—worked in the same capacity, treating shell shock victims with such occult techniques as automatic writing. (We will examine the Surrealists in more detail in a later chapter.)

Another celebrated therapist of the First War was one W.H.R. Rivers, who exerted considerable influence over the lives and thought of such important individuals of the time as the poet Siegfried Sassoon and the poet, novelist and mythologian Robert Graves (who was also a confidant of Sargant, another therapist who specialized in shell shock and the application of psychotherapy in a military setting). Rivers had spent some time studying the enigmatic Toda tribe of India, a strange ethnic group that seems to trace their origins to the ancient Middle East, including—according to some observers—ancient Sumeria. Rivers treated Sassoon at a military hospital for shell shock (or, as it seemed to some critics, malingering) and began to derive a philosophy of the mind from the experience as well as from his background in ethnology and the study of primitive cultures.

In a lecture given after the War, he had this to say about the relationship between mental illness and combat:

> Perhaps the most striking feature of the war from the medical point of view has been the enormous scale upon which its conditions have produced functional nervous disorders, a scale far surpassing any previous war, although the Russo-Japanese campaign gave indications of the mental and nervous havoc which the conditions of modern warfare are able to produce.
>
> —W. H. R. Rivers to the John Rylands Library, April 9, 1919

This idea that modern warfare contributes to a serious rise in mental disorders is one that would influence William Sargant and others following in the footsteps of the great therapists of the first decades of the twentieth century. Rivers would devote a great deal of his time towards an understanding of the relationship between "Medicine, Magic and Religion" (as a collection of his essays is entitled), looking for a solution to the problem of the mind-body dichotomy. This, of course, is the bedrock of what would become the mind-control programs of the Americans, the Soviets, the Chinese and others, although Rivers—a humanitarian and idealist—would presumably have been horrified to see his insights result in such experimentation.

As World War I became World War II—and "shell shock" became "battle fatigue"—military authorities were under pressure to counter the growing incidence of soldiers unfit for combat due to mental disturbances. This situation became quite severe during the Korean War, when a new wrinkle—"brainwashing"—was added to the mix. In November 1951—the height of the Korean conflict—the very first edition of the *DSM* was finalized.

By the time we were coming out of the Vietnam War, the *DSM* had gone through several editions. "Battle fatigue" had become institutionalized as "post traumatic stress disorder" or PTSD, in *DSM-III.* And suddenly the era of the "crazed Vietnam veteran" was upon us, introducing a new breed of menace in American streets: the lonely, alienated warrior who had seen and experienced too much in the Southeast Asian jungles, had taken too many drugs, had killed too many people, had learned loyalty and sacrifice under fire only to see these values mocked by his Stateside friends and family. He hallucinates, has flashbacks of the jungle, cannot relate to his wife or girlfriend, and winds up wandering the streets at night, stoned, armed, and believing he is back in the jungle. A killing machine. A powder keg ready to explode.

It was an urban myth to a certain extent, of course, pumped up and exploited by the media in novels, movies, and television shows, but it was a short slide from the "crazed Vietnam veteran" to a particular refinement of the archetype in the more robust "serial killer." With the serial killer, we forgot all about the crazed Vietnam vets and began worrying about the quiet, soft-spoken, socially inept young white man next door with the foul body odor, the rotting teeth, the uneducated English, and the basement full of corpses. It was a pop-culture segue from the Age of Manson to the Age of Lucas, Dahmer, Gacey, and Bundy. Manson had a retinue of young women and men to carry out his bizarre plans; the serial killers worked alone, or in pairs. They derived pleasure from committing the acts directly, themselves, and would never have dreamed of "farming out" the work to a "Family." The body count of a single serial killer such as Dahmer or Gacey would be far greater than that of a Manson. And what's more, they were solo acts.

For some reason, the serial killer captured the American imagination. Murder has always been interesting to people, but usually in the slightly-claustrophobic and socially-refined venue of the detective story. The stories of Agatha Christie, Arthur Conan Doyle, and Edgar Allan Poe (the father of the detective story) defined our notion of how to handle the grotesque and the morbid: we have brilliant amateurs who trace minute specs of evidence or apply an unassailable logic to the conditions of the crime to identify and apprehend the perpetrator. They are crimes solved by science and logic tables.

With the serial killer, however, we enter the world of the motiveless crime, a world where the abilities of a Sherlock Holmes or a Miss Marple would shatter like a stained glass window in the rays of a hideous insanity, a lust for blood, a ritualistic slashing of the carving knife. We are desperate to understand the serial killer, finding in him a fascinating and compelling introduction to the dark corners and fetid basements of our own troubled psyches. And, just as Freud sought to understand the human mind by examining its pathologies, we come to understand not only the substance of our own souls by studying the serial killer but—as authors of serial killer fiction such as Thomas Harris have implied—also the possibilities of our transformation. We seek, in the blood and madness and gore of the serial killer's frenzied occupation, the rites of the shaman, the illumination of the magician, the ecstatic trance of the medium, the possession by a god.

The hallmark American film which sensationalized the serial killer was Alfred Hitchcock's masterpiece, *Psycho* (1960). It was based, loosely, on the case of a genuine serial killer, Ed Gein, who murdered women and saved their skin to sew together as garments, creating a kind of "woman suit" that he could wear. The character of Norman Bates—played by Anthony Perkins—is in the grip of what would come to be known as multiple personality disorder (MPD). He is sometimes Norman Bates, and sometimes his abusive (and dead) mother. The idea that Norman grew up in a physically-abusive household which molded his personality—or, to be more precise, dissociated his personality—is hinted at in the film but not emphasized. It is Norman's own insanity that confronts us, not that of his mother.

As the psychiatric profession developed its theories of personality disorders, it abandoned the concept of "multiple personalities" to embrace one of "dissociated personalities," i.e., taking the philosophical stance that there is only one personality allowed per human being but that it can, at times, become dissociated: splinter into several parts, as it were. Whatever name we give it (and some psychiatrists are not happy with the dissociative identity disorder—DID—classification and retain MPD as their preferred nomenclature), the disorder is easily confused with what our ancestors thought of as demonic possession, for in a case of DID the personality undergoes a profound change, sometimes even in front of the therapist. The patient will speak in a different voice, perhaps that of a different sex, different age group, act differently, use a different vocabulary and "present" differently from the other personality or personalities. Each personality may remember what has happened to the other personalities, or more usually may not. This type of amnesia is common in cases of DID, and was of intense interest to the CIA scientists of MK-ULTRA.

Yet, involved with the already heady experience of dealing with a serial killer who may be suffering from DID, we also have—in the fictional case of *Psycho* but also in the actual case of Ed Gein—the concept of transformation.

This idea that one can transform oneself spiritually (or physically) through murder and mutilation was explored by novelist Thomas Harris in his famous *The Silence of the Lambs*, since made into a film (1991) starring Jodie Foster as FBI Special Agent Clarice Starling and Anthony Hopkins as Dr. Hannibal Lecter. In this story, the serial killer is a virtual Ed Gein, capturing women and starving them so that their skin would become loose on their bodies, and then killing them and removing the skin. His goal—after being turned down by several sex-change clinics—was to become a woman, and to do this he would don a woman's actual skin, or a skin suit composed of pieces of various women.

That this smacks of pure lycanthropy, as practiced by shamanistic cults the world over, albeit with animal skins, usually goes unnoticed. Yet, to further drive home his message, Harris has his serial killer insert the larva of a specific type of moth into the mouths of his victims when he dumps their bodies. The moth, of course, is a symbol of transformation. The mythology is carefully worked out and, it must be said, beyond the imagination and creativity of most serial killers one comes across in the news. That does not mean, however, that the genuine serial killer is not (subconsciously at least) seeking transformation. But we must ask ourselves, Is transformation a code word for psychic integration? Or does it mean something more?

THE MANCHURIAN SERIAL KILLER

A favorite topic in the underground press is the concept that some serial killers are the victims of a government mind-control project run amok.

With the Rockefeller Commission investigations in the 1970s and the subsequent revelation that the United States had carried out a number of experiments on violent offenders—dosing them with enormous amounts of LSD, for instance—one comes to the natural conclusion that the experience must have made a deep and serious impact on the already fragile psyches of these dangerous felons. Did they get religion? Did they become mystics, eschewing their former lives of murder and rape, under the benign energy flowing into their souls from the kindly government medical men in their white robes and insincere smiles, hypodermic syringes raised to the heavens? Or, as is more likely, did the intense psychological pressure of the massive dosage of hallucinogens force some other, less savory, response of these men in prison cells and iron shackles? Unfortunately, we shall never know. The files have been destroyed. We don't even know their names. We don't know what streets they wander, or what diseased daydreams occupy them as they gaze upon the rest of us in their madness.

As we saw in Book II, Congressman Leo Ryan believed that the leadership of the Symbionese Liberation Army might have been victims of an MK-ULTRA program during their incarceration at Vacaville prior to their assault on California banks and the kidnapping of Patty Hearst. Congressman Ryan would be murdered in the presence of the local CIA *resident* only a few months after he made his inquiries of the CIA.

A more pressing case before us, however, is that of convicted serial killer Arthur Shawcross. In Shawcross we have all the elements of a paranoid fantasy that even Hollywood would find a hard time digesting. A Vietnam veteran, child molester, rapist, and murderer who is set free only to kill again. A man who claimed a history of violent encounters in Vietnam ... but whose official Army records deny any substance to the stories. A man whose brain shows evidence of surgical intervention, but whose Army medical records were classified and not permitted to be reviewed by his own defense team. A man who claimed he heard voices, haunted by ghosts no one else could see.

A common defense for serial murder—entertained, if not actually implemented at trial—is the insanity plea. We will look at that more closely a little later, but for now it is enough to know that this plea (with its origins in nineteenth century British jurisprudence) is honored more in the breach than in the observance. The insanity plea is rarely used, not quite so often as Hollywood would have us believe, but it is a tantalizing plea nevertheless. As in the Fritz Lang film mentioned above, society seems to realize that there exists in the world the "involuntary" killer, the man (or sometimes the woman) driven to kill by uncontrollable impulses; a man who is not whole, or not wholly human. A man who cannot be held accountable for his crimes.

A traditional tactic of the defense attorney—and defense psychiatrist—in attempting to convince a judge and jury of the insanity of their client is to demonstrate the existence of some kind of organic mental illness, something that can be proven in the laboratory: a chemical imbalance, say, or severe brain damage. Perhaps a tumor, or lesions in the temporal lobe. Many of our most famous serial killers have, indeed, such a medical history. Bobby Joe Long of Kenova, West Virginia had been hit on the head as a child, beaten with an iron pipe. The damage was severe, and could be seen in X-rays of his head. He also had a demonstrable chemical imbalance and all sorts of hormonal problems. Bobby Joe Long had to have sex many times during the day, and when no sexual partner was available he resorted to constant masturbation. Eventually, he became known as the Want-Ad Rapist in southern Florida, a man responsible for the rape and murder of many young women. Incidentally, Long served some time in the US Army before being discharged due to his peculiar personal habits and his violence towards authority.

When the mental disorder is not organic, it is not uncommon for the defense to wonder if their client is the victim of multiple personalities, the Dissociated Identity Disorder of the *DSM-IV*. In the case of a true "multiple," the perpetrator of the crime is only one of the many personalities inhabiting the defendant. The others may have no knowledge at all that a murder has been committed, much less that they are actually responsible. They have total amnesia of the event, and only the personality who actually committed the murder will know anything about it. This, of course, is exactly what the CIA wanted to achieve in the MK-ULTRA experiments.

What many casual observers do not realize is that the "not guilty by reason of insanity" defense was, itself, originally a politically-motivated one. Like the *DSM*, and so much else in American science and psychiatry, it had its origins in politics.

Not Guilty By Reason of Insanity

Some criminals in the United States and in other countries have managed to escape a harsh penalty—death or life imprisonment—due to this strange, even profound, concept. It is understood that moral responsibility and madness do not mix; therefore, the insane can only be hospitalized and not penalized. Readers may be forgiven if they believe that "insanity" is a clinical term, a medical designation. It is not. It is a legal term, and pretends to describe a state of mind in which the accused is unaware of the difference between right and wrong and therefore incapable of making moral choices. There is even a special subset of this condition, known as "temporary insanity," in which the accused was in this state of mind only during the time necessary to commit the crime and was remarkably "sane" later. In this latter case, there is no need for either hospitalization or prison; the accused often walks.

In Malaysia, a particularly ugly episode took place in 1969. It is known as the "May 13th Incident." Without going into detail about Malaysian politics, suffice it to say that the Malay racial hegemony over this multi-ethnic society was briefly challenged by a coalition of opposition parties chiefly composed of ethnic Chinese, who in Malaysia are generally either Christian or Buddhist. Rather than celebrate their victory indoors, out of sight of the restless Malays, the Chinese supporters decided to stage an ad hoc parade through their neighborhoods. The ethnic Malay (and religiously Muslim) politicians began churning up their followers, fanning the flames of fear, paranoia and hatred. What happened next is a matter for the history books, and has been told to me by many persons who lived through it. Malay men—some of them in uniform, troops called out to quell the violence but who, instead, found themselves contributing to it—fell upon the Chinese with knives, both the long, machete-like *parang* and the wavy-bladed *kriss*. Thus began hours and then three days of terror as ethnic Malays attacked ethnic Chinese in the streets and in some cases house to house. More than 6000 Malaysians—90% of them ethnic Chinese—were homeless in Kuala Lumpur by the end of this savagery, as their houses and shops were burned to the ground; the official government statistic shows 178 dead although this figure is challenged, many critics insisting the death toll was much higher.

No one was ever brought to trial for this outrage. The reason? The Malays had "gone *amok*." *Amok* is one of a handful of Malaysian words that is familiar to Western audiences, being rather colorful and exciting. It is classed nowadays as a kind of momentary pathological state of blood lust. Like going "berserk"—a mental state closely related to "amok"—the victim is possessed by an insensible violent spirit that can only be diminished over time. Since the Malays were amok at the time of the massacres, they could not be held accountable for their actions. It was a group version of "not guilty by reason of insanity," and temporary insanity, at that; it was used to excuse an outbreak of politically, racially and religiously-motivated violence that is still remembered with horror today.

The first case in which the verdict "not guilty by reason of insanity" was pronounced was not during a normal criminal trial, but in a notorious political assassination scandal. In 1843 the accused, a Mr. Daniel M'Naghton, had attacked British Prime Minister Sir Robert Peel. M'Naghton—a Scotsman and a wood-turner—believed that the British Prime Minister was oppressing him. Knowing the historic relationship between the people of Scotland and the people of England, we must at least admit this was a theoretical possibility.... Be that as it may, Mr. M'Naghton believed that demonic forces were bent on his destruction and that they were personified by Sir Robert. He fired into a carriage carrying both Sir Robert and his secretary. He mistook the secretary for Sir Robert (there being no television in those days and precious little photographic coverage, so mistaken identity was perhaps more of a problem then than now) and the secretary was wounded. The secretary walked to his home after the attack, so he was not in mortal danger at that time. However, he had very poor medical care and died shortly thereafter from complications. Sir Robert managed to survive the attack. The Queen was outraged, and was looking forward to the death penalty for such an outlandish and willful attack on her ministers, but Mr. M'Naghton was sent to the mental asylum known as Bedlam after having been judged not to be in the possession of all his faculties. The verdict? *Not guilty by reason of insanity.* This has since become known as the M'Naghton Rule, after the famous would-be assassin. And, at the same time, the stereotype of the "crazed, lone assassin" was born.

In the United States, we marginalize political assassins. They are either crazed loners—like Oswald, Hinckley, Chapman—or they are marginal people, such as the Palestinian Sirhan B. Sirhan. The established ruling class of a country cannot accept a sane, reasonable assassin any more than they can accept the points of view of their political or military enemies. Assassins are, by definition, insane or somehow racially or ethnically "other," if not actually inferior. They do not come from the body politic. They are outsiders, and their outsider status is what causes them to commit these crimes. We cannot afford to give these assassins a soap box from which to convince us of the rightness of their actions, because we may be swayed by a person who is so consumed by political conviction that he picks up a gun and rids the country of someone we may be tempted to realize was a tyrant, and by extension therefore to question the present government altogether.

So, we eventually accept a subliminal message every time an assassin is murdered or otherwise silenced before he or she can stand trial: *to attack the king is insanity.*

Oswald was a perfect case. A misfit, a loner, a defector who had spent time in the Evil Empire (the Soviet Union, which had a practice of putting political dissidents in mental institutions, thus implying that *the entire non-Communist world* was psychotic). He returned to America with his Russian wife and shortly thereafter found himself in Dallas, accused of killing the President. Well, anyone who desires to attack and kill the ruler of a kingdom is, by definition, unhappy. A misfit. Someone who feels he has already been marginalized by a state that has no room for him; or by life itself, perhaps, which is so full of contradiction and hypocrisy that the only healthy state of mind may be insanity (*vide* psychiatrists Laing and Szacs, not to mention visionary literature from Gogol to Vonnegut and Tom Robbins). The assassination of a president may, from this point of view, be an act of clarity cloaked in ritual: an attempt to awaken a sleeping population and, at the same time, to exact revenge for an unimaginable list of perceived crimes against humanity.

Those who may be scandalized by the above few lines should realize that there is no truly objective state of sanity; that the psychological states so carefully enumerated and tabulated in *DSM-IV* are so socially-loaded that it becomes obvious that the people who threaten us or our perceptions of life are the ones we declare mentally ill. As in Euclidean geometry, there are certain—in this case, unspoken—axioms which we take to be self-evident, such as "parallel lines do not meet" or "sociopaths feel no guilt." In other words, what we have determined to be mental disorders are reflective of a certain point of view about society itself and not about the human mind or the human spirit, which is (or perhaps should be) much more than merely its social function.

As mentioned, "insanity" is a legal term, not a medical one. It is a complex knot of moral, social, cultural and behavioral assumptions; much more so "temporary insanity." But it can be an excuse for some of the most hideous crimes ever committed. In our society, a man who kills and eats his enemy can be pretty safely considered "insane." Serial killer Jeffrey Dahmer had a collection of body parts in his apartment, and had built an altar there to display them, after the fashion of a Borneo headhunter. These actions revolted us, and with good reason. But in the case of the Kwakiutl Cannibal Societies of North America mentioned in Eliade, for instance, such behavior was *central to the rites of transformation* and accepted by these societies as such.[11] Talking to spirits may provide one's peers with enough cause for certification to a mental hospital, but many primitive (and not so primitive) religious societies could not exist without this essential component. And what of Catholics who believe that they are eating the flesh and blood of a man who died on a cross two thousand years ago … and that they are partaking of his divinity, his godhead by doing so … and that he rose from the dead and ascended bodily into heaven?

To be 'crazy' is a social concept; we use social restrictions and definitions in order to distinguish mental disturbances.… It is not an absolute increase in insanity that makes our asylums swell like monsters, it is the fact that we cannot stand abnormal people any more, so there are apparently very many more crazy people than formerly.

—C.G. Jung[12]

One of our more famous serial killers of the past century—Earl Nelson, who was charged with committing more than 20 murders over a period of only 18 months—was the subject of an intense debate over the insanity plea. He was charged in Canada in 1927, where some of his murders were committed, and subject to the British legal system which gave us the M'Naghton Rule. Insanity was invoked as a possible defence, but no one could agree on just what insanity (or sanity, for that matter) meant. The two prevailing opinions were that "insanity" only meant not knowing right from wrong; or that insanity was of a "cyclic" nature and knowing right from wrong one moment did not mean that one knew right from wrong at another moment (hence, "temporary insanity"). The issue, though is with "right" and "wrong."

Normally, it seems to be the case that these are interpreted in a purely legal way. In other words, insanity is an inability to understand what society considers legal and illegal. I submit that in this rapidly shrinking world where it is possible for me to be in Beijing at 10 A.M. and in New York City at 5 P.M. the same day due to jet travel and time zones, that not knowing what is legal in one country does not necessarily mean one is insane. Of course, many readers will object to this oversimplification; obviously, killing another human being is wrong anywhere, it is illegal everywhere. But that itself is an oversimplification and begs the question: what does it mean to be insane? Killing the enemy on the battlefield is considered legal and sane; killing the same man a year later on a city street is illegal, and if the person who commits that crime does not realize this, then he is insane. Is it perhaps a problem of society itself, that sanity is a moveable feast to be determined not by science but by politicians? And that somehow the State has managed to arrogate to itself the power to determine the state of our souls?

Clearly what is needed is a new approach to the concepts of sanity and insanity, as well as of blood lust, psychopathology and sociopathology, even transformation, initiation, and spiritual growth. We are accustomed to believing that spiritual growth is possible only by prayer and meditation and good works. Unfortunately, the record of the world's religions will show that spiritual growth may be dependent on such horrors that we may be forgiven for relinquishing advanced states of spirituality, exchanging the possibility for a new lawn mower, video game or the latest Britney Spears CD.

Susan Sontag has given us a brilliant invitation to the world of the insane in her article on the French actor, playwright, author and director Antonin Artaud, "Approaching Artaud." She discusses the provincial nature of the concept of madness and cites the outrage over the practice in the (now former) Soviet Union of locking political dissidents up in insane asylums as "misplaced." Further along she states,

> In every society, the definitions of sanity and madness are arbitrary—are, in the largest sense, political.[13]

And further,

> Artaud … saw the insane as the heroes and martyrs of thought, stranded at the vantage point of extreme social (rather than merely psychological) alienation, *volunteering for madness*—as those who, through a superior conception of honor, prefer to go mad rather than forfeit a certain lucidity … (emphasis added)[14]

Far from being the province of privileged academia, however, the study of madness and politics has a more pedestrian, more utilitarian purpose. Madness, you see, can be harnessed for political ends … if only we know how to induce it, how to maintain it, and how to get rid of it when necessary.

In other words, we need to know how to become shamans.

Artaud saw his own escalating mental disorder as just such a path towards illumination. While Sontag, above, interprets madness as a political term in her discussion of Artaud, Artaud himself writes,

> My confinement was thus a religious matter, an affair of initiation and spells, of black magic and also most importantly of white magic, however unpopular that may be.[15]

Without realizing what they were doing, this is precisely what the CIA attempted to do from 1950 to 1973, and probably much more recently than that. This is also what the military tried to do beginning roughly at the same time and continuing for an unknown period, possibly even to the present day. The goal was to create the perfect spy and the perfect assassin. The CIA claims they did not succeed at either, at least not through their mind-control projects which fit under the umbrella of MK-ULTRA. However, when we examine the claims and counterclaims of those involved in debunking or supporting the "repressed memory syndrome" concept, we will see that someone, somewhere must be lying.

The central concept behind the shamanistic initiation is the controlled derangement (reorganization?) of the human mind in such a way that it follows a predictable and useful pattern. I use the term "shamanistic" in the sense that Mircea Eliade and others have done: not to devalue the process or to attribute it only to "primitive" peoples or practices, but to refer to a natural and vibrant mystico-psychological process to accomplish what Jung might have termed "individuation," but which (because of the paranormal abilities involved) might be closer to the presumed accomplishments of certain yogis. The descriptions of the torments the shamanic initiate had to undergo are close in feeling and content to those of an early Christian ascetic in the desert: everything from a sensation of dying to complete dismemberment, decapitation, disembowelment, and worse. What is interesting is that this process is undergone voluntarily and willfully, and this fact perhaps more than any other points out how relatively easy it must be for any of us to go "insane." As Eliade writes,

> The strange behavior of future shamans has not failed to attract the attention of scholars, and from the middle of the past century several attempts have been made to explain the phenomenon of shamanism as a mental disorder. But the problem was wrongly put. For, on the one hand, it is not true that shamans always are or always have to be neuropathics; on the other hand, those among them who had been ill *became shamans precisely because they had succeeded in becoming cured....* But if shamanism cannot simply be identified with a psychopathological phenomenon, it is nevertheless true that the shamanic vocation often implies a crisis so deep that it sometimes

> borders on madness.... But I should like even now to stress the fact that the psychopathology of the shamanic vocation is not profane; it does not belong to ordinary symptomatology. (emphasis in original)[16]

One is reminded of the case of August Strindberg, the Swedish playwright who descended into madness for a period of years (fueled by occult and alchemical researches, by the way; he claimed to have made gold from base metals and there was talk of proposing him for a Nobel Prize in science) and then came out on the other side, "sane" and productive. Others were not so fortunate: Nietzsche, Artaud, Van Gogh are easy examples. Eliade wrote the above passage in 1958, when MK-ULTRA was in its heyday. It is tempting to wonder if the G-scale experimenters were familiar with his work, and if they understood what they were doing to the psyches of the subjects—both willing and unwilling—at their disposal. The evidence we have suggests not. Both in the LSD testing that was conducted on violent offenders—with huge doses administered over days and weeks—to the notorious "psychic driving" systems developed by Dr. Ewen Cameron in Montreal, it is obvious that there was no thought at all to what the procedures were doing to the mental, emotional or (dare we say it?) spiritual states of the unwitting test subjects. In fact, the CIA (and the military) were opening a Pandora's Box of demonic forces: the black box of consciousness. It is the story of a modern day Dr. Frankenstein, or a laboratory full of Drs. Frankenstein, and the monsters they made: monsters that wander the streets of our cities today. The complexity of the human experience is such that we can only wonder what trigger mechanisms exist in the environment—on television, in newspapers and magazines, and even the Internet—that suggest modes of behavior to these victims that are dangerous to themselves and to us. The records of these experiments were destroyed. The names and identification of the test subjects have been erased. Those few who have come forward with bizarre memories of mind-control scenarios are laughed off the stage; they are so obviously deranged that no one can take them seriously. Or they are in prison for committing various crimes—some of them violent—so their testimony is ignored as tainted. Isn't it ironic? Don't you think?

POSSESSION, DEMONIACAL AND ... OTHER

The question as to what extent the investigator, the exorcist, the therapist or even the community generally contribute towards the creation of multiple personalities is by no means an easy one even to formulate satisfactorily ...

—T. K. Oesterreich, *Possession, Demoniacal and Other*[17]

Madness is rare in individuals—but in groups, parties, nations, and ages it is the rule.

—Friedrich Nietzsche[18]

A reading of *DSM-IV* is an education, though not necessarily in the way intended by the authors of this grimoire of mental illness. When we look at some of the more infamous disorders—such as sociopathy, psychopathy, dissociative identity disorder (the old "multiple personality disorder")—we see lists of symptoms that could easily apply to our most cherished Hollywood film characters ... or the protagonists of some of our most popular novels. Certainly one could make a case for some of our revered political leaders being absolutely off their rockers, according to the list of symptoms given in the *DSM*. Nixon comes to mind when we discuss the Paranoid type, for instance.

The psychotic have always made good copy, and great movies. Hannibal Lecter, for example, as the cannibalistic psychiatrist and serial murderer; the psychotic arch-enemies in the James Bond films; Anthony Perkins as *Psycho*, itself a film based on the real-life serial killer Ed Gein. *Dracula* has been identified by many authors as a thinly-veiled sexual psychopath. And, of course, the mad scientists of *Frankenstein, Dr. Jekyl and Mr. Hyde*, and a host of others spanning the history of cinema, and of Romantic-era literature generally, attempting to penetrate the mysteries of nature by taking the most awful risks and jeopardizing the very nature they are trying to understand. They go insane, eventually, either because of their blasphemous studies (most of which are being undertaken quite blandly today in the world's most modern laboratories) or because of the guilt that overcomes them when they realize what they have done.

But the factor that most interests us in this case when speaking of mental illness is the use made of mental disorders by shamans and the proverbial "witch doctors," who see this type of (sometimes voluntary) madness as a prerequisite to spiritual understanding and occult power. And in order to understand that, in context, we have to look at how thinking about mental illness in the ages before psychiatry was often confounded with thinking about demonic possession.

Since we have access to the unconscious only through pathological material, our efforts arouse the resistance of the conscious, awake individual. Yet all this is inconsequential compared with the one great fact which [Freud] did not mention: that it is of the essence of his simple and ingenious approach to make something unconscious comprehensible by grasping it in illness and kindred states. Only through pathological material could sure knowledge be won ...

—Lou-Andreas Salome, *Freud Journal*, Oct 26, 1912

According to Oesterreich, in his landmark and definitive study *Possession, Demoniacal and Other*, the phenomenon of possession is a central element to religious faith, because it seems to offer concrete proof of an afterlife, and of the existence of spiritual forces. Whether the possession is by a demon, an animal spirit, or a divine being, the displacement of a human's personality by the personality of an Other is considered by most to be proof positive of the existence of spiritual forces. This type of phenomenon is very hard to discredit, because in so-called "actual" cases of possession, the new personality is so alien to the original that the only explanation that comes to mind is that the old personality has been evicted, so to speak, from the organism and a wholly new—i.e., "other"—personality has taken its place. This other personality must therefore be a spirit that is lacking a physical body, and therefore there must exist spirits in addition to whatever animates our bodies while we are alive.

Demonic possession became a household phrase in the 1970s with the publication of the novel *The Exorcist,* written by William Peter Blatty, a Hollywood screenwriter. As is well-known by now, the novel was based on an actual case of possession that took place in a small town in Maryland while Blatty was a student at Georgetown University. What is not so well-known is that Blatty himself had been an intelligence officer, specializing in psychological warfare, in the years before writing his famous novel. It was Blatty who also wrote the screenplay for a film that came to be known as *The Ninth Configuration* (1980) after his original novel *Twinkle, Twinkle Killer Kane,* a book and film that come as close to describing the arcane world of military psychiatry as any (imagine *Catch-22* meets *The Manchurian Candidate*). It was Blatty who took us through the strange and horrifying world of possession and gave it a scientific-sounding name—briefly—before taking it away again: *somnambulaform possession.* Not exactly a genuine scientific term, it can be found in Oesterreich's work, which was a source for Blatty when it came to organizing the material around a scientific viewpoint, but it will not be found in *DSM-III* or *-IV.* Unfortunately, in the novel, the scientists cannot help the possessed girl later played by Linda Blair, and priests—exorcists—are called in to perform the rituals that will drive out the demon and save the child.

There are many interesting points of contact between *The Exorcist* and Stoker's *Dracula,* and this is probably not the place to go into them. One could suggest wondering why the demon is invisible in *The Exorcist* even though we have a young girl in mortal danger being rescued by an older expert in occult phenomena who is also a scientist; in *Dracula,* the demon—this time in the form of Count Dracula, the vampire itself—is very much visible. Does Regan's demon represent an element in ourselves—psychological or cultural—that we do not wish to face, or admit?

No matter. What is interesting is that the novel, and then the film, sparked a nearly global interest in demonic possession and kept movie theaters—and churches—filled for some time to come.

Until the devil we knew was replaced by a devil we didn't know.

We have become accustomed by now to accounts of Multiple Personality Disorder (MPD), what is now also known as Dissociative Identity Disorder (DID). The former designation implied the existence of more than one personality in a single human being; the new designation implies a breaking down of the unitary personality into a group of fragmentary personalities. Regardless of the mechanism behind the phenomenon, what we have in this type of condition is the invasion of a human's consciousness by an alien personality. Now, this personality may be a fragment of the original, or it may be a kind of "split" from the original now functioning independently of the original. In any case, it could appear to be demonic to the lay observer and the person could seem to be suffering from an involuntary possession.

The new personality or personalities often has information that the original personality does not; is able to speak in different accents or even in different languages and even to be conscious of much biographical information of which the original was not. In the case of MPD or Dissociative Identity Disorder, this may only be a temporary or fluctuating situation; i.e., the new personality is in control for a short period of time and then retreats into the background, allowing the original personality—or another personality—to regain control. It is typical of these cases that the original personality has no memory of what transpired when the "alter" was in control.

This condition would have been of utmost interest to the mind-control researchers for all that was implied in terms of memory and control. If the scientists could create an alter personality in a given subject, for instance, they could create a robot. This would be true only if the scientists were able to control the alter themselves. This would probably be difficult to do, since the evidence at the moment suggests that the alter is a defense mechanism of the original personality, to protect it against a traumatic episode (child abuse, for instance, being the most common and most documented cause). Also, there is a danger that the alter—possessed of a perfect memory—would not be the ideal mechanism for creating spies and assassins.

Yet, the basic functions of multiple personality disorder would have attracted the scientists and they would have sought ways in which they could create and/or manipulate multiples. Fortunately for them, there is a large literature on voluntary possession. As documented by Oesterreich and in other places, this experience is worldwide, and the author has been privileged to witness this phenomenon firsthand in various countries, notably in Haiti, in the United States, and in parts of Asia.

What is perhaps not so widely known to the general public is the fact that the very concept of multiple personality disorder (and its recent incarnation as dissociative identity disorder) has led to a schism among psychiatric professionals. There are those who deny that the disorder is genuine, and accuse either the psychiatrists of fraud or gullibility, or the patients of malingering. There are those—also professionals in psychology and psychiatry—on the far opposite side of the spectrum who feel that MPD and DID are proof of the existence of an afterlife, of reincarnation, and the like. There is even one psychiatrist who has alleged that a woman suffering from multiple personalities was a witch and had cursed him, causing his ulcer to flare up.

The division between those who "believe" in MPD/DID and those who do not seems to be a function of whether the therapist had ever confronted such a case. Those who have treated this disorder claim that there is no way their patients could pretend to have multiple personalities, that the personality changes are so defined, so extreme, as to be beyond the capabilities of all but the most accomplished, Oscar-winning actor. In addition, there is the problem that some of these "alter" personalities may have powers and abilities—such as in foreign languages, or certain of the sciences—that the other personalities do not have, and which the "core personality" has never studied or learned. There is also the question of amnesia, with some of the personalities remembering events in the person's life and others not—which has led to a controversy over legal responsibility in the case where a person suffering from MPD/DID has committed a crime and only one of the personalities is aware of this.

Those who snicker at the claims of MPD/DID do so based largely on the philosophical platform that each person has only one personality, i.e., that there is only one personality allowed per body. In other words, the argument runs (as it does for most subjects considered even remotely "paranormal") from the conclusion backward to the proof. The assumption is that no two personalities can inhabit the same consciousness, much less fifteen or twenty or more in some documented cases of MPD/DID. And the fact that spiritual possession occurs in so many "primitive" cultures does actually provide an argument *against* the validity of MPD/DID, since the medical professionals point to what they interpret as the natural credulity and superstition of these cultures as being the breeding ground for this particular form of "hysteria." If the condition can be acquired voluntarily, they argue, then it is obviously not a unique psychological disorder but a simple case of delusion, paranoia, or hysteria. But, if the condition can be *acquired*, then the mind-control researchers of MK-ULTRA had something to work with.

Those who submit to the voluntary form of possession are doing so in order to contact the world beyond life; to speak with spirits; to effect material changes in this world by utilizing supernatural "connections." Voluntary possession—such as that made famous by the practitioners of *voudoun* (or "voodoo," as it is usually spelled) seems to our eyes a kind of sorcery. The possession is of a controlled nature: there is a limited hierarchy of spiritual forces that can possess the devotee, and each member of this hierarchy can be recognized by certain visible signs. For instance, someone possessed by Baron Samedi will be seen to smoke cigars, drink rum, walk with a limp, and comport him- (or her-)self in an old-worldly, gentlemanly way. Erzulie, the Goddess of Love, is obvious by her behavior and her love of flowers, etc. It is to be noted that these cases of possession only occur within the rigidly controlled and structured environment of the ritual itself. That being said, another phenomenon does take place—again, witnessed by the author, both in Haiti and in New York City's borough of Queens—in which a bystander, heretofore unexposed to this type of experience, is himself or herself possessed by one of the Haitian gods, or *loa.* This "contagious" aspect of possession is remarked upon by Oesterreich, and perhaps the most famous example in literature is that reported by Aldous Huxley in *The Devils of Loudon,* in which nuns, priests and the exorcists themselves became possessed by an epidemic of demonic forces. Actually, in the case of the voudoun rituals, the dynamics of the rituals themselves are catalysts and can conceivably act upon anyone, even uptight middle-aged white executives from Silicon Valley. The timbre and rhythm of the drums, for instance, and the dark, candle-lit *peristyle* with the waving of flags, the chanting, the sacrifice of animals, etc. all contribute to a kind of psychodrama in which this author believes subtle levels of consciousness are triggered, possibly due to the effect of some of these elements on the autonomic nervous system (the drum beats, for instance, causing the drummers to gain control over the pulse rate of the listeners and slow it down or speed it up as the ritual demands).

It would be the contagious form of possession that would crystallize this phenomenon for the men of MK-ULTRA. A contagious psychological condition is analogous to a contagious biological agent, and both were under examination and trial by the CIA and the military in the years after World War II. For, if we look at the scientific reactions to cases of possession and reincarnation (in which a living person suddenly "remembers" another life and can speak in a foreign tongue, etc.) and take the time to see these cases as the mind-control experimenters would, we notice a glaring admission which is not framed as such. In these cases—especially when the subject speaks in a foreign tongue—we are told by the psychiatrists and the scientists that this is *not* evidence of a spiritual agency; rather, the subjects had been exposed to this material at some point in their childhood and subconsciously recorded it before forgetting all about it. While that explanation may satisfy the need of a rationalist approach to paranormal phenomena, it is a double-edged sword, because it admits that these unconscious powers exist ... with the implication that they could be harnessed in service to the government, or to some faction thereof. None of the phenomena associated with either possession or "reincarnation"-type personality changes are accepted as spiritual or metaphysical evidence; the same phenomena, however, have to be explained and categorized in some way that does not invalidate the modern scientific model. When the scientists—and Oesterreich included—came to the conclusion that this type of phenomenon had a basis in scientific reality they unwittingly opened the door to the men of MK-ULTRA. In both cases of involuntary and voluntary possession, memory is tapped in its deepest layers and everyday consciousness is suspended while this powerful new entity controls the subject, sometimes even wiping the memory of the subjects so that they have no recollection of what they were doing while "under the influence." In cases of voluntary possession, the condition is easily reversible; even in cases of involuntary possession, exorcism sometimes works, rendering the condition equally reversible. And in the case of multiple—or dissociative—personality disorder, it is possible to exert some control over the manifestation of the alters, but only at considerable expense of time and money, which would not be an attractive proposition to the government scientists who, after all, had a Cold War to win.

Therefore, it would be only a matter of time before the mind-control researchers began to scour the records of occultists, magicians, witches, voodoo priests and Siberian shamans to isolate the techniques that were used since time immemorial to supplant a person's normal, comfortable, everyday consciousness and replace it with a powerful, all-knowing (and sometime violent, and always deceptive) alter personality; and to use those alters to uncover the action of deep memory, for MK-ULTRA was, at its core, an assault on the Land of Memory: the creation of new, false memories and the eradication of old, dangerous ones.

The techniques included drugs, various types of hypnosis including autohypnosis (as pioneered by CIA psychiatrist George Estabrooks, among others, who saw occult phenomena as evidence of MPD), and even more extreme measures such as those developed by Dr. Ewen Cameron in Montreal, procedures known as "psychic driving," which involved drastic sensory deprivation sessions in an effort to wipe the consciousness clean and record a new consciousness over the old, much the same way we record over a used cassette tape or floppy disk file. But even more distressing and bordering on the incredible are reports that are starting to surface of a systematic effort to create perfect assassins and espionage agents from the ground up … using children.

One of the salient features of multiple personality disorder is that its major predisposing factor is childhood trauma, particularly physical and sexual abuse. What this told the researchers was that the human child was an eminently malleable subject, and with the right sort of conditioning a child could be turned into virtually anything the researchers could come up with. We, as Americans, cannot give credence to these stories because we do not believe that such activities ever took place within our shores. And we may be right. The bulk of the evidence that is coming to light is that the worst of these excesses took place under CIA aegis and completely within the parameters of the CIA charter: i.e., the CIA is forbidden to conduct its intelligence gathering activities in the United States; that is properly the jurisdiction of the FBI. By running operations of questionable morality in foreign countries, the CIA was able to avoid a great deal of oversight. It was also able to keep the operations "legal" in the sense that they did not take place in the United States, but abroad. Further, by using a number of cover or front organizations it was able to utilize that wonderful elocution, "plausible deniability."

That children are routinely used and abused all over the world outside the United States is beyond any reasonable doubt. Child prostitution has become a plague, especially in Southeast Asia, where the prepubescent prostitutes (male and female) of Thailand, the Philippines and now Cambodia, Burma, Vietnam and other countries are infamous. This prostitution takes place with the tacit approval—and sometimes the insistence and cooperation—of local government agencies, such as the military in Burma. The murder of orphans and "street Arabs" in the city streets of Central and South American countries is a tragedy of epic proportions, even as many of these murders were—and are—carried out by members of the military and police forces of those countries. As if that wasn't enough, children are being increasingly recruited into army organizations in Africa and Asia. It has become a staple of television news to see children under the age of twelve holding Kalashnikovs and taking fire from the treeline. This has become such a global problem that the United Nations has considered a treaty that would forbid the recruitment of any child under the age of eighteen. (Oddly enough, one of the main opponents of such an agreement has been the United States, which wants the option of bringing seventeen-year-olds into the Army.) The Chinese organized crime clans—known as the Triads or sometimes the Tongs—routinely use children as assassins, as they cannot be tried as adults in many American states, even for murder. That horrendous and appalling medical experimentation was carried out on children in Nazi Germany and the Nazi-occupied territories within the living memory of many adults is also without question. Yet, somehow, we tend to disbelieve that all of this could be taking place today and in our own country or under the supervision of our government agencies, (even though we imported many Nazi medical scientists as part of Operation Paperclip and other operations after World War II). This type of blindness could only exist in a culture where we have begun to believe our own propaganda, since it is so much more attractive than the awful, the heartbreaking, truth.

As stories surface concerning something called Operation Monarch, and as these stories are blasted by critics because of the outlandish claims being made—high government officials sexually abusing the young children of military families in controlled settings; young children being programmed as assassins; etc.; etc.—there appears substantiating evidence of an even more troublesome (because perfectly believable) nature. Although there are many documented cases of children being trained as fanatic soldiers and killers—especially in Asia, in some celebrated cases in the Golden Triangle, and in Africa—we choose to believe that this is a bizarre aberration. Yet, as we investigate the evidence in the following pages, we will walk into the center of a nightmare of unbelievable proportions because this single, documented, *American* case contains within itself all the elements that we—as serious researchers, journalists and historians—have been taught to treat with skepticism and condescension. We will uncover an organization that was trolling for child subjects (victims) all over the globe; that used these children in strange rituals involving animal sacrifice; that sent these children to secret schools abroad; and that—when on the verge of discovery and exposure—was finally protected by the CIA.

FINDERS, KEEPERS?

On February 5, 1987 the US Customs Service received a phone call from Sergeant JoAnn VanMeter of the Juvenile Division of the Tallahassee Police Department in Florida. Six very young children—aged 2 to 7 years—had been found in the apparent custody of two well-dressed men. The children were scampering in a park in Tallahassee, but they appeared to be ill-fed, ill-clothed—some not wearing underwear—and filthy. An anonymous tip to the Tallahassee PD was enough for the police to undertake a routine investigation, questioning the adults and the children. When the adults proved to be evasive, and their van—a 1980 blue Dodge with Virginia license plates—which was as filthy and foul-smelling as the children, was discovered to be full of books, maps and a single mattress, the police had enough to charge the two men with child abuse.

One of the two men now in custody gave the police a business card with a statement on one side saying that the "bearer knew his constitutional rights to remain silent and that he intended to do so." The children could not name the two men either. In fact, they didn't know the "function and purpose of telephones, televisions and toilets" and further stated that "they were not allowed to live indoors and were only given food as a reward."

They further said that they were on their way to Mexico to go to a school for smart kids. Tallahassee PD phoned the Customs Service to see if they had any information on the adults, the kids, or the alleged school in Mexico and to determine whether or not there were grounds for holding the men on a federal charge. The Tallahassee police suspected that the children were being used in a child pornography ring, and the Customs Service has a database devoted to collecting information on international child pornography operations. The fact that Mexico was stated as their destination aroused the suspicions of both TPD and the Customs Service even further; Mexico is a haven for every type of pornography production, including child pornography—still photos and films including child prostitution—as well as for purported "snuff" film factories south of the Rio Grande.

Customs said they would investigate the links of the men to an address in the D.C. area, discovered through a check of the license plate on the van.

And this is where it all came together … and then exploded apart.

The Tallahassee Police Department and the Customs Service coordinated their efforts with the Washington D.C. Metropolitan Police Department (MPD), as the van was traced to an address in the District and other identification was found in the van leading the detectives to two addresses in Washington. A search warrant was obtained, and a Detective Bradley of the Washington MPD informed the Customs agents that an informer reported that a cult known as the Finders was operating out of those addresses, and that the Finders were involved in blood sacrifice, sex orgies involving children, etc. The two men in custody were determined to be known members of the Finders, and several of the children were identified as "belonging" to the cult.

By the time the warrant was served, there were no children at the cult headquarters at 3918/20 W. Street, NW, but a large quantity of children's clothing was found, including diapers and other clothing, though nothing for children past pre-school age. The worse was yet to come, however.

In another part of the building, filled with computers and files, the detectives found detailed instructions for "obtaining children for unspecified purposes." I will let Special Agent, US Customs Service, Ramon J. Martinez continue in his own words:

> "The instructions included the impregnation of female members of the community known as the Finders, purchasing children, trading, and kidnapping. There were telex messages using MCI account numbers between a computer terminal believed to be located in the same room, and others located across the country and in foreign locations. One such telex specifically ordered the purchase of two children in Hong Kong to be arranged through a contact in the Chinese Embassy there.... Other documents identified interests in high-tech transfers to the United Kingdom, numerous properties under the control of the Finders, a keen interest in terrorism, explosives, and the evasion of law enforcement."

The next day, Friday February 6, 1987, Martinez and Bradley then proceeded to the Finders' warehouse at 1307 4th Street, NE. If anything, the take in the warehouse was more horrifying than what was discovered at cult headquarters. Again, to quote Special Agent Martinez:

> "I was able to observe numerous documents which described explicit sexual conduct between the members of the community known as Finders. I also saw a large collection of photographs of unidentified persons. Some of the photographs were nudes, believed to be of members of the Finders. There were numerous photos of children, some nude, at least one of which was a photo of a child "on display" and appearing to accent the child's genitals. I was only able to examine a very small amount of the photos at this time. However, one of the officers presented me with a photo album for my review. The album contained a series of photos of adults and children dressed in white sheets participating in a "blood ritual." The ritual centered around the execution of at least two goats. The photos portrayed the execution, disembowelment, skinning and dismemberment of the goats at the hands of the children. This included the removal of the testes of a male goat, the

> discovery of a female goat's "womb" and the "baby goats" inside the womb, and the presentation of a goat's head to one of the children."

There can be no doubt, therefore, that what was discovered in the photographs satisfies the criteria for a "satanic" cult involving blood sacrifice and children. The graphic nature of the photographs emphasizes still further that no mere ritual sacrifice of the goats was intended, but a complete disembowelment and dismembering, including a concentration on the sexual organs of the animals. A ritual sacrifice would have been bad enough; hideous, even, for children to be forced to take part. But to carry the bloody ritual to its specific conclusion of the mutilation of the bodies seems to be an attempt to either traumatize the children to an extent that dissociative identity disorder would be a likely outcome, or to anesthetize the children against the performance of bloody and barbaric acts. The author can think of no other purpose that would be served.

However, in fairness to the reader it should be mentioned that the author has spent many years in Asia and in countries and regions where Islam and Hinduism are popular religions. In both these world religions, animal sacrifice is an accepted part of ritual practice and male children of a certain age can be seen participating in or observing these rituals. And, during a Shi'ite festival which commemorates the martyrdom of a Muslim saint, it is not uncommon to see fathers cutting the heads of their own children with swords or machetes to the extent that the children are screaming and covered in blood, as a sign of their grief over the death of Ali.

I submit, however, that the practice of animal sacrifice in a community where there is general support for this practice within the context of an accepted religion has a different effect on a child's understanding than the barbaric butchering and mutilation of an animal in secret, in a country, a city and among people for whom the closest they would normally come to animal sacrifice is the meat counter at their local supermarket. (And isn't this the point, that "insanity" is a social concept, dependent on the mores of the society in which one finds oneself?)

The discoveries at the Finders warehouse were not over, however.

> "Further inspection of the premises disclosed numerous files relating to activities of the organization in different parts of the world. Locations I observed are as follows: London, Germany, the Bahamas, Japan, Hong Kong, Malaysia, Africa, Costa Rica, and "Europe"…There was one file entitled "Pentagon Break-In," and others referring to members operating in foreign countries."

What the agents faced was a mountain of evidence pointing to an international trade in children and the use of children in horrible rituals which were photographed for posterity. They found passports and other travel documents, details for trafficking in foreign currency and in high technology transfer to foreign countries. In effect, they had a gold mine and what could have been the most scandalous, most astonishing case in the history of modern jurisprudence because it has it all: child abuse, slavery, rituals, sex, money, and power. But the Finders case had still another aspect, one which the Customs agents could not have predicted.

Martinez arrived at MPD to discuss the case with Detective Bradley, as pre-arranged. Bradley was unavailable. Instead, Martinez was asked to speak to an unidentified third party who could only speak "off the record."

And what he told Martinez was the last straw.

All passport data had been turned over to the State Department, who told MPD that the passports and the travel represented by the passports was "within the law," even though this involved "travel to Moscow, North Korea, and North Vietnam from the late 1950s to mid 1970s." Further, Martinez was told that "the investigation into the activity of the Finders had become a CIA internal matter. The MPD report has been classified SECRET and was not available for review."

A cult. Kidnapped children. Sexual abuse. Blood sacrifice. Mutilation. A world-wide organization. Covered up by the CIA. This sounds like a bad Ludlum novel, but it was reality. In Washington, D.C. In 1987.

In *Unholy Alliance*, I wrote extensively of another such cult, this one based in Chile. Called Colonia Dignidad, it was run by a former World War II Luftwaffe officer and defrocked (?) Baptist minister, and was involved in the trafficking of children from various countries, torture of political prisoners, and other Nazi pastimes. It was covered up by the Pinochet government and by its secret service, the dreaded DINA. It was finally uncovered, raided several times, and its back broken. We think. Its owner and founder was apprehended and is now awaiting trial as you read this.

There is a lot of hysteria on the subject of "satanic cult survivor syndrome," and much of the skepticism which greets these claims is well deserved. However, when confronted with a real-life children-sex-sacrifice-CIA cult what are we to believe? How do we answer the skeptics who insist that it's a figment of overactive imaginations and underactive libidos? How do we answer the believers who accept that there is a world-wide satanic conspiracy involving stolen children and cult members impregnated to give birth to sacrificial babies? The Finders case has robbed us of the luxury of disbelief. And the CIA has robbed us of the answers we need to put the Finders in some sort of perspective, some method in which to handle this bizarre information in a way more suitable to our early 21st century sensibilities.

One set of sinister questions remains, and has yet to be answered: not in the Customs documents, not in any of the news reports. The answer may be buried Bobby in the MPD files marked SECRET (if they still exist at all) or in the CIA's own files on the matter.

What did the Finders do with the children after they"found" them? Where did they go? Where was the school in Mexico? What did they do there? How many more were there?

And ... *where are they now and what are they doing?*

And to whom?

Item: When Lee Harvey Oswald made his famous trip by bus to Mexico City in 1963, ostensibly to obtain a visa for Cuba, he sat next to an Englishman by the name of John Howard Bowen, alias Albert Osborne. Bowen was an "itinerant preacher" of the Baptist persuasion, an elderly gentleman who traveled frequently to Mexico, according to Warren Commission exhibits (mostly FBI interrogation reports). When confronted by the FBI, Bowen claimed he had borrowed the identity of Albert Osborne, an Englishman who was also an itinerant Baptist preacher, when investigated by the Mexican authorities at a time when he couldn't find his own identification. He claimed that Osborne was an Englishman but that he, Bowen, was born in the United States. Unfortunately, the other passengers on that fabled bus trip to Mexico City identified Bowen as an Englishman, and eventually the FBI concluded that Bowen and Osborne were one and the same.[19] What is interesting is the fact that Bowen-Osborne was a devoted Nazi both before and during World War II, opposing America's entry into the war, and ran a fascist camp for boys in rural Tennessee until it was closed down in 1942.[20]

At the time of the Kennedy Assassination in 1963, there were persistent rumors that Bowen-Osborne was running a school for assassins in Mexico, somewhere in Pueblo, under the guise of a "missionary effort." (When Bowen was first interrogated by the FBI, he claimed that he had been ordained a minister in 1914 by the Plymouth Brethren in Trenton, New Jersey. The Plymouth Brethren is the sect to which Aleister Crowley's parents belonged and from whom he "discovered" his true identity as the Great Beast 666.) Even the Warren Commission could not accept the testimony of Bowen-Osborne, and they were easy marks. Gradually, stories of Bowen's connections to American paramilitary organizations began to circulate, including his involvement with the Minutemen. It was Fred Crisman's purported relationship to the same paramilitary group that led to his interrogation by Jim Garrison in 1968.

A Mexican school for assassination. The recruitment of young boys. Nazis. The Christian Right. 1963.

Item: Los Angeles, May 13, 1964. Less than six months after the Kennedy assassination. The 19th Annual Convention and Scientific Program of the Society of Biological Psychiatry takes place. During the convention, it is reported that 450 children, aged 4 to 15, at Creedmore State Hospital have been subjected to a massive program of hallucinogen experimentation, incorporating everything from LSD to psilocybin to various other drugs. Doses are 150 mcg of LSD or 20 mg of psilocybin, daily, "for periods up to several months." The children ranged from autistic to "slightly schizophrenic" (whatever that means).

WHOEVER FIGHTS MONSTERS

Whoever fights monsters should see to it that in the process he does not become a monster. And when you look long into an abyss, the abyss also looks into you.
—Friedrich Nietzsche[21]

It wasn't until the mid-1970s that the term "serial killer" became the household word it is today. Coined by FBI profiler Robert K. Ressler, it has taken on a life of its own. Often, the term is applied when it shouldn't be, but we still understand the basic concept: a repeat murderer who doesn't kill for money or for revenge or some other, commonly understood, motive but to satisfy a deep need, a "lust to kill." Serial killers come in two basic flavors, organized and disorganized, but there are killers who partake of both characteristics and are therefore sometimes more difficult to capture. Typically, a serial killer is a young white male, although there have been female serial killers and serial killers of other races.

(As I write these lines, Pakistan has just convicted a serial killer in their country. Their mode of justice? They will strangle him in front of the parents whose children he himself had strangled to death, and then they will destroy his body with acid, again as he did to his victims.) But in the United States, which has become a kind of serial killer capital of the world, we have hundreds on the streets at any given time and they are all mostly young white males.

Many theories have been advanced to explain their strange behavior: the rituals of killing, the cycles or periods, the trolling for victims, the fugue state before the kill and its aftermath, the sometimes gruesome souvenirs, the taunting of police officers, etc. Psychoanalysis of some of our most famous 20th century cases reveals a depressing similarity among these "monsters": horrible childhoods, in some cases horrible beyond description; physical abuse, including severe head traumas and sexual abuse; perhaps one absentee parent. In fact, many of these events are also characteristic of cases of dissociative identity disorder ("multiple personalities"), so it should come as no surprise that the insanity defense is often invoked for crimes committed by serial killers. We want to classify these people as something other than human, and in the last hundred years or so the easiest, most "politically correct" way to do this has been to use insanity as an excuse.

But when we examine the individual cases we see that there is a social component to the genesis of their mental condition. It seems that serial killers are not born, they are made: in much the same way dissociative identity disorder is a creature of a hideous childhood and a violent upbringing. That presents a problem for the death penalty lobby, because if the development of a personality into a serial killer is not a matter of choice (such as, for instance, dealing drugs, etc.) then how can we punish the offender? If the shrinks are correct, then the killers have no conscious control over their actions. And it would certainly seem to be the case, since the pattern is so well-known by now: the early days of torturing small animals, sexual abuse of children or other vulnerable persons, the first kill which leads inevitably to the second, and then the cycle increasing in intensity with the time period between each successive kill growing shorter and shorter until it seems that the killer will explode in a homicidal frenzy. It has all the hallmarks of a psychological syndrome, a psychopathology that demands treatment instead of punishment.

But we have no way to "treat" a serial killer; by the time he has begun killing he is usually too far gone to be treated. The best we can do is jail him, hospitalize him, or execute him. There is no other alternative; he certainly can never be returned to society. And we can't treat a serial killer because—even with all the understanding of how a serial killer is "made" in childhood—we feel he is beyond salvage. He is too cunning for psychoanalysis, a cunning born of survival in the "straight" world. He will say what the analyst wants him to say; he will appear ingratiating, accommodating, perhaps feigning sanity or insanity as the situation warrants, playing with his captors. Intelligence is one of the characteristics of the serial killer: usually above-average and sometimes even genius-level intelligence, particularly in the case of the so-called "organized" killer. We have the modern-day icon of Hannibal Lecter as a model for this type of highly intelligent, highly organized killer. It also reinforces an attitude Americans have towards the intelligent, that they are somehow "different" from the rest of us. It makes us feel better to see the intelligent as psychotic, or—as pointed out in *Unholy Alliance*—Nazis. At the same time, serial killers are obsessed with their dark yearnings. They have somehow equated sexual gratification with violence and murder, arousal with the blood and pain and fear of their victims. And we abhor the crime and the criminal especially because of the sexual aspect of this disorder, an aspect that can include necrophilia and worse.

There is another aspect of this phenomenon, however, that concerns us more closely because it may hold a clue not only to the serial killer himself but to the human condition in general. A careful examination of many of the more famous cases in the last one hundred years will reveal that many of these killers had a religious or occult obsession that ran parallel to their lust-murder obsession. This combination has lent some of these killers a superior attitude towards their captors, an air of smugness and complacency, as if they were in possession of secret knowledge. Certainly, a man who has killed dozens of victims in cities across the country, constantly evading capture and baffling law enforcement, probably feels a little superior to his captors. More importantly, the actual act of murder itself—especially in this case, in taking the life of another human being without motive but by deeds of unspeakable violence—must cause a strange disorientation in the murderer, a kind of twilight state in which reality is distorted. A killer *is* different from the rest of us: he has performed an action that is the ultimate in what society considers heinous. A serial killer's experience is even more bizarre, more outlandish. He kills a string of people for no socially-identifiable purpose. He takes their lives himself, one after the other, repeatedly, in a complex ritual that has meaning only for him. He has stared into the eyes of his victims as they expire. In many cases, he defiles their bodies, or dismembers them, keeping parts as souvenirs; Jeffrey Dahmer and Edmund Kemper come readily to mind.

We have not had these experiences. We know nothing of this. We can read the words, or hear them spoken, but we cannot imagine the sensations; we cannot put ourselves in the killer's place, although we can probably identify with the horror of the victims. There is nothing in our experience, generally, to equate with a lust killing. Most of us have never killed a human being under any circumstances, including war. We certainly have no psychological analog to a lust killing, unless it is lust—sexual desire and arousal—itself. Those of us who feel guilty about our own sexual desires may believe they can understand to some extent the sexual component of the serial killer's strange actions. Think again. *DSM-IV* has no category for this. Thus, the superior (even smug) attitude of the serial killer towards the rest of us. He has walked with demons. He has defiled himself in the most extreme manner possible for a human being. He has seen deeply into the abyss. The problem is, he is still there and cannot get out.

If the CIA in their desperate zeal to combat a perceived brainwashing threat from the Chinese or Russians had attempted to open the black box of consciousness in order to create the perfect assassin—a man or woman who would kill as programmed and forget why (which could be a clinical description of the serial killer's functions as well)—then they were also experimenting with the same mechanism that creates serial killers ... and shamans. The horrifying visions of the shaman-in-training are nearly identical, if not exactly identical, to those that obsess the serial killer: the dismemberments, the excruciating pain, the visions, the voices in the head, the blood lust. It is, as Eliade points out, tantamount to psychopathology. In the case of the shaman, he is eventually cured of this disorder even though it may last for a long time. His society understands what is going on, and they have mechanisms for dealing with it; the shaman will be a valuable addition to their society after the cure, because then he will be able to communicate with the spirit world, to intercede for his neighbors and to foretell the future. The crucial difference between a shaman and a serial killer may be that the latter has *externalized* the psychological process. What for a shaman—as well as for the artist, the poet, the musician—is an internal nightmare of hallucinogenic proportions becomes, in the hands of the serial killer, a dreadful reality. In another example, Christianity teaches that Jesus was beaten, and crucified, and then had his side pierced with a spear. The terrible tortures (analogous to the tortures of the shaman) happened *to* him; he did not visit them upon his fellow human beings. But a serial killer enacts these same crimes, which first began as childhood or adolescent fantasies, upon innocent victims, one after the other, until he is stopped.

Is a serial killer a shaman who has not made it back?

In 1998, the following was reported in the Indonesian press as well as by the Agence France Presse: An Indonesian practitioner of black magic—a type of sorcerer called a *dukun*—one Ahmad Suraji, was sentenced to death for the murder of forty-two women. He claimed that his father came to him in a dream and told him if he killed seventy women and drank their saliva, his magic powers would be increased and he would—paradoxically—become a better healer. The bodies of all forty-two women were found in a sugar cane field, most of whom had been strangled by the man they came to for help with love and money problems. In a separate trial, one of Suraji's three wives was named as an accomplice.

Obviously, there is a logical problem with a shaman who has to kill seventy people in order to become a better healer! But in any event, we are faced with this instance of a serial killer who is a shaman, albeit a poor one. Southeast Asia is still full of examples of shamans, dukuns, bomohs, and other types of sorcerers who resort to murder in order to enhance their occult abilities. There are many examples in Indonesia, as well as in Malaysia, Thailand and the Philippines. While these shamans may be nominal Muslims, Buddhists or Christians, they are really animists at heart: pagan occultists for whom their religious affiliations are more of a vehicle for reaching more people in their role as healers or witches. Serial murder is not unknown; a case in Malaysia of sorcerers who killed a number of foreigners in an attempt to use their skulls to gain greater powers was reported in the press around the same time as the Suraji case in Indonesia.

Thus, in Asia, we have compelling evidence of a link between serial murder and occult practices. What we do not know is if this is a cultural phenomenon, or if the type of killer such as Suraji fits the accepted FBI profile of a serial or "lust" killer such as a Dahmer or a Gacey … or if this is a different phenomenon altogether. We do know that Dahmer, for instance, was fascinated by occultism and believed that he could create zombies from his victims, and also had an altar adorned with the skulls of his victims when he was finally apprehended. Yet, in Dahmer's case, we don't know if the occult beliefs preceded the lust for murder, or if they were only window-dressing, a ritualization to heighten the sexual pleasure he derived from his actions. Perhaps a closer look at Dahmer's case would be revealing of larger issues.

PROM NIGHT

I saw and think 'The Exorcist' was the best saterical comedy that I have ever seen.

—letter from the Zodiac Killer to the San Francisco *Chronicle*, January 30, 1974 (Candlemas), misspelling in the original.[22]

Jeffrey Dahmer was the prototypical awkward teenager, but one with a secret. According to FBI interview transcripts, Dahmer knew he was homosexual since he was about thirteen years old. In 1970s small-town Ohio, that meant that he had to disguise his sexuality and pretend to be as heterosexual as everyone else. For someone like Dahmer, however, that was not going to be easy.

Thin, shy, and nervous, Dahmer would never come across as a macho man. Nevertheless, he had a date for the high school prom in June of 1978. The unfortunate lady was Bridget Geiger, and she would later participate in a séance in Dahmer's home.

According to press reports published at the time of the grisly Dahmer revelations, Ms. Geiger described herself as an unpopular high school sophomore, and Dahmer was equally unpopular as a senior. A mutual friend had arranged their "date" for the prom, during which Dahmer ignored her for hours, ostensibly to go out and get hamburgers. He was obviously painfully shy around girls, and could not even bring himself to pin the obligatory corsage to her prom dress, but had to enlist the aid of her mother.[23]

The prom took place in May 1978. A month later, Jeffrey invited her to a party at his house. It was not much of a party, according to Ms. Geiger, but just a half dozen people sitting around with no food, no music, not much of anything. At one point during the evening, Dahmer decided he wanted to have a séance to contact the spirit of someone who had died in the house. According to Dahmer, an evil spirit had contacted him and spoken to him, asking him to do things that scared him. As the candles were lit and started to flare up and sputter, Bridget Geiger realized that Dahmer was not joking, and she fled the house, never to see or speak to Dahmer again.[24]

That same month, Dahmer claimed his first victim, the young hitchhiker Steven Hicks.

It is important to put the events in perspective. Dahmer—described variously as a loner and as the class clown, capable of practical jokes but never having any close friends—attends his senior prom, probably through social pressure from his parents or what he felt society expected of him. Although he knew he was homosexual at this time, he had not actually acted out any homosexual acts with others (except for a brief interlude as a younger child with a friend which did not progress beyond some mild groping or fondling). He attended the prom with a young lady who described herself as unpopular as Dahmer himself. One would have thought that Dahmer would have been eager to put that episode out of his mind, but a month later he invites the same girl to a "party" that is not a party at all, but a prelude to a séance to contact an evil spirit; moreover, an evil spirit that has been telling Dahmer to do things that scare him. The séance seems to have proceeded without Ms. Geiger's participation. What occurred, we do not know; but that same month, possibly only days or at most weeks later, Dahmer is cruising a country road and finds his first victim.

Steven Hicks was a personable nineteen-year-old, socially adept, and according to Dr. Joel Norris the diametric opposite to Dahmer in terms of personality. Hicks was on his way to a rock concert, and Dahmer picked him up and convinced him to return with him to Dahmer's home for a drink. What transpired next is subject to some controversy, as Dahmer has given conflicting accounts. We do not know if Dahmer had sex with Steven Hicks, but what is certain is that when Hicks attempted to leave Dahmer went berserk and killed him with a barbell.

He then proceeded to the next phase of his pattern, which was the dismemberment of the body.

Mircea Eliade has described the curious process of "election" of a shaman; it begins with some notification from the spirit world that the subject has been "elected" to become a shaman. In other words, there is a spiritual force—demonic or angelic or simply an amoral spiritual entity of some kind—which makes its presence known to the future shaman. If we take the above story at face value, this is exactly what happened with Dahmer. As an outsider, a loner, he fit the bill in every other respect. Even as someone sexually confused, or homosexual, or a transvestite: all of these sexually ambiguous or "deviant" behaviors were evidence of a shamanistic vocation in some cultures. The process of initiation begins immediately upon notification to the future shaman that he or she has been elected.

This initiatory process involves a gradually worsening stage of mental disorder and illness, as described above. This includes a sensation of being murdered and dismembered, of having one's organs removed, of being reduced to a skeleton. In some cases, as in Siberian shamanism, it was not unusual for the fully-initiated shaman to wear a coat covered in animal (or human) bones, as a marker of his initiatory death and dismemberment. These are all steps taken by Dahmer himself in the intensification of his disorder, as he began to kill and eviscerate and dismember his victims. To a shaman, it would appear as an externalization of what should have remained an internalized experience.

Dahmer had dismembered and eviscerated animals before, always "road kill" that he found on the highway. According to Dahmer, he never killed an animal himself. What argues against this, however, is the scene close to his house of a kind of ritual setting in the woods in which it seems dogs were killed as part of an occult rite. This had taken place the previous year, in 1977, amid reports of missing dogs in the Bath, Ohio neighborhood where he lived. The scene was described by Jim Klippel to the *Akron Beacon-Journal*:

> "Somebody must have had a lot of fun with that dog...if that's what you want to call it. It was skinned and gutted. And about a hundred yards away there had been a large fire and thirteen little fires around it. It looked so much like cult worship that it scared us to death."[25]

The dog that Klippel referred to had been found nailed to a tree.

It fits the profile of a serial killer that Dahmer would have started torturing animals, eventually moving up to humans. Dahmer insists that he did not kill any animals himself, that he did not want to inflict pain. His human victims were said to have been drugged first before he killed them—usually by strangulation—so that they would not feel pain. It is possible that the drugging only made it easier for Dahmer to subdue and murder his victims, and that pain (or the avoidance of it) had nothing to do with it. In any event, the disappearing and murdered dogs in 1977 pointed to a disappearing and murdered Steven Hicks in 1978.

It is worthwhile to note here that missing dogs—especially German shepherds—are a recurring theme around cult murders and cult activity, and that the slaughter of dogs was an element of the cult surrounding the Son of Sam killings that we will investigate shortly. (About a year before the Son of Sam killings began, the author lived in Brooklyn Heights and heard stories of dogs being tortured and killed in a warehouse near the Brooklyn Bridge. This is the same neighborhood where the Warlock Shop once stood, the occult store referred to by Maury Terry several times in *The Ultimate Evil* as an informal meeting place for some of the Sam cultists.)

Dahmer disposed of Hicks' body, burying the pieces in the earth near his home (where they would be found thirteen years later), and went about his life as if nothing had happened. He enrolled in college, but was kicked out due to his excessive drinking, a habit that began when Dahmer was still in high school. At the end of 1978, we find Dahmer enlisting in the Army and being sent to Germany.

His military record, obtained by the FBI and part of his declassified FBI file, shows that Dahmer had severe problems in the Army, problems with drinking and problems with authority. He was eventually discharged from the Army when they realized they couldn't do very much for him, and he could do nothing for the Army. So many of our nation's most famous serial killers have spent time in the Armed Services: Dahmer, David Berkowitz, Bobby Joe Long, Arthur Shawcross ... the list is long and gruesome. Dahmer may be relatively unique in that he began killing *before* he enlisted; the others did not begin until after they had been in the service.

What transpired after his discharge is by now well-known among aficionados of the bizarre and the morbid. He returned home, eventually found a job or series of jobs in Milwaukee, and began trolling for victims. He honed his skills, and refined his rituals. His victims were all gay men, of various races—Black, White, Asian, Hispanic—mostly young, people he met in gay bars as far away as Chicago. He would work during the week, and then go crazy on the weekends, drinking and hanging out in gay strip clubs, gay discos, adult movie theaters and bookstores, and when he was finally apprehended the body count came to seventeen, including his first victim, Steven Hicks. Their bodies had been dismembered, dissolved in vats of acid in his apartment, stored in a large freezer. Their skulls had been retained, cleaned and defleshed and in some cases painted, and were adorning his altar, his "power altar."[26] The number of skulls on the altar has been given variously as six (Ressler) or ten (Norris), along with a planned hanging skeleton on either side, a central hanging lamp, and two griffins. The altar was not complete at the time of his arrest, but some of the skulls and the two griffins were in place, as well as candles, incense, and other vaguely occult paraphernalia.

The griffins are interesting, only in that we encountered a pair of griffins in Book I: atop the incredible wandering house in Ashland, Kentucky, where—it was claimed—they had the power to ward off evil. In Dahmer's case, the griffins had names: one was Leon and the other was Apal, according to an FBI report on an interview with Dahmer on August 3, 1992. These words were written on the griffins themselves, which were knocked over during his session with victim Curtis Straughter who rolled off the bed and crashed into the altar, alarming Dahmer. According to the FBI report,

> DAHMER stated that these griffins were part of the occult, and symbolized personal power and made it that he did not have to answer to anyone. DAHMER stated that there were words written on each griffin, one had Leon and the other had Apal. DAHMER again stated that this symbolized personal power, and he felt that this was a sign to show that he was losing control.[27]

For those interested in these things, the names of the griffins may provide a type of clue. "Leon," of course, is simply the Spanish word for lion, and, of course, the lion represents the kind of strength and power that attracted Dahmer. "Apal" is somewhat more problematic. It could simply be the Hebrew word אפל which means "darkness, gloom," in which case the combination of lion with darkness is most apt.

When asked about his occult beliefs, he made an interesting revelation. Again, according to the FBI:

> DAHMER was asked if he was involved in the occult, and DAHMER stated that he started dabbling in the occult and reading, and his favorite movie was EXORCIST III, because it helped fit into his fantasy. DAHMER

> stated that in the movie EXORCIST III the guy could create illusions, and DAHMER felt that he himself could create illusions.[28]

For those who have not seen this film (*Exorcist III,* 1990), or who don't remember it, it is a sequel to the original William Friedkin film, and was actually directed by Friedkin himself. (*Exorcist II* was not a Friedkin production.) In addition, it had some members of the original cast. The important thing about this film, however, is that *it links serial murder with demonic possession,* something which the earlier *Exorcist* films did not do.

That this was Dahmer's favorite film is very revealing. The throwaway line about "creating illusions" is just that, a decoy. As we read famed FBI profiler Robert K. Ressler's interview with Dahmer, the reason Dahmer was fascinated by *Exorcist III* was the power the possessed had over reality, over the minds and bodies of the rest of the world.[29] The element of "creating illusions" was only a tool, a means to an end. There are many films concerned with the creation of illusions, but only *Exorcist III* marries this theme with that of demonic possession and serial murder. Dahmer went so far as to procure yellow contact lenses, to give his eyes that feral, haunted glow when he trolled the bars, looking for victims. He believed that they "exuded power."[30]

Further evidence of this is given by an intended victim who escaped, one Tracy Edwards.

Edwards had been invited back to Dahmer's Milwaukee apartment, and during a drinking session managed to have one hand handcuffed at knife point but retained enough common sense or sobriety to refuse to have the other hand cuffed. Dahmer, however, although angry, was calm because he had drugged Edwards' drink. His victim would soon be unconscious, and a little later dead.

While waiting for the drug to take effect, and with knife in hand, Dahmer demanded that Edwards watch a videotape with him. It was *Exorcist III.*

Dahmer watched the film intently, at times rocking back and forth, chanting in a humming sound, and seeming to go into a trance (as described in Book II, the same process was used by Mark David Chapman when invoking Satan or talking to his Little People). Then a personality change would take place during the parts of the film that depicted possession sequences. At this time, Dahmer himself would become aggressive and demand that Edwards place the other handcuff on his wrist. Then, as the filmed possession sequence would change to something more mundane, Dahmer's mood also shifted and he began to complain about his life and his loneliness.

Eventually, Edwards escaped through a combination of luck and intelligence. He played Dahmer's moods and in a moment of inattention managed to hit Dahmer with enough force that he fell to the side, allowing Edwards to escape out into the night, running as fast as he could.

The mood changes may indicate some form of dissociation on Dahmer's part, such as we have already discussed, although Dahmer never presented as a sufferer from DID or MPD at the time of his arrest or subsequent medical examinations. Indeed, psychiatrists were never able to completely analyze Dahmer, as Dahmer himself complained. They could point to his necrophilia (he would have sex with the corpses of his victims before they were dismembered, copulating with them or even drawing slits in their chest for this purpose) or his other symptoms, but never be able to integrate these symptoms into a single diagnosis. FBI profiler Ressler would say that Dahmer represented a new phenomenon, and partially blamed Hollywood (even though he himself had been a technical adviser on *Silence of the Lambs*). He saw *Exorcist III* as some kind of triggering mechanism for Dahmer, as something that gave the killer a kind of validation.

I believe this is a hard point to prove, as one would have to show other instances in which this film instigated murder, dismemberment and cannibalism. Nonetheless, by blaming cinema and also to an extent pornography for the Dahmer phenomenon, Ressler was raising the ante: he was stating, simply, that American culture had contributed to the creation of Dahmer. If we look at other instances of serial murder around the globe, however, including the Indonesian case mentioned above as well as Chikatilo in Russia, and cases in Pakistan, China, and everywhere else, it is obvious that it is not American culture that creates serial killers—not even of the cannibalistic variety—but perhaps culture in general offers a social medium for the phenomenon. In Indonesia, it manifested as witchcraft; in Milwaukee, as a string of homosexual and racist hate crimes. The common denominator, however, in so many cases of serial murder and other vicious crimes seems to be theological. There is a supernatural element wherever we look, if we look deeply enough. A taste for ritual, for horror films, for spiritual evocation, for demonology. A taste for Satan.

In a macabre example of art imitating life imitating art, we have *The Exorcist*, which was a favorite film of the man eventually identified as the Zodiac Killer, and then *Exorcist III*, in which the demon-possessed serial murderer, the Gemini Killer, is based on the same Zodiac Killer (who, unknown to the film's writer, director and producer, was a fan of the first *Exorcist* movie). This real-life connection then leaps into Jeffrey Dahmer, who is mesmerized by the character and who probably does not realize that the fictional Gemini Killer is based on a real person, a genuine serial murderer such as he himself is becoming, a famous murderer with a taste for the occult and for Satanism, as Robert Graysmith's sequel to his definitive work on the Zodiac killer, *Zodiac Unmasked*, amply illustrates. And this, a movie based on a book written about a genuine case of demonic possession … a book written by a psychological warfare officer, a man himself laboring in an occult tradition of Giordano Bruno, as identified and clarified, by poor, murdered Professor Culianu. The links examined by Culianu—of eros and image, of magic and sexuality—are in this single example drawn so carefully and completely that I feel it safe to say that no one would be able to ignore the obvious conclusion that both Bruno and Culianu were correct and saw the inner workings of the sinister force with tremendous clarity, as we shall soon see.

The cannibalism factor increased the fascination the public has had with Dahmer. The killer admitted that he ate various body parts of his victims, so that he could feel them as part of him. It gave him a sexual thrill, but was obviously satisfying on some deeper level as well. Like the fictional Hannibal Lecter he would fry pieces of his victims on a skillet over a stove.

I would ask the reader to stop for a moment, inundated as we are with all of this hideous detail, and try to imagine the atmosphere of Dahmer's apartment. It was not a large place. It was a one-bedroom affair of the type one would see in most large cities: a sitting or living room, a bedroom, a toilet, not much else. In this apartment was a giant freezer filled with body parts. There was a vat containing acid and more body parts. There was a pot in which he cooked pieces of his victims. And there was the altar with its complement of skulls.

He *lived* in that apartment; it was not a kill zone, a special secret place hidden away in the woods like the witch's house in Hansel and Gretel (another example of murder, witchcraft, cannibalism and child abuse). It was where he went to sleep and woke up every morning. Showered. Shaved. Left everyday to go to work, or to find more victims. Once he had killed them, and had sex with their bodies, he would begin the laborious process of cutting them up into smaller pieces, some of which he would eat and some of which he would freeze for later. The rest would get dissolved in acid, and the blood and offal poured down the normal bathroom drains. Police investigators found pots in the apartment containing severed hands, genitalia, and other body parts, like something out of a nightmare. Or a children's fairy tale.

Put yourself there. Try to imagine Dahmer—a chain smoker—standing over his latest victim, a large sharp kitchen knife in his bloodied hand and a cigarette in his mouth, spilling ash, as he sawed away at someone's thigh or arm. Someone with whom he had had sex—alive and dead—perhaps only hours before. Try to tell yourself that this is life, this is how some people live, that this is an experience to which a human being can become inured, accustomed, habituated. With the black walls and dark furniture and altar of skulls and griffins, the lighting must have been dim. There were blood stains on the carpet. At times, the giant freezer leaked. There was a smell.

And the next weekend Dahmer would go out again.

There was a great distance between Dahmer's childhood home in Bath, Ohio and the apartment in Milwaukee, a spiritual distance most of us will never cover. We can talk about isolation, about confused sexuality, about alienation, even about multiple personalities and sexual dysfunctions. We can try to *reduce* this phenomenon to something we can live with, something within the boundaries of the reality we know, rather than the reality we suspect exists.

Adolf Eichmann, the prototype and exemplar of Hannah Arendt's "banality of evil," rarely saw the victims he consigned to the death camps as part of the Third Reich's "Final Solution." He did not wallow in their blood and gore. He did not dismember his victims, much less devour their flesh. He was an accountant, making sure quotas were filled and trains ran on time. If the evil that Eichmann represents is, indeed, "banal" or at least masquerades as banality, then what do we make of the evil represented by Dahmer?

What do we make of evil itself?

Dahmer, with his thin build and owlish, bespectacled appearance could have been Ohio's answer to Eichmann. They were both matter-of-fact during their respective interrogations. Eichmann's responsibility was for the deaths of millions of people; Dahmer's for seventeen. Do we measure evil in terms of body count? This question has never been answered. It seems beyond human ability to answer. Were Eichmann and Dahmer evil? Were they sane? Were they *equally* evil, equally sane or insane? What does this question demand of us as human beings? Does it demand that we question … no, that we *examine* the consequences of our actions, no matter how "banal"? Do we have to kill, dismember and devour our victims before society can pass a judgment of "evil" upon us? Or is it enough simply to sign the execution orders? Or to pay the taxes that will pay for the construction of missiles, or for the covert actions of anonymous assassins in Third World countries?

Or is it enough to *imagine* acts of evil, like a Stephen King or a Clive Barker, or a Thomas Harris? Or an H.P. Lovecraft?

Or like you? Like me?

In an American court of law, it is enough to be convicted of *responsibility* to deserve the death sentence, as in the case of Charles Manson; but that is, in itself, not enough of a verdict of evil. It is a verdict of guilt in the eyes of the law, but not necessarily of evil, or of sanity.

In Dahmer's case, we have what appears to be an unequivocal example of pure, unadulterated, evil. Yet, his defense attorneys attempted to win their case on the basis of diminished capacity, i.e., the insanity defense. Dahmer had already confessed to the crimes, including that of Steven Hicks thirteen years previously. There was no doubt in anyone's mind that Dahmer had actually committed these crimes. What the trial was to determine, before a jury, was whether or not Dahmer was "insane."

Dahmer's meticulous planning of each crime and the effort he made to dispose of the bodies before going out again to perform the same actions were enough for the jury to come back with a verdict of "sanity." There were, of course, other social issues surrounding the trial, including the Rodney King case in which a black man was beaten by Los Angeles Police Department officers and the entire episode captured on videotape. Much was made of

Dahmer's victims, that they were all homosexual and that eleven of the seventeen were black. Dahmer's crimes were painted as "hate crimes," i.e., that Dahmer—conflicted about his homosexuality—took out his shame and rage on homosexuals and extended that via a basic racist streak to include blacks. To equate Dahmer's murder, dismemberment and consumption of his victims—not to mention his attempts to turn at least one of them into a zombie by drilling holes in his skull while he was still alive and filling the holes with acid—to the LAPD brutality in the case of Rodney King, was quite a stretch. Although both crimes were hideous, the case of Dahmer reveals a sickness and depravity that even the LAPD could not match on its best days.

The expert witnesses and other observers on the case admitted a degree of bafflement when it came to Dahmer. The language became, in fact, embarrassingly theological.

John Liccione, the chief psychologist of the Milwaukee County Medical Health Complex at the time of the Dahmer arrest, claimed, "We may think we know the person, but rare is the case we really know what a person feels and thinks deep down in the bowels of his soul.... Soul can be concealed. Who knows what is in there?"[31]

Theresa Smith, the sister of Dahmer victim Eddie Smith, put it more succinctly when she said, "I just know Dahmer's evil.... And if they had a plea for that, that's what he'd get—evilness."[32]

The drawing Dahmer made of his proposed Power Altar included a black table with ten painted skulls, a standing skeleton on either side of the altar, what appear to be incense burners on top and at either side of the altar, and an overhead hanging lamp with four blue globes. The four globes (or six globes, according to Ressler, p. 128) are the mysterious element; they don't seem to fit the overall layout of death and darkness. There might be a clue—however tenuous, but we *are* in very murky territory—in several works by noted occult scholar and head of one of Aleister Crowley's Ordo Templi Orientis (OTO) organizations in England, Kenneth Grant.

Quoting from the Lovecraft tale, "The Lurker at the Threshold," he writes (in 1980),

> The globes, or bubbles, comprise 'that tentacled amorphous monster ... whose mask was as a congeries of iridescent globes, the noxious Yog-Sothoth, who froths as primal slime in nuclear chaos beyond the nethermost outposts of space and time'.[33]

And previously, in 1972, quoting the same story and linking it to a design in Crowley's own Pantacle:

> Not stars, but suns, great globes of light ... and not these alone, but the breaking apart of the nearest globes, and the protoplasmic flesh that flamed

> blackly outward to join together and form that eldritch, hideous horror from outer space …[34]

Had the stories of H. P. Lovecraft influenced the dreams and forbidden fantasies of the introverted young Ohio homosexual who held séances in his home as a teenager to confront the evil spirit who, he said, was telling him to do "scary things"? We shall probably never know.

Jeffrey Dahmer was beaten to death in prison in November 1994 by a black inmate, Christopher J. Scarver, who was serving a life sentence for murder.

Scarver said that voices in his head told him that he, Scarver, was the Son of God.[35]

MURDER AND TRANSFIGURATION

We are accustomed to thinking of the fictional killer as someone who is in fiendish pursuit of a kind of transformation. The killer in Thomas Harris' famous *Silence of the Lambs* is trying to transform himself into a woman by sewing the skin of his victims together to make a kind of suit, à la real-life serial killer Ed Gein; the symbol of that novel-turned-movie is a moth: a motif of transformation from caterpillar to pupa to winged creature. How much more interesting an evil character who is in search of self-transcendence! It elevates the discussion beyond a mere carnal craving for blood; and why? Because we want to elevate our own sexual urges into something more … divine? A tantric take on lust murder? Or is there something fundamentally correct in the assumption that the serial killer—like the shaman—is in search (consciously or unconsciously) of a kind of transformation? Before our minds were filled with stories and images of vicious and depraved serial killers, there was in North America an institutionalized form of murder, evisceration and dismemberment: the ritual killings that took place among the Aztecs and Mayas, and all as part of public displays that merged religious intensity with dramatic scenes of bloody knives and hearts, still beating, ripped from the chests of victims. This linkage of hideous slaughter with communication with God and the preservation of society was not exclusive to the ancient Mexican civilizations, of course. Jesus is another such example. Transformation by way of torture, bloodshed, and murder.

Is this what compelled the CIA to dig deeper into the mentality of violent offenders and psychopaths? Not because they wanted to see God, but because they wanted to control that urge for transformation, for transcendence and re-direct it towards a more politically useful target?

Critics of Thomas Harris' novels point to an obvious "flaw" if his work is to be taken scientifically, and that is that serial killers by and large do not have the intellect, the control, and the deep inner resources of a Hannibal Lecter; they are usually underachievers, usually white men who are marginal in society due to physical or mental defects or social ostracism, a lot closer to the brutal redneck antagonists in *Deliverance* than the urbane, literate Lecter.

Yet it is just these men who, in other societies, may find themselves called to the position and function of shaman, and not to the role of the intellectually-astute, the suave, cultivated man of science and society.

David Sexton—literary editor of the *London Evening Standard*—has written a thoughtful and stimulating book on Thomas Harris and the themes in his novels: *The Strange World of Thomas Harris.*[36] In this tightly-focused essay, we are startled to read that the themes we have been pursuing are echoed quite clearly by this British critic, for he draws a comparison between the mind of Hannibal Lecter and *The Art of Memory* by Frances A. Yates,[37] showing that the number and type of connections and correspondences in Harris' work is a deliberate creation of a kind of memory palace, and that numerous Web sites have sprung up devoted to unraveling these connections and demonstrating the superb depth of erudition and culture that permeate the Lecter novels, giving them a resonance far beyond that of a traditional thriller or horror story. Hannibal Lecter is, himself, a kind of memory palace, which is why he is able to spend long days, weeks and months in his cell without his books as he pores over a vast mental library and museum that is his own memory. Further, while giving homage to Sherlock Holmes, Harris also draws his inspiration directly from Edgar Allen Poe and the American traditions of the detective story and the horror story (as did Sir Arthur Conan Doyle), traditions steeped in that peculiar American culture that European critics deny we possess while they simultaneously admire and emulate it, for it is, after all, a tradition born in the darkest of human impulses: conquest, heresy, the ripping of the veils of Temple and Kingship.

It was Ioan Culianu who revealed the close association between eros and magic, and called it the birthplace of the modern sciences of propaganda and advertising. The serial killer is, after all, a "lust" killer; his crimes are referred to as "sexual homicides" and it is for this reason that we have become fascinated with the serial killer, as he represents the "link" or "bond" between sex (eros) and magic, sex and transformation. The transformation that is so much a part of the Harris novels is also the core impulse behind the shaman; it was also a major factor in the thinking of serial killers such as Jeffrey Dahmer.

Yet, before we examine the deeper processes of the shaman and the serial killer, let us remind ourselves of the political uses of psychology and of "brainwashing," so that we can put this all into some kind of context. It would be useful to understand that there exist in the United States—and probably in many other countries as well—two "sciences" that run parallel to each other. As James Bamford described in his definitive study of the National Security Agency, *The Puzzle Palace*, in 1982, the scientific establishment is not necessarily completely up-to-date on new developments that affect national security considerations. Much science is conducted behind closed, locked, and even hidden and disappearing doors. The NSA itself has had an enormous influence on the development of computer science, as they needed more and more powerful machines to create cyphers and to decrypt the cyphers of other countries. The NSA also had a tremendous influence on the development of space science, as they struggled to design spy satellites that could eavesdrop on conversations many miles below their orbits. The NSA—and similar organizations around the globe—of necessity have to be several years, or even several generations, beyond what is taking place in the civilian scientific community.[38] The same, it may be safely assumed, is true of psychiatric science as well.

Psychiatry being generally beyond the purview of the NSA, the military intelligence groups and the CIA had a monopoly on new developments in this area, as we have seen. Like the NSA and computer technology, the CIA financed many specific psychiatric projects but always with an emphasis on memory and control. The creation of amnesia, the embedding of secret orders via hypnosis, or drugs, or "brainwashing" or some combination of these or other techniques, were all vitally important to intelligence organizations, and CIA-funded research made its way into the general literature (just as NSA-funded research contributed to the explosive growth of computer science and telecommunications; just as the Army's Psychological Warfare effort funded and directed the new science of communications; just as the military directed the creation of the *DSM* with its tremendous influence on generations of American psychiatrists). Other authors—such as the psychiatrist and hypnosis expert George Estabrooks, who worked for CIA—have described how the CIA was interested in the creation of multiple personality disorder. As we uncover more and more concerning the parallel interests of the Army and the Navy in these matters, we can only assume that they were also fascinated by this disorder and the potential uses to which it could be put.

Item: Lt. Commander Dr. Thomas Narut—a US Navy psychologist—claimed before a NATO conference of psychologists in Oslo that ONI (the Office of Naval Intelligence) had been using convicted murderers in a bizarre scheme to create the perfect commando. These were men from military prisons who were sent to various US embassies abroad after having been "treated" with behavior modification techniques and turned into assassins "who could kill on command." Narut was later reprimanded by the Navy and forced to retract his statement, but the cat was already out of the bag.[39]

While disturbing and possibly unethical, this program used individuals who were already murderers. In another program, it is possible that the CIA actually contributed to the creation of a famous killer:

Item: It is revealed that Ted Kaczynski, the famed "Unabomber," had been a test subject in a CIA mind-control project during his university days. A brilliant mathematician, Kaczynski would escape from society and hole up in a cabin in the Montana woods until his capture by federal agents, after his letter bombs killed three people and wounded twenty-three over a course of seventeen years. The man who experimented upon him was none other than Dr. Henry A. Murray, the former OSS psychiatrist for whom Timothy Leary had developed a psilocybin experimentation program at Harvard in 1960 after his return from a trip to Mexico. Kaczynski was one of only twenty-two Harvard undergrads who were part of this secret project from the fall of 1959 to the spring of 1962, a program based loosely on OSS interrogation methods and designed to break down the student's personality. The personality assessment tests devised by Murray for the OSS during the war were conceived as an attempt to find out which candidates would do well under interrogation and torture; some OSS candidates broke down even *before* the tests were administered, so frightening were the rumors about their intensity. Kaczynski, who needed the money and volunteered for these tests without being told what to expect, began to develop signs of emotional stress and a hatred for society as his Harvard years progressed. Eventually, less than ten years after the completion of the Harvard tests, he disappeared into the Montana woods, wrote his journals and a long Manifesto that some critics have called "brilliant," and mailed bombs all over America.[40]

MISBEGOTTEN SONS

Stuart Clark, a Professor of History at the University of Swansea (and winner of the Royal Historical Society's Gladstone History Prize in 1997) has written a book that examines the politics of witchcraft. Entitled *Thinking With Demons: the Idea of Witchcraft in Early Modern Europe*, it is a thorough examination not only of the political issues surrounding the idea of witchcraft but also of politics and religion in general, especially the uncomfortable relationship between political institutions, and particularly political leaders, and the Church, and how witchcraft at once tested and in some cases validated the supernatural role of the King. Although he is writing of a time hundreds of years in the past, his theme could just as easily be ported to a modern context:

> To add confessional uniformity to institutional centralization—to control minds as well as bodies—was an understandable ambition of governments, and the pursuit of spiritual dissidents in the courts could be its practical outcome. Control of political loyalties was, after all, felt to rest on control of denominational ones.[41]

It is this strange alliance between political loyalties and denominational ones that paved the way for the excesses—not only of the Inquisition, which began after all with the persecution of the Cathars, a heretical sect that threatened political hegemony in France—but also of the mind-control efforts of modern governments. In the last hundred years, as psychiatry became become more popular and influential, especially as it tried to mimic the scientific method on which so much technology is based, the social role of religion in the West came under increasing pressure. Religious beliefs were considered in the light of psychopathologies, for instance in William Sargant's study of religious conversion and "brainwashing," but also in the Soviet Union, which saw religious affiliation in the same light as political dissidence, both of which were cause for commitment in a mental institution. Religion—at least in the eyes of those psychologists and psychiatrists working for the government—was seen in mechanical terms, as a kind of hysterical reaction, a nervous disorder; and, just as psychopathology could be put to the service of the State (such as in the case of multiple personality disorder), so also could religious sentiment which, after all, was only a complex of mental disorders as seen in the light of psychiatric illumination.

In the West, religious affiliation implied political loyalty, and still does to some extent (witness the abortion controversy as a test not only of religious commitment but also of political action and party loyalty). In the Communist East, to be religious at all was tantamount to treason. Instead of burning the religious (or politically dissident) at the stake, they were committed to institutions or, in China, to re-education camps.

That does not mean, however, that the powers unleashed by intense religious devotion would be ignored. Neither in the West nor in the East could governments afford to disregard the weapons potential of the "disordered" mind. Strip the denominational dogma from the religious experience and one can see a range of striking similarities among the spiritualities of many cultures and beliefs. These similarities are the bedrock of the psychological approach to religion, a wellspring of unconscious mental ability that finds expression in religious sentiment, but which can just as easily be molded to other beliefs, other … loyalties. But to do that, to at once evoke and control, *manipulate*, this power one has to dig down and get one's hands dirty. And, it should be stressed, bloody.

Nietzsche wrote that what we perceive as higher culture is nothing more than the elevation of our innate savagery to a divine state. He wrote of the canonization of evil, the social consensus that transforms acts of hideous cruelty into spiritually redeeming metaphors. Society has this power, the power to bless barbarity. The early history of Christianity—of Jesus, of the Martyrs, all those dead Virgins—is of the sacralization of the Victim; the later history of Christianity is of the sacralization of the soldier, the witch-burner, the firebrand: of the Inquisition and the Crusades. Saint Ignatius Loyola, he of the Counter-Reformation, said that to give him a child for a year was to bind that child to the Church for life.

Take a child, then. As young as possible. Remove him from his family, from his parents, and bring him up in a commune with other children. The only adults are the wardens of this commune, the "trainers." Authority figures, authority without love. Keep him isolated from the rest of the world. Do not give him a name; do not allow him to develop an independent personality. Feed him poorly; dress him poorly. Keep him hungry and cold. Subject him to scenes of bloodshed and violence; make him partake in these scenarios. Brutalize his consciousness. You will be creating a monster, who will one day go out and kill … or self-destruct in some addicts' hallway. A terrorist, an assassin, a psychopath … a killer.

The serial killer fixates on a certain type of victim, a type that makes sense only to him. Someone who reminds him of his mother, maybe, according to the stereotype. Or women with long hair. Or white women only. Or prostitutes only. Or young boys.

What if—in the course of this "instruction" in our special school for children—we implant a different fixation? What if we create the psyche of the child from the ground on up? This, as discussed in Book I, is what Dr. Ewen Cameron of Montreal had pledged to do, and with CIA funding, until that fateful day in November 1963 when his services were no longer required. Like Otto Rahn, the reluctant SS officer and historian whose goal was the Holy Grail, Cameron died on a mountaintop. His records and documentation were seized by CIA officer William Buckley, who later found himself at the mercy of Arab terrorists who worked on him the same foul black magic that Cameron had used on his victims. Cameron created the technique of "depatterning," which—in its application as well as its theory—could just as easily be called "dissociating": a subject had his or her mind methodically erased, broken into pieces and scattered to the winds. Long established patterns of thought and behavior were disassembled, the patient reduced to a blank slate on which Cameron could write anything he wished. Tapes played constantly, day and night, with speakers under the patient's pillow, formulating a new purpose, a new identity, a new set of learned behavior. Like the central character in *A Clockwork Orange*, the patient would become a "New Man."

But the interest of the CIA was not in developing a technique for the soul's individuation. That would have no military or intelligence value at all. The CIA's approach was purely mechanical: how do we turn an ordinary person into a killer, in fact a killer with selective amnesia? Cameron claimed to be able to create selective amnesia. A combination of drugs, sensory deprivation, monotonous tape recordings of command phrases … but were the side effects too cumbersome? What about surgery? What if we did a little nip-and-tuck in the cerebral cortex? What then?

The example of Arthur Shawcross may be a case in point. A convicted serial killer and rapist, Shawcross had spent time in Vietnam. He claimed to have seen bloody combat in the jungles, and to have first cannibalized his victims there. The Army denied that Shawcross was anywhere near combat, and instead insisted that throughout his tour he had remained "in the rear with the gear."

When he was finally apprehended for a string of ghastly homicides in and around Rochester, New York, his defense team were not allowed copies of his military medical files. Pictures of his brain, however, showed evidence of medical intervention: symmetrical scarring that his team believed had to have been the result of surgery and not from natural causes. It was Shawcross who claimed to hear voices in his head, ghostly spirits urging him to kill. To the prosecution, he was simply malingering and faking mental illness. To the defense, he was a cipher. They needed the medical files. They could not get them.

The perspective of modern science and modern jurisprudence seems to be that, for the most part, killers are killers because they want to be killers. They have chosen evil as a way of life, and for that reason they should be punished if not executed. Society agrees in principle, of course; who needs killers loose on the streets? But when it comes to the serial killer, we are on shaky ground. As queried earlier, is a serial killer a voluntary or an involuntary murderer? Who are these "misbegotten sons"?

Any answer depends, first of all, upon determining who is, and is not, a serial killer, because the loose application of this term has caused some confusion in the popular media. By simple arithmetic, a serial killer is a killer who kills more than once; i.e., who kills victim after victim over a period of time. Obviously, hired assassins or Mafia hit men are not included in this category. That is because the term "serial killer" is a more modern term for what used to be termed a "lust killer." In other words, the criteria for labeling a person a "serial killer" is more complex than simply a long hit list of victims. A serial killer—popularly understood—is someone who kills more than one person over a period of time (i.e. "in series") due to an emotional urge (a "lust") to kill. These killers are very personally involved in their crimes; they need to see the victim up close, to spill blood with their own two hands. The act of murder is for them a kind of sexual act, and quite often the crime scenes show evidence of sexual activity with the victim, pre-mortem and/or post-mortem. The victims are all selected according to a pattern that involves either their profession (prostitution, for example) or their physical appearance, or some other quality known only to the killer.

In this way, we can see that killers such as Charles Manson do not fit the profile. The crimes for which Manson was convicted were all committed by other people, the members of his "Family." No self-respecting serial killer, motivated by the lust of killing, would assign murders to other people to carry out. Nor would they attack at a distance.

> In most serial murders, then as now, the weapon of choice was the knife, with the second most favored method being strangulation and the third, suffocation. Serial murderers, in general, do not use guns, which kill people from a distance; serial murderers want the personal satisfaction of causing death right there at hand.
>
> —Robert K. Ressler[42]

The same may be said for David Berkowitz. Try as they might, psychologists working on the Son of Sam case could not squeeze the round peg that is David Berkowitz into the square hole that is the "lust" or serial killer. While Berkowitz admits to several of the killings, he insists that he did not commit all of them and that the murders were, in fact, carried out under the orders of a cult to which he belonged. As he is in prison for life with no possibility of parole, he has no ulterior motive for making this claim. Nothing that he says at this point will reduce his sentence and he has, as mentioned, freely admitted to committing some of the murders anyway. By pleading guilty immediately after his apprehension, he denied the rest of us an examination of the available evidence which would have pointed to the existence of the murderous cult to which he belonged. In fact, the evidence collected in the twenty-five years since the time of the killings is now leaning heavily to support this allegation of a cult of murderers operating in the New York metropolitan area as well as in other parts of the country, including North Dakota and California. While many critics sincerely doubt the claims of Maury Terry and others who point to a vast conspiracy of Satanic killers (and some of Terry's claims *are* weak and poorly supported), the preponderance of the evidence in the Son of Sam case is strong enough to suggest that what Berkowitz is saying is, in fact, true.

Thus if we include Manson and Berkowitz in any study of serial murder, the statistics will become skewed and much valuable data will be lost. Whatever the psychic disorders suffered by Manson and Berkowitz—and they may be legion—the label of serial killer cannot, in all honesty, be used in their cases. In fact, Terry's evidence goes far to suggest that the Manson and Berkowitz cases may actually be related; that the cult to which Berkowitz belonged in New York City was a branch of the one to which Manson had allegiance. Just as in our study of coincidence and politics, when it comes to serial murder the coincidences also pile up, suggesting that the same dynamic applies. It is but another indication of the existence of a powerful, hidden force in nature that surfaces in time of tremendous stress in the fabric of reality.

For although there are definite and critical differences between Manson and Berkowitz on one hand, and Dahmer and Gein (for example) on the other, there are certain deeper threads that can tell us a great deal about these killers as well as about the forces they represent. In the case of Manson and Berkowitz, we can point to the dim outlines of a cult of killers using occult jargon and ritual to buttress what may have been simply a drug-related criminal operation, much the same way the Matamoros killers used *palo mayombe* as a front for what were essentially normal, criminal operations. The killers themselves believed in their respective cults (whether or not their leaders did), and committed their crimes out of a sense that they were being initiated into a circle of tremendous occult power.

In the cases of both Jeffrey Dahmer and Ed Gein—killers who operated alone and not as part of any cult or criminal organization—they were still interested in ideas of transformation (and, in Dahmer's case, occultism) and in the techniques of empowerment that murder would afford them both. In Ed Gein's case, he wanted to transform himself physically into a woman; in Dahmer's case, he simply wanted more power than he had: he wanted to create a zombie that would be his personal sex slave, a human being devoid of will who would simply not exist if Dahmer was away but who would become his plaything when he was home. On the other hand, and in the context of our argument, neither Manson nor Berkowitz were "shamanistic"; that is, they were carrying out the murderous wishes of a cult to which they belonged in the expectation (perhaps) of attaining some degree of occult power in the process, power that would be bestowed by the cult leadership as a reward for their efforts, or obtained through the very act of killing in a cult context. This is similar to the mechanism of normal initiatic cults the world over, where certain tests and trials are administered to the initiand, both to test the candidate's loyalty as well as to cause emotional and psychological stress conducive to illumination. (Even in Freemasonry, one is initiated at the point of a sword—blindfolded and bound—and made to swear all manner of frightening oaths.)

But both Dahmer and Gein were prime examples of loners, outcast from any kind of society, people with sick fantasies of blood, dismemberment, cannibalism and necrophilia, as well as confused sexual identities. They had secret chambers to which non-initiates were not allowed, places reeking of gore and offal that were monuments to their dreams of godlike power and psychic integration.

Shamanism and Serial Murder

Neurosis and initiation are the same thing, except that neurosis stops short of apotheosis, and the tremendous forces that mold all life are encysted—short circuited and turned poisonous.

—Jack Parsons

As the West became increasingly Judeo-Christian, and a split was created between humanity and nature, with nature being suspected of harboring evil, the role of the shaman was relegated to the dustbin of personal spiritual illumination. Church and temple were organized, social places that contained all the spirituality that any normal human being could ask for. They channeled the spiritual desires of men and women into socially-acceptable forms, cookie-cutter spirituality. In the process, Westerners began to lose their contact with nature, their reverence for nature, and by so doing became alienated and desperate. Jung said somewhere that Christianity caused Europeans to become schizophrenic, and perhaps he was right. We lost the ability to nurture the shamanic impulses into mutually beneficial manifestations. The pseudo-shamans we produce—the Dahmers, the Geins, the Gaceys, the Bundys—know only the impulse, but not the technology, for spiritual integration. They experience the nightmare of the "future shaman," but not the communication with God.

Sexuality was another victim of the rise of Christianity in the West. The expression of sexuality was severely suppressed by the Church, and a caste of celibate priests and nuns was created—after a period of hundreds of years as the Church consolidated its political and economic power in Rome—and sex was considered to be a kind of necessary evil, useful only for procreation. To enjoy sexuality was to be sinful. Women were characterized as wanton sexual creatures, whose constant thirst for sex made them easy prey for the Devil, who turned them into witches and made them kiss his buttocks as a sign of their submission to his infernal will.

The sexual content of serial murder is well-known. Virtually all serial killings have a strong sexual element, whether it is actual sex with the victim before or after death—or during the murder itself—or sexual mutilation, or display of the victim's genitalia, etc. Why, then, is serial murder not simply serial rape? Why does murder become involved in what seems to be only a sex crime, a mutation of normal sexual affection and desire into something violent and morbid? Is it because we in the West have associated sex with punishment, with death—with spiritual death—for so long that our serial killers are only demonstrating to us our own repressed desires? Perhaps. And perhaps there is even a deeper context in which to look at serial murder.

Human sexuality is, quite apart from Christian repressions, a highly questionable phenomenon, and belongs, at least potentially, among the extreme rather than the ordinary experiences of humanity. Tamed as it may be, sexuality remains one of the demonic forces in human consciousness—pushing us at intervals close to taboo and dangerous desires, which range from the impulse to commit sudden arbitrary violence upon another person to the voluptuous yearning for the extinction of one's consciousness, for death itself.

—Susan Sontag[43]

The historian of religion Mircea Eliade has written about sexuality and shamanism, albeit briefly. In his monumental work entitled *Shamanism,* he has examined the role of sexual energy and gender-transfer in shamanistic circles around the world. Some shamans are called to change their sex; to wear the clothing and adopt the mannerisms of the other sex and even to marry as if they had truly changed gender. It is interesting to note that in some cultures, although the call to switch gender is understood to occasionally be part of the initiatic process, some "future shamans" prefer suicide.[44] Thus, the call is seen as powerful and demanding, and the shaman sees no way out of his predicament other than self-extermination. Eliade goes on to state that "transvestitism and ritual change of sex are found, for example, in Indonesia (the *manang bali* of the Sea Dyak), in South America (Patagonians and Araucanians), and among certain North American tribes (Arapaho, Cheyenne, Ute, etc.)."[45]

In a later chapter, one devoted to Asian shamanism, Eliade confronts certain shamanistic cults of Tibet in which the identical stage of decapitation, dismemberment, and cannibalism is undergone by an initiate—albeit in a state of meditation and trance and not in actuality—at the hands of a goddess, brandishing a sword. The flesh and blood of the initiate is given to demons and wild beasts, and eventually the initiate is reborn after this horrifying experience.[46] Eliade sees in tantrism remnants of ancient shamanistic practices concerning sex and sexual energy, such as the Tibetan practice of "mystical heat" in which the initiate is made to conserve his sexual energy and transform it into a kind of bodily heat so intense that he is able to dry wet blankets on his skin outdoors in the winter.[47] This idea of "mystical heat" was not unknown to shamans of various other countries and climates, and was inextricably linked to healing of physical illnesses in others, and in a bizarre form of self-mutilation in which the body of the shaman is "heated" in this mystical fashion, as well as his knife. When both knife and body have been heated to the right temperature, the shaman opens a wound in his own abdomen without pain.[48]

The shamans may also be the sexual partners of spiritual forces, spirits of the opposite sex who come to the initiate on his sick-bed (for the initiation always begins in illness of some kind) and tell the future shaman that he has been selected as a husband. To refuse is to die. The shaman thus selected may find himself unable to satisfy a mortal woman, or to refuse all sexual contact except with this ethereal entity who nonetheless teaches him shamanism over a period of years. Many of the public rituals performed by shamans are sexual in nature, using elaborately carved wooden phalluses for example, accompanied by the beating of the drum and hypnotic incantations.[49] We are reminded of Dahmer on his couch, in trance, in mystical communion with the demon who tells him to do "scary things."

We may also remember Foucault and his "blood and sex" theory. Does the shaman live on the tangent between blood and sex? Is the "place between the worlds" that is symbolized (or actualized) by the magic circle, the *hounfort*, the temple, the place between blood and sex, between death and rebirth, between nature and … murder? Is the magic circle really a place of healing, not only of physical ailments and mental disorders, but of the rift between who we are and who we wish to become, between what is our nature and what society demands of us? Possibly the only way for the sick, the disturbed, to become whole—to become healed—is to communicate directly with God.

If the shamanistic process is allowed to continue on its normal route, the future shaman will recover from his illness after an experience of ascending into the heavens and becoming reborn as a shaman. It is an ecstatic journey that puts the shaman into contact with higher forces, centering him and empowering him not only as a shaman but as a human being, as a productive and important member of his tribe: someone who has been to the Other Side and come back with the ability to predict the future and heal the sick. And if the shamanistic process is not allowed to continue?

The total crisis of the future shaman, sometimes leading to complete disintegration of the personality and to madness, can be valuated not only as an initiatory death but also as a symbolic return to the precosmogonic Chaos, to the amorphous and indescribable state that precedes any cosmogony. Now, as we know, for archaic and traditional cultures, a symbolic return to Chaos is equivalent to preparing a new Creation. It follows that we may interpret the psychic Chaos of the future shaman as a sign that the profane man is being "dissolved" and a new personality being prepared for birth.

—Mircea Eliade[50]

For modern psychiatry, every mental breakdown—every mental illness, every mental disorder—has its origin somewhere in the patient's life. A person does not go insane for reasons that are not part of his personal history. Therefore, what Eliade is saying would be considered suspect by psychiatrists. How could a person go insane—how could his personality disintegrate to that extent—due to an *external* influence? There is either an organic reason (such as a hormonal imbalance or some other chemical reason, or physical trauma of some sort, such as a blow to the head), or there is a precipitating cause in the patient's immediate environment. Yet, in the context of shamanism, the precipitating cause is the summons of a spirit. Even more threatening, the shaman is a person who has gone "through" madness and has become "cured" without the benefit of modern psychiatric technique. Even more astonishing, this person who had once been mad is now a valued and even a revered member of his society, and *all due to the fact of his madness and subsequent cure.*

The controversial Scottish psychiatrist (and sometime visitor to the Timothy Leary/William Hitchcock estate at Millbrook) R. D. Laing wrote in 1967, in *The Politics of Experience,*

> When a person goes mad, a profound transposition of his place in relation to all domains of being occurs.... *Nevertheless, he can often be to us, even through his profound wretchedness and disintegration, the hierophant of the sacred.* An exile from the scene of being as we know it, he is an alien, a stranger signaling to us from the void in which he is foundering, a void which may be peopled by presences that we do not even dream of. They used to be called demons and spirits.... Madness need not be all breakdown. It may also be breakthrough. (emphasis added)[51]

Madness and psychic disintegration (dissociation?) leading to ... spiritual breakthrough, psychic powers, attainment, illumination: the shaman, the medicine man, the magician.

When the governments of the world undertook their various and individual programs for exploring the possibility of mind control, they were seeking a way to "disintegrate" the personality of a subject and then rebuild it in some other, more convenient, form. The efforts of Dr. Cameron in Montreal were certainly perfect examples of this approach. If the government—or, at least, its intelligence agencies—could arrogate to themselves the power of initiation then they could indeed create a "cult of intelligence" to which their most valuable members would not even be aware they belonged. In Eliade's world of shamanism, the shaman-to-be began in illness—mental illness or even epilepsy or some epileptoid disorder—and found his personality "disintegrating," his body being dismembered and disemboweled on some level, and then gradually became whole again and the proud owner of a "new" personality. The problem with this process—in the eyes of government agencies—would be the time it took to develop this new personality and the ambiguity of that personality: why not design the new personality from scratch and drag the unsuspecting "shaman" through the entire initiatic process in record time with drugs, sensory deprivation, and all the other tools of the trade? To that end they explored the shamanistic repertoire of hallucinogenic drugs, ritual, hypnosis, and whatever else they could find, not realizing that they were—in the eyes of shamans, mystics, magicians everywhere—becoming "black magicians" in the process. Just like every other wistful and lazy would-be occultist with the flowery titles and advanced degrees of imaginary spiritual attainments, the CIA psychiatrists wanted all the benefits of the initiatic process but without the expense of time and effort required to do it right. They also wanted complete control over the finished product; this, from people who had not been through the process themselves and had no idea what changes it would create in the minds—dare we say "souls"?—of their subjects. They were wading into deep waters, the same waters that could create a shaman … or serial killer.

The real problem is that people like Dahmer present a dilemma for society, which has not evolved proper ways to deal with them. Focusing on notions of right and wrong does not begin to approach the complex reality of what Dahmer did.

—FBI Profiler Robert K. Ressler[52]

It is a cliché of modern psychiatry that a child who has been abused will grow into an adult who abuses children. What about the serial killer? Obviously, he was not "killed" as a child, was not dismembered or eviscerated. What causes the escalation from physical and sexual abuse into serial murder, into lust killing? If an adult abuser is only "acting out" what he has experienced as a child, is the serial killer acting out a different experience, a different reality? What were the nightmares of Jeffrey Dahmer like? Did he wake up one morning, feverish and shaking, from a vision of hell? Did he truly hear a voice telling him to do "scary things"? A normal therapeutic course would probably not have helped Dahmer very much; he would have known to keep the darker elements of his nature quite hidden. Patients fool therapists all the time, particularly sociopathic patients. Perhaps what Dahmer needed was not therapy, but initiation.

If, as Mircea Eliade said, those who were mentally ill "became shamans precisely because they had succeeded in becoming cured," then I submit that those who were mentally ill (like Dahmer, like Gein), became serial killers precisely because they had *not* succeeded in becoming cured. I submit that the shamanic impulse has not died, it has only been suppressed in our society, and thrown in with diagnoses of schizophrenia and other mental disorders; that characterizing what used to be understood as a mystical state as, instead, evidence of psychosis has robbed us of any hope of spiritual comprehension. And generations of psychiatrists and psychologists since at least the time of Freud have warned us what to expect when strong emotional impulses are denied.

This is not to suggest that serial killers are somehow holy or spiritual beings; far from it. The call to become a shaman is not necessarily divine; it could as easily be demonic. How would we know the difference? We have lost our moral compass in a society that tolerates priestly pederasty, the avarice of televangelists, the cupidity of politicians. We get our education in ethics from made-for-tv-movies and obnoxious political talk show hosts. Our spiritual lives have been canned for so long, we wouldn't recognize "fresh" if it grew in our backyards. The spiritual aspirations of Americans—like that of most Westerners—have been manipulated by social forces for so long, it would be amazing if modern America could produce a single person worthy of canonization by a church worthy to canonize. Monotheism brought with it a political structure that mimics that of the monarchy; even Hell, in the medieval grimoires, is peopled with kings and dukes and princes and, yes, presidents. More than anything else, the Postwar 1950s brought with it not only the man in the grey flannel suit, but the priest, the minister, and the rabbi in the grey flannel suit. The excesses of the 1960s were an obvious and predictable reaction against the stifling of the spiritual impulse to celebrate, to worship life in all its forms, to experience spiritual ecstasy.

The serial killer is the dark side of that force, the symbol of a twisted and corrupt spiritual desire forced to feed in silence and solitude on its own flesh and blood.

And when the CIA began to experiment on the minds of violent offenders with drugs and behavior modification and God knows what else, they were playing hide-and-seek in the dungeon with Hannibal Lecter. And when they experimented on children, dosing them with huge amounts of LSD and other hallucinogens, they were opening the very gates of hell itself. This is not to apportion blame, but to state a simple fact regardless of who or what is to blame, if anyone, if anything. With respect to the study of serial murderers and shamans, the CIA was contributing with ravaged minds and body bags, courtesy of Doctors Cameron, Gottlieb, Estabrooks, and so many others.

Imagine a government-run Zen monastery in which the penalty for not solving your koan is execution by a firing squad.

Endnotes

[1] Mircea Eliade, *Rites and Symbols of Initiation*, Harper Torchbooks, NY, 1965, p. 88
[2] Stuart Clark, *Thinking With Demons: The Idea of Witchcraft in Early Modern Europe*, Oxford University Press, Oxford, 1999, p. 554
[3] Peter Dale Scott, *Deep Politics and the Death of JFK*, University of California Press, Berkeley, 1996, p. 17 and 21
[4] Aleister Crowley, *Moonchild*, Mandrake Press, London, 1929, p. 29-30
[5] Colin A. Ross, *Dissociative Identity Disorder: Diagnosis, Clinical Features, and Treatment of Multiple Personality*, John Wiley & Sons, NY, 1997, p. 6
[6] *Diagnostic and Statistical Manual: Mental Disorders*, American Psychiatric Association, Washington, D.C., 1952, p. vi
[7] Ibid., p. vi-vii
[8] Ibid., p. vii
[9] Ibid., p. vii
[10] Crowley, op. cit., p. 179
[11] Eliade, op. cit., p. 68-72
[12] Carl G. Jung, *Analytical Psychology, Its Theory and Practice*, Vintage Books, NY, 1970, p. 38
[13] Susan Sontag, "Approaching Artaud," *Under The Sign of Saturn*, Farrar, Straus, Giroux, NY, 1980, p. 64
[14] Ibid., p. 64-65
[15] Bettina L. Knapp, *Antonin Artaud, Man of Vision*. Discus, NY, 1971, p. 183
[16] Eliade, op. cit., p. 88-89
[17] T. K. Oesterreich, *Possession: Demoniacal and Other*, University Books, NY, 1966, p. xiv
[18] Friedrich Nietzsche, *Beyond Good and Evil*, Vintage, NY, 1966, p. 90
[19] Warren Commission Exhibits 2196 and 2443
[20] Anthony Summers, *The Kennedy Conspiracy*, Warner Books, NY, 1996, p. 344
[21] Nietzsche, op. cit., p. 89
[22] Robert Graysmith, *Zodiac Unmasked*, Berkley Books, NY, 2003, p. 151
[23] Milwaukee *Sentinel*, 7/27/91, page 5, Section A; and Joel Norris, *Jeffrey Dahmer*, Pinnacle Books, NY, 1992, p. 79-80
[24] Norris, op. cit., p. 80
[25] Ibid., p. 65
[26] Ibid., p. 280
[27] FBI transcript dated 9/11/92, File # 7-MW-26057-83, p. 10
[28] Ibid., p. 10
[29] Robert K. Ressler & Tom Schachtman, *I Have Lived in the Monster*, St Martin's, NY, 1998, p. 150-1
[30] Ibid., p. 151
[31] Milwaukee *Sentinel*, Sept 12, 1991, page 10A, by Joe Manning

[32] Milwaukee *Sentinel*, Sept 11, 1991, Final Edition, page 1A, by Rick Romell
[33] Kenneth Grant, *Outside the Circles of Time*, Frederick Muller, London, 1980, p. 206
[34] Kenneth Grant, *The Magical Revival*, Frederick Muller, London, 1972, p. 116
[35] Ressler, op. cit., p. 160
[36] David Sexton, *The Strange World of Thomas Harris*, Short Books, London, 2001, ISBN 0-571-20845-2
[37] Ibid., p. 152 and see Frances A. Yates, *The Art of Memory*, University of Chicago Press, Chicago, 1966
[38] James Bamford, *The Puzzle Palace*, Penguin Books, New York, 1983, p. 507-511
[39] Martin, Harry V. and Caul, David, "Mind Control," *Napa Valley Sentinel*, August-November, 1991
[40] Alston Chase, "Harvard and the Making of the Unabomber," *The Atlantic Monthly*, June 2000
[41] Clark, op. cit., p. 554
[42] Ressler, op. cit., p. 54
[43] Susan Sontag, "The Pornographic Imagination," in Bataille, *Story of the Eye*, Penguin, London, 2001 p. 103 (originally published in 1967, in synchronicity with Laing, below)
[44] Mircea Eliade, *Shamanism*, Arkana, NY, 1989, p. 258
[45] Ibid., p. 258
[46] Ibid., p. 436
[47] Ibid., p. 437
[48] Ibid., p. 256-257
[49] Ibid., p. 71-81
[50] Eliade, op. cit., p. 89
[51] R.D. Laing, *The Politics of Experience*, Pantheon, NY, 1967, p. 133
[52] Ressler, op. cit., p. 160

Death is the focus of many known secret society group occult rituals, such as the current Bohemia Grove's Cremation of Care Ceremony, which includes a realistic immolation in front of a giant stone owl, and the many Masonic bloody oaths and staged ritualistic murderous dramas. The Order of Skull and Bone's Temple, commonly known as the Tomb, is where initiates may fathom their mortality snugly ensconced within a coffin, and chants about death are part of the initiatory experience. Unwitting initiate, Dr. Frank Olson pulled into one of Dr. Sidney Gottlieb's CIA mind-bending misadventures and, without the proper set and setting, lost his life … for real.

Chapter Seventeen

Voluntary Madness

The deliberately induced psychotic state, which in certain unstable individuals might easily lead to a real psychosis, is a danger that needs to be taken very seriously indeed. These things really are dangerous and ought not to be meddled with in our typically Western way. It is a meddling with fate, which strikes at the very roots of human existence and can let loose a flood of sufferings of which no sane person ever dreamed.

—C.G. Jung, "Psychological Commentary" to the *Tibetan Book of the Dead*, p. xlvi

… what we are basically talking about is an activity which took place in the country that involved the perversion and the corruption of many of our outstanding research centers in this country, with CIA funds, where some of our top researchers were unwittingly involved in research sponsored by the Agency in which they had no knowledge of the background or the support for. Much of it was done with American citizens who were completely unknowing in terms of taking various drugs, and there are perhaps any number of Americans who are walking around today on the east coast or west coast who were given drugs, with all the kinds of physical and psychological damage that can be caused. We have gone over that in very careful detail, and it is significant and severe indeed.

—Senator Edward Kennedy, during 1977 Senate Hearing Testimony of CIA Director Stansfield Turner on MK-ULTRA, August 3, 1977

The notion that unreason as well as reason rules us from above is psychologically painful. This intolerability has given rise to the consoling world-views of religion …

—Peter Dale Scott, *Deep Politics*[1]

The séance was the true laboratory for the study of multiple personality.

—Daniel Lomas, *The Haunted Self*[2]

We in the West have always had a hard time with madness. We can't define it, but we know what it is when we see it. Like the term "insanity," it is not a clinical definition of a mental state or disorder, but a general epithet or legal characterization. Michel Foucault has written extensively and eloquently about the ways in which the West has viewed and treated the "mad," and we are all familiar with the cliches that tell us that primitive people believed the mad were "touched by the gods," and were therefore revered.

Mircea Eliade has written at length about the shamanistic vocation and has described the agonies of the shaman-to-be as a psychopathology, thus linking the rituals of initiation with the frightening madness of the berserker and "witch doctor." Yet, Eliade was not the only one to see something redemptive and salvageable in the acute mental disorders of the primitive occultists. Government leaders and military men also found reason to rejoice in the gibberings of the hopelessly insane.

While a detailed examination of the official attitudes towards mental illness is beyond the scope of this work, a brief look at the unwholesome way in which mental illness has been confused with both government policies and tactical weapons is in order.

What we undertake to show in this chapter is nothing less than a technique for going insane. So far, most discussions of this topic have been general and allusive. We will attempt a more direct approach here. Based on the practices of voluntary madmen going back millennia, and refined by modern psychiatric and behaviorist methods as shown in the papers and reports coming out of military and intelligence agency mind-control and behavior-control programs, the goal of this technique is to go mad *temporarily* and return in one piece.

Because this is probably the first time such a technique has ever been described fully, the vocabulary and concepts may appear strange at first, bordering on the superstitious. Remember that this is a process of going insane, and a bizarre or off-beat appearance should not be demoralizing.

What we are going to do is utilize the methodology of the shaman and the magician, the artist and the visionary—who have made a kind of science out of this temporary insanity—but within the framework of the projects of Cameron, Estabrooks, Gottlieb, et al. In other words, we will use occultism and mind control to describe each other and so come to a better understanding of both. Once the basic method of "voluntary madness" is understood by examining the actual processes, then we can better understand how it is being used today.

Merely reading the following pages will not cause madness; but putting the methods into practice in a serious attempt will cause serious psychic dislocation. Therefore caution is necessary.

SET AND SETTING

Magick is the art and science of causing change to occur in conformity with will.
—Aleister Crowley

Many of our more famous artists, writers and musicians have had serious mental problems. We can think of Van Gogh, Artaud, Nietzsche, and many others who have gone insane, either temporarily or permanently. It almost seems a prerequisite for creativity. What is not so well known, though, is that there was a tendency among artists of the past hundred years or so to court insanity as a means of reaching altered states of consciousness. The boundary between the artist and the psychopath is a shifting one, more of a twilight horizon in which it is difficult to separate sea and sky than a solid firebreak designed to protect hearth and home. What is even more interesting is that the same concept is at the heart of mysticism and magic. Shamans, artists, mystics … and psychopaths.

When the CIA began to unravel the smoking entrails of consciousness, they understood that the artistic community was an obvious medium for their experimentation. After all, didn't novelist and philosopher Aldous Huxley—a colleague of CIA drug experimenter and psychic researcher Dr. Humphrey Ormond, who provided some of the drugs Huxley took—write the seminal manifesto for the drug culture in *The Doors of Perception*? And didn't the cult-rock band The Doors take their name, inspiration and modus vivendi from Huxley's work? And didn't Jim Morrison of The Doors eventually become initiated into witchcraft? Just pulling at that single thread is suggestive enough. See what happens when we pull at the entire tapestry.

The psycho-biographies of artists and writers—full of alcohol, drugs, sex, and "derangement"—are rarely informative when it comes to the actual processes that led them on their individual paths to perdition. We can read a biography of August Strindberg and still be no closer to the process he (successfully) followed that led him into insanity and back out again. Yet, if we take a page from the acid book of the Sixties, we just might be able to understand what happened to these people and what really goes on in the heart and soul of creative thinkers when they decide to test the boundaries of reality and consciousness.

Anyone who went through the Sixties (and can still remember them) will find the phrase "set and setting" very familiar. Basically, it means that before one takes an acid trip—before, that is, one ingests a tab of LSD-25—it is vitally important to ensure that the environment is conducive to the "trip" and that one's mental state is likewise calm and receptive. This "hallowing" of the space before a religious ritual (and, indeed, before the twentieth century the only people who took hallucinogens were those being initiated into shamanistic cults, in Europe, Latin America, Africa, and Asia) is something we come across in every instance of occult and religious practice. While this is perceived by anthropologists and archaeologists as a kind of superstitious identification of the city-state or the temple with heaven itself, when we apply this same reasoning to the acid trip or the psilocybin experience, we discover that it is vitally important to the success of the undertaking that the environment within which one "drops acid" has been carefully selected and prepared beforehand. It was not unusual in the Sixties to see the environment prepared with burning incense, candles, soft music, etc. And, as in the tantric and yogic ashrams of the East, there was generally also a Guide.

The guided trip was a mainstay of the acid culture in the early days of the Postwar era. It was patterned—consciously or unconsciously—after the rites of the Mexican shamans who performed their initiations with peyote (mescaline) or mushrooms (psilocybin). Naturally, as acid became more and more popular and easily available, it lost its "sacramental" allure and simply became another drug, another escape valve from society and the environment, and then we experienced the burn-outs and the suicides and all the trauma of the "bad trip."

There was a precedent for all of this in the workbooks of the European ceremonial magicians, the mysterious *grimoires.* While it was believed that the druggies who were going "voluntarily mad" were some kind of modern social aberration, the grimoires were evidence that going insane voluntarily was a long and serious tradition going back for nearly a thousand years. Before the medieval grimoires, however, there were books of magic spells in ancient Egypt and even spells carved into wet clay cylinders in the firelight of Mesopotamia and Sumer. Yet, the casting of spells is not, in and of itself, the central element of ceremonial magic, and these practices—while cognate with magic—are not what we seek, for a successful practitioner of magic is one who has made some contact with the Other. The spells and workbooks of the sorcerer and witch are only recipes to assist one who has already become a "cook."

In the grimoires, we find the same reliance upon set and setting that we will come across again, hundreds of years later in a different context. (Set and setting will also be recognized as a crucial element in psychological warfare and interrogation techniques. The process is all of a piece, and we may be able to understand the entire gestalt better if we look at how each of these practices describes and reinforces the others.)

In order to become a successful magician—according to the grimoires—one must first evoke spiritual forces. One must make contact with the spirit world. This is identical to the training of a shaman, the more primitive and even pre-literate school of magic. For the ceremonial magician, "set and setting" is crucial. It lays the groundwork for the ritual to follow, and if it is not meticulously planned beforehand then the entire endeavor is doomed to failure. The day and time for the ritual of evoking spiritual forces must be selected long in advance. This will be based on the nature of the spiritual force to be evoked. For the European ceremonial magician—as for the Asian fakir, tantrist, saddhu, or Daoist—this is linked to astrological data. For instance, there are spiritual forces (angels, demons, elementals) that have particular affinity for one or other of the stars or planets or zodiacal signs or elements. Once the appropriate spiritual force has been identified, and its affinity understood, then a day and hour appropriate to that affinity is selected for the ritual.

This is "set and setting" taken to an extreme, perhaps, but it is based on an assumption that was quite common in medieval times and, actually, for thousands of years of recorded human history before then: the doctrine of correspondences. This doctrine may fairly be said to be the doctrine of "co-incidences" as well, as we shall see, and is very probably the key to the entire realm of what we have been calling "sinister forces."

The Romanian-born historian of religion, Ioan Culianu, was probably the first to delve deeply into the medieval doctrine of the occult link and to show its relevance not only to the history of the Renaissance but to modern history as well. His published writings on the subject are nothing short of revolutionary, both for their breadth of scholarship as well as for the brilliant way he expresses his theories. It is a serious and tragic loss to the history of religion that he was murdered at the University of Chicago in 1991, a crime that has remained unsolved but, which has been laid at the door of the Romanian secret police.

Culianu's most fascinating contribution was *Eros and Magic in the Renaissance*, a work that is based in part on the writings of the philosopher-magician Giordano Bruno and particularly on his *De vinculis*, a work that surpasses Machiavelli's *The Prince* in its sheer audacity. *De vinculis*—or "Of the link"—is a virtual operating manual for consensus reality. While it appears on its face to be an introduction to a method of conjuring demons, it is also a guide to psychological warfare, probably the earliest ever written. Culianu understood the relationship between magic and politics as no other before him, and while his scholarship may be daunting to a non-academic it is nonetheless a valuable contribution to this discussion.

There is no space to go into a detailed exposition of *Eros and Magic*, but instead we will focus on *De vinculis* and Giordano Bruno, because *De vinculis* is about more than just the magical link, and Giordano Bruno is more than just a philosopher who ran afoul of the Inquisition. In fact, Bruno was himself a magician-spy, in the mold of the English magician-spy John Dee, and their paths crossed more than once.

Giordano Bruno was a Neapolitan philosopher, writer, former priest, heretic, and was excommunicated from the Church when he wrote his literary masterpieces. Bruno is probably the closest the western world has come to the living embodiment of the satanic priest, a character that Dennis Wheatley has created in several of his occult novels and which seems fantastic in the present-day. He "aspired to the mantle" of Dr. John Dee,[3] the magician, mathematician, astrologer and spy in the service of Queen Elizabeth I of England, a man renowned throughout Europe for the breadth of his knowledge of both the mundane and the spiritual realms. It was to the same service of Elizabeth I that Giordano Bruno once worked as a deep-cover intelligence officer, uncovering Catholic conspiracies against the Queen during his stay at a house in London.

Bruno's hatred of the Catholic Church ran very deep. He had been a Catholic priest himself, one who abandoned the Holy Orders and "defrocked" himself, becoming in the process excommunicate and forbidden by the Church to even attend Mass, much less celebrate it. His hatred of what he saw as Papal idiocy and criminality led him to support various Protestant groups and operations at every opportunity, although he did not consider himself a Christian at all much less a Protestant, and could be more correctly identified as a kind of pagan, a New Age philosopher quite ahead of his time; certainly, he was a magician, and the bulk of his writings after the "Embassy affair" of 1584—in which his espionage activities against French Ambassador to England Michel de Castelnau resulted in the arrest and execution of various individuals who were conspiring with the Church against the Queen—were about occultism.[4]

Bruno is described as using or contemplating four "arms" or methods of toppling the Papacy: armed force, fraud (or, as Bruno called it, the "art of dissimulation" which, in Bruno's case, included espionage), ridicule, and magic.[5]

> ...his last works ... are indeed about magic ... showing that he intended to pull off the ultimate coup against the papacy by personally enchanting Pope Clement VIII ... one might well think that having failed to shake the papacy by force, fraud or ridicule he was driven to magic as a last resort. And I doubt that we can use against it the history of a cool-headed secret agent we now know, for it seems fairly clear to me that, in exploring in *De vinculis* the ways by which affinities personal and cosmic might be manipulated for political ends, Bruno was thinking of his management of Castelnau as a model of how the thing should be done.[6]

In *Giordano Bruno and the Embassy Affair*, John Bossy records several instances in which Bruno and Dr. Dee met each other, either at Dee's home in Mortlake or in Prague. Dee was reputed to have the best library in England, and they shared a common interest in the occult as well as in espionage. As mentioned in *Unholy Alliance*, there is no doubt now that John Dee was a spy for the court of Queen Elizabeth I at a time when religious, colonial and territorial wars were rampant. The original 007—literally—Dee was involved in espionage for the queen during his visits to the Continent, where he ran into Bruno once again in Prague, the site of the famous evocation of the angelic forces that has come down to us as the system of Enochian magic, a system very badly understood by many of today's practitioners.

Bruno would eventually be captured by the Inquisition and put to death by being burned at the stake in Campo dei Fiori in Rome on February 17, 1600, on orders of the same Pope Clement VIII he had attempted to destroy through magic. To understand what Bruno was up to—and to understand even better how this system has been used since then by politicians, military strategists, spies and terrorists—we will look at *De vinculis*, which gives the show away.

As far as I know, this small book has not been translated into English although both Latin and Italian copies exist. I base my brief discussion on my own translations of same as well as on Ioan Culianu's extended study of Bruno and his work.

Is the Western State, in our time, a true magician, or is it a sorcerer's apprentice who sets in motion dark and uncontrollable forces?
—Ioan P. Culianu[7]

Ioan Culianu (whose patronymic is spelled variously as Culianu, Coulianu, Couliano) was born on January 5, 1950 in Romania at a time of tremendous political upheaval in that country, due to the Communist takeover of the government and the abdication of the young King Michael. His story is one familiar to many Eastern Europeans of a certain age: political repression, poverty, lack of exposure to the West and its suspiciously alluring ideas of democracy and capitalism. The man who would become his mentor, the extremely influential Mircea Eliade, was also a Romanian, and one who had made his home in the West … specifically at the University of Chicago where he made a name for himself as an authority in the history of religions. Eliade's books—notably *Shamanism, The Myth of the Eternal Return, The Quest* and *Images and Symbols*—have been and will be cited many times during the course of this work.

Eliade was a hero to the young Culianu, who worked assiduously to get himself noticed by the master with an eye to working with him in the United States. Emigrating to Italy—actually overstaying on a special exit visa from Romania that allowed him to attend a seminar there—he wound up in a camp for displaced persons and even attempted suicide, driven to despair over his lack of legal status and any way to earn a living, coupled with increasingly dismal news from home. Eventually, however, he managed to work his way out of his depression and through a series of contacts and clever networking his brilliance came to the attention of the University of Milan, and he began to write many excellent articles, reviews and monographs on Renaissance studies, philosophy, religion, and related subjects during his tenure there and at the Netherlands Institute for Advanced Study, where he was a Fellow.

This outpouring of work and garnership of professional accolades finally earned him the attention of Mircea Eliade, and he eventually wound up in America with a professorship at the same University of Chicago in 1985.

This was largely due to the impact of two important works published by Culianu in 1984. One was a study of shamanism and ecstasy; the next was *Eros and Magic in the Renaissance*, a work begun when Culianu was only nineteen. It is on the basis of this last work that his reputation was assured, both in Europe (where it was first published in France) and then in the United States when *Eros and Magic* became available in English translation. (It was also in 1984 that Archbishop Valerian Trifa of the Romanian Orthodox Church was finally deported, when it became known that he had been a Nazi and member of the Iron Guard during the war; in fact, it fell upon Culianu's shoulders to defend his mentor, Mircea Eliade, from the same claim, once it was revealed that Eliade—à la Carl Jung—had written admiringly of the Iron Guardists, albeit before their name became synonymous with the worst sort of atrocities.)

Culianu himself was fascinated by the occult and what occultism says about reality and consciousness. He studied the medieval witchcraft trials, Renaissance magic, the Tarot, even conducting seminars on the symbolism in the popular David Lynch television series *Twin Peaks*. He wrote about gnosticism, shamanism, the use of drugs in altered states of consciousness ... and all from a serious, academic viewpoint with virtually every line buttressed by extensive citations and primary sources in Latin, Italian, German, English, and many other languages. He was at once serious and playful, a man who felt that modern society had lost its connection to the miraculous, to the metaphysical, and that because of this loss we were in no position to understand the writings of men like Bruno who formulated entire technologies for reorganizing the human mind, beginning with memory and extending to every mental and psychological faculty.

Eros and Magic in the Renaissance concentrates on three seminal figures in Renaissance philosophy, magic, and—at least in Bruno's case—politics. Aside from Giordano Bruno, Culianu discusses Marsilio Ficino and Pico della Mirandola: three men who had an enormous influence over the development of hermetic thought during the Renaissance. Pico della Mirandola was a student of Ficino, and Giordano Bruno drew his inspiration from both.

Although Bruno had written a number of famous and influential works, Culianu concentrates on *De vinculis en genere*, sometimes referred to simply as *De vinculis* or "Of Links." These links, according to Bruno, are those between human beings, but they could just as easily be those that link God to humans; the links to which he refers are any connections that could be made between any created objects at all. Magic is the art of manipulating these links, links which have been activated through the desire of the magician; thus magic is, in other words, *eros*.

Eros forges connections between human beings, as we have all witnessed and as we are all the tangible result. Eros is a field of attraction between two objects; in human terms, we may call this attraction "love" or "fascination" or "chemistry," etc. When the attraction exists between inanimate objects, other terms might be used, but according to Bruno (and the generations of hermeticists before him) they are all variations of the same theme. This is magic, pure and simple. Even Aleister Crowley was not able to refrain from using a verse from the *Book of the Law* as a kind of slogan: *Do what thou wilt shall be the whole of the Law; Love is the law, love under Will.* This is an accurate summation of Bruno's technology, and what Culianu discovered, for Culianu—in describing Bruno's contribution to occult philosophy—states that Bruno's ideal magician "*epitomizes the most perfect, hence the least human, product of the age of phantasms: a person capable of free will untrammeled by the turgid forces of his nature, which he has learned to dominate*" (emphasis in original).[8] This is virtually identical to Crowley's much-overused and misunderstood slogan, and reveals that both the late-Renaissance magician Giordano Bruno and the early-twentieth-century magician Aleister Crowley were in agreement on the core issue of magical technology. What is important for us to consider is whether or not the knowledge of this technology was disseminated more widely than the narrow and shadowy corridors of the secret societies.

For Bruno took this hermetic concept one step further, to the realm of politics. And so did Culianu.

Securitate, a friend once said, they're all mystics.
—Ted Anton[9]

It is no secret that the goal of the Nazi Party under Hitler, Hess and Himmler was nothing less than the creation of a "new man." Hitler mentioned this repeatedly, and corroborating evidence is given in the author's previous work. The goal of the occult and political programs of the Third Reich was the jump-starting of human evolution to the next stage. Whether or not such a process is possible is beside the point; what concerns us here is what the leaders of the Reich understood this next stage to be.

Throughout the writings and declarations of the "theologians" of the Third Reich—everyone from Eckart to Rosenberg to Darre to Rahn to Wiligut—there is an emphasis on the idea of the lost psychic powers of the Aryan race due to pollution of the blood. That the New Aryan Man would be possessed of these powers was taken for granted by Wiligut and his protégés. That the Third Reich itself was perceived to be the result of a "triumph of the Will" is clear, both from the writings of Hitler and his colleagues as well as from that famous film by Leni Riefenstahl. The early anti-Semitic mystics—men like Lanz von Liebenfels and Guido von List—wrote of the seductive charms of the Jewish woman, and of the enslavement of Aryan men to these erotic creatures; and of the necessity to reject their advances and to gain control over one's own libidos: to put one's emotions and sexuality under direct conscious control. In this sense, the phenomenon of the Third Reich can be seen as a validation of the occult theories of Bruno and others; indeed, the attraction of Jung, Eliade and others to the initial appearance of the Nazi Party is most likely due to this transcendental nature, this occult platform of the Party that was so much in agreement with the technologies of the Hermeticists. It was an error to suppose that just because a political party—or, more correctly in this case, a cult—should have adopted such theories and technologies, they were, therefore, spiritually enlightened or illuminated. When the horrors of the Third Reich became known, men like Jung and Eliade distanced themselves from it as much as possible and came away with a rude awakening: that not everyone who puts occult theories into practice is a "white magician," and that having occult abilities does not automatically imply moral superiority. If anything, one lesson of the Third Reich can be summarized as the realization that occult technologies can be utilized by any individual or group, regardless of their political affiliation or spiritual growth. This was a lesson that was taken to heart by Soviet intelligence, Chinese and Korean intelligence, the Romanian secret police (the Securitate), Hamas, Hizbolleh, Al-Qaeda, and by the men of MK-ULTRA.

But before terrorism became an accepted tool of international diplomacy, and interrogation refined to the astonishing degree that it has been in the twentieth century, there was the Renaissance. At that time, the West was divided by religious wars. Catholics and Protestants were the main combatants, although the Jews were still being persecuted as well. And even among the Protestants there was conflict, with various groups claiming to be the sole authority on the pure, unadulterated practice of Christianity. The Catholic Church, with special emphasis on the Pope in Rome, was considered to be a great evil: a debauched, degenerate, corrupt organization that was more interested in material wealth and temporal power than in spiritual attainments. By the time Martin Luther nailed his famous ninety-five theses to the door of the cathedral (October 31, 1517 … Halloween and the day the gates of the underworld are opened), the Reformation had begun.

While authorities are divided as to the dates when Renaissance and Reformation both began and ended (and, indeed, the dates are different for different countries, with England coming in later than the Continent), it can be said that the Renaissance began in Italy either as early as the twelfth or as late as the fourteenth century, as Europe shrugged itself awake from the so-called Dark Ages, and reached its height with the fall of Constantinople in 1453 and particularly with the discovery of America and the expulsion of the last Muslim Caliphate from Spain in 1492. Thus, Martin Luther's attack on the Catholic Church took place in a time feverish with theological, philosophical, metaphysical, artistic and political changes.

For Marsilio Ficino, it was the rebirth of Platonic philosophy that characterized the era, a kind of pagan sensibility that was refined and redefined by Pico della Mirandolla and then, eventually, by Giordano Bruno himself. This amalgamation of Greek and Byzantine philosophy and metaphysics with Arab science, Jewish mysticism and Catholic ritual and liturgical practices created an explosion of consciousness among the intelligentsia of Europe. The Greek gods were rediscovered and became a kind of esoteric shorthand for the artists, poets, and philosophers of the time; Egyptian religion—particularly the as-yet undeciphered hieroglyphics—became a fascination for many, as it seemed to be a kind of system that communicated directly to the soul, to the unconscious mind. The Renaissance was a time of Image, both in the Art of Memory and in the Art of Magic, and at the time of the Inquisition's investigation of Bruno it was believed that there was really no difference between the two. Indeed, Bruno was hard put to defend the Art of Memory as a science that had nothing to do with Magic; a sly dissimulation by the master of the art of subterfuge, since he knew as well as anyone else that the two practices are mutually dependent.

That the manipulation of a human being's memory is tantamount to control over his consciousness is something that was clearly understood by the magicians of the Renaissance and rediscovered by the intelligence officers of the twentieth century; but while the latter threw the entire weight of hypnosis, drugs, electroshock and other heavy-handed machinery at their subjects, Bruno cautioned a lighter touch. It was necessary that his subjects be unaware of his intentions, that they be *charmed* into performing those actions he required. You couldn't accomplish this with drugs and psychotherapy unless you wiped the memory and consciousness of the subject clean, as Ewen Cameron tried to do, and that took a lot of time and energy and resources, and the results were never very reliable or consistent. Bruno's approach might today be called "subliminal," that is, below the threshold of conscious awareness. While the operator may train himself in these techniques while in a heightened state of awareness brought about by meditation, ritual, drugs, "Tantric" sex and other devices, it was necessary that the target be free to go about his life uninterrupted and oblivious. Just as one is not aware of the process of falling in love—of all the thousand impressions and subconscious signals that are sent and received in the course of a relationship—just so the target of Bruno's magic would not be aware that he was being "bewitched," i.e., psychologically manipulated, until it was too late. The process, according to Bruno and those before him, was virtually identical. Hence, eros *is* magic because eros charges or activates the link.

According to Bruno, there is a network of "links" (or we may call them "connections") that "fills the universe." This is actually a sophisticated concept for a fifteenth century philosopher to expound, for it turns up again in the idea of the "matrix," both in quantum physics as well as in the popular motion picture series of the same name. These links may be activated by a force that resides in the body and that proceeds from the body, what Bruno calls metaphorically the "hand that binds" which "throws out its snares" (*De vinculis*, I).

No one is immune from this phenomenon. Every type of person may be affected by the judicious application of this technique. The type of "knot" or "binding" used depends on the target; the use of images is especially employed as a mechanism for attracting the binding energy. According to Bruno, one must study one's target carefully and create what today we would call a psychological profile of the intended victim. This will give an accurate picture of the state of the victim's consciousness: the mental images with which he surrounds himself, images that can be manipulated by the magician. The Chinese philosophers say that in order to know someone or something, "know what it eats"; Bruno would have said, "know what it loves," for in that love is the key to its submission.

For Bruno, love is the occult force that binds the universe together, and if one can understand love and understand how others love and what they love, then one can control them through their passions and their appetites. If reality is what our conscious minds make of it—a deliberate ordering of sensations in categories of priority, translated by our brain as images of light and dark, color, sound, dimension, etc.—then the way into the mind of another is through the images he or she manufactures. Rather than create a whole, complex reality that will be translated and identified by the subject's brain, one simply creates the images of the desired reality, working backwards from the image to the result desired.

Bruno understood that thought is a succession of images in the "mind's eye"; that memory is a storehouse of images, as his promotion of the Art of Memory exploits. Culianu calls the magician the "artist of memory," and this is an extremely important point; else, why did the mind-control experts concentrate so profoundly on ordering and redesigning the memory of selected subjects? Bruno's strategy employed a technique of going directly to the brain through the use of images, creating an alternate reality over which he was the master. In order for this system to work, it was necessary that the target be "seduced" by the images, i.e., "fall in love" in a sense with the image presented by the magician and thereby allow it to work in his consciousness. For this to happen, the magician himself must expend great amounts of energy—of passion, really—through that image in order to create the "link," in order to "enchain" the other person or persons and make them instruments of his will. As a corollary, Bruno insists that the magician not allow himself to fall in love with his own images, lest he become enslaved by them and ultimately destroyed. Thus, the magician places himself above love—above all the human passions and desires—so that he is not enchained in turn. Culianu understands that this seems at first glance to be a contradiction: the magician employs love and all the machinations and subterfuges of love, of eros, of passion and desire in order to seduce—to enchain or enslave—the will of others; he must experience love deeply, that "derangement of the senses" of which Rimbaud is the most famous exponent; yet he must not be affected by love, not "fall in love" himself even as he seems to be the ultimate lover, the most desirable suitor, working on the sensory apparatus of his victim with all the stored erotic energy at his disposal for, finally, the perfect magician is one who remains celibate, who retains his seed and uses the accumulated energy to power his magic. *He must believe he is in love with his subject at the time he works his magic, and not at any other time.* This is our introduction, not only to the

Manson Secret, but also to the television preacher, the popular politician, the salesman, the advertising executive. Culianu understood all of this, and was perhaps the first person to clarify and enlarge upon this idea.

At least, until he was murdered on May 21, 1991 at the age of 41.

Culianu's political involvements were largely unknown or misunderstood by his colleagues. One would have had to have a good working knowledge of the Byzantine conspiracies and intrigues of Romanian politics to get an inkling of Culianu's dangerous activities. He could not resist writing against the dictatorial Ceaucescu regime, although at times his writings were more in the way of a *ludus serius*, a kind of game involving symbolic figures, than they were out-and-out broadsides against the Communist leader and his secret police, the Securitate. But Culianu was a living symbol of the rewards that freedom of thought, freedom of expression, and the free and open exchange of intellectual ideas could bring. Further, he was a problem for both sides of the Romanian problem: right and left. Although there is no doubt that he was a sincere anti-Communist—living and suffering under a Soviet-style Eastern European dictatorship is enough to convert anyone to democracy and the free-market system, without even knowing what those concepts really represent—he was also anti-Nazi. This, in the context of Eastern European politics, was a difficult position to maintain, for it meant that he attracted enemies from both the Securitate and from various underground movements that had their origins in the ideas, if not in the actual membership roles, of the Romanian Nazi Iron Guard.

Six years previously, Valerian Trifa had been deported from the United States. This former Iron Guard leader and dedicated anti-Semite had come to America and taken by force the Romanian Orthodox Church, proclaiming himself its archbishop and leader. This was a man who had never been ordained a priest, nor had he any theological or ecclesiastical training whatsoever, a man who was little more than a violent thug and ringleader of a network of Iron Guardists from North America to South America, Europe, and Australia. When some US government officials discovered that Trifa had actually been a Nazi, they worked at getting his citizenship revoked, which resulted in his eventual deportation in 1984. Although Trifa himself was deported, he was not removed as the head of the Romanian Orthodox Church nor is there any evidence that he relaxed his control over the global Iron Guard network.

At the same time, Romanian secret police were active in the United States; thus, Culianu was surrounded by enemies who would have stopped at nothing if he was identified as a threat to the regime, or to the underground Iron Guard network. As Mircea Eliade's literary executor after his death in 1986, he also had access to documents concerning his mentor's Iron Guard affiliations, evidence that he had written articles in the 1930s supportive of fascism and the Iron Guard itself, evidence that troubled Culianu deeply.[10]

Culianu himself had written articles condemning the right-wing in Romania, which enraged the fascists who had thought he was one of them. Truly, the shots that were fired in the men's toilet at the University of Chicago from a .25 caliber Beretta—killing Culianu execution style, to the head—could have come from anywhere. Although the crime remains unsolved to this day despite heavy FBI involvement in the case, it is a certainty that what killed the young professor of religion was the very force he had been studying and writing about so extensively and with such penetrating insight.

INITIATION, INTERROGATION

The doctrine of correspondences assumes that everything in reality is somehow linked to everything else in some way; that the microcosmic world is a perfect image of the macrocosmic world; and that if we can cause a change to occur in the microcosm it will reflect in a corresponding change in the macrocosm. This is the essence of practical magic, and it is nothing less than a realization that there is a way to defeat the space-time continuum. It is an attempt to understand—and to exploit—"non-locality," a concept familiar to quantum physicists and which we shall examine in a later chapter. For now, suffice it to say that for the magician there is no such thing as a coincidence; for the magician, every coincidence is the manifestation of a subtle correspondence. While we experience coincidences in life as if they were accidents, the magician turns the tables and utilizes coincidence *proactively* as a way of causing change to occur in the real world.

We will examine this mechanism more fully a bit later on. For now, let us look at the technology of magic where we will see some parallels in modern psychology, particularly in multiple personality disorder and other forms of psychosis.

The magician, having selected the day and time of his ritual, must also select the appropriate location. Many grimoires give suggestions ranging from abandoned churchyards to lonely forests to a room in one's own home that has been stripped of all ornamentation. The idea behind each of these recommendations is particular to the type of ritual being performed. In the evocation of demonic forces, for instance, a graveyard would be an appropriate locale because it would cause feelings of dread and heightened anxiety in the magician, sentiments which are conducive to the experience of confronting evil firsthand. Even more importantly, such an environment would be a reminder to the magician that what he is undertaking is a dangerous endeavor and that he should not turn his back for a moment on the forces thus externalized.

There is another reason for choosing an outdoor site, and that is one of simple expedience: spiritual forces need to clothe themselves in bits and pieces of reality in order to become "visible" to the magician. This is known as the "material basis" in modern occult parlance. Something must be available for the force to "inhabit," if only briefly, so that it may become sensible to the magician. This can range from the smoke of burning incense to a drop of ink in a bowl of water, to the rustling of leaves on a nearby tree or even a hapless forest animal who may be in the vicinity.

In a closed room, where the environment is one hundred percent controlled and designed by the magician, this basis may be incense smoke or ink in water, as mentioned, or may even be a pure hallucination caused by the sensory deprivation techniques we will examine shortly. Whatever the case, the environment for the ritual must be carefully chosen in advance and prepared for the ritual by the magician.

Space and time, the ritual location and the day and hour of its performance, have now been manipulated by the magician to a certain extent, based on the doctrine of correspondences. That is "setting." Now the magician must concern himself with "set."

"Set," in this case as it is in the case of the LSD trip, is the mental state of the person undergoing the experience. The grimoires usually specify a period of fasting, celibacy and prayer to precede the actual performance of the ritual. This period may be anything from a few days before the ritual to months in advance. During this time, the magician must concentrate on the ritual to be performed, and must become "inflamed with prayer." As the day and hour of the ritual approaches, the praying and fasting is stepped up. The entire being of the magician—body and soul—is devoted to the ritual and everything else, every extraneous thought and desire, must be eradicated from his consciousness. This is a kind of controlled fanaticism, fanaticism focused towards a specific goal at a specific time and place.

The shaman, for his initiation, becomes ill at first: feverish, delusional, near dead, psychotic. The magician also becomes deranged, for as elevated as this spiritual state may seem—constant prayer, celibacy, fasting—it shares a great deal with the psychotic state. After all, this entire uncomfortable existence is surrounded by images of spiritual forces, by the manufacture and preparation of exotic instruments designed to force obedience from those forces, by the creation of a blank book in which to record the experience and—in the case of some grimoires—to actually receive the signature and seal of the spirit evoked. After a long period with very little food, no sexual activity of any kind, and constant focus and concentration on invisible beings, one could safely say that the magician is entering a state of controlled psychosis, a state leading deliberately up to the evocation of one of these invisible beings to visible appearance. What the shaman was doing in the forest or jungle by himself, at the mercy of visions of hideous torment, the magician does to himself deliberately in his European city or town, driving himself slowly insane, loosening his grip on "reality" so that he may catch a glimpse of the sinister forces that operate below the radar of even our most sophisticated science. The very predicate that these forces exist, and can be summoned, would be enough to sentence many a modern man or woman to thirty days of observation in a mental ward. The investment of time, money, and consciousness in the effort to summon, and to communicate with, these forces contribute to a state of mind in the magician that is difficult to describe. He builds up within himself a determination to know the unknowable, to see the unseeable, to do the undoable, and this sets up a psychic tension in the magician that can easily lead to a nervous breakdown, or worse.

One of the most accessible of the modern practitioners of this art was the late Francis Israel Regardie, one time secretary to Aleister Crowley and—oddly enough—one-time associate of Kennedy assassination researcher Mary Ferrell. Regardie went on record several times insisting that anyone desiring to go on the path of occult attainment represented by ceremonial magic first undergo a period of psychological analysis and therapy.[11] A disturbed mind would find the ceremony and ritual of magic too comfortable, and would find itself a prisoner of the unreal, of the Other. The practice of magic by such a mind would further its derangement, but without the hope or expectation that a state superior to sanity would be achieved; rather, the health of such a mind would be forfeit if it undertook a practice of magic alone, without the benefit of a strict and observant guide. The resultant anxiety—in which the "magician" would see signs and portents everywhere, in a chaos of iconography that is perhaps best represented by the type of conspiracy theorist who believes that the goal of all those wealthy men and government acronyms is to destabilize *him* personally—leads easily to what the *DSM* calls "paranoid schizophrenia," from which the road back to mental health is long and painful. This is because magic, as it is known in the West, is a highly intellectual art. The psychological edifice created by a knowledge of ancient tongues and scripts, the minutiae of astrology, the language of symbolism, all combine in a structure whose internal logic serves as a means by which one can both create the ritual *and* decipher its outcome. A certain objectivity is required, and this is why a strong grasp of the principles of the doctrine of correspondences is so necessary, for this is the alphabet and the vocabulary of visions, dreams, nightmares, and the disturbing coincidences that surround the magician once embarked on this mysterious quest.

To make matters even more confusing, the set of correspondences is not identical from culture to culture, from society to society. A Siberian shaman may use one set of correspondences familiar to him due to the flora, fauna and folk religion of his environment; the European ceremonial magician will use another, even more elaborate, set; and the voodoo priest yet another. However, attempts have been made to show that these different sets of correspondences do share some basic information, that there is a common denominator to all cultures and practices even though they may seem to differ widely. The Golden Dawn of the late nineteenth century sought to do just that, by using the Jewish Qabala and Tree of Life as a template upon which to "fit" the belief systems (and, thus, the correspondence systems) of every known culture, past and present. Aleister Crowley, himself an initiate of the Golden Dawn, attempted to perfect that system with the help of several of his friends, and the result is the impressive *Liber 777*. This is nothing less than a kind of database of religious and occult beliefs and practices, all set out on the 10 spheres and 22 paths of the Qabalistic Tree of Life. Thus, we can see at a glance how specific symbols in religious processes as disparate as Hinduism and Islam, Christianity and Buddhism, Greek and Roman mythology, etc. all correspond to each other in some way. While this was intended both as an aid in understanding different religions and as a means of creating occult rituals that would take into consideration a profound depth of meaning cutting across geography and millenia, it is also a useful place to begin comprehending the activity of what the Dutch novelist Couperus called "the hidden force." An understanding of the system of correspondences enables us to grasp the mechanism of what we have become accustomed to call "coincidence."

We will investigate coincidence and synchronicity in greater detail in a later chapter. For now, we should understand that—for the occultist—there is truly "no such thing as coincidence," or, more accurately, that coincidence is a clue that deeper connections exist between observable phenomena, that another force of nature is at work that we don't understand, but which has something to do with what quantum physics means when they refer to "non-locality." To New Orleans District Attorney Jim Garrison, the accumulation of coincidence in the Kennedy assassination case meant that intelligence agencies were at work behind the scenes. That he was correct should be beyond doubt, regardless of whether or not you believe Oswald acted alone. What we will do in this chapter, and in this entire book, is to go a layer deeper than political conspiracy and examine a mysterious and dangerous structure of sinister forces that "conspire" at a level where science and magic, magic and politics, meet.

That is our "set and setting."

The magician's magic circle is designed with a dual purpose in mind, and that is perhaps why it is usually portrayed as two concentric circles. In a sense, the magic circle—the setting—is needed to contain the mental focus of the magician within a narrowly structured (nine foot diameter, according to many of the grimoires) space; in another sense, the circle is also designed to keep everything else *out*. The grimoires are full of the direst warnings should the circle ever be breached: such an accident would prove the destruction of the magician. For the duration of the ritual, the magician stays inside the circle and ensures that its physical integrity is maintained.

The famous Beat poet and novelist William Burroughs, in a letter to the editor of the *Necronomicon*, wrote that the magician is like a mafia don, safe within his magic circle, sending spiritual forces to do his bidding and not getting his hands dirty. In a very real way, that is the idea. The magician, by expending huge amounts of energy and intense mental focus during the days and weeks leading up to the culmination of the ritual, is creating a psychological state in which the energy must be directed somewhere. To a psychologist, this may mean that the energy is directed inwards, leading to an imbalance in the psyche of the operator. To an occultist, however, while there is a very real danger of just that, the structure of the ritual is such that channels are designed to move this energy away from the conscious mind of the operator and outwards, into a specific space for a specific goal or target. The success or failure of the occult ritual largely depends, therefore, on the ability of the operator to externalize this accumulated energy: whether in an evocation of spiritual forces to visible appearance, in an attempt to heal someone of an illness, to find money, or to cause physical or mental harm to another.

In order to properly focus the mind and will of the operator, then, the magic circle and its environment—the setting—must reflect the nature of the specific ritual being undertaken. This is where the doctrine of correspondences comes into play. We have seen that an appropriate *time* is selected for the ritual, based on astrological principles that correspond to the nature of the ritual or to the spiritual force being evoked. We have seen that a *space* is also selected that would be conducive to the performance of such a ritual. Now that space and time must be manipulated in such a way that only the stated purpose of the ritual—and nothing else—will be permitted in the consciousness of the operator. The selection of the appropriate space and time is already half-way there; it is as if we have chosen a specific highway to a specific town. The performance of the ritual itself is akin to driving the car along that highway to reach that town.

By beginning at the right time, at the precise moment specified by the ritual, the magician "stops time" in a sense. The magic circle is commonly thought of as a place between two worlds, a place where the usual laws governing space and time are waived. As long as the ritual begins at the right time, and no matter how long the ritual lasts, it is still "that time" in the sense of the ritual. Just as a human being, born at a specific time, is said by the astrologers to bear certain characteristics of that day and year and hour no matter how long he lives, so the ritual is "born" at a specific time and place and contains within itself the characteristics of that time and place. In fact, occultists routinely draw up horoscope charts for the proposed rituals in advance, as if the rituals were persons.

Before we go much further in this examination, let's stop here for a moment and look at how set and setting are used by interrogation experts the world over.

It is a truism that the first duty of an interrogation specialist is to disorient his subject. The idea is to make the subject feel as uncomfortable as possible, and to become confused as to the time and place he is being held. Lights are turned on and off at whim; meals are served at random intervals; sounds are broadcast in close proximity, from the screams of the damned to the shouts and commands of the interrogators/torturers. This is the "softening up" process, designed to make the subject more malleable during the actual interrogation itself. From a combination of fear, anxiety, and confusion it is hoped that the resistance of the subject is broken down. Rarely is it necessary to apply actual physical torture to a prisoner to gain cooperation. Those who torture their prisoners usually do so because they enjoy it, and not because it is necessary. Psychological torture is much more powerful, and is easier to regulate. Physical torture can result in the death or incapacitation of the subject, rendering the whole exercise a failure.

While the magician needs to control every aspect of his environment prior to undertaking the ritual, the interrogator needs to control every aspect of the environment of his subject prior to the actual interrogation itself. He begins with the physical environment and, if he is skilled or lucky, moves on to the mental environment. He begins perhaps as an adversary, and then transforms himself over time into a kind of "accomplice" of the subject, someone the subject can trust. The interrogation subject has become a kind of "material basis" for the information the interrogator needs; he is a medium through which the information will "speak." The actual subject himself is of no real use to the interrogator; his only concern is for the information the subject is hiding.

Let us look at a recently declassified CIA manual on interrogation, the famous "KUBARK Counterintelligence Manual," which was originally circulated (internally at the CIA) in July 1963 and was declassified (albeit with heavy censorship) in January 1997.[12] The following is from Chapter VII: "Planning the Counterintelligence Interrogation," Section C: "The Specifics":

> 3. The Interrogation Setting
> The room in which the interrogation is to be conducted should be free of distractions. The colors of walls, ceiling, rugs, and furniture should not be startling. Pictures should be missing or dull. Whether the furniture should include a desk depends not upon the interrogator's convenience but rather upon the subject's anticipated reaction to connotations of superiority and officialdom. A plain table may be preferable. An overstuffed chair for the use of the interrogatee is sometimes preferable to a straight-backed, wooden chair because if he is made to stand for a lengthy period or is otherwise deprived of physical comfort, *the contrast is intensified and increased disorientation results....* If a new safehouse is to be used as the interrogation site, it should be studied carefully to be sure that *the total environment can be manipulated as desired.* (emphases added)

As we can see from the preceding, the goal of the interrogator in designing the "setting" for the interrogation is virtually identical to that of the magician. Total control of the environment is uppermost in the mind of the careful interrogator. As the document goes on to describe in much more detail, everything from telephones to electrical generators to a "do not disturb" sign on the door of the interrogation room is taken into consideration to eliminate every single instance of interruption and distraction. The need for the disorientation of the subject is also noted. This type of disorientation will also take place as a result of the occult ritual, properly performed. It is nothing less than the "derangement of the senses" demanded by the French poet Rimbaud and echoed throughout the surrealist movement; or the dictum of Timothy Leary, "Turn On, Tune In, Drop Out," to which it may be compared. The difference is that the interrogator is using these techniques on an unwilling and resistant subject; it is the application of a very old occult technique for modern, intelligence-gathering purposes.

In a chapter of the manual entitled "IX. Coercive Counterintelligence Interrogation of Resistant Sources" we find the following, very revealing, paragraph:

> 1. The more completely the place of confinement eliminates sensory stimuli, the more rapidly and deeply will the interrogatee be affected. Results produced only after weeks or months of imprisonment in an ordinary cell can be duplicated in hours or days in a cell which has no light (or weak artificial light which never varies), which is sound-proofed, in which odors are eliminated, etc. An environment still more subject to control, such as water-tank or iron lung, is even more effective.

The purpose of all this sensory deprivation is further clarified:

> 4. The deprivation of stimuli induces regression by depriving the subject's mind of contact with an outer world and thus forcing it in upon itself. At the same time, the calculated provision of stimuli during interrogation tends to make the regressed subject view the interrogator as a father-figure. The result, normally, is a strengthening of the subject's tendencies toward compliance.

And there is the crux of the matter: "regression." As the authors of the manual state at the beginning of the section, "All coercive techniques are designed to induce regression." Even hypnosis is considered a means to this end. On page 96 of the manual, reference is made to the work of Merton M. Gill and Margaret Brenman, who state, "The psychoanalytic theory of hypnosis clearly implies, where it does not explicitly state, that hypnosis is a form of regression." In other words, the idea is to regress the subject to "a level at which the resistance can no longer be sustained. Hypnosis is one way of regressing people."

Therefore, the interrogation environment is designed to disorient a subject and then regress that subject to the point where he or she has become, in a psychological sense, a child. This is clear from the statement above that "the regressed subject view the interrogator as a father-figure." The subject becomes a child, the interrogator a father; or the subject becomes a candidate for initiation, and the interrogator, the initiator.

The blindfolding and binding of the Masonic candidate (from which we get the word "hoodwinked"), the mock burial of candidates in the European mystery religions, the isolation of the shamanic candidate and his reduction to a childlike state of helplessness by his mental or physical illness, are all means of reducing sensory stimuli and regressing the candidate to a childlike state, in order to be "reborn."

In occult matters, this disorientation is a preliminary phase. Like the shaman in the forest, sick and hallucinating, this initial period serves to "unlock" normal mental and psychological perceptions. We have all heard of the expression "to change one's mind," and of the difficulty of "changing the mind" of a particularly stubborn person (or resistant interrogatee). The purpose of the disorientation phase is to allow the mind to be more easily changed. This is as true of the CIA's interrogation methods as it is of spiritual or occult initiation. In the case of the shamans, this disorientation was achieved by illness—either physical or mental, or a combination of both—as well as by the future shaman's isolation in the wild. In the context of modern Western occultism, this disorientation is achieved by a refinement of the "sick in the woods" shamanistic type, and involves sensory deprivation. The Masonic initiate is brought in blindfolded and bound; without sight, and without the unrestricted use of his limbs, he is reduced to hearing and smell: the chants of his fellow Masons and the aroma of incense. All other sensory input has been—as the CIA manual would have it—"manipulated." In the more ancient mystery religions—as well as in some initiatory cults in the West today—the candidate for initiation was buried alive, his sensory input slowly reduced to nothing as he lay in a grave or a tomb, awaiting his rebirth or "resurrection." This is mirrored in some Eastern Orthodox ceremonies in which the candidate for the bishop's mitre spends the night in the church, prone on the church floor, and covered with a sheet as if dead; heavy candlesticks hold down the four edges of the sheet. At dawn, he is "risen," the sheet and candlesticks removed, and he joins the company of his fellow bishops for the formal consecration ceremony.

It is perhaps this state of disorientation that enables the interrogation to proceed more smoothly as the subject searches for the next stage of initiation: "rebirth" is not putting too fine a point on it. The subject is expected to do the unthinkable: to give his enemy vital information that may lead to the arrest or death of his colleagues or cause some danger or threat to his country. He must find a way to do this, to live with this decision to side with his enemy, even if under coercion and torture.

The CIA manual contains bibliographic information for the interrogator's reference, including many of the "usual suspects" (such as works by Lawrence

Hinkle and Harold Wolff, Robert Jay Lifton, Margaret Singer, and *Brainwashing: A Guide to the Literature*, published by a CIA front, the Society for the Investigation of Human Ecology) plus an interesting offering by psychiatrist James Clark Moloney, "Psychic Self-Abandon and Extortion of Confessions," included in the January/February 1955 edition of the *International Journal of Psychoanalysis*. This article, according to the CIA manual, relates the "psychological release obtained through confession (i.e., the sense of well-being following surrender as a solution to an otherwise unsolvable conflict) with religious experiences generally and some ten Buddhist practices particularly."[13] Thus, even as early as 1955, it was realized by some observers that there is a distinct relationship between the gestalt of the interrogation room and that of the meditation chamber or other religious experience. The CIA held a dim view of Moloney's work, even as they cited it in the Bibliography of the interrogation manual; they recommended the serious interrogator read *Hypnosis and Related States: Psychoanalytic Studies in Regression*, by Merton Gill and Margaret Brenman.

Also cited in the annotated CIA bibliography was an obscure article by John C. Lilly, he of "talking with dolphins" fame. This article—entitled "Mental Effects of Reduction of Ordinary Levels of Physical Stimuli on Intact Healthy Persons," in the *Psychological Research Report #5* of the American Psychiatric Association (1956)—is devoted to a study of sensory deprivation: "The effect was to speed up the results of the more usual sort of isolation (for example, solitary confinement). Delusions and hallucinations, preceded by other symptoms, appeared after short periods. The author does not discuss the possible relevance of his findings to interrogation."[14]

In one of the many coincidences that shadowed the writing of this book over the years, there is another worthwhile to mention, as it occurred as these words were being written.

In order to identify the source of my information that Francis Israel Regardie recommended a course of psychological analysis prior to undertaking occult practice, I located a copy of *An Interview with Israel Regardie: His Final Thoughts and Views*, edited by Christopher S. Hyatt, buried deep within my library, and found the relevant quotation. Scanning through the book, however, I came upon an article by Regardie at the rear of the book which is an attack on James Clark Moloney and is entitled "Cry Havoc!" This attack is due to Moloney's published distaste for the practice of chiropractic, which was of serious interest to Regardie.

Thus, I read the references to Moloney in at least two places: in the CIA document,[15] and then immediately—the same day, perhaps an hour or so later—another in a book so far removed from the subject matter of the interrogation manual as to render the occurrence even more meaningful. As if to emphasize the bizarre nature of this "coincidence," the preceding article in the Regardie collection is entitled "What Is Psychotherapy?" and contains, on page 113, a reference to (actually, a quotation from) that notorious and by-now-familiar CIA mind-control psychiatrist and inventor of "psychic driving" and "depatterning" techniques, Dr. Ewen Cameron! Although the collection of articles and the interview was published as a book in 1985, there is no mention of when the articles in question first appeared in print, nor is there a source for the Cameron quotation, alas.

Before we close the section dealing with "set and setting" it will perhaps be useful to look once more at the CIA interrogation manual, in the section dealing with "coercive interrogation," i.e., where the subject is resistant to interrogation, such as a political prisoner might be. The CIA manual quotes at length from Lawrence Hinkle (who, with Harold Wolff, was asked to study brainwashing at the request of Allen Dulles, becoming, in the process, "the chief brainwashing studiers for the U.S. government")[16] and then again from Lilly. The CIA found Lilly's description of the sensory deprivation experienced by, for instance, arctic explorers to be particularly fascinating and relevant, especially the passage from his article that states, "The symptoms most commonly produced by isolation are superstition, intense love of any other living thing, perceiving inanimate objects as alive, hallucinations, and delusions."[17]

These are all symptoms that we may, with confidence, also ascribe to heightened states of mystical or occult awareness. Unfortunately, the terms "hallucination" and "delusion" are, of course, emotionally loaded. We may wish to substitute terms like "vision" or "altered mental state," or even the Golden Dawn's suggestive "evocation to visible appearance," in the cases where these experiences are the result of a deliberate attempt to penetrate other levels or modes of consciousness. It is interesting that Lilly discovers superstition as one of the side effects of lengthy isolation and sensory deprivation; this may be understood as the willingness of the subject to see relationships between events that are not seen or not recognized by the mentally healthy. These relationships, of course, are precisely what the occultist is seeking to understand; Jung called this phenomenon "synchronicity" and science calls it "coincidence."

The setting of the occultist is just as consciously controlled and manipulated as is that of the interrogator. Every detail must be considered, and the entire environment must reflect the purpose of the ritual. In the case, for instance, of a ritual designed to evoke spiritual forces which may be represented by the planet Venus—a planet that represents for the occultist, as for the mythologian and the anthropologist, ideas cognate with love, luxury, beauty, fine arts, etc.—the color scheme must represent what his culture identifies with Venus. In Europe, this would be the color green; the metal would be copper; sweet incenses would be burned; the entire environment of the ritual chamber would reflect the concept of Venus and no other. For Mars, these elements would be replaced by the color red, iron as the metal, and so forth. These correspondences may be found in any work of ceremonial magic such as those by Agrippa, pseudo-Agrippa, pseudo-Solomon, or in *Liber 777* aforementioned. This is a type of sensory deprivation, in which all extraneous ideas and mental triggers are removed from the chamber and replaced by a single, strident pulse in which sound, sight, smell, touch, and even taste are of a piece: one insistent message being broadcast from the environment back onto the senses of the magician or operator. Further, the operator has himself designed the room or chamber to reflect this purpose, so the message has gone out from the operator to the environment and back again. The chamber thus designed acts as a kind of externalization of the inner thoughts and desires of the operator, much the same way we decorate our homes to reflect personal taste. Yet, this chamber's design is temporary; it will serve for the performance of a single ritual—or ritual series—only. On another day, it will be completely re-arranged to reflect a different spiritual force.

Thus, the magician is at once interrogator and interrogatee; he is the one in charge of manipulating and controlling the environment, but not for the effect it will have on someone else, but on himself alone. What the CIA has done in its interrogation manual—itself the product of MK-ULTRA, as is obvious from the works cited in its Bibliography, entire entries of which have been redacted while the others are overwhelmingly works by MK-ULTRA and military mind-control specialists—is to separate the magician from the ultimate goal of all occultism, which is a kind of spiritual perfection and elevated consciousness, and instead focus all the powers of occult technique on an unwilling and uninformed subject, to manipulate him as well as the environment, to change the subject and transform him into something more useful to the interrogator and of mortal danger to the subject's own people. It is, in the jargon of occultism, black magic; and black magic in the service of the State.

The interrogator himself must be of a very special and unique character. He must be capable of what Robert Jay Lifton has called "doubling." That is, a CIA interrogator must be capable of being two persons at once. Lifton used the "doubling" metaphor to describe those German scientists who—although from gentle and cultured backgrounds, with wives and children of their own—were able to become monsters in the service of the Nazi state. They had, in effect, two totally distinct personalities, which was the only way they were capable of carrying out the horrendous experiments they did while at the same time considering themselves human beings and men of science. While Lifton stops short of calling this a case of multiple personality disorder or dissociated identity disorder, it is so borderline a state as to be confusing to the non-professional. The CIA interrogator, as per the declassified manual, must also be capable of this type of "dissociation":

> Once questioning starts, the interrogator is called upon to function at two levels. He is trying to do two seemingly contradictory things at once: achieve rapport with the subject but remain an essentially detached observer. Or he may project himself to the resistant interrogatee as powerful and ominous (in order to eradicate resistance and create the necessary conditions for rapport) while remaining wholly uncommitted at the deeper level, noting the significance of the subjects [*sic*] reactions and the effectiveness of his own performance. Poor interrogators often confuse this bi-level functioning with role-playing, but there is a vital difference. The interrogator who merely pretends, in his surface performance, to feel a given emotion or to hold a given attitude toward the source is likely to be unconvincing; the source quickly senses the deception. Even children are very quick to feel this kind of pretense. To be persuasive, the sympathy or anger must be genuine; but to be useful, it must not interfere with the deeper level of precise, unaffected observation. Bi-level functioning is not difficult or even unusual; most people act at times as both performer and observer unless their emotions are so deeply involved in the situation that the critical faculty disintegrates. Through experience the interrogator becomes adept in this dualism.[18]

If some careful reader sees in the above an echo of the Stanislavski Method, he may be forgiven. As we will see in a following chapter, the Method resonates quite well with both occult practices and intelligence work.

Thus, we have examined set and setting; set is the mental state of the occultist and of the interrogator, a mental condition conducive towards obtaining a desired result. Setting is the environment, which is designed, controlled and manipulated in such a way as to reinforce the mental set. Mind control and magic: not very far apart at all. It is perhaps a natural reluctance on the part of many government scientists and brainwashing experimenters to take occultism and its literature and practitioners seriously that has prevented the CIA and the military from becoming even more powerful and omniscient than they have been; or, perhaps, we don't know the half of what they have already achieved and the lengths to which they have gone to achieve it. That the literature of occultism, spiritual initiation, and shamanism could contribute greatly to mind-control programs was acknowledged by some specialists. As we have seen, Moloney noticed it; and some of the operations already described in this work involved consultation with psychics, magicians, and others of that industry. It is the fact that the initiatory process itself is time-consuming and highly subjective that probably prevented its use as a mind-control weapon; however, the rites and methods of the occultist and shaman were scoured carefully by the men of the CIA to see if there were short-cuts and indications of other technologies that might be employed, such as, of course, hallucinogens.

That there are no short-cuts to either initiation or occult abilities—whether one chooses to believe in them or not—did not occur to them, however.

Techniques and tools were taken out of context and bent to serve the urgent needs of the state. This is similar to a prince hiring an alchemist to churn out gold; or a monarch hiring a seer to divine the intentions of an enemy. While occult abilities have always, since the dawn of recorded history, been used in the service of the state, there used to be an acknowledgment of the spiritual nature of these powers on the behalf of the rulers, and of the necessity of appeasing the spiritual forces thus evoked. Today, with a totally mechanistic and technological approach to science, this basic perspective has been lost, and with it the moral imperative to treat the use of these powers (and, by extension, the hearts and minds of human beings) with care and respect.

BORN AGAIN

Eliade and other commentators on initiation myths have remarked often that the goal of the initiation is to cause the initiand to be "reborn"; the symbolism of wombs and tombs, of death and resurrection, all point to a dramatic rebirth of the initiand before he or she can take a place among the members of the cult. Naturally, this rebirth experience is quite different from an actual birth; after all, one undergoes this process voluntarily with the expectation of a great reward at the end of it. One is reborn with all one's memories intact. One has been conscious of the progression from lay person to initiand to initiate, which is more than can be said for most of us who have only been born once, the normal way. Yet, this insistence on the rebirth of the initiand into a "new life" is so widespread among so many cultures around the world, that it must have something important to convey to us. This may reside in the concept of a new *identity*.

When one is baptized in the Catholic faith, one is given a "Christian" name. When the author was a child, this had to be the name of a saint. One could not be baptized as "Phoenix" or "Serendipity" or "Moon," there being no Catholic saints with those names.

But then came the rite of Confirmation. This is the ritual where a Catholic child must repeat the baptismal vows which were said on his behalf by his godparents when he was an infant. Now that the child is of age—usually around ten or eleven years old and safely before the actual onset of puberty—he or she is expected to participate in this ritual which "confirms" those vows. Dressed in white, carrying a candle or a flower, the child makes his way to the communion rail of the church where a bishop confirms the child in its vows, *slaps the child on the cheek*, and then calls the child by a *new name*. This is probably as close as traditional Roman Catholics ever come to a "born again" experience. It is a replay of Baptism but with a totally conscious and aware child taking the place of the infant. The slap has been described as a means of warning the child that he or she will not have an easy road ahead as a Christian. I am not so sure if this is its true intention. But it is the new name that concerns us, because after all the child already has a Christian name, conferred at the time of Baptism. Why another name?

Of course, since the child is now conscious and capable of making moral decisions and knowing right from wrong, it is expected that the child will also take another name as an indication that he or she is fully conscious in a moral sense. The child selects this name beforehand. It also must be the name of a saint, preferably a saint whose example the child admires and emulates.

This rite may have had as its inspiration the Jewish ritual of the bar mitzvah, in which a Jewish boy of thirteen years or so "becomes a man" and is introduced to the community of men as a full-fledged member. Whatever its origin, it is the bestowal of a new name that concerns us.

When one converts to Islam, one is also expected to take a Muslim name, which is usually Arabic and is usually either the name of a prophet or other holy figure, or which means something appropriately spiritual. (We are reminded of the prizefighter Cassius Clay becoming Mohammed Ali.)

The same is also true of virtually every occult society. The name is selected by the initiand beforehand, and may be in any language. In the tradition of the Golden Dawn, this new name was usually in Latin but may also have been in Greek, Sanskrit, Hebrew and even Gaelic. The name was believed to be especially meaningful and to contain within itself an entire occult program. Its numerology was carefully examined, as well as its linguistic roots and occult "heredity." Within the cult's chambers, the initiate was only known by his or her cult name.

In the Manson Family this was not unusual, either. Lynette Fromme was "Squeaky," Ruth Ann Moorehouse was "Ouisch," and there were "Gypsy," "Sexy Sadie," and so many others. This idea of naming served the purpose to unite the group but also to delineate its boundaries from the rest of society. To Ms. Fromme's parents, she would always be Lynette. To the police, to the government, she would always be known by her "Christian" name. But to her friends and colleagues, she was Squeaky, even as she attempted the assassination of President Ford long after the Tate/La Bianca killings.

And, of course, in the intelligence community, false names and code names are a commonplace. In this instance, it is to protect the user and conceal his or her identity from those without a "need to know"; but it has the same psychological effect on the agent who must use that name as his identification within the "cult of intelligence." His membership in the elite group of intelligence officers is known only to his colleagues; he must use a different persona when outside of that charmed circle. Another case of "doubling"?

A book could be written on this topic of identity, and the reader will be relieved to learn I am not going to explore the theme thoroughly here. I am only pointing out the obvious, that the tradition of taking a new name begins in religion and culminates in the cult—whether of murderers, such as the

Manson Family, or of intelligence, such as the CIA—and that the psychological effect of this new name has not been fully investigated.

We understand that the person suffering from dissociative identity disorder or multiple personality disorder also uses a multiplicity of names. Each "alter" personality has its own name and its own identity, usually vastly different from every other alter. The goal of MK-ULTRA was, of course, the creation of this type of disorder in its subjects in the search for the perfect—and perfectly deniable—assassin. In the case of DID or MPD, this disorder is the result of a trauma inflicted from outside the subject: an abusive parent or other older person, usually. In the case of the cult, this name is often bestowed upon the subject by its leader or guru or, as in the case of the Golden Dawn or the Catholic Confirmation ceremony, chosen by the subjects themselves. Again, the emphasis is on willing versus unwilling participation in the rituals of consciousness. The CIA wished to manipulate the subject completely, physically and mentally. They and their agents were mostly unaware that this could also lead to a spiritual crisis in the subject, one from which most people would not recover; one from which it was almost impossible to claim a heightened spiritual state or initiation. When they incorporated drugs into the program and, as in the case of Dr. Cameron, bizarre sensory deprivation techniques coupled with the endlessly droning tape players—a suggestion first bruited about by Aldous Huxley—we had all the elements of a serious occult experience, but man-handled by men of science and government who had no interest in the spiritual dimensions of their work, nor in the spiritual state of their subjects, and whose own level of spiritual development and awareness would have been equally suspect.

I have witnessed what may happen to a person when unwittingly "possessed" during the course of a voodoo ceremony. At times, uninvolved observers of such a ritual will, themselves, fall into a state of possession even though they are not members of the cult nor are believers in possession specifically or voodoo in general. The person becomes a danger to themselves and to others. The voodoo priest in charge of the ritual will usually bring this unfortunate person out of the trance (I have seen this done with a whispered prayer and a spray of rum in the subject's face), whereupon the person is led back to their seat in a dazed state, remembering nothing of what has transpired. Possession, trance, amnesia. In the case of Dr. Cameron and the other practitioners of this "black art," there was no attempt to bring the subject out of trance, or to protect the subject from the consequences of accidental "possession." The trance was the thing; the creation of multiple personalities was the goal; selective amnesia was a necessary side effect. Anything that stood in its way was, of course, anathema, but whatever contributed to these strange and dangerous psychological conditions was welcomed and enhanced.

To understand why this effort by Cameron was so evil, it is perhaps a good idea to compare Cameron's methods with normal psychotherapy. There are many forms of psychotherapy, of course, but the most common is what is sometimes referred to as the "talking cure." For fifty minutes a day, several days a week, a patient goes to see a psychiatrist or a psychotherapist, sits on a chair or lies on a couch, and talks. The therapist is usually silent, or perhaps gently prods the patient with a mumbled "hmmm" or "ah" or "how does that make you feel?" This can go on for years. It is used to treat various low-level neuroses; nothing life-threatening, no voices in the head or snakes on the walls. This is the type of therapy we are accustomed to hearing about when we read the gossip columns or the movie star magazines. The regularity of the therapy—a strict fifty minute hour, according to a strict schedule laid out in advance—is designed to give some order and structure to the patient's life. The patient, after all, is in the midst of chaotic feelings, confused emotional responses, anxieties, mood swings, depression. The unvarying routine of the therapy sessions forces a kind of artificial edifice within which these emotions are contained; it is like telling the patient that, no matter how chaotic life becomes, tomorrow at precisely four o'clock and for precisely fifty minutes, he will have the undivided attention of his therapist, just as he has had for the past three years and can reasonably expect to do for the next three or thirteen or thirty. It is also a safe environment in which to externalize these deeper emotions, anxieties, rages. The therapist will never criticize the patient, or laugh at him, or humiliate him in any way. And, at the end of the fifty minutes, no matter what is being discussed or how emotionally charged the atmosphere has become, the session is over and the patient must leave to make way for the next patient. While that seems harsh and annoying, it is actually part of the "cure": it once again reminds the patient that no matter what he or she is going through, there is a structure and routine to life and tomorrow is another day.

There are, of course, other therapies and therapeutic techniques. There is primal scream therapy in which patients are encouraged to re-live the moment of their birth as mewling infants, screaming in a kind of frenzied catharsis to overcome feelings of abandonment by the mother, etc. There is Jungian therapy, in which great attention is given to dreams and other symbolic material. Strict Freudian therapy, of course, involves the therapist speaking very little while the patient does all the talking, or doesn't talk at all. And so it goes. But the constant in these therapies is the sense that the therapist is a safe and trustworthy person, and that the therapeutic environment is a safe haven in which it is permissible and encouraged to reveal one's innermost thoughts, dreams, desires.

Therefore, when this environment is used for an attack on the mind and body of the patient, a grievous harm has been committed. The sense of betrayal of trust is enormous. Imagine going to a doctor with a minor ailment and leaving his office with a mortal disease, deliberately injected into your skin by the man or woman you trusted with your life. The same was taking place at Cameron's clinic in Montreal. Many of his patients became vegetables; some never recovered. When the CIA manual on interrogation was first promulgated within the Agency—in July 1963—Cameron's experiments were still ongoing, as was MK-ULTRA. Instead of his patients being "born again" into a healthy, robust psyche, they were being psychically murdered.

I hasten to add that some therapies may require confrontational techniques, such as in the use of psychodrama by some therapists. Again, this is done within the context of a therapeutic setting, and the patients are not strapped down to a hospital bed, fed drugs intravenously, and made to listen to subliminal messages on endless tape loops for days on end, like a scene out of *A Clockwork Orange*. In the case of Cameron—and in other cases in which helpless victims were made to suffer the very pains of hell at the hands of men and women of science—the patients were, quite simply, guinea pigs. They had become objects, and had lost their humanity. Isn't this how the serial killer views his victims? How the Nazi doctors viewed their prisoners?

What MK-ULTRA and the other government mind-control programs revealed was that the techniques of occult initiation and psychotherapy could be used not only to elevate a human being and sanctify his life; they could also be used to maim and kill. This was analogous to the relatively secret methods of using acupuncture (for instance) as an instrument not only of healing, but of torture.

The spiritual rebirth promised by the secret society, the mystical cult, the shamanistic initiation is not the end of the road for the initiate. It is a necessary prerequisite to greater accomplishments, and the path of the initiate is never-ending. While many professional skeptics—such as the Amazing Randi, among others—take delight in debunking the paranormal, there are aspects of occult initiation that transcend sleight-of-hand and legerdemain. While Randi has gone to great lengths to try to debunk the powers of Uri Geller, for instance, his own demonstrations of Geller-like abilities have always been weak. Yet, it is in the incredible mental abilities of the more "primitive" cultures that we find the greatest expression of what can only be called paranormal abilities, even as we try to define them using outmoded scientific vocabulary.

For instance, every year in Southeast Asia and parts of India there is the celebration of the Hindu festival of Thaipusam. This is the day when devotees fulfill promises made to the gods by having their half-naked bodies pierced with long needles from which are hung heavy fruits and other equally weighty objects. The devotees feel no pain, and there is no blood from these wounds. They walk in the tropical heat in a trance, their chests, cheeks, and other parts of their bodies run through with needles. Some of them carry huge float-like ornaments on their heads, secured by more needles run through their skin. This is a common festival, drawing crowds every year, and yet no one has been able to adequately explain how these people—no Uri Gellers or Amazing Randis among them—are able to enter into the kind of hypnotic trance necessary to demonstrate these startling abilities. They are under the tutelage of a guru, of course, who cautions the bystanders that no attempt must be made to break the trance of the devotees, for if they were to "snap out of it" they would find themselves in excruciating pain.

When the rite is accomplished, the needles are removed and there are typically no scars to show where the needles had been inserted and, of course, no evidence of bleeding. In Kuala Lumpur, where the author lived for several years, this rite takes place annually at the Batu Caves, a Hindu shrine devoted to the goddess Kali. In Singapore, the same festival is celebrated with the devotees walking on hot coals, showing neither pain nor burns or blisters. These feats of paranormal control over the body's natural responses—responses of pain, blistering, bleeding, etc—all take place within a religious context. Apologists for the scientific viewpoint would try to extricate the phenomena from their context, and explain them away as a kind of autohypnosis; yet, the field of hypnosis itself is not without its critics among the scientific community. What is the state of mind of the devotee during these painful (to watch) proceedings? Some have described it as a kind of "out of body" experience, as if they were watching what was being done from afar; what some theorists have called "splitting." The "center of gravity" of their consciousness is removed from a physical locale and suspended somewhere over their head. It is a trance, very much like a hypnotic trance, and indeed some of this same phenomena may be duplicated in the hypnotist's parlor. In a famous scene from Edgar Cayce's life, this "sleeping prophet" would go into a trance and critics would poke needles through his skin. No blood, no pain, no scar tissue.

In China, dedicated practitioners of the martial arts show the same abilities to ignore pain and stop the flow of blood, using swords to make their "point." What would be the therapeutic value of these techniques to modern medical science, one wonders?

In Africa, in the "village of the sorcerers" at Yho, in the Ivory Coast, there is a reported birthing ritual in which small children are put into a hypnotic trance and tossed into the air like sticks, from one man to another, each holding a sharp knife. The children have their eyes wide open, but are frozen solid, deep in trance. This tossing of the children from one man to another outside the hut where a woman is in labor continues as long as necessary, until the woman actually gives birth. The children in the air, the men with the knives, are said to simulate the actual moment of birth and to facilitate the entry of the child into the world. Like most such explanations, it has lost something in the translation, I am sure.[19]

The fact that hypnotic trances have been used in various ways by cultures around the world—as the above, very few, examples illustrate—indicates a knowledge of the powers of the mind that is at least as extensive as that of modern psychiatry, albeit in different, culturally-specific, garb. The "splitting" of consciousness necessary for the Thaipusam devotee or the Shaolin Temple monk or the Yho village sorcerer all represent a kind of voluntary madness, a temporary state of dislocation, of dissociation, of the personality that is considered useful and appropriate under certain, socially-approved, conditions. The example of spirit possession—such as that in Haitian voudoun as well as in African religious rites, Chinese Daoist mediumship, Siberian shamanism, and the more genteel European séance—is another type of dissociation, one that has been classified as "hysteria" by early modern psychiatry, but one which is a core element of much spiritualism and occult practice. The body is seen as a vehicle for spiritual forces, a kind of horse that can be mounted by the spiritual force evoked. Indeed, in Haitian voudoun this is the symbolism employed, for the possessed person is called a horse. In Malaysia, there is a virtually identical ritual—called *Kuda Kepang*—in which men carrying large wooden horse figures (similar to the western "hobby horse") dance around in a circle until they become possessed by spirits, all under the watchful eye of the shaman, or *bomoh* as he is called in the local language.

This leads us to the next element of the occult ceremonies in which forces are evoked: the "material basis."

Having regard to the nature and antecedents of the Intelligences with which Black Magic professes to be concerned, it must be highly important that the operator should know the kinds of apparitions which may be expected.... According to the Grimorium Verum, the spirits do not invariably manifest under the same forms ... being disengaged from all matter, they must of necessity borrow a body in order to appear before us, and then they assume any shape and figure which seems good to them. Beware, however, lest they affright thee ...

—A.E. Waite[20]

We have seen how the belief systems of ancient peoples allowed for the temporary possession of human beings by spiritual forces. This is a belief that persists to this day, from the Caribbean to Africa to Asia, and in virtually every continent and among virtually every race. The conscious evocation of forces, the invitation to these forces to inhabit a human being, is as commonplace in Haiti as it is in Malaysia and Africa. While spirit possession may also occur without conscious invitation—such as in the cases of demonic possession to which Oesterreich refers in his monumental *Possession, Demoniacal and Other*—we will focus for the moment on the voluntary kind. Normally, this takes place in an environment that has been under the conscious control of a shaman of some sort; the shaman provides a physical area that has been "blessed" or sanctified in some way, an area that will contain the forces summoned. This is as true for European ceremonial magic as it is for Haitian voudoun. Then, the shaman or magician begins the ceremony that will summon these forces into the bodies of the worshippers. The worshippers then become possessed by these forces under the watchful eye of the shaman, and depart as well under his supervision and observation.

In the jargon of modern ceremonial magic, the person thus possessed would be considered a "material basis."

This is a well-known idea in European magic. In some of the early grimoires, we read of the advisability of having a young boy act as a seer under the control of the magician; the boy should be a virgin (perhaps to ensure that his emotional state was unencumbered by the heavy calculus of adult desires and worries), and at or below the age of puberty. In the literature concerning poltergeist activity—the "noisy ghost" phenomenon in which household implements are thrown through the air, furniture levitated, bangs and explosions and all sorts of startling occurrences take place without any obvious human or mechanical agency—it is believed that the presence of young children reaching the age of puberty are (unconsciously) at fault. There is a tentative theory that children reaching that age possess telekinetic powers due to some hormonal imbalance taking place as their bodies prepare for the onslaught of adolescence.

In other, more recent, cases we have the example of Aleister Crowley and his sometime disciple, the poor doomed Victor Neuberg. In the sands of northern Africa, Crowley and Neuberg were involved in the evocation of spiritual forces using basic ceremonial techniques. In these experiments, a magic circle was drawn within which the chief operator or magician would stand throughout the ceremony. A triangle was drawn outside the circle, and in this figure the "material basis" would sit during the same period. This "material basis" could have been anything from an animal to a magic mirror to a brazier of burning incense, but in the case of at least one of the operations carried out in the north African desert, Crowley himself sat in the triangle while his assistant, Victor Neuberg, stood in the circle and recorded everything that transpired. During the course of this ritual, it seems Crowley became possessed by a spiritual force—in this case, identified as Choronzon, the Beast of the Abyss—and attacked Neuberg, leaving the triangle and jumping inside the magic circle whose integrity had been breached by Crowley/Choronzon throwing small amounts of sand over the circle, obliterating it in places. Neuberg reacted quickly, stabbing outward at the "apparition" with his magic dagger, and Crowley/Choronzon retired to its triangle as Neuberg repaired his circle.

A "material basis" is a medium whereby an invisible, formless spiritual force may manifest itself in three-dimensional terms. This basis can be anything malleable enough for a force to inhabit and animate in some way. Billows of incense may collect themselves into the semblance of a demon or a genie, much the way children see faces in clouds. Images may coalesce on the surface of a magic mirror or crystal ball. A cat on a leash or a bird in a cage may, when planted within the magic triangle, become agitated in ways that evince an occult, occupying force. And a human being, especially one mediumistic, artistic or sensitive enough to begin with, can also become a material basis for the occupation of a spiritual force. This happens with regularity among people all over the world, but usually in a socially-powerful setting like a voodoo ceremony or shamanistic séance. In Western ceremonial magic, the same goal is desired but within a very strictly controlled setting and with a very specific force in mind. The rituals of ceremonial magic are less Dionysian than those of Haitian voudoun; they are more ponderous, more complicated, and are created with the evocation of a particular entity in mind, to the exclusion of all others. The Haitian ceremonies are like occult cocktail parties to which a variety of guests are invited and the music and the drums are an integral part of the "entertainment." By comparison, the ceremonies of western magic are more like job interviews. But in either case, the material basis is necessary.

A more detailed description of this concept may be found in a novel by English magician Aleister Crowley: *Moonchild*. In this work, a room is fitted with decorations all designed to invoke lunar qualities, so that a young woman may become pregnant therein and give birth to a child of lunar characteristics. It is a concept that has its origins in the idea of sensory deprivation, but of a more refined type in which every sensory stimulus is removed save the ones most conducive to the desired goal of the ritual. It is a study of the complete control of a physical environment in order to similarly control the mental and emotional state of a human subject, so that the subject becomes the "material basis" for a spiritual force that has been summoned by the operator. Just as a woman becomes the material basis for the soul of the child she is carrying—so goes the argument—other physical media can become (temporarily or permanently) the material basis for other "souls" or spiritual forces.

If we stop to consider for a moment how this works, we will see at once an analogy to the theme of this book, for the spiritual forces are invisible, yet we know they are there. To evoke them only needs a suitable medium, and the will to summon them. They will then clothe themselves in the molecules of whatever medium is available, arranging them around themselves into a semblance of what they are and what they represent, a kind of mask or persona, much the same way we dress ourselves in our everyday costumes, making a statement with every article of clothing we wear. The intelligence agent does the same thing, of course. Beginning with the assumed name, he is "born again" as someone else. He dresses the part, speaks the part (possibly even in a language foreign to him), and acts the part. He occupies a space in front of his enemies, but they know him not. He is, essentially, a spiritual force moving through their environment: the physical representative of the will of some other government, some other country, some other agenda, some other reality. Some of these agents may simply be gathering information; others may be bent on more sinister ends: assassination, sabotage, the overthrow of a political regime. They are analogous to spiritual forces, sent by magicians to investigate the

"Other Side." And when they are discovered, it is usually by the enemy's own "magicians," who understand the secret world of the spies and who can read the signs they leave on the aether.

When the interrogator begins his ceremony, the subject is brought into a controlled environment and his entire consciousness is manipulated coldly and effectively by the interrogator. The subject has information the interrogator needs. The subject is the "material basis" for the information; the poor wretch destined to occupy the dread Triangle of Art while the magician—the interrogator—is safe within his magic circle.

The interrogatee has been unwillingly led onto an initiatory path from which—according to the point of view of the theologian, the mystic, the occultist—he may not escape. Irrevocable forces have been set in motion; the interrogatee has been forced to see inside himself, to witness profound truths about the state of his soul and, by extension, the state of the world—of reality—as well. His world has been turned inside out: an adult, he has become a child again; an enemy, he has become a collaborator; a man who thought he understood how the world works, he has become an initiate into a deeper, darker mystery.

When these techniques have been amplified by the use of drugs, hypnosis, and the other paraphernalia of medical men like Ewen Cameron or Sidney Gottlieb, they become intensive initiatory experiences, but without the saving graces of a spiritual context that would permit some kind of growth. Instead, it is as if the initiation chamber had been taken over by the sorcerer's apprentice: a non-initiate with no real, personal knowledge of the initiatory process but who managed to get hold of the book and recite the incantations carelessly, thus damning both himself and whoever happened to be in close proximity. It is no accident, I believe, that Dr. Frank Olson—arguably one of the first victims of the CIA's mind-control program—was made to visit an important stage magician in the hours before he plunged to his death from a window at the Statler Hotel. The reason for this unusual visit has never been satisfactorily explained.

L'Art Magique

If within the last century art conceived as an autonomous activity has come to be invested with an unprecedented stature—the nearest thing to a sacramental human activity acknowledged by secular society—it is because one of the tasks art has assumed is making forays into and taking up positions on the frontiers of consciousness (often very dangerous to the artist as a person) and reporting back what's there.

—Susan Sontag[21]

Le Poete se fait voyant par un long, immense et raisonne dereglement de tous les sens, toutes les formes d'amour, de souffrance, de folie; il cherche lui-meme, il epuise en lui tous les poisons, pour n'en garder que les quintessences. Ineffable torture ou il a besoin de toute la foi, de toute la force surhumaine, ou il devient entre tous le grande malade, le grand criminel, le grand maudit—et le supreme Savant!—Car il arrive a l'inconnu!

— Rimbaud, letter to Paul Demeny, 15 May 1871[22]

How, then, to compare the "sacramental human activity acknowledged by secular society" with a sacramental human activity *not* acknowledged by secular society, such as magic, Tantra, shamanism, etc., which has the same ends and often very similar means? If, as Rimbaud insists above, the duty of the Poet is to become a seer, by "an immense and systematic derangement of the senses," and thereby arrive at sure knowledge of the Unknown, then where do we draw the line between art and shamanism, between poetry and psychological warfare? We have spoken in previous volumes about the strange interrelationships that exist between certain films and actual political events, such as *The Manchurian Candidate*'s director John Frankenheimer being the host of Bobby Kennedy's last meal. Film, of course, is an art form and—as stagecraft by other means—one of the oldest forms of art in the world, and one of the most sacred in a mystical and religious sense, the actors inviting possession by the gods they represented in the theater, a sacred space. Can art be used to understand magic, and vice versa? Or can the lives and techniques of the artist be used to reinterpret the lives, techniques and even address the accomplishments of the magician? The reader may be surprised to learn that there is a body of literature on the subject of art as occultism, and art as psychology ... with very revealing things to say about all three. The application of this literature to our theme will become obvious in the following pages.

We saw in Book I how communication science developed out of the requirements of psychological warfare, or what the Germans called "world-view warfare." We have also seen how the bible of modern psychiatry, the *Diagnostic and Statistical Manual, Mental Disorders (DSM)*, arose from US military requirements. While we have not yet investigated the impact of psychological warfare concepts on the most pervasive artistic media of modern times—music and cinema—we will first examine the development of one influential artistic movement and its relationship to both modern psychiatry and modern occultism: surrealism.

There have been several attempts to understand surrealism from the point of view of psychology and of occultism. An excellent example of the former is *The Haunted Self: Surrealism, Psychoanalysis, Subjectivity* by David Lomas. Published in 2000 by Yale University Press, it is a profound study of the cross-pollination of surrealism, psychoanalysis and various "fringe" practices, such as hypnosis and automatic writing. As an example of the latter, we have Nadia Choucha's *Surrealism and the Occult: Shamanism, Magic, Alchemy, and the Birth of an Artistic Movement.* Published in 1991, it covers much of the same ground as the later work by Lomas, but with a more specific—and equally revealing—focus.

The man largely considered to be the father of the surrealist movement is Andre Breton. During World War I, he worked in a military hospital treating victims of what is now known as post-traumatic stress disorder (PTSD). A medical student at the Sorbonne, he was heavily influenced by the writings of Pierre Janet, the famous psychologist who also exerted a great influence over Freud and Jung and a generation of philosophers and thinkers. Janet's work *Psychological Automatism* was a seminal study of the role automatic writing and free association could play in an understanding of the unconscious mind. Breton took this technique to heart, and used it in his treatment of shell-shocked veterans.

Automatic writing is a technique whereby one either closes his eyes or is otherwise distracted from what his hand is writing on a sheet of paper, the idea being that the hand will write words that come directly from the unconscious mind, sneaking in below the super-ego, the radar of consciousness. To the spiritualists, automatic writing was a form of communicating with the Other World, the spirit world, and mediums would use this as a means of obtaining messages from deceased loved ones. (This technique was dramatized in the Nicole Kidman film, *The Others.*) Breton and many of the other Surrealists, however, denied the existence of spiritual forces, ghosts, etc. and insisted that automatic writing—like all of the occult arts—was only a means towards releasing images and information, even heretofore hidden powers, from the unconscious mind. Although heavily involved in occult studies—as Nadia Choucha demonstrates—they were unconvinced of the existence of the spirit world per se, and instead preferred to conceive of the occult arts as a kind of proto-psychology:

> The surrealists all rejected the idea of spirits, believing that these messages and drawings came from the unconscious mind of the medium as a result of dissociation of the personality.[23]

This idea of the "dissociation of the personality" was as important to the surrealists as it was for later generations of psychiatrists and mind-control experimenters. To the surrealists, the human consciousness was *normally* in a state of dissociation and it required techniques such as automatic writing and other trance-states to unify the unconscious material with consciousness; that is, they believed dissociation was a sign of the breakdown in communication between the conscious and unconscious minds. They sought to re-integrate, individuate, the human personality (in much the same way as did the psychoanalysts and the shamans) by uncovering repressed unconscious data and making it available to the consciousness. Yet, while the psychoanalyst worked one-on-one with a patient, the surrealists intended to explore the mind's potential in their poetic and artistic expressions and thus, perhaps, instigate a move towards illumination among larger numbers of individuals.

The study of cases of double and multiple personality (so-called 'disaggregations of the personality'), of which there was a near epidemic in the late nineteenth century, caused a number of investigators to raise doubts about the philosophical premise that the human subject is a unity.

—David Lomas[24]

Breton was heavily influenced by the writings of the French symbolist poet, Arthur Rimbaud. He believed, like Rimbaud, that a "derangement of the senses" was necessary before true illumination could be obtained. At the same time, he was as strongly influenced by the writings of Janet, who believed that hysteria was caused by dissociation, or by the dissociation of a traumatic episode in the patient's past, with a host of related ideas that could only be accessed through such methods as free association and automatic writing. This equation of dissociation with hysteria is important; after all, modern psychiatry has insisted that the incidence of witchcraft in Salem—for instance—was simply a manifestation of hysteria; and writers on demonic possession put forth the theory that possession is either a form of hysteria or of dissociation. A person suffering from dissociative identity disorder may appear to be "possessed"; a possessed person may only be suffering from a form of what Janet or Freud would call hysteria. This complex of ideas surrounding what other cultures believed to be a spiritual phenomenon is at the core of shamanistic practices, just as it is of the CIA's MK-ULTRA and similar programs for unlocking the secrets of the mind. To Breton, surrealism was nothing more or less than "a form of psychic automatism"[25] and "magic dictation." The use of what had originally been an occult technique—automatic writing, a mediumistic method of contacting spiritual forces—to understand hysteria and dissociation (which had originally been believed to be evidence of possession by spiritual forces) is revealing, for not only the symptomatology of the mental disorder had its origins in witchcraft and magic, but the method for treating it also claimed similar origins. All that changed, really, was a set of labels.

The surrealists as a group struggled with the relationship between word and image; they felt that language was paramount (after all, automatic writing is writing, not drawing), but those who were artists rather than poets were confused as to how the newly discovered ideas of psychology, science and philosophy could be expressed through image. There was a great deal of struggle between the poet-surrealists and the artist-surrealists at the birth of the movement, the poets claiming that the artists could not hope to duplicate their efforts since the mind was, at its heart, verbal. "In the beginning was the Word." Much of what Janet and, later, Freud wrote concerning the functions of the mind stressed the verbal quality of consciousness. To Breton, the spiritual mentors of the movement were Rimbaud and Baudelaire, and of course Lautreamont: poets, not painters.

Asian languages, however, show that frequently both word and image are combined. Chinese characters have their origin in hieroglyphics, and there is little in a Chinese character to indicate its pronounciation. Ancient Egyptian writing was, of course, pictographic and evolved into the famous hieroglyphs we all know. Ancient Mayan writing—only recently deciphered—was also hieroglyphic. The idea that a word could also be an image, or could contain an image inside of it somehow, was also the essence of Qabala. As Hebrew letters were also numbers, which meant that each Hebrew word contained within itself hundreds or thousands of associations, that also meant that each Hebrew word contained within itself images corresponding to those associations. The Golden Dawn used a technique for "translating" Hebrew words into images, as a kind of coding system. They further refined this method as the Enochian system, in which the four elements each have their symbolic animals (the Eagle, the Lion, the Bull, the Man, representing the four fixed signs of Scorpio, Leo, Taurus and Aquarius respectively, which themselves represent Water, Fire, Earth and Air respectively), and combinations of the elements meant one could combine the four elemental "animals" into various configurations, producing what were certainly "surreal" images: perhaps the head of a Man, the body of a Bull, the legs of an Eagle and the tail of a Lion? Using the Hebrew alphabet, one could also translate that combination into a word using the Hebrew letters for the four elements as found in the unpronounceable name of God, YHVH.

One of the surrealist artists connected with the occult was Austin Osman Spare. Spare was also concerned with the connection between word and image, and in his work (what he called "automatic drawing") he created a "magical alphabet" that used Roman letters arranged in such a way as to create occult symbols or "sigils." Spare claimed to have been initiated into witchcraft by a descendant of the original Salem witches, and was also a member of Aleister Crowley's occult society, the *Argenteum Astrum* or A.·. A.·.. His work has also had a profound influence on occult author and Crowley-initiate Kenneth Grant. Spare believed that the method of automatic *drawing* was "a means to art," as an essay of his—published as a chapter in his *The Book of Pleasure (Self-Love): The Psychology of Ecstasy*—attests. What Spare and many other surrealists had done was to take the essentially passive approach of Breton—as reflected in their fascination with automatic writing and the hypnotic trance—and raise the stakes by incorporating a more aggressive approach to unlocking the secrets of the mind by using formal occult methods involving spirit conjuration, drugs, and sexually-oriented rituals. It was taking Rimbaud's "derangement of the senses" much more seriously, much more energetically. It was the "voluntary madness" of Artaud, which even Artaud understood in occult terms.

The list of surrealist painters who were also occultists is actually quite long, and many art critics are not aware of this relationship, just as many occultists are not aware that some of the more well-known authors on occult subjects were also surrealist painters. Spare is only one example of an occultist who was an acknowledged surrealist artist. There was also Ithell Colquhoun, who wrote a history of the Golden Dawn entitled *The Sword of Wisdom.* There was respected surrealist painter Kurt Seligmann, who wrote a history of occultism: *Magic, Supernaturalism and Religion.* Aleister Crowley himself was a painter, although one hesitates to classify him as a surrealist.

The other surrealists who were fascinated with occultism and incorporated occult themes in their works or occult knowledge in their approach to art include virtually every famous name of the movement: Max Ernst, Antonin Artaud, Marcel Duchamp, and many others were heavily influenced by occultism and read avidly in the subject, and were, in their turn, subject to occult "analyses" by art historians and critics who came after them. Kandinsky, a kind of proto-surrealist, was also very involved in occult theory and Theosophy and was on familiar terms with the works of Blavatsky, Rudolf Steiner, and Maurice Maeterlinck, as his own writings demonstrate. He, too, wrote of art as a revolutionary act, equating mysticism, revolution and art, with references to Nietzsche, Blavatsky, and the other "revolutionary" thinkers of the day. Picasso was considered by Breton to be a forerunner of surrealism, and Picasso's interest in primitive art parallels that of Freud as well as the surrealists'.

The primitive, the childlike, the insane: these were the vocabularies that Breton wanted to investigate, like a fortune-teller over a pack of Tarot cards, for their hidden meanings and their clues to the unconscious world; and these three categories of being represented opposition to the social status quo.

There can be no doubting that Breton's wartime experience as a medical auxiliary predisposed him to view hysteria as a form of insubordination—a protest, albeit a mute one, against military and medical authority.

—Lomas[26]

The surrealist perspective is echoed in that of Scottish psychiatrist R.D. Laing who, in his controversial and thought-provoking essay *The Politics of Experience*, makes many of the same points concerning schizophrenia and the possibilities of spiritual growth through madness. It should be noted that Laing also began his medical career in the army, in this case the British Army, where he worked as a psychiatrist before going on to the Tavistock Clinic. Laing agrees with the surrealists when he states that "... we are bemused and crazed creatures, strangers to our true selves, to one another, and to the spiritual and material world—mad, even, from an ideal standpoint we can glimpse but not adopt,"[27] and, "We are potentially men, but are in an alienated state, and this state is not simply a natural system."[28] *The Politics of Experience* includes a final section, entitled "The Bird of Paradise," that would have satisfied many a surrealist, as it seems to be a free-association-like account of a journey into and out of madness. Concerning the voyage into madness, Laing is unequivocal:

> We can no longer assume that such a voyage is an illness that has to be treated.... Can we not see that this voyage is not what we need to be cured of, but that it is itself a natural way of healing our own appalling state of alienation called normality?
>
> In other times people intentionally embarked upon this voyage.
>
> Or, if they found themselves already embarked, willy-nilly, they gave thanks, as for a special grace.[29]

Thus Laing, more than forty years and a World War after the first *Surrealist Manifesto,* is seen endorsing what is really a surrealist agenda, except he is doing so as a trained, experienced, and respected member of the psychiatric profession and not as an artist. He recognizes that "in other times people intentionally embarked upon this voyage," the condition of voluntary madness that is a hallmark of poets like Rimbaud and Artaud, as well as of occultists and shamans, and people like Breton, Masson, Ernst, Duchamp and so many others. The energy of the surrealist movement perhaps finds its culmination in Laing; we are certainly living now in a state of *denouement* in which the ideas of Laing have been discarded or ignored by a profession that seems to have found its savior in chemical therapies that treat symptoms, and make the neurotic and psychotic more productive members of an increasingly unhappy and alienated society.

It was not only Laing who represented this new appraisal of surrealist ideas. Even Mircea Eliade—cited earlier for his insights into the link between shamanism and madness—speaks directly to the problem, writing in 1969:

> It is naively believed that six months of "field work" among a tribe whose language one can scarcely speak haltingly constitutes "serious" work that can advance the knowledge of man—and one ignores all that surrealism or James Joyce, Henry Michaux, and Picasso have contributed to the knowledge of man.
>
> The contemporary artistic experiments are capable of aiding the historians of religions in their own research ... It is not without interest to note, for example, that in their revolt against the traditional forms of art and their attacks on bourgeois society and morality the surrealists not only elaborated a revolutionary aesthetic but also formulated a technique by which they hoped to *change* the human condition. (emphasis in original)[30]

Eliade recognized the attempt by the surrealists—more than any other "artistic movement"—to actually *change* humanity. This historian of religion, mysticism and shamanism saw kindred spirits among the surrealists, and wondered openly about the value of his anthropological colleagues living with primitive tribes for short periods and writing up elaborate explanations of their culture and beliefs, when there was such a rich storehouse of knowledge about the human condition sitting ignored in the texts and artworks of the surrealists and other voluntary madmen. He goes on to state in the same paragraph that the exercises of the surrealists "recall certain Yogic or Zen practices" and that the effort of the surrealists to enter into a state of consciousness that combines both the sleeping and the waking states—à la the hypnotic trance—was nothing less than "the desire to effect in concrete the coincidence of opposites, the hope of being able to annul history in order to begin anew with the original power and purity—nostalgia and hopes rather familiar to historians of religions."[31]

Did the surrealists succeed? Did they leave a map for others to follow?

I will take a very big chance of alienating many people by stating that it may be wrong to consider surrealism as simply another artistic movement. The stated goal of the surrealists—as revealed in the succession of manifestos that appeared in the 1920s and 1930s, usually from the pen of Andre Breton, but signed and ratified by the surrealist luminaries of the time—was nothing less than open communication between the conscious and unconscious minds, and the expected resultant freedom and empowerment of the individual. They intended to accomplish this in ways that were, in a sense, anti-intellectual, although the literature of surrealism see-saws between the intensely intellectual and the playfully poetic. In a sense, the surrealists used artistic media as weapons in their revolutionary struggle to liberate human consciousness. As a social movement—that is, as a movement with the intention of affecting as many members of society as possible, rather than through a slow and arduous process of initiation—they did share a few elements in common with both the psychological warfare officers (engaged in "world-view warfare") and the men of MK-ULTRA.

The surrealists sought to tap the powers of the mind using psychiatry and occultism (whatever would work, whatever would help them break through the barrier between consciousness and unconsciousness), and in this they are not very different from shamans, not very different from the men of MK-ULTRA. Art—painting, sculpture, poetry, fiction, and even (with Bunuel and Dali) cinema—happened to be the medium in which they worked, but surrealism was born on the battlefields of World War I, as the confrontation between life and death, between existence and non-existence, forced a generation of artists to chose between the dangerous ignorance of a cultivated sanity and the seemingly crystal clarity of madness. The hideousness of that conflict, the first "high-technology" war using tanks, airplanes, mass communications, and chemical weapons, traumatized a generation. Breton began life as a medical student, and worked with shell-shocked soldiers at the front. Andre Masson, another important surrealist, fought in the War and spent agonizing hours wounded, lying in a ditch face-to-face with a dead German soldier, literally "facing death." Using automatic writing, hypnosis, and later various occult techniques and occult studies such as alchemy and ceremonial magic, the surrealists tried to penetrate the secrets of the mind; this endeavor would be repeated by the CIA a few years after World War II, continuing for decades until fear of discovery made them either cancel their projects or disguise them in some way. The preliminary goals of the surrealists and the spies were the same: unlock the secrets of the unconscious mind, understand amnesia, hypnotic trance, hysteria, dissociation, multiple personalities and "the self," and the human will. Yet, the ultimate goals were quite different. For the surrealists, the liberation of humanity—the perfect freedom of men and women—was their target, their *raison d'etre*. For the CIA and the military, the aim was the enslavement of those minds and the harnessing of consciousness to political and military purposes. The surrealists used the garret, the artist's studio, the writer's desk; the CIA used the laboratory, the interrogation room, the torture chamber.

This is not to say that the surrealists were apolitical. A little-discussed and perhaps consciously-ignored aspect of the surrealist movement is the strength of their political commitment. Art historians tend to avoid political analysis as much as military historians ignore the religious or spiritual framework of combating forces (such as the occult nature of much of the Third Reich, and especially of the SS). However, the widespread and energetic political involvement of the surrealists is as important to a complete understanding of what they were as are their psychic explorations. As early in the movement as 1925, when the French government began to suppress Moroccan tribesmen in their African colonies, the surrealists expressed a political agenda that was anti-authoritarian, anti-colonial and—eventually—anti-fascist as well. Breton's *Manifesto of the 121*, for instance, was an attack on the Algerian war of the 1950s.

Most importantly, though, was surrealism's clear-cut opposition to both fascism and Stalinism. While they supported revolution against oppressive authority in general, and could be considered a kind of socialist movement in sympathy with Marxism-Leninism, they opposed totalitarian governments. Their aim, after all, was the liberation of the human soul. Breton spoke out publicly against fascism in the 1930s (for instance, in Belgium in 1934), and surrealism eventually came to the attention of the Nazis. The Nazi "art exhibit" of 1937, *Degenerate "Art,"* was a clear attack on the surrealist movement which was, after all, an affront to fascism not only politically but also "spiritually." The surrealists were on the Nazi death lists, and they had to flee.

As noted in Book I, virtually the entire surrealist movement managed to escape the Third Reich and go into exile abroad: Breton, Ernst, and so many others avoided the death camps through the assistance of Valerian Fry and others, the same people who helped Hans Habe escape to America. It is of great interest to this study that the artistic movement most singled out by the Nazis for destruction was surrealism, for the surrealists may have been polar opposites of the Nazis when it came to political ideas, but they were just as fascinated by the occult and by the possibilities of human consciousness. The Nazis, however, were a cult, and cults can admit of no competing cults. While it would be rash to label surrealism a "cult," it was not purely an artistic movement, either. Art was their medium of expression, but the experiments entertained by the movement—including in one case hypnotic trances carried out every day for more than a year by surrealist Rene Crevel—were more in line with psychic research and psychoanalysis than sculpture.

In 1938, Breton famously met exiled Russian revolutionary Leon Trotsky in Mexico, accompanied at the time by painter Diego Rivera, and they penned yet another manifesto, this time on revolution and art. It was an attack on Stalinism, of course, and the photo that exists of Trotsky, Breton and Rivera standing around in Mexico, chatting, tells us more about why the surrealists were despised—and why they were important—than any volume of art analysis. From Breton the medical man, Breton the psychotherapist in the trenches, Breton the poet and founder of the surrealist movement, Breton the psychic researcher, to Breton the anti-fascist and revolutionary: a single man can so succinctly represent the entire flow of ideas in this work:

He managed to escape the Nazis during World War II and wound up in exile.

In December 1945, he gave a speech on surrealism in Haiti.

A few days later, the Haitian government was overthrown in a popular uprising.

John Lilly on sensory deprivation and hallucinations; James Clark Moloney on the similarities between interrogation and religious experience; the surrealists and the occult … and anti-fascism. Perhaps the reader will agree that the thesis I have been promoting is not so far-fetched after all. Intelligence agency and secret military mind-control programs, psychological warfare, and … art and … religion. In Books I and II we have looked at CIA programs affiliated with MK-ULTRA which investigated paranormal phenomena as well as occultism of various types. We have examined the CIA's promotion (and investigation) of hallucinogens such as LSD-25, as well as shamanistic resources like psilocybin and mescaline and the *Flesh of God.* We've watched as OSS scientists such as Henry Murray became involved in drug research (with Timothy Leary) and interrogation techniques (on Ted Kaczysnki, the Unabomber). If we match what the CIA was doing under BLUEBIRD, ARTICHOKE, and MK-ULTRA with religious conversion phenomena, mystical practices, shamanistic rituals, and the initiatory cults of Europe, Asia, Africa and other areas, we will better understand the role of psychology, philosophy, and organized religion in modern American politics.

In Book I we saw how Nazism infected many American political and industrial leaders, and in another place (*Unholy Alliance*) I showed how Nazism was (and is) in fact a cult, with an ideology all its own. We have seen how the Christian Right has supported a political agenda at home in America and abroad in the developing nations. We have witnessed the merger of organized religions such as Roman Catholicism and Eastern Orthodoxy with both fascist and Nazi political parties and with "ethnic outreach" programs in Europe and the United States. We saw how the churches helped many Nazi war criminals not only escape justice, but thrive and prosper in their new countries.

We will also see how this moral blindness has contributed to the phenomenon of the serial killer, the mass murderer, and to the present state of world affairs. I apologize if this perspective is disturbing, and I am sensitive to the criticism that there may be other explanations for the data I have already presented, as well as the data I am about to describe. However, the state of the world today requires us more than ever to seriously consider these strange arguments, for they offer an explanation for modern events that no other, less controversial, course of study so far has been able to contribute.

There is no such "condition" as "schizophrenia," but the label is a social fact and the social fact is a political event.

—*The Politics of Experience* (emphasis in original)[32]

Endnotes

[1] Peter Dale Scott, *Deep Politics and the Death of JFK*, University of California Press, Berkeley, 1996, p. 12

[2] David Lomas, *The Haunted Self*, Yale University Press, New Haven, 2000, p. 67

[3] John Bossy, *Giordano Bruno and the Embassy Affair*, Yale University Press, New Haven, 1991, p. 101

[4] Ibid., p. 154

[5] Ibid., p. 146-154

[6] Ibid., p. 154

[7] Ioan P. Couliano, *Eros and Magic in the Renaissance*, University of Chicago Press, Chicago, 1987, p. 105

[8] Ibid., p. 69

[9] Ted Anton, *Eros, Magic, and The Murder of Professor Culianu*, Northwestern University Press, Evanston, 1996, p. 123

[10] Ibid., p. 135

[11] Christopher S. Hyatt, ed., *An Interview with Israel Regardie*, Falcon Press, Phoenix, 1985, p. 31-34, ISBN 0-941404-31-5, LOC 84-80967

[12] This manual is available in many places on-line, and was originally generated in July 1963 as *Kubark Counterintelligence Interrogation*, KUBARK being an internal codeword referring to the CIA.

[13] Ibid., p. 116-117

[14] Ibid., p. 116

[15] Ibid., p. 31, p. 116

[16] John Marks, *The Search for The "Manchurian Candidate,"* Times, NY, 1979, p. 127-130
[17] *Kubark Counterintelligence Interrogation*, p. 88
[18] Ibid., p. 48
[19] Hassoldt Davis, *Sorcerers' Village*, Little, Brown, Boston, 1955, p. 304-305
[20] A.E. Waite, *The Book of Ceremonial Magic*, Dover, NY, p. 193-4
[21] Susan Sontag, "The Pornographic Imagination," in Georges Bataille, *Story of the Eye*, Penguin, London, 2001, p. 92
[22] Reprinted in p. 11, *Rimbaud, Collected Poems*, introduced and edited by Oliver Bernard, Penguin Books, London, 1962.

> "The Poet makes himself a seer by a long, immense and reasoned derangement of all the senses, all forms of love, of suffering, of madness; he searches within himself, consuming every poison and retaining only their quintessence. Ineffable torture, where he needs all his faith and superhuman strength, and during which he becomes the great patient, the great criminal, the great accursed—and the supreme Wise Man! —among all men, because he arrives at the unknown!"

[23] Nadia Choucha, *Surrealism and the Occult*, Destiny Books, Rochester VT, 1992, p. 53
[24] Lomas, op. cit., p. 59
[25] Ibid., p. 22
[26] Ibid., p. 56
[27] R.D. Laing, *The Politics of Experience*, Parthenon, NY, 1967, p. 13
[28] Ibid., p. 13
[29] Ibid., p. 167
[30] Mircea Eliade, *The Quest: History and Meaning in Religion*, University of Chicago, Chicago, 1975 edition, p. 65
[31] Ibid., p. 65
[32] Laing, op. cit., p. 121

Chapter Eighteen

Hollywood Babalon

Babylon was Bab-ilani, a "gate of the gods," for it was there that the gods descended to earth.... But it is always Babylon that is the scene of the connection between the earth and the lower regions, for the city had been built upon bab apsi, the "Gate of the Apsu"—apsu designating the waters of chaos before the Creation.

—Mircea Eliade[1]

Now that we have succeeded in breaking down the atom the cosmos is split wide open.... We have arrived, possessed of a power which even the gods of old could not wield. We are there, before the gates of hell. Will we storm the gates, burst hell itself wide open? I believe we will. I think that the task of the future is to explore the domain of evil until not a shred of mystery is left.

—Henry Miller[2]

Evil has become a determinant reality. It can no longer be dismissed from the world by a circumlocution. We must learn how to handle it, since it is here to stay. How we can live with it without terrible consequences cannot for the present be conceived.

In any case, we stand in need of reorientation, a metanoia. Touching evil brings with it the grave peril of succumbing to it. We must, therefore, no longer succumb to anything at all, not even to good.

—C.G. Jung, (in reference to Nazism)[3]

Sinister forces are at work!

—Peter Sellers as Inspector Clouseau in *The Pink Panther Strikes Again* (1976)

One might have guessed that I am the type of movie-goer who sits in the theater at the end of the film and reads the credits. Naturally, I am interested in the actors, character actors, director, producers, cinematographers, and writers; but I am also interested in the locations, the musical score (the composer, the arrangers, the selections of pre-recorded music and their performers and composers, etc.), as well as in the organizations and people thanked by the producers, usually at the end of the long list of credits and just before the copyright notices. This means I am usually the last person sitting in the theater when the house lights go up.

Now, with the advent of video tape and especially of DVD technology, I am able to watch these credits more carefully, rewind and re-read, and generally perfect my education. What I am doing with film is what I do with novels, non-fiction, government files, police reports, interviews and news reports: data mining. It's hard on the eyes and taxes the brain—and the patience of those around you. When you discover connections no one else has, you are elated until you find yourself greeted by annoyed glances of "so what?" and "here we go again." Yet, the rewards can be great if your prey is the dark matter at the heart of existence.

I grew up watching old films on a small black-and-white television. These were mostly gritty gangster flicks and propaganda films from World War II. My mother would share bits of information about the personal lives of some of the actors, and this made me aware of another world hiding behind the celluloid world. I watched James Cagney, Errol Flynn, Humphrey Bogart, Ronald Coleman … *A Tale of Two Cities, The Light That Failed, Casablanca*, and all the sentimental, swashbuckling tales of the 1930s and 1940s. *Singin' in the Rain, Easter Parade, Oklahoma!, The Wizard of Oz, The Bells of St. Mary's, Boy's Town* … Like it or not, the themes and attitudes of these films helped mold a certain way of looking at the world, a way of expecting heroism, self-sacrifice, humor, gallantry, and resolve in the face of danger. *A Passage to Marseilles, The Cross of Lorraine* … I learned how to be a gentleman watching performances by Ronald Coleman, Michael Rennie and George Sanders … and then learned that there was no room for gentlemen in the Postwar world. Gentlemen, I discovered, were dinosaurs: obsolete, like the black-and-white screen I grew up watching, in which the world itself was reduced to a case of black versus white, of evil versus good.

When I left home at the tender age of eighteen, I moved to a tiny studio apartment in Brooklyn Heights not far from the legendary haunts of Henry Miller, Walt Whitman, and Norman Mailer. I did not have a television set, and would not own or watch a television set for another ten years, all through the decade of the 1970s. Co-workers felt this was an indication that I was some kind of subversive, or perhaps an alien. Others would say I had not missed a thing.

Instead, I went to the movies.

Things had changed since the propaganda flicks of the 1940s. Now we had a more sophisticated medium, offering us *Catch-22, A Clockwork Or-*

ange, The Kremlin Letter, Anne of a Thousand Days, Joe, The Revolutionary, The Strawberry Statement, Slaughterhouse-Five. And then I discovered foreign films. *Murmur of the Heart, Sunday Bloody Sunday, Belle de Jour, Satyricon, Roma, La Nuit Americaine.* Suddenly I had developed a taste for Truffaut, Malle, Fellini, Bunuel. When a new film was screened in Manhattan—usually on a Thursday—I would take off work, call in sick, and be the first one into the theater for the first run of the film in New York. Sometimes I would see two films on the same day, an unheard-of luxury for a young man working at minimum wage as an inventory clerk who sometimes had to walk to work across the Brooklyn Bridge and up to 32nd Street—a jaunt of several miles—just to save the subway fare to buy an ice cream for lunch at Grand Central Station on 42nd Street. At night, I would return home to my studio apartment—really a former pantry that had been blessed with a modern bathroom, the largest and most comfortable room in the damp, freezing studio—and work on my short stories, which were experiments along the line of surrealism.

I foraged for Grove Press books at a store in a subway arcade under Madison Square Garden, and began to read Burroughs and Kerouac and Ginsberg. I was alone, my parents had separated, my brother and sister were still in high school and living with our mother in the Bronx, and the books—and the movies—were my company and my education and culture. The artistic nudes in *Evergreen* were my introduction to the female form. Paperbacks by Abbie Hoffman and Regis Debray and Chairman Mao were my introduction to subversive politics, politics as a kind of culture, a kind of artform. Movies, books, politics all became a homogenous mass, a black mass of revolution, freedom, exhilaration. I wore a beret, and read French newspapers. I made friends in Brooklyn Heights and spent time in sidewalk cafes, talking about Vietnam and Palestine, assassinations and rebellions, art and film and poetry. I might as well have been in Paris. Or Barcelona. Or Prague, until that deadly Spring.

But underneath all of that was another reality, one I had suppressed; a reality of séances and Ouija boards, churches and liturgical celebrations, Russians and Syrians and spies. I had befriended students of similar ethnic background as myself, people of Czech and Slovak ancestry who spoke the languages and had one foot in the Old Country. I was introduced to the world of the Eastern Orthodox churches, a demimonde in the middle of New York City populated by exiled countesses and bearded archimandrites, of low-level agents and fascist sympathizers. It was a fascinating, glamorous world for a sixteen- and seventeen-year-old boy from the Bronx and one in which I easily fit. I was desperately hungry for culture, for knowledge, for an explanation of the things I had lived through in my life so far. America did not provide much in the way of culture beyond television and sports, or so I thought, and the exiled European communities presented me with entire, fully-articulated cultural experiences involving languages, cuisines, religions and politics. I soon began to study Church Slavonic, to the point where I could read it effortlessly and chant along with the monks in the Russian, Ukrainian, Serbian, Bulgarian, Slovenian, Carpatho-Russian orthodox churches of New York City.

And one day, in the company of one of my friends, I went to see a film starring Anthony Quinn and Michael Caine, *The Magus*. Based on the best-selling novel by John Fowles, the film made a great impression on my young mind. I left the theater wondering if everything I saw around me was an illusion; if the people around me were merely actors, playing a role designed to elicit from me some specific reaction, like the Michael Caine character in the film who is an Englishman living on a Greek island, befriended by the mysterious Anthony Quinn character who stage manages an entire experience for him, to the point where Caine does not know if he is going mad.

Film had that ability, I realized. An ability to alter perceptions of reality, if only for a moment. What power! And this was long before I ever heard of subliminal messages in advertising or films: little snippets of film, a few frames long, inserted into the tape so that your conscious mind did not record the images but your unconscious mind—which sees everything—did. No, this was simply the artistry of the motion picture, the power of actors and plot and lighting and music to work on your mind to such an extent that you lost contact with your historical world and entered into one invented by the filmmakers. An *unconscious* suspension of disbelief. An open challenge to your "worldview." Mind control.

My father had been an actor for a while, and had copies of Stanislavksi's writings on the Method, alongside a complete set of the works of Edgar Allan Poe. Maybe, I thought, there was more to this than simply memorizing lines and pretending to be someone else and looking pretty while doing it. As I grew older, I discovered that the writings of Stanislavski were applicable to a wide range of human experience. No wonder Hollywood actors feel they have something to say about everything, I thought, even if they don't! Stanislavski makes them believe they do, makes them believe that acting gives them an insight that is relevant to all of human experience. The true Method actor is a kind of initiate, a voluntary madman, and opens himself or herself up to forces he or she does not understand, but which are potent nonetheless. And these forces—being summoned—then act upon those in close proximity. That was the point, after all, of the very first theatrical performances in ancient Greece, which were sacerdotal in nature, a conjuration of the gods. That was why theatrical performances were banned by the medieval Church as occasions of sin and tools of the Devil. And that is why the American film industry is seen as such a threat to the cultures and mores of people living in developing nations around the world. It is, as the splendid German phrase has it, "world-view warfare."

THE METHOD

Let me remind you of our cardinal principle: through conscious means we reach the subconscious.

— Stanislavski[4]

"They told me that you had gone totally insane, and ... uh... that your methods were unsound."

"Are my methods unsound?"

"I don't see any ... method ... at all, sir."

—an exchange between Colonel Kurtz (Marlon Brando) and Captain Willard (Martin Sheen) in Francis Ford Coppola's *Apocalypse Now!*

On October 7, 1947—a few months after the first modern American UFO sighting in June and the Roswell "crash" in July—the Actor's Studio was opened in New York City. An organization dedicated to teaching actors the Stanislavski "Method," it was mentored by Lee Strasberg and Sandy Meisner, both strong adherents of the Method who at the same time became mortal enemies due to "artistic differences." Thirteen days later, on October 20, 1947 the House Committee on Un-American Activities or HUAC began its investigation into Communist infiltration of the Hollywood movie business. Ronald Reagan (FBI agent T-10) was one of the first to betray his friends as Communists, thus paving the way for a career in American politics, first as Republican Governor of California and later as President of the United States. Walt Disney was another one eager to cooperate with the Committee, as was Jack Warner of Warner Brothers and Louis B. Mayer of MGM. While the two events are seemingly unrelated, it is ironic to realize that Stanislavski—a Russian who stayed in Russia after the Revolution and who died in Moscow in 1938—would wield such an influence over American acting and filmmaking even as HUAC was attempting to clean out Hollywood of Communists, Communist sympathizers, and fellow travelers.

Eventually, one of Lee Strasberg's most famous pupils at the Actor's Studio would be Marilyn Monroe.

Konstantin Stanislavksi was born Konstantin Sergeyevich Alekseyev in Moscow in 1863. The child of a wealthy family of manufacturers, he had the freedom to choose his career and went wholeheartedly into acting, forming—in 1897—the celebrated Moscow Art Theater or MAT. His performances as an actor in roles by Chekhov and Ibsen, as well as Shakespeare's *Othello*, earned him renown not only in Russia but throughout Europe. One of his other, more famous, accomplishments as a director includes Maurice Maeterlinck's *The Blue Bird*, and of course with that, as detailed in Book I, we are back at the ranch. *The Blue Bird* would once again be performed in Moscow, but this time in 1976 as a film directed by George Cukor and starring Elizabeth Taylor, Jane Fonda, Ava Gardner, Cicely Tyson, and many others in a star-studded cast that was the first ever US–Soviet joint film production. It was not, however, the first film version of Maeterlinck's play, but it has been the last to date. (Oddly enough, the first was a 1940 offering by Walter Lang starring Shirley Temple, released just one year after *The Wizard of Oz*.) Stanislavski was evidently very much taken with Maeterlinck, for he mentions him and *The Blue Bird* several times in *An Actor Prepares*. As Maeterlinck was well-known as a mystic, an astrologer, and a spiritualist as well as a Nobel-Prize winning author, we should not be startled to realize that Stanislavksi's "method," for all its naturalistic emphasis, has its roots very firmly in the occult tradition, particularly that represented by the surrealist point of view.

Consider the following:

> I have no desire to prove whether Prana really exists or not. My sensations may be purely individual to me, the whole thing may be the fruit of my imagination. That is all of no consequence provided I can make use of it for my purposes and it helps me.[5]

In discussing Prana—the Sanskrit term for "the breath of life" or spirit, power, vitality, etc.—Stanislavski was applying yoga and yogic techniques to husbanding this energy and using it in performance for everything from breath control to physical presence on the stage. (Is it a coincidence that the film company that produced the first vampire film, *Nosferatu*—a company created by German occultists—would also be named Prana?) Stanislavski's approach is a common-sense one that the surrealists would have approved, for he does not care if Prana exists in an objective sense, only that he can use the concept to help him in his work. This fits in very well with Breton's insistence that there was no such thing as a ghost, but that mediumship was useful and interesting.

Stanislavski was clear about the cardinal principle of the Method: "through conscious means we reach the subconscious." This was, of course, the surrealist agenda, except that for Stanislavski it was dangerous and pointless to penetrate the subconscious realm directly. One had to approach it obliquely, to coax it into making an appearance, and then when it did, not interfere. This ability of the subconscious he called "intuition," and it was an actor's greatest asset.

In order to summon intuition—in order to consciously reach the subconscious, in his words—he made use of physical gestures and of providing background stories for the characters portrayed, thereby developing actors' sense memories. One of the most difficult aspects of the Method for many actors is this delving deeply into one's past, dredging up past traumas in order to use the energy, the gestures, the reactions constructively in a role.

It is a type of psychoanalysis, after all, in which an actor is made to undergo painful experiences from his past in a classroom full of his fellow students. This conscious invocation of pain and memory is an echo of the shamanistic initiations we discussed briefly in the previous chapter. It is a deliberate attempt to induce a kind of hysteria in the student-actor while maintaining his or her conscious control over it. A very difficult and very demanding process, and one that does not have psychological integration as the goal. Rather, this system can be used to create a kind of dissociation necessary for the kind of spectacular performances we have come to expect of a Brando, a Pacino, a DeNiro. A Christopher Walken.

For what is an actor but a person who specializes in multiple personalities? Who deliberately invokes—on a stage, night after night—an alien presence into his body, his consciousness?

The structure of the play, the static form of the lines to be recited, the necessity to react to the other actors in the right time and place, act as a kind of ritual, enabling the performers to retain their sanity to the end. (My mother told me the story—certainly apocryphal, for I have found no record of this—that the Broadway theater cast of Erskine Caldwell's *Tobacco Road* had gone somewhat insane as a result of portraying the same miserable, defeated characters night after night, and could not "get out of character" once the performance was over. Such was the reputed pernicious power of the "Method.") As noted previously, theater was originally presented not as entertainment but as education and illumination. It was sacerdotal in nature, a religious and mystical experience, and the actors prepared for this accordingly. What Stanislavski did was to put down on paper and in practice a codified form of this ancient system, for acting had in a sense degenerated since that time into one-dimensional pantomime. Actors no longer thought of their function as sacred or mystical, but as a vehicle for ego, for self-dramatization at the expense of the play. Stanislavski brought the actors back to a realization of the importance of their art by speaking of the subconscious and of "psychic processes," thus elevating acting to a kind of priestly role.

> Our subconscious is inaccessible to our consciousness. We cannot enter into that realm. If for any reason we do penetrate it, then the subconscious becomes conscious and dies.[6]

What Stanislavski means here is that the raising of the subconscious to consciousness robs the subconscious of its energy. Freud understood that subconscious (or unconscious) material drew energy into itself from the very fact of its suppression. Stanislavski did not want perfectly individuated and psychically integrated actors, for they would not have the artistic temperament required to make their performances come alive. Yet, he did want to tap that energy in a conscious way. He wanted, in other words, to play with fire: to have his cake and eat it too.

> Fortunately there is a way out. We find the solution in an oblique instead of a direct approach. In the soul of a human being there are certain elements which are subject to consciousness and will. These accessible parts are capable in turn of acting on psychic processes that are involuntary.
>
> To be sure, this calls for extremely complicated creative work. It is carried on in part under the control of our consciousness, but a much more significant proportion is subconscious and involuntary.
>
> To raise your subconscious to creative work there is a special technique. We must leave all that is in the fullest sense subconscious to nature, and address ourselves to what is within our reach. When the subconscious, when intuition, enters into our work we must know how not to interfere.[7]

What he is discussing are the physical gestures that can "accidentally" release subconscious energy, and the evocation of personal memories which are "accessible" and which can act on involuntary psychic processes. He is asking his students to allow themselves to become vehicles for the roles to be performed. This can have its dangerous aspect, but the method used by Stanislavski—while much more intense than normal acting classes which rely on basic stagecraft—is primarily safe insofar as it goes, although in unstable people some of the exercises could cause emotional distress if the teacher is not experienced enough to handle the rough psychological fallout. In any event, the Method is a viable means of awakening the unconscious, and it does so within a socially-acceptable context of theater arts.

The problem—from the point of view of initiation—is that the unconscious is awakened and put to use for different roles, different performances, in a consciously-controlled environment that is not conducive to spiritual growth in and of itself. Today you are Othello, tomorrow Romeo. You have no control over the order or nature of the roles you take on. Unlike a magician or shaman who has a set path to follow and a set order of experience, an actor puts on and takes off personalities like a voodoo practitioner who becomes possessed by different gods. The spiritual growth of a voodoo devotee (from the point of view of shamanistic initiation) is not clear. His ability to become possessed by his gods does not immediately suggest that he has entered upon a spiritual path with integration or individuation (to use the Jungian term) as its goal. The voodoo *priest*, however, is another matter, and in order to be successful and attain credibility among his congregation he must have passed through a complete initiatic program, much as his ancestors and present-day counterparts in western Africa.

The Method actor is—for all his preparation and soul-searching and intensity of concentration—still at the whim of the demands of the theatrical world. It is a business, a job, and requires one to be able to be different people at different times, all on command. The audience is in a similar situation. They do not progress through a set program of theatrical events, rising in spiritual or psychological understanding with each passing performance. Instead, their experience is as willy-nilly as that of the actors themselves. Unlike the calendar of ritual used by the Catholic Church, for instance, in which Epiphany follows Christmas with unerring regularity and the Christian year moves slowly into Lent and then Holy Week and Good Friday and Easter, a theatrical calendar can be anything, in any combination, at any time. It is considered "entertainment," but those of us who have witnessed great performances—whether on stage or screen—instinctively know that entertainment is a weak description of what has transpired. For westerners in the 21st-century world, theater and especially cinema is the closest thing to a spiritual experience many of us will ever have. That is why we so easily misunderstand and miscalculate the tremendous influence of religion in developing countries that do not have their own movie industry … and the horror with which many non-westerners view Hollywood Babylon.

ANGER MANAGEMENT

"The only performance that makes it, that really makes it all the way, is the one that achieves madness."

—Mick Jagger as "Turner" in *Performance* (1968)

Filmmaker Kenneth Anger (1929 -) began his career as a child actor in a production of *A Midsummer Night's Dream* (1935)—the only sound film ever made by Max Reinhardt, the Austrian stage director, which was also the film debut of Olivia de Havilland, and featured an all-star cast including James Cagney, Dick Powell and Mickey Rooney (as Puck). He eventually moved behind the camera to write and direct such cult classics as *Kustom Kar Kommando* (1965) and *Scorpio Rising* (1963), *Invocation of My Demon Brother* (1969), and *Inauguration of the Pleasure Dome* (1954-56). Some critics have insisted that Anger is the precursor of—and inspiration for—such directors as David Lynch, Pier Paolo Pasolini, Martin Scorcese and Francis Ford Coppola. His involvement with Thelema—the cult founded by Aleister Crowley—is clearly evident in everything from *Pleasure Dome*, which featured Anais Nin and Marjorie Cameron (Jack Parsons' wife) to *Demon Brother*, which featured Manson Family member and convicted murderer Bobby Beausoleil as well as Anton LaVey of the Church of Satan. When we search for links and connections between the Ordo Templis Orientis (OTO), the Church of Satan, the Manson Family, Hollywood, and Sixties rock 'n' roll, we can do worse than to begin with Kenneth Anger.

> The '69 Tate massacre was not Old Hollywood. What befell the red house on Cielo Drive resembled the devastation caused by a jet plane crash: the

> Bad Ship Lollipop piloted by Uncle Sugar. Charlie Manson—programmed puppet, *deus ex garbage can.*
> —Kenneth Anger[8]

Now more than 75 years old, Anger made his impact on Hollywood with a film entitled *Fireworks*, which was released in 1947 and caught the eye of French poet and filmmaker Jean Cocteau. Cocteau (1889-1963) was one of the earliest "surrealist" filmmakers, with his *Le Sang d'un Poete* (*The Blood of a Poet*) released in 1930, and he was part of the symbolist entourage around such notables as Claude Debussy, designing the sets for Debussy's *Pelleas et Melisande*, which was itself an operatic version of a Maeterlinck play on Merovingian themes. He is perhaps better known for his film *Orphee* (*Orpheus*), released in 1950, which received wide critical acclaim and which was an interpretation of the myth of Orpheus who descended into the Underworld, certainly an initiatic theme. Even more importantly for us, Cocteau was identified as one of the leaders of the Priory of Sion (the French society which, it is claimed, holds secret information concerning the bloodline of Jesus Christ) by the investigative team of Baigent, Leigh and Lincoln in their controversial bestseller based on documents found in the Bibliotheque Nationale in Paris, *Holy Blood, Holy Grail*,[9] and for some background on the French occult societies that interpenetrated French artistic circles, *Holy Blood, Holy Grail* is a good introduction, and shows how deeply artists like Cocteau and Debussy were involved in everything from Rosicrucian mysteries to Cathar revivalism. (Cocteau's design for a mural of the crucifixion in the Notre Dame de France cathedral in London is a blatant Rosicrucian—and Templar—allegory which would have appealed to Anger, with its hints of Egyptian and occult symbolism.)

Anger followed *Fireworks* with *Rabbit's Moon* in 1950 and *Eaux d'Artifice* in 1953, having become deeply involved in occultism of the Aleister Crowley variety during his high school years. One of his films, the early *Les Chants de Maldoror*, now lost, was based on the famous pre-surrealist "prose poem" of the same name by the doomed visionary, Lautreamont, who was such an influence over Breton and the surrealist movement. This fusion of occultism with art and cinema places Anger firmly within the surrealist category, at least for a time early in his career.

With his critical *bonafides* supplied by Cocteau, he spent time in France working for the director of the *Cinematheque Francais* and wrote what would become an underground classic: *Hollywood Babylon*, published originally in French in 1959. This was an exploration of Hollywood's seamier side, revealing scandal after scandal, murder, suicide, drugs and sex, which opens with a famous quotation from Aleister Crowley's *Book of the Law*, the "Bible" of his religion of Thelema: "Every man and every woman is a star." A sensation in France, it eventually made it into an English version in the United States in

1975. In the interim, Anger had become part of the Rolling Stones' entourage and had traveled with them on tour, finding time to cultivate friendships within the sinister nexus that accumulated around Charles Manson, the Church of Satan, and the OTO. Manson Family member Susan Atkins had already performed for the Church of Satan as a vampire in a black mass, an effort that was caught on film and preserved for posterity.

In fact, it is with Anger that we gain a backstage pass to the ebb and flow of the sinister forces at work in America, for he seems to be either at the center or the periphery of some of America's most pivotal cultural events from the 1950s through the 1970s, and beyond. From his early film starring Marjorie Cameron and Anais Nin, to films featuring performances by Bobby Beausoleil, Mick Jagger, Keith Richards, Anton LaVey, and so many others, we find that Anger is there for everything from the doomed Thelema Lodge of the OTO to the Magick Powerhouse of Oz to the Church of Satan to the Charles Manson Family to Altamont and "Sympathy for the Devil." For a while, death and destruction seemed to hover around Anger like demented groupies at a Megadeth concert.

In 1955, Kenneth Anger went to Cefalu, Sicily, the site of Aleister Crowley's Abbey of Thelema during Mussolini's rule, with the intention of doing a documentary on the place, and found it essentially intact, from an occult and artistic point of view anyway. Many of the murals painted by Crowley were still in evidence, albeit whitewashed over by nervous villagers who had the place exorcised after Crowley's departure, much as the cottage where Stephen Ward resided at Cliveden was exorcised, and Anger shot a lot of film on-site, at one point escorting famed sexologist Alfred Kinsey around the place.[10] This was a year after he had released *Inauguration of the Pleasure Dome* featuring Marjorie Cameron. Thus, by the mid-1950s, Anger was thoroughly in the midst of a magical quest, and used his preferred artistic medium—film—to record, celebrate, and illuminate the fact.

This fusion of occultism and film was not the first attempt to use the medium to promote a surrealist agenda, but it was one of the more accessible to avant-garde American audiences. By the 1950s, it is doubtful whether surrealism, *per se*, was still a force to be reckoned with in the artistic world; the Beats were taking over the imagination of the disaffected young with poetry by Ginsberg and Ferlinghetti, fiction by Kerouac and Burroughs, and a generation of the beret-wearing, black-turtlenecked, finger-snapping, bongo-playing, professionally-alienated "artistes," so charmingly portrayed by the cartoon character GoGo Man Van Gogh in the bizarre animated series *Beanie and Cecil*. The difference between Anger's offerings and surrealist art in general was that Anger's was a specifically occult production, attempting to convey occult ideas, as well as other "marginal" concepts such as homosexuality, sadomasochism, etc. Whether or not Anger deliberately attempted to cause change in human consciousness with his films (most of which were quite short) or whether his goal was simply self-expression in the context of a radical approach to filmmaking cannot be easily understood. What is easier to trace is his involvement with occult organizations, especially as they connect to the arts in general.

Among the most influential rock bands of the late 1960s and early '70s were the Rolling Stones, Led Zeppelin, and The Doors. All three of these bands had very strong links with occultism. Jim Morrison, the leading light of The Doors, married Patricia Kennely, a Welsh Traditionalist witch whose Craft genealogy can be traced directly back to Gerald Gardner and Aleister Crowley. Led Zeppelin's Jimmy Page became so involved with Crowley's occultism (some say, due to Kenneth Anger's proselytizing) that he bought Crowley's old estate in Scotland: Boleskine. Even the Beatles would put a picture of Aleister Crowley on the back of their *Sergeant Pepper* album among the "People We Like," and we remember their pilgrimage to India to sit the feet of the Maharishi (along with Mia Farrow, of *Rosemary's Baby* fame).

But it is the relationship of the Rolling Stones—and specifically of Mick Jagger and Keith Richards—to hard-core occultism and satanism that fascinates us, and the compelling figure of Kenneth Anger who lurks at the center of this uneasy alliance.

One of the Stones' most famous songs is "Sympathy for the Devil," an intelligent and sinister paean to "his Satanic majesty." It was the song being performed at Altamont when the Hell's Angels killed a man in front of the stage before thousands of witnesses. What only serious followers of the Stones already know is that the strange "wooo-wooo" backup vocals are being performed by Anita Pallenberg and Marianne Faithfull, the lovers of Keith Richards and Mick Jagger, respectively. These two ladies were also very involved in occult practices, under the tutelage of Kenneth Anger, and had appeared in his Crowley-themed films. Pallenberg would later become involved in the suicide of a young man at the home she shared with Keith Richards; Faithfull would record a song in honor of witchcraft, and would appear in the magazine published by the Process Church of the Final Judgement.

One of the entourage around Anger, Pallenberg, Faithfull and the Rolling Stones was a somewhat more successful filmmaker, Donald Cammell (1934-1996). Cammell is interesting in this context because his father was none other than Charles J. Cammell, a biographer (the first) of Aleister Crowley. C.J. Cammell was a friend of not only Crowley but a whole coven's worth of occultists, including Victor Neuberg, the man we discussed in the previous chapter as working at rituals with Crowley in North Africa. Donald Cammell grew up around occultists of every variety due to his father's interests and claimed that he sat on Crowley's lap at least once when he was a child (surely a cause for parental alarm?). Cammell directed Pallenberg and Mick Jagger—as jaded rock star "Turner"—in his acclaimed film *Performance* (filmed in 1968, released with heavy cuts in 1971), and Julie Christie in his bizarre *Demon Seed* (1977), about a computer that impregnates a young woman played by Christie. His film *Wild Side* (1996)—starring Christopher Walken, Anne Heche and Joan Chen—never saw theatrical distribution due to artistic differences between the director and the studio, NuImage, which was looking for something less artistic and less different, and so retained final cut and made a mess of Cammell's vision. *Wild Side* eventually made it into the cable-tv world, albeit heavily cut and edited.

His last completed work was *White of the Eye* (1988), about a serial killer and the woman who loves him. Although it died at the box office, it was considered an artistic success.

Four films in his entire career, the themes running from a gangster and rock star ménage à trois in *Performance*, to a computer fathering a child in *Demon Seed*, to another gangster and another ménage à trois in *Wild Side*, to a serial killer in *White of the Eye*. He had false starts such as *Ishtar*, (a film that would have starred William Burroughs, Mick Jagger and Norman Mailer, about the Babylonian goddess returning to earth) and *Fan Tan* (a Marlon Brando project about piracy in the South Pacific). For various reasons, these projects never came to fruition. *Performance*, which made his name as a director to watch, was heavily influenced not only by the Rolling Stones and the rock 'n' roll world of London in the late Sixties, but also by occult mythology, in this case the world of Hassan i-Sabah, he of the Assassins cult which figured so prominently in Book II. In addition, the shadows of Genet, Borges, the artist Francis Bacon and themes of death, identity transfer, gender transfer, and transformation generally haunt this production from the very beginning. His cast included Mick Jagger and Anita Pallenberg, already wired into the British occult scene, and James Fox (the brother of actor Edward Fox) who would do an about-face and begin working for a Christian missionary organization right after filming was complete on *Performance*. He would not return to acting until 1983, even though he was a well-known actor who had starred in such films as *The Chase* (1965) with Jane Fonda.

Donald Cammell came to the attention of Kenneth Anger early on, and played the role of Osiris in Anger's *Lucifer Rising* (1970), made during Anger's Rolling Stones period. Anger said it was "type-casting." Cammell was already well on the way to making surrealist films, and admitted his influences were Antonin Artaud and Jorge Luis Borges, the famous Argentine writer who gave the world some of its most interesting and unearthly prose, fortified by prodigious learning and intellectual vigor, made all the more remarkable considering that Borges was blind.

It is said that Cammell's last words were about Borges, as the bullet that entered his skull did its damage and slowly dimmed the light of one of Hollywood's least appreciated and certainly least understood directors, reprising the scene in which Turner is killed in *Performance*, as the camera shows us the bullet entering his skull (from above, the same awkward angle Cammell chose for his own death) and culminating in a picture of Borges. Cammell committed suicide on April 23, 1996 when on the verge of revitalizing his career, and it took him forty minutes to die in the arms of his wife, China (Patti Kong) Cammell.

In his final years, Cammell—son of an occultist and a crypto-occultist himself, surrounded by witches and magicians—became mentally unhinged. He developed an alternate personality, called "the uncensored Cammell," who did outrageous things in public (such as driving at high speed in the Hollywood hills, completely naked) that the other Cammell would never have done, and never remembered afterward. This was a clear sign of dissociated identity disorder, and his friends asked him to seek medical help but it was no use. He claimed the anti-depressants he was prescribed actually made his situation worse. It is not known whether the doctor he visited for only a few sessions was aware of Cammell's increasing dissociation, or if he was just being treated for depression. It is also entirely possible that Cammell was right, and that the anti-depressants made things worse by empowering the "uncensored Cammell." Alas, we shall never know.

In the same category of actors plagued by their art to the extent that they do themselves damage is a more recent case, that of Hong Kong actor and singer Leslie Cheung, who committed suicide on April 1, 2003 by plunging from his Hong Kong hotel room window to the streets below. Mr. Cheung—a handsome young man with an intelligent and knowing visage, an idol to Chinese men and women alike for both his immensely popular songs and his movies—had starred in a recent string of hits, including *Double Tap* (2000) and *Inner Senses* (2002). In *Double Tap* he had portrayed a gunsmith and expert marksman who kills a man in an effort to save lives, only to discover that he enjoys killing, becoming, in effect, a serial murderer. It was a powerful performance by the boyish-looking singer, and led to *Inner Senses,* his last film.

In *Inner Senses*—one of a growing number of excellent Asian horror films—he portrayed a psychotherapist who tries to help a young woman who is being driven insane by visions of ghosts. As he cures her, he becomes "haunted" himself. The film explores themes such as suicide, spiritual possession, the paranormal, and madness with a rare, deft touch, and we watch as Mr. Cheung's character goes slowly insane from guilt over the suicide of an old girlfriend when he was still in secondary school. He begins the film by stating that repressed memories should stay repressed, as they have been repressed for a reason (an odd position for a psychoanalyst!); and, in a kind of corollary, that "there are no such things as ghosts," that ghosts represent useless information that cannot be accommodated in other ways. As the film progresses to its climax, the Cheung character's own memories come to haunt him and nearly kill him. The penultimate scene is of the psychoanalyst, confronted with the ghost of his dead girlfriend, at the edge of a tall building saved at the last minute from falling to his death by neutralizing his feelings of guilt over her suicide in a conversation with her ghostly form. It's the type of ending that would make sense to a psychotherapist, but perhaps not to Leslie Cheung himself, who became strangely withdrawn and isolated after the completion of the film.

The rumors in Asia at the time of his death were that the film had so shattered his psyche that he did not recover from its effects, and that the Hollywood-style ending—so Western in its resolution of the problem by making the ghost and the analyst "talk out" the problem, so that both ghost and analyst come away whole—was so artificial in an Asian context that Leslie Cheung could find no other way to resolve a deeper, mysterious personal problem except by resolving the film's central problem with his own death, in exactly the same way as it would have happened in the film: falling from a tall building. No one knows why the actor committed suicide, and it shocked and saddened the entire Chinese-speaking world to an extent reminiscent of the death of Rudolph Valentino nearly a century earlier. While in the West ghosts are the stuff of legends and scary movies, in Asia ghosts are taken very seriously, and it is perhaps this cultural disconnect that opened a door into Mr. Cheung's sensitive nature and caused a psychic imbalance. While James Fox left filmmaking altogether after *Performance* in order to become a Christian missionary and sort out his inner turmoil in a more constructive manner, Leslie Cheung was not so fortunate. And, as it turned out, neither was Donald Cammell.

It is interesting to think of the two director-occultists together on the same set, as they were for *Lucifer Rising*: Donald Cammell, the pedigreed visionary whose father knew Aleister Crowley and who himself met Crowley when he was a child in his Edinburgh home filled with art, music, fantasy, and magic; and Kenneth Anger, the black magician wannabee who came at the occult from the dark side of satanism, sadomasochism, and sexuality. While neither man could claim to be a Hollywood success story, it is clear that, from the point of view of the studios, Cammell had somewhat more going for him. His four completed films were full-length Hollywood movies with intricate plotting and character development and a profligate use of flashbacks, intercutting and hallucinogenic cinematography and special effects. By contrast, Anger's films are short subjects on interesting themes, with some recognizable actors and film scores by Jagger and Bobby Beausoleil, but on the whole curiosities of the art and extremely experimental, rather more in the line of filmed rituals, no matter how beautifully realized. Both directors have become cult idols, of course, and critics point to the influence of both Cammell and Anger over generations of new directors.

Cammell himself confessed that he was an admirer of Anger and that *Performance* was largely inspired by Anger's work. At the time *Performance* was being filmed, Cammell was part of the entourage around the Rolling Stones including Pallenberg (who was leaving Brian Jones for Keith Richards), Marianne Faithfull (who was supposed to have played Pallenberg's role—Pherber—in the movie, but who had to leave the production due to pregnancy by Mick Jagger), Mick Jagger, Keith Richards and Brian Jones themselves, and Anger. It was also the year that "Sympathy for the Devil" was released, a song sung by Satan himself which became the soundtrack for the Altamont homicide the following year. It was Pallenberg and Faithfull who came up with the idea to use the "woo-woo" chant as background vocals to the song and it is the two witches who actually perform it in the 1968 recording. On a more recent note, the music of the Stones was employed almost as a physical presence in the occult thriller *Fallen* (1997), starring Denzel Washington as a police detective attempting to solve a series of murders which are, in fact, being committed by a demon. In the beginning of the film, the demon has possessed a serial killer, who sings "Time Is On My Side"—a song made famous by the Stones—during his execution, and this song is picked up and used throughout the film as the signature tune of the demon. The credits go up, however, not with "Time Is On My Side" but with that other classic, "Sympathy for the Devil." The idea of a demonically-possessed serial killer was first introduced to American audiences with *Exorcist III* (1990), however, and is a theme whose powerful attraction is difficult to describe, but whose affect on genuine serial killer Jeffrey Dahmer has already been noted.

It is claimed by music historians that the Stones' fascination with Crowley, magic and satanism ended with the tragedy at Altamont, a rock festival that was promoted as a kind of "Woodstock West," but which somehow degenerated into a catastrophe culminating in murder. That did not affect Anita Pallenberg or Marianne Faithfull in quite the same way, however, and there is no evidence that they abandoned their occult beliefs or practices after 1969. While there is a lot of speculation that Kenneth Anger had relationships with members of the Process Church of the Final Judgement, I have been unable to verify this. However, his close relationships with the Church of Satan and with the OTO is beyond doubt, as they are heavily documented in Anger's own films.

With Pallenberg and Faithfull, however, we are on firmer ground, as we know that Faithfull, for instance, once posed for the Process in a photo published in their magazine (the same magazine that featured writing by Charles Manson in one of their issues). Thus, through Faithfull and in the same time period as *Performance* and *Lucifer Rising*, we have solid Process connections. In fact, a 1999 update of Maury Terry's 1987 book on the Son of Sam and Manson cases, *The Ultimate Evil*, shows that Manson met the Process as early as 1968—the same year *Performance* was being filmed—and in one case actually met Process members in the Tate-Polanski home on Cielo Drive before the doomed actress moved in.[11] While Terry's conclusions are not always to be relied upon, his raw data is usually trustworthy. I believe it is safe to say that the circle around Anger knew the Process fairly well and had contacts with them. To what extent exactly these contacts involved the darker side of both the Process and the Anger circle is subject to speculation.

Pallenberg for her part was involved in a death that took place at the home she shared with Keith Richards in 1979. The death is startling enough, but it took place in an area that was known as the "eastern headquarters" of the Process, in upstate New York near the Connecticut border, in the town of Pound Ridge. According to Terry, the Process had their headquarters nearby in the appropriately-named Salem, New York. The victim was a seventeen-year-old caretaker, Scott Cantrell, who shot himself to death in her bed. The death was ruled a suicide, but for a while it looked as if Pallenberg would be accused of manslaughter. It seems that Cantrell was talking of playing Russian Roulette. The nexus of events surrounding this location is compelling, however, for the small and remote area around Pound Ridge comes up several times in this investigation, showing the twisting threads of coincidence and conspiracy wrapped around themselves in a Gordian knot of sinister forces.

For instance, actress Ali MacGraw (*Love Story*, *Goodbye Columbus*) grew up in the same area—in the town of Bedford Village—which is not unusual in and of itself; but her father *was* rather unusual. A failed artist, he cultivated an interest in UFOs, Egyptian hieroglyphics, the mysterious Easter Island script, and many other languages.[12] He was a genius, born a little too late to be recognized in a world that does not value arcane erudition, or, indeed, erudition of any kind at all. An embittered, angry man, he made life unpleasant for his family, even as his gaze was turned towards a borderland reality they could not see.

Ms. MacGraw's first brush with the movie industry came in 1967 when she was part of the entourage around *Barbarella*, which was being filmed in Italy at the time. She met Jane Fonda and Anita Pallenberg off the set of that strange piece of science-fiction erotica; ironically, Fonda had already turned down the leading role in *Rosemary's Baby*, the part that would eventually go to Mia Farrow. (Pallenberg's role in *Barbarella* was as the Great Tyrant, a black-robed queen of the night.) Our interest in Ali MacGraw does not end there, however, for she brings us into the world of *Rosemary's Baby* producer Robert Evans, a man briefly believed to have been responsible for a murder connected to both the Son of Sam cult *and* the Manson Family.

Another link with Pound Ridge is a scandal that brewed there a few years ago, when local parents and teachers were upset over what they perceived to be a cult operating among their schoolchildren. As it turned out, this "cult" was based on the card game *Magic*, and Pound Ridge residents were convinced that the game was teaching its children occult ideas and practices. Perhaps the good citizens of Pound Ridge were a little sensitive on the issue, considering the suspected satanic activity of their neighbors, from Anita Pallenberg to the Process.

Before we leave Kenneth Anger, a closer look at two of his films—among the three involving overt occult themes—is well-deserved, for they will set the stage for what is to follow.

In *Invocation of My Demon Brother*, released in August 1969 (the same month as the Tate/La Bianca murders in Hollywood), Anger himself plays the role of the Magus; Anton LaVey of the Church of Satan portrays Satan; and Bobby Beausoleil (one of the convicted Manson murderers) is the Trickster, smoking a pipe in the shape of a skull. The Rolling Stones make an appearance in the film, in footage shot in Hyde Park three days after the death of their colleague Brian Jones. All this, in a film only eleven minutes in length. Anger's portrayal of himself as the Magus—as the master magician in control of the environment—could be interpreted as everything from wishful thinking and cinematic hyperbole to a darker (perhaps unconscious?) statement of moral responsibility. The year 1969 is, after all, the year the energy summoned by the Summer of Love two years previously began to die out, turn sour, and putrefy. The Manson murders in Hollywood, Altamont ... all this counter-culture evil taking place the same year that human beings first set foot on the moon in answer to the call of a martyred president.

For *Lucifer Rising*, released definitively in 1980, Anger had a more ambitious agenda. The producer of this film was none other than Anita Pallenberg, with Anger's credits as director, editor and the film's creator. Music was provided by Bobby Beausoleil, then in prison for life for the crime of murder (of musician Gary Hinman) in the first degree. Actors included Marianne Faithfull (as Lilith), and Donald Cammell as Osiris opposite his sometime lover Miriam Girbil as Isis. Kenneth Anger once again assumes the role of Magus.

The footage was shot in various potent locations, from Gizeh, Luxor and Karnak in Egypt to Stonehenge in England ... to Externsteine in Germany, the sacred pagan shrine so venerated by the Nazis. Anger, Faithfull and Donald Cammell were along for the ride, shooting in the Egyptian desert at the foot of the pyramids at Gizeh or at the temples of Luxor and Karnak. One can be reasonably certain that more than just filmmaking was taking place during this time. Bobby Beausoleil was originally cast as Lucifer, but his incarceration made shooting a trifle difficult, and a total of five "Lucifers" were cast over the years—including Mick Jagger—before Anger settled on Leslie Huggins in the title role. Jimmy Page of Led Zeppelin was writing music for the soundtrack, but he and Anger fought over various issues, with Anger famously cursing Page and—according to the tabloids—causing all sorts of evil things to befall the Crowleyan musician and resident of Boleskine, where some of the footage was shot. Anger was upset over the music Page had produced, and dismissed him as a mere occult dilettante. When this author met Anger—in the company of the OTO in New York City about the time of the release of *Lucifer Rising*—he appeared rather quick to denounce those with whom he disagreed.

One of the myths surrounding the film is that of the stolen footage, buried in the California desert by an irate Bobby Beausoleil and never seen again. Beausoleil denies this episode, but Anger has claimed that it is true. Beausoleil, in an interview published on his own Web site, beausoleil.net, claims that no film footage ever existed, and implies that Anger was trying to placate his "German backers" by saying that the film was stolen, when, in fact, he hadn't shot a single frame. In any event, the production was beset by all sorts of difficulties and would not appear for more than ten years. Beausoleil, it should be remembered, had appeared in films before, notably as an Indian brave in the soft-core porn epic *Ramrodder*, shot in Topanga Canyon not far from the Spiral Staircase in Malibu, the strange house where both the Process and Manson used to hang out. Appearing with him in *Ramrodder* was Catherine "Gypsy" Share, another Manson Family member, who would be involved in a shootout with police after a failed attempt to rob a gun store. Their plan was to break into prison, rescue Manson and head for the desert and freedom.

Lucifer Rising—only twenty-nine minutes long—concerns the invocation of Lucifer by Isis, Osiris, Lilith and of course the Magus. The characters play humans possessed by these gods at the various sites of power in Egypt, Germany and England, and the scenes are intercut with various images Anger found compelling, such as a solar eclipse, fires, volcanoes, and a goat. The finale of the film is a shot of a flying saucer sailing over the Sphinx. A pink flying saucer.

This identification of Lucifer with the God of Light—essentially the same as the Egyptian god Horus—is a familiar one, found in Theosophical writings as well as Nazi ideology. Indeed, the name "Lucifer" is Latin for "Light-Bringer," an echo of the belief that Lucifer was the brightest of all the angels and rebelled against God due to his sin of pride. Others have tried to show how Lucifer is merely another manifestation of Prometheus, who stole fire from the gods to give to humanity and was punished for his transgression. In a sense, then, Lucifer and Prometheus are both personifications of an older myth, perhaps reminiscent of Adam in the Garden of Eden, who disobeys God in order to know both good and evil and then is also punished.

Anger's only other film to incorporate occult themes is his earlier production, *Inauguration of the Pleasure Dome* (1954), with Anais Nin as Astarte. This is the film that boasts Marjorie Cameron—the widow of OTO's self-appointed Antichrist, Jack Parsons—in a cameo role. Ms. Cameron remained involved in occult practices long after the death of her husband in 1952, and various works by British OTO leader Kenneth Grant mention her writings and activities since that time. While Anger was interested in invoking Lucifer, Parsons was dedicated to Babalon, the Crowleyan Goddess, and was sure she had been incarnated sometime in the immediate Postwar era. As described in Book I, some of Parsons' letters to Marjorie Cameron on a variety of occult themes have survived, and they provide insightful, intelligent commentary on the entire movement.

It would be Parsons and Cammell who would die violently, both consumed by their esoteric visions; Beausoleil and Manson who would live on, but in prison, as murderers; Pallenberg and Faithfull who would survive addiction and worse and come out the other side. Jagger and Richards were never touched deeply enough by the forces swirling around them to derail them from their careers. And Kenneth Anger is now in his seventies, contemplating a filmed version of Crowley's Gnostic Mass and a second sequel to *Hollywood Babylon*, the Magus safe in his California home and surrounded by the ghosts of so many dead and dying gods.

Was Manson a "programmed puppet"? Of course, that is the thesis of this book as well as a throw-away line of Anger's. My information, however, comes second-hand from primary sources: from memoirs, police files, declassified government documents, and the like, seasoned with an extensive background in the esoterica of many countries. Anger was part of Manson's circle, or perhaps we should say Manson was part of Anger's. More importantly, Anger refers to the Tate killings as a plane crash of the "Bad Ship Lolllipop" being piloted by "Uncle Sugar," a nickname for Uncle Sam or the United States government. What does Anger know about the Manson killings? What does he suspect?

One wonders if he thinks back to the days of The Magick Powerhouse of Oz, Bobby Beausoleil's band in California during the "Equinox of the Gods" ceremony at the Straight Theater on September 21, 1967? Or of the Himalayan Academy that he helped to establish with Timothy Leary and, it is said, Abigail Folger, who would die so violently and hideously at the hands of the Manson Family at the Polanski-Tate residence? Or of Altamont and "Sympathy for the Devil" in 1969 and yet another murder, this time of a black man by Hell's Angels gang members? Or the even more bizarre story circulated on the Internet that Kenneth Anger met Mark David Chapman in Hawaii six weeks before the Lennon assassination in 1980; to accentuate the eeriness of the tale, it is insisted that Chapman gave Anger a gift of some live bullets. It *would* account for Chapman showing up in New York City with a gun but no ammunition.

Regardless of the fact or fiction of the stories woven around Anger—many woven on Anger's own loom—it may be agreed that he has staying power. Whether he is still the Magus, still ordering the universe to fit his peculiar Gnostic vision, remains for history to decide.

Queen of the Night

At one of the Polanskis' wild, drug-fueled bashes at 10050 Cielo Drive in tony Brentwood, the housekeeper could not get into the bathroom and began pounding on the locked door.

Eventually, the door opened and out came Jane, hair mussed and clothing askew, with another male guest.... "I hate it," she said, "when something's half finished." A guest recalled that the mysterious "other man" may have been handsome millionaire hairstylist Jay Sebring, who had been Sharon Tate's lover before she met Polanski.[13]

"You know you're only allowed out on Halloween!"
—Jane Fonda as "Night" in *The Blue Bird*, 1976

One of Jane Fonda's more bizarre cinematic appearances is as Night in the film version of Maurice Maeterlinck's play, *The Blue Bird*. We discussed this work extensively in Book I, due to its compelling relevance to (and possible inspiration for) the CIA mind-control program of the same name. Maeterlinck's play was first performed in Russia, and was important to Konstantin Stanislavski. It was only fitting, then, that a film version be made in Russia once again, this time starring Elizabeth Taylor, Jane Fonda, Ava Gardner, and a host of other bright Hollywood lights and using a local Russian film crew. By all accounts, the film was a disaster. George Cukor had never made a fantasy film before, being remembered more for classics such as *Gaslight*, and this lavish attempt seemed doomed to failure even before the rushes were in. Fonda spent six weeks filming in Moscow, only to find that the bulk of her performance wound up on the proverbial cutting-room floor.

It is the fact that the film was made at all that interests us, for the only other time anyone had filmed *The Blue Bird* (in 1940), it had starred Shirley Temple, who eventually wound up as the American Ambassador to Czechoslovakia. This time, the film was being made in the Soviet Union as a gesture of détente, and thus rife with political undertones. Fonda was known in Russia only barely, and primarily for the fact that she had visited Hanoi during the Vietnam War. Her husband, Tom Hayden, accompanied her for a while to Moscow, only to become disgusted at the bourgeois appetites of the Muscovites, who seemed more interested in blue jeans than politics. What is not discussed in any of the sources I have been able to locate is the extent to which American intelligence used this first American–Soviet cinema co-production to advance their own agenda in Russia. It seems like a heaven-sent opportunity to infiltrate an agent or two into the entourage, using the production as a cover for more nefarious activities, but, alas, there is no documentation to support such a contention.

Yet, how *The Blue Bird*—the operational name for the CIA's first mind-control effort—came to be associated with Russia and filmed in Moscow (the evil empire, after all, that had used mind control on Cardinal Mindszenty to force him to make outrageous confessions before television cameras) is one of the "coincidences" in this study that hum beneath the threshold of our hearing. One has to ask why it was important to Cukor and his producers to make the film at all, and at considerable expense. It must have seemed an eccentric choice. As it was filmed on location in early 1975 and released in 1976, seven years after the Manson killings and the year of the U.S. bicentennial, I like to think that *The Blue Bird* production was Jane Fonda's wake-up call, literally. After all, as detailed in Book I, she was likely present—along with husband-director Roger Vadim—at the Polanski home on the day that a drug dealer was pistol-whipped in front of Polanski's guests, only days before the actual murders of Sharon Tate and her friends. She studied Krishnamurti for a while, largely due to her brother's influence, but generally avoided occultism (according to one of her biographers, Christoper Andersen[14]), even though it was very popular in her circle and especially among the Polanski clique.

The Blue Bird is about memory, and fear, and conspiracy, and ultimately salvation. It is about innocence, and about traveling far and wide, only eventually to find happiness at home. Like the *Oz* books—the stories by Frank Baum that inspired the name of Beausoleil's band, The Magick Powerhouse of Oz—its message is faintly fascistic: "there's no place like home." To get to this primeval state of bliss, one has to proceed through a nightmare of anxiety, mortal attacks, and terror. The children do this in *The Blue Bird*, just as Dorothy does in *The Wizard of Oz*. (Strangely, and again according to Maury Terry's informants, one of the cults connected to the Son of Sam operation was called "The Children.") It is a spiritual voyage straight from the world's shamanistic traditions, and at least in Maeterlinck's case the analogy was probably deliberate.

Maeterlinck wrote extensively on occult themes, as we have seen, and was a believer in spiritualism and psychic phenomena in general. His influence over Stanislavski was due at least as much to his spiritual worldview as it was his Nobel Prize in Literature. Maeterlinck was a man with a mission, a believer. *The Blue Bird*—while seemingly a story for children—is, like most fairy tales, a coded message for adults, one the CIA took very much to heart, ransacking it for technique and theory while ignoring its higher meaning.

While the Cukor film is worth mentioning simply because we have spent so much time with Maeterlinck and the play before—in the context of the CIA—Fonda's role in it is compelling for two reasons: one, she was obviously very close to the circle around Sharon Tate and Roman Polanski and was even suspected of having had sex with Tate's former lover, Jay Sebring, as well as of having been present for the unfortunate punishment of the drug dealer at the Polanski home: connections that lead us straight back to Charles Manson and the Family. But the other reason is perhaps even more bizarre. It involves her brother, Peter Fonda, and his marriage to Susan Brewer.

Peter Fonda, of course, became a film idol with the release of *Easy Rider* (1969), another film that has become a cult classic. With co-stars Dennis Hopper and Jack Nicholson—"Indians!"—Peter made his indelible mark on Hollywood history and personified a generation of young Americans during the time of the Vietnam War. (According to audio commentary on the DVD release by the film's director, Dennis Hopper, the famous LSD scene towards the end of the movie was based on the Gnostic *Gospel of St. Thomas* found at the Nag Hammadi library.) One Jerry Kay, the art director for the film, was—according to the first edition of Ed Sanders' *The Family*—a member of the infamous Solar Lodge of the OTO, the Thelemic organization that was involved in the "boy in the box" affair that caused Grady McMurtry to reactivate his OTO status and fly to California to ward off the sudden interest of the FBI in the Order and deflect it towards the "unofficial" OTO lodge, a series of events that were put in motion during a police raid on the Solar Lodge on July 26, 1969 to investigate charges of child abuse ... the day before Bobby Beausoleil murdered Gary Hinman.[15] There was also circumstantial evidence linking Charles Manson to the Solar Lodge, and much stronger evidence showing his relationship with the Process. It is strange, then, in the context of our study, to discover that Peter Fonda—in New York City in October 1961—would marry the stepdaughter of Noah Dietrich.

Noah Dietrich was probably the one man on earth who knew Howard Hughes inside and out. An employee, and CPA of the Hughes empire for thirty-two years after 1925, he ran Hughes Tool and, according to former Hughes insider and CIA Castro-assassination plotter Robert Maheu, delivered "net profits as high as $55 million annually."[16] Dietrich was the steady, efficient businessman and financial genius behind the Hughes empire, but when Dietrich asked for the stock options he had been repeatedly promised by Hughes, Hughes fired him in May of 1957. To be sure, this was also at the height of Hughes' troubles with TWA. Hughes had wanted to buy more planes, and needed the support of the banks to do so. They refused to put more money into TWA, and it seemed that Dietrich also refused to cooperate with the scheme. No matter which way the story played out, by the end of 1957 Howard Hughes had retreated from public view, by his lights abandoned by his friends and cheated by the courts and the government. It was the beginning of the great Hughes disappearing act.

Dietrich eventually published his memoirs, *Howard: The Amazing Mr. Hughes*, but not before it became something of a cause célèbre. A circulating manuscript of the book was supposedly used by Clifford Irving to forge the infamous Hughes memoirs.

Strange, then, that Peter Fonda would marry Dietrich's stepdaughter four years after the 1957 debacle with Howard Hughes. No, not evidence of any kind of conspiracy, but the nexus of Hughes-Dietrich-Fonda is fascinating, because it connects us—matrix-like—to Fonda-Polanski-Tate-Manson and, of course, *The Blue Bird*, which is, after all, the "Manson Secret." Remember also that Jack Parsons worked for the Hughes Corporation for a while, and the strong links between the Hughes Corporation and the CIA on the one hand (particularly with regard to the Glomar Explorer and the raising of a sunken Soviet submarine) and the Mormons on the other, with tendrils that slither out and wrap around the Watergate office building in 1972.

Conspiracy theorists usually concentrate on political phenomena and criminal suspects at the expense of other types of information, but if we extend our search to include Hollywood on the one side, and religion and even mysticism on the other, we can come up with revealing angles to every political event that are nowhere else considered. We have to dig down deeply in the evidence lockers, looking at the inventories of books, films, and documents from the crime scenes, ones that were rejected by the detectives and inspectors as irrelevant to the cases, if we want to understand the sinister forces that flow beneath the surface of public events. No political event exists in a vacuum; no politician is only a politician. The one-dimensional approach to history has hobbled us for so long that the history books in our schools have become little more than fleshed-out chronologies. The very idea of "history" itself is suspect, now that we understand a little more about time, space, consciousness, psychological warfare, and the quanta. It is my hope that this "deconstruction" of some of Hollywood's famous (and not so famous) films will lend itself to a new approach to history, one that is as firmly based in culture, science and—what we call for want of a better word—"religion," as it is in politics.

There were mysteries at the Polanski house, most of which have never been revealed publicly, and these mysteries are germane to the wilder of the Maury Terry and Ed Sanders satanic conspiracy theories. Terry Melcher, who had lived in the Polanski residence shortly before the Polanskis moved in, stated that Roman Polanski had made unusual films there involving sadomasochism, pornography, etc.[17] A friend of the Manson Family, Charlene Cafritz, claimed to own motion picture footage of the Manson clan that the police did not have and of which they were not aware.[18] At the time of the trial, Cafritz was at St. Elizabeth's Hospital in Washington, D.C., the same hospital from which James Forrestal plunged to his death, and where poet Ezra Pound was kept after the War. It was where Dr. Winfred Overholser worked on truth serums for the OSS and, later, the CIA. Ms. Cafritz died soon thereafter, of an overdose of Nembutal, and was buried in the D.C. area without ever having revealed the location of the famous Manson films.

One of the strange twists of fate that link two otherwise unrelated events is the person of Min S. Yee, a reporter who—with rock star John Phillips of The Mamas and The Papas, a close friend of Sharon Tate—visited a "voodoo astrologer," who told them that the night of August 8-9, 1969 had been a perfect time for a sacrifice. Also, it seems a "voodoo adept" had threatened the life of Wojciech Frykowski, one of the Tate murder victims.[19] This prompted Polanski and Phillips to fly to Jamaica to conduct their own investigation of Caribbean voodoo and some other, possibly drug-related, Jamaican links to the murders, apparently without success.

This same Min Yee later collaborated with Dr. Thomas N. Layton on a book about the Jonestown massacre and his family's role in it: *In My Father's House* (1981).

It was Dennis Hopper who insisted to police after the killings at the Polanski residence that a lot of very strange activity took place there, and that some of the stranger episodes were actually filmed. Hopper was close to Jane Fonda and her circle: he attended her Las Vegas wedding to Roger Vadim with his wife and Peter and Susan Fonda, and of course co-wrote and co-starred with Peter Fonda in *Easy Rider*, released the same year as the Tate/La Bianca killings. He attended the raucous parties at the Polanski residence on Cielo Drive, and was in a position to know what went on there. Jane Fonda has not gone into any detail as to what transpired among the Polanskis, and all we surmise about her participation in their weird scenes is second-hand.

I don't know how close Susan Brewer was to her stepfather, Noah Dietrich; but the Tate/La Bianca killings took place in August 1969, and by November 1970 Clifford Irving had been approached by the powerful people who wanted him to work on a special project, ostensibly involving Howard Hughes and the fraudulent biography, a biography that would be based largely on Noah Dietrich's memoirs.[20] This undertaking would be fraught with danger, since it involved parties "who would stop at nothing to achieve their own ends—even murder."[21] Hughes had officially "disappeared" that same month, on November 25, 1970, an event that was recorded with some fanfare in Hank Greenspun's *Las Vegas Sun* on December 2.

The Manson trial was still in progress at that time, and would not be over until January 25, 1971, when the jury returned a verdict of "guilty" for all four defendants, returning on March 29, 1971, in the penalty phase of the trial, to pronounce "death" for Manson and the convicted members of his Family.

BELL, BOOK ... AND CANDLE IN THE WIND

I have the most wonderful memory for forgetting things.
—Marilyn Monroe[22]

Director Luis Bunuel was one of the clique of surrealist film directors around such leading lights as Jean Cocteau and Salvador Dali. One of his screenwriters (on the acclaimed *La Cucaracha*) was a young Mexican man of great good looks (of the "Latin leading man" type) known as Jose Bolanos. During the McCarthy Era, when so many Hollywood stars, writers, and directors were either being blacklisted or blacklisting, Mexico became a safe haven for people like Bunuel and Bolanos, particularly as both could speak Spanish, of course, and would find themselves in a congenial environment. Mexico was friendly to socialists and socialist governments, and the Cuban

Government of Fidel Castro had an embassy there, as did the Soviets. Lee Harvey Oswald (or someone pretending to be Lee Harvey Oswald) would visit the Soviet Embassy in Mexico City in 1963, just a few months before the assassination of the late Marilyn Monroe's putative lover, John F. Kennedy.

By 1962, though, the year that concerns us in this section, Castro was in firm control of his island nation and had "outed" himself as a Communist. It was bad news for the United States, and especially for those who had supported Castro in good faith … including everyone from CIA agents to movie stars like Errol Flynn. The Mafia was faced with the sudden loss of their casinos in Havana, and they were busy plotting revenge against "the Beard." Khrushchev was beaming, godfather-like, down at this tropical paradise only ninety miles off the coast of his arch-enemy, the United States of America. What a good place to plant a few ICBMs, he thought.

At this time, young writer Bolanos found himself in very good company, indeed. After an intense courtship involving flowers presented on a family heirloom silver plate, numerous mariachi bands, drinking, dancing, and god knows what else, Bolanos had managed the dream date: screen legend and would-be socialist Marilyn Monroe.

When we talk about politics and Hollywood, we cannot avoid the seemingly surreal. Weirdness is the order of the day, and truth is always much, much stranger than fiction. Lee Harvey Oswald was captured in a movie theater, as an example. It was showing a Van Heflin film, *Cry of Battle* (1963), about insurrection in the Philippines, which would have been interesting to Oswald under kinder circumstances, since he spent some time there as a US Marine. Abraham Lincoln was assassinated in a theater while watching a stage play, *Our American Cousin*, shot in the back of the head by a famous actor and leading man, John Wilkes Booth. The movies gave us Ronald and Nancy Reagan—both Hollywood actors—as President and First Lady.

Yet, not many people know that Fidel Castro himself was once a film actor in Hollywood. In the October 30, 1997 edition of *Zenit*, Uruguayan film critic Alvara Sanjurjo confirmed persistent rumors that Castro did, indeed, have a fledgling start as an actor in two George Sidney productions, *Bathing Beauty* (1944) and *Holiday in Mexico* (1946). Sanjurjo is an intimate of Alfredo Guevara Valdes, the head of the Cuban Instituto Cinematografico de Cuba, who himself is a close friend of the Cuban leader, and should know. Even the current owner of *Holiday in Mexico*, Turner Classic Movies (TCM), states, on its Web site, TCM.com:

> Pasternak and Sidney released their third film in Technicolor, the sizzling *Holiday in Mexico* (1946). Starring Walter Pidgeon as the U.S. Ambassador, *Holiday* promised fun in the sun when his daughter (Jane Powell) falls for a Latin lover (Jose Iturbi). In addition to a bossa nova score, *Holiday*

> *in Mexico* featured a young Fidel Castro in a bit part—look close for the future dictator!

Even such definitive biographies of the great Cuban dictator as that of Tad Szulc do not include this bizarre stage in his development, yet the data is available. Castro made several trips to the United States before he became a guerrilla leader and eventual *El Lider*, one of which was for a honeymoon after his marriage on October 12, 1948 (yes, Columbus Day and Crowley's birthday) to Mirta Diaz-Balart, and, during another trip a year later, he stayed in a small apartment at 155 West 82nd Street in New York City for a few months and haunted Marxist bookstores, like so many other students and would-be revolutionaries of the author's own acquaintance during the 1960s. Although these two trips are well-documented, the appearance of Castro in *two* Hollywood films—both made by George Sidney, who also directed *Pal Joey* (1957) and other Sinatra vehicles (oddly enough, considering that the Rat Pack, and particularly Sinatra, were major supporters of the Kennedy presidential campaign in 1960) goes virtually unnoted in biographies of Castro and histories of the Cuban conflict. (Sidney would retire from Hollywood at the age of 49 and become a respected paleontologist!) Castro did himself make one sly reference to his earlier career during a visit to Princeton University in 1959, shortly after he marched through Havana at the head of the victorious revolutionaries:

> In response to an implied accusation that his motives were less than altruistic, Castro reportedly rejoined with the following assertion: "I could be rich … You know how? By writing the history of our revolution for Hollywood."

This curious circumstance lends itself to all sorts of semiotic possibilities. Castro as young Hollywood extra in wartime California, between bouts of baiting the politicos in Havana. Since it is now known for certain that Castro did, indeed, have a bit part in *Bathing Beauty*, one wonders why he returned to Hollywood for *Holiday in Mexico*. Was he called back? Did he have an agent? Did he go out of his way to show up for an audition? (Castro at a cattle call!) Did he briefly toy with being an actor instead of a politician or, as has been suggested, a professional baseball player?

Regardless, Castro came to understand the power of Hollywood, and it should have come as no surprise when movie stars and directors began showing up in Havana in the late 1990s for heart-to-heart talks with Fidel.

But was screenwriter Jose Bolanos a Fidelista? Or was Bolanos—the last known lover of Marilyn Monroe—working for another organization altogether?

In the months leading up to the death of Marilyn Monroe on August 4-5, 1962, the United States was engaged in a serious struggle with the Castro regime in Cuba. The Bay of Pigs invasion had failed disastrously on April 17, 1961; the world was only months away from the Cuban Missile Crisis of October 1962. Throughout the spring of 1962 the operation that would become known as Mongoose consumed more and more of the Kennedys' time: Jack and Robert, the President and the Attorney General. Declassified State Department files show that meetings were held weekly and almost daily at the State Department and the CIA on the subject of destabilizing the Castro regime by using everything from psychological warfare to sabotage and assassination. The largest domestic CIA operation ever was mounted in Florida, with a recruitment of anti-Castro Cubans and fellow travelers, including mysterious Mafiosi with exploding cigars, courtesy of the CIA's Technical Services Division and the collaboration of Robert Maheu.

Yet, at the same time, documents and published eyewitness interviews will confirm that Ms. Monroe was seeing both of the Kennedy brothers romantically. In fact, there have been persistent rumors that Christine Keeler of the Profumo Affair had seen Jack Kennedy in July of 1962 during a visit to the United States with her friend, Mandy Rice-Davies. This would have been less than a month before the death of Monroe, and during the lead-in to the Cuban Missile Crisis that October. While there is no documentation to support that either Kennedy ever actually met—much less romanced—either Ms. Keeler or Ms. Rice-Davies during that time, the mere possibility was giving American intelligence nightmares, as Keeler had been sleeping with both British War Minister John Profumo and the local Soviet GRU *rezident* at the time of the October crisis. This was magnified by what they *did* know concerning the Kennedys' involvement with Marilyn Monroe, who, from about February 1962 on, became involved with a group of Communists living in exile in Mexico City.

As recounted in several modern biographies of Monroe—notably by Anthony Summers, who also did a comprehensive job on the Kennedy assassination, and Donald E. Wolfe, whose research is based in part on Summers' interviews—there was a hotbed of Communists, socialists, and assorted left-wingers in Mexico City in the early 1960s, some of whom had been in self-imposed exile since the start of the HUAC investigations, and many of whom had Hollywood connections. During this same period, relations between the United States and Cuba had become dangerously heated, with the US secretly (and sometimes not so secretly) aiming raids, sabotage, and agent infiltration at Castro's island, and attempting to assassinate the leader using a wide variety of toxins developed by the CIA and agents-in-place, all part of "Operation Mongoose." Mexico City in those days was like a western hemisphere Vienna: a place of fragile neutrality, teeming with spies, in which agents from the opposing camps—Soviet, Cuban, American—could watch each other come and go in the Zona Rosa. One of these was the famous "silver spoon Communist": Frederick Vanderbilt Field.

Coming from a wealthy background as a right-wing American, Field's political faith wavered, and then finally fell on the side of the left. Around him in Mexico City was a gaggle of left-wingers who professed everything from diehard Communism of the Soviet Communist International or "Comintern" model to revolutionary Castroism—liberal dilettantes who were excited to be this close to real socialists and Communists and who, anyway, professed humanitarian principles ranging from racial integration to a change in American foreign policy in Latin America. In the midst of this cocktail circuit could be discerned such influences as artist (and Communist) Diego Rivera—the aforementioned comrade of Trotsky and Andre Breton—as well as filmmaker Luis Bunuel. As always, surrealism found itself in support of radical political solutions, even as it decried "Soviet realism" in art. It was an eclectic group of people from various backgrounds, and it is in this mélange that we find Marilyn Monroe in February of 1962.

Introduced to Field via her psychiatrist, Ralph Greenson, and his homunculus, Eunice Murray, Monroe and Field became fast friends. (At the time of her death, Field was even staying at Monroe's New York City apartment.) Indeed, Field's Mexican wife had been an artist's model for Diego Rivera. Field offered instant entrée into leftist artistic circles, something that was noticeably missing (or, at best, underground) in Hollywood. Monroe was impressed by the strong emotional feelings she encountered among the exiles: a typical liberal fascination with their idealistic *fervorinos* against American hegemony, racial segregation, and political hypocrisy in high places. Communist propaganda of the time appealed to a paranoid, conspiratorial view of politics, in which the rich oppressed the poor, the whites oppressed the blacks, and the wealthy American oligarchy did what it could to extend that dynamic overseas, by oppressing poorer "third world" nations. Racial segregation was an easy target, and demonstrated to the liberal elite that at least part of what the Communists were saying was obviously true. Support was especially high in favor of Castro's Cuba.

Of course, the exiles were equally charmed by the presence in their midst of such a famous and glamorous superstar as Marilyn Monroe. It was one thing to hobnob with the likes of Diego Rivera and Luis Bunuel, arch intellectuals and artists bathed in a kind of fashionable cynicism among a fawning expatriate community of many nations; it was quite another to be seen in the company of the world's most famous woman, a person who was at the same time relatively naïve about politics, yet open to new information and new points of view. She was also quite vulnerable, having gone through a series of famous (and not so famous) husbands, in an endless, desperate search for true love and emotional fulfillment. Her ex-husband Arthur Miller, for instance, was known to be sympathetic to the Left, and his famous play, *The Crucible*, is a thinly disguised attack on the McCarthy hearings … as seen from the point of view of the witchcraft trials in Salem. As always, we keep coming back in a smaller and smaller spiral linking politics, the occult, and culture. It is a volatile formula, and one that very possibly led to Marilyn's death.

She was also surrounded by Communists at home, even between husbands. This preponderance of closet Communists around Marilyn Monroe is a fact that deserves much more scrutiny than it has been given so far—except by Summers and Wolfe, aforementioned. Even her psychiatrist, Dr. Ralph Greenson, was a Communist, and was approved by the Party as a politically-reliable shrink, a functionary of an organization infiltrated to an extent by European émigrés who owed their allegiance to both Freud and Marx. This organization, known as the Psychoanalytic Institutes, with offices in most major American cities,[23] and which contained within its ranks members of various political affiliations, served as a secure means for Communist Party members to meet and exchange information. Psychiatry, in general, was a wonderful mechanism for running "cells" in a foreign country. No one would question why a person had to meet secretly with a psychoanalyst or psychiatrist; in fact, many psychiatrists' offices are designed to permit only one person at a time in the waiting area, and each patient leaves by a separate exit so that no patient need be seen by another.

This situation is perfect for debriefing agents, and for discovering the innermost secrets of others, and may have been one of the reasons why the Watergate Plumbers broke into the office of Daniel Ellsberg's psychiatrist, Dr. Lewis Fielding. As the man who leaked the Pentagon Papers to the press, Ellsberg's motives seemed highly suspect, and Ellsberg himself was targeted as a Communist. That suspicion might have extended to his psychiatrist, in a replay of what had been going on in the early 1960s. After all, Lewis Fielding was a close friend of Marilyn Monroe's analyst, Dr. Greenson, and the FBI maintained a file on Greenson, a file that is still classified to this day. The story of the "Communist-cell psychiatrists" is one that has not been told, and the implications of the story are alarming. Much of this history is still classified, but what we do know has serious implications for the Marilyn Monroe story.

For instance, Dr. Greenson was the leader of the Arts, Sciences, and Professions Committee (ASPC), which was a front organization for Communist infiltration of the media. Within the ASPC were a number of other organizations, including the Doctors Professional Group, and the People's Educational Center, "which was established and funded by Frederick Vanderbilt Field."[24] The founder of the ASPC, Louis Budenz, was "a Communist Party leader and one time managing editor of the *Daily Worker*" (Wolfe, p. 474). Many of these men were openly Communist in the immediate pre-War days, but went underground once the Senate and HUAC hearings began. As Wolfe relates,

> One of Greenson's contacts within the hierarchy of the Comintern was Frederick Vanderbilt Field. As the director of the American Russian Institute, Field was also associated with Greenson's mother, Katharine Greenschpoon,

> who was on the board of directors, according to the Senate Fact Finding Committee on Un-American Activities in California bulletin of 1948.[25]

And again,

> Field was closely monitored by the FBI in Mexico City, and ... continued his links to the United States through the Comintern leader in Los Angeles—Dr. Ralph Greenson.[26]

Field (and many others) had to flee to Mexico once Louis Budenz defected and began giving the Senate the names of other Communists in California as the McCarthy investigations intensified. Gradually, Marilyn became aware that there was something sinister about Greenson's attentions (and those of his spy, Eunice Murray), and by July 1962 she was openly revolting against them. By then, of course it was too late.

Just as the CIA was in full throttle on MK-ULTRA, the Soviets were using traditional psychiatric and psychoanalytic settings in the United States to serve as Comintern fronts and, perhaps, to condition and control certain select patients. When we see the degree to which Monroe depended upon Greenson, and when we learn of Greenson's bizarre "anti-analytic" approach with Monroe in direct violation of his own, published therapeutic principles, we can easily understand how a charge could be made that Monroe was being deliberately manipulated by the Comintern.

And when we learn that E. Howard Hunt—former CIA agent, formerly stationed in Mexico City, one of the Watergate Plumbers himself, and present during the break-in at Fielding's office—was a good friend of the last man to call himself Marilyn Monroe's lover, Jose Bolanos, we are forced to take a completely different look at the events of 1962 and 1963.

Bonafide Communist Frederick Field was highly suspicious of Bolanos, and warned Monroe against seeing him. He believed that Bolanos had infiltrated into the left-wing community in Mexico, an insincere Communist with a hidden agenda, "distrusted by the real left."[27] As revealed in Wolfe's analysis of the death of Marilyn Monroe, Bolanos and E. Howard Hunt were friends.[28] Hunt traveled frequently to Mexico City—either in official or unofficial capacity (he was still with the CIA at the time, although David Atlee Phillips was CIA station chief in Mexico City during this period)—and the two would occasionally meet. Hunt, a writer, considered himself a kind of Ian Fleming, but was actually quite a bit more like the Cigarette Smoking Man, the *X-Files* character based on Hunt. He was also interested in Latin occult practices (as evidenced in his novel *The Coven*), so it is possible that his interest in Mexico City and the Zona Rosa was more of a literary one, slumming with the glamorous expats.

But I don't think so.

I believe that Bolanos was Hunt's man in the Zona Rosa, and once it became known that Marilyn Monroe was hanging out there—at the suggestion, no less, of her Communist Party-approved psychiatrist, Greenson—alarm bells should have gone off at Langley. Unknown to Monroe, Frederick Field knew her housekeeper, Eunice Murray, quite well, and Murray was the conduit to both Field and Greenson. Her husband, John Murray, had been a labor organizer in Hollywood in the 1940s and a dedicated Communist Party member. When the Murray family underwent a reversal of fortune after the War, John Murray sold his home (the site of many Party meetings) to Dr. Greenson, a man he knew from Communist cell gatherings in Hollywood. (It was to this house that Marilyn Monroe would go for her psychiatric meetings with Dr. Greenson.) It was Dr. Greenson, in fact, who ordered his patient to fire her loyal friend and masseur, Ralph Roberts, and replace him with the sinister Ms. Eunice Murray, without telling Ms. Monroe that Murray was a psychiatric nurse, and a Communist at that.[29]

The FBI had surveillance on Peter Lawford as well as Marilyn Monroe—according to its own documents—which in some instances refer to a mysterious confidential informant, who (on the basis of internal evidence) can only be Bolanos. At the same time, the CIA was of course also surveilling Field as a suspected Soviet agent, and CIA Counterintelligence Chief James Angleton confirmed that Marilyn's home was bugged.[30]

So, as you can see, Marilyn never had a chance.

In 1962, Operation Mongoose was in full swing, as the US government ramped up to destabilize Cuba and assassinate Castro. The missiles were starting to arrive in Cuba, smaller tactical missiles at first and then the ICBMs. By late 1961, incoming CIA Station Chief in Mexico, David Atlee Phillips, already knew the first of the missiles were there. By July 1962 everyone at Langley knew. Hunt was still the CIA liaison with the Cuban exiles, trying to keep up their spirits after the failed Bay of Pigs invasion. And here was Marilyn Monroe, drinking mezcal with the Reds and—who knows?—maybe eating the worm. She was already friendly with Robert Kennedy, and had been asking him a great many leading political questions, questions provided to her by a suspiciously helpful Dr. Greenson. She would then report on these meetings, in all innocence, in the Zona Rosa to Comintern member Frederick Field, to E. Howard Hunt intimate Jose Bolanos, and from there to …?

In addition, Robert Kennedy would be informed sometime in 1962 that the CIA under General Lansdale (whom we encountered in Book I in his incarnation as a psychological warfare expert) was subcontracting the Castro assassination to the Mafia, using the ever-helpful Robert Maheu as cutout. Ms. Monroe's friendship with Mafiosi Johnny Roselli and Sam Giancana—themselves deeply involved in these same clandestine arrangements and directly involved with both Richard Nixon and E. Howard Hunt—went back a ways as well, dating from the beginning of her Sinatra period, and this just wove the noose around her neck a little tighter. All around her were some of the seminal figures in the history of modern American covert operations and the Cold War. And, it was suspected, she was writing it all down in her ever-present red-bound diary.

Marilyn Monroe had direct access to the President of the United States and the Attorney General of the United States on the one hand, and to the Communist Party on the other, not to mention the Mafia on still another appendage of what murdered investigative journalist Danny Casolaro would call "the Octopus." That made her the Christine Keeler of America. But while Ms. Keeler's interests in John Profumo and Yevgeny Ivanov were purely materialistic, Ms. Monroe's interest in the Kennedy brothers, and particularly in Bobby Kennedy, was purely romantic. As far as we can discern from witness interviews at the time, Marilyn Monroe was despondent over her relationship with the Attorney General, whom she believed would leave his wife and children in order to marry her. They had argued about a number of political issues, however, including nuclear testing and Cuba as it turns out, with Bobby Kennedy eventually accusing her of turning Communist on the basis of her leftist views.[31]

So, who wanted Marilyn dead? As in the case of the John F. Kennedy assassination a year later, the list of suspects is a long one. At one time, her home was being bugged and her phones tapped by the FBI as well as by an "independent investigator," whose employer might have been either the Mob or the CIA. She was under surveillance by them all. Her association with both the Kennedys and with the Comintern made her a dangerous woman; had the CIA succeeded in assassinating Castro, it is entirely possible that Ms. Monroe would have gone public with what she knew. She was already feeding information to the Mexico City Communists, as well as to Jose Bolanos who, we suspect, was working for E. Howard Hunt. She was a liability to the Kennedys, to the FBI, and to the CIA—specifically, to Operation Mongoose; and, to the extent that she could jeopardize Operation Mongoose, she was a liability to the Mafia. The only people who did not want Marilyn Monroe dead would have been the Communists themselves, since she was so close to the President, the Attorney General, Sam Giancana, Johnny Roselli, "Operation Mongoose," etc., etc. It would have been insane to kill the goose that was laying golden eggs.

However, by July of 1962 and only weeks before her death, she had realized that something wasn't right with Greenson and Murray. She told her ex-husband Robert Slatzer that she was going to fire them all. Was a decision made to silence her before she could reveal the existence of this clandestine Communist cell in Hollywood and Mexico City?

Robert F. Kennedy arrived with his family in Los Angeles on August 3, 1962. There is a great deal of speculation—supported by some fragile circumstantial evidence and the testimony of eyewitnesses—that Kennedy visited Marilyn Monroe sometime between August 3 and August 5, the day of her death. The existence of her diary was well-known, and she had made it understood that she had potentially explosive information. Was a decision made to murder Marilyn Monroe when it was known Bobby Kennedy was in town, as an attempt to embarrass or possibly ruin the Attorney General, the one man Jimmy Hoffa and other union-mafiosi hated the most?

Some authors support the Mafia-Killed-Marilyn theory; others the Kennedys-killed-Marilyn theory; still others the FBI/CIA-killed-Marilyn theory. That she was murdered and did not commit suicide seems, at this point, a safe inference, based on forensic evidence and crime scene photographs, as well as conflicting witness testimony. Whatever the truth may be, one thing is for certain: her diary was never found, even though it was the target of a search by James Jesus Angleton, the CIA's Chief of Counterintelligence, the man responsible for hunting the famed Soviet "mole" within American intelligence. Angleton would become enmeshed in another hunt for the diary of a Presidential lover, this time in 1964 with the death of Mary Pinchot Meyer, as described in Book I.

Monroe's diary, however, was without a doubt political nitroglycerine. Referred to as her "book of secrets," it contained information on everything from the Mafia, Hoffa, and the Bay of Pigs to the CIA assassination plots against Castro, all culled from conversations with Jack and Bobby Kennedy.[32] Monroe kept all of this written down because, as revealed in her conversations with her ex-husband Robert Slatzer only weeks before her death, Bobby Kennedy would get mad at her for not remembering "anything he told me" concerning political issues.[33] During this conversation with Slatzer, in which she allowed him to browse through her "book of secrets" and "handwritten notes from Bobby Kennedy—some of them on Justice Department stationery,"[34] she spoke of the possibility of holding a press conference in the event that either the President or the Attorney General refused to speak with her. Convinced that her phones were tapped (they were), she met Slatzer outdoors where they could speak in private.[35] This was in late July 1962.

The weekend of July 28-29 probably holds a key to what transpired only days later. Ms. Monroe spent the weekend at the Cal-Neva Lodge in Lake Tahoe, and the mystery that surrounds this weekend is impenetrable. That something loathsome did take place, and that it involved Marilyn Monroe who was only now making an important comeback, is certain, if only because of the reticence of eyewitnesses to discuss it.

Wolfe makes a good case that she was invited to the Cal-Neva Lodge—Sinatra's unofficial headquarters—in order to be pressured into not going to the press with what she knew about the Kennedys and that those present on that weekend were Sinatra, Peter and Pat Lawford, her friend Gloria Romanoff ... and Sam Giancana. It was Giancana's presence there that weekend that wound up costing Sinatra his gaming license, so we know that much is true. What has been revealed since then by eyewitnesses who did come forward is almost too much to believe, a horror that goes beyond anything we might comfortably imagine.

Her ex-husband, Joe DiMaggio—icon of American baseball and one of the men who truly loved Marilyn—arrived unexpectedly at the scene. No one knows how he knew his ex-wife would be there, but he showed up and was not allowed inside the complex of bungalows that had been reserved for Monroe, Sinatra, and Giancana, on orders from Sinatra. Instead, he had to take a room at a nearby motel. Marilyn Monroe herself was not actually registered at the Cal-Neva, a precaution that now seems much more sinister in retrospect; instead, she was put into the bungalow complex and kept watch over the entire time.

When DiMaggio returned from Lake Tahoe, he told his friend Harry Hall that he was furious with what had happened, that Sinatra had kept Monroe on drugs, and that they had "sex parties."[36] To clarify what was meant by that, photographer Billy Woodfield was quoted as saying that Sinatra gave him a roll of film from that weekend. When Woodfield developed the roll, he evidently found photos of Marilyn being sexually abused by, or at least in the presence of, Sam Giancana and Frank Sinatra.[37]

In other words, Marilyn Monroe was likely drugged, raped, and photographed; the photos would be used as blackmail against her if she decided to come forward with what she knew about the Kennedys, the Mafia, and Castro.

A drugged Monroe was returned to Los Angeles late the night of July 29-30, in the company of Peter Lawford. Monroe was returned to her home in a limo, but Lawford rode with the flight crew to his beach home. Before arriving home, he asked the crew to stop for a moment so he could make a call from a pay phone (knowing his own home was bugged and his phones tapped). He made a mysterious phone call that lasted about twenty minutes before finally going home in the early hours of that morning.

That phone call was logged into the White House, a call that went directly to the President.

Marilyn's last days were a turmoil of political intrigue. It seems the blackmail effort was not panning out the way everyone thought it would. She was threatening to go public with what she knew; she was also on the verge of firing Dr. Greenson and Eunice Murray who, she finally realized, was sent to spy on her by Greenson.[38] She had made an appointment to see her attorney, Mickey Rudin, the following Monday in order to change her will. Mickey Rudin was Dr. Greenson's brother-in-law, and Frank Sinatra's attorney as well, so the circle grows increasingly smaller … and tighter. She had already "fired" her friend Paula Strasberg, of the Actor's Studio Strasbergs. Her efforts at learning the Method had worked well, according to Lee Strasberg, and she was becoming a serious, accomplished actress, and not merely someone to be cast in comedy roles or fluff pieces. But the influence of the Strasbergs had proved pernicious; while they had managed to avoid the worst of the HUAC excesses, they were still considered "Reds" and the Method was, after all, a psychological conditioning process, what A.O. Scott of the *New York Times* has recently called "a mode of psychological melodrama, a means by which the obscure, private noise of the soul is transformed into speech and gesture."[39] Add to this sex, drugs, and politics, and you have a volatile mixture, an initiatory explosion in the making. According to Anthony Summers, Monroe had built up"a considerable library. Marilyn had a lifetime interest in the occult, and she often visited astrologers and psychics."[40]

This tantalizing bit of information is left there. As in so many biographies of the famous, the celebrated, the influential—such as in biographies of Hitler, for instance—a fascination with the occult is mentioned, briefly, and then glossed over. No one seems willing to offer more than a few words on the subject, even as they dissect every other aspect of the person's private, personal life. Her longtime friend and one-time husband, Bob Slatzer, devotes a short chapter in his biography of Marilyn to her interest in the occult,[41] and even reproduces an astrological chart cast for her by Laetitia "Tish" Leroy.[42] But between her interest in the occult on one side, and her early involvement with leftists and others who came afoul of the Senate and Congressional committees on the other, she was already peering behind the veil of American politics and American reality.

Marilyn Monroe had already penetrated the mysteries of the Kennedy Administration: she, herself, had become one of those mysteries. She was being groomed and trained—via the Method and via psychiatry—by a cabal of Communists with a hidden agenda, such as Dr. Greenson, who told her what friends to have, what film roles to take, and who generally abused the oath of a physician by doing everything contrary to established psychiatric procedure when it came to the screen goddess. (As if to underscore the connection, her code name when calling the President was "Miss Green."[43])

She was *their* initiate, sent into the opposing camp; they had made this vulnerable, talented woman a Discordia, Goddess of Confusion and Disharmony, the unwitting spy of a Soviet cabal. But she was turning on everyone: Mafia, Kennedys, Communists alike, in a desperate attempt to hold herself together, to integrate her personality and become the strong, even happy, woman she knew herself capable of being.

She had become that dangerous entity, the student who has surpassed the need for a master. On August 4, 1962—at the age of only thirty-six—she died. The crime scene was a mess; forensics were a joke. It was the proverbial "locked room" mystery, in which the victim was murdered in a room that was locked from the inside. She was said to have overdosed on sleeping pills

... but none were found in her digestive tract. There was no glass of water in that locked room to enable her to swallow what were estimated to be nearly 50 capsules. And no hypodermic syringe. Her psychiatrist Dr. Greenson and her physician Dr. Engelberg (who were, after all, close friends) waited hours before calling the police. It was Engelberg who prescribed the Nembutal that was said to have resulted in her death. It was Engelberg who gave her mysterious injections the week she died.

Shortly thereafter, other women began dying. Mary Pinchot Meyer was murdered on a street outside her home in 1964. This was the ex-wife of an important CIA official, who was also a lover of President Kennedy and the woman who turned him on to drugs, courtesy of Dr. Timothy Leary; she was the woman who called Leary shortly after the assassination, possessed of guilty secrets.

On November 8, 1965, columnist and reporter Dorothy Kilgallen died under mysterious circumstances, soon after she had visited Jack Ruby in prison in Dallas. She was conducting her own investigation of the Kennedy assassination, and had been in possession—through her lover, Ron Pataki—of some secret information concerning Marilyn Monroe, with whom she had also been friendly.[44] Her notes of the interview with Jack Ruby disappeared after her death. Pataki had seen them, however, but refuses to discuss their contents, so once again we are cheated of knowing the truth about America, the truth about our history, by people who arrogate to themselves the title of well-intentioned guardians of our memory.

But it was not only the women who died.

After Marilyn Monroe's death in August 1962 came the Cuban Missile Crisis in October, the Profumo Affair the following year with the suicide of Dr. Stephen Ward, and the Kennedy assassination in November 1963. Ironically, the John Frankenheimer film starring Frank Sinatra and Angela Lansbury, *The Manchurian Candidate*, was released in 1962, the year Marilyn was murdered, and pulled from distribution after the assassination of the President in 1963.

And then Bobby, a man racked with guilt over the death of his brother, if not also for the murder of Marilyn Monroe, who decides to make a run for the presidency and try to make America a better place, to end the war in Vietnam, to ensure racial integration and equality, is gunned down on the day of his California victory in June 1968.

Darkly, like the wings of a deeper conspiracy, flickered the faces of Roman Polanski and Sharon Tate at the Frankenheimer dinner table for Bobby Kennedy's Last Supper that night. The following year, almost on the anniversary of Marilyn Monroe's death and in the same town, Sharon Tate herself would be horribly butchered, and the man accused of masterminding that crime would be held in the same jail cell that had been especially designed for Bobby Kennedy's putative killer, Sirhan Sirhan.

Another man, perhaps satisfied with the death of the screen legend, would go on to greater glory: E. Howard Hunt. The Watergate affair would dredge up all kinds of ugly secrets, prompting Richard Nixon to famously worry about exposing "the whole Bay of Pigs thing." Hunt and Jose Bolanos. Hunt and the break-in at Dr. Lewis Fielding's office: the close friend of Marilyn's Comintern analyst, Dr. Ralph Greenson. Hunt as "action officer" on the Bay of Pigs invasion. Hunt as CIA icon to the anti-Castro Cubans in Miami. Hunt as mastermind of the Watergate break-in. And Bolanos as FBI informant *and* CIA informant? The middle man between Marilyn Monroe and E. Howard Hunt? Bolanos as screenwriter to surrealist Bunuel, hovering around the edges of the Mexican surrealist community that included Bunuel, Dali, Diego Rivera and Frida Kahlo, meanwhile spying on them for the Company. *La Cucaracha*, indeed.

It's possible that the men who killed Marilyn were concerned about national security; it's possible that they were protecting American secrets from leaking to the press, or to the Soviet Union. It's possible they told themselves, these grey-souled men of the CIA, the FBI, the Mob, the anti-Castro Cubans, the Sinatras, the Giancanas, the Hunts, that Marilyn Monroe was just a weak-willed, inconvenient woman who was in the way, a dumb broad with a big mouth, a slut who slept her way to stardom, a woman scorned, a mistress dumped.

I submit—after my own, twenty-five-year-long investigation into American politics and American culture—that all these men taken together, all these Hunts and Sinatras and Giancanas and Bolanos, and Greenson and Murray and all the rest, were not worth one Marilyn Monroe, whatever the official or unofficial reason for her execution.

I found out something I never knew. I found out that my world was not the real world.
—Robert F. Kennedy, shortly before he was assassinated[45]

Me And The Devil (Blues)

I do enjoy the Beatles however; their music has a definite beat and in many ways their music is good music.
—Rudolf Hess[46]

Me and the Devil
Was walking side by side ...
—Robert Johnson, "Me and the Devil Blues"

Although every form of music has had its satanic influences—and music probably its origins as drum beats and chants in primeval rituals performed in the same darkened caves where the first art was painted and the first theater enacted—in the present era we can trace the fusion of music and madness to the blues composer and guitarist, Robert Johnson.

Johnson (1911-1938) began playing the juke joints and roadhouses of Mississippi during the Depression in the early 1930s, after a tragic life in which his sixteen-year-old wife and newborn baby both died in childbirth, an event that came in the wake of Johnson's own illegitimate birth, his childhood at a variety of homes and under a variety of names, but always to the soulful sound of the Mississippi Delta blues. He was murdered—poisoned with strychnine—by a jealous husband on August 16, 1938 at the age of 27, but not before he had recorded some famous and influential tracks, like "Terraplane," "Hellhound on my Trail," and "Little Queen of Spades."

But it was the dark, and darkly sardonic, anthems that reached the souls of modern rockers and opened their eyes to the sinister that is an inextricable element of all music, but especially of any music that pretends to speak directly to the soul. Readers may wonder at my identification of the "sinister" with music, but "sinister" is a word with many meanings and implications. It can represent the sense of awe we feel at the approach of a divine mystery as much as it can mean an unsettling feeling in the presence of the demonic. The word "sinister" refers, after all, to things of the "left hand," and the left side of the body is controlled by the right side of the brain. It is fascinating to learn that the Italians speak of the paranormal, and conspiracy theories in general, as *dietrologia*, or the "science of the left hand side."

To Jungian analyst Adolf Guggenbuehl-Craig—author of the aptly-titled *From the Wrong Side: A Paradoxical Approach to Psychology*—the sinister has celestial associations:

> The sinister is always the unintelligible, the impressive, the numinous. Wherever something divine appears, we begin to experience fear.[47]

And further:

> I assume that an encounter with God or with the transcendent, per se, can only then occur when we experience the violent side of God, creation and mankind as well. We meet God and the world just as much in the horrific as in the beautiful and sublime.[48]

Many music critics might agree that the sinister and the sublime meet in the works of Robert Johnson. Only twenty-nine Johnson titles still exist on vinyl, and they were compiled into *Robert Johnson: The Complete Recordings* on the Columbia label in 1990. These recordings were all made in Texas, some in Dallas, from November 23—27, 1936, and their influence has been enormous.

In fact, Eric Clapton—in an essay on Johnson published in the liner notes to Johnson's complete recordings—states,

> Up until the time I was 25, if you didn't know who Robert Johnson was, I wouldn't talk to you. It was almost like that. *It was as if I had been prepared to receive Robert Johnson, almost like a religious experience* … Even then I wasn't quite ready. (emphasis in original)

In another essay in the liner notes, Keith Richards of the Rolling Stones relates how he heard Johnson for the first time at the home of Brian Jones:

> To me, Robert Johnson's influence—he was like a comet or a meteor that came along and, BOOM, suddenly he raised the ante, suddenly you had to aim that much higher.

And, of course, he did. From "Me and the Devil Blues" by Johnson to "Sympathy for the Devil" by Jagger and Richards, there is a continuum of fascination with evil, and the use of music to *evoke* those sinister forces that has so frightened Fundamentalist Christians and the Christian Right in general. Rock 'n' roll as early as Elvis Presley was considered satanic, inspired by the Devil himself to instigate revolution against authority, sexual liberation, and "dirty dancing." Johnson threw down the gauntlet with his songs about women, violence, and despair as a master of Delta Blues, and the gauntlet was picked up and passed around by generations of serious musicians to follow.

While we can see the "satanic" influence of Johnson over the Rolling Stones—the Stones certainly had their share of occult influences and connections, from Anger and Cammell to Pallenberg and Faithfull—occultism was never very far from the other icons of '60s rock. While the Beach Boys were hobnobbing with Charlie Manson, who himself was reading arcane messages into Beatles lyrics, and Jimmy Page of Led Zeppelin was starring in and scoring Anger films and living at Crowley's Boleskine estate in Scotland, Jim Morrison of The Doors was marrying a witch.

The marriage was a pagan version of the same, known as a "handfasting" in Wiccan circles, and thus had no legal standing, which has led to some animosity among Morrison's girlfriends and fiancées. To understand where this is going, we have to rely upon reminiscences by the witch in question, one Patricia Kennealy or Patricia Kennealy-Morrison as she prefers to be known. Writing in her autobiography, *Strange Days*, she describes a great deal about her pagan experiences and philosophy, and she gave an abridged version of same to interviewers from a pagan publication, *Pagan Muse and World Report*, in their Fall 1996 edition and since reprinted on Ms. Kennealy's own Web site. This marriage of rock-icon Morrison to Kennealy was covered briefly in Oliver Stone's film about the group, *The Doors*, which does emphasize a mystical quality of The Doors and of Morrison himself.

Morrison died tragically in a bathtub in a Paris apartment of a friend in 1971, only a year after he and Kennealy were handfasted in a pagan ceremony. At the time, Kennealy was a member of a coven of Celtic witches she had joined in 1966 (the same year as the formation of the Church of Satan), becoming high priestess in 1969, the same year she met Morrison. She had been working for a rock music magazine, which is how she came to meet him. She was "married" to Jim Morrison on Midsummer's Day, 1970, before the members of her coven. He would die in July of 1971, a little over a year after the handfasting, and under mysterious circumstances. The French forensics—as in the case of LAPD's investigation of the death of Marilyn Monroe—were a farce; no one really knows how Morrison died or who might have been responsible. What is known is that there was a quantity of drugs in the apartment where he died, and that he had snorted heroin and probably overdosed in the bathtub, according to Pamela Susan Courson who was snorting heroin with him at the time. Ms. Courson, with whom Morrison was staying, had his body wrapped in plastic and packed in dry ice, and she slept next to his body for three nights until someone sent over a coffin. Ms. Courson had a lover, a French count, whom she shared with Marianne Faithfull, who was also in Paris that week. Courson told the count that it was a heroin overdose that killed Morrison, warning him because they all—Pamela Courson, the count, Morrison, and Faithfull—had scored off the same dealer. The count returned from Courson's apartment, told Faithfull what had happened, and the two of them—count and witch—left immediately for Morocco to avoid being interrogated by the French police.

Morrison was quickly buried in a cheap coffin during a funeral ceremony that lasted all of eight minutes and with only a handful of mourners. Eventually, his gravesite would be placed under tight security, replete with motion sensors and CCTV cameras, due to the incidents of attempted grave robbing by hysterical fans and venal ghouls. It is now one of the most famous tourist attractions in Paris.

After his death, Ms. Kennealy avoided the coven for several years in her grief, eventually becoming involved with Margot Adler's Pagan Way celebrations in New York City and from there joining a Welsh Traditionalist coven until it fell apart shortly thereafter (in or about 1977). (Dr. Adler is the author of *Drawing Down The Moon*, a study of modern American paganism, and a descendant of famous psychoanalyst Alfred Adler.) According to Ms. Kennealy, Jim Morrison had fully intended to be initiated into witchcraft upon his return from Paris, but fate had other ideas.

Morrison took the name of his group from Aldous Huxley's *The Doors of Perception*. More than any other rock band of the era, The Doors were famous for mystical lyrics and haunting, dreamlike melodies. There is no doubt that Morrison was fascinated with alternate forms of spirituality, expressed in eerie, stream-of-consciousness verse and alchemical allusions. Kennealy who, after all, began her career as a rock critic, describes Morrison as a shaman and The Doors concerts as rituals:

> The audiences were actually participants in Doors concerts, not just spectators. Those shows were mystical occasions. It sounds like so much hooey now, but you really had to be there, 'cause they absolutely were.... It was all absolutely there for you to grab onto. Because Jim made sure it was there for you to grab. Because he put it there. He really did see it like that, and he consciously tried to make it happen.... He saw it as actively functioning as a living link between people and the creative power ... where you represent the people before the gods and the gods before the people.[49]

Ms. Kennealy herself later went on to become the successful fantasy and science fiction author of a series of books known as the Keltiad, and was knighted in the Ordo Supremus Militaris Templi Hierosolymitani (the Sovereign Military Order of the Temple of Jerusalem) in September 1990 at Rosslyn Chapel in Scotland, sponsored by fantasy authors Katherine Kurtz and Scott MacMillan. Rosslyn Chapel is a mecca for New Agers interested in the Templar tradition, as it has been mentioned in books supporting the theory that some Templars escaped to Scotland after the disbanding of their Order by the Pope and the King of France in the fourteenth century. The Chapel itself is at least as strange in its architectural details as that other infamous and possibly Templar edifice, Abbe Sauniere's strange church at Rennes-le-Chateau in the Pyrenees, also a must-see on any serious New Age tour. The Order into which she was knighted is a repository of some of these legends and mysteries surrounding the original Templars. Ms. Kennealy, through her initiation into a Celtic coven, then a Welsh Traditionalist coven, and then a Templar Order, manages to represent for us the pagan, Crowleyan and Masonic strains of modern western occultism. Welsh Traditionalist witchcraft is a form of Gardnerian "Wicca" and, as such, is heir to the Crowleyan tradition. The Sovereign Military Order of the Temple of Jerusalem is, by intention, a resurrection of certain Templar ideas and principles which predate Crowley, and the OTO to which he belonged, and which contributed to the creation and survival of the phenomenon of Freemasonry. All of this, and a handfasting to Jim Morrison of The Doors.

At the time that Ms. Kennealy was working with Margot Adler and a Welsh Traditionalist coven in New York City, the Son of Sam murders were in full swing. The witches of Ms. Kennealy's acquaintance were customers of that venerable institution, the Warlock Shop/Magickal Childe Bookstore in both its Brooklyn Heights and then West 19th Street, Manhattan incarnations. Herman Slater's remarkable store was a meeting place for witches of all persuasions, as well as for Satanists, Thelemites, the odd alchemist, Scientologists, and members of the Process. Members of the Son of Sam cult also visited the store on occasion, and several of the young women mentioned in Maury Terry's book on the Sam case—*The Ultimate Evil*—were known to frequent the shop. One day, perhaps, its story will be told in detail. While Terry's book has been ridiculed on pagan and occult Web sites (and often for good reason), much of his data is known to be accurate, even if his conclusions are occasionally off-the-mark or off-the-wall. We will return to this story in the following chapter, but for now let us conclude our study of sinister forces in Hollywood with a look at the background of the Son of Sam cult, as seen through the life and times of one of Hollywood's most famous producers.

Along the way we will look at the film that put serial killer Jeffrey Dahmer into a murderous trance, and discover a director whose work could only be called initiatory in the strictest sense of the term.

BAD TRANSFORMERS

I learned that just beneath the surface there's another world, and still different worlds as you dig deeper.

—David Lynch[50]

A recurring feature of David Lynch films is the flickering electric light, result—as we are told in the pilot episode of his television series, *Twin Peaks*—of a "bad transformer." This flickering electric light will appear again in such Lynch films as *Mulholland Drive*, to announce the appearance of the Cowboy: a bizarre character who speaks in gnomic riddles, like a cross between Gary Cooper and David Carradine. In *Twin Peaks* it is the light in the morgue over the place where the body of Laura Palmer had been kept, and which is then visited by Mike, the one-armed man, who recites the famous poem:

Through the darkness of futures past
The magician longs to see;
One chants out between two worlds
"Fire, walk with me."

There, in a strange little verse, we have the key to unlocking the mystery not only of *Twin Peaks* but of virtually all of Lynch's films: the suspension of normal laws of time ("futures past") and the idea that the magician lives "between two worlds." The suspension of a normal, linear narrative event in favor of a dreamlike, hallucinatory set of images that are taking place all over the fourth dimension is part of Lynch's appeal as a director, and part of what makes his films so frustrating to the average filmgoer. His realization that there are two worlds, and a place to stand between them, is what contributes to his aura as a modern, twenty-first century initiate of the Mysteries, for that is what his "mystery" films are: elucidations of the core Mystery behind reality.

> We all find this book of riddles and it's just what's going on. And you can figure them out. The problem is, you figure them out inside yourself, and even if you told somebody, they wouldn't believe you or understand it in the same way you do. You'd suddenly realize that the communication wasn't 100 per cent. There are a lot of things like that going on in life, and words just fail you.[51]

And one of the keys to the mysteries—in fact, their *raison d'etre*—is the very idea of transformation, and of the sinister implications of a "bad transformer." In the same pilot episode of *Twin Peaks* where this throwaway line is used, the conversation is between the one-armed man, Mike (who knows where the serial killer, Bob, is hiding), and FBI Special Agent Dale Cooper. As we discover towards the very end of the very last episode of *Twin Peaks*, it is Cooper himself who becomes a "bad transformer" and who winds up in the "place between the worlds," the dreaded Lodge. Transformation is a central theme of Lynch's films, as characters change identities and places in the space-time continuum with astonishing regularity; and it is closer to an initiated understanding of how reality works than a standard linear narrative could ever be. In Lynch films, there is no such thing as coincidence. The universe is not that lazy, events not that meaningless. Behind every event there lurks a world of information, of relevance, of mysterious connections that link one seemingly innocuous image with another. Telephones, lampshades, ashtrays, coffee cups, dripping water, the wind in the trees … everything becomes fraught with sinister, cosmic significance.

One could devote volumes to describing and "decoding" the astrological, alchemical, historical, and political references in Lynch's work, especially in *Twin Peaks*, which is the closest thing we have in modern America to the *Chymical Wedding of Christian Rosenkreutz*. Some professors of religion—such as Mircea Eliade's brilliant Romanian protégé Ioan Culianu—did just that, in Culianu's case holding weekly student seminars on the subject, until his murder in a restroom of the University of Chicago.

It is the idea of transformation that concerns us most at the moment. It was, after all, the principle goal of alchemy to be able to effect transformations, whether of lead into gold or of base humanity into a heightened spiritual state. Jung's interpretation of alchemy tended towards the psychological, of course, and for him the idea of transformation was emblematic of spiritual and psychological growth. His famous forward to a translation of a Chinese alchemical text—*The Secret of the Golden Flower*—is evidence of this, as is the bulk of his considerable writing on the subject of alchemy and on the similarity of alchemical symbols (so beloved of the surrealists) to the drawings of patients undergoing psychotherapy.

Spiritual possession is also a form, albeit temporary, of transformation. From the days when shamans wore animal skins and turned lycanthrope, to the ecstatic dances of Haitian voudoun or Malaysian *kuda kepang*, this type of transformation was temporary in time, but its effects on the psyche of the possessed must be of a long-term nature, setting them apart from other human beings and allowing them to visit, if only for a moment, the "place between the worlds," or what Lynch calls "the Lodge." This concept received a sudden impetus from the research of Charles Darwin concerning evolution, and of Madame Blavatsky's framing of evolution in spiritual as well as racial terms. All at once, the ancient occult and alchemical dream of transformation became respectable: transformation was not only possible, the descent of man through various stages of animal life including most recently those of the simian variety was evidence that even greater evolutionary stages were possible. But ... evolution, transformation into what? Would humanity one day be considered nothing more than a temporary phase of evolution before an even greater advancement?

Fundamentalist Christianity could not accept Darwinian evolution because it disagreed with the Biblical account of the creation of man; yet, even worse, an acceptance of the possibility of evolution carries with it a greater danger. If humanity is destined for a more perfect modification or more refined mutation in the future, then the incarnated Christ of two thousand years ago was inhabiting an inferior vessel, one that was not made in the "image and likeness of God," for that is yet to come. This is another reason why those who believe in the literal word of the Bible—whatever that is, as one must select from a bewildering array of Biblical translations—cannot accept evolution, and why secret societies embrace it with open arms. They believe it is the soul or spirit that is eternal, that is in the "image and likeness of God," and that the body is a material basis for that spirit, only: a machine, a device that enables the spirit to function in this hostile world. That the machine was perfectible, or at any rate mutable and subject to transformation, was a given, and irrefutable evidence of the possibility of spiritual attainments.

I have declined to quote much Jungian material in this work so far, even though the subject matter practically screams out at times for a Jungian perspective, because it may seem too scholarly or academic an approach to take, and because Jung—as valuable as his insights may be—is too controversial a source. However, we would be amiss if we did not take into consideration what he has said about alchemical transformation, as he was one of the first to realize the psychological nature of the alchemical texts.

In describing one early text, one of the visions of Zosimos, he tells us, concerning transformation,

> The drama shows how the divine process of change manifests itself to our human understanding and how man experiences it—as punishment, torment, death, and transfiguration. The dreamer describes how a man would act and what he would have to suffer if he were drawn into the cycle of the death and rebirth of the gods, and what effect the *deus absconditus* would

> have if a mortal man should succeed by his "art" in setting free the "guardian of spirits" from his dark dwelling. There are indications in the literature that this is not without its dangers.[52]

In a footnote to this text, he writes,

> The element of torture, so conspicuous in Zosimos, is not uncommon in alchemical literature.[53]

Indeed. As we have seen, torture—specifically including dismemberment and cannibalism—is a common element in shamanistic initiation traditions, although the experience is usually an internalized affair or, as in the case of the Kwakiutl tribe of North America, enacted in ritualized pantomime in memory of a time when it was performed in fact. Transformation comes at a price, a price that can be too heavy for many to bear.

We discussed Mormonism in Book I of this study; we return to it again for confirmation of what we are discussing here. Mormonism shares many beliefs in common with the Gnostics, and many that are diametrically opposed to orthodox Christianity, especially with regard to the possibilities of transformation and of individual human beings attaining Godhead.

As cited in the book *Mormon America: The Power and The Promise* by Richard N. Ostling and Joan K. Ostling (considered a "definite introduction to the Church of Jesus Christ of Latter Day Saints" by *Library Journal*), Mormon apologist B. H. Roberts, in a dialogue with a Jesuit critic, defined three points on which Mormons differ from "traditional" Christians (and, we may assume, traditional Jews and Muslims as well):

> First, we believe that God is a being with a body in form like man's; that he possesses body, parts and passions; that in a word, God is an exalted, perfected man.
> Second, we believe in a plurality of Gods.
> Third, we believe that somewhere and some time in the ages to come, through development, through enlargement, through purification, until perfection is attained, man at last may become like God—a God.[54]

There is nothing in the above statement that conflicts with occult beliefs, but much that conflicts with the great monotheistic religions. Whether Joseph Smith formulated these ideas before or after his involvement with Freemasonry is moot; he was a practicing magician from early adolescence. In Mormonism, American religion has adopted many occult and hermetic beliefs, including Gnosticism and a belief in transformation. The above statement does not admit to the possibility that today, in this lifetime, a human being may become

God; it purposely postpones that possibility until "some time in the ages to come," but at the same time admits that God is "an exalted, perfected man," implying that some of these transformations have—in however isolated a fashion—already taken place. It is not known whether or not Mormonism, perhaps in its more secret conclaves, ever considers the possibility that techniques exist for attaining this goal in this lifetime, but the mere fact that they accept this type of transformation as dogma is intriguing.

Serial killer Jeffrey Dahmer was fascinated with the concept of transformation, for he believed that with transformation came spiritual power. His favorite film was *Exorcist III*, as we have seen, and it is a proper sequel to *The Exorcist,* with some of the original cast and with the original director, William Friedkin. In *Exorcist III*, we meet the demon who was exorcised in the first film, entering the body of a serial killer at the moment it leaves the body of little Regan. The demon has returned as a serial killer, and it was this element of possession/transformation that transfixed Dahmer. Every time the demon would make an appearance on the screen, Dahmer would go into a kind of trance ... as if willing the demon to enter *him.*

What many people already know is that the original book by William Peter Blatty is based on a genuine case of demonic possession. Dahmer would have known this as well, and his attraction to the theme of *The Exorcist* is at least partly based on the idea that demonic possession is genuine and that the events in the first film were based on reality. The events of the third film became reality ... through Dahmer, serial killer and cannibal, himself. Is it only coincidence, then, that Blatty was a psychological warfare officer for the US military in the 1960s before he wrote his bestselling novel? And that another Blatty novel, *Twinkle, Twinkle Killer Kane*, was about a military mental hospital, with hints of a mind-control program run amok? Further, that this novel was also made into a film, *The Ninth Configuration* (1980), starring Stacey Keach as the new director of the hospital (set in a castle) who is if anything even more insane than his patients; and that the film was directed by William Peter Blatty himself, and featured Jason Miller: the "Father Damien" of *The Exorcist.* It is as if Blatty is trying to tell us something.

The Exorcist, of course, started all sorts of demonic possession hysteria. One writer who contributed to this sense of the sinister all around us was Malachi Martin, a former Catholic priest, whose book on possession and exorcism in America, *Hostage to the Devil*, was praised by some clergymen even as it was attacked by others. Martin's book begins with a vignette of an Irish Catholic priest in Nanjing at the time of the Japanese invasion. The priest is trying to exorcise a demon from the body of a Chinese Catholic man, a man who has been identified by the Chinese police as ... a serial killer.

Malachi Martin's *bona fides* have been challenged by Robert Blair Kaiser, a former *Time* Vatican correspondent, who claims in his autobiography that Martin stole his wife and had him committed to a mental institution in order to get rid of him. It is a nasty attack on the late Martin, and represents what has become a general whiff of opprobrium where the former priest is concerned. While the Catholic Church has been officially silent on the matter of Malachi Martin, his books have been popular among a certain segment of the Catholic population, who believe that there is an evil, Satanic element within the Vatican that has hijacked the Church for its own purposes. Martin was writing about this years before revelations exploded about the Vatican banking scandals, the Masonic P-2 society infiltration of the Vatican as high as cardinal level, and the alleged murder of Pope John Paul I after only thirty days as Pontiff.

Thus, it is entirely possible that there are at least two factions within the Church, and that one faction supported Martin's researches and that another firmly opposed them. Martin also alleged that there existed within the Church something he called the "Superforce," which was the name he gave to the cabal of evildoers within the Vatican that perpetrated not only political and financial crimes, but which was also involved in pedophilia and other sexual scandals, some under the guise of a satanic cult of sex abusers. Recent revelations concerning the widespread cover up of pedophilia and other forms of sexual abuse within the Church—a cover up that begins at the highest levels of the Vatican bureaucracy—seem to support Martin's contentions, particularly as, in some cases, this abuse was connected with vaguely ritualistic settings and ceremonies. Whatever the truth behind the mysterious Malachi Martin—who, at one point, had a correspondence with our dear friend Rayelan Russbacher of Barbara Honegger, October Surprise, wandering bishop, and *Les Dances Enchants* fame—his most vocal opponent and the source of the scurrilous rumors about him is Robert Blair Kaiser, in his autobiography *Clerical Error*.

Kaiser's book has been both praised and attacked by Catholics, largely depending upon where they stand where the subject of Father Martin is concerned. Having begun his career as a candidate for the priesthood, spending eight years at a Jesuit seminary, Kaiser abandoned Holy Orders and eventually won a posting with *Time* magazine in Rome, covering the controversial Second Vatican Council ("Vatican II") of Pope John XXIII and winning awards for his reporting in the process, reporting that was assisted in no small part by Malachi Martin. In *Clerical Error*, Kaiser accuses Martin of abusing their relationship by sleeping with his wife while he was a houseguest of the Kaisers. The whole sordid story is there—published, of course, after Martin's death from a stroke in 1999—and it confirms the suspicions of many in the New Church that Father Martin was a sexual predator of vast proclivities who betrayed Church and friend, alike, with reckless abandon.

Yet, defenders of Father Martin point to a paucity of documentation supporting Kaiser's contentions and insist that his period spent in a mental institution—where he was diagnosed as suffering from acute paranoia and schizophrenia—has contributed to a wild tale without foundation, fueled by unresolved psychological issues concerning the Church, the Jesuits, celibacy, and a host of other problems that, perhaps, only lapsed Catholics can fully understand.

How strange, then, that we find Mr. Kaiser three years after the close of Vatican II back in Los Angeles working as a stringer when the Robert F. Kennedy assassination occurred, jumping at the chance to become involved in Sirhan's defense team and gaining unprecedented access to Sirhan for the ostensible purpose of writing a book and some articles as a means of raising money for the defense lawyers.

His book on the case, *RFK Must Die!*, is an oft-cited source for material on the assassination. In fact, according to such authorities as William Klaber and Philip H. Melanson (*Shadow Play: The Untold Story of the Robert F. Kennedy Assassination*), Philip H. Melanson (*The Robert F. Kennedy Assassination: New Revelations on the Conspiracy and Cover-up, 1968-1991*) and William Turner and John Christian (*The Assassination of Robert F. Kennedy: The Conspiracy and Coverup*) there is a lot of speculation about Kaiser's true role as part of Sirhan's defense. Kaiser shifted gears numerous times during the investigation and subsequent trial, going from conviction that there was a conspiracy involved and that Sirhan was a hypnotically-programmed assassin, to his final verdict that Sirhan acted alone and fired all the shots that killed the Senator.

Reading the Turner and Christian book is an exercise in frustration when it comes to Kaiser's role, for he so obviously had virtually unlimited access to the defendant, the defendant's family, and to investigative intelligence, yet seems to have shared little of this with anyone else, even after the publication of his book on the subject. He can't seem to get to the bottom of Sirhan Sirhan, and admits as much, leaving us to wonder if Kaiser was the right man in the right place at the right time. Courtroom observers have often wondered at the strategy employed by Sirhan's defense team, which did not try to work the evidence in their client's favor, instead working out a plea bargain in advance and permitting Sirhan to hang himself in court with his own words. Even the transcripts of Dr. Bernard Diamond's efforts to hypnotize Sirhan to get at the truth of the assassination read more like a text on brainwashing than an attempt to penetrate Sirhan's unconscious and reveal what actually had taken place, and with the hypnotist leading the subject every step of the way.

Assassinations, demonic possession, serial killers, transformation, Hollywood. It gets stranger.

According to interviews with Malachi Martin and other sources—some available on religious Web sites on the Internet, some via Art Bell's syndicated radio talk shows—self-confessed serial killer David Berkowitz of the Son of Sam killings asked to speak to Fr. Martin while in jail before his sentencing. Martin obliged, and subsequently refused all offers of a book deal or other financial gain from the fruits of that meeting, and probably for good reason.

Fr. Martin, after all, concluded that Berkowitz was possessed by a demon.

THE ULTIMATE EVIL

...and it is in the humble opinion of this narrator that this is not just "something that happened"; this cannot be "one of those things"; this, please, cannot be that. ... this was not just a matter of chance. Huh! These strange things happen all the time.

—"The Narrator," *Magnolia* (1999), Paul Thomas Anderson

The essential magical work, apart from any particular operation, is the proper formation of the Magical Being or Body of Light.

—Chapter XI, "Of Our Lady Babalon and of the Beast Whereon She Rideth. Also Concerning Transformations." *Magick in Theory and Practice*, Aleister Crowley[55]

It may seem odd that this look at sinister forces at work in Hollywood would lead us to the Son of Sam cult, but that is the nature of the Beast. We, as humans and especially as historians, academics, etc., think in terms of genre, of categories. Life, however, does not itself fit so easily into categories. Neither does our experience of life. The forces at work in assassinations manifest just as easily in works of art, for instance. The goal of alchemy is something called the Great Work, or *Magnum Opus.* This Great Work is symbolized by the production of the Philosopher's Stone, the object which effects transformation. The Great Work itself is not necessarily a purely alchemical accomplishment; it can be attained by other means. It is, from the point of view of modern western occultists, the perfect uniting in oneself of macrocosm and microcosm: mastery over one giving you automatic mastery over the other. This can be accomplished through yoga, for instance, as much as through alchemy, or ceremonial magic, or musical composition, painting, literature, architecture, or many other pursuits. That is why the great accomplishments of the artist are called by the same name—*Magnum Opus*, or Great Work—as the great accomplishment of the alchemist and magician.

Two types of individuals can lay claim to the status of those who have attained the Great Work. There are the public figures who, by virtue of their obvious attainments and contributions to society, seem destined to achieve the Great Work: presidents, generals, movie stars. Their intense personal focus on the Work in their lives leads them through fields of obstacles and to confrontation with the darker forces at work in the world even as they insist on continuing their quest regardless of the dangers. They typify for us what mythologian Joseph Campbell called "the hero with a thousand faces."

There is another type, however, and this individual may remain completely unknown and unrecognized until that moment in time when something exceedingly brilliant—or, more often, exceedingly vile—occurs as a result of the pressure-cooker nature of internalizing the psychological process, the intense focus, to a point of no return. This type of individual is just as focused as the first type, just as inexorable in his pursuit of the Work, but the result is usually an explosion, a slaughter, a catastrophe.

The Great Work is not an end in itself. It is a preliminary to greater accomplishments, but those which cannot be easily described or categorized. A person who has accomplished the Great Work may remain completely anonymous; conversely, he or she may dive deeply into society and work very hard to improve the lives of others. In any case, the fact that someone has accomplished the Great Work will not be obvious to those who have not, themselves, done the same. In fact, accomplishing the Great Work does not automatically imply a future of good works and good thoughts. There are those who have chosen an evil path, according to the literature, and use their hard-won knowledge and insight to further their own, very personal and often very sinister, ends. These are known as "brothers of the left-hand path" or "black magicians." It is generally acknowledged that further spiritual growth is impossible for them; however, they themselves often do not recognize any possible growth beyond what they have already accomplished.

This is obviously a discussion for initiates … or, at least, people who consider themselves initiates! For us, it is enough to track the existence of those who have accomplished the Great Work, who are adept at transformation, and who understand the workings of reality to such an extent that they can make use of what appear to the rest of us to be useless information, useless objects, meaningless events. Because to become a master of these sinister forces is to become a master of the phenomenon of coincidence, of correspondences, of synchronicity.

And, as such, of memory.

The "art of memory" was investigated in recent times by Dame Frances A. Yates, who understood the intricate "memory palaces" as having links with Renaissance magic, and how the art of memory itself was accused of being a "black art,"[56] even as Aristotle professed to find God resident in memory.[57] Describing in some detail the memory systems of Giordano Bruno, Raymond Lull and Robert Fludd—all famous occult scholars who wielded enormous influence over generations of hermeticists—she demonstrated how closely related were the *ars memorandi* and mystical thought. In addition, and clearly pertinent to our study, is her discovery of the fact that Robert Fludd's theater of memory is based on the actual Globe Theater of Shakespearean fame … or, conversely, that the Globe Theater was, itself, designed along hermetic lines in accord with occult principles: another instance of the close relationship between dramaturgy and thaumaturgy.[58]

> Thoughts occur to one of the possibility of using Fludd's revelations, not only for the understanding of the actual staging of Shakespeare's plays, but also for an interpretation of the relative spiritual significance of scenes played on different levels. Is the Shakespearean stage a Renaissance and Hermetic transformation of the old religious stage?[59]

In regards to this virtually lost art, it can be described simply: one trained one's memory by imagining a vast hall or other building filled with niches, columns, and levels into or onto which one put an element of the thing one was trying to memorize. It could be a line from a speech, or a mathematical formula, or anything at all. For convenience, one would choose an existing building, such as a cathedral, and memorize its architecture carefully. Then, one would take pieces of the thing to be memorized and associate them in turn with the statues, the columns, the entrances and exits, and other ornamentation, with each statue, etc. calling forth the associated idea in one's memory. In this way, the theater of memory would be filled with images corresponding to the target memories. The theater of memory served as a template, with the memories assigned to their respective positions on the template.

In the days before teleprompters, computer disks and PDAs, a powerful memory was an enormous asset in business, politics and, of course, the theater. Memory also permitted one to see associations that others would miss, because recurring patterns of behavior and natural events would become clear if one remembered past incidents and could relate them in some way to present issues. It was a means of reducing the pernicious effects of chance, much the same way card-counters win at blackjack.

Occultists already had such a system in place, the product of their efforts to reduce all of creation onto, or into, a kind of map. Qabalists had already contributed to this concept by asserting that the Torah contained encoded information that could be understood only by converting the Hebrew letters of the sacred texts to their numerical equivalents and discovering associations between words that had the same numerical value; from there, they went on to create the map of creation known as the Tree of Life upon which all things could be found.

In medieval Europe, as in India and China, the human body was also a map that could be studied for clues to how the universe worked. By associating various planets and stars with individual organs and limbs, the ancients could duplicate celestial events on a very human scale. The Hindu system of *chakras* is just such a map, with mystical and astrological associations developed for neurological centers along the spinal column, each with its own colors, letters, mantras, etc. "Raising the serpent Kundalini" along this path was tantamount to walking to the stars, each step bringing with it greater insights and greater powers. *Chakra* means "wheel" or "sphere," and the Qabalists likewise called their stations along the Tree of Life *sephira*, the Hebrew for "sphere," and often depicted their Tree of Life overlayed on an image of a man, the "perfect man" or "Adam Kadmon." The similarities between the Indian and the Qabalistic systems are very compelling, and they are joined by an almost identical system of the Daoist Chinese, that of the *Shangqing* school of Daoist alchemy.

Lest readers wonder at the relevance of Qabalism and Hindu mythology to this subject, let us point out one exemplar of modern culture's appropriation of these ancient mystic beliefs. There is probably no person of 1980s and 1990s American popular culture that represents better the conflicting spiritual forces we are discussing than Madonna. A young woman of Italian-American descent who became a huge force in popular music and the MTV age of the music video, Madonna shocked the world with the video accompanying her song "Like A Prayer" as the 1980s came to a close. While the lyrics to the song itself are not overtly religious or spiritual in nature—they are more like a traditional love song—the music video was another matter. Shot in a church, with Madonna in her usual *deshabille*, it features scenes of a statue of a black saint coming to life and kissing Madonna on the lips while outside the church white thugs attack a young black man they mistakenly believe has committed a murder. By combining elements of race, religion and even sex in one video that takes place in a Catholic church, with a choir singing backup, no less, it was a forceful attack on the Church, and moreover one that used only images and rather inoffensive lyrics to make its point.

Madonna later followed this up with a collection of her "hits" under the title *Immaculate Collection*, an obvious allusion to the Catholic doctrine of the Immaculate Conception. And when Irish pop singer Sinead O'Connor tore up a photograph of the Pope on live television and in front of a stunned audience (on NBC's *Saturday Night Live*) with the admonition "Fight the real enemy," basically stealing Madonna's thunder, Madonna herself responded humorously and intelligently the following week by tearing up a photograph of Joey Buttafuocco (of the infamous "Long Island Lolita" attempted-murder case) with the same pithy admonition.

But what makes all of this much more interesting is the fact that a decade later Madonna began a serious study of the Qabala at a Los Angeles temple. From a Catholic upbringing, to an attack on the organized Church, to a study of the Qabala ... this is essentially the same route many lapsed Catholics have taken since the Second Vatican Council of the early 1960s, and it smacks of a return to Gnosticism. The Catholic and the Qabalist mindsets are entirely different: the difference between faith and curiosity, perhaps. It also reveals a sense that there are underlying forces at work in the universe that traditional religious instruction never adequately addresses, and for which it certainly never provides theory and practice. That Madonna has also studied yoga and other Eastern philosophies is well-known; some of her later music videos depict her in Hindu dress, while another has her hands bearing the henna tattoos of the Middle East.

A common factor underlying these systems in vastly different cultures is the idea that there is another world, another reality, either parallel to ours or at times (and places) tangential to ours, and that subjecting the human body to tightly-focused control by a trained mind can open the gate to this other reality as the body's resources—neurological, biochemical—are diverted towards this end. The other means of opening the gate is, as we have already shown, the "derangement of the senses" championed by the surrealists and the shamans. The lack of conscious control in the latter method is considered quite dangerous by adepts, although it is a faster route. For that reason, the "fast approach" is usually undertaken in groups, so that there is the possibility of intervention by a more experienced practitioner should an emergency arise. The first method can be undertaken by a solo operator as long as a strict regimen is followed, gradually building up conscious control of what are, after all, unconscious processes. In his excellent forward to the collected works of alchemist Thomas Vaughan, Beat hero Kenneth Rexroth describes this process "conscious control of the autonomic nervous system"; this it is, of course, but such control is not the goal but only the tool, the instrument, to the opening of this "gate."

We have shown in the previous chapter many points of similarity between the serial killer and the shaman, even to the extent of demonstrating how—in some cases, at least, for which we have adequate documentation—they share a fascination with the idea of transformation. The Behavioral Sciences Unit at the FBI's training academy at Quantico has been credited with developing the distinction between the organized and the disorganized serial killer, and with creating the famous "profiles" which aid local law enforcement personnel in their hunt for this most difficult of murderers to apprehend. Often, as in any other science, evidence is sometimes bent to fit a theory, however. It is the contention of this study that Charles Manson and David Berkowitz were not serial killers in the classic sense. They represent a different phenomenon entirely, and one that we will examine in this and the chapter to follow.

Maury Terry has insisted that there is a connection between Charles Manson and David Berkowitz, and he has based this conclusion largely on jailhouse confessions and some controversial interviews with convicted felons. His research has been attacked in many cases, especially as it has contributed to the rise of "satanic cult survivor hysteria" in the 1980s and 1990s in the United States. Some of his conclusions have been drawn from an idiosyncratic decoding of the "Son of Sam" letters to the press and by a loose association of the dates of the Sam murders to dates with alleged occult significance. In this regard, Terry has followed (probably unconsciously) in the footsteps of more venerable scholars of the occult, people like Dame Frances A. Yates and, more recently, David Ovason who, in books such as *The Zelator* and *The Secrets of Nostradamus*, discusses something he calls the "green language" (after Fulcanelli), and which former AP reporter and right-wing conspiriologist Michael A. Hoffman II calls "twilight language."[60] These authors find that the enigmatic references in everything from the prophecies of Nostradamus and modern political propaganda to the gnomic alchemical and Rosicrucian texts conceal a deeper meaning which is easier to understand once you have the key. Both Terry and Hoffman understand—from their radically different perspectives—that language conceals as much as it reveals, and that occultists have made liberal use of this characteristic to disguise more profound, more sinister truths about everything from world events to inner, psychological states. The problem, as always, lies in interpretation.

When Charles Manson "deconstructed" the lyrics to the Beatles' *White Album,* he was employing his own version of the "green language," believing that the Beatles were, in some way, mystical adepts who were communicating with their followers directly in coded messages in their songs. Thus, the song "Revolution 9" became, for Manson, "Revelations 9," a Biblical reference to the Apocalypse. The socio-political agenda of the Manson Family became "Helter Skelter," a reference to the title of another *White Album* song, etc.

Terry is guilty of the same type of deconstruction attempt on the Son of Sam letters, and for this he has been criticized by people claiming to be occultists. A long and detailed attack on Terry's book by someone named G. M. Kelly and posted on the Internet by something called the "Castle of the Silver Star,"[61] is a case in point. We are to understand that Kelly is a Thelemite, a follower of Crowley, as he begins his review of Terry's book with the salutation "Do what thou wilt shall be the whole of the Law," which is standard among members of the OTO and other followers of Thelema. Kelly is not, however, a member of the Grady McMurtry faction of the OTO which he terms the "Caliphate pseudo-o.t.o." and an "enemy of human evolution." (The insertion of human evolution into the argument supports my thesis that occult organizations tend to believe in the fact or possibility of human evolution, as opposed to more traditional organized religions that either oppose the idea or are sceptical about it.) Thus, his perspective is that of one who has been (deliberately or inadvertently) attacked by the conclusions printed in Terry's book and who is thus defending occultism (and specifically the Crowleyan kind) from Terry's shotgun approach.

Kelly argues, and quite rightly, that Terry goes overboard in his analysis of the Son of Sam letters and other details about the Son of Sam killings and related matters including—and most importantly—Terry's understanding of the nature of cults. To Terry, virtually everything that is not a socially accepted organized religion in America is a cult. This is a trap into which many have fallen at one time or another, including Attorney General Janet Reno in her doomed opposition to the Branch Davidians in Waco, Texas. How do we define a cult in a country that celebrates freedom of religion and which was, itself, founded by members of what was, essentially, a cult? From the Puritans who managed the first Thanksgiving to Freemasons such as George Washington, America was seeded with cults. To the English government, the fleeing Puritans were certainly heretics and cultists, as were eventually the Huegenots, the Plymouth Brethren, and—to the Catholic Church—the Lutherans, Presbyterians, etc.

Without going into the minutiae of the various murders and other phenomena that Kelly analyzes—putting off until the next chapter a more penetrating look at the Son of Sam case—let us look at what he says concerning the Son of Sam letters.

As is well-known, during the crime spree known as the Son of Sam killings, someone sent letters to the newspapers boasting of the crimes, much in the same way the Jack the Ripper killings were accompanied by letters from the murderer to the police and the newspapers a hundred years earlier.

One of the letters, known as the "Borrelli letter" and supposedly written by David Berkowitz and dropped at the Suriani-Esau crime scene for the attention of NYPD Captain Joseph Borrelli, states,

> *I am the "Son of Sam."*

And,

> *I am on a different wave*
> *length then everybody*
> *else—programmed to*
> *kill.*

And,

> *I am the "monster"—*
> *"Beelzebub"—the*
> *"Chubby Behemouth."*[62]

A programmed killer who is also a demoniac. Clearly, the writer was working within a venerable tradition!

The NYPD released a psychiatric profile of the Sam killer on May 26, 1977, after analyzing the Borrelli letter and coming to the conclusion that the killer was:

> ... neurotic, schizophrenic and paranoid—dime-store definitions resulting from remote analyses by the psychiatrists. The profile also suggested that the killer might regard himself as a victim of "demonic possession."[63]

PAGING FATHER MARTIN

Terry's book describes a conversation between him and Larry Siegel, a "well-informed researcher and professional writer," who, at Terry's suggestion, began to investigate the occult with an eye to unlocking the secrets of the Sam letters. They latched immediately onto the references to Beelzebub and "Behemouth" in the Borrelli letter, as they were Biblical demons; but where the conversation turns "green" or "twilight" is in their interpretation of Behemouth (or, actually, Behemoth) as a demon represented as an elephant, and the name of the Elephas Disco near where one of the Sam killings took place. As the letter to Borrelli was dropped weeks before the Elephas attack—and *elephas* being the Latin for "elephant" and hence, by association, to the "Chubby

Behemouth"—Terry and Siegel felt they had proof that the killings were planned in advance, not random, particularly as the writer of the letter stated that the "wemon of Queens are z prettyest of all," even as the letter itself was dropped at a *Bronx* crime scene and Elephas was in Queens.[64]

This does seem to strain "coincidence," but Kelly does not mention this in his lengthy attack on *The Ultimate Evil*, only pointing out that Beelzebub and Behemoth were more likely references to a Judeo-Christian context than a satanic one ... even as he decries satanism as nothing more than an "extreme overreaction to extreme Judeo-Christian religious ethics and restrictions"! Kelly is trying to have his cake and eat it, too. Satanism and Judeao-Christianity are inextricably linked, the one a reaction to and defiance of the other, so it is natural to expect Biblical references in satanic literature. Kelly is correct in attempting to distance Thelema and modern, New Age paganism from Judeo-Christianity, of course; but his case is made more difficult by Crowley himself, who incorporated a "Gnostic Mass" into his repertoire of occult ceremonies and constantly referred to himself as the Great Beast mentioned in the Apocalypse and to his consorts as "Scarlet Women." The fact is that it is extremely difficult to extricate Judeo-Christianity from Thelema, especially in view of Crowley's own writings on occult themes, which are hardly ever purely pagan or non-Judeo-Christian.

Kelly's problem with Terry's book is probably less with Terry's leaps of logic than with the possible reaction to Terry's thesis by people who would "use books like Maury Terry's to evoke a new form of the Inquisition."[61] Kelly, as a self-described "serious student of the so-called 'occult' now for at least two decades" can "definitely say that there is nothing whatsoever in the Borrelli letter to indicate any great knowledge of any esoteric or occult subject,"[61] Yet, the unusual references to "Chubby Behemouth" and the "wemon of Queens" and a subsequent attack at the Elephas Disco in Queens weeks later, implies someone with a somewhat deeper understanding of occultism than the somewhat airy phrases of the Borrelli letter initially suggest, regardless of Kelly's demurral.

I believe the problem lies in affiliations.

G.M. Kelly firmly defines his identity as a Thelemite and a serious student of the occult for decades; normally, this implies a certain tradition that can be traced through the OTO and the Golden Dawn, back to Freemasonry and the Rosicrucians and the Knights Templar. It is a specific train of esoteric thought and practice, and the various branches share a common language, even as they may be at loggerheads with each other over minutiae of ritual or interpretation.

But there are other organizations that have only the most tenuous of affiliation with the standard occult secret societies, and which determine their own "tradition" without regard to the standard texts. There is certainly nothing in the available literature on the hermetic secret societies of the West to show that human sacrifice was an acceptable part of the ritual, yet to deny that ritual murder ever has taken place in the past is to deny a healthy part of human history. Recently, in fact, we have the Matamoros cult that was responsible for a number of ritual murders in Mexico and Texas: a group that was supposedly practicing a form of Latin shamanism known as *palo mayombe*, even as "legitimate" practitioners insisted that the Matamoros group had no legal standing within their religion. The Matamoros cult—which involved trafficking in illegal drugs across the Mexican-Texas border—was only revealed in 1989, two years *after* the publication of Terry's book insisting there was an occult "culture" surrounding certain elements of the international drug trade. Thus, if we posit a secret society—a cult, if you will—that engages in this type of ritual murder, then we must expect that they do not take their ceremonial guidance from the same sources wherein Mr. Kelly finds his spiritual comfort, or that, if they do, their interpretation of these sources is at wide variance from those enjoyed by Kelly and other Thelemites.

The "great satanic network" described by Maury Terry has nothing to do with the OTO as it is known today. As I say in *Unholy Alliance*, the McMurtry version of the OTO, at least, could not organize a bake sale much less a calendar of premeditated murder. But individuals who had once been members of the OTO could have become involved in any kind of criminal activity; and this is where the rules of evidence are necessary in order to define what was cult activity and what were simply the actions of people who had once been involved with a cult. And, in the case of the Son of Sam cult and its alleged connections with Charles Manson and other murders throughout the United States, we have to accept that we may be dealing with a stranger phenomenon that simply a gaggle of self-involved, poor-complexioned, wide-eyed, robe-wearing adolescents waving fancy cutlery and howling at the moon.

What captures our attention here, however, is the way Terry has interpreted the Son of Sam letters, looking for occult content to support his idea that a nationwide network of satanic killers was involved in the Sam killings. The fact that one of the probable members of this cult, Michael Carr, was born on October 12—the same birthday as Aleister Crowley—is taken as relevant, as if Mr. Carr had been able to choose his birthday with that in mind. Also, as Kelly points out, October 12 is Columbus Day in America, the day Columbus first set eyes on the New World—a mission influenced, as we saw in Book I, by a desire to mount another Crusade to take Jerusalem away from the Muslims. In any event, being born on Crowley's birthday does not imply satanic tendencies!

Another piece of "green interpretation" is Terry's wild analysis of a phrase in the "Breslin letter," a letter from the Sam killer to *Daily News* columnist

Jimmy Breslin. The phrase that bothered Terry was a simple one, but set apart from the rest of the letter by quotation marks, as were other suggestive phrases:

> *"Keep 'em*
> *digging, drive on, think*
> *positive, get off your*
> *butts, knock on coffins, etc."*[65]

Terry "deconstructs" what seems to be a simple and obvious sentence into actual directions to David Berkowitz' apartment! He begins by stating that he uses two techniques, one a kind of "crossword puzzle type of system"[66] and what he calls a "common satanist trick: spelling words backwards."[67] The latter he probably derives from that standard novelistic description of a Black Mass which has its participants reciting the Lord's Prayer backwards, but ... who knows? In any event, the method bears bizarre fruit.

By spelling "keep 'em" backwards, he gets "peek me"; "digging" he believes is a reference to "digs" or home. Thus, he translates this first phrase as "LOOK FOR ME HOME."[68]

Again: "drive on" becomes "drive no" the "no" meaning "north," so that he gets "drive north" or "NORTH AVENUE."[69]

For "think positive" he eventually derives "HEAD RIGHT."[70]

For "get off your butts" he translates "butts" as cigarette butts and therefore as "ash," obtaining "GET OFF ASH."[71]

Finally, "knock on coffins" becomes "KNOCK ON PINE," since a coffin is a "pine box."

To continue with Terry's own words:

> ...to reach David Berkowitz's apartment from any of the major routes out of New York City—site of the investigation—one would exit the parkways or thruways, drive across Ashburton Avenue, head right off Ashburton onto North Broadway and proceed to Pine.[72]

Realizing, perhaps, that he was straining credulity with this analysis, he goes straight to Benoit Mandelbrot, he of the Mandelbrot Set and discoverer of fractals, a famous mathematician, who looked over the Sam letter and Terry's accompanying analysis and concluded,

> The odds against one phrase being accurate were small; against two being on target they increased dramatically; and so forth. Finally, the odds against all five—in order—leading step by step to the right address were almost impossible to calculate as a coincidence or an unintentional happening.
>
> "So, " Mandelbrot intoned, "it's not a coincidence. What you have done is correct. If you sent me a letter, what do you think the odds would be

that I could get step-by-step directions to your house out of five successive phrases if you didn't intend to word your writing in such a manner?"[73]

There are many more such leaps of logic in Terry's work, and we won't go into them all. However, instances like the several mentioned above demonstrate the activity of something deeper at work than mere chance or coincidence, popularly understood. Occultists like Kelly ignore this type of evidence, even as it supports their core contention: that there is an alternate reality parallel or tangential to our own that manifests in symbols, whether of events, dates, places, objects, etc. This reality may be an artificial construct of some group or "cult"; or it may be a physical, "objective" reality. Or there may be no difference between the two. But this reality, whatever its theoretical basis, may be manipulated, and so cause change to occur in this world, even as the other world is changed in turn. The evidence points to only two possible conclusions: that there is at work in the world a relatively sophisticated conspiracy of occultists involved in ritual murders, or that there is in operation a force behind events in the world that we don't understand.

It was this blurring of boundaries between David Lynch's "two worlds" that led to a murder scandal surrounding *Rosemary's Baby* producer Bob Evans, a sophisticated drug-running operation, political and police corruption, serial murder, mysterious cults, and the existence of a "Manson II." It will even lead, however briefly, straight back to Ashland, Kentucky.

Fire, walk with me.

Endnotes

[1] Mircea Eliade, *The Myth of the Eternal Return*, Bollingen Series XLVI, Princeton University Press, NJ, p. 14-15

[2] Henry Miller, *The Time of the Assassins: A Study of Rimbaud*, New Directions, NY, 1962, p. 33

[3] Carl G. Jung, *Memories, Dreams, Reflections*, Vintage Books, NY, 1963, p. 329

[4] Konstantin Stanislavski, *An Actor Prepares*, Routledge/Theatre Arts, NY, 1989, 1936, p. 176

[5] Ibid., p. 199

[6] Ibid., p. 13

[7] Ibid., p. 14

[8] Kenneth Anger, *Hollywood Babylon*, Dell, NY, 1981, p. 413

[9] Michael Baigent, Richard Leigh, Henry Lincoln, *Holy Blood, Holy Grail*, Dell, NY, 1983, p. 157-158

[10] Sandy Robertson, *The Aleister Crowley Scrapbook*, Samuel Weiser, NY, 1988, p. 83-87

[11] Maury Terry, *The Ultimate Evil*, Barnes & Noble, NY, 1999, p. 533-534

[12] Ali MacGraw, *Moving Pictures*, Bantam, NY, 1992, p. 41

[13] Christopher Andersen, *Citizen Jane: The Turbulent Life of Jane Fonda*, Henry Holt, NY, 1990, p. 180-181

[14] Ibid., p. 180

[15] Ed Sanders, *The Family*, E.P. Dutton, NY, 1971, p. 164

[16] Robert Maheu & Richard Hack, *Next To Hughes*, HarperCollins, NY, 1992, p. 87
[17] Ed Sanders, *The Family*, (Revised and Updated Edition), Signet, NY, 1990, p. 404
[18] Ibid., p. 405
[19] Ibid., p. 294-295
[20] Stephen Fay, Lewis Chester, Magnus Linklater, *Hoax*, Viking, NY, 1972, p. 309 and p. 240
[21] Ibid., p. 340
[22] Donald H. Wolfe, *The Assassination of Marilyn Monroe*, Warner Books, NY, 1998, p. 541
[23] Ibid., p. 477
[24] Ibid., p. 475
[25] Ibid., p. 476
[26] Ibid., p. 476
[27] Ibid., p. 487
[28] Ibid., p. 487
[29] Ibid., p. 468-471
[30] Ibid., p. 538-539
[31] Anthony Summers, *Goddess: The Secret Lives of Marilyn Monroe*, Indigo, London, 1985, p. 540
[32] Wolfe, op. cit., p. 452, 540-1
[33] Ibid., p. 541
[34] Ibid., p. 540
[35] Robert F. Slatzer, *The Life and Curious Death of Marilyn Monroe*, Pinnacle, NY, 1974, p. 6-23
[36] Wolfe, op. cit., p. 547
[37] Ibid., p. 547
[38] Ibid., p. 557
[39] A.O. Scott, *International Herald Tribune*, April 22, 2003, p. 18
[40] Summers (1985), p. 41
[41] Slatzer, op. cit., p. 156-168
[42] Ibid., p. 281
[43] Wolfe, op. cit., p. 450
[44] Ibid, p. 555
[45] From David & David, *Bobby Kennedy, the Making of a Folk Hero*, cited in Gus Russo, *Live By The Sword*, Bancroft, Baltimore, 1998, p. 381
[46] Eugene K. Bird, *Prisoner #7: Rudolf Hess*, Viking, NY, 1974
[47] Cited in *Skull Session* by Daniel Hecht, 1998, Signet, NY
[48] Adolf Guggenbuehl-Craig, *From The Wrong Side*, Spring, Woodstock CT, 1995, p. 78-79
[49] From "Opening Her Own Doors: Patricia's Portrait, Jim Morrison—A Shaman's Showman," *Pagan Muse & World Report*, Fall, 1996
[50] David Lynch, in *Lynch on Lynch*, Chris Rodley, Faber and Faber, London, 1997, p. 8
[51] Ibid., p. 25-26
[52] C.G. Jung, *Alchemical Studies*, Bollingen Foundation, NY, 1967, p. 105
[53] Ibid., p. 105
[54] Richard N. Ostling & Joan K. Ostling, *Mormon America: The Power and the Promise,* Harper-SanFrancisco, 2000, p. 297

[55] Aleister Crowley, *Magic In Theory and Practice*, Dover, NY, 1976, p. 88
[56] Frances A. Yates, *The Art of Memory*, The University of Chicago Press, Chicago, 1966, p. 42-43
[57] Ibid., p. 47
[58] Ibid., p. 342-367
[59] Ibid., p. 365
[60] Michael A. Hoffman II, *Secret Societies and Psychological Warfare*, Independent History and Research, Coeur d'Ilene, Idaho, 2001
[61] http://www.geocities.com/Athens/Parthenon/7069/index.html
[62] Maury Terry, op. cit., p.44-45
[63] Ibid., p. 47
[64] Ibid., p. 164-166
[65] Ibid., p. 50
[66] Ibid., p. 119
[67] Ibid., p. 119
[68] Ibid., p. 119
[69] Ibid., p. 119
[70] Ibid., p. 120
[71] Ibid., p. 120
[72] Ibid., p. 120
[73] Ibid., p. 121

POLICE DEPT.
DES PLAINES, ILL.
NYS DOCS
78A1976
BERKOWITZ, DAVID R
5'8"   225lbs
DIN # 78A1976

Chapter Nineteen

An American Dream

"I saw a man once just after he came back from a killing. You looked like he did."
"How did he look?"
"Like he'd been painted with a touch of magic."
—Norman Mailer, *An American Dream*

In the previous chapter we discussed some of the occult influences swirling around the Hollywood music and movie scene, focusing on the 1960s and 1970s. Readers may wonder why I bother to mention Hollywood at all, since it seems somewhat out of place in a book that takes history seriously, and history is the stuff of dictators and armies, kings and presidents, economic boom and bust. As I hope I have indicated—and supported—adequately thus far, it is as impossible to extricate the arts from politics as it is religion from politics. Indeed, one may say that religion occupies the middle pew between art and politics, partaking as it does of the powers and conceits of both. So much more so the phenomenon of the secret society, the mystic cult.

If we—in concert with Giordano Bruno and with Professor Culianu as our guides—understand that the power behind the connections between events and persons, the fuel of the magic link itself, is *eros*, then we can come to no greater comprehension of American history over the past century than to realize the central position occupied by sex, and how quickly and almost effortlessly sex leads us to art on the one hand, and to murder on the other.

Thus, critical to our thesis is the story of the interpenetration of Hollywood and homicide, for the "scarlet thread of murder" that is woven through the fabric of history is one of those elements that reveals to us the existence of the sinister forces of which we speak. Murder makes everything relevant: blood samples, blood patterns, body temperature, time of day, day of year, hair, semen, cloth, fur, positioning of body, placement of body in relation to other objects, rigor mortis … in short, the entire crime scene—like those medieval woodcuts of the human body showing signs of the zodiac representing various organs—takes on cosmic significance; and the doctrine of correspondences is probably nowhere as prominent in the thinking of scientists as it is in that of criminologists, and no crime scene is as pregnant with meaning—deep, profound meaning—as that of the serial killer, whose mental images, whose fantasies, fuel the act itself and are revealed in its arrangements. For both murder and sex, the human body is at once the *image*, the representation of either hatred or lust, and the place where the desired act is performed, the object upon which it is perpetrated, the physical *link* itself. Often, movie stars themselves are hunted, stalked and slain by deranged fans who have no real idea of who the star is, of the star's actual personality or genuine nature, but only what was visible on the screen, the image of the star, so powerful is this new medium, so ancient in its origins among the rituals and magic of our ancestors.

It is for this reason that we are compelled to look closely at a series of murders that took place between 1977 and 1983, and also beyond. These killings involved some of the most powerful, most famous names in the movie business … and some of the least known, least respected as well. The culture of drugs, cults, and death overtook the culture of the screen, and for a brief moment the veil of the dark temple was lifted by a corner, and a whiff of sulphur and satanism escaped into the disbelieving world. Appropriately enough, the central character in this episode was the producer of Roman Polanski's film, *Rosemary's Baby*: Robert Evans. Evans would go on to marry Ali MacGraw—the actress whose father was the mystic of Bedford Village—and Phyllis George, a former Miss America who later married a governor of the Commonwealth of Kentucky, a governor involved in the drugs and money scandal surrounding an organization known only as "the Company."

Evans was involved in a homicide, one with tentacles reaching from New York to Los Angeles, from Miami to Bogota … and from Charles Manson to a second killer known as Manson II … and a spate of homicides known to the press as the Son of Sam killings. What we have read so far about occultism and Hollywood finds its epitome in this single example, as so many of the characters overlap between the Roy Radin homicide case in 1983 and the Manson Family environment in 1969, with the Son of Sam murders taking place in the interim. As with every facet of American history we have investigated so far, we will see that the coincidences pile up in remarkable ways and considerable volume, and we have to ask ourselves again that question: is all this the result of a conspiracy, as many would have us believe? Or is it the result of something deeper and more mysterious, but no less threatening?

Is it the Manson Secret?

A Bronx Tale

Maury Terry, the investigative journalist whose *The Ultimate Evil* started a landslide of satanic cult hysteria in the United States in the late 1980s, as he delved deeply into the Son of Sam murder mystery, discovered that he had actually gone to high school with John Carr, one of the suspects in the re-opened case who was killed by a shotgun blast to the head at an Air Force base in North Dakota. In the spirit of historical accuracy and complete disclosure, therefore, I must make a similar declaration.

I am a graduate of Christopher Columbus High School, in the Bronx. This institution boasts at least two well-known alumni. One is pioneer transsexual Christine Jorgensen. The other is confessed Son of Sam killer David Berkowitz.

I cannot claim to have known Berkowitz in high school, since I graduated in 1968 and he started at Columbus in 1969, but he would have read my article on alchemy and the transmutation of metals in the school's "literary-arts magazine," *Horizon*, which was published that year. In fact, Berkowitz lived for a while on Barnes Avenue in the Bronx, a few blocks from where I lived on Revere Avenue. And he worked as a security guard at Co-Op City, very close by.

And we had friends in common.

During my last two years at Columbus, I was friendly with a number of people who lived in and near Pelham Bay Park, which is in the same area of the northeastern Bronx as Barnes and Revere Avenues, a few subway station stops north of Westchester Square and at the end of the Number 6 line (the famous "Pelham 1-2-3"). In those years, 1967-1969, there was a lot of mysticism going on in the United States, and the Bronx was no exception. These individuals were very involved in ritual practices, as they understood them. (Some were even teachers at the high school.) We held séances together in Pelham Bay, near where Co-Op City now stands; some of us even tried summoning demons. As a text, we relied upon A. E. Waite's *Book of Ceremonial Magic* (or, in its more ominous incarnation, *The Book of Black Magic and of Pacts*). Vietnam was in full heat, and there were many of us who would go off to the jungles, never to return. We wanted to know what was really "out there," of what strange stuff reality was really composed. We knew the Church was not telling us everything; we knew the government was lying to us about so much, starting with Dallas in 1963. We questioned all authority, and with reason. Authority had let us down; authority was sending us to die in a war no one understood. We knew there were secrets, and we resented that, resented the fact that we could die without knowing the Truth. To that end, we read the works of Marx and Engels, Mao and Angela Davis and Abbie Hoffman, side by side with Aleister Crowley, Eliphas Levi, and MacGregor Mathers.

To that end, we scrupulously copied down arcane ceremonies and mispronounced Greek and Hebrew incantations (although we could be counted upon to get the Latin right, altar boys as some of us had been before the days of Vatican II and the vernacular Mass). We made our own instruments and tools "of Art": wands, knives, swords, robes, and censers.

We stalked the dead lands of pre-Co-Op City in the middle of the night, lit candles in the dark and chanted to the Moon.

We tugged at the veil of the Temple, hoping to rip it from its moorings and reveal the Light once and for all.

We gathered strange herbs from the roadsides and the park grounds, burned them in our censers or drank them as sacraments.

We stood on a rock at dawn and worshipped the Sun and reached out to touch the face of God.

This was the Bronx in 1968.

Many of the people mentioned in Maury Terry's book were either known to us, or known to friends of ours. This web of relationships would increase once Herman Slater opened his famous store on Henry Street in Brooklyn Heights in 1972, like a crazy little magnet that attracted only those on the very fringe of society. From that year until 1984 I found myself in the center of many of the incidents recounted in Terry's book, at least those that involved the Warlock Shop, Brooklyn Heights, the OTO, and the various other secret societies and cults with their tenuous connections to the Scientologists, the Process Church of the Final Judgement, the Church of Satan, the Ku Klux Klan, the National Renaissance Party, and all the various witchcraft covens and personalities, from the Gardnerians to the Alexandrians and Welsh Traditionalists, from Raymond Buckland to Leo Martello and Margot Adler, from covens gay and straight and mixed, to covens clothed and "sky clad." What was going on was much more blatant, much more vigorous, than even Terry suspected. There was *a lot* going on in those days, and much of it was open and covered by a skeptical but eager press, while the rest could be discovered with a little patience and good humor.

Raymond Buckland had already appeared on television talk shows as early as the late 1960s, sometimes opposite popular witch and author Sybil Leek. The American Society for Psychical Research was flourishing under the leadership of Dr. Karlis Osis, and I was a member … even though I was only sixteen years old, attending ASPR meetings at night in Manhattan with my mother, and once taking the train to Brentwood, Long Island to spy on the home of Raymond Buckland, author, leader of a coven of witches, proprietor of a witchcraft museum … and owner of the hearse parked in his driveway.

Samuel Weiser's in those days was a second-hand bookstore just below Union Square, with a basement section, dimly lighted, devoted to the occult and orientalia where you would find herbals, Tarot decks, grimoires, incense sticks, ephemerides, Sanskrit dictionaries, and a very strange clientele. It moved several times thereafter, dumping the second-hand stock and specializing in both selling and publishing occult arcana, each time the premises becoming smaller and smaller, finally reduced to the size of the original occult section in the basement of the store off Union Square.

Zoltan Mason's store was near Bloomingdales, uptown and second-storey, a quiet, dignified shop that specialized in astrological literature but which also boasted a decent alchemy section and some odds and ends on ritual magic. They frowned on walk-in trade, were not really interested in the retail business, but held classes in astrology. Zoltan Mason himself, noticing my serious demeanor and ambitious book selections—the *Turba Philosophorum*, the *Chymical Wedding of Christian Rosenkreutz*, the *Christian Rosenkreutz Anthology* in a large, beautifully printed and very expensive hardcover edition—took me inside to the back room (in actuality, his well-appointed office and secret storeroom, an elaborate Zodiac hanging on the wall behind his desk) and asked me what languages I spoke, and if I could help him with some translations from Latin, Russian, Church Slavonic …

It was an era of tea rooms and card readings, horoscopes and spells.

And, under it all, a seething political revolution in the making.

It was the height of the Vietnam War, but also of US government penetration of the anti-War movement, as well as of the Black Panthers, the Ku Klux Klan, the Weathermen, and the cults. In 1968, Martin Luther King, Jr. was assassinated in Memphis, Tennessee. Columbus High School held a moment of silence as we sat, stunned, in our seats during home room. A few months later, Bobby Kennedy was shot in Los Angeles, California. We were reeling from one assassination then another, to the backbeat of our neighbors dying in Vietnam. During the funeral service for Bobby Kennedy at St. Patrick's Cathedral in Manhattan, Andy Williams sang *The Battle Hymn of the Republic* as the mourners began to file out, one by one, into the June sunshine and Leonard Bernstein powered up the Hallelujah Chorus from *The Messiah.*

Two months later, in Miami, *The Battle Hymn of the Republic* was played once again, this time at the Republican National Convention that nominated Richard Nixon as their candidate for the Presidency. The obscenity of that event—if not its implicit symbolism—should have put us all on notice, those of us who needed to be warned.

James Earl Ray—the putative assassin of Dr. King—co-authored a book on the King assassination with anti-tax activist Frederick Saussy, *Tennessee Waltz,* with an afterword by Mr. Saussy entitled "The Politics of Witchcraft."

Politics and witchcraft were in the air, not as mutually exclusive themes but as two ways of looking at the same phenomenon. With this in mind, we can proceed safely to an analysis of the Son of Sam killings and, by extension, the weird and highly "coincidental" Roy Radin homicide. As in the case with the assassination of President Kennedy, we will uncover so many corpses along the way, so much "collateral damage," that we will be forgiven if we come to the conclusion that the reason our criminal justice system is so flawed is that our scientific method of forensic investigation does not allow for something as ethereal as moral responsibility, much less a close definition of what constitutes good and evil.

OCCULT CALENDARS AND MOVEABLE FEASTS

One of the essential elements used by Terry and others to define what constitutes evidence of an occult crime spree is the use of an alleged occult calendar as a timing device for ritual murders. They point to Halloween as a "sacred day" in the calendar of the occultists or satanists, and a few other days as well, and then try to fit the dates of the murders to the so-called satanic or pagan calendar. Some of their efforts have been correctly held up to ridicule; the pagan holidays are astronomically determined, and there is not a lot of temporal leeway for their celebration. However, having witnessed the lax attitude of many self-proclaimed pagans and satanists in the past—and sometimes the necessity of holding ritual holidays on days when most of the participants would be free from obligations at the office—I can attest that, to the less serious among the pagans, these days are *somewhat* moveable. The question then arises: would a cult devoted to ritual murder and human sacrifice actually postpone a homicide to a convenient weekend or bank holiday? Serial killers like Dahmer did most of their killing on days off; would the same hold true for an organized cult? The answer: not likely.

That said, let us examine the occult holidays in question beginning with the traditional pagan and occult holidays, and then comparing them with the table in Terry's book.

Traditionally, the most important days on the occult calendar—and this is demonstrated by cultures as disparate in time and space as the Stonehenge cult, the American Mound Builders, and the ancient Egyptians—are those that mark the solstices and the equinoces: sacred space aligned with sacred time. Thus, the first days of Spring, Summer, Fall and Winter are the most important and are called the Quarter Days as they divide the year into fourths. The great stone calendar of Stonehenge is so oriented, for example.

Then, the next four days of occult importance—and considered by some to be more important than the Quarter Days—are the Cross Quarter Days. These are the days that divide the previous quarters, appearing (for instance) halfway between the first day of Spring and the first day of Summer. These are:

- April 30, called *Walpurgisnacht* in Germany and *Beltane* in the Celtic countries;
- August 1, called *Lammas*;
- October 31, called Halloween or *Samhain* by the Celts; and
- January 31, called Candlemas or *Oimelc* by the Celts.

There are other days of importance to various cults, and these should not be ignored. They would include—but are not limited to—October 12, which is the birthday of Aleister Crowley; December 1, which is the day Crowley died; July 23, which is the birthday of Crowley's wife, purportedly the woman indirectly responsible for bringing Crowley's attention to the presence of the extraterrestrial intelligence known as Aiwass during their honeymoon in Cairo in 1904 (and, also, the day of the rising of the Dog Star, Sirius: a date sacred to the ancient Egyptians, source of much modern occult symbolism), and many others, including dates of importance only to Thelemites, or to Anton LaVey's Church of Satan, or Michael Aquino's Temple of Set, etc.

It is to be stressed that these are all dates of importance to those using the Western, Gregorian Calendar. There may be cults in Russia and some of the Eastern European and Balkan countries that use the older, Julian calendar. Asians have their own sacred holidays and these are usually moveable with regard to the Western calendar, based as they are on the lunar cycle. So, the type of cult one is dealing with will predict how it will use the calendar; conversely, if one knows the calendar being used, one can identify the type of cult involved with reasonable assurance.

It should be pointed out that lunar cycles are also important. The Full and New Moons especially are trigger dates for the celebration of pagan rituals, especially for the Wiccan cults that are based on a ritual they call "Drawing Down the Moon," which is quite possibly the relict of an old Thracian ritual, and possibly also an elaboration of Gerald Gardner and Aleister Crowley, although we have to admit that any witchcraft cults that pre-existed the Gardnerian versions would have also worshipped the moon.

The Quarter Days are normally celebrated at dawn on those days, and are rituals oriented towards the sun and towards the solar calendar, as evidenced by Neolithic structures such as Stonehenge and the American earthworks of the "mound builders" culture. The Cross Quarter Days, by contrast, are normally celebrated at night, most appropriately at midnight. Taken together, the Quarter and Cross Quarter Days would be known as "sabbats" to the witch cult and to some of the satanic organizations as well; the lunar rituals based on the Full or New Moons are considered "esbats" in the literature, a type of lesser sabbat. There are normally thirteen lunar months of roughly twenty-eight days each in a solar year of twelve months, but a solar year can only contain four Quarter Days and four Cross Quarter Days. As the full and new moons are also of great importance and significance to Islam, Buddhism, Hinduism and Daoism, we can safely say that a knowledge of the lunar calendar as well as the Quarter and Cross Quarter Days would be sufficient to cover most bases.

The Son of Sam killings began, officially, with the attack on Donna Lauria and Jody Valente on July 29, 1976. Donna Lauria died in the assault. As the pagan festival of Lammas begins officially on the eve of August 1, we may agree that this event is quite close to fitting the occult calendar as envisioned by Terry and described above. According to Terry's research, and Berkowitz' own admission in the Epilogue to Terry's book,[1] the attack on Donna Lauria was a deliberate one, and not a random attack as were some of the other killings. Therefore we must assume that—if a cult were involved—this date would have some special significance. The fact that it happens on a Thursday, rather than on a more convenient weekend night like most of the others, should compel our close attention. Also present at the murder was Michael Carr, according to Berkowitz, although Berkowitz admitted he did the actual shooting. Several other members of the cult—which Berkowitz readily identifies as such—were also present as observers.

Terry goes further, however, by insisting that the murderous assault on Arlis Perry in a church at Stanford University—a truly hideous killing that incorporated many ritualistic elements—was a killing by the same cult as that responsible for the Son of Sam killings three years later in New York City. There is greater weight to this conviction for several reasons (as we will see below), but the fact that the murder took place on the night of October 12, 1974—and thus Crowley's birthday, a day that is celebrated by some Thelemic groups—already forces us to consider that the killer or killers were familiar with this date and chose it deliberately.

Of course, some critics of this approach have stated that it is also Columbus Day, and that it would be equally credible to say that Arlis Perry was murdered by a crazed Genoan, or by someone upset with Columbus' invasion of the Native American territories, etc., or even by a Norwegian who wanted to bring the country's attention to the fact that Lief Erikson was the first to discover America and not Columbus, etc. However, the selection of a church as the murder site, the insertion of a candle in the victim's vagina with another between her breasts, and the strange placement of her bare legs and the blue jeans positioned over them, forming a kind of diamond pattern (or a six-pointed star), suggested to many investigators that this was a cult crime.

The time frame October 12-13 is important for another reason which is largely ignored by writers on cult crime, for it was Friday, October 13, 1307 when the Knights Templar were arrested throughout France in an attempt—orchestrated by Pope and King—to destroy the Order. It is possibly the event that gave rise to the idea that Friday the 13th is unlucky, and which has made Friday the 13th such a popular date among occultists and horror movie directors. More than that, it is an important date for Freemasons and modern-day Templars who derive their heritage from the famous Order.

(For those interested in such things, March 18 is also notable as the date on which Templar Grand Master Jacques de Molay was burned at the stake in 1314. It is also the birthday of "sleeping prophet" Edgar Cayce, as well as alleged Kennedy assassination conspirator and wandering bishop David Ferrie.)

The next Son of Sam attack took place on October 23, 1976, a Saturday. This date has no particular occult significance, and is not near enough to another date to be remarkable. It is over a week early for Halloween, for instance. In addition, Terry believes that the targets in this case—Rosemary Keenan and Carl Denaro—were chosen randomly, even though Ms. Keenan was the daughter of an NYPD detective and Mr. Denaro was a security guard who had just joined the Air Force. According to Berkowitz, the shooter was a woman.[2]

Next, we have the attack on Joanne Lomino and Donna DeMasi on November 27, 1976, also a Saturday. Conceivably, this could have been a date chosen for its proximity to December 1, the day of Crowley's demise, as it is the closest weekend night; a weak theory, but possibly one that would obtain. Both were wounded. Both saw their killer before he opened fire, and their description of him was as different from that of David Berkowitz as it was possible to be, although virtually identical to that of the Donna Lauria assailant: slim, blonde, with a high-pitched voice. Berkowitz claimed it was John Carr.[3]

Then we have the attack on Christine Freund on January 30, 1977, a Sunday. This is identified by Terry—for completely different reasons—as a deliberate Son of Sam target rather than a random shooting. This is also a date comfortably close to Candlemas and the pagan festival of Oimelc. Thus, the dates match in this case as well as they do for Arlis Perry and for Donna Lauria. Christine Freund died on her way to a Masonic dance with her boyfriend, John Diel, who was unhurt in the attack. It would be the Freund case that would lead some investigators towards a possible motive for some of the killings that did not fit a "crazed, lone gunman" scenario. According to Berkowitz, an "out of town" shooter was brought in for this one, although there were a total of five cult members present for this attack. The shooter in this case was identified by Berkowitz as "Manson II," who also claimed responsibility for the Arlis Perry attack.

The next Sam attack took place on March 8, 1977, a Tuesday and another anomaly in the calendar. This was the shooting of Virginia Voskerichian. March 8 has no particular significance in the calendar, so this attack is a mystery. Bulgarian-born Voskerichian died instantly when the slug from the .44 Charter Arms Bulldog revolver passed through her skull as she walked down the Queens street on her way home from Columbia University. Berkowitz claims a woman committed this murder.[4]

This is followed by the attack on Alexander Esau and Valentina Suriani on April 17, 1977, the Sunday after Easter, taking place along the Hutchinson River Parkway in the Pelham Bay section of the Bronx, not far from where David Berkowitz (and the author) used to live. Again, no occult significance, but both were slain and a letter left in the car to the attention of Queens Detective Captain Joseph Borelli, the letter that would state for the first time "I am the 'Son of Sam.'"[5] However, there were indications in that letter that the murders had been planned for Easter, a week earlier, and were supposed to have taken place in Queens. From internal evidence, it seemed to the police that the letter itself had been written more than a week earlier, designed to be left at a Queens crime scene and not at one in the Bronx … which leaves us with the question, who was the intended target for Easter Sunday? Berkowitz admits to having committed this crime, although other cult members were, as usual, present.

On May 30, 1977, a letter was mailed to *Daily News* columnist Jimmy Breslin from the "Son of Sam." This letter contained many specific references to people who would later become identified once Berkowitz was apprehended, including John Carr. It was a well-written, creepy letter that ignited the imagination of New Yorkers, and put them on alert that something more than your everyday, crazed killer was on the loose. The letter contained occult references as well as building upon the vampiric symbolism of the first letter left at the Esau/Suriani crime scene. It was, in fact, an intelligent piece of work and was the first communication bearing the Son of Sam "logo," a grouping of astrological symbols that had some investigators wondering at a link to California's Zodiac killer.

June 26, 1977—a Sunday—is the day of the attack on Judy Placido and Salvatore Lupo outside the Elephas Disco in Queens. This date is somewhat problematic. Was it chosen because it is the closest weekend date after the summer solstice, which would have been on or about June 22? Both survived this attack. (Ironically, Judy Placido had attended Son of Sam victim Valentina Suriani's funeral two months earlier.) Michael Carr committed this murder, again according to Berkowitz.[6]

But the final confirmed Son of Sam murder was that of Stacy Moskowitz (and the blinding of her date, Robert Violante) in Brooklyn on July 31, 1977—virtually the first anniversary of the Sam killings as well as Lammas in the pagan calendar and a Sunday. And a full moon. This attack had a plethora of eyewitnesses who saw more than one participant in the killing and at least two vehicles: one, a Ford Galaxie, was Berkowitz' car, the one identified by a parking ticket that night. The other was a Volkswagen Beetle.[7] Although Berkowitz was present at this killing, evidence shows he could not have committed it and, indeed, once he knew his car had just received a parking ticket, tried to call it off, knowing where that clue would lead. However, the killing went ahead as planned, committed—according to Berkowitz—by a friend of John Carr's from North Dakota.[8]

As you can see, not all of the killings were timed to the official pagan calendar. In fact, most of them could not be successfully placed near enough to a cult date to be significant. Yet, is there a pattern we could be missing? Or is the lack of a pattern in some killings an indication that they were committed merely to confuse the issue, or conversely that they are evidence of a second killer or killers?

One possible pattern is the astrological one.

If we consider the Arlis Perry homicide first, we are relatively secure in that this murder took place on Crowley's birthday, a date of considerable significance to his followers. But if we look a little deeper, from the point of view of a sophisticated cultist with a hidden agenda, we may find something more than we bargained for.

Arlis Perry was killed on or about midnight of October 12-13, 1974. An astrological chart drawn up for that place and time would reveal that there was a conjunction of the Sun and Mars in Libra at the Lower Heaven (the point in space opposite the Midheaven where the Sun is highest at noon). This conjunction is squared by Saturn in Cancer, and "semi-sextiled" (an angle of thirty degrees) by the waning Moon in Virgo. To reinforce the imagery, there were also significant angles between Pluto, Neptune and Jupiter that night. In fact, virtually all the "angles" that night were squares, conjunctions or oppositions: all considered "hard" aspects in astrological circles. In other words, it was a potent night for a ritual murder and may have been selected with that point of view in addition to the fact that all of these aspects were taking place on Crowley's birthday.

One does not need to believe in astrology at all to understand that others do. One does not have to believe in the efficacy or value of human sacrifice to understand that others do. As pointed out in *Unholy Alliance*, even British Intelligence understood that the Nazis were astrology-crazed, and worked up several propaganda and psy-war campaigns to turn that belief against them, realizing that no matter how you view astrology, there is a certain internal consistency to its methods that can be exploited by a clever astrologer-turned-intelligence officer.

Could an astrological perspective assist us in analyzing the other Son of Sam homicides?

For one thing, charts drawn up for all the murders indicate that only one—that of Virginia Voskerichian on March 8, 1977—did not take place during a waxing moon. (In fact, the Voskerichian attack was very anomalous in other regards, taking place much earlier in the evening than the others.) The other shootings took place either on New or Full Moons or when the Moon was somewhere between New and Full. In fact, the attack on Alexander Esau and Valentina Suriani on the strange date of April 17, 1977 (a date with no known pagan or occult significance) took place during the New Moon. The attack on Rosemary Keenan and Carl Denaro on October 23, 1976 (again, a date with no known occult significance) not only took place on the night of the New Moon but also when both the Sun and the Moon were entering conjunction with Uranus and Mars and the Moon's North Node (traditionally an indicator of an eclipse).

The attack on Stacy Moskowitch—the last of the official Son of Sam murders—took place not only on Lammas but also on the night of the Full Moon.

If one believes in astrology, then one can say that the murders happened on those dates and times because the "stars were aright." And if one does *not* believe in astrology, then one can still say that someone else, someone who *did* believe in astrology, chose those dates and times deliberately. It is not a conclusive piece of evidence, but the astrological character of the murder calendar is suggestive. Berkowitz told Terry that he was not aware of the reasons for the murders, or why some victims were chosen for death; he was simply told what to do and he did it.

Then, however, we have the collateral damage, the deaths of people who were close to the suspects or the investigation. These include:

September 20, 1977: Andrew Dupay—a mailman who worked the Yonkers route where Berkowitz and the Carrs lived—goes downstairs to the basement of his home while his wife is bathing their two daughters, writes a hasty suicide note, and kills himself with a shotgun. It is the autumnal equinox. No one knows the motive for the suicide, except that in the days immediately before and after Berkowitz' arrest, co-workers say Dupay began acting fearful, gradually becoming consumed with panic through the month of August and into September. One informant wrote Terry that Dupay had met someone in Pelham Bay Park the day before his suicide. Pelham Bay Park, of course, is the same area of the Bronx where Berkowitz had lived a few years earlier. The man he met was not identified.[9]

October 31, 1981: the murders of Ronald Sisman and Elizabeth Plotzman on Halloween. Sisman was a photographer who claimed to have possession of videotapes made by the Son of Sam killer(s), notably of the murder of Stacy Moskowitz. Sisman was planning on giving this evidence to the authorities, but he and his girlfriend were executed. It was Sisman who introduced actress (*Welcome Back, Kotter*) and model (*Playboy*) Melonie Haller to producer Roy Radin, who was himself murdered by the Son of Sam cult according to Terry. Melonie Haller was savagely beaten at Radin's Long Island estate and claimed that the beatings and possible rape were videotaped by Radin and/or his accomplices.

Craig Glassman, on October 31, 1991: again, Halloween. Glassman, an important witness to the goings-on in and around the Yonkers apartment of David Berkowitz, who had received threatening letters and was the target of an arson attack by Berkowitz, died on the Taconic State Parkway in a bizarre auto accident.

There were numerous other murders and violent deaths surrounding the Son of Sam cult, much as we saw in the case of the Kennedy assassination, lending credence to the conspiracy theory proposed by Terry. A further piece of evidence, circumstantial as it may be, is that of the dates of the famous Zodiac killings in California.

The Zodiac killer began his murderous spree on October 30, 1966—again, uncomfortably close to Halloween and very suggestive of cult involvement. (In fact, this date is interesting for another reason, for it is the very same day that President John F. Kennedy's brain was discovered missing from the National Archives; within two weeks New Orleans DA Jim Garrison would begin his own investigation of the assassination and, at the same time, the Mothman sightings would begin in West Virginia.) The murders continued until May 20, 1981 … a period of nearly fifteen years. The Zodiac killer was never apprehended and the case remains open, although there have been one or two very good suspects. What is important for our investigation, however, is the fact that the Zodiac killings stopped from October 16, 1975 until starting up again on February 24, 1979, a quiescent period of about three and half years. This period of Zodiac inactivity dovetails with the Son of Sam murders, which took place from July 1976 to August 1977, and the murders of alleged Sam accomplices John Carr in February 1978 and Michael Carr in October 1978.

In fact, the murder of Arlis Perry in Stanford on October 12, 1974 also fits neatly into the Zodiac framework, as the killer was operating mostly in and around the San Francisco area at this time. If the Zodiac murders were the result of a cult in operation, then it is reasonable to assume that the Son of Sam cult—on the East Coast as opposed to Zodiac's West Coast sphere of influence—was picking up *when* Zodiac left off, for whatever reason, and that Zodiac picked up shortly after the last Sam killing in late 1978, thus perpetuating a calendar of murder for reasons at which we can only guess.

There are many similarities between the Zodiac case and the Son of Sam case. The definitive study of the Zodiac killings—*Zodiac* by Robert Graysmith—tells us that the killings took place "on weekends when the moon was new or full."[10] In addition, Graysmith has linked the killings to the Quarter Days: the summer and winter solstices and the spring and autumn equinoces.[11] Further, Zodiac sent taunting letters to the press, as did the Son of Sam killer(s) as well as probably the most famous serial killer of all time, Jack the Ripper. Like the Ripper, the Zodiac's identity is unknown.

There was a Zodiac murder in 1974, only a few weeks before Arlis Perry's. This took place "six days after the Autumnal Equinox in 1974," when a fourteen-year-old girl was killed.[12] The Zodiac used a wide variety of murder weapons, making his identification and apprehension even more difficult. Then, after October 1975 there seems to be little or no more activity from the Zodiac until February 1979: virtually the same time frame in which the Son of Sam murders took place, including the violent deaths of John and Michael Carr.

In Graysmith's sequel, *Zodiac Unmasked* published in April 2002, he identifies the Zodiac Killer as one Arthur Leigh Allen, and notes that the period of Zodiac inactivity matches the years when Allen was in prison … specifically the Atascadero State Hospital for the Criminally Insane, convicted of child molestation.[13] Strange, then, that the Son of Sam cult would begin operation when he was incarcerated, and then stop shortly after he was released. If this is coincidence, then it is evidence of a deeper historical force at work.

Maury Terry has linked the Son of Sam killings to the operation of a satanic cult; indeed, David Berkowitz has admitted as much and in some detail in the Epilogue to Terry's book. The Zodiac used occult symbols, astrological symbols, and ciphers in his letters to the press. Even his *nom de guerre*, "Zodiac," is of course astrological.

Of course, as always, the alternative explanation is "coincidence." As we have seen, coincidence can be evidence of the operation of something deeper behind historical events. Although every historical event—and many, smaller, personal events—can be shown to demonstrate a certain degree of "coincidence" in action, it is when we discuss murder, from presidential assassinations to mass murder to serial murder, that we find the frequency and specificity of coincidence increasing dramatically. We see that events have been presaged by webs of convenient accidents, bringing specific people into specific places at specific times. It is perhaps the inclusion of *people* into this time-space continuum that has something to do with the mechanism of coincidence, as people have the ability to remember the past, and to predict—with various degrees of accuracy—the future.

The interface between consciousness and physical space is one that we will examine in the final section of this work, because it, quite simply, gives the game away. However, the conclusions to which I am drawn will not make much sense unless you witness for yourself the operation of this mysterious, sinister force for yourselves.

As an example, and considering dates of pagan significance, the famous Texas Tower Sniper case took place on Lammas, that is on August 1, 1966 at Austin (this is a Cross Quarter Day; the next Cross Quarter Day would be October 31, 1966 when the Zodiac killings began). Charles Whitman was an ex-Marine who somehow lost his mind and began shooting at random targets from the top of a tower at the University of Texas, hitting forty-five people in ninety-six minutes and killing fourteen of those. Whitman had had trouble in the Marines, and had been court-martialed in November 1963. He had served in Guantanamo Bay, Cuba beginning in December 1959 when Castro's revolution was in full swing and the island nation was transferring its political allegiance to the Soviet Union. In June 1961 he was sent to a college preparatory school in Bainbridge, Maryland, eventually enrolling in the University of Texas in September 1961 under a special program designed to enrich the Marine Corps' scientific and technical capabilities by training selected Marines in engineering, mathematics and science.

It was a prestigious assignment, and one that Whitman eventually flunked, in tandem with a gradual deterioration of his mental state. He lost his scholarship, and had to report to Camp Lejeune in North Carolina in February 1963.

He was court-martialed in November for an assault on another Marine, and his fiancée showed up for the trial. She thought she had become pregnant the night of November 23, 1963—according to Whitman's journal—but it was a false alarm. It is interesting to note the similarities between Whitman's career and the American political experience of the time. Whitman, a Marine, is stationed in Cuba at the time of the Castro revolution; Lee Harvey Oswald, another Marine on active duty the same time as Whitman, is tested in Russian in February of 1959, but is released from active duty on September 11, 1959 before Whitman arrives in Cuba. Oswald (who would eventually campaign for the Fair Play for Cuba Committee) will renounce his American citizenship in Moscow on October 31, 1959 (Halloween).

Oswald, either a very poor Marine or a deep-cover intelligence asset depending on whom you believe, is accused of assassinating President Kennedy on November 22, 1963 from the Texas Schoolbook Depository in Dallas, Texas using a poorly made sniper's rifle. The following night, Marine Charles Whitman is having sex with his fiancée while awaiting a court martial, an act the fiancée later believes to have impregnated her. The following day, Oswald is killed by Jack Ruby.

Three years later, on August 1, 1966, Charles Whitman becomes the second ex-Marine accused of sniping at people from a high place in Texas, after first murdering his wife and mother the previous evening. All of this would just be interesting and perhaps even ironic, were it not for a book that had been published a few years earlier describing the same scenario: *Open Square.*

Like the Maeterlinck play that prefigured the Kennedy assassination in Dallas, this paperback thriller by Ford Clark prefigures the Texas Tower case. It tells the story of Ted Weeks, a student and a psychotic, who climbs a tower in a Midwestern university town and begins shooting at random targets below.

The definitive story of Charles Whitman, *A Sniper In The Tower: The Charles Whitman Murders*, by Gary M. Lavergne, has this to say about the startling similarities between Clark's novel and the real-life events that unfolded a few years later:

> … the sniper's nest had food; Weeks had an overly loving mother and a perfectionist for a father; he could not live up to the expectations of his father; he was trained to shoot in the military (ROTC); he hauled his supplies in a suitcase, the contents of which included water, gasoline, and five hundred rounds of ammunition; and he used ventilation slits as portholes to fire through. Astoundingly, the fictitious sniper Ted Weeks was killed by a police force headed by a "Chief Miles."[14]

In other words, the details of the fictional sniper matched perfectly those of the real sniper, *even down to the name of the chief of police* which, in the real-life case was Chief Robert Miles.

Of course, efforts were made to discover whether or not Whitman had read the Clark novel. No copy of the novel was found in his home after the shootings; no one could remember him ever reading it, or mentioning it. He had not taken it out of the library. It was not a well-known book, not a bestseller likely to have been on everyone's nightstand. In fact, Whitman is said to have looked at the tower years earlier—perhaps even earlier than the book's publication—and remarked that one could "hold off an army" from up there.[15] And, anyway, Whitman could not have arranged for the chief of police to be named Miles.

So, it was "just one of those things."

A coincidence, however, is frequently a glimpse of a pattern otherwise hidden. His heart tells him indisputably what his mind resists: This is no random event, but part of the elaborate design in a tapestry, and at the center of the design is he himself, caught and murdered.

—Dean Koontz[16]

To return to Terry's cult calendar analysis,[17] it shows that he arrived at similar conclusions where dates of cult significance are concerned, but used far too much leeway in his calculations, thus opening himself up to criticism from those who study occultism seriously.

For instance, he mentions the October 23 shooting and links it to Halloween, a conclusion I think is too far-fetched, as Halloween is over a week later. We can't use more than a day or so on either side of a specific date to show relevance, I believe, otherwise virtually any date you would care to mention is close enough to a cult "holiday." November 27 he links to November 30 (St. Andrew's Eve) and a date that does not seem to have any significance taken that way, but which does link successfully with December 1, the date of Crowley's death which he does not mention. As November 27 fell on a Saturday, it may indeed have been used as the closest weekend date to December 1, if our cultists were constrained to use weekends for hits for the most part due to day jobs or other obligations, or perhaps the convenience of using the weekend as it would be a time when their targets would be out late at night. He also refers, on the same page, to December 21 as St. Thomas' Day, a "satanic feast"; I believe he really wants to point out the significance of the winter solstice rather than a saint's day. The one that puzzles Terry most of all—as it does me—is the Virginia Voskerichian homicide of March 8, which seems to be the one anomalous shooting of all, even taking into consideration lunar phases; further, it took place on a Tuesday rather than a weekend, and much earlier in the evening—7:30 P.M.—than the other homicides, which all took place between midnight and 3:00 A.M. Terry's partner in the investigation opines that it might have been the cult leader's birthday, but that does not account for the early evening shooting unless it was timed specifically to coincide with other data (such as the putative cult leader's birth time) to which we have no access.

A search of my records and a large timeline developed for the purpose of tracking these events has revealed virtually nothing of significance for March 8 in any era. However, March 8, 1990 *was* chosen as the date of the *first* New York City "Zodiac" murder; the fourth and last New York City "Zodiac" killing was on June 21 that year: the summer solstice. It is possible that the March 8 date was selected deliberately to reinforce a link with the Son of Sam attack on Voskerichian, but there is no evidence to support this, either. Thus, the March 8 date remains a mystery.

There are other resonances to the "occult calendar," however, and these may be of interest to some readers:

Candlemas—1/31/1865: the 13th Amendment to the US Constitution is passed, abolishing slavery in the United States.
1/30/1933: Adolf Hitler seizes power in Germany.
1/31/1958: America's first satellite, Explorer I, built and controlled by the Jet Propulsion Laboratory, discovers the Van Allen Belt; the American space age begins.
1/30/1972: "Bloody Sunday," the massacre of 13 marchers in Derry, Northern Ireland by British troops during a protest of Unionist rule.
1/31/1976: George H.W. Bush becomes Director of the CIA.
Vernal Equinox—3/21/1973: The George Stano serial killings begin, in Gainesville, FL (thus giving more support to a cult calendar theory).
Beltane—5/1/1960: Francis Gary Powers shot down over the USSR.
Summer Solstice—6/21/1972: the date of the famous 18 ½ minute gap on the Nixon Oval Office tapes, giving rise to the suspicion of "sinister forces."
6/21/1975: Self-proclaimed satanist Michael Aquino is visited by the Egyptian deity Set during an occult ritual, giving birth to the Temple of Set.
6/22/1979: the Susan Reinert "Mainline" murders in Philadelphia, believed to have been part of a satanic sacrifice.
Lammas—8/1/1914: Germany mobilizes against Russia; World War I begins.
7/29/1921: The Council on Foreign Relations incorporated in New York.
7/29/1958: NASA created.
7/31/1980: The children of slain Congressman Leo J. Ryan file suit against the US government over the Jonestown murders.
Crowleymas—10/12/1962: Lee Harvey Oswald gets a job at Jaggers-Chiles-Stovall, a company whose name has Thelemic resonances.
10/12/1964: Mary Pinchot Meyer, confidant of John F. Kennedy and Timothy Leary, is murdered in Washington, DC.

10/13/1968: Clida Delaney and Nancy Warren are murdered near Ukiah, California, believed to have been the work of the Manson Family.
10/12/1979: Doreen Levesque murdered by Carl Drew in Fall River, MA as part of a cult sacrifice
10/12/1988: Patricia Ann Cantero murdered by her son, Jonathan, in Tampa, FL as part of a satanic ritual

A note to the first entry, the passing of the anti-slavery amendment to the US Constitution on January 31, 1865: General Lee of the Confederacy surrendered to General Grant at Appomattox on Palm Sunday, 1865, thus ending the Civil War; President Abraham Lincoln was assassinated less than a week later, on Good Friday, by an actor in a theater. It was as if America was acting out its own version of the Passion Play, with Lincoln as Christ. It is no wonder, then, that so many parallels would be found between Presidents Lincoln and Kennedy, and that their deaths would be elevated to the status of iconic events in the eyes of many observers. On the other hand, perhaps the driving force of some other intelligence below the conscious threshold of the American psyche manipulates these events, and their ancillary coincidences and correspondences may be the evidence of this arcane activity.

As can be seen from the above, very small sampling, a number of occult murders and serial killings were begun or committed on important dates on the cult calendar, many more than Maury Terry was aware of when he wrote *The Ultimate Evil.* The dates with political overtones were included only to show how politics and the occult intermingle and to stimulate further research (if warranted), as well as to show how easily conspiracy theories can spin out of control.

A Different Wave Length

Murder is a recent interest of mine.
—David Berkowitz[18]

David Richard Berkowitz was born on June 1, 1953 in Brooklyn, New York. He was conceived in a parked car, the natural child of Betty Broder of Brooklyn and Joseph Klineman of Long Island, a married man who was having an affair with Ms. Broder. Ms. Broder herself had been married before, to a Tony Falco, who left her. On David Berkowitz' adoption papers, it is Tony Falco's name that appears as the natural father, even though it was Joseph Klineman who was responsible. Betty Broder had a daughter, Roslyn, with Falco: David Berkowitz' half-sister.

Both Joseph Klineman and Betty Broder were Jewish.

"Richard David Falco" (to give David Berkowitz his name as it appears in the adoption records) was then adopted by Nathan and Pearl Berkowitz, who lived on Stratford Avenue in the Soundview section of the Bronx. Nathan Berkowitz had a hardware store on Melrose Avenue in the Bronx. They renamed the baby David Richard Berkowitz and everything seemed to be fine until October 1967, when Pearl Berkowitz died of cancer. David was fourteen years old.

Late in 1969, David and his father moved to Co-Op City in the Bronx, a housing development that was just being completed and touted as one of the largest in the world at the time, with its own shopping center, movie theater, etc. David Berkowitz enrolled in Christopher Columbus High School that year. He was sixteen.

The following year, he joined the Auxiliary Police force of the New York Police Department, out of the 45th Precinct in the Bronx. The Auxiliary Police force (to which the author belonged for a while in the summer of 1980) is a civilian patrol unit, a separate division of NYPD that helps the regular police monitor neighborhood activity, help out in directing traffic at public events, and generally make an appearance as the "eyes and ears" of the police department. They dress in standard NYPD uniforms, carry a baton (a nightstick), and a distinctive shield (badge). They carry radios but are not authorized to carry firearms. They are not peace officers per se, but assist the police in day-to-day activities, usually in the evenings or on weekends, since most of the civilian police—or APO's (Auxiliary Police Officers) as they are known—either have day jobs or are, like David, busy at school. David joined the volunteer fire department at Co-Op City, which is ironic (or cynical) considering his penchant for committing arson.

Around this time, his adopted father Nathan married Julia, a woman who had children of her own from a previous marriage. One of these children, David's stepsister, is a witch of some description, and taught David about the occult.

He graduated from Columbus High School in June of 1971, and immediately enlisted in the Army.

This was deep into the Vietnam conflict, when many young men were looking for ways to avoid service. Berkowitz, however, had spent time in uniform as an APO and as a volunteer fireman. Restless, he is a joiner, seemingly trying to compensate for an imagined flaw. He will spend the rest of his life in one kind of uniform after another, as he moves from the Army to work as a security guard and finally as a mailman, at which point he is arrested for the Son of Sam killings and begins wearing a prison uniform.

In the Army, Berkowitz is stationed not in Vietnam but in Korea, spending a year there and taking LSD during his tour. Not much is known about his life in the Army at this point, only that after his hitch in Korea he is transferred to Fort Knox, Kentucky in January 1973.

This is where David Berkowitz goes off the rails.

Although Berkowitz is Jewish—his adoptive parents are Jewish, his natural parents are Jewish—David suddenly becomes a Christian upon his return from Korea. While stationed at Fort Knox—the site of the nation's heavily-guarded gold repository—he begins attending the Beth Haven Baptist Church in Louisville and becomes a fanatic Christian. He tries to convert both civilian and military personnel, even preaching (à la Jim Jones in Indiana) on street corners. Again, there is insufficient data to make any kind of assumption here about what motivated Berkowitz to become religious, much less Christian. Did it have something to do with his discovery that he was adopted? Did the LSD he took in Korea have anything to do with this sudden spiritual awakening?

In June 1974 he is discharged from the Army and moves back to the Bronx, to 2161 Barnes Avenue, and enrolls in Bronx Community College. At the same time, he gets a job as a security guard for IBI Security, working in Manhattan.

Arlis Perry is murdered in California on October 12, 1974.

Early in 1975, his adoptive father, Nathan and Nathan's wife Julia leave the Bronx and move to Boynton Beach, Florida. David's stepsister—the would-be witch—decamps for a commune in California. In April 1975, Saigon falls to the Communists.

In May, David Berkowitz takes an important personal step. He joins ALMA, the Adoptees Liberty Movement Association, in an effort to come to terms with his adopted status, something that has obviously been bothering him. That Mother's Day, he sends a card to his natural mother, Betty Falco. This leads to an emotional meeting with her, during which he discovers that she has remarried (to a man named Leo). More disturbing to David is the fact that she reveals he was born illegitimately and moreover that she has other children she has not abandoned. This must contribute to seeing himself as worthless and unwanted.

Thus begins a strange odyssey with so many false starts and red herrings that we are forced to sit back and wonder at what was really going on.

In February of 1976, Berkowitz moves to New Rochelle from the Bronx, to an apartment that is much farther away from both his college and his job and which is more expensive. No one knows why he does this. It makes no sense. The apartment was only advertised in a local Westchester newspaper, not something Berkowitz would have normally seen in the course of his days in the Bronx and Manhattan. It is in a private home owned by one Jack Cassara. At that time, Cassara is working at the Neptune Moving Company in New Rochelle. One of his co-workers is Fred Cowan, a neo-Nazi who would go amok and, during a siege at the moving company, kill six people before killing himself on Valentine's Day 1977. Later, clippings would be found in Berkowitz' Yonkers apartment covering the Cowan case in detail. Berkowitz would refer to Cowan as "one of the Sons."[19] Later, during a court-ordered interrogation in October 1978, Berkowitz would reveal that he knew Cowan personally. He obviously knew Cowan's co-worker, Jack Cassara.[20]

Then, the following month, he applies for an apartment in Yonkers, on the other side of New York from New Rochelle, at 35 Pine Street, even though he has a one-year lease with the Cassaras that is only a month old. Again, why?

In April 1976, he moves to 35 Pine Street. Again, this move makes no sense for someone working and studying in the Bronx. Not only is the time it takes to commute a factor, but also the additional cost of commuting; plus, the rent is one hundred dollars more a month than the original place he had in the Bronx. One hundred "1976" dollars. This is the apartment where he would eventually be arrested on August 10, 1977.

On May 13, 1976, the house of a Yonkers neighbor is firebombed, part of a pattern of firebombings in the area.

In June 1976, Berkowitz travels to Florida to visit his father, and then drives on to Houston, Texas to visit an Army buddy—Billy Dan Parker—who buys him the .44 Bulldog revolver that was used in at least some of the Son of Sam shootings. Outside of Houston, in the town of Beaumont, lives the ex-wife of John Carr. Beaumont is also believed to be a cult center, one referred to by serial killer Henry Lee Lucas.

He returns to the Bronx and gets a job as a cabdriver in Co-Op City, making the long commute from Yonkers every day.

On July 29, 1976 the first Son of Sam shooting takes place.

Maury Terry's thesis is that the Son of Sam killings were committed by more than one person, and that David Berkowitz was only one of perhaps as many as three different shooters. Based on that theory—and it is a good one, and fits the eyewitness evidence as well as a lot of circumstantial clues—there was a conspiracy to commit these murders. Of what was this conspiracy composed?

When Berkowitz was finally arrested for the crimes on August 10, 1977 (for those following this sort of thing, the anniversary of the La Bianca killings in 1969) he pled guilty, thus avoiding a trial. This had happened before, of course, such as in the cases of accused Martin Luther King assassin James Earl Ray and John Lennon assassin Mark David Chapman. I don't want to elevate David Berkowitz to the same level as a political assassin, but will only point out that when the public is deprived of the right to see the evidence laid out in a trial, the public is similarly robbed of a chance to understand the crime and to benefit from the investigative resources of a defense team which might uncover a deeper, darker truth. I believe this is something which we should not allow to happen when a case is as important as a political assassination, or a serial murder spree that held a major city hostage for more than a year.

When the Sam killings were taking place, and the taunting letters received and printed in the newspapers, many of us New Yorkers were convinced at the time that more than one shooter was involved. The timing of the murders was very suggestive of more than one killer, and the various eyewitness descriptions of the shooters were so different that it naturally raised a lot of speculation about multiple killers. But this had not been experienced before in the United States: a group of murderers carrying out seemingly pointless and random homicides. It was easier to believe that one, crazed gunman was responsible. So, when Berkowitz was arrested and pled guilty, the entire case was swept under a rug. And there it stayed for quite some time.

But an examination of the letters sent by the Son of Sam killer(s) pointed to other connections, and more correspondence both from Berkowitz himself and from other convicts began to reveal a strange set of correspondences between the Son of Sam killings and murders taking place as far away as California and as long ago as 1969. And when Berkowitz associates wound up dying violently all over the United States after Berkowitz was in prison and could not conceivably have committed these additional killings himself, alarm bells began to go off. In addition, the very bookstore to which Terry refers several times in his book as being a central meeting place for members of this murderous cult was the same bookstore around which the author and several of his friends congregated from time to time during the Son of Sam killings, a store rapidly becoming notorious as a kind of occult clearing house for pagans, witches, satanists, magicians, and assorted other fringe religionists.

It is possible that Terry jumped to a lot of conclusions in the Son of Sam case, and that some of his theories about a proposed network of satanic killers are a little thin. It is also more than likely that some of the felons (including Berkowitz) who confided in him, telling tall tales of cult rituals in the moonlight replete with the sacrifice of dogs and humans, were doing so for ulterior motives or just having fun at Terry's expense. However, a few pieces of evidence militate against this point of view.

In the first place, Berkowitz has absolutely nothing to gain by spreading stories of a murderous cult to which he claimed to belong, and by admitting that he committed *some* of the killings but not *all.* That he is a self-confessed murderer is beyond doubt, and he does not try to backpedal from that fact. Berkowitz is in prison for life, and he knows it. There is no possibility of parole for David Berkowitz. His much-publicized conversion to Christianity (a re-conversion, actually, considering his activities in Kentucky a few years before the murders) does not buy him any time outside his prison walls. He has his own Web site now, and tries to impart uplifting spiritual messages via that medium, tranquilly acknowledging that he was a murderer who will never see freedom, who is only interested in being an example of redemption for other felons like him, as well as for those on the "outside." He cannot gain financially from any of these activities, for it was because of Berkowitz that we have the famous "Son of Sam laws" that forbid a convicted felon from benefiting from his crimes by selling the rights to a book publisher or movie producer, etc. Thus, he has no ulterior motive that we can see for finally coming forward and telling Maury Terry that he belonged to a satanic cult that was a splinter group of the Process, and that there were links between his group and the Charles Manson Family.

In the second place, the letters Terry received contained much internal evidence to suggest that his correspondents knew more about various other murders committed around the country than could be gleaned from newspaper reports. This includes Berkowitz, but also other inmates and other informants who claimed to have befriended Berkowitz inside, and who had heard of substantiating evidence that could be checked by Terry and other investigators.

Where Terry is on shakier ground is his analysis of occultism and the activities of various cults and secret societies. His background in this field comes strictly from a handful of very poorly-composed occult books designed for popular audiences that were themselves written by people with very little direct knowledge. This has happened to many investigators, of course, who come upon occultism for the first time and have their eyes opened wide at this strange demimonde in their own communities, and thus begin to believe everything they read on the subject, growing more and more nervous with each purple page of sensationalist prose, not realizing that the reality behind most of what comprises the modern manifestation of occultism is usually a lot less exciting and a lot more tawdry, about one step up from the standard established by Star Trek conventions, but minus the sophistication. Thus, it is possible for Terry—in *The Ultimate Evil*—to confuse the Golden Dawn with satanism, or the OTO with the Process, etc. Although we can easily show a "line of succession" leading from the Golden Dawn to Aleister Crowley, and from Crowley to the OTO and from the OTO to Scientology, and from Scientology to the Process Church of the Final Judgement, and eventually from there to Charles Manson, the so-called "Solar Lodge of the OTO," and even cult killers such as Clifford St. Joseph and others, we certainly don't have enough to show a deliberate conspiracy on the part of all these organizations in the Son of Sam case, and certainly not enough for calling all of these groups "satanic" or "murderous." Perhaps, from a very narrow Fundamentalist Christian point of view, Terry could be forgiven for making these assumptions, because to a Fundamentalist anything smacking of the occult is automatically from the Devil and satanic. This includes rock music, homosexuals, prime time television and your daily horoscope. All the evidence shows, however, that Terry is not a Fundamentalist Christian with an axe to grind against alternative religions, so we have to be a bit more selective and astute when it comes to investigating the occult aspect of the Son of Sam case, and this is what we mean to do, armed with such evidence as is available and beyond doubt. It will take us back to Charles Manson, and ahead to Manson II and a nexus of drugs, rituals, pornography, prostitution, and politics in low places. It will help reveal the Manson Secret.

Return of the Process

Your process is all fucked up!
— Brad Pitt to Bruce Willis in *The Twelve Monkeys*

There are other Sons out there—God help the world.
— David Berkowitz[21]

A key element in Terry's thesis is that the Process Church of the Final Judgement is alive and well, and involved in nefarious activity stretching from drug-running to child prostitution to murder. This was also asserted in Ed Sanders' study of the Manson Family, *The Family*. Sanders was successfully sued (in the United States) and references to both the Process and the OTO—so prevalent in the first edition of his book—were expunged by the time the book was republished. (This was not so in the United Kingdom, where the courts decided in favor of the publisher and author.) However, Terry recounts in *The Ultimate Evil* his discussions with Sanders concerning these cults. Terry makes no bones about mentioning both the Process and the OTO in *The Ultimate Evil*, and has evidently resisted any legal attempts to get him to change his story.

What initially bothered Terry about the Process was the appearance in one of their issues (the "Death" issue) of an article written by Charles Manson. Critics of the Terry thesis have scoffed at this, saying that such persons as Marianne Faithfull and Salvador Dali also appeared in the Process magazine; my reaction is simply this, however: what was Charles Manson doing in such august company? Further, Marianne Faithfull (as we have seen) had a long association with occultists of the Crowley dispensation through her relationship with Kenneth Anger. Dali himself was very involved in occultism, was well-known in several occult milieus, and his paintings—true to his reputation as a surrealist—reveal many occult and alchemical themes. There is a certain cultural or spiritual consistency to those who graced the pages of the Process magazine, and to dismiss Manson's appearance there as of little import is to be quite naïve. Further, as we have already learned, Manson told prosecutor Bugliosi that he and Robert Moore (the founder of the Process) were "the same." In addition, members of the Process on a mysterious mission visited Manson in prison after his arrest for the Tate/La Bianca killings, after which he no longer referred to the Process in any way. It is doubtful that Manson would have been worried about a lawsuit for slander, so we have to assume that something more was at stake.

In addition, we also have the visits by Manson Family member Bruce Davis to England on at least two occasions; as discussed in Book I, the British police agencies identified Davis as visiting the Scientologists and/or the Process on each visit. In fact, we also have the murders of former Scientologists in England at this time, members connected with the Manson Family and, as we will see, yet another Scientologist was killed, this time in connection with the Son of Sam case.

That there was a connection—however tenuous one believes it to be—between Manson and the Process is known and documented, even in the Process' own publication. The neo-gnostic theology of the Process would have appealed to Manson, extolling as it does both Jesus and Satan—Manson thought he was both, anyway.

The next step is to find any relation at all between David Berkowitz, the Son of Sam murders, and the Process. If this can be done, then we have left the realm of pure speculation and have entered the world of logical possibility.

Let's begin with the dogs.

For some reason, there have been reports of sacrifices of large numbers of dogs, mostly German shepherds, throughout the United States in the past thirty-odd years, but notably in areas where we discover confirmed cult activity. This was as true in Berkowitz' Yonkers neighborhood as it was in Walden, New York, where a "total of eighty-five skinned German shepherds and Dobermans were found" in a single year "between October 1976 and October 1977."[22] The day after Berkowitz' arrest in Yonkers, the bodies of three slain German shepherds were found in an aqueduct behind his apartment. Two had been strangled with chains; the third had been shot in the head.

Two days before his arrest, someone phoned an animal shelter using his name and address, inquiring about adopting a German shepherd that had been advertised in a local paper. A few hours later, someone else called from the same street in Yonkers, also inquiring about the dog. This caller said he was "fixing some cars" on Pine Street; an allusion that Terry believes actually refers to the Carr family who figure so prominently in this case.[23] As it turned out, two men did visit the shelter, including one who resembled Berkowitz, but according to Berkowitz himself it was not he, although he acknowledges that someone may have been impersonating him on the phone.

Why? This was *before* his arrest and identification in the press as the Son of Sam.

Remember that serial killer Jeffrey Dahmer's first "kill" was the ritual slaughter of a dog behind his home in Ohio, which culminated in his placing the dog's skull atop a stake hammered into the earth; and, around the time of the Sam killings, the author heard convincing rumors of the abuse and slaughter of dogs in a warehouse near Brooklyn Heights, within walking distance of the Warlock Shop, before Berkowitz was arrested and the connection with dogs was made.

Terry connects the German shepherd sacrifices with the Process, due to their fondness for the animals. Members of the Process in those halcyon days of the 1960s were to be seen around San Francisco dressed in black and leading shepherds on the leash. The "Fear" issue of the Process magazine featured a photo spread of twenty German shepherds in a menacing pose. It doesn't automatically follow, however, that the Process would sacrifice the animals.

Another symbolic association that should be mentioned is the fact that Hitler favored German shepherds above all other animals. That there might be a Nazi or neo-Nazi element to the Son of Sam cult should not be ignored, especially as mass murderer Fred Cowan—one of the "Sons" according to Berkowitz—was a neo-Nazi. Further, the Process symbol was a stylized swastika: what some members referred to as "four P's"; these "four P's" later contributed to the name of a Process splinter group called "Four P" after the same symbol. It was this group that remained behind in California after most of the regular Process decamped and went to New York City following the assassination of Robert F. Kennedy. Four P—and its reputed leader, the Grand Chingon—has been implicated in a number of vile acts, including animal and human sacrifice, in northern and southern California. Convicted serial killer and cannibal Stanley Baker claimed to belong to this cult, and Manson Family members were known to refer to Charles Manson as the Grand Chingon, even though the organization was supposedly so secret that its very existence was unknown to all but a few.[24]

The Devil does not exist. It is a false name invented by the Black Brothers to imply a Unity in their ignorant muddle of dispersions. A devil who had unity would be a God.... It is, however, always easy to call up the demons, for they are always calling you ...

—Aleister Crowley[25]

I'd say anybody who worships the devil is not a nice person.

—David Berkowitz, court-ordered interrogation, October 26, 1978[26]

Aside from the famous statement in letters and in person by Berkowitz that he alone committed the Son of Sam murders because he was ordered to do so by Sam Carr's dog—who was actually an ancient demonic force, according to Berkowitz—there was much more in the letters and in documentation found in Berkowitz' apartment after his arrest to suggest that he was part of a larger organization. In fact, in his letters to the press, he alludes to some of these participants by name, although his references were not understood at the time.

The most important from an investigative point of view was the name of "John Wheaties," identified in the letter to Jimmy Breslin as a "Rapist and Suffocater of Young Girls."[27] It was the investigative work of Terry and his associate (and former police detective) Jim Mitteager that uncovered the identity of this person as John Wheat Carr, a son of Sam Carr of the infamous demonic dog. John Carr led to his brother Michael Carr, a high-level Scientologist, and to Wheat Carr, their sister who worked for the Yonkers Police Department and who was married to a police officer. In a court-ordered interrogation of David Berkowitz in October 1978 at the Marcy Correctional Institute near Utica, New York, Berkowitz revealed that he hated the Carrs. In that same interrogation, he grudgingly (almost accidentally, due to clever questioning by a Legal Aid lawyer representing Terry's associate Mitteager) revealed the existence of the cult to which he, the Carrs, and probably Fred Cowan belonged.[28]

Critics of these revelations point to the fact that Berkowitz appears not to know very much about occultism or satanism in this lengthy exchange, often quoting lines out of context to prove their point. Anyone reading the entire Q&A, however, will recognize that Berkowitz was being cagey and evasive, even at times arrogant or flippant, in his answers; the fact that he would admit to knowledge and then take back the admission, and flip-flop like this several times during the interview, eventually breaking down in front of the interrogators, is more than enough to support the point of view that Berkowitz was afraid for his life. He was also being "handled" quite effectively by the prison doctor, who, it appears, spoke with him during a lunch break and managed to get Berkowitz to retract everything he had said in the morning, and to refuse to answer any more questions. When this did not work—when Berkowitz eventually relented and began talking again—the interrogation was interrupted by both the aforementioned doctor and a representative of the New York Attorney General's office, who ordered that the interrogation be stopped immediately.[29] Why this occurred is open to a great deal of conjecture, of course. It is possible that the authorities did not want the Son of Sam case reopened, as it would make a lot of detectives and prosecutors look inept or incompetent when so much additional evidence pointing to a conspiracy was revealed. It is also possible that the cult to which it is alleged Berkowitz and the Carrs belonged exerted pressure behind the scenes to ensure that Berkowitz—and only Berkowitz—took the fall for the Sam killings.

This latter theory does not seem so far-fetched when we consider some further facts.

John Wheat Carr, a career member of the Air Force who was discharged for drug related offences, died violently on February 16, 1978 at the airbase in Minot, North Dakota, the victim of a shotgun wound to the head. OSI—the Air Force's internal police agency—initially determined that the death was a probable homicide, changing that determination to suicide when the investigation took on national proportions with inquiries from Westchester County and New York City police departments and prosecutors' offices. He had been in Yonkers, at Sam Carr's home, only a few days before and unexpectedly flew back to Minot on Valentine's Day, after phoning his girlfriend at the base and telling her that the police were after him and things were too hot in New York. John Carr was on the run, but he never made it. Terry is convinced that Carr was murdered, and the evidence at the scene certainly points in that direction.

The murder of John Carr establishes the fact of conspiracy in the Son of Sam murders; John Carr's death was the conspirators' attempt to silence someone who might conceivably talk to the authorities. Carr had been the subject of a manhunt by police all over New York City and Westchester once it had been realized that he was the "John Wheaties" of the Son of Sam letters. If someone killed John Carr—while David Berkowitz was sitting in prison—then the implication is that there was at least one more conspirator out there: the one doing the mopping up. To make matters more interesting, John Carr's description fit perfectly with eyewitness reports of the Son of Sam killer seen at more than one crime scene, down to the color of his hair, his build, and his left-handedness. Evidence gathered since then shows that Carr was in New York City for at least four of the shootings, even though he lived in Minot, North Dakota at the time. He was also present in Houston, Texas on June 12, 1976: the day Billy Dan Parker bought the .44 Charter Arms Bulldog for Berkowitz in that city.

John Carr—who was born on October 12, 1946 (Aleister Crowley's birthday, as Terry points out)—was interested in the occult. Growing up in Yonkers, he was a schoolmate of Maury Terry in high school, as Terry himself reveals in *The Ultimate Evil*[30]—an odd parallel to the fact that *this* author went to the same high school as David Berkowitz. Carr traveled the world with the Air Force, spending time in Thailand and Korea, before returning to the Strategic Air Command base at Minot. But his involvement with drugs led to his downfall with the Air Force. He was hospitalized several times for drug overdoses, and was taking Haldol at the time of his death. Haldol is usually prescribed for psychiatric disorders.

Carr was discharged from the Air Force on October 13, 1976, due to his drug-related problems, after twelve years in the military. He, of course, does not sound like a sophisticated cult hitman, but then we are not watching a Hollywood movie version of a satanic cult. If we posit the existence of a daring group of Satan-worshipping killers then the position of John Carr in this group must have been relatively the same as that of Berkowitz: they were both expendable, sent out to kill specific targets on specific days, both psychologically damaged in some way and vulnerable to manipulation by more sophisticated—more motivated—leaders who had done all the planning and who probably wrote the famous letters to the press, for it would eventually come out that Berkowitz did not write them himself. With Berkowitz silent in prison, and the police onto John Carr's involvement and looking for him everywhere, these mysterious leaders only needed to tie up loose ends, beginning with John Carr but not ending there.

While John Carr's familiarity with the occult is documented in Terry's book (everything from keeping a list of demons with him to burying dog excrement in the yards of people he was trying to curse), it receives further confirmation from Berkowitz himself, who characterized him as a "devil worshipper" during his interrogation at Marcy ... oddly enough not including himself in that category.

Later, police in the Minot, North Dakota area acknowledged that John Carr was a member of a satanic cult that operated there, that John Carr himself was not only using drugs but dealing (not an uncommon combination), and that he told police detectives that members of the cult had to drink their leader's urine from a chalice, among other unsavory details. (He had been rousted by the police in October 1976 on a street in Minot for being under the influence of drugs.) Even more importantly, the Minot police agencies knew that Carr and Berkowitz were acquainted and that both belonged to the same cult, based on voluminous testimony from friends, including a fellow airman and roommate, Jeffrey Sloat, who eventually had John Carr committed to a mental institution for a while due to the latter's strange behavior, which included chanting in an unknown tongue and talking to a picture of Abraham Lincoln. The police involved in the investigation in North Dakota forwarded this information to their New York City and Westchester County counterparts, and never heard back from them.[31] The details on the existence of the cult and the participation of more than one person in the so-called Son of Sam murders was deep-sixed by the New York authorities; in essence, allowing the cult to continue its operation unhindered, possibly even to the present day.

In the months leading up to his capture, Berkowitz was engaged in a campaign of terrorism in his neighborhood designed to get him arrested on lesser charges before he was apprehended for the Son of Sam murders, and before he would be expected to commit more. He was firebombing houses, shooting dogs, and sending hate mail to all and sundry ... with return addresses that would only point back to him. The inability of the Westchester Sheriff's Department and the Yonkers police to put all of this together—even when Sam Carr himself walked into a police station with the evidence long before the last two Son of Sam attacks—drove Berkowitz crazy. He wanted to be taken off the streets before more people were killed; rather than simply walking into a police station and saying, "I'm the Son of Sam," he preferred to be picked up on lesser charges so that when the next Sam killing took place he would have an alibi, and the attention would drift away from him (if, indeed, it would ever focus on him in the first place). That was his plan. But it was not working.

Shortly before his arrest, he scouted another murder site, this time on Long Island. Feeling the pressure of another upcoming murder, and knowing it was only a matter of time before the police analyzed the parking tickets issued at the time and place of the Stacy Moskowitz killing, he placed a rifle in his car in full view and a Sam letter in the glove compartment. His apartment had been cleaned out a week or so earlier, and most of his furniture and an expensive stereo set purchased in Korea had been left in front of a Salvation Army storefront. He then proceeded to decorate the walls with weird writing in Magic Marker, making references to "the children" and "the little ones" becoming murderers. And he sat and waited for the cops to show up.

After his arrest, he would eventually be interviewed by Dr. David Abrahamson, to determine if he was mentally fit to stand trial. Abrahamson wrote a book about the experience, entitled *Confessions of Son of Sam* and published in 1985. In this book, we learn that Berkowitz recognized Abrahamson when they were first introduced, as he had read Abrahamson's *The Murdering Mind* prior to his arrest! He also read a number of books about murderers such as Richard Speck and Nathan Leopold that he took out of the Yonkers Public Library, telling the doctor, "Murder is a recent interest of mine."[32]

In the same book, we find a poem written by Berkowitz as the killings were beginning, entitled "Mother of Satan" and dated September 22, 1976: the autumnal equinox and one of the Quarter Days. It reads (with the original spelling):

Old Mother Hubbard
Sitting near the cubbard
with a hand grenade
under the oatmeal.

Who will you kill now
Daughter of Satan?

In the image of the
Virgin Mary—pure and innocent
The Great Impersonator—
Is that you? "Yes."
How many have you decieved—
lured to slaughter like a
fat cow?[33]

The first stanza is compelling, humorous and well-written, despite the misspelling of "cupboard" unless, of course, the misspelling was intentional and yet another piece of coded information. Also, in the earliest versions of "Mother Hubbard" we find that her dog is her master.

But one cannot help wondering if Berkowitz wrote this with a specific person in mind, someone from the cult. Someone, a woman, "in the image of the Virgin Mary" and a "Great Impersonator," who deceived many and lured them to slaughter "like a fat cow," is also the "Daughter of Satan." A woman, rumored to belong to the cult, was present at some of the Sam killings according to eyewitnesses. Was this another gofer of the cult, or someone more important?

Abrahamson, however, did not address himself to the idea of a cult behind the murders. He was only concerned with Berkowitz' mental state, as far as the courts asked for his opinion. Berkowitz was given a battery of tests, including the MMPI, and Abrahamson came back with the following diagnosis:

> Clinical scales indicated pathological elevations regarding the following scales: schizophrenia; paranoia; psychopathic deviation; depression; hypomania; psychasthenia and social introversion.[34]

Abrahamson also reveals that Berkowitz lay claim to setting numerous fires in the years 1974–77. We know he firebombed his neighbors' homes in the months leading to his arrest, but that was for a specific purpose: to get himself arrested. Abrahamson reveals a much longer career as an arsonist, however, beginning on May 13, 1974 with a rubbish fire set in the area of Co-Op City. This is odd, since supposedly Berkowitz was still in the Army at the time, stationed in Kentucky.

Then, Abrahamson says that Berkowitz had a detailed list of the fires he set, a total of 1,411 fires from 1974 until his arrest in 1977; the list includes the date, time, street, borough, weather, firebox number and Fire Department code.[35] This incredible assertion is nowhere else mentioned in connection with Berkowitz and the Son of Sam case, and the sheer number of fires beggars belief. 1,411 fires in three years? Anyone doing the math will realize that means he set roughly 1.25 fires per day, every day, for that period … and was never caught. Further, Berkowitz states that he committed no arsons in the period December 25, 1974 to June 6, 1975 (this was the period when he was searching for his birth mother). So, he had to have committed 1.50 fires per day in the time available. One senses that Berkowitz was having some fun with Dr. Abrahamson; either that, or the 1,411 fires were the total of a group effort and not Berkowitz acting alone.

Another startling revelation from Abrahamson's book is the acknowledgment by Berkowitz that he attacked a young, fourteen-year-old girl on Christmas Eve 1975 between 10:30 and 11:00 P.M. on Baychester Avenue in the Co-Op City area of the Bronx. This was done with a 3-1/2 inch long hunting knife and, according to Berkowitz, he stabbed her repeatedly but she survived. If true, this would be the only attack by Berkowitz that did not involve a .44 Charter Arms Bulldog revolver.

The problem I have with this information stems from a telling revelation at the very beginning of the book: that Berkowitz had read Abrahamson's text on *The Murdering Mind* long before he met the doctor, and that he had also studied Richard Speck and other murderers. He may have gleaned from these texts the classic symptoms of the serial killer: beginning with arson, graduating to a disordered attack (the Christmas Eve assault on the young girl) and from there to a more orderly, more sophisticated pattern of murder.

The fact that we have a growing mountain of evidence—including eye-witness testimony, circumstantial evidence, and crime scene evidence—that point to a conspiracy in the Son of Sam murders strongly implies that they were *not* the work of a lone serial killer at all, and that Berkowitz was simply tailoring his story to fit what he knew Abrahamson's assumptions would be. It is interesting that in his discussions with the doctor he did not abandon his "Son of Sam" story, replete with demon-possessed dog, which since then has been acknowledged to be a fabrication designed by Berkowitz to insure himself an insanity plea. There *were* dogs, there *was* a Sam Carr, and there *were* devil worshippers, however. It's just that Berkowitz used the *literal* interpretation of the Sam letters to convince the doctors that he was insane.

On July 10, 1979, David Berkowitz was attacked by a fellow inmate, his throat slashed, but he survived.

A few weeks later, a friend of his was shot to death in his apartment in Flushing, Queens. Howard Weiss was a fellow member of the police auxiliary unit in Co-Op City to which Berkowitz and another colleague, a former Yonkers police officer who is not identified in Terry's book except for a pseudonym, belonged. These three men had attended a wedding of a friend in Maryland in 1976, before the Son of Sam killings began: a wedding that was captured on videotape, showing all three men present. Another link between them was the fact that the Yonkers police officer knew the Carrs, and that all three men were known to have owned .44 Charter Arms Bulldog revolvers.[36] Sources would confirm that all three men (as well as the Carrs and many others) belonged to the same cult, and were even involved in multiple arson attacks—thus confirming the author's suspicion that the fires Berkowitz claimed he set were, in reality, set by more than one person—but these sources are not identified in Terry's book, and nothing more about them is known. Regardless of this nagging problem, the fact that Berkowitz' friends begin dying (violently) all over the place is enough to give one pause. Like all those violent deaths that surround the Kennedy assassination and its aftermath, it points to the existence of a powerful conspiracy. (Should these deaths be unconnected to each other in any way, however, then we are looking at a different phenomenon entirely, and one that cannot be explained away by pious invocations of "coincidence.")

In the background of all of these killings, Terry and a few of his contacts in law enforcement began to search strenuously for links between John Carr and David Berkowitz in an effort to understand how these two men would have known each other and influenced each other. With Berkowitz in prison and John Carr murdered in North Dakota, it seemed more urgent than ever to uncover other friends and associates common to these two men.

When they spoke by phone to Minot, North Dakota law enforcement they were shocked to learn that Minot knew all along about John Carr's occult involvements as well as the existence of a cult in Minot that, among other things, sacrificed German shepherds. Terry and another investigator, NYPD detective Harry Cinotti, flew to Minot to discover for themselves what the cult is like, who are its members, and what is its murderous agenda. Cinotti is a strange character; although a police officer he is also a very religious, very Roman Catholic, devotee of a woman of local Queens celebrity, Veronica Leukens, who channels the Virgin Mother every year at a gathering in Flushing Meadows and has a devoted following. Cinotti is the Van Helsing in this case, a man who one suspects travels with crucifixes, holy water, and a set of wooden stakes packed next to his service revolver and shield. On an expedition one evening to the strangely beautiful Untermyer Park in Yonkers where cult activity was known to take place—cult activity connected with Berkowitz and the slaughtered German shepherds—Cinotti prepared his fellow investigators with spiritual advice on how to protect oneself against the dark forces of Hell, thus both alienating and freaking out his fellows in equal measure.

Once in Minot, a town less than a hundred miles from the Canadian border and about a hundred miles from Bismark (and fifty miles from the edge of nowhere), Terry and Cinotti met the local law enforcement personnel and learned about John Carr's cult in disturbing detail. Several members of the cult were identified—some of whom would die violently before the investigation concluded—and some were interviewed for background on John Carr and David Berkowitz. There were many confirmations of the Carr/Berkowitz relationship, and an equal number of confirmations concerning John Carr's involvement in the occult, including a blatant admission from his own sister back in Yonkers.

Cult involvement *per se* is no reason to get excited. Defining what a cult is and isn't has kept theologians, historians of religion, psychologists and even criminologists busy for years. In addition, there are many relatively benign alternative religious organizations in the United States and abroad that may qualify as someone's idea of a cult, but which do not engage in anything remotely nefarious. The problem with the putative Son of Sam cult is that evidence began to mount that it was a cover for drug-running, child prostitution, pornography and murder-for-hire. The circumstantial links to the Process are what made Terry take special notice that what he was investigating might turn out to be a very sophisticated, very well-managed criminal enterprise that spanned the globe; moreover, one in which devil worship comprised the organization's "mission statement."

Why should this be a special problem?

Criminal organizations are businesses like any other. They sell a product or service, and exist for profit. What makes them criminal is the product or service they offer: drugs, guns, or sex, for instance. Otherwise, though, they are usually rational groups of like-minded individuals who understand the world in terms of cause and effect, and moreover who are willing to go to extremes to defend their business from competitors. Extremes like murder. Because they are involved in trade in illegal commodities, they are vulnerable to more than market forces. They are also vulnerable to law enforcement agencies, making their business more complicated and more difficult to manage and defend. Therefore, the type of person who becomes involved in criminal enterprises has already placed himself outside the social milieu in which the rest of us live, and experiences life in a more desperate, more emotionally-charged way than we do. Although we may take advantage of the products and services offered by the criminal organization from time to time—and thereby support the criminals with our own, honestly earned, money—we do not murder our competitors, or steal from banks and armored cars, or fence stolen property, or deal drugs or guns or rent our bodies for sex. Thus, we can go to church on Sunday feeling suitably redeemable from our petty sins, sheep who have strayed perhaps, but who are nonetheless members of the flock. Not so the criminal.

Criminals have seen life the way police officers do: from the bottom, up. They see life the way it really is, behind closed doors. They know the weaknesses of their fellow humans, because they cater to them. They know the judge with a gambling problem, or the priest who prefers sex with underage boys. They see beyond the façade of society, and what they discover is no more elevated or spiritual than their own, tawdry, experience has taught them. The criminal feels that he or she is a realist, is in fact honest because he or she does not disguise the fact of belonging to a race of beings that is inherently … evil. To a criminal, nothing is beautiful, nothing is innocent, nothing is pure. The priest at Mass is a pederast, a bigot, a hypocrite. The same hands that touch the sacred Wafer, transforming bread and wine into the Body and Blood of Christ, had just last night touched the genitals of an altar boy in the sacristy. "Where was Jesus?" the criminal laughs.

The criminal, then, is a satanist. The criminal respects only power and the only powerful person the criminal respects is the one that demonstrates that power on a regular basis. The Mafia chieftain ordering the death of a subordinate, the pimp beating the reluctant or lazy prostitute, the drug dealer wiping out a competitor. To a criminal, murder is the ultimate demonstration and exercise of power; in a way, then, the criminal worships the one who dispenses death and fear.

To the criminal, sex is a commodity and there is no love to redeem it. The criminal respects lust. Everything else is a romance novel, suitable for children (those he has not already corrupted). Women are inferior beings, dangerous at times, but like children should be seen and not heard.

Drugs are for the weak, a product to enslave the masses and take their money.

Gradually, we can understand the attraction Satanism would have for a criminal. Not that the criminal himself would be a pious Satanist, spending hard-earned money on building chapels devoted to Hell; but he would understand that devotion to Satan would lead automatically to an acceptance of the criminal's lifestyle and perspective. The Satanic perspective would allow and encourage drug use, all types of sexual acts with all types of partners, willing and unwilling, and the forceful suppression of dissent, the aggressive enslavement of the weak. Satanism is not about worship or devotion; it is about power, and about power as manifest on both a physical and a spiritual level.

That is not to say that the Satanic cult attracts only the powerful. In fact, the opposite is true.

The people who worship power are those who do not have it. The vast majority of people who have been attracted to Satanic cults have been—in the author's experience as an observer of the occult environment—the weak, the desperate, the downtrodden, the impoverished … the petty criminal, the drug addict. They become the playground for a handful of people at the top, who manipulate their willing servants, exploiting their submission and devotion, and turn them into drug couriers, pornographers, and murderers. The glue that binds these groups together is the ritual held in the dead of night in abandoned parks and ruined buildings, the shedding of innocent blood, and the promise of eternal reward in a Hell of their own devising.

The Process Church of the Final Judgement made Satanism fashionable to an extent, and if not glamorous, then a bit more intellectually honest. Robert Moore's neo-Gnosticism was a refinement of Anton LaVey's blatantly commercial approach to Satan. While LaVey's showmanship attracted a certain element that was ready to dip their toes into the thrill of actually participating in a Black Mass, Moore's Process Church strained for a more severe aesthetic. Moore had a mission, and a program. Moore *believed.* LaVey did not. Moore came from a Scientology background, in which the possibilities of human programming, of mind control and ritual, were vigorously explored. LaVey's "do your own thing and don't let guilt or shame or other people get in your way" was little more than warmed-over Rabelais and a dose of Dale Carnegie. It was not intellectually ambitious, but an approach designed to appeal to the greatest number of people, and thus based on a few simple ideas. The Church of Satan was a kind of psychotherapy clinic dressed up in Gothic robes and black candles. Psychodrama for the counter-culture that was just coming into its own in 1966. It was "the Power of Positive Thinking" meets *La-Bas.*

The Process, on the other hand, was a genuine cult. The early days of their group, flying from London to Mexico *en famille* with guard dogs and black jackets, blending Jehovah with Lucifer and then adding a strong dose of Satan as they germinated in San Francisco a few blocks up the street in the Haight from where Manson was staying, is evidence that what Moore was up to was much more than LaVey ever had in mind. Moore was undergoing his own shamanistic initiation at the expense of his followers; his magazine, *Process*, with its issues devoted to "Death" and "Fear," was riding a wave of disintegration and dismemberment, albeit in an artistic way replete with photos of pop icons like Dali and Faithfull, not to mention epistles from Manson himself.

And that is what eventually happened.

The Process splintered in the years after 1968. The three main bodies within the Process—the groups devoted to Jehovah, Lucifer, and Satan—broke apart from each other and attempted to retain independent status. Moore himself left the Process (or, as some say, was kicked out in a kind of palace coup orchestrated by his wife) and melted into obscurity; the same might be said for the Jehovah and Lucifer contingents, as the Process reinvented itself and tried to hold onto what they could from the old days, amalgamating what they could of the older membership. The Satan contingent, however, seems to have survived.

Rumors of a cult calling itself the Four P surfaced in California shortly after the Process disappeared from that state. "Four P" was a name taken from the Process symbol, which resembles four "P's" in a circle forming a kind of swastika figure. Then there was the Grand Chingon, said to be the leader of the Four P. Manson Family members used to claim that Charlie was the Grand Chingon, but that was empty boasting. No one seems to know who the Grand Chingon was, or even what "Chingon" means, except that it may not be a real title but a kind of epithet. In Mexican Spanish, the verb *chingar* means "to fuck" and is used as an expletive, such as in the word *chingada* for "fucking" or *chinga su madre*, a common curse. Thus, the word *chingon* could mean "the fucker." As the Luciferian element of the Process was the one involved most directly in the lascivious aspects of the cult—the purely sexual component, rather than the more intense power component of the Satan element—it is possible that the Grand Chingon was leading a group of dissident Luciferians, except for the fact that the Four P group and the Grand Chingon were implicated in several vicious murders in the California area in the late 1960s and early 1970s, including the one involving Stanley Baker, the aforementioned cannibal.

Remaining behind in California, at a time when the film *Rosemary's Baby* had just been released, another Kennedy slain, Dr. King assassinated, the Days of Rage raging in Chicago, the infamous Tet Offensive ongoing in Vietnam, etc., cult members and those who lived on the fringes of the cults still sought to stay active and to survive. California to most people is Hollywood, the City of Dreams. The free-wheeling lifestyle of movie stars, directors, producers fit perfectly with the "nothing is true, everything is permitted" school of born-again Ismailism which became—at least in California—a kind of neo-gnostic Satanism. After all, in Hollywood one had access to all the things that cults are today accused of exploiting: drugs, pornography, prostitution, and extravagant dreams of wealth, fame and power. Scientology deliberately targeted movie stars, and the current membership lists bear out this strategy: John Travolta, Kirstie Alley, Tom Cruise, and Nicole Kidman are all Hubbard alumni, as well as many lesser-known dream factory employees. With celebrities, Scientology could buy respectability.

But people like Charlie Manson were fishing in the same waters. Charlie, with his close relationship to Dennis Wilson of the Beach Boys and his on-again, off-again partnership with Terry Melcher (son of Doris Day), and his de facto guardianship of DiDi Lansbury, was prowling the fringes of the Hollywood boondoggle. There are fortunes to be made in Hollywood, and fortunes to be lost. It is a high-risk, high-stress environment that has seen its share of murder and suicide, long before Charlie Manson and long after. Those who work this industry know where to score drugs, where to pick up sexual partners for a price, and where to hire a hitman.

One of the many theories about the Manson killings is that they were murder-for-hire. This is the field that Maury Terry has plowed so earnestly, for it leads him back to one of the more spectacular Hollywood murders of recent years, that of Roy Radin and the hired hitman known as Manson II.

The Cotton Club Murders

And it shall come to pass, that thy choicest valleys shall be full of chariots, and the horsemen shall set themselves in array at the gate.

—*Isaiah 22:7*, in a King James Bible opened to this page and found at the Roy Radin crime scene by Maury Terry [37]

We can't really talk about this aspect of the case without talking about Robert Evans, for Evans will lead us to Roy Radin and Elaine Jacobs and Manson II. Bob Evans is a famous Hollywood movie icon, a producer who was responsible for such box office hits as *Rosemary's Baby* and *The Godfather*. In fact, this axis of directors Roman Polanski and Francis Ford Coppola is one that will surface again in his career, as he went on to produce both *Chinatown* and the doomed *Cotton Club*.

Robert Evans has been married to some of Hollywood's most celebrated leading ladies in his time, including Ali MacGraw and former Miss America Phyllis George. It was Ali MacGraw who served as our guide into the Process-infiltrated area of upstate New York, where we found Pound Ridge, Salem and Brewster in the midst of satanic skullduggery, including the presence of unapologetic occultist Anita Pallenberg and a dead seventeen-year-old boy in her bed, and a flap over satanic activity in the area that continues to the present time. Phyllis George will introduce us to her former husband Kentucky Governor John Y. Brown and a scandal surrounding the governor, Colombian drug runners in northeastern Kentucky and a bizarre paramilitary drug cult known as "the Company." More importantly, Evans will meet and—some say—eventually propose to one Elaine "Laney" Jacobs, the wife of several drug runners in her time with a trail that leads directly back to crazed *narcotraficante*, worshipper of John Lennon, and neo-Nazi, Carlos Lehder, currently a guest of the US federal prison system. The number of associations that swirl around Robert Evans is astonishing; the fact that he was arrested and convicted once for cocaine possession is only the tip of a very old and very cold iceberg. He was a suspect in a homicide, and it was this homicide that brought the Son of Sam cult to the surface.

As with most "deep politics," the connections between these individuals and events are murky, but definite. These are all people who knew each other, did business together, did drugs together, and in some cases committed murder. It is a matter of the public record. What has not been revealed until now is the extent to which these events are linked below the surface to each other and to darker forces at work in the collective American psyche.

There are several books which can introduce the reader to the broader aspects of these cases, even though they do not reference each other and seem on the surface to be unrelated. They are, in addition to Maury Terry's *The Ultimate Evil*, Ali MacGraw's *Moving Pictures*, Sally Denton's *The Bluegrass Conspiracy*, and Steve Wick's *Bad Company: Drugs, Hollywood and the Cotton Club Murder*. The latter is a review of the murder case involving Bob Evans and as such is a bit less self-serving than Evans' own autobiography, *The Kid Stays In The Picture* (later made into a lugubrious documentary with a running Bob Evans voice-over whose only saving grace is the hilarious impression of Evans by Dustin Hoffman over the closing credits).

The following is a précis of the facts of the case as represented in the above works and the public record.

Orson Welles may seem like a strange person to introduce this story, but once again we are faced with deep resonances and incredible Brunoesque "links." Welles, one of the pioneers of the motion picture and an incredible artist (as evidenced by his *Citizen Kane*, which is the focus of many filmmaking courses and books of cinema criticism) was also fascinated with the occult and the power of mass media. His infamous broadcast of H.G. Wells' *The War of the Worlds* over the radio on Halloween 1938 is part of American history; the broadcast seemed so genuine to listeners that it caused a panic as people believed the Earth had actually been invaded by creatures from Mars. His aborted attempt to make a film in Brazil about Latin American witchcraft led to his being cursed by a local shaman, something Welles took very seriously.

But Welles is important to us at this juncture for another reason entirely. He was Roy Radin's mentor.

Roy Alexander Radin was born to impresario Alexander Radin and his wife Renee, a former stripper, on November 13, 1949. The elder Radin had been a confidant of Welles, and Welles took over the education of the teenaged boy when Al Radin died. Al Radin had been a fixture on Broadway, a man who knew all the players from the actors and actresses to the producers, directors, agents and other hangers-on and could make or break a career. His son looked up to him, and considered his father "the greatest man in the world." He inherited some of his father's contacts and clientele, even so far as to include former Rat Packer comedian Joey Bishop as emcee for some of his roadshow extravaganzas. (With Frank Sinatra and Peter Lawford deeply involved in the Marilyn Monroe/Kennedy brothers affair, that would leave only Dean Martin and Sammy Davis, Jr. of all the Rat Packers relatively unscathed from conspiracy associations … except for the fact that Sammy Davis, Jr. *did* join the Knights of Malta, long rumored to be a hotbed of intelligence activity and Illuminati-type machinations.)

Overweight, with a pudgy face framed by a short beard, and always well-dressed in public (while preferring a bathrobe at home in his huge Southampton mansion, Ocean Castle), Radin was a show business entrepreneur who managed talent that others wouldn't touch or know what to do with. He represented such acts as George Gobel, Georgie Jessel, Red Buttons, Demond Wilson, and Tiny Tim, sometimes ganging up a few dozen acts and taking the whole geriatric entourage on the road, doing policemen's clubs and other small venues from New England to the Midwest and up and down the Eastern seaboard by bus. Magicians, ventriloquists, dancing poodles and has-been actors and comedians from the 1950s were his stock-in-trade and, incredibly, Middle America loved it and made him a wealthy man.

And with the wealth came the drugs, lots of drugs.

When we speak of cults, particularly satanic cults, we have a picture in our mind of black robes, burning candles, sexual orgies, and strange drugs burning in the censers, sending clouds of potent smoke flowing through the ruined chapel, further enflaming the strange desires of the participants, urging them onwards towards greater depravities. We remember the command of Rimbaud, to "derange the senses" as prerequisite to insight, to spiritual understanding; it was a command the surrealists took to heart, and one that became almost a commonplace among the Hollywood crowd of the 1960s and 1970s. Sexual "deviance" was a necessary tool, as necessary as the drugs; and this is not to make a moral observation or a value judgment on what type of sexuality is "deviant" or "perverse," but only to acknowledge that sexuality is technology in the hands of the mystic as well as of the satanist. The deliberate pursuit of whatever type of sex is considered deviant by one's own culture is part of the program of spiritual seekers as far removed from each other in time and space as Tantric Hindus, California Satanists, Daoist sorcerers, Siberian shamans, and paunchy English "witches" with their scourges and "sky-clad" rituals in the New Forest. To break tabu is a necessary stage in *vama marg* tantra ceremonies, for instance, in which dietary and sexual tabus are deliberately broken, one after another. It is recognized by these technologists of the spirit that deviation from socially-acceptable mores is a powerful tool for awakening the sleeping powers within us, provided that this deviation takes place within the occult engines they have designed.

In the Roy Radin case, sex and drugs combined in the usual ways, but with the addition of cult practices on the one hand, and videotape technology on the other. To show how far we worship the image, merely participating in extreme sexual activity was not enough anymore for people of Radin's circle. It became necessary to record the images on tape so that the events could be relived or—and this is more likely—could be examined and studied from a different perspective, a different angle than the lenses of our own eyes permit us, like seeing yourself talk on television for the first time. To watch yourself having sex with another on tape is to sink a well into your subconscious. It is a point of view normally reserved for your sexual partner; by breaking that parameter you have changed the dynamic of the act completely. While you have *performed* as a sexual being until that time—from the inside, out—you are now a sexual *image*, from the outside, in. You have reversed polarity. And if this is done without the proper safeguards, you can spin out of control.

It is no wonder, then, that all of the high-profile cult scandals of the last thirty years have involved videotaped sex acts: from the much-rumored sex tapes of Sharon Tate and Roman Polanski to the missing videotapes of the Manson Family, to the Sisman videotapes of the Son of Sam killings and the Roy Radin videotapes, sex and murder have become images, have become magical glyphs and sigils in a modern-day grimoire. And, as usual, there is always an organization in place to take control of these images: a cult, a gang, a government. In Radin's case, it was all three.

Radin had made the shrewd choice to hire as many off-duty police as possible, and always threw benefits for the local police departments, thus ingratiating himself with law enforcement, who looked the other way when he was buying cocaine (even having it delivered to his mansion like take-out pizza) or who would give him a head's-up when they knew he was about to be raided. What they did not know was that his godfather—his literal godfather—was Johnny Stoppelli,[38] a soldier in the Genovese crime family who maintained an upscale lifestyle in Manhattan's Murray Hill section. Radin referred to Stoppelli as his "muscle," and when Ron Sisman was murdered along with his girlfriend Elizabeth Plotsman on a Halloween night it was rumored that Radin (and, possibly, Stoppelli) had something to do with it. That's because Sisman had been the one who sent Melonie Haller down to Ocean Castle one night, thus threatening Radin's reputation and lifestyle when she was found, unconscious, on the Long Island Railroad.

Melonie Haller had posed nude for *Playboy* magazine after her appearances on the network television sit-com *Welcome Back, Kotter* in the 1970s. It was Ron Sisman, a photographer with numerous contacts in the entertainment industry in New York, who suggested she visit Radin at his Long Island home. Radin would be able to help her career, he explained, and she should bring along her portfolio to show him.

Haller showed up at Ocean Castle on April 11, 1980 with a friend, and had dinner with Radin, Radin's second wife Toni Fillet, and two men who were actually police detectives from Rhode Island. Haller's friend was telling stories of cocaine buys he had made, not knowing that his dinner companions were cops. It made for an interesting evening. Once the police had left, Haller and her friend stayed behind and—during the course of an alcohol- and drug-filled evening—wound up donning skimpy leather Nazi uniforms and whipping each other for the benefit of their host. According to various eyewitness testimony—supplemented by a lot of rumor and innuendo—Radin had a movie camera set up in his bedroom where much of this activity took place.

When Haller later told this story, she said her rape had been caught on video, and when the police eventually raided Ocean Castle, they seized what turned out to be a blank (erased) tape from the machine in Radin's bedroom. Whether or not Haller was actually raped or if she did, in fact, willingly participate in sex acts with Radin or other parties is not known for certain. What is known is that, on the following day, when she tried to interest Radin in her portfolio he was less than attentive. She became either unstable or simply upset and angry (depending on which version of the story one believes) and Radin ordered her out of the house. Her companion of the previous evening—a management consultant, no less—is said to have beaten and kicked her, and to eventually have her taken to a local train station and put on the LIRR for Manhattan, where she was found unconscious and heavily bruised.

The tabloid press was gleeful, of course, and Haller rewarded their joy by insisting to the police that she had been drugged, raped and beaten by Radin and his associates and that everything had been captured on videotape. No such tape was found, but then Radin had ample advance warning from the local cops and would have been able to erase any incriminating evidence. As it was, he had the household staff clean the rooms thoroughly and dispose of any drugs, weapons, stains, etc. By the time the police arrived, all they could find was a pistol in Radin's closet, for which he was eventually indicted on a misdemeanor charge of possession of an unregistered weapon.

Whether Radin blamed his predicament on photographer Ron Sisman is not known; what is known is that Sisman was murdered shortly thereafter. The talk on the street, however, was that Sisman was killed for another, even more sinister, reason: he claimed to have possession of a videotape showing the murder of Stacey Moskowitz, the last Son of Sam victim. Appropriately enough, Sisman and his girlfriend were executed in their townhouse on Halloween night 1981, and no videotape was found at the scene.

After the scandal of the Melonie Haller episode—which was followed extensively by the New York tabloid press—Radin had to rebuild his reputation and his business. He had expensive tastes, and so did his *arriviste* wife, Toni Fillet, who fancied herself a society matron and whose ultra-thin and boney physique reflected her maiden name. It would take him two years of turmoil, but in 1982 he sold his Southampton estate for eight million dollars (he had paid only $300,000 for it in 1978) and began his run at Hollywood. In his briefcase was a batch of screenplays that had been sent him over the years. One was a musical he liked about a Harlem nightspot, and it was called *The Cotton Club.*

The same year (and in the same state) that Radin was being investigated over the Melonie Haller affair, Hollywood producer Robert Evans was having his own problems with law enforcement. He had been arrested and convicted for cocaine possession, a charge Radin himself narrowly avoided by flushing his drugs down the toilets minutes before the police raid on Ocean Castle. Evans had been the *enfant terrible* of the Hollywood movie industry in the late 1960s and 1970s, producing a string of box office smashes that included *Rosemary's Baby, Love Story,* and *The Godfather.* He was wealthy, self-assured, powerful, and attractive in a boyish sort of way. He charmed Ali MacGraw, to whom he was married for a while, as well as Phyllis George (who would go on to marry Kentucky Governor John Y. Brown) whom he divorced in 1978. He was a regular on the cocktail and cocaine circuit. Evans became dependent on cocaine, and this led to his eventual arrest and conviction for possession of five ounces of the powder in New York, where Radin was having his own problems with the law. This arrest came after a series of financial and critical failures for Evans at the box office, which included, incidentally, the first film made of a Thomas Harris book, *Black Sunday.*

Evans avoided an actual prison term by plea-bargaining his way out of it, producing instead a television special with an anti-drug message: *Get High On Yourself.* Like the previous string of Evans releases, this was also a flop.

Evans and Radin: both in trouble with the law, both at the lowest ebbs of their respective professional careers, reputations in tatters, friends not returning calls, money dwindling, yet neither having ever met the other. It would take a woman with millions of dollars in cocaine money to bring the two together, to essentially seduce both men, becoming in the process a real-life *femme fatale.* By the time a year was over, one of the men would be dead, the other would be questioned by homicide investigators, and Laney Jacobs would be married yet again.

Karen DeLayne Jacobs was born in the third week of June 1947, at the moment UFOs were skimming across the skies of the northwest United States, confusing Kenneth Arnold, and giving rise to the term "flying saucer." She was born in the state of Alabama to an auto mechanic and his wife. Her father eventually became an auto salesman and their financial lives improved, but at the expense of their homelife. Her parents divorced when "Laney" (as she was known) was only nine years old, and in spite of careful upbringing by her grandparents in Georgia she became a willful and wild child, even though her school records were impressive and she had joined a number of clubs and was considered popular, that Holy Grail of teenaged girls. After school she held a number of jobs, but her restless nature was not satisfied with being a legal secretary, and she soon started hanging out in the Latin demimonde of South Florida.

A brittle-looking brunette and at times peroxide blonde with a tight smile and a ferret's features, she was nonetheless as popular around the Cuban and Colombian *narcotraficante* circuit as she was in her Georgia high school Pep Club. Known as *La Rubia* ("the Blonde"), she began cutting deals behind the backs of her drug-dealing boyfriends and was soon running coke in quantity from Miami to Los Angeles. Sometimes loud and abrasive, bordering on the vulgar, she was also smart and cautious with a bookkeeper's approach to the drug business, keeping careful records of all her deals and building a substantial fortune in the process. She loved hanging out in Latin discos and clubs, and her stable of boyfriends was almost exclusively Cuban or Colombian or of other Latin American ancestry; in addition, what they had in common was a love of the drug trade and the fabulous wealth it represented to the otherwise unaccomplished, uneducated, and underprivileged of *norteamericano* society, Latin or *gringo.*

She had gone through a long succession of marriages before her fateful trip to Los Angeles in 1982 (poor Laney, always a bride, never a bridesmaid!) but her most recent liaison was with a powerful trafficker, one Milan Bellechasses. Bellechasses, a native of Santiago de Cuba, worked for the Medellin drug cartel and specifically for Carlos Lehder Rivas, one of the most colorful of the three men who made up the cartel. Lehder was not only a drug trafficker (who had spent time in the Bronx as a teenager, dealing marijuana and boosting cars), but he also considered himself a political activist dedicated to the overthrow of North American hegemony in Colombia and the rest of Latin America through the exportation of illegal drugs to the States: weapons of mass addiction, perhaps. He was also a worshipper (there is no other word) of former Beatle John Lennon, and erected a statue of him outside a hotel he owned in Colombia. The statue shows Lennon completely nude, except for a Nazi helmet, a guitar, and a hole where his heart would be. Lehder's fascination with Nazism perhaps stems from his own background: his father had been a German engineer who emigrated (mysteriously) to Colombia around the time of World War II.

It would be Lehder who would eventually give evidence against Panamanian President Manuel Noriega, after the latter's abduction from Panama by American troops. (Lehder himself had been captured in Colombia and extradited to the United States by the Colombian government on US federal drug charges, a situation that caused tremendous dislocation in New York City as rival gangs fought over his territories, leaving scores of people dead in an underground war that was never reported by the English language press, although it was extensively covered in Spanish language newspapers for weeks. The remaining cartel members offered to pay off all of Colombia's national debt—in cash—if they would be assured that they would not also be extradited. The Colombian government, to its credit, did not entertain the offer.)

This was the milieu in which Laney Jacobs moved and operated. When Miami got a little too hot for her—and her husband and the father of her unborn child was arrested in a drug raid—she decided to decamp to Los Angeles, a dream of hers since childhood. She wanted to be in the movie business. She wanted to be a producer. She could not completely sever the ties that bound her to the drug trade, however, and she really didn't want to. The money was too good, and besides she also had a serious coke habit to support. Then there was Milan Bellechasses, always lurking in the background, a man to whom Laney was inexplicably attracted, and with whom she did millions of dollars of business over the years.

How Laney met Bob Evans was pure serendipity. She had rented a limousine in LA from a company in which Evans was a part owner, Ascot Limousine, and the chauffeur heard her talking about investing some of her money in a movie project. The chauffeur knew that Evans was looking for backers for new projects of his own, and offered to put Laney Jacobs in touch. He was as good as his word, and soon Evans was sending flowers to Laney and taking her out on the town, introducing her to his Hollywood world. The fact that they had cocaine in common didn't hurt the relationship, although Evans would always, incredibly, claim that he did not know that Laney Jacobs was a dealer or that the money she was considering investing in his various projects was drug money. Friends and acquaintances, of course, insist otherwise.

Evans was at his wits' end at the time, trying to jump-start his stalled career when into the midst of his purgatory wandered Jacobs, a brash player in a tight red gown and a bulging purse who single-handedly gave the term "powdering one's nose" a whole new meaning. It was a marriage made in some perverse kind of heaven, where the angels play maracas instead of harps, and the clouds have a street value of a hundred bucks a gram.

For a brief time, one of his financial backers was Adnan Khashoggi.

As revealed in Ronald Kessler's biography of the international arms dealer, *The Richest Man In The World*,[39] Evans had been introduced to Khashoggi by a mutual friend, Melissa Prophet, "a former Miss California who portrayed a tennis groupie in his 1977 movie *Players*."[40] Prophet heard that Evans was having trouble raising money for *The Cotton Club*, and contacted Khashoggi who suggested that they meet immediately and discuss the deal. Khashoggi agreed to provide $750,000 up front, with another $1,250,000 when Evans managed to sign a few more backers. It was with this money, according to Kessler, that Evans hired Mario Puzo to write the script. Melissa Prophet got a credit as an associate producer.

However, Khashoggi (a failed producer himself, whose movie about the Prophet Muhammad starring Anthony Quinn—*The Message*—was banned in Muslim countries and actually caused riots) eventually wanted to own more than 50% of the film, and was prepared to invest an additional ten million dollars for the privilege, but Evans turned him down and eventually bought him out for one million dollars cash.[41] Kessler's book is thin on dates, and unfortunately we don't know exactly how these events tied into those that follow. Khashoggi's original offer of two million dollars is suggestive, as we shall see, as well as Evans' ability to buy him out for a cool million when, according to all accounts, he was flat broke at the time.

Laney Jacobs and Roy Radin both arrived in Los Angeles in January of 1983, and it was shortly thereafter that Laney met Evans and then met Radin, who was interested in renting or buying her house in Benedict Canyon. Radin and Jacobs hit it off immediately, Radin inviting Jacobs to his temporary, serviced apartment, where his assistant prepared a light supper for them.

As their relationship blossomed, Jacobs confided to Radin that she wanted to be a movie producer. Since Radin was in Hollywood on the same mission, they could pool their resources. When Jacobs mentioned her friendship with Robert Evans, however, that took the dialogue to a whole new level. Radin was ecstatic at the possibility of working with a legend like Evans, and when a meeting was finally arranged, Radin talked to him about the various scripts he was interested in promoting.

One of the projects in question was *The Cotton Club*. The story of a Harlem nightclub, Evans had wanted to do a film about the history of the club himself, but more as a drama, while Radin was favoring a musical (true to his Vaudeville roots). The script would eventually go through several hands including Mario Puzo and Francis Ford Coppola. As the story unfolded, Evans would turn Hollywood upside down looking for backers, even interesting international arms dealer (and eventual Iran-Contra figure) Adnan Khashoggi. Finally, he garnered the support of the Doumani brothers, Las Vegas businessmen and casino owners (El Morocco) who were inclined to help finance the project if they had some control over the script and the casting. It was just as the Doumani deal was in danger of falling through that Laney Jacobs brought Roy Radin to meet Evans; was it synchronicity that both Evans and Radin were interested in making a film about the Cotton Club? That Evans had already started raising funding and doing rewrites of the initial script when Radin walked in with another Cotton Club treatment under his arm?

Radin was elated; he was finally in the big leagues. Further, Evans was a known coke-head and even the Doumani brothers were fed up with his habit. Radin had experience with cokeheads and felt he could control Evans to a certain degree. He could coast on Evans' legendary reputation in the movie business (even though that legend was largely tarnished) and create a new reputation for himself. And everything would have been fine, had it not been for Tally Rogers.

Rogers was Laney's drug courier, and the man who had installed the safe in her house. After an argument about the amount he was to be paid for a Miami-Los Angeles round trip, he rifled her safe and her stash and made off with a million dollars' worth of cocaine and cash, and then promptly disappeared.

Radin by this time was back on the East Coast temporarily tending to some business, when he received a hysterical phone call from Laney accusing Radin of being partners with Rogers in the crime. Radin, of course, had nothing to do with it. He had bigger fish to fry, and was eager to be rid of Laney Jacobs if at all possible and get down to business with Evans. But Jacobs was having none of it. She began phoning all over the country in an effort to locate Rogers.

The coke business in those days was done largely on credit. The cocaine Jacobs had in her home—and she had stacks of it from floor to ceiling in her closet—had not been paid for. It had been extended on credit to Milan Bellechasses from his Colombian suppliers, and from Bellechasses to Jacobs. Jacobs would have to make good on the coke, in cash. Hence, the hysteria. If she didn't, the Colombians were notoriously lacking in a sense of humor, and would deal with her harshly. To compound matters, her small son was living with her and could also conceivably become a victim in some hideously operatic act of revenge.

Tally Rogers *had* taken the coke and the cash, angry at the way he had been treated by Jacobs, and was now driving around the country, moving from place to place and keeping a low profile, believing it would eventually blow over. Roy Radin shared this point of view, and concentrated on his production career instead, ignoring Laney's screams over the telephone.

Jacobs, terrified that either Rogers would come back to steal the rest of her stash or that the Colombians would show up, all firepower and fatal finery, went to a friend of hers and asked him to help her find a bodyguard. The friend introduced her to one Bill Mentzer and one Alex Marti, both former bodyguards of *Hustler* magazine publisher Larry Flynt, who had been wounded in an assassination attempt a few years previously. Laney took them to her house to guard her home and coke, and eventually began "dating" Mentzer. Marti, an Argentine and reputed former death squad member was the more violent of the two, and also a Hitler devotee who had a portrait of the Fuhrer in his home, a Third Reich library, and who admired the Nazi method of execution: a single gunshot to the back of the head.[42]

In the meantime, Radin was going forward with his movie deal with Evans. Jacobs found out that she was going to be cut out of the deal, less a finder's fee, and she was livid. Cocaine makes one paranoid as it is, but is it paranoia when everyone really is plotting against you?

Jacobs and Radin agreed to a fifty thousand dollar finder's fee upon signing of an agreement between Evans and Radin (something which had been going nowhere since both coked-out producers could not manage to write a single declarative sentence that made any sense). Radin did his best to ignore Laney Jacobs, and was busy investigating a mysterious burglary of his office in Manhattan when, unknown to him, Bob Evans and Laney Jacobs traveled together from California to New York and from there on to Miami, where Laney was introducing Evans to her circle of friends.

Laney had managed to get Evans to agree to disassociate himself from Radin, at least on principle. Radin was still insisting he could raise thirty-five million dollars, and Evans could not afford to ignore that. However, Laney wined and dined and bedded Evans in Miami, showing him that it was possible to raise cash as easily in Miami as it was from Roy Radin. Evans already had Mario Puzo and Francis Ford Coppola lined up to make the Cotton Club movie, and these were bankable names.

During this visit to Miami, Laney Jacobs introduced Robert Evans to Milan Bellechasses.

At the same time, Radin was actually accomplishing something on his own. He had managed to convince the Puerto Rican government to raise the thirty-five million dollars through an industrial bond offering. The idea was this: Evans would make the film in Puerto Rico and the Puerto Rican government would build a Hollywood-class studio to accommodate him (and many future films), and would even make Evans a professor of film at the University of Puerto Rico. In other words, there was serious and reputable money behind the scheme. For his part, Evans had to raise money through the sale of foreign rights, and Radin had to front another eight million dollars of his own money, which he felt he could do through the sale of his Long Island mansion. Radin would own 45 percent of the deal, Evans another 45 percent, and their Puerto Rican attorney the remaining ten percent. It seemed like a done deal.

On the New York side, pre-production was already in progress at Astoria Studios on *Cotton Club*. People were being hired, money was being spent, there was still no official screenplay, but the show must, as they say, go on. The Doumani brothers were still in for $1.6 million and had not been paid back, and there was fighting over the script that seemed to go on forever, but at least the movie was being made.

Then, in April of 1983, it all went wrong.

Visiting Evans at his home one evening, Radin learned that Laney Jacobs was back in the picture, literally. Evans tried to convince Radin to give Laney half of his 45 percent. If he had done that, of course, Radin would have lost any control he had over the project. Evans would keep 45 percent, the lion's share, and if he formed a bloc with Laney (as it appeared to be the case), then Radin was reduced to a minor role. This was not what Radin had in mind, especially since he had been the one to set up the Puerto Rican deal in the first place.

On May 5, 1983, and in the midst of the accusations and recriminations that were flying around the New York City townhouse of Robert Evans that week, Radin managed to bring his "godfather," Johnny Stoppelli, to one of the meetings, hoping that they could work something out between Radin and Evans. However, they had just begun to talk when Laney walked in with her Miami attorney, Frank Diaz, and the fighting began again. Radin was adamant about not letting Jacobs have any percentage of the deal. He did not want to have to deal with her at all. Even more compelling, however, was Johnny Stoppelli's reaction: he recognized Jacobs for what she was, and told Radin that he would not do business with drug dealers and warned Radin to forget the whole thing. That, if he did not, he was asking for trouble.[43] Radin felt he could not abandon the project completely, and was still committed to doing something in Hollywood.

On May 7, 1983 Roy Radin flew to Hollywood to attend the bar mitzvah of comedian Red Buttons' son, Adam. He was still anxious about the *Cotton Club* deal and felt, understandably, that he had put the whole deal together from financing to studios and should be allowed to have a greater say in the future of the project. He felt he did not owe Laney Jacobs anything beyond the finder's fee, since all she did was introduce him to Evans. He had done the rest.

When he was out one afternoon, he received a call at his Los Angeles hotel on his private line. It was a New York mobster, warning him to keep his mouth shut and to get out of town. The call was taken by Radin's assistant, Jonathan Lawson, who was appropriately alarmed and urged Radin to heed the advice. It had been a warning—the last one.

Radin called Stoppelli in New York City and asked about the call, but Stoppelli hadn't a clue. He only reiterated what he had told Radin before: get out of LA and forget the movie business. He was involved with drug dealers and it could only mean trouble. Radin promised he would return to New York on Friday, after the bar mitzvah.

Immediately, the issue began to heat up. Evans offered to buy out Radin for two million dollars cash, but Radin declined. (Where did Evans get two million dollars in cash, if not from Laney Jacobs?) Evans called the Puerto Rican attorney and asked if the deal could still go through without Radin. The attorney preferred that both Evans and Radin be involved; however, if someone could come up with the financing that Radin was due to invest—eight million dollars—then it was possible. A girlfriend of Radin's—and a close friend of Laney Jacobs—warned Radin that there was heavy muscle in town around Jacobs and that Radin should under no circumstances agree to meet with her. Most curiously, Evans had not been able to post the performance bond necessary to get the movie contract signed with the Puerto Ricans, but somehow had two million dollars cash to give Radin. Evans' insistence that he did not know Laney Jacobs was involved in drug-dealing begins to look very weak at this point.

But the die had been cast. Laney Jacobs had called and asked for one last meeting to try to sort out the *Cotton Club* mess. Radin, pushed to the wall but still believing he could salvage the deal, agreed.

The date was set for Friday, May 13.

That night, Laney Jacobs arrived in a limousine to collect Radin and drive to the La Scala restaurant in Los Angeles. Radin's assistant, Lawson, did not trust the arrangement at all. Instead, he had one of Radin's long-time friends and fellow coke user, actor Demond Wilson (*Sanford and Son*, *The New Odd Couple* television sitcoms), tail the limo to the restaurant. Wilson, according to all accounts, was armed. Lawson stood in the lobby of their hotel and watched as Jacobs and Radin drove off in the limo, driven by one Bob Lowe. Prior to that, Jacobs had tried to get Lawson to drive to her house to pick up some cocaine but Lawson, smelling a rat, refused and stayed behind. It was a decision that saved his life, for Jacobs had two men waiting for him in a pickup truck outside her house.

Wilson, who had already done at least two lines of cocaine in the car, began following the limousine but not before another car swung out behind it, a black Caddy driven—as it was later discovered—by Bill Mentzer, with Alex Marti riding shotgun, appropriately enough. The two cars lost Wilson in traffic, taking evasive measures and running a red light, so that Wilson wound up driving directly to La Scala to wait for Radin and Jacobs to appear. The plan was that Wilson would take another table and watch the proceedings from a safe distance.

They never showed up. After a few hours, Lawson called La Scala to see what was going on and was informed that Radin and Jacobs never arrived. He asked to speak to Wilson, and was dumbfounded to learn that Wilson was just sitting in the restaurant all this time, waiting for the friend he would never see again.

Wilson, terrified by now, disappeared that night. It would be two days before Lawson could locate him, but by that time Radin had already been reported missing.

Wilson has since left show business and refuses to talk about that night. Instead (like so many others who have been touched by the cults), he became a Christian minister and now preaches the Gospel, trading cocaine for the "opium of the people."

Lawson, confronting Jacobs, got two different stories, neither of which made much sense. Either Radin left the limo before arriving at La Scala after a fight with Laney, or Jacobs did. No matter, they were both lies. That same week she had her infant son and her maid fly back out to Miami, and she put her Los Angeles home up for sale, telling everyone she was going to New York to work for Robert Evans. Events had been set in motion behind Radin's back.

The full story would not come out until much later, after several years of investigation, but on June 10, 1983—less than a month after Radin's disappearance—a bee-keeper by the name of Glen Fischer wandering in the rough country near Gorman, California came across a body that was partially buried in a ravine, the fingers of one hand clawing upward from the ground, its skull almost completely destroyed, its jawbone several feet away from its head, pumped with twenty-eight shots at point blank range, and dressed in an expensive three-piece suit and a Pierre Cardin tie. Glen Fischer had found Roy Radin.

It is at this point in the story that we must rejoin our previous protagonists, who had been searching zealously for evidence of just such a crime before it was even reported. Maury Terry, acting on the basis of information obtained from an informer—"Vinny"—who had known David Berkowitz in prison, was looking at Roy Radin as the possible East Coast connection for the Son of Sam cult. Why? There was more to Ocean Castle than the Melonie Haller incident. It seems that police had been called out to the Castle several times in the past, acting on complaints of sexual assault. There was a strong rumor that many of the parties and other activities there had been videotaped; and that photographer Ronald Sisman was more deeply involved with Radin and with cult activity than others had suspected. Vinny had actually named Radin—knowing him only as "Rodan" and "Rodan the Flying Monster"—as well as Sisman and others involved in the case. Radin was said to be involved with "Dale Evans," another code name, and in this case Roy Radin was referred to as "Roy Rogers."

"Dale Evans," then, was possibly Bob Evans … but some of this information went back long before Evans and Radin were thought to have met, implying a deeper involvement between the two men, something that Evans has always denied. In fact, Evans would only admit that Radin was merely an acquaintance and not a business partner, a statement that was patently untrue, as signed copies of their movie agreement exist to disprove this allegation beyond any doubt. To be sure, "Roy Rogers" could also have been a reference to Tally Rogers who, as Laney Jacobs' drug courier, was driving between Miami and Los Angeles twice a month and could conceivably have been more than simply a drug courier, and used to transport information between the Los Angeles branch of the Sam Cult and the East Coast. (When the investigators finally caught up with Tally Rogers, he was serving time in the Louisiana prison system for child molestation, having sexually abused two young sons of his then-current girlfriend.)

Vinny insisted that Radin had close connections to Los Angeles and the Son of Sam cult supposed to be headquartered there. Terry's information included reports of satanic activity at Ocean Castle along with all the drugs and polymorphous sexuality. David Berkowitz himself was known to have visited Ocean Castle at least once, which was explosive information as it was … but then Berkowitz also had been seen in Minot, North Dakota, the other Sam cult site. Terry tried connecting all the dots, but he did not have identities for some of the players, and in other cases he was dealing with ongoing police investigations and could not reveal more specific information, or possibly such information was not available to him.

Terry has been criticized a great deal by both occultists and others for some of his conclusions, as I have mentioned, but a close reading of *The Ultimate Evil* and collation with other documentation of these cases shows that Terry has been reliable where names, dates and places are concerned. He has reproduced documentation received from his informants and others, including Berkowitz, and these bear out the basic facts of his theory: that there is (or was) a nationwide network of criminals either using satanic activity as a front, or a satanic cult using criminal activity to finance their operation. In any case, murder is an essential part of their business plan, either "for hire" or for reasons of ritual magic and sacrifice. There is no way some of his informants would have had the information they had—in advance of any media accounts—unless they were "connected" in some way to the events described.

Once Radin's body had been found, Terry was notified and prepared to fly to Los Angeles to examine the crime scene himself, certain he was that Radin had been part of the Sam cult he was investigating. That is when he received another note from "Vinny," who told him to look at the scene carefully, for the killers would have left a cultic clue behind. Terry had a lot of clues in his hands, but until Roy Radin's body was found he didn't know what to do with them. As the Radin murder became news, Terry realized that the scenario fit all the details of the cult organization and activity he had been hearing about. He flew to Los Angeles and drove out to the canyons around Gorman, convinced he would find what Vinny had been telling him was there: evidence of cult involvement in the murder of Roy Radin.

And that is when he found the Bible, buried underneath a bush next to where Radin's body had been found, opened to the twenty-second chapter of Isaiah.

The murder of Roy Radin, while solved, is not wholly explained. There was the angle that Laney Jacobs believed Radin had ripped off her drugs and cash to the tune of one million dollars; killing Radin would not get that money back and, in fact, everyone knew who had taken the drugs anyway: Laney's drug courier Tally Rogers. Radin had been buying drugs from Rogers, but giving him checks made out to Laney Jacobs, making it clear that he expected Laney to be paid back for the money Rogers stole from her. Thus, the drugs-and-cash angle for Radin's murder did not make a lot of sense: he was the only one playing straight with her on that score.

Then there was the movie angle. Was Radin murdered so that Laney Jacobs could enjoy greater participation in the Evans venture? This is possible, of course, although it does give a whole new meaning to the phrase "termination clause." Why was it necessary to kill Radin? In the first place, if Evans felt strongly enough about having Jacobs involved in the production (perhaps due to her ability to provide huge amounts of drug money to finance his projects) he could have simply given her part of his share rather than insisting that it come from Radin's end. Of course, that would mean less control for Evans and more for Radin, and that was unacceptable.

So, Evans actually had a motive for getting rid of Radin; but he pled the Fifth Amendment, answered no questions in court, and was never charged. Other than Jacobs and Evans, who else would have wanted Radin dead?

The mystery man behind Laney Jacobs is, of course, Milan Bellechasses. It is reported in Steve Wick's account of the murder that Bellechasses was quietly involved in the Puerto Rican movie studio project with Radin and Evans, using his girlfriend Laney Jacobs as a front. Bellechasses thought that a movie deal with the Puerto Rican government would enable him to launder drug money easily. Money laundering is an essential part of the drug trade: profits from the sale of illegal narcotics is collected in cash, and even one neighborhood in a busy American city can net millions of dollars in cash profits in a single month. Counting this cash, transporting it and, eventually, banking it is an arduous task which requires its own specialists and its own network of couriers, accountants and compliant banks in countries with flexible banking systems.

According to this theory, Bellechasses would have viewed the Evans-Jacobs-Radin arrangement as tailor-made for his purposes. In order for this to work, he would have to retain—through Laney Jacobs—a percentage of the company; a finder's fee, such as Radin was offering, just wouldn't work.

Evans had to have known about this, and Wick's book suggests as much (along with a disclaimer that Evans has denied knowing anything about this, even though he was identified by Bill Mentzer on the witness stand as the man who gave the orders to kill Radin). Evans has never been convicted of a crime in connection with the *Cotton Club* murder, although he has been a suspect. On the basis of the information in Wick's book and much else uncovered by Terry and others, I think it is safe to say of Evans that "the kid stays in the picture."

Wick also mentions that the name "Rodan" was given to Roy Radin by his neo-Nazi killer, Alex Marti, who also called Radin "a big, fat Jew." Terry's informant on the East Coast knew the nickname Rodan before Radin was killed. Since Radin was known as "Rodan" to the Son of Sam cult (via Vinny's information), the only possible conclusion to draw is that Marti and his partner Mentzer were either members of that same cabal or had been hired guns of the cabal. All Terry needed to confirm the stories he had heard was proof at the crime scene of cult involvement, as the Sam cult usually left a "signature" behind.

Terry, wandering around the Radin crime scene on two separate occasions, found the Bible on the last day of his visit to Los Angeles, steeling himself to dig under a bush close by the scene that had been overlooked by police. The Bible was not buried in the sand, but simply sitting at the root of the bush, opened to the page mentioned above. It was straining credulity to believe that the positioning of the Bible in that place, miles from civilization and in the middle of the desert, was simply a coincidence. It had to have been planted. As the investigation progressed and Bill Mentzer, Alex Marti, Bob Lowe and, finally, Laney Jacobs were identified as the co-conspirators in the murder of Roy Radin, it only made Terry more convinced that the Son of Sam cult was behind the murder, and that there might have been other motives for Radin's messy extermination.

That "Vinny"and "Danny"—Terry's prison informants—would have known details about Radin, Evans, Ocean Castle, Sisman, Berkowitz, drugs, videotaped sexual acts, and much else besides, clearly implies (but does not prove) that they were right in other areas as well, including the satanic cult angle. The author himself can attest that Roy Radin had expressed interest in filming occult rituals being performed in Manhattan by the magicians and other self-styled sorcerers hanging out at the Magickal Childe bookstore on 19th Street, identified by Terry (although not by name) as an important locus for the Sam cult. And an address book in Berkowitz' possession did show an entry for Ocean Castle. Sisman did introduce Melonie Haller to Roy Radin, and Sisman and his girlfriend were murdered on Halloween; police—aware of the relationship between the two men—questioned Radin about the murder, but he claimed ignorance. Sisman was also rumored to have in his possession the all-important Stacey Moscowitz murder videotape ... if, indeed, such ever existed.

Return of the Family

For reasons why this murder neatly fits a theory of a nationwide satanic cult, we only have to look at Terry's evidence concerning Bill Mentzer and his early years in California, including his relationship to the Manson Family. Mentzer is a link that ties together not only Charles Manson and the Roy Radin murder, but also those separate cases and the Son of Sam murders in New York City, as well as other murders across the country. While the author does not wish to re-ignite the "satanic cult hysteria" of the 1980s, it is important to look at this evidence soberly, for the murders in question are not the key reasons why an understanding of the Manson/Sam cult is critical; rather, the murders—while vile enough in and of themselves—are only one aspect of the group's activities.

Bill Mentzer—Terry's pick as "Manson II," a much-rumored hitman with cult credentials—has the necessary pedigree. According to Terry's informants within the Los Angeles police, federal agencies, and the criminal subculture (very few of whom are named, making independent corroboration or confirmation difficult if not at times impossible), Mentzer had been a friend of both Charles Manson and, most importantly, Abigail Folger in the late 1960s. Although much has been made of the Sharon Tate murders, which were ghastly, the focus has been primarily on Sharon Tate herself, her filmmaker husband Roman Polanski (who was in Europe at the time of the killings), and Wojciech Frykowski, who was a known drug dealer and a friend of Polanski's from their early days in Poland. There has not been a lot of light shed on Abigail Folger, even though she was arguably the wealthiest person among the victims, and had bankrolled numerous New Age-type projects in California in the 1960s.

Heir to the Folger Coffee fortune, Abigail had made a practice of financing worthy causes, and these included the Himalayan Society (to which it is said Manson himself belonged) and the Straight Theater in San Francisco, which was the scene of the famous Magick Powerhouse of Oz performance that brought together Kenneth Anger and Bobby Beausoleil, as well as other Manson Family members. An informant who had penetrated the anti-war movement in America on behalf of the federal government told Terry that he had been present at a meal that included Abigail Folger and Bill Mentzer. Mentzer obviously had a soft spot for the counter-culture, for he wound up working for *Hustler* publisher Larry Flynt later on in the '70s.

While Mentzer had a criminal record and had been involved in questionable and illegal activity for a while, what does not ring true about Mentzer being the much-vaunted "Manson II" is that, for a hitman, he evidently has a rather weak stomach. On each occasion where we know Mentzer was present at or committed a murder he had to drink himself into the role. That is, he had to be pretty drunk before he could carry out the killings, whereas his associates—men like Argentine assassin Alex Marti—carried out these missions with glee, and needed no "Dutch courage" to get them in the mood. In the case of Roy Radin, it is agreed that Mentzer did not fire the shot that killed the producer. It was Marti who fired some twenty-seven rounds into Radin's skull; Mentzer only delivered the twenty-eighth and final shot, a kind of *coup de grace*, and that only after he had been drinking. While he may have been a willing hitman—at least theoretically—it would take him some time to work up the nerve. This does not sound like a "Manson II," but it is possible I am reading too much into the sobriquet for, after all, Manson himself was never convicted of actually committing a murder, but only of having ordered them to be carried out. If the Manson killings were murder-for-hire, Manson acting on instructions from another source, then the Mentzer killings were certainly hired hits. The murder of Roy Radin was carried out on Laney Jacobs' instructions. Another murder, that of a transvestite in Los Angeles who was allegedly blackmailing a wealthy family, was also murder-for-hire, a contract fulfilled by Mentzer.

Thus, we have to look a little deeper into the Manson and Mentzer killings to understand that they were not the result of crazed dope fiends going on a murder spree, but possibly contracted killings, paid for or at least ordered by person or persons unknown. In the case of Roy Radin and the Los Angeles transvestite, the contracts are clear. They were murders for specific motives. In the case of the Manson Family, we do not know who contracted the Tate/La Bianca killings (if indeed they were contracted), but, on the basis of much evidence and assorted testimony by those close to the case, we are safe in making the general assumption that Manson was carrying out assassinations at the behest of others.

That Manson and Mentzer knew each other in California in the 1960s is now virtually a certainty. That they were both involved in cult activity is also something for which Terry makes a very good case. We have already looked carefully at Manson's career and his cult involvements, which are beyond dispute. In addition, Terry has Mentzer not only friendly with both Charles Manson and Abigail Folger, but in the days after the Manson killings he places Mentzer at cult sites in California, Texas, and on the East Coast.

If we understand that the Son of Sam killings also included some specific hits, possibly ordered by an organized crime lord (as intimated by David Berkowitz himself, who has never avoided responsibility for his participation in these murders), and if we understand that Manson, Mentzer and Berkowitz are linked quite specifically via their respective cults, we have to come to the inescapable conclusion that a cult exists whose members are available for contract killings, and that this cult has existed since at least the late 1960s through the late 1970s, and likely beyond. We have also to understand that some of the Son of Sam killings were cult sacrifices, chosen to take place on days selected in advance according to an occult calendar or to some other, more esoteric, method. These killings were probably arranged to "blood" the new recruits: to acquaint them with the act of murder and to win their loyalty through fear of exposure to the authorities. This implies a well-organized and disciplined operation with, indeed, national coverage, as murders connected to this cult have taken place all over the United States.

As we mentioned, however, murder is only one aspect of this cult's activities. Drug-running is another, and probably provides much of the operating income for the group. Prostitution—both male and female, adult and child—is also a function of the group, as well as pornography and particularly child pornography.

While we have looked at both the Manson-Mentzer-Berkowitz connections and the Robert Evans-Laney Jacobs-Mentzer connections, what the reader may find startling are connections to still yet another group of organized killers and drug runners, the infamous "Company."

When Laney Jacobs was asked about her sources of income, she would usually tell people that she had made investments in the Suzy Creamcheese line of women's fashions and was a part-owner of the franchise which was famous in Las Vegas and among Hollywood celebrities. We don't know if Jacobs did indeed own a piece of the Suzy Creamcheese action, but she is known to have taken friends to visit Las Vegas and stay at Suzy Creamcheese owner Leslie DeKeyser's house, and to buy them clothes at the boutique. Jacobs spent a lot of time traveling to Vegas from both Florida and California, and we remember that Bob Evans was trying to raise money from casino owners there, the Doumani brothers.

Suzy Creamcheese had another illustrious client, and this will lead us back to Ashland, Kentucky and—strangely enough—back to Bob Evans, drugs, and murder. This time the main character is a bizarre figure who was part-commando, part-mystic, and total criminal, a man who leaped to his death on September 11, 1985, when his parachute didn't open because the $75-million worth of cocaine he had strapped to his body proved too heavy: Andrew Carter "Drew" Thornton II.

THE BLUEGRASS CONSPIRACY

Suzy Creamcheese was the brainchild of one Leslie DeKeyser, a flamboyant man with outrageous taste in fashion who created outfits that even a Vegas showgirl might have been embarrassed to wear. (The name came from a famous Frank Zappa song, whose most memorable lyric "Suzy Creamcheese, what's got into you?" became a rallying cry for a certain type of hippie-chick/rock groupie of the 1960s.) Although he boasted such ... luminaries as Charo and Cher among his satisfied customers, his most devoted client was one Anita Madden, nee Myers, a woman who was raised in Ashland, Kentucky on the wrong side of the tracks, but who clawed her way to the top by marrying the heir to the Madden horse-raising fortune. Sharing a great deal in common with Laney Jacobs, another poor white Southern girl who made it a habit to marry wealthy men, Anita Madden's parties became scandalous affairs in the late 1960s (and through to 1998, the year of the last Madden Kentucky Derby-Eve bash), with Ms. Madden decked out in the latest Suzy Creamcheese outrage, all leathers and feathers, and surrounding herself with show business and sports personalities, in a determined effort to invade and hold hostage the society columns of the Kentucky newspapers, struggling against those other blue-blooded clans, the Whitneys, the Vanderbilts, and the Barnstables who looked down their noses at the noisy bottle-blonde with the trashy, Frederick's of Hollywood *couture.* Ms. Creamcheese "herself" would show up at these galas—particularly the pre-Derby extravaganzas that are a mainstay of Kentucky society—resplendent in whips and chains, while nude mermaids and muscular men in sadomasochistic gear wandered the grounds of Madden's estate, Hamburg Place, making sure all the guests were properly lubricated.

All of this is recounted in greater and fascinating detail in investigative journalist Sally Denton's *The Bluegrass Conspiracy*, and it makes for compelling reading, especially as we begin to come across familiar names and suggestive time frames.

For instance, we don't know if Laney Jacobs and Anita Madden ever met; we do know that one of Anita Madden's closest friends married one of Laney Jacobs' husbands, however. Although Laney Jacobs herself is not mentioned in Denton's work, even though her story dovetails neatly with that book's drugs-murder-conspiracy saga, and neither is her lover and putative fiancé Bob Evans, Phyllis George makes an important appearance, she who was once married to the Hollywood producer. The Laney Jacobs-Suzy Creamcheese-Anita Madden nexus catapults us to the Laney Jacobs-Robert Evans-Phyllis George nexus and the *Cotton Club* murder, with Kentucky Fried Chicken along the way.

Confused?

Like her compatriot, Charles Manson, Anita Madden grew from a poor white background in Ashland to become figurative head of a social demimonde that rejoiced in free love, drugs, and dangerous alliances. While Charlie's girls were putting out in hot, dirt-floor shacks in the desert for Charlie's unhygienic guests—usually the Hell's Angels or some other motorcycle gang running LSD and pot through the American landscape like Wells Fargo on angel dust—Anita Madden's parties were a bit more upscale, the guests generally bathed, and the Dom was always properly chilled. But beneath the social register veneer lay the same sinister forces that suppurated so openly among the Family. While Charlie courted Terry Melcher and the Beach Boys on the West Coast, Anita Madden was hosting Sissy Spacek, Ann-Margaret, Connie Stevens and Larry Flynt (employer of convicted Radin assassins Bill Mentzer and Alex Marti) in Kentucky; but for both there was violence and bloodshed just below the surface. At the end, there would be many dead—both the innocent and the guilty—including the first assassination of a federal judge in a hundred years. And we will incredibly find ourselves back at Dealey Plaza on November 22, 1963, with a wisp of smoke rising from the Grassy Knoll.

The complex mystery begins with a bizarre paramilitary operation known as the "Company" a nickname not to be confused with that of the CIA … maybe. As it turns out, the Company was involved in more than what was originally suspected by Kentucky law enforcement, which was drug-running, pure and simple. Sally Denton's book is virtually the only text anywhere that exposes this operation, and Ms. Denton found herself being squeezed out of mainstream journalism largely due to her insistence (and evidence) that Kentucky politics was dirty with drug and arms deals. Ms. Denton again went against the establishment with her oft-cited piece "The Crimes of Mena" (co-authored with Roger Morris), an article on a covert government drugs- and arms-smuggling operation, an exposé that was spiked by the *Washington Post* at the last minute, and wound up instead in the pages of *Penthouse.* The Mena article is an account of an Iran-Contra operation in the tiny town of Mena, Arkansas during the Reagan-Bush years, while Bill Clinton was governor of the state. Denton would go on to investigate both the criminal history of Las Vegas (also co-authored with Roger Morris) as well as the Mormon Mountain Meadows Massacre of September 11, 1857, thus illustrating once again that independent investigation into America's history keeps pulling one back to the same topics.

Kentucky has a tradition of smuggling that goes back more than a century, making it the Paraguay of the South. With the Ohio River on one side and the Big Sandy on the other, and a stretch of the Mississippi on the western border, Kentucky has seen more than its share of strange water traffic, with contraband running as far south as the Gulf of Mexico. Running slaves, then liquor, and finally drugs and guns, Kentucky's history as a smuggler's state is almost genteel, serving as an unofficial frontier between the Northeast, the South and the Western parts of the United States.

The police investigation of the Company revealed a state whose politics—from the Governor's Mansion on down through the various local and state police departments—was corrupt to the extent that its reputation is only surpassed by that of Louisiana and Rhode Island. There were so many former and current law enforcement officers as part of the Company that for a while many investigators were under the assumption that it was a covert federal operation, perhaps something linked to arms deals with the Contras. Indeed, Iran-Contra figure Adnan Khashoggi makes an appearance in this story, too, as a frequent visitor to Kentucky whose own company's name—the Triad Corporation—was echoed in the name of the farm that served as the Company's headquarters: Triad. The logo of the Triad Farm was a pitchfork, and locals insisted to police and federal investigators that it was used not only for paramilitary training but was also the headquarters of a satanic cult.[44] In fact, it was during the search for a missing friend of Company members, Melanie Flynn (sister of baseball player Doug Flynn of the Mets and later the Cincinnati Reds), that a psychic was eventually called in, and without prompting led police to the site where they privately believed Flynn had been killed; the same psychic told the investigators that she believed a cult was behind the murder. She identified Drew Thornton as one of the persons responsible for Flynn's murder, and the heavy occult "vibes" she received chilled her to the bone.

There is a strong tradition linking Kentucky and the casinos of Las Vegas. Kentuckians are inveterate gamblers; after all, their state boasts the prestigious Kentucky Derby, and many fortunes are won and lost on a single race. Several important Vegas casinos were run by Kentuckians, and they favored people from their home state as dealers in their employ. There is also a link between Kentucky and Florida, and that is the drug trade.

In the 1970s, Kentucky became infamous for activity of the Company, a network of illegal trade in drugs, arms and prostitution. The Company was largely composed of former law enforcement officers, and had intelligence resources high up in several federal agencies, notably the Drug Enforcement

Agency, or DEA. It was widely rumored that the Company had CIA connections, and that they were part of the infrastructure that eventually began supplying the Contras in the 1980s. With planeloads of weapons and high-technology gear such as night-vision scopes and other James Bond paraphernalia (either stolen from US military bases such as China Lake, or actually supplied by the government, the truth is a little hard to find), the materiel wound up supporting Latin American military regimes, and the planes would fly back into the United States with shipments of marijuana and, later, cocaine. Shipments worth millions of dollars a flight.

One of the central figures of this organization—believed by federal agents to have been the most dangerous, most highly-organized and tightly-controlled illegal operation in the country—was Drew Thornton, a former Lexington, Kentucky police officer and martial arts specialist. Thornton's parents were Northerners; his father was from New Jersey and his mother from Connecticut, but they assimilated quickly into Kentucky society by the expedient of raising racehorses on a small ranch near the town of Paris. Thornton joined the Army at the time of the Vietnam conflict, and then rotated back to the States and became a police officer, eventually working Narcotics as well as Intelligence. He formed alliances at this time with an entire brotherhood of police officers who had no problem with selling the dope they confiscated, usually long before it made its way to the evidence locker.

The Lexington police department became notorious for dirty cops during this period, and evidence began to accumulate showing that they were actually being protected by the local DEA chief, giving rise to speculation that the "dirty cops" were working on a larger, more covert, operation on behalf of the DEA and, possibly, the CIA; conversely, other speculation was simpler and more direct: the DEA chief in Kentucky was corrupt. The reality is probably a combination of both.

At various times in her book, Denton mentions the fact that Drew Thornton believed himself possessed of supernatural powers, but she does not delve any deeper into this except to imply that it was a mélange of Asian mysticism and martial arts philosophy, and that Thornton had become a kind of David Carradine (of television series *Kung Fu* fame) at least in his own mind. (His first wife also professed to be psychic, able to predict future events.) This mysticism was wedded to his paramilitary exploits, and his Triad Farm became a venue for both occult practices of some description and commando training. It was also a center for the trade in illegal narcotics, and more than one eyewitness reported seeing aircraft flying low over Triad and dropping bundles that were believed to be drugs. In other cases, federal agencies reported suspicions that arms, including tanks, were being smuggled into and out of Triad Farm. When State Police investigator Ralph Ross attempted to learn more, he was warned off the case by Lexington police officers … even though they had no jurisdiction over the territory. Ross was eventually set up by his own men in a desperate effort to silence him, and thus remove the threat of an investigation which was lapping gently around the doorway to the Governor's Mansion.

The investigation into the clandestine affairs of the Company eventually went as high as the governor of the state, who at the time was John Y. Brown, a successful Democratic businessman who had parlayed the Kentucky Fried Chicken franchise into a hugely successful operation (and would later become involved with Kenny Rogers Roasters and the Roadhouse Grill franchises). Harlan Sanders, who had created Kentucky Fried Chicken and become an honorary "Colonel" in the process, harbored ill feelings towards the deal, believing that he had been cheated out of money that was rightfully his. "Colonel" Sanders had developed the business from a mom-and-pop operation to over six hundred outlets by 1963. In 1964, John Y. Brown arranged a buyout of Sanders, a deal in which the "Colonel" felt manipulated into selling, and said as much to the newspapers.[45] The deal, however, made Brown a multimillionaire once he brought the company public, and he gave jobs in KFC to friends of his who would later become notorious in the Company investigation, including Dan Chandler and Jimmy Lambert. Chandler would become an "unindicted co-conspirator," and Lambert would face a criminal indictment over the affair. They were all part of the Anita Madden social circuit, including Governor Brown himself.

There were (and are) other "social circuits" in Kentucky society, of course, and Madden was viewed as something of an interloper at first, her personal pedigree not being up to the local standards of old money and Southern antebellum aristocracy. But Anita was a force to be reckoned with, as she trucked in the bodybuilders and the strippers and the rock bands and the outrageous costumes and "theme" parties. It was to this particular circuit that we trace all the movers and shakers of the Company and its ancillary characters and operations, however, and not to the Vanderbilts, Whitneys or Barnstables. There is a certain cachet that comes from having worked your way up from the bottom, a certain pragmatic if not pugnacious view of life and how best to meet its challenges, that attracts the adventurer, the politician, and the criminal. Also, the business of the Madden dynasty was the raising of thoroughbred horses, not an industry defined by the mint julep and the shy Southern belle, but by hard choices and fierce competition. Thus, it was to Anita Madden and her Hamburg Place estate (and what they represented) that men like Brown, Chandler, Lambert, Barry Bryant and Drew Thornton would gravitate.

Brown was married to former Miss America Phyllis George (after her divorce from producer Robert Evans), united by their mutual love of sports. Brown would go on to become owner of various ball teams, and Ms. George would go on to be a television announcer. They would eventually divorce after some twenty years of marriage, and Brown would go on to marry (and divorce) another beauty pageant queen in the late 1990s.

The story of the Company is much too long and complex to be discussed here in its entirety, and readers are urged to find a copy of *The Bluegrass*

Conspiracy and prepare to be stunned at the breadth and depth of political corruption that reaches from the bottom-feeder nickle-bag street dealers to the cops who bust them and on up to Colombian drug lords, crooked DEA chiefs, and gun-running mercenaries and suspect spooks. The time frame of *The Bluegrass Conspiracy* parallels that of the Son of Sam killings and the Roy Radin murder, however, and stretches across the same real estate: South Florida cocaine circles, the Medellin cartel, Las Vegas money-laundering, the use of prostitutes to blackmail political leaders, and the rise of Los Angeles as cocaine-central after Miami. We have David Berkowitz in Kentucky preaching on street corners at the same time Drew Thornton is busting radicals and dope dealers there, in an eerie replay of the Jim Jones and Dan Mitrione "relationship" in Indiana; we have Laney Jacobs staying with Suzy Creamcheese founder Leslie DeKeyser at the latter's home in Las Vegas, at the same time that she is plotting the Roy Radin murder and is involved with Robert Evans[46]; Leslie DeKeyser is also an intimate of Anita Madden and a regular at her parties; Laney will later marry Larry Greenberger, a famous South Florida cocaine dealer and lieutenant of Medellin cartel *narcotraficante* Carlos Lehder Rivas; Greenberger himself is later murdered either by his wife, Laney, or by one of her lovers, before she herself is arrested and convicted for her role in the Radin homicide. We have Larry Flynt, the man who employed Radin assassins Bill Mentzer and Alex Marti, attending Anita Madden's pre-Derby parties at Hamburg Place … and we have the assassination of federal judge John Wood at the orders of drug kingpin Jimmy Chagra, an assassination carried out by hitman Charles Harrelson, father of actor Woody Harrelson ("Woody" on the television sit-com *Cheers*, who later portrayed a serial killer in Oliver Stone's *Natural Born Killers* and … Larry Flynt, in *The People vs. Larry Flynt*). When arrested, Charles Harrelson will confess to having been the man on the grassy knoll in Dallas on November 22, 1963; he will confess to having assassinated President John F. Kennedy. He will quickly retract that confession on the advice of his attorney, and he has never spoken about it again.

The assassination of US District Judge "Maximum" John Wood took place on May 29, 1979 in San Antonio, Texas, on the day that Jimmy Chagra was due to appear in his courtroom for the beginning of his trial on charges of drug trafficking. Jimmy Chagra was an American of Lebanese ancestry whose brother, Lee Chagra, had been a famous defense attorney for drug dealers, until a drug bust in 1973 attracted the attention of the DEA. Jimmy Chagra eventually began running his brother's operation—which included masterminding a drug operation that extended from Lebanon to South America, an operation that used Caesars Palace in Las Vegas as its unofficial headquarters.

At the time, Caesars was being managed by Dan Chandler, the friend of Kentucky Governor John Brown, to whom he owed the position. Chandler would introduce the Chagra brothers to Barry Bryant and Drew Thornton, the two partners running the Company. The Chagras were tied to the more prosaic organized-crime families of the Patriarcas in New England and Spilotros of Chicago,[47] so the meeting and eventual partnership between the Chagras and the Company signaled a crime empire that would literally span the globe and extend the reach of both organizations considerably, with old-time Vegas-style Mafia wheeling and dealing on the one hand, and "New Age" paramilitary and covert ops on the other. In addition, federal officials believed that the Chagras also had ties to Middle Eastern terrorist organizations, ties that probably involved the trade in heroin from Mideast markets such as Afghanistan, Pakistan, and the Levant.[48]

By 1978, it was virtually impossible to tell the two operations apart. Jimmy Chagra was experiencing a lot of heat from federal attention, leaving the Company to take advantage of his organized-crime connections and grow exponentially. They developed important links with the intelligence community, as they crossed paths in the underground world of arms dealing and money laundering, and of course the international trade in narcotics.

Then, on December 23, 1978, Lee Chagra was murdered, the victim of a .22 calibre bullet fired at close range in his law office.

A few months later, and his brother Jimmy would be arrested on four counts of drug trafficking from Colombia, his bail set at one million dollars.

Then, on the day he was due to go to trial, his mortal enemy—Judge John Wood—was assassinated, killed by a single shot from a sniper's rifle. According to FBI Director William Webster, it was "the crime of the century" (which probably shows their bias when it comes to the assassinations of John F. Kennedy, Robert F. Kennedy, Dr. Martin Luther King, Jr, Medgar Evers, Malcolm X … etc., etc.). As the investigation into the judge's assassination progressed from Chagra, Bryant and others involved with the Company, a suspect was eventually identified and arrested, a man who confessed to the killing: Charles Voyde Harrelson.

When Harrelson was arrested, he also confessed to the assassination of JFK, and, indeed, photographs of the famous "three hoboes" arrested that day in Dallas do seem to show a somewhat younger Harrelson in the lineup, and forensic experts from the Houston Police Department evidently agree. A book written about the assassination and focusing on one of the other co-conspirators—Charles Rogers—by John R. Craig and Philip A. Rogers tells the story in some detail.[49] Although it lacks documentation and source material, and for that reason cannot be taken as "gospel," it does name names and gives dates and places for many of the events described, particularly those leading up to Dallas in November 1963.

Harrelson's life as a professional hitman is not in question. He had been arrested for various crimes involving firearms all his life, and was an acknowledged killer in several unrelated cases. He is presently in prison for the rest of his life, due to the Judge Wood assassination. He has refused to discuss anything more about the Kennedy assassination after that one day in which he admitted he was on the grassy knoll with another assassin, suspected murderer Charles Rogers.

Rogers came to the attention of researchers because of the murder of his parents on Father's Day, June 20, 1965 in Houston. They had been murdered and dismembered, some body parts flushed down the drains and the rest stuffed in the refrigerator, wrapped in plastic, à la Jeffrey Dahmer. Rogers, who lived with his parents, was nowhere to be found and would never be found again. According to the authors, his parents had been killed because they suspected their son's involvement in the assassination. This was due to—again, according to the authors—both Charles Harrelson and Lee Harvey Oswald turning up one day in September 1963 at the parents' church a few blocks away, asking to wait there for a mysterious "Carlos" who would turn up later: a "Carlos" who knew the minister and his wife very well.

The day after the Kennedy assassination, the minister and his wife recognized the photograph of Lee Harvey Oswald as the "Lee" who had visited them a few months earlier. They already knew who "Carlos" was, as they spotted him outside the church talking with Oswald and Harrelson. It was their congregants' son, Charles Rogers.

The authors make many connections between Charles Rogers and David Ferrie, Lee Harvey Oswald, Charles Harrelson, the Civil Air Patrol, the CIA, etc., even going so far as to tie Rogers in with the man who executed Che Guevara in Bolivia. Some of the data is verifiable, such as Rogers enlistment in the Navy, his work for ONI (the Office of Naval Intelligence), and his academic career, as well as his brief employment with Shell Oil before his ostensible recruitment by the CIA. Although Rogers was obviously a suspect in the murder of his parents, he was never sought by authorities and the case remains open and unsolved to this day. Not so the John Wood assassination, however, for which Charles Harrelson is doing life without parole in Marion.

Years later, Sally Denton would return to the drugs and arms conspiracies of the South with her fabled article in *Penthouse*, co-authored with Dr. Roger Morris, a Harvard professor who had worked in the National Security Council during both the Johnson and the Nixon administrations. Ms. Denton herself was head of UPI's investigative unit and had written for the *Washington Post* and other mainstream media before the guns-for-drugs conspiracy among Kentucky's law enforcement elite grabbed her attention, and lost her the support of the system. "The Crimes of Mena" tells the story of Barry Seal, an admitted drug smuggler who—as all evidence now shows beyond any shadow of a doubt—worked for the federal government, specifically for the CIA and the DEA and possibly other agencies as well, at the same time he was running drugs from South America. Later, he would be murdered by the Medellin cartel in Baton Rouge, Louisiana, where he was giving evidence against the drug lords. Seal was part of an operation that was set in motion by forces within the White House that wanted to support the Contras in Nicaragua by any means necessary, an operation that became known to the world at large when another smuggler, Eugene Hasenfus, was shot down over Nicaraguan airspace in a plane that was once owned and flown by Barry Seal. The trail of drugs and arms smuggling led from that Hasenfus crash along a moral fault line that terminated at Oliver North and the Iran-Contra scandal.

The Denton/Morris article never mentions Kentucky and the famous "Company" of Drew Thornton detailed in Denton's earlier book on the Bluegrass Conspiracy, but the conclusion is inescapable. All of the theories being tossed around at the time of the Company investigation by federal investigators included the same guns-for-drugs scenario that eventually defined the Barry Seal case and, indeed, both operations were running concurrently … if they were, in fact, different operations and not part of a single, overall clandestine project to finance and supply the anti-Sandinista forces in Nicaragua using funds provided by the sale of cocaine in the United States.

Nothing more has been heard of Mena. The right-wing cartel in the United States has tried to pin the blame on Bill Clinton, of course, claiming that since he was Governor of Arkansas at the time that Barry Seal was using the small town of Mena as the headquarters for his vast criminal empire he should have done something about it. The blame backfired, however, when it was realized that this was a program begun under the Reagan and Bush administrations and could not properly be laid at the Governor's door. (In fact, readers may remember the story of Larry Nichols, the man fired by then-Governor Clinton because he was using the state's telephones to raise money for the Contras, and who later parlayed his termination into the "Clinton Chronicles," financed by Richard Mellon Scaife.) Those who insisted that Clinton should have done something about Mena when he was governor miss the essential element in all of this: the Barry Seal operation had the blessing of the White House. As Denton and Morris make very clear, nothing connected to Seal could be investigated: not by the FBI, not by the IRS, not by US Customs, not by the DEA … by no one. Had Clinton forced the issue and brought it to the attention of the media, he would have been pilloried by the very same people who now blame him for *not* doing so, the people who believe that Oliver North is a hero, that ignoring Congressional regulations such as the Boland Amendment was admirable, and that Iran-Contra was justified.

And so it goes.

David Berkowitz. Charles Manson. Roy Radin. Robert Evans. Bill Mentzer. Laney Jacobs. Anita Madden. Leslie DeKeyser. John Y. Brown. Phyllis George. Larry Greenberger. Carlos Lehder. Drew Thornton. Barry Seal. Charles Harrelson. Drugs. Guns. Assassinations. Cults. Hollywood. Miami. Las Vegas. Lexington. Mena. And behind it all, a vast criminal enterprise that had its roots in the White House and its branches in nearly every state in the Union, and in so many Latin American countries that it was a virtual NAFTA agreement, so much so that the "loud, sucking sound" so beloved of independent candidate H. Ross Perot's aborted 1992 presidential campaign may have been nothing more than lines of coke being hoovered up the collective American nose.

These are the trivia, the minutiae that give conspiracy theorists anxiety attacks, and for which there is no satisfying explanation other than the ubiquitous "coincidence," a word that is meaningless because it is *supposed* to be meaningless: a word intended to represent a pointless concurrence of two events, which presupposes that events can occur at the same time or the same place or to the same people, or some combination of these, and yet have no possible relation to each other. It is a way of avoiding a question and, by extension, the uncomfortable answer to that question. Yet, they are "links" in the Brunoesque sense of the word, in Coulianu's sense of the word. They may be thought of as synchronistic, in Jung's sense of the word. Something at the edge of quantum physics, perhaps, or something peculiar to depth psychology or social anthropology.

Or they may be evidence of genuine political and criminal conspiracy.

Or something darker, more dangerous: a sinister force that has festered within the soul of America for many, many years.

Sometimes I think there's a buried maniac who runs the mind of this city. And he sets up the coincidences.

—Norman Mailer, *An American Dream*

As Denton and Morris reveal, among Eugene Hasenfus' personal effects when his plane crashed in the Nicaraguan jungle, thus initiating the Iran-Contra investigation, was documentation showing his involvement with the controversial and top-secret Area 51 in Nevada …

Endnotes

1 Maury Terry, *The Ultimate Evil*, Barnes & Noble, NY, 1999, p. 529
2 Ibid., p. 529
3 Ibid., p. 529
4 Ibid., p. 530
5 Ibid., p. 44
6 Ibid., p. 530
7 Ibid., p. 64-72
8 Ibid., p. 531
9 Ibid., p. 149-151
10 Robert Graysmith, *Zodiac*, Berkley Books, NY, 1987, p. 248

[11] Ibid., p. 254
[12] Ibid., p. 254
[13] Robert Graysmith, *Zodiac Unmasked,* Berkley Books, NY, 2003, p. 160-162
[14] Gary M. Lavergne, *A Sniper In The Tower,* Bantam Books, NY, 1997, p. 341
[15] Ibid., p. 342
[16] Dean Koontz, *One Door Away From Heaven,* Bantam, NY, 2001, p. 76
[17] Terry, op. cit., p. 170
[18] David Abrahamson, *Confessions of Son of Sam,* Columbia University Press, NY, 1985, p. 15
[19] Terry, op. cit., p. 154
[20] Ibid., p. 224
[21] Ibid., p. 147
[22] Ibid., p. 162
[23] Ibid., p. 158-162
[24] Ibid., p. 179
[25] Aleister Crowley, *Magic In Theory and Practice,* Dover, NY, 1976, p. 193
[26] Terry, op. cit., p. 228
[27] Ibid., p. 50
[28] Ibid., p. 228
[29] Ibid., p. 229
[30] Ibid., p. 184
[31] Ibid., p. 249-256
[32] Abrahamson, op. cit., p. 2, 14
[33] Ibid., p. 87
[34] Ibid., p. 151
[35] Ibid., p. 180
[36] Terry, op. cit., p. 257-258
[37] Terry, op. cit., p. 462-463
[38] Steve Wick, *Bad Company: Drugs, Hollywood, and the Cotton Club Murder,* Harcourt, Brace, Jovanovich, NY, 1990, p. 64
[39] Ronald Kessler, *The Richest Man In The World: The Story of Adnan Khashoggi,* Warner Books, New York, 1986
[40] Ibid., p. 130
[41] Ibid., p. 131-132
[42] Wick, op. cit., p. 112
[43] Ibid., p. 131
[44] Sally Denton, *The Bluegrass Conspiracy,* Doubleday, NY, 1990, p. 102-103
[45] Ibid., p. 147
[46] Wicks, op. cit., p. 105
[47] Denton, op. cit., p. 66
[48] Ibid., p. 67
[49] John R. Craig and Philip A. Rogers, *The Man On The Grassy Knoll,* Avon, New York, 1992

CHAPTER TWENTY

COMMUNION

Behind the scenes high-ranking Air Force officers are soberly concerned about the UFOs. But through official secrecy and ridicule, many citizens are led to believe the unknown flying objects are nonsense.

—Rear Admiral Roscoe Hillenkoetter, former Director of the CIA, in a memorandum to Congress dated August 22, 1960

The UFOs reported by competent observers are devices under intelligent control.... These UFOs are interplanetary devices systematically observing the earth, either manned or under remote control, or both.

—Colonel Joseph J. Bryan III, Chief and Founder of the CIA's Psychological Warfare Staff, former Special Assistant to the Secretary of the Air Force, in a 1960 letter to Major Donald Keyhoe

We deal now not with things of this world alone. We deal now with the ultimate conflict between a unified human race and the sinister forces of some other planetary galaxy.

—General Douglas MacArthur, 1962

We can study files for decades, but every so often we are tempted to throw up our hands and declare that history is merely another literary genre: the past is autobiographical fiction pretending to be a parliamentary report.

—Julian Barnes[1]

...given that in the course of history many have acted on beliefs in which many others did not believe, we must perforce admit that for each, to a different degree, history has been largely the theater of an illusion.

—Umberto Eco[2]

For not all true things are to be said to all men.
—Bishop Clement of Alexandria (c. A.D. 150-215)

At the very heart of the UFO controversy is the question of Truth. Like the fictional FBI Agent of *X-Files*, Fox Mulder, we are inclined to believe that "the Truth is out there," but even Mulder eventually lost the faith. That is the crux of the problem, isn't it? Faith?

Many Christians do not realize that the parameters of their faith were established by the Council of Nicea in 325 A.D., a Council controlled by Emperor Constantine through his emissary Bishop Eusebius. In other words, a political leader would decide core issues of what would become a world religion. This Council decided the question of Jesus' divinity once and for all, and it was the men who composed this Council who decided which texts would comprise both the Old and the New Testaments. The decision—which resulted in the modern Holy Bible—was both a religious and a political issue. To summarize, doctrines held by groups believed not to be "team players" were denounced as heretical, and the relevant texts omitted from the final Scripture. Especially dangerous to the development of a "state church"—which is what Constantine was creating, even though he would not actually become baptized until his death bed—was the phenomenon of Gnosticism. Gnostics embraced the Christian message, but in a way inimical to authority. They believed that everyone should approach God directly.

As Biblical scholar Elaine Pagels writes,

> … when we examine its practical effect on the Christian movement, we can see, paradoxically, that the doctrine of bodily resurrection also serves an essential *political* function: it legitimizes the authority of certain men who claim to exercise exclusive leadership over the churches as the successors of the apostle Peter. From the second century, the doctrine has served to validate the apostolic succession of bishops, the basis of papal authority to this day. (emphasis in original)[3]

She goes on to clarify:

> … orthodox teaching … legitimized a hierarchy of persons through whose authority all others must approach God. Gnostic teaching … was potentially subversive of this order: it claimed to offer to every initiate direct access to God of which the priests and bishops themselves might be ignorant.[4]

And:

> … when gnostic and orthodox Christians discussed the nature of God, they were at the same time debating the issue of *spiritual authority.* (emphasis in original)[5]

Thus, matters as diverse as the Nicene Creed, which emphasizes the physical reality of Jesus' resurrection, and the actual books included in the Bible, were the result of political issues being decided at the time: an attempt to create a state religion with an identifiable hierarchy that was amenable to control. Obviously, a religion in which every member had direct access to God was a threat not only to the concept of an ecclesiastical hierarchy, but was also subversive of the State itself. How could any person with direct access to God also pay the appropriate homage to a temporal leader, to an Emperor? Thus, matters of faith and matters of truth became tools to be used in order to manipulate the citizenry.

Bishop Clement of Alexandria, quoted above, a powerful figure in second century Christianity, wrote pragmatically on the question of truth and faith. Like an ancient precursor to Machiavelli, Clement understood that truth was dangerous and not to be entrusted to just anybody. Clement's fears about the special volatility of truth may be evidence of some deeper, darker secret at the heart of Christianity, a secret to which he was privy. As we uncover more scrolls and decipher more arcane texts from Biblical times, often against enormous opposition from the Church (as described in Baigent and Leigh's *The Dead Sea Scroll Deception*),[6] we are gradually getting used to the idea that the last two thousand years of Western history may have been based on a magician's trick, a bit of misdirection and legerdemain, concealing a closely-guarded secret of which underground societies and some high-level clerics have long been aware.

What does this have to do with UFOs?

No, I am not about to insist that Jesus was an astronaut or some kind of space alien. What I am going to suggest is that we in the West have become accustomed to accepting a great deal at face value, on "faith." After all, we are heirs to easily the most bizarre set of beliefs among all the world's major religions: that a man—or someone who seemed very much like a man—was executed in Roman-occupied Palestine two thousands years ago, and then rose from the dead, disappearing after a short time into the heavens. Christians are required to believe this; it is central to their faith and is represented in the Nicene Creed, and in the celebration of the Mass (or Divine Liturgy) in which believing Christians partake of the body and blood of Jesus, substances that have been transformed from bread and wine through some occult agency, thus adding a form of cannibalism to the already heady mix of crucifixion and resurrection. When it comes to Jesus, Muslims are ready to accept him as a prophet; when it comes to his resurrection, they demur. The same with the Jews. But there are over a billion people in the world who believe—or who belong to religious sects which insist they believe—that Jesus was born of woman, lived to the age of 33, then was crucified, experienced death, was buried, and rose from his tomb "on the third day," or actually about 39 hours after he was taken down from the cross.

The Swiss psychoanalyst and philosopher C.G. Jung once commented that Christianity had, in effect, turned the Western world schizoid. Forced to accept an impossibility as the truth, and forced in turn to repress natural instincts in the service of this impossibility. Western civilization since the time of Constantine has been struggling with itself. To complicate matters, the doctrine of Original Sin—that all humans are born with a blemish of sin on their soul due to the original defection of Adam and Eve—means that we are all guilty, from birth; indeed, we are also guilty to some extent of the sufferings and death of Jesus, who "died for our sins." Christians, and especially Roman Catholics, are awash in guilt, and conflicted over their true desires and the extent to which those desires are at odds with Christian doctrines of personal behavior and sin. Yet, to deny the Risen Christ (or to refute any of these individual doctrines) was to invite personal disaster in the form of Inquisition and the stake. Thus, many otherwise decent and intelligent people learned to dissemble from a very early age. They learned to lie, either to themselves or to others, in order to survive.

But ... miracles do happen. Strange things do occur. And to deny the Risen Christ may be to throw out the Baby with the baptismal water. If we insist that resurrection from the dead is an impossibility in this world, do we entertain the idea—even for a moment—that it might be a reality in another world? Do we insist that the "real world" we see around us is the one, sole, objective truth and there is no other even though we know—intellectually—that what we experience with our senses is largely a creation of our nervous systems? When we say that resurrection is impossible, upon what do we base that assumption?

Upon science. Upon scientific evidence. Thus the war between science and religion, a war that reached its climax in the Renaissance, when the occult, the mystical, made one last brave attempt to redeem civilization for the dreamers, the artists, the believers.

Belief is love. The very English word "belief" is related to the German verb *lieben* ("to love"). To *believe* something is to *hold dear* that idea, to prefer it to others, to feel emotional about it, maybe even passionate. That is why "true believers" scare us so much: they seem to have abandoned rational thought and to have fallen in love with a fantasy.

Bishop Clement was very clear about this, in his own way:

> For even if they should say something true, one who loves the Truth should not, even so, agree with them. For not all true things are the Truth; nor should that truth which seems true according to human opinions be preferred to the true Truth—that according to the faith.[7]

We can see the seeds of the Baltimore Catechism being sown even then! The "true Truth"—according to the good bishop—is that "according to the faith."

This is why we have such a difficult time resolving the UFO issue.

Eugene Hasenfus was shot down over Nicaragua during his mission to supply the anti-Sandinista Contras. He was part of a wide-ranging network of self-anointed patriots and right-wing zealots who were championed by General Singlaub and the various Republican Party ethnic outreach groups. (Incidentally, Clinton antagonist Larry Nichols was a self-admitted member of one of these groups). Hasenfus is the sort of man typified by "Jack D. Ripper," the commander in charge of an Air Force Base in the Peter Sellers comedy *Dr. Strangelove*, who believes fluoridation of water to be a Communist plot to deprive Americans of their "precious bodily fluids," and thus instigates World War III. In Hasenfus' possession were documents linking him to Area 51 in Nevada.

Area 51 is the scene of a great deal of controversy among the UFO enthusiasts, as they believe that captured alien spacecraft are taken there to be "re-engineered" by American engineers and scientists. Another engineer, one Bob Lazar, has insisted that he himself witnessed this procedure in operation at Area 51.

Area 51—known as Groom Lake, and Dreamland, and a host of other appellations—is without a doubt a top-secret US Air Force facility where, it is said, "stealth" bombers and other military aircraft are designed and tested. The facility is so secret that for years the government would not even admit it existed, even though its presence there was announced by the barbed wire fencing and the warning signs advising that anyone breaching security would be shot.

Why a member of the Contra supply network would have connections of any kind to Area 51 is a question that has not yet been answered. Hasenfus was a pilot and a mercenary; he was not an aerospace scientist with a top-secret classification. We are in the uncomfortable position of having two mysteries wrapped around each other, and neither giving us much room for deduction: first, we don't really know what is going on at Area 51, so we can't imagine what Hasenfus would be doing flying over Nicaragua for the Contras and having Area 51 phone numbers in his possession; in the second place, we don't know much about the background of Eugene Hasenfus himself, and details about the day-to-day operation of the Contra effort are shrouded in similar mysteries. If we knew more about Hasenfus, we might piece together some important information about Area 51; if we knew more about Area 51, we might understand why Hasenfus was linked to it. As it stands, we know virtually nothing about both pieces of this puzzle, for—as it is written—"not all things are to be said to all men."

CONTACT

Is this the devil? What the hell is this?

—Whitley Strieber, under hypnosis to recall details of his abduction[8]

Whitley Strieber was born a Roman Catholic. Although, as we see from his writings both in print and on his Web site, he and his wife were involved with the Gurdjieff Foundation for a while (and he also admits that he has attended witchcraft ceremonies, of the "New Age" pagan variety[9]), he nonetheless retains a great deal from his Catholic upbringing. A gifted storyteller, several of his novels have been made into movies (including *The Wolfen* and *The Hunger*) and, indeed, he worked as a screenwriter for a while (*The Owl and the Pussycat*). But Strieber came to international prominence largely on the strength of one book, a non-fiction bestseller in which he claimed to have been abducted by an alien force.

Communion: A True Story was not only a bestseller, but it became a feature film starring Christopher Walken as Strieber, a film that was unsettling and eerie to many audiences and made even more so by the filmmakers' insistence that it was based on actual events. That the title, *Communion*, has special resonance for Catholics should be obvious: it is the name for the ritual involving consumption of the body and blood of Jesus. It is one of the seven sacraments in the Catholic Church, and signifies full membership in the Church.

Yet "communion" also means "communication," albeit on a deeper level, and this is the emphasis of the film and especially of the book, as well as of all the others from Whitley Strieber that have followed *Communion*, and which deal with the same phenomena. In fact, one of the sequels to *Communion* is *Confirmation*, a word that describes another Catholic sacrament, this time the ritual in which a young boy or girl reaffirms the vows made by their godparents at their baptism; i.e., *confirms* that they renounce Satan and believe in Jesus. The titles of the other sequels are not so openly sacerdotal, however, being *Breakthrough*, *Transformation*, and *The Secret School*. (One does suspect that it would be difficult to use *Extreme Unction* as a title, although *Penance, Baptism* and even *Matrimony* have possibilities, not to mention the potentially sinister *Holy Orders*.)

Briefly, the story is this:

On the night of December 26, 1985 Whitley Strieber—on holiday at his cabin in the woods in Ulster County, upstate New York—was awakened by a strange noise in the living room. It would later be recorded that a UFO had been sighted in the area that night, but at the time Whitley had no knowledge of this and did not associate his experience with UFOs and alien visitors until months later.[10] He sat up in bed, startled, but then lay back down to return to sleep. He says that this type of strange behavior would be "repeated many times,"[11] a kind of nervous reaction to events so out of the ordinary that there does not seem to be an appropriate response based on the usual fight or flight instincts of our lower brains.

Then he is visited by several creatures who surround his bed, and who seem to carry him aloft and out of the cabin.

It should be noted that both his wife and his young son are with him in the cabin, but they do not seem to have been awakened by the strange noise or by the visitors at this time.

He then winds up in a "messy round room,"[12] and then observes many tiny people rushing about and finds that he is in a state of abject terror. Other events are taking place, but he cannot recall what they are, ascribing this lack of detail to a form of amnesia brought about either by sheer terror or, somewhat more prosaically, by drugs. While neither Whitley Strieber nor his wife, Anne, are drug takers, he implies that he may have been deliberately drugged with some exotic narcotic by the creatures who abducted him and took him to the "messy room."

He describes having his cranium penetrated by a long, thin needle, and then the insult of the infamous "rectal probe." Soon thereafter, his memories end, and he wakes up to a winter morning in the New York woods with a vague recollection of something having happened during the night, but unsure what it was.

During the following weeks, he feels a general mental and physical deterioration as he struggles with the fallout of that night, still unaware of what really happened and equally unaware of an "extraterrestrial" element to the experience. It merely seems to him that he is going insane.

Back in New York City on February 6, 1986, he came across the name of UFO researcher Budd Hopkins in a book about UFOs he had received as a Christmas present but which he had been too afraid to read before, for reasons then unknown to him. Discovering that Hopkins lived in New York City, not far from his own Greenwich Village apartment, he decided to call him although he wasn't quite sure what to say. The images he recalled from the "event" of that night were so abnormal that he did not know if they fit the now-familiar pattern of a close encounter.

Hopkins invited him over and the two spent a few hours discussing the event, and then Hopkins asked whether Strieber had had any similar experiences in the past, and that is when he suddenly remembered an event in October of 1985, an event that was experienced by other witnesses.

It took place in the same cabin in the woods, but this time he had houseguests as well as his wife and son: two authors—one a Romanian immigrant and the author of an account of his experience in a Romanian work camp, and the other an American-born intellectual. His houseguests were aware of a strange light—an unearthly glow—all around the cabin the night of October 4, a light so bright that it woke them up. Whitley thought the cabin was actually on fire, but of course there was no damage. They discussed it—as well as a loud bang the same night, a sound of unknown origin—the following morning, but then thought nothing more about it.

Prompted by Budd Hopkins, Whitley asked his family what they remembered of that night. Whitley's son Andrew said it was the night of the bang, when his father threw his shoe at a fly. When asked who told him about throwing a shoe, Andrew remarked that it was "Just a bunch of people. People who were around."[13] When pressed for more details, specifically about any strange dreams from that period, Andrew readily replied that he had a dream about "little doctors" who put him on a cot and told him not to worry.[14] As one might imagine, this was unwelcome news to Whitley Strieber! What he was dealing with, if it was a hallucination, was a hallucination shared by his family. Either they were all going insane, or there was some external force prompting these strange recollections.

Asking his friends about what they remembered about that October night, they verified the existence of a bright light in the woods and a loud explosion, and Whitley's telling them it was all right: "The light is gone. Go back to sleep."[15]

Eventually, Strieber would seek a hypnotist to enable him to recall more details of the two experiences and transcripts of the sessions are given verbatim in *Communion.* The experience was obviously terrifying, with visions of the world being destroyed and his son being killed, all suggested by the strange beings who had abducted him and forced him to see these images and to react violently toward them. There was also a vision of his father, on a train, surrounded by soldiers in uniform. Whitley later states that this had to be a memory of 1957, returning on a train from a vacation in Madison, Wisconsin back to Texas, where Whitley was born and where the family lived. (This link between Whitley's abduction experiences and a sudden vision of his father in a way that seems out of context will turn out to be quite important, and what eventually led Whitley Strieber to contact this author some years later, as we shall see.)

While Strieber's story in *Communion* refers to events that took place while he was an adult and spending holidays at his cabin in the woods of upstate New York with his family and friends, it becomes clear through his writings that he links that experience with older, more unsettling ones from his childhood. Whitley Strieber has never insisted that he was abducted by what the popular imagination terms "space aliens." He is not convinced that the UFO phenomenon is, strictly speaking, the visitation of the earth by beings from another planet, or that he (and others like him) have been periodically kidnapped by these beings and used in gruesome medical experiments. He keeps an open mind, and as far as I can discern is sincerely seeking to understand what his experience really was, what it represents. While he has interpreted it in spiritual terms, and more so as the years have gone by, he seems nonetheless perfectly willing to accept the beings as space aliens if it could be proved; he is just as willing to accept a verdict of angels or spirits or extra-dimensional creatures of some sort, or even subconscious material surfacing in a unique and powerful way. The important aspect to the case is how the interaction between human beings and these "aliens" is handled, and what changes it can cause in the human psyche. Does "contact" enable a person to become more centered and at the same time more aware? Does it ennoble a person? Does it cause significant psychological change or growth?

Or does it represent something else, something more dangerous?

Harvard professor and psychiatrist John E. Mack, M.D. concludes that those who have experienced "alien abduction" are genuinely suffering from post-traumatic stress disorder (PTSD).[16] That is, they have had an experience which has caused all the psychological and organic reactions typical of soldiers who have been in battle, or people who have witnessed a particularly upsetting event, such as violent death. We may remember that it was just this illness that gave rise to the creation of the *Diagnostic and Statistical Manual* by the US Army; and that Surrealist author Andre Breton used automatic writing to treat soldiers suffering from this disorder. We remember that brainwashing expert William Sargant cut his medical eye teeth on the same disorder. It is—whether one gives it the clinical name "post-traumatic stress disorder" or the more colorful "shell shock" or "battle fatigue"—a virtual mother-lode of inspiration for artists and G-men alike. Mack, who won a Pulitzer Prize for his psycho-biography of Lawrence of Arabia (*A Prince of Our Disorder*), was roundly criticized by his peers for accepting the testimony of abductees at face value; but all he was really doing was explaining to the world at large that these people had apparently suffered from some appalling treatment, since they were exhibiting all the same symptoms as people suffering from shell shock or battle fatigue. Yet, there was nothing in their backgrounds that could account for the experiences. Thus, Mack was inclined to believe that the abductees had experienced something so unusual, and so stressful, that to call it "alien abduction" was not far from the truth.

Malachi Martin also makes a brief appearance in this story, in an encounter he had with a former *Newsweek* journalist, Bruce Lee, who one day was inspecting racks of *Communion* in a bookstore shortly after its release and saw what appeared to Lee to be … well, aliens: short beings dressed oddly, as if in disguise, and laughing at details in the book, complaining of what Whitley "got wrong."[17] The experience unnerved Lee, who later was visited by Fr. Martin, who was one of his authors. (Lee by this time was an editor at publishing house William Morrow.) He told Martin about this strange encounter, at which point Martin—suddenly quite nervous—asked Lee, "Does this experience disturb you?" to which Lee responded, "No." Martin then told him that "they exist."[18] It should be pointed out that Father Martin disturbed Lee more than the aliens; after working with Martin on his book about demonic possession, *Hostage To The Devil*, Lee had to resort to an exorcist himself, because the experience, he said, left him feeling "unclean."

This association of aliens with demons has occupied many writers and thinkers over the past fifty years since the days of Kenneth Arnold, Fred Crisman, and Roswell. (Conceivably, an encounter with either one—I mean aliens and demons, not Arnold or Crisman—would be sufficient cause for a case of post-traumatic stress disorder.)

Eventually, as Whitley Strieber's memories became clearer, he remembered some salient points from his own childhood that could have important bearing on this case, and could explain some of what Mack's patients were experiencing.

At this point, and in the spirit of full disclosure, I have to say for the record that Mr. Strieber contacted me via email a few years ago, after reading my first book, *Unholy Alliance.* His question to me was quite specific: an inquiry concerning Operation Paperclip and the identity of some German officers who had been stationed at Randolph AFB in the 1950s. Since I had spent years researching Nazi Germany and particularly those who escaped justice and wound up in the Americas, it was natural enough that he would contact me for this information.

But as we communicated further, and at length, concerning this period of American history, it became clear that Strieber believed that he may have been a victim of some sort of medical treatment or experiment at the hands of these men. He further believed that some sort of connection existed between the Randolph AFB group and a school in Mexico, and this is where the story came unnervingly close to actual events which are only now coming to light.

For this, we must go back to Whitley's own childhood and the state of the world, and particularly of the United States, in the early 1950s.

We must go back to the Secret School.

THE SECRET SCHOOL

Si la bomba no ha destruido al mundo, ha destruido a nuestra idea del mundo. ... Redescubrimos un sentimiento que acompano siempre a los aztecas, a los hindues y a los cristianos del ano mil. La tecnica comienza por ser una negacion de la imagen del mundo y termina por ser una imagen de la destruccion del mundo.

—Octavio Paz[19]

... Sade was still haunted by the fear of what he called "the black men" who lay in wait to put him away.

—Michel Foucault[20]

Whitley Strieber was born on June 13, 1945 in San Antonio, Texas. The war in Europe was over, but the war in the Pacific was still two months away from its complete and dramatic conclusion, with the dropping of the atomic bombs on Hiroshima and Nagasaki. His father, Karl Strieber, was a well-known and respected attorney who specialized in the petroleum industry, a common-enough occupation in Texas. His mother, Mary, was the daughter of a wealthy businessman. All in all, his home life could be described as "comfortable."

San Antonio—one of the most agreeable of Texas cities—is surrounded by military bases, from the US Army's Fort Sam Houston to several Air Force bases, such as Randolph Air Force Base, which served as the headquarters for the "aviation medicine" effort of the US Army Air Corps (which became the US Air Force). This program was largely staffed by Nazi scientists brought over after the War's end, as recounted in Book I. The most prominent among them, of course, was Dr. Hubertus Strughold, a man who should have been sentenced at Nuremberg, but who was rescued by American military scientists eager to make use of his expertise in the relatively new field of "aviation medicine" ... a field whose guinea pigs had been chosen from the death camps of the Third Reich. Strughold paid it forward, and rescued in turn a number of his own colleagues, falsifying documents and *curricula vitae* so that the cream of the crop could accompany him to relative security and luxury in the United States. The end result was that Randolph AFB became a kind of sanctuary for scientists who were used to experimenting on living human subjects.

This type of experimentation was not limited to testing the limits of physical endurance at zero-g, but also included psychological and neurological testing. Hallucinations are a natural part of the isolation of a high-altitude pilot, due to the sensory deprivation and lack of oxygen that occurs from long periods of solitude in the air, and experiments were conducted to determine how long an individual pilot can remain sensory deprived before hitting the panic button. Incredibly, many test subjects reported the same hallucination: little yellow men in black hats. This gave rise to speculation that the visions are triggered by some sort of neurological factor, thus far unknown and unidentified.

In Whitley Strieber's communications with me, he expressed a suspicion that perhaps he himself had been a test subject at Randolph. He mentioned Dr. Strughold by name, and also a mysterious Dr. Antonio Krause, whom I have so far been unable to identify, but who figures strongly in Strieber's memories as related to me and on his own Web site. To understand why he would have come to that conclusion—and why it could be seriously entertained—we must understand what the climate was like in the United States at that time: the immediate Postwar period.

America had gone from the universally-acknowledged victor of World War II to the first atomic superpower in the same year, 1945. America had done the unimaginable: it had developed a weapon of mass destruction, a bomb so powerful that one dropped from a plane could level an entire city, killing hundreds of thousands of people in the process and guaranteeing generations of hereditary illnesses from exposure to high doses of radiation. Then, almost immediately, America found itself facing its greatest enemy to date: the threat of Communism.

It was General Patton who is famously quoted as saying that America had fought the wrong enemy in the war; that the true evil was that represented by the Soviet Union and, later, Red China. In 1950, the Korean War began, as North Korean troops—supplied and supported by Mao's China—began an assault on Seoul, with the aim of creating a Communist Korea. United

Nations troops—largely composed of American soldiers, but including combatants from many nations—fought a desperate and harrowing struggle to help South Korea repel the invaders, and a few years later the war came to an uneasy truce with a country still divided.

At the same time that the Korean War was coming to a close, Vietnam had become another flashpoint, with the defeat of the French military forces at Dien Bien Phu and the eventual splitting of the country into a Communist North Vietnam and a democratic Republic of Vietnam in the South.

The war against Communism was an ideological conflict; the Communists were atheists who persecuted religion, and this was generally enough to turn most Americans into rabid anti-Communists. The American government did not shy away from using whatever tools came to hand in this life-and-death struggle for the planet. As we have seen, these tools included Nazi scientists, spies, mercenaries, and medical men; but these tools also extended to American children.

As a child growing up in America in the 1950s, the author experienced some of this first-hand. We were taught to expect an aerial attack at any time, and were trained in how to protect ourselves from a bombardment: the old "stick your head between your knees and kiss your ass goodbye" position. We rehearsed this every week, as air raid sirens went off in the city like something out of a World War II propaganda film. Of course, this could be construed as a kind of psychological warfare, conducted by the government on its own citizens, since it is doubtful that in the 1950s the Soviet Union possessed the military capability necessary to invade the United States or bomb Chicago (where I lived for a while as a child and learned to "duck and cover."). They had been devastated in the war, lost more than twenty million of their people to fighting and starvation, and had their hands full in Eastern Europe. No matter; as a child I was taken to visit Nike missile bases and given lectures on the Communist threat. We were told to be aware, and to report suspicious activity. In some cases, children were encouraged to spy on their neighbors, or even on members of their own families; certainly, they were keeping an eye on their teachers.

We grew up with the Bomb. It was always there, in the background, ready to destroy the world's civilizations at only a few moments' notice. We were told what it would be like: the intense flash of light, the hurricane-force winds, the disintegration at ground zero, the blowing out of windows and destruction of buildings miles from the center of the blast. We were shown how people in Hiroshima had been reduced to photo images: shadowy shapes on walls and bridges made by the brilliant blast, all that was left of the people who, a moment earlier, had been standing in those spots. We grew up with Armageddon a sudden plausibility ... and the end of the millennium was less than fifty years away. The end of the world seemed like something one reasonably should plan for.

We grew up with air raid shelters. There were those in our city neighborhoods: basements of churches and schools with the familiar yellow-and-black signs and the stockpile of medicines and canned food. Outside the cities, people began building their own shelters: in their backyards or below their homes, concrete bunkers with candles, flashlights, bottled water, and transistor radios (a new invention). America was preparing for a pre-emptive first strike, nuclear winter, and possible invasion.

With all of this threat and perceived threat in the air, a daily experience for most of us, it was natural that red-blooded American citizens should be prepared to make the necessary sacrifices to defeat the Communist enemy wherever it could be found. Communism was sneaky; it wasn't quite the same as the German-American Bund of the 1930s, holding marches in the Yorkville section of New York City to support the Nazi Party in Germany. Communism was more covert; people spoke of "Communist infiltration" and "fellow travelers." People spoke of something—a newspaper article, a book, a movie—as being "Communist inspired." When some Americans came to their senses and started calling the Army–McCarthy hearings a "witch hunt," they were more right than they knew. Arthur Miller saw it, and wrote *The Crucible*, a play ostensibly about the Salem witchcraft trials but seen—more correctly—as a parable about the anti-Communist hysteria gripping America at that time. We saw how this theme influenced Miller's wife, the actress Marilyn Monroe, who became more sympathetic towards Communism as the years went on.

It was understood that the Soviet Union—and those countries identified as "satellites" of the Soviet Union, i.e., Eastern European countries such as Poland, Hungary, Czechoslovakia, and East Germany—brainwashed its children and taught them to spy on their own parents. Whether this was true or not, it was a powerful image when seen in the United States, which had just come from confronting brainwashing first hand in Korea. The CIA went to great pains to find a way to counteract this threat, focusing on the soldier in the field at first; but it has always been whispered that the intelligence agencies—either the CIA or the military intelligence organs, or both—experimented in some way or form on children in the United States in the 1950s.

Only scraps of evidence have ever come to light. As mentioned in Chapter Sixteen there is published documentation proving that children were used in drug experiments in the United States, drugs that included LSD. In Montreal in the 1950s, we know that children in orphanages were used experimentally, particularly in those orphanages run by the Catholic Church, once they had been diagnosed as "retarded" or categorized with some other mental illness as a ruse for the institution to earn additional government funds. We also know that Montreal in the 1950s was the scene for some of the CIA's most imaginative and chilling psychological experiments, those of Dr. Ewen Cameron at his Mount Royal "Ravenscroft" clinic. This precedent—that of the CIA using medical institutions in foreign countries as contractors for their psychological experiments—is worthwhile studying, for it may reveal a pattern.

While the hideous example of Dr. Cameron's psychic driving and other programs in Canada is by now well-known to those who study this field, there is virtually no information about similar programs undertaken south of the border, in Mexico.

But there is the Finders case.

As we saw earlier, when US government officials were called in on February 5, 1987, due to the arrest of two men in Florida in connection with the suspected trafficking of children to Mexico, with the subsequent discovery that a group called "Finders" was involved in everything from ritual sacrifice to international travel to proscribed destinations (like North Korea and North Vietnam), and had ties with Chinese embassy officials in Hong Kong, among other things, the lid was clamped down tight and the American public was not allowed to know anything more about this group that had ties to the CIA. Since then, the entire case has been stonewalled and whitewashed; we have been presented with a picture of Finders that is innocuous and bland, and the arrests just a big misunderstanding. But there is no misunderstanding what Washington, D.C. area police discovered at the Finders headquarters, or the fact that several small children were in the charge of two well-dressed men who were taking them to a "special school" in Mexico, a school for very bright children. This report of the school in Mexico has never been followed up; that part of the story died when the police were told—by the CIA—to keep away from it. Strangely, the news media also dropped the story.

No one knows what happened to the children who were picked up in Florida: filthy, in tattered clothing, ignorant about things like television and computers but nonetheless quite intelligent, they disappeared from view as surely as the story disappeared from the newspapers. To put together a scenario of what might have happened all we have is the inventory list of what police found at Finders headquarters, and that included photographs of children participating in animal sacrifice; copies of communications between Chinese nationals and Finders on the subject of trafficking in human beings and "obtaining children for unspecified purposes"; instructions on money laundering; and more.

Since then, some (but not all) of this has been explained away by the Finders leader, Marion Pettie, who has put a benign and eccentric spin on the facts. Context is everything, and Pettie paints his organization in a kind of loopy, New Age light that has nothing to do with espionage, psychological warfare, brainwashing, or any of that Cold War impedimenta. Yes, he and his family have CIA connections going back to the 1950s. Yes, they killed a goat, and children *were* present. But this is all being taken out of context, he insists. The reality is really quite boring.

Yet, he has never answered any questions concerning the travel to Communist countries in the 1950s through 1970s, or the telex traffic with the

Chinese embassy in Hong Kong concerning the purchase of two children, or the fact that Finders had files on their activities and the activities of their members all over the globe. As a matter of national security, we are not allowed to ask these questions or to reopen the case. The matter is closed, and the US Customs and Metropolitan Police Department files are locked away in a file marked SECRET.

What happened to the children? Where were they going?

As Maury Terry continued his investigation of the Son of Sam cult, an investigation that became more linked with the Process or one of its offshoots—through statements made by former Process members—he kept hearing the cult called by a peculiar name, "The Children." David Berkowitz knew the cult by this name, and it was stated by Terry that a wealthy émigré from Postwar Germany who lived in the Yonkers area was an important leader. This man has since died. Terry, who knows the man's name, did not divulge it in his book, but he did attend the wake and saw the proliferation of black flowers around the man's coffin.

The Children.

A noted psychotherapist and expert on hypnosis, D. Corydon Hammond, has also insisted that a satanic cult exists in America that was begun by Nazi émigrés after the war, and that this cult abuses and even sacrifices children as part of its ritual.[21] If we put this together with Terry's discovery, we begin to see a pattern emerging … particularly as the Nazis could not have come to America and begun developing their network without at least preliminary support by American intelligence officials. It is possible that the tales of a nationwide Nazi–Satanic cult that sacrifices children is only the smoke from a much smaller, but potentially more dangerous, fire.

The facts that we have to hand may be of help:

We know, for instance, that Nazi scientists and medical professionals were allowed to emigrate to the United States after the war as part of Operation Paperclip and succeeding efforts to rescue as many Nazi professionals as possible in the effort to contain Communism. We also know that American intelligence hired an entire network of Nazi spies to assist them in combating the Soviet Union, a network known as the Gehlen Organization. We also know that many Eastern European Waffen-SS and other Nazi troops, including high-ranking officers, were allowed to emigrate to America after the War, and in some cases (such as that of Valerian Trifa of the Romanian Orthodox Church and the Iron Guard) became prominent in Eastern Orthodox churches in the United States, either as clergymen or as financial supporters, and wound up holding positions of prominence in American political organizations. We also know that CIA Director Allen Dulles had a critical role to play in covering up details of his involvement with Nazi officials. All of this has been covered in detail, and fully documented, in Books I and II.

Knowing all of this, is it so far-fetched an idea that some of these Nazis were allowed—or encouraged—to continue their medical and psychological programs in America? Or, where it was considerably safer, in Canada or Mexico under CIA or military intelligence auspices?

What Whitley Strieber describes—the involvement of Nazi scientist Hubertus Strughold in the experimentation program—is not beyond the realm of possibility. That Randolph AFB would have been chosen as the site of this activity is logical, as it was the center for aviation medicine research, a broad category that included virtually anything having to do with neurological, biological, and psychological testing. It was also close to the Strieber home in San Antonio, Texas.

However, how can we accept that the young son of a prominent San Antonio attorney would have been selected for psychological experimentation by the US Army?

The answer lies in the context of the times.

In the immediate Postwar years, as the Soviet Union gradually assumed the mantle of our cosmic enemy, Americans were called as never before to do what they could to contain and eventually destroy this threat. It seemed as if Communism was erupting all over the world, from Asia to Europe to Latin America. Educators, scientists, journalists, and businessmen were called to the service of the CIA, enlisted in the global fight against the Red Menace and the Yellow Peril. It is hard for those who did not grow up in those times to realize just how much this sentiment insinuated itself into the lives of those who did. The orgy of red-baiting, loyalty oaths, and purges of government agencies, and the entertainment and other industries, was a constant backbeat to the news reports of new Communist successes, of falling dominoes around the world. All Americans were expected to do what they could to help in this Manichaean struggle between West and East, between Capitalism and Communism, between Democracy and Dictatorship.

Many children in those days were tested for intelligence, and some were selected for further tests. We only have bits and pieces of information about these programs available to us now, some only on the basis of personal testimony. The memories recorded by Whitley Strieber of his childhood encounters with the "visitors" at the secret school hidden within San Antonio's Olmos Basin *may be*, he admits, screen memories of actual psychological testing that was done on behalf of American intelligence and conducted by the Nazi doctors of Randolph AFB, tests that could have included hallucinogenic drugs such as LSD and psilocybin. We know that such testing was done on children, for instance at Creedmore in the 1960s. We do not know how much drug testing was done by the military at this time, although we do know that such men as Andrija Puharich were conducting all sorts of psychological and chemical tests on behalf of the US Army in the 1950s. We also know that, at that same time, the CIA was not above dosing its own employees and contractors with LSD and other substances without their knowledge, as the Frank Olson tragedy clearly demonstrates.

Without going into a discussion of whether or not Whitley Strieber's experiences with the visitors were actually memories of medical experimentation by the Nazi doctors of Randolph, or were genuine experiences of alien abduction and mental programming, we can accept—at least theoretically—that there is a basis for believing that young Whitley (or others like him) were subjected to some form of psychological experimentation during the 1950s, and that this experimentation may have included the use of psychotropic substances. We can accept this, because there is enough documentation to prove that programs like this were already in existence, and that the American government agencies and private medical teams involved were not above employing these tests on unwitting human subjects, including children. San Antonio, Texas was a military town. Many of the local people owed their jobs to either the military or to the petroleum industry. There were Army bases and Air Force bases, and the mysterious Randolph AFB with its coterie of unrepentant Nazis. Patriotic American parents might have been willing (or even proud) to have their children placed in experimental programs, assured by their own government that the testing would be passive, non-invasive and benign, especially if their children had shown a high IQ or other abilities on standard tests administered by the school system.

In that context, and in the 1950s, anything was possible.

Nuclear physicist Jack Sarfatti (intimate of Saul Paul Sirag, Andrija Puharich, Uri Geller, Ira Einhorn, Philip K. Dick, Carlos Castaneda, Barbara Honegger, and many others) has written about a similar experience he had as a primary school student around the same time, in 1952, an experience in which he places a lot of stock and which was obviously a seminal event in his life. He had been identified as boy with a genius IQ, and preparations would soon be made to send him to Cornell University on a full scholarship at the age of 17. In the meantime, however, he received a strange phone call at his home in the Flatbush section of Brooklyn.

According to Sarfatti's own account in *The Destiny Matrix* (1995), and also available on the Internet,

> The telephone rings. I pick it up. I hear curious clanking mechanical sounds like relays clicking. A distant cold metallic voice speaking numbers gets louder.
>
> "Who are you?" I ask.
>
> "I am a conscious computer on board a spacecraft … We have identified you as one of four hundred young bright receptive minds … You must give us your decision now. If you say yes, you will begin to link up with the others in twenty years."

After a few seconds, young Sarfatti agrees, and the voice replies,"Good, go to your firescape [*sic*]. We will send a ship to pick you up in ten minutes.

Nothing happened.

Sarfatti then goes on to explain how he later became a member of a group of gifted children, an after-school coterie led by one Walter Breen (1928-1993), "a graduate student at Columbia and well known Numismatist associated with psychologist William Shelden."[22] Walter Breen is a fascinating person in his own right. His *Complete Encyclopedia of US and Colonial Coins* is the definitive volume on this subject, and retails today for $135. But he was also very familiar to the science fiction circles of the 1960s, and was a co-founder of the Society for Creative Anachronism (SCA). He also wrote, under the pseudonym J.Z. Eglinton, *Greek Love*, a text that has been referenced by the North American Man Boy Love Association (NAMBLA) as supportive of their philosophy concerning sexual relationships between men and boys. Breen had been arrested before for child molestation, and would be again at the end of his life.

But the gifted children group to which Sarfatti belonged was somehow linked with the Sandia Corporation, now part of Lockheed Martin, a charter member of the Defense–Energy establishment. In an email posted on a Web site (http://groups.yahoo.com/group/ItalianPhysicsCenter/message/79) and dated July 16, 2001, Sarfatti writes, "Breen was talking about extra dimensions, telepathy, remote viewing, UFOs, mutant humans, contact with aliens ... Sandia was trying to develop us as super-kids to have paranormal powers and to deal with extra-dimensional intelligence." Sandia is still involved with gifted children to this day, in cooperation with a "super kids" program that selects very bright students to work with its supercomputer.

As for Walter Breen, he eventually married Marion Zimmer Bradley (1930-1999), the science-fiction author of *The Mists of Avalon* (and author of much lesbian fiction besides, who was very active in gay counseling as well as a contributor to *The Mattachine Review*) who would bear two children (in addition to a child by her first marriage) while they were married and before their separation in 1979. Even more fascinating is the fact that, in 1980, both Marion Zimmer Bradley and Walter *Breen would be ordained as priests in the Eastern Orthodox Church by Bishop Michael Itkin,* making their line of apostolic succession (via Bishop, and now "Saint," Carl Stanley) the same as David Ferrie's! (As you can see, it is virtually impossible to extricate the material of this book from the moist-palm grasp of the ubiquitous wandering bishops.)

The data in Sarfatti's article/book-in-progress reads like a history and who's-who of American (and foreign) alternative culture in the 1970s. Twenty years after his strange phone call (and, as we discover later, there were more than one) he was indeed linked with some of the brightest and most creative minds on the planet. He has considered whether or not the phone call was some kind of hoax, but he is reluctant to accept that explanation. Others have had similar phone calls, he tells us, and—of course—the spaceship-computer scenario was playing out even then with Andrija Puharich and his circle in their evocation of The Nine (albeit unknown to young Sarfatti—or anyone else—at the time). Incidentally, and congruent with our overall thesis, Sarfatti was also heavily influenced by the surrealist film *Orphee* by Jean Cocteau.

He became involved with the Stanford Research Institute at about this time (1973), and with Hal Puthoff and Russel Targ, scientists who were involved in SRI's "remote viewing" and other paranormal experiments. Until this association, Sarfatti considers himself to have been"anti-mystical" (Sarfatti Web site), but during his time with SRI he begins to realize the importance of those mysterious phone calls made twenty years earlier. He also discovers that artist and remote viewer Ingo Swann "channeled" a "cold, metallic voice from a saucer 100 years into future" at Stanford Research Institute (SRI), along with our friend Barbara Honegger (she of the "October Surprise" episode). SRI, of course, was also the place where Israeli psychic Uri Geller was tested in 1973.[23] In 1975, in a separate series of tests of Uri Geller's psychic abilities by a team at Lawrence Livermore Laboratories (where much of America's nuclear weapons research takes place; the scientists were worried that someone with Geller's abilities would be able to trigger a nuclear device or scramble a computer system using only his mind), scientists recorded another "distinctive, metallic-sounding voice, unheard during the actual experiment but now clearly audible."[24] Among the few words that could be made out, however, was "the code name of a very closely held government project. The project had nothing to do with psychic research, and neither it nor its code name was known to … Livermore."[25] More about the Lawrence Livermore incident in the following chapter, but in line with the experience of Sarfatti, one of the Livermore scientists actually received a phone call from the "strange metallic voice," which told him and the team to cease the experiments with Uri Geller. They did, and were left alone after that.[26]

(In a side note, Sarfatti also reveals that he had been a member of the Civil Air Patrol (CAP) in New York at the age of fourteen. In attempting to put together his timeline, it occurred to me that he was in the CAP at the same time as David Ferrie and Lee Harvey Oswald, but of course a thousand miles away from the New Orleans operation. At that same time, my parents were also members of the CAP, but in the Cook County, Illinois area. Considering that my father had right-wing sentiments and a history as a segregationist … well, you can see where I'm going with this!)

Thus begins a personal odyssey, during which Sarfatti discovers he is descended from a Knight Templar, hangs out with science-fiction authors Philip K. Dick and Robert Anton Wilson, meets Carlo Suares (*The Cipher of Genesis*), is told by some Theosophists that he is the reincarnation of their

Bishop Leadbetter (the gay and "wandering" bishop who on a beach in India discovered the young boy who would become future spiritual guru Krishnamurti), and on and on.

Sarfatti is a scientist, and if you read some of the email exchanges posted on the Internet between him and other physicists and physicist-wannabes, you will become very quickly bogged down in a quagmire of calculus and contempt. The internecine wars between physicists are as unseemly as those between Kennedy assassination theorists or battling UFO apologists; but in the end the fact that Sarfatti *is* a scientist is what stands out. And while his childhood experiences do not match, chapter and verse, those of Whitley Strieber, there are very strong and suggestive parallels between the two. Both are contacted by alien intelligences; both are linked to spacecraft; both are "identified" by these intelligences while they are quite young: Whitley was nine years old, and Sarfatti was about twelve. Both had their experiences in roughly the same timeframe: the early 1950s. Sarfatti was "contacted" in 1952/53; Strieber in 1954. Both were members of a "secret school" that had associations with paranormal abilities and UFOs.

Sarfatti mentions in another email exchange, from June 2002, that he had been "studied" by the US Army in the late 1940s, and goes on to describe the after-school group led by Walter Breen as the "McDermott-Sheldon-Breen 'Columbia-Sandia eugenics' connection of 1953-56."[27] Again, this is a very suggestive timeframe in which to be placing events so similar as those related by Sarfatti and Strieber.

In yet another place Sarfatti goes into more detail about this observation by the Army.[28] He claims it occurred at "US Army Quarter Masters in Lower Manhattan in the late 1940s soon after the alleged Roswell incident," and mentions that his mentor Walter Breen told him that he (i.e., Breen) had been in a plane crash in 1947 and had complete amnesia of the event, only coming to later in an Army hospital. 1947, of course, was the year of the Roswell incident. Sarfatti wonders if there was a connection between Breen and Roswell. (Breen would later go on to become a charter member of the American MENSA organization.)

It is not only Sarfatti who has a single degree of separation between himself and the UFOs, however. One of Whitley Strieber's neighbors was the Colonel in charge of the air base from which Captain Mantell went on his fateful chase of a UFO, and became the first ever military casualty of a UFO in American history. (More about this in a bit.) Young Whitley used to play in the Colonel's swimming pool with the Colonel's own son.[29]

(And, in the spirit once again of full disclosure, the author must acknowledge that he was approached in 1961-62 after an intelligence test of some kind administered by his school in the sixth grade. I was never told the results of this test, but a parade of teachers and other, unidentifiable, persons coming into my classroom to stare at me made me aware there was something odd going on. Later that same school year, after a science fair in which I made an exhibit out of CAP navigational materials such as maps, plotters, etc., men representing Cornell University came to visit my teacher and to speak with my parents about my attending a special class there. I never knew the outcome of those visits, but suspect that—due to my father's FBI records—I was rejected as potentially subversive!)

Whatever opinion one may hold of Whitley Strieber—fraud, psychotic, contactee, abductee, mystic, trickster, or honestly concerned about inexplicable events in his own life and the life of the world—one is hard put to categorize Sarfatti the same way. Yet they both share an experience of alien contact while children, an experience that neither yet fully understands: Was it a hoax? Was it "real"? Were the perpetrators aliens? US government officials? Something else?

Sarfatti's involvement with the Columbia–Sandia "superkids" program is no mystery, and neither is the existence of Walter Breen. Strieber's difficulty lies in the fact that there is very little corroboration of his experience, aside from some other children (now adults) in the neighborhood in those years who used to disappear for hours at a time in the Olmos Basin, and aside from Whitley's discovery of the buildings used by the "secret school" during a taping for a television series, *Contact,* right where he had always claimed they would be.[30]

What seems a certainty is that both men had something done to them as children during the Cold War, something that may have been government-sanctioned. And if we find that theory far-fetched, we only have to remember how the CIA covered up the Finders revelations in the name of national security. Whatever happened to Sarfatti—and what seems to have happened to Strieber—it bore fruit. Sarfatti has become well-known as both a scientist and as a popularizer of quantum physics through his books and collaborative efforts with other scientists, writers, and thinkers. He has pursued the idea of alien intelligence relentlessly, searching for the physics that would make stellar travel possible and stretching the limits of quantum mechanics to break Einstein's "wall of light," i.e., to find a way to travel faster than the speed of light and thus master the space-time continuum.

Strieber has heroically recorded his experiences with "the visitors," knowing full well that he was subjecting himself to near-universal ridicule and humiliation. He was (and is) a successful novelist whose books become movies; like Philip Corso, he had no need to jump into this particular fray and take a stand one way or another. Yet, while Sarfatti pursues the science behind the alien experience, name-dropping like mad (and why not?) and trading good-natured insults with some of the world's most intelligent human beings, Strieber is struggling to find a meaning to all of this that transcends science, a spiritual or perhaps existential paradigm lurking behind the flashing lights, the speeding saucers, the bug-eyed monsters of our nightmares.

Both men were touched by something supernatural in their childhoods during the Cold War that led each on his own path, paths that converge—perhaps—during recess at the secret school.

A COLD, METALLIC VOICE

A clean mind is one that has been brainwashed.
—Walter Breen

Sarfatti is obviously convinced that the "cold, metallic voice" he heard over the phone was some type of paranormal communication, either of alien beings actually hovering overhead in a spacecraft of some kind or something that has yet to be fully identified and described. He admits it *may* have been part of an ultra-secret government program, a kind of brainwashing or mind-control experiment, but he insists that it was not a hoax or a prank. In this, he is running parallel in his thinking to that of Whitley Strieber, who also heard a "machine-like voice" during his contacts with the Visitors.[31]

What many UFOlogists and "fellow travelers" may not realize, however, is that this "cold, metallic voice" has an impressive pedigree in the United States, even before computers, radios, and other modern communications media existed to give us an idea of what that kind of voice would sound like.

In M.V. Ingram's ambitiously entitled *An Authenticated History of the Famous Bell Witch. The Wonder of the 19th Century, and Unexplained Phenomenon of the Christian Era. The Mysterious Talking Goblin That Terrorized the West End of Robertson County, Tennessee, Tormenting John Bell to His Death. The Story of Besty Bell, Her Lover and the Haunting Sphinx*, published in Clarksville, Tennessee in 1894, we read of an encounter between General Andrew Jackson and the famous Bell Witch. One section is worth quoting here, and takes place when General Jackson is on the move through Robertson County, Tennessee in the vicinity of the Bell Witch. His wagon freezes on a level road, and no amount of coaxing the horses or pulling by his troops will enable the wagon to move an inch. The wheels are removed, the axles inspected, and there is no indication of a problem with either the wagon or with the road. It is a bizarre situation in and of itself, but then:

> All stood off looking at the wagon in serious meditation, for they were "stuck." Gen. Jackson after a few moments thought, realizing that they were in a fix, threw up his hands exclaiming, "By the eternal, boys, it is the witch." Then came the sound of a sharp metallic voice from the bushes, saying, "All right General, let the wagon move on, I will see you tonight." The men in bewildered astonishment looked in every direction to see if they could discover from whence came the strange voice, but could find no explanation to the mystery. Gen. Jackson exclaimed again, "By the eternal, boys, this is worse than fighting the British." The horses then started

> unexpectedly of their own accord, and the wagon rolled along as light and smoothly as ever.

Jackson's entourage arrived later that night at Mr. Bell's home, where they sat up waiting for the witch to keep her promise. They had with them a self-described "witch layer," or exorcist, who kept a pistol loaded with a silver bullet, ready to destroy the phantom.

> Presently perfect quiet reigned, and then was heard a noise like dainty footsteps prancing over the floor, and quickly following, the same metallic voice heard in the bushes rang out from one corner of the room, exclaiming, "All right, General, I am on hand ready for business."[32]

The "witch layer" then tried to shoot in the direction of the voice, but his pistol would not fire. Eventually the Bell Witch grabbed the man by his nose and threw him out of the house, much to the consternation as well as the amusement of General Jackson and his men, who could nonetheless not actually see what was causing the witch layer so much discomfort. The Witch then assured Jackson that it would return the following night, but Jackson could not convince his men to hang around much longer and they left with daybreak.

This account is that of one Colonel Thomas L. Yancey, a lawyer in Clarksville, who compiled this story from surviving eyewitnesses, and then sent the report to M.V. Ingram for inclusion in his book in 1894. What is interesting is the statement—made twice—that the Bell Witch spoke in a "metallic voice." One wonders what that meant to people living in 1894? Was that the phrase used by his eyewitnesses, who would have heard that voice during Jackson's lifetime (1767-1845), more specifically in the early decades of the nineteenth century? The Witch evidently possessed paranormal abilities, was invisible, but spoke English tolerably well despite the strange sound of her voice. This would seem to fit neatly with the characteristics noted by Sarfatti.

To be sure, the UFO phenomenon itself is not new. Strange lights in the sky have bedeviled humanity for centuries, if not millennia, and so have the strange creatures who either pilot the craft or are just along for the ride.

French scientist Jacques Vallee has seriously studied this phenomenon for many years ,and discusses his findings in a series of books, most notably among them *Messengers of Deception* and *Passport to Magonia.* He admits that it is foolish to discount the thousands of UFO reports as nothing more than mistaken sightings of the planet Venus, or swamp gas, or the other frankly unbelievable "scientific" explanations of the events. Researcher John Keel, whose book *The Mothman Prophecies* was eventually made into a film starring Richard Gere, is even more forward when he claims that our planet is "haunted." He sees—as does Vallee and many others—the UFO experience as analogous (if not identical) to the experience of demons, fairies, and other monsters from other times. The fact that we now describe these events in terms that make it sound as if the "visitors" are space travelers may be more a reflection of how our culture is oriented in the aftershock of nuclear explosions and lunar missions than of any kind of "objective" reality. It may be the same experience as seeing demons, or fairies, only filtered through a modern consciousness and more "scientific" sensitivity.

Keel reports many instances of strange phone calls connected to UFO activity and UFO "contactees." He himself was the recipient of many such strange calls, and at one time the number of strange calls to members of UFO groups around the country reached such a crescendo that it contributed to the eventual breakup of many of these groups. The calls would range from electronic beeps and clanking noises—such as Sarfatti first experienced with the "spaceship" call—to threats, to persons imitating the voices of friends, to static … and in some cases the caller would play back taped conversations the recipient had moments or days ago with other parties, as if to demonstrate that the phone lines were tapped. This indicates either that the government was behind this elaborate campaign of intimidation and disinformation, or that some other force with unlimited resources was the culprit. No private organization or company—no Minutemen or Michigan Militia, Ku Klux Klan or Black Panthers, Weathermen or Conservative Coalition—has the ability to mount such an aggressive campaign against the UFO groups, and more importantly no motivation to do so. If we accept the data given in Keel's book—and in so many other reports published over the last thirty to fifty years—then we are forced to assume that the American government was responsible for the phone calls, the mysterious "men in black," and other related phenomena associated with the UFO experiencers. If the American government was *not* responsible, then we have a potentially more serious problem on our hands.

It is not the intention of this author to weigh in on one side or the other in the UFO controversy. I have never seen a UFO, have never been abducted by aliens or had any analogous experiences. I have seen the fabled "men in black," however, when an old black Cadillac drove up in front of my home one afternoon and the driver aimed a camera with a telephoto lens at me. When I tried to confront them, the vehicle drove away quickly and was replaced by another, this time containing two rather short women instead of two men, who drove into my driveway—blocking my car and preventing me from chasing the Cadillac—left their vehicle, and stood before me asking me sweetly if I knew where a "Mr. Devilbis" lived. Startled, I responded in the negative although the name was familiar to me: it was that of a manufacturing company somewhere in the Midwest to which, a few weeks earlier, I had been referred by a former co-worker as a possible client for some electronic work. There was no Devilbis anywhere in the immediate vicinity of the town where I lived, however, and none for almost fifty miles in any direction. It wasn't until years later that a "deconstruction" of that event led me to the amusing revelation that "Devilbis" was actually two words: "devil" and Latin "bis," meaning "the second devil" or "the devil, again."

Why this visitation should have taken place is beyond me. As I said, I am not a UFO contactee and have never belonged to any of the UFO groups or really had anything at all to do with UFOs. My specialty has always been history and culture, specifically the history of religions and mystical movements. But this was the winter before the Gulf War began, and it is possible that my 1960s experiences with a variety of anti-war groups and other radical associations would have flagged me in some kind of government computer. At least, that is what I told myself in those days even though, on reflection, it doesn't make any sense. It is quite costly to maintain a surveillance operation using two cars and four agents for a single individual who has had nothing to do with politics in over twenty years. Of course, my business took me all over the world, and especially to China, but that still does not rate me two cars, four agents, a telephoto lens and "Devilbis." I have never been able to determine the cause of the event, or the identities of the individuals involved or the organization, if any, to which they belonged. I did have another similar run-in years later, however, at Changi Airport in Singapore, when a young woman appeared from out of nowhere, dressed like a 1950s spy in a trenchcoat—totally inappropriate for Singapore weather!—and who smiled at me and tapped me on the shoulder, gave me a little wave, and disappeared again.

And so it goes.

THE STARGATE CONSPIRACY

... *NASA is the disturbed child of two dysfunctional parents—paranoia and war.*
—Graham Hancock[33]

In 1999, the authorial team of Lynn Picknett and Clive Prince published *The Stargate Conspiracy*,[34] an exposé of what appeared to be a US government conspiracy to control access to the type of information that people like Jack Sarfatti, Hal Puthoff and others were accumulating on their own. Picknett and Prince connected this conspiracy to activities surrounding the Pyramids and the Sphinx in Egypt, but focused as well on the circle of mystics around Andrija Puharich and the alien intelligences known as "The Nine." Missing the most crucial connection of all, however—that of Arthur Young, Ruth Paine and Lee Harvey Oswald—they ended their book with the breathless expectation that something of awesome global importance would occur at or near the millennium at the site of the Pyramids at Gizeh. Nothing of that nature transpired ... at least, not that we know of, anyway!

But their research is valuable in other ways. Picknett and Prince have been rummaging through the Catholic closet for a while, coming up with new spins on the Shroud of Turin (*Turin Shroud—In Whose Image?*) and the Knights Templar (*The Templar Revelation: Secret Guardians of the True Identity of Christ*), going to the same well as the team of Baigent, Lincoln and Leigh before them (*Holy Blood, Holy Grail*). What makes *The Stargate Conspiracy* unique is the level of research into lesser known realms, less well-trod paths of arcane knowledge and secret societies with political connections. For many readers, it might have been the first time they came across the names that were once household words among the New Age crowd of the 1970s: Uri Geller, Andrija Puharich and the rest. The fact that the event of momentous import at the millennium apparently did not occur when they said it would is no reason to ignore this book, which is full of detail concerning some of the most colorful individuals of our time, and some of the most sinister associations. It is also useful for its introduction into the world of Egyptology, and the political machinations that take place both within and without the Cairo Museum.

The reason for this is a belief—held by some individuals and groups, including (the authors insist) elements of the US Government—that the Egyptian gods were extra-terrestrial beings. Aliens. And that the Pyramids of Gizeh and the Sphinx somehow conceal evidence of this, either in their construction or in whatever may be buried beneath them, or both. Indeed, "The Nine" itself is a reference to the council of Nine Gods—the Ennead—in Egyptian religion, and thus reinforces the links between ancient Egypt, alien civilizations, and the séances with The Nine conducted (on behalf of the military?) by Andrija Puharich and his group totaling nine members.

The field of paleo-astronomy is esoteric in itself; when you mix it up with eccentric ideas about history and archaeology you are only asking for trouble. Academia will either ignore you (at best), or ridicule you. You will be lumped in with the cranks and the crackpots, the un-credentialed and un-accredited "amateur historians," who have no business kicking sand at the tenured bullies who occupy their privileged positions in sunny safety from the deep water of rushing currents of controversy and treacherous whirlpools of contradictory and anomalous evidence, rather like beached whales. Yet, as the decades have gone by, it has become more and more obvious that many of our ancient structures—Stonehenge, the Pyramids, the Adena and Hopewell mounds—were astronomically oriented. Academia will grudgingly accept that some of these edifices were built in such a way that the rising of the sun on the summer or winter solstice was accommodated in their design, so that rays of the sun would fall through a specific aperture in the stone or wood or earthen construction (as is obvious to anyone who has been there at the time). The ultimate purpose for this, of course, is a matter of some debate. Those academics who wish to support this theory will go so far as to state that these astronomically-oriented creations were used as a kind of calendar, telling primitive man when to sow and when to reap. The problem with this uneasy concession is that the constructions are often much more elaborate than that, and consumed a great deal of primitive society's time and resources to build.

In the case of the Pyramids, a serious attempt has been made to associate their design and orientation with the constellation Orion.[35] In the case of the Gothic cathedrals of France, Louis Charpentier (*Les Mysteres du Chartres*) has put forward the theory that they were built in imitation of the zodiacal sign Virgo (for "virgin," since each of these cathedrals were known as a "Notre Dame" or "Our Lady"). This approach to archaeology and "sacred architecture" was anticipated in that classic of the scientific interpretation of myth, *Hamlet's Mill*,[36] in which the authors deconstruct many famous world myths to demonstrate that they had astronomical significance and were referencing events that had taken place in the heavens.

A full discussion of these ideas is outside the scope of this book, and the interested reader is encouraged to seek out *Hamlet's Mill* in particular for an engrossing and illuminating exposition of these themes, before going on to the more popular *The Orion Mystery* and some of the other titles fighting for shelf space in either the New Age section, the Ancient History section, or somewhere in between. One would be amiss not to mention R.A. Schwaller de Lubicz' works in this context as well, such as *The Temple In Man* and *Sacred Science*. Of course, the works by former OSS officer Peter Tompkins are also valuable, such as his *The Secrets of the Great Pyramid*.

It is enough to say for now that these theories of the inter-relationship between ancient buildings and monuments and the stars—and the even more esoteric correspondences between both buildings and stars and the human body and its processes and systems—were taken seriously by agencies of the US (and other) governments, if not by academia itself. The design of these edifices and their orientation to the compass points were thought to either *symbolize* a kind of divine geometry, inherent mathematical formulae embedded deep within nature, or to actually *cause* the building in question to function as a kind of machine. We know that the ancient Egyptians placed great store in the idea of resurrection; whether of the physical body or of some spiritual analogue is still open to furious debate. We also see, from a careful and "astronomical" reading of the Coffin Texts and other elements of what is sometimes called the Egyptian Book of the Dead, that the Egyptians were very conscious of the stars, and had developed an entire liturgical culture around the stars and the transportation of the soul of the dead pharaoh to a place in the celestial firmament. Thus, the idea of space travel is at least as old as ancient Egypt, if not much, much older.

The Germans had come closest to the dream of space travel during World War II. The rocket factories were cranking out missiles like the V-1 and V-2, but designs on the boards covered everything from jet aircraft to "flying saucer" prototypes. In the immediate postwar years, various Germans approached American intelligence (CIC) officers in Germany professing to have details of the saucer effort, including the Horten brothers who were part of Operation Paperclip,[37] and the bizarre case of Guido Bernardy. On August 5, 1947, Bernardy approached the US Army in Frankfurt in an attempt to see General Lucius Clay to warn him about Nazi secret weapons, the development of flying saucers by Hitler's scientists, Hitler's survival in a submarine sailing in the Southern Hemisphere and about to launch these weapons against the US and Europe, and the appearance of "two gentlemen, with no special talent in their lives, [who] discovered they did have extraordinary powers and capabilities which made it possible for them to communicate and contact the spirit world."[38] The agent who interviewed him, one Albert Goldstein, added, "Subject seemed entirely sincere, and the strong possibility that he is merely a crackpot is not apparent."[39] A few months later, the Horten brothers became an issue once again, as the Roswell case and the multiple sightings of "flying saucers" in the United States caused the Deputy Director of Intelligence, European Command to send a memorandum—dated 21 October 1947—to the American Chief of Staff about information received from Wright Field "concerning the flying saucers recently sighted over the UNITED STATES.

"For your information, the Air Materiel Command at WRIGHT FIELD is making a study of this subject and is constructing models to be tested in a wind tunnel.... The Air Materiel Command is of the opinion that some sort of object, such as the flying saucer, did exist" (Document declassified 5 July 1994). It would seem from the context of the accompanying documentation that the Horten brothers were assisting the US government in this assessment. It is known that the Operation Paperclip scientists had been sent to Wright Field (which would become Wright-Patterson AFB) in July 1947 at the time of the Roswell incident. Although Roswell is not mentioned in the declassified documents, it is nonetheless remarkable that the engineers and scientists of Wright Field were testing models of flying saucers in a wind tunnel there a few months after the incident (which the military had ridiculed as being the mistaken identification of a weather balloon, and which later researchers identified as artifacts of Project Mogul) and that this testing involved de-Nazified scientists under Paperclip, and that their preliminary conclusion was that a flying saucer "did exist."

Hitler kept waiting to the very end for the coveted "secret weapon" that would decide the war, and he would remain disappointed, but Wehrner von Braun and Walter Dornberger fled to the United States with the designs in their files and in their heads, and eventually with hundreds of their fellow scientists in tow managed to fill in the gaps and create the American space program, a military endeavor which later became NASA.

One of the amateur, popular and revisionist historians and archaeologists to draw the attention and suspicion (perhaps unfairly) of the Picknett and Prince team is Graham Hancock, who caused a worldwide sensation with the publication in 1992 of *The Sign and the Seal*, a book in which Hancock claimed to have discovered the resting place of the Ark of the Covenant. Hancock is a respected journalist and expert on East Africa, who worked for *The Economist* and *The Traveler*. He also won honorable mention in the 1990 H.L. Mencken journalism award for his book *Lords of Poverty*. Thus, Hancock is not an amateur journalist or armchair anthropologist, but a credible field observer of the cultures on which he reports. Yet, like Howard Blum, Jim Marrs and the other members of the "brotherhood buried alive," he has drifted from purely political reportage to the arcane. Since *The Sign and the Seal*, he has authored many hefty tomes on the subject of alien influence on ancient civilizations, such as *The Mars Mystery* (1994) and *Fingerprints of the Gods: A Quest for the Beginning and the End* (1995). In the former, he writes,

> NASA was formed in 1958 at the height of the Cold War when all advances in space science were spin-offs from the development of more efficient killing machines. The exploration of space itself was directly linked to defense policy.[40]

This is something which many Americans forget, just as they forget that everything from their superb interstate highway system to the *Diagnostic and Statistical Manual of Mental Disorders* was the result of defense policies. Military policies. War.

NASA was created around the dark genius of a coven of Nazi scientists who first tested their designs and discoveries on the civilian population of London during the Blitz. While many may feel that Hancock's characterization of NASA as a "disturbed child" is overstating the case, the preponderance of men who should have been standing trial for war crimes instead working for NASA in those days—men who had used slave labor to build bigger and better rockets—certainly goes some way to justify a verdict for moral imbecility, and the network that existed in the 1950s between the rocket scientists on the one hand and the "psychic scientists" like Andrija Puharich on the other—including the presence of the Nazi doctors at Randolph AFB—is clearly evidence of a hidden agenda. When Puharich went to Brazil to investigate Arigo, the "psychic surgeon," it was in collaboration with his friend John Laurence, an engineer specializing in satellites and telecommunications and one of the founding members of NASA.

Clearly, whoever was working with or for NASA in the 1950s and 1960s had to be able to accept the presence—let alone the dominance—of the many Nazis on their team and, as we have seen in previous volumes, those Nazis would not have been able to emigrate safely to the United States much less serve in positions of tremendous prestige and authority if it were not for the unwavering support and material assistance of men like Allen Dulles and Richard Nixon. As unpalatable as this idea seems, and as outrageous as it will appear to many, the facts speak for themselves and are incontrovertible. The same men who went after spirited anti-Nazis like Helen Gahagan Douglas in political campaigns, using Red-baiting and anti-Semitism as their weapons, also did their best to defend the active involvement of committed Nazis in the most sensitive, most secret caverns of American military technology, aviation medicine, and intelligence.

When Jack Sarfatti and Whitley Strieber were getting their marching orders as children from "the visitors" or perhaps "The Nine," NASA had not yet been created. *All* American space research before October 1, 1958—the date the National Aeronautics and Space Act was signed, creating the National Aeronautics and Space Administration, or NASA—was in the hands of the military, or under military contract at places like the Jet Propulsion Laboratory, which would become part of NASA very quickly. All investigation of the UFO phenomenon was in the hands of the FBI, the CIA, or the military. And the military departments responsible for space research were dominated by the Nazis they had brought over after 1945, Nazis who would eventually become an integral part of NASA, an agency that was created in response to the launching of the first earth-orbit satellite by the Soviet Union in 1957, *Sputnik*. Who can extricate their memories of America's early space programs from the image of affable Wehrner von Braun, a man who once wore the uniform of the Third Reich? Indeed, who among us who were alive at the time can forget Tom Lehrer's 1965 song "Wehrner von Braun," which, while a humorous satire on the former German officer, was nonetheless asking an important question: is it ethical to have former Nazis running our space program?

While the military and intelligence organs dominated UFO research—and kept sightings investigations, recovered evidence, and eyewitness testimony (particularly with regard to radar observations and encounters with military and commercial pilots, etc.) under wraps, thus robbing civilian groups of the chance to evaluate much UFO evidence—these military and intelligence organs also dominated psychic research and mind-control programs. Thus, on the one hand you had the Pentagon and the CIA monitoring UFO reports and massaging data, and on the other hand you had the same agencies racing to dominate inner space, as well. If the UFO phenomenon partakes of both the scientific (space flight, faster-than-light travel, alien visitations) and the psychological (hallucinations, visions, spiritual encounters and illumination), then the US government had all the bases covered. About all civilians could do was point to the sky and say they saw a UFO, or point to some burned grass on their lawn, or recount a tale of alien visitation; the civilians would have no access to the government's files on their experience, would have no opportunity to evaluate their experience in terms of ongoing military or intelligence operations, or in the context of data on similar experiences already in the government database, etc. The civilian would have had one of the most profound experiences of his or her life, and be unable to put it into *any* kind of context. Worse, individuals would be subject to ridicule if they opened their mouths. Further, this experience was either "real," i.e. had a scientific basis in objective reality, or was "spiritual" and had a more psychological dimension; the civilian would have no knowledge of how to interpret the event, and would thus be left in the dark having received no input from either the government or the scientists ... or the church.

In the early Postwar period, as we can see from the quotations that open this chapter, some of America's most powerful individuals were convinced of the reality of the UFO phenomenon, not as some kind of mass delusion among the credulous elements of the population, but as a scientific fact: even more, as a problem that had to be evaluated from a military perspective. Generals, admirals, high-ranking CIA officials all believed in the potential threat posed by the phenomenon and then, abruptly, they grew silent; but not before the childhood experiences of Jack Sarfatti and Whitley Strieber, and not before the creation of NASA. In fact, one could reasonably say that the statements by credible, trained military and intelligence observers supporting the view that UFOs represented an alien civilization, a "sinister force" to use the words of General MacArthur, came to a halt after the Kennedy assassination in 1963. Odd, then, that we would find Fred Crisman and Guy Bannister in at the very beginning of the twentieth century's UFO flap—two stalwarts of the assassination conspiracy as viewed by Jim Garrison, and both former intelligence officers (Crisman for OSS and eventually the CIA, Bannister for the FBI and, at one point, as the boss of FBI Special Agent Robert Maheu, who would go on to organize the Mafia–CIA assassination attempts against Castro).

Odd, then, that we would find many of Lee Harvey Oswald's co-workers at the Reily Coffee Company in New Orleans leaving that firm after the assassination and getting jobs with NASA and its subcontractors.

Coffee company employees. NASA.

Odd, then, that the Oswalds' Texas benefactors—the Paines—would have strong ties to the aerospace industry, and that Michael Paine would work for General Walter Dornberger at Bell Aerospace.

NASA was only one side of the story. Operation BLUEBIRD and, eventually, MK-ULTRA were the other. During 1954 alone, the year that Whitley Strieber recalls as being the first year he was brought to the "secret school," a total of seventeen MK-ULTRA contracts were signed, including everything from hypnosis (Projects 25, 29) to stage magic (John Mulholland's projects, including Projects 15 and 19) to drugs (Projects 26, 27, 28, 37, 38). These projects included testing of hallucinogens and narcotics on human subjects, as well as John Mulholland's specialty, which was training agents in how to dose unwitting subjects in the field. The following year saw the start of the Ionia State Hospital program of massive dosing of prisoners with LSD as well as the use of hypnosis in interrogations (Project 39) and, in 1956, Louis Jolyon West's experiments in "dissociated states" under the auspices of the University of Oklahoma (Project 43). Unfortunately, we have very little information on analogous *military* research taking place at the same time. We know that the Air Force contracted with the CIA in 1959 to conduct studies of "the Nature and Uses of Hypnosis as a Control Technique" (contract AF 49(638)-72B), and that the Navy had similar interests in 1964 (contract Nonr-4731(00)), and that the Air Force again commissioned the CIA to investigate the relation between sleep and hypnosis (contract AF-AFOSR-707-67) from 1964-1971. The only reason we know about any of this was because four boxes of MK-ULTRA files were found to have escaped the shredding frenzy of Richard Helms and Sidney Gottlieb. We did not learn of this from the Armed Forces directly, which is generally under no pressure to open its research files to the public. Not on mind-control programs. Not on UFO sightings. Elements of both fall under the heading "national security."

Thus, the American government had a stranglehold on research exploring the nature of consciousness, of memory, of deception, of manipulation—using drugs, hypnosis, and occult techniques—at the same time as they were performing damage control on the UFO flap. If these efforts were not coordinated at some level—if the research products of both were not being sent to the same, anonymous office in Arlington or Langley or Washington for analysis—then a tremendous opportunity was lost: an opportunity to learn, once and for all, what the UFO sightings (and especially the abductions and other "close encounters") represented. At the same time, if these efforts *were* coordinated, then the American people were being well and truly "controlled," and important information, central to our understanding of who we are and the place we have in the world, was being withheld.

The comedy *Men In Black*, a film starring Tommy Lee Jones and Will Smith as government agents keeping a lid on alien "immigration" to the United States, features a device which erases a contactee's memory: of both the alien experience as well as of the MIBs themselves. One imagines there are government agents who would have given their right arms for a device of that nature. One has no need to wonder if time and money was spent in pursuing that technology, since we have shown in Books I and II that the government was committed to achieving just that sort of power over the minds of its citizens, and over the minds of selected foreign citizens and populations as well.

At some point, the exploration of outer space extends into an exploration of inner space. This was perhaps the message of the experiences shared by Strieber and Sarfatti, a message both are still trying to communicate and to understand to this day. In Strieber's case, it comes with a warning: the entities we discover on our journeys may not always be altogether benign.

The Nine, The Process, and The Visitors

Despite what they had done to me, I did not hate the visitors. Because I knew their strength but not their motives, they frightened me.... That they represented a real, living force seemed hard to dispute. But that this force might be essentially human in origin remained a definite possibility.

—Whitley Strieber[41]

It may seem incongruous to try to contact aliens aboard their spaceships through the means of a séance. After all, the séance is the proper environment of the ghost and the disembodied spirit. The assumption one makes about aliens is that they are, at least, alive. (Although, considering that, is it not possible that perhaps dead aliens who have visited this planet would have left behind a similar effluvium, some alien ectoplasm, a Martian ghost haunting our planet, moaning unintelligibly in alien dialects, and able to be contacted with Ouija board and medium? Is Roswell thus haunted?) Nevertheless, the séances conducted by Andrija Puharich and his blue-blooded colleagues from December 31, 1952 through June 27, 1953 with the mysterious Dr. Vinod, Arthur Young, Ruth Forbes Paine Young, and Alice Astor were just such instances, and they were taking place during the same period that Sarfatti and Strieber were each, in their own way, making contact. (Although Strieber places great emphasis on 1954 as the year he was admitted to the "secret school," his memories of childhood encounters stretches from 1951 to 1957.) As we have seen earlier, these séances gave rise to the concept of The Nine, and these forces—speaking through Dr. Vinod—established themselves as living entities, as alien visitors aboard a spacecraft that was hovering over the earth. Indeed, Whitley Strieber himself speaks of hearing "nine knocks" associated with visits by his alien stalkers, and Sarfatti is likewise aware of The Nine, although at times in his lengthy email exchanges one sees them referred to as the "Alien Raj." Uri Geller also claimed to have been contacted by The Nine, as we see from Andrija Puharich's book on the Israeli psychic, *Uri.*

These are the associations that give Picknett and Prince some anxiety, for they understand The Nine to be a hostile agency (no matter whether it be an alien menace or a clandestine psy-war campaign) and the covert cooperation with The Nine—or with what they interpret as the hidden agenda of The Nine—by government and science as a betrayal of humanity. If we are to believe Robert Temple, for example (and there is no reason why we should not), then the US government was extremely interested in his research into the African Dogon tribe—the primitive tribe that knew of the existence of both Sirius A and Sirius B, including having much detailed information about the physical and chemical composition of both, as well as an accurate calendar of the double star's movements—and attempted to keep Temple from publishing his results in *The Sirius Mystery*, an attempt that obviously failed. Whether or not the attempt was a genuine, albeit half-hearted, effort on the behalf of the CIA to stop Temple from publishing, or was itself part of a disinformation campaign or some other psy-war experiment, is not known. What is known is that the CIA knew in detail of Temple's research long before he had gone to press. If we trace Temple's research in a "chain of custody," we find that it leads to the artist and occultist Harry Smith (so beloved of the OTO) and directly from Smith back to ... Arthur Young, Smith's mentor and benefactor. Temple himself studied with Arthur Young. And when we deal with Arthur Young, we are dealing with The Nine.

The "nine knocks" of Whitley Strieber's experience is related both in *Transformation* and in his later book, *Breakthrough*. They took place on the evening of August 27, 1986 while he was at his upstate New York cabin. There was a definite series of three distinct sets of three knocks, for a total of nine knocks, coming from a corner of the ceiling. Strieber seemed to understand this as an invitation to go outside and meet "the visitors" ... an invitation he declined, from fear. His cats also reacted in terror, staring at the spot the knocks came from.

Then, as he relates in *Breakthrough*, exactly eighteen months to the day from his experience of nine knocks, an entire town—Glenrock, Wyoming—was awakened at 2:45 A.M. on February 27, 1988 by the same phenomenon: nine knocks in three groups of three on the sides of their houses, their cars, their doors. This was related in the local newspaper, but no one ever discovered the cause of this bizarre event.

And when Strieber wrote *The Secret School* in 1997, it contained nine "lessons" divided into three "triads."

One would tend to dismiss these strange matters as having nothing really essential to do with The Nine, other than the mere fact of number, except for the peculiar association that three groups of three knocks would have for someone who had studied Western occultism.

First, magician Aleister Crowley, in his amusing and informative *Magick In Theory and Practice*, states,

> The general object of a knock or a knell is to mark a stage in the ceremony.... The sudden and sharp impact of the sound throws the mind into an alert activity which enables it to break loose from the obsession of its previous mood. It is aroused to apply itself aggressively to the ideas which had oppressed it. There is therefore a perfectly rational interpretation of the psychological power of the knock.[42]

Crowley belonged to the Golden Dawn, the British secret society that gave him the theoretical framework for much of his occult knowledge. Recourse to the rituals of the Golden Dawn—as published in Crowley secretary Israel Regardie's *The Golden Dawn*—will show us one way three groups of three knocks may be employed.

The ritual in question is that of the Neophyte Grade, the very first initiation in the Golden Dawn scheme. The temple is arranged, according to Regardie, in Egyptian fashion, and the whole rite recalls the weighing of the soul of the recently departed against the feather of the Goddess Maat. The Neophyte wears a black hooded robe. The other officers of the temple are dressed according to their rank, but again the regalement includes Egyptian motifs.

To one side is a representation of the Evil Triad of the Egyptians: gods who are prepared to devour the entrails of the Neophyte should he be found wanting. Surrounding the Neophyte are four benevolent gods, who will protect him from the savage hunger of the Evil Triad.

At one point in the ceremony, the three main initiators perform a "battery" of nine knocks, three knocks each, while uttering the formula "Khabs Am Pekht. Konx Om Pax; Light In Extension," one knock for each word. The initial phrase is Coptic, thus reinforcing the Egyptian character of the ritual, while the second phrase is in a "corrupt Greek" form. As for the meaning behind this, Regardie states,

> This affirms the establishment of the White Triangle and therefore the Completion of the Opening Ceremony. The Mystic Words "Khabs Am Pekht" which accompany the knocks seal the image of the Light.[43]

The Egyptian tenor of this rite is immediately suggestive to those who have read the Picknett and Prince book, because Egypt is at the heart of this mystery of The Nine.

However, the way in which the knocks are sounded is quite important; the interval between each knock is as essential as the knock and number of knocks itself. In the case of the Strieber/Glenrock events, the nine knocks are given in three groups of three, thus: 3—3—3. The number 333 has enormous significance for Qabalists (such as Madonna and Demi Moore!) as well as for ceremonial magicians in general, for it represents Choronzon, the Beast of the Abyss.

We have all heard of the significance of the number 666 as the number of the Beast of the Apocalypse. Some of us have wondered at the significance of 555 which, as I mention in *Unholy Alliance*, is the number of Hitler's original membership in the Nazi Party, as well as the height (in feet) of the Washington Monument, the altitude of Ashland, Kentucky above sea level, and the number of the Greek word *Necronomicon*.

In the case of 333, we are dealing with a suspiciously empty section of the Qabalistic Tree of Life. The Tree consists of ten *sephiroth* or spheres, each representing some facet of creation. Dividing the top three spheres from the lower seven is what occultists refer to as Daath, or the Abyss. It represents for some the "dark night of the soul," a necessary purging of the soul's sins, its karma, its dross before it can continue to the three "supernals" and complete its journey to Nirvana (to mix theologies for a moment). Just as there is an "Evil Triad" waiting for the Neophyte at the very first grade of initiation—demonic forms that wish to devour the unworthy aspirant—there is a Beast waiting in the Abyss itself, as if for a second and more brutal initiation. The number of Choronzon (derived from Qabalistic numerology) is the number of that particular Beast: 333.

Yet, as Masonic and other lore will remind us, these fierce creatures only appear fierce to the unclean. To those who have been purged of self-interest, self-consciousness, and the ego in general, these hideous monsters appear as angelic beings: the fierceness was one's own gross nature reflected on the faces of the guardians.

It is to this sector of the Tree of Life that Crowley successor Kenneth Grant has applied so much of his learning and exegesis. Grant believes that what the Qabalists consider the Abyss is actually a Gate, a way out to the zone of the stars, and a way in for the alien intelligences that have been summoned by magicians. While he devotes nearly an entire book to this thesis (*Nightside of Eden*), he covers the theme in many of his other works as well. In *Outside the Circles of Time*, he states that Choronzon "creates the event-act known as The Beast, viz: the creative vortex in the Aether that gives rise to the manifestation of phenomena *via* the mechanics of atavistic resurgence."[44] In *Hecate's Fountain*, he writes, "To enter into consciousness of this mystery is to become ashes to one world, but living and eternal fire to the next …"[45] In reference to studies by fellow occultist Michel Bertiaux, he writes (in *Cults of the Shadow*), "Choronzon, as the guardian of the gate *between* the known universe and the unknown universe—A and B—equates with ideas shared by all cults of the Shadow …," linking Choronzon and the Abyss to Haitian voodoo, for instance.[46] Finally, Grant defines the Abyss as "the Gulf between the unreal and the real, i.e., between phenomena and noumenon. Crossing the Abyss is the most critical event on the Spiritual Path.… Only the total abolition of the ego, or limited individual consciousness, makes a successful crossing possible."[47]

As mentioned in an earlier chapter, Grant also makes note of the fact that the drawing of one of Crowley's alien intelligences, Lam, is virtually identical to the famous portrait of one of the Visitors that adorns Whitley Strieber's *Communion.* If we posit, for a moment, the idea that all of the theories of Kenneth Grant and Aleister Crowley refer to specific phenomena—however they interpret them—then we have a sudden resurgence of those phenomena in the events experienced by Whitley Strieber, as well as by others before and since.

Ed Conroy, the reporter who researched Whitley Strieber's claims for a book entitled *Report On Communion: An Independent Investigation of and Commentary on Whitley Strieber's* Communion, also noted the correlations between Strieber's experiences and western occultism in general, taking particular care to cite Kenneth Grant, and Grant's views on the UFO phenomenon as an occult event of great importance, and then spends pages discussing Aleister

Crowley's invocation of Choronzon … without being aware at this time of Whitley's experience of the nine knocks.[48]

For me, the nine knocks were personal confirmation.
—Whitley Strieber[49]

Indeed.

To an occultist, the "nine knocks" may appear sinister, heavy with foreboding, for it serves in its grouping of three triads as an invocation of Choronzon; or is it perhaps a signal from the Abyss that the "Portal" is open. The Portal is the gateway to the Inner Temple, the Holy of Holies, and of this Israel Regardie writes,

> We are told in the Portal that the nine months' wait which must intervene before the Portal is again opened for the Aspirant has a correspondence to the nine months of gestation before birth.[50]

(It was eighteen months to the day between Strieber's "nine knocks" and the "nine knocks" of Glenrock, Wyoming: two times nine months. One wonders how the Portal was opened nine months after Strieber's experience and nine months before Glenrock's? And what did Glenrock do to deserve this in the first place?)

For years I have told of being present at the University of Texas when Charles Whitman went on his shooting spree from the tower in 1966. But I wasn't there.
Then where was I?
—Whitley Strieber[51]

Strieber's experiences are certainly bizarre enough by themselves, but when related to other events occurring at the same time they take on larger, more cosmic overtones. Strieber's books vacillate between "Gee, I have no idea what is happening to me," and "Gee, this must be an event of momentous importance!" as well they should. We are in no mood for prophets these days, unless they can give us the winning lottery number, so those who have been touched by supernatural forces are generally encouraged to keep silent and pass the butter.

For instance, as quoted above, he firmly believed for years that he had been at the University of Texas when Charles Whitman began sniping at innocent civilians from the Tower. Yet, as he discovered later to his chagrin, he was never there. He did attend UT, but a year or more *after* the event in question, and he doesn't know why he believed he was there, with such vivid memories of what went on.

In other cases, he has no memories of entire weeks of his life, weeks that have disappeared and for which he has only scraps of information, none of which seem to make sense when strung together (as he himself admits). The year 1968 is a case in point, and one with extreme relevance to our story.

In January of 1968, Strieber left Texas to go to London. He had been accepted at the London School of Film Technique, and the twenty-two-year-old was looking forward to spending time in England. But after about six months, he finds himself taking a train to Italy from London and meeting on the train a young lady. The couple decide to travel together and somehow they wind up in Rome, but after a stop of a few days? six weeks? in Florence. Once in Rome, they break up (for whatever reason, Strieber does not remember) and Whitley takes another train, this time bound for Strasbourg. From Strasbourg he goes by rail across France, winding up at the Spanish border at Port Bou, where he takes yet another train and winds up in Barcelona, booking a small room on the Ramblas. All this time he is in a state of fear, but we never learn the object of that fear, only that it may, somehow, have to do with the Visitors. He eventually returns to London, but has been gone for much longer than he thought: about six weeks is the best guess.[52] Further, he also has memories of attending some kind of "ancient university" at this time, and of seeing adobe huts which made him think of North Africa (an easy trip from Spain).

What are we to make of this?

During Whitley Strieber's radio interview of this author about *Unholy Alliance*, he mentioned in passing that he had visited the headquarters of the Process while he was in London that year, and that of course made my ears prick up even as the revelation caught me off guard. 1968 was a particularly volatile time for the Process, and it was during this year that Manson Family member Bruce Davis was known to have paid a visit or two to Process headquarters in London. Further, Sharon Tate and Roman Polanski were wed in London in January of that year, the same month Strieber flew to London from Texas. (In the spring of 1968, both Sirhan Sirhan and Naomi Judd would, at different times, visit Theosophical Society headquarters in Los Angeles.) Dr. Martin Luther King, Jr. was assassinated that April, and his putative assassin, James Earl Ray, escaped to London in May, visiting first Portugal and then returning to London to buy tickets for Belgium. He was arrested in June of that year in London and extradited back to the United States. Bobby Kennedy was assassinated a day or two earlier, and the Process went underground almost immediately in Los Angeles.

On July 29, when Whitley was presumably on the Continent, scientist Dr. James McDonald—a former US Navy intelligence officer during World War II—testified before Congress on the reality of the UFO phenomenon. (He would commit suicide some time later.) And, in November of 1968, Bruce Davis visited the Process in London. Whitley Strieber was still in London, and did not return to the United States until December of that year.[53] There is, of course, no evidence at all that Strieber ever met Davis, or that the two men were ever in Process headquarters at the same time. That is not the point I am trying to make, however.

Whitley Strieber, who for a long time inexplicably believed (erroneously) that he had been at the University of Texas on the day that Charles Whitman began shooting people at random, *was* in London when James Earl Ray was there after the Martin Luther King assassination; he *was* in London, visiting the Process, the same year that Manson Family member Bruce Davis was in London visiting the Process; he *was* in London when Sharon Tate and Roman Polanski were married there.

We would not consider all of this as evidence of anything at all, except that Whitley's behavior during 1968 was bizarre by his own admission, and that he had also visited the Process—for whatever reason—that same year. The author believes that Whitley's odyssey probably had nothing at all to do with the Process *per se*; that his visiting their headquarters in London might have been motivated more by simple curiosity than anything else. Yet, placing the young—by now, twenty-three-year-old—Whitley Strieber at the Process headquarters in London at the same time that they were forging some kind of link with the Manson Family is suggestive of some deeper influence, for the Process would later leave California for New York City, which is where Whitley wound up after leaving London and at the same time. They also had operations in Texas, principally Houston, where Maury Terry opines they were working with the Son of Sam cult—if, indeed, the two groups could safely be considered separate by that time, the 1970s.

No, Whitley Strieber is not some crazed Process/Son of Sam hitman; rather he was a contactee, vibrating like a tuning fork with all of the resonant associations taking place around him. One would have probably thought nothing at all of these coincidental links except for that one, salient piece of data: that he had visited the Process in London in 1968. For someone who had been at the mercy of the "secret school" since the age of six, and particularly since the age of nine, dealing with God-knows-what (military mind-control experiment or alien abduction), it comes as something of a shock—like a significant plot twist in a cinematic drama—to find him wandering into Process headquarters only a few months before Bruce Davis makes one of several known appearances there. After that episode, however, things quieted down for Whitley. At least for a while.

In 1970, Whitley and Anne Strieber were married and lived in New York, on West 55th Street in Manhattan. Strieber cannot recall much of significance until April of 1977, when more strange occurrences began to take place. This time, both he and Anne heard a voice coming out of their stereo. This in itself is not a strange occurrence in New York City, where police and taxi radios frequently come in over stereo receivers in the home, but in this case the voice had a conversation with the young couple, something which is certainly *not* possible under ordinary circumstances.

After a series of moves back and forth to Connecticut they eventually settled for a time in New York City, and maintained the famous cabin upstate where the most dramatic of the "visitations" took place. At some point during these early years of his marriage, however, Whitley Strieber and his wife Anne became involved with the Gurdjieff Foundation.

The Gurdjieff Foundation can hardly be considered a cult. During the same time that Whitley was a member, this author was in contact with a few other members in New York, who held the organization in high esteem and virtually spoke of it only in whispers. It operates relatively secretly, and is devoted to the teachings of both the Georgian mystic G.I. Gurdjieff and his most famous disciple, P. D. Ouspensky. Interested readers are encouraged to read their works, as there is no time or space here to go into much discussion of their philosophy.

Suffice it to say that it is hermetic, and metaphysical. There are physical exercises, chants (in particular the Gurdjieffian "double tone" chant) and meditations, as well as teachings on a wide variety of subjects pertaining to an illuminated understanding of nature and consciousness, including Gurdjieff's famous insistence that most people are "asleep," and need to "wake up." It is a method to integrate the dissociated parts of one's personality, much like Jungian depth psychology but in a more active way (the passive Jungian system having a great deal in common with Freudian psychoanalysis). By all accounts, Gurdjieff himself was a powerful occultist, and had been trained at various places in Asia Minor and the Caucasus. He was also a trickster, and used paradox and practical jokes in the way Jesus used parables and miracles. In the end, those of his followers who adhere strictly to his teachings are generally considered to be forces for good in the world, and only the most doctrinaire of Christian theologian would go so far as to condemn them as "cultists."

One knows that Strieber gained very much through his fifteen-year association with them; unintentionally perhaps, they gave him tools for understanding his alien experiences, and methods for safeguarding himself and his family from the fallout of the traumatic processes to which he was subjected.[54] At one point, in his mid-thirties, he also found himself "working with young people" at the Foundation, and that must have struck a subconscious chord with his repressed memories of the "secret school."

Around the time he parted ways with the Gurdjieff Foundation, he had the terrifying series of experiences in the New York cabin that he relates in *Communion.* Since that time, he has created a virtual cottage industry in contactee experiences and has developed that theme into something more baldly spiritual and metaphysical, in books such as *The Key* and *The Path* which he markets on his own Web site, www.unknowncountry.com. Although he has always stressed the spiritual side of the Visitor experience—even from the early days of *Communion*—the importance of the esoteric as it relates to the Visitors has become more pronounced in his writings in the past few years. That said, he has not abandoned the traditional areas of UFOlogy, such as saucer sightings and cattle mutilations, even as he has expanded into new realms, including some conspiracy literature and secret society lore. The interrelationship of all of these fields is something of which Strieber is keenly aware, and he links it to apocalyptic presentiments of global destruction and the possibility of a major appearance by the Visitors in the near future.

The Swiss psychiatrist C.G. Jung wrote a book devoted to the UFO phenomenon, entitled *Flying Saucers* and published in 1958 in German, and in English the following year. Jung is also the source for the concept of synchronicity, and we will address this more fully in the following chapter. What he has to say about those who have witnessed UFO contacts or sightings is actually quite apt in this case, and bears quoting:

> The empirical man extends beyond his conscious boundaries, his life and fate have far more than a personal meaning. He attracts the interest of "another world"; achievements are expected of him which go beyond the empirical realm and its narrow limits.... This numinous transformation is not the result of conscious intention or intellectual conviction, but is brought about by the impact of overwhelming archetypal impressions.[55]

And:

> An experience of this kind is not without its dangers, because it often has an inflating effect on the individual. His ego fancies itself increased and exalted, whereas in reality it is thrust into the background.... It is not the ego that is exalted; rather, something greater than it makes its appearance: the self, a symbol that expressed the whole man.[56]

This could go a long way toward explaining Whitley Strieber's development from a writer of horror fiction to the promoter of a kind of New Age mysticism based on his memories of the Visitors and the integration of them into his personal spirituality. Strieber himself writes of the phrase he heard during his abduction in the New York forest: "You are the chosen one," a phrase he immediately rejected as a little too hokey, but one that would have been in line with Jung's evaluation. Jung, of course, was inclined to reject the UFO phenomenon as simply a psychological matter for interpretation, until he had to admit that there was sufficient evidence to show that these sightings were not the result of mere hallucination, but had been tracked on radar and witnessed by military observers who were (in 1958) taking it seriously.[57]

Behind all of this is the lurking suspicion that some of these experiences may not be the result of benign forces looking to improve the lot of mankind, or the natural process of Jungian individuation. Again, it may be useless—psychologically speaking—to draw a sharp line of distinction between an actual alien visitation and the inner, spiritual experience it initiates. But can we be sure that the initiatory process (when put in motion by an experience of the Visitors) is "benign"? After all, just because a civilization is more advanced than we are technologically does not mean it has our best interests at heart. If nothing else, the history of colonialism would tell us that. That an alien race may be neither benign nor hostile, but simply self-interested, is an idea not normally entertained by the UFOlogists. Indeed, the world could be in the position of the Native American population of Manhattan Island, who sold their birthright for a string of beads. (The experience of aboriginal populations when it comes to the advent of colonial powers is worthwhile revisiting for the lessons it can teach us: powerful invading forces that sweetly smile on the natives and assure them that they mean no harm, and then proceed to rape the country, exploit its natural resources, and enslave or slaughter the residents as they go along. How could the aboriginals understand the mentality of the colonial powers, when they had no social context in which to place such an "otherworldly" event? How could they defend themselves, or even understand that they had to do so?) Even more troublesome, genuine contactee experiences may be mixed up with nefarious government disinformation programs, thus corrupting the entire contactee "database."

A Secret Bruise

If mine was not an uncommon experience, it might be that we live in a society that bears a secret bruise from it.

—Whitley Strieber[58]

It's not as if there were *no* evidence that the planet has been visited by *something.* The number of sightings that have taken place that have never been satisfactorily explained as due to atmospheric anomalies, swamp gas, the planet Venus, etc. is quite large. The number of sightings that have been tracked by the military on radar is also large enough to warrant some serious investigation. The number of sightings by commercial airline pilots is also worth consideration. And that is not counting sightings by citizens, people the government and the scientists do not deem "credible" because they have no training in celestial observations. In other words, the UFO phenomenon has been hijacked by the very establishments we have reason to believe may be responsible for at least some of the disinformation and misinformation that has gone on for so long in connection with the "flying saucers." There is no question that eyewitnesses make mistakes; there have been many studies in the psychological and criminological literature proving just that. However, what those studies do not prove is that while eyewitnesses may differ on the size and shape of a criminal, the clothing he was wearing or the color of his eyes, they normally agree on the fact that a crime has been committed:

a gun did go off, a car was stolen, a man was beaten, a woman was raped. As Dr. James McDonald relayed in his Congressional testimony: "Those eyewitnesses don't come in from, say, a street corner accident and claim they saw a giraffe killed by a tiger.... There is legally confusing difference of timing and distance, and so on; but all are in agreement that it was an auto accident."[59]

In the case of the UFO phenomenon, eyewitnesses may differ as to the number of colored lights, or the sound or lack of sound, or the shape of the craft; they agree, however, that something strange was in the sky that night. The weakness of eyewitness testimony is something that conservative scientists and scientific observers and skeptics—like the late Carl Sagan, for instance—rely upon to bolster their *a priori* judgment that the craft seen was not a craft at all because the witnesses cannot agree on specific details. They have become, in effect, defense attorneys poking holes in the testimony of witnesses in order to protect their client, in this case the scientific (or military) establishment. To be sure, as Sagan said "extraordinary claims require extraordinary proof"; but who decides what is ordinary and extraordinary proof? And, really, what is an extraordinary claim? Since the time of the Renaissance, science has usurped the role of religion and has relegated to itself the right to decide upon matters that were once the province of faith: specifically, the nature of reality, of creation itself. When science demands physical evidence of alien contact—evidence beyond the scorched circles in the farmyards, the blips on the radar screens, the affidavits by eyewitnesses, the photographs of celestial anomalies taken during nighttime and daylight—it has slyly changed the rules of the game. Evidence good enough for a court of law is no longer evidence, which, of course, calls into question the truth of other verdicts handed down by those same courts.

Science, quite rightly, places itself above and beyond such political decisions. Like Supreme Court justices, scientists reserve the right to tell the truth no matter what the effect will be on popular ideas of what is real and what is not, what is fact and what is fiction. Yet, in actual practice, the reality is somewhat different. The history of science is the history of the relationship between scientists and politicians, between men of science and men of *realpolitik* who hold the purse strings on the government grants so desperately needed for research. The history of science is the history of scientists: men and women so fiercely competitive that they will falsify data and steal the research of others to further their own agendas, their own careers. In other words, scientists are people prone to the same vanities and cardinal sins as the rest of us, and this humanity colors their perceptions, particularly of the unanswerable questions which—since they are unanswerable—serve no pragmatic purpose for a scientist who must earn a living doing useful work. Let's look for our keys under the streetlamp because there's more light there, even though we lost them across the street.

This blindered view of scientists toward the UFO phenomenon has worked extraordinarily well for the government and the military, for it means they have the ability to study the problem at their leisure, without having to explain anything to the populace at large. They can simply refer the curious to the scientists, who will tell them that there is nothing to worry about.

There have been exceptions of course.

It is unfortunate that Dr. McDonald couldn't understand or adjust to the political-military situation, and chose instead to act only according to strict scientific dictates.

—Dr. J. Allen Hynek[60]

On July 29, 1968, Dr. James E. McDonald—Professor in the Department of Meteorology at the University of Arizona and a Senior Physicist at the Institute of Atmospheric Physics, former US Naval intelligence officer during World War II, member of various scientific associations, husband, and father of six children—testified before the Committee on Science and Aeronautics of the U.S. House of Representatives during their Symposium on Unidentified Flying Objects. In a very thoughtful, reasoned way—both in his oral testimony and in the prepared statement that was inserted into the Record—Dr. McDonald came out in support of the extraterrestrial origin of some of the UFOs seen over America and the rest of the world. As a meteorologist, he was well-equipped to dismiss some of the "atmospheric" explanations of the phenomenon, such as ball lightning or swamp gas. After describing several convincing cases of UFO sightings and activity, and attacking positions taken by other scientists who were not meteorologists and therefore who made mistakes in their evaluations of the evidence, he addressed a famous UFO debunker, Philip Klass of *Aviation Week*, who specialized in ridiculing UFO reports, saying that Klass' explanations of UFO sightings as "atmospheric-electrical plasmas" just "do not make good sense."[61] Then, rather than beat around the bush with the type of vague statements we too often expect from our professional class, he was quite straightforward in his estimate of the situation:

> To conclude, then, my position is that UFO's are entirely real and we do not know what they are, because we have laughed them out of court. The possibility that these are extraterrestrial devices, that we are dealing with surveillance from some advanced technology, is a possibility I take very seriously.[62]

He then answered a number of questions put to him by the assembled Representatives.

> Representative Bell asked, "What leads you to believe that whatever these phenomena are, they are extraterrestrial?

"What facts do you have?"

To which Dr. McDonald replied:
May I say that I wouldn't use the word "believe." I would say the "hypothesis" that these are extraterrestrial surveillance, is the hypothesis I presently regard as most likely.

He then clarified his statement by referring to the evidence he had examined over the previous two years of intense study:

> It is this very large body of impressive witnesses' testimony, radar-tracking data on ultra-high-speed objects sometimes moving at over 5,000 miles an hour, UFO's, combined radar-visual sightings, and just too much other consistent evidence that suggests we are dealing with machine-like devices from somewhere else.[63]

McDonald's testimony was valuable, and his verbal statement before the Committee plus the appended report makes an interesting contribution to the rational discussion of the UFO phenomenon. Unfortunately, Dr. McDonald was ridiculed for taking an unabashed "pro-UFO" stand. His testimony before Congress on other issues—such as the danger to the ozone layer posed by the supersonic transport, or SST—was greeted with derision by some Congressional committee members, who described him as "the man who believed in little green men." Philip Klass, who somehow saw McDonald as a kind of nemesis, is known to have planted false information with investigative journalist Jack Anderson, claiming that Dr. McDonald used US Navy funds illegally to study UFOs. Although this claim was later disproved by Navy auditors, the pressure of public humiliation and ridicule became too much.

On June 13, 1971 his body was found in the Arizona desert, an apparent suicide. There was a revolver next to his body, and a note. Dr. McDonald had been silenced forever. But he was not the first.

Morris K. Jessup was another scientist whose support of continued UFO research very probably cost him his life. An astrophysicist with degrees in astronomy and mathematics, who had served with the US Army during World War I, Jessup was a generation older than James McDonald. He spent time in the Union of South Africa in the 1920s, and then in Brazil during the Depression, and later with an archaeological expedition in Central America studying Maya ruins, a junket funded by the Carnegie Foundation. The ancient ruins fascinated the young astronomer, and he would make a return visit there in the 1950s to determine how the huge monuments were built without the aid of machines. At the time, the UFO phenomenon had reached epidemic proportions, with massive sightings throughout the world, but particularly in France and the United States. Jessup studied the available evidence, and eventually—in 1955—published *The Case for the UFO.* In addition, Jessup felt that some of the geological anomalies he had discovered during his visits to the Mexican and Central American jungles and ruins were consistent with some types of lunar cratering, and that they could only have been made by an intelligent, albeit alien, race.

Jessup would have joined the ranks of the other scientists who took UFOs seriously and been laughed out of existence had it not been for the so-called "Allende letters," and the insistence of a strange, probably crank, correspondent that the US Navy had conducted an experiment in "electronic camouflage" during World War II at the Philadelphia Navy Yard, with disastrous results. According to the correspondent, who identified himself as "Carlos Miguel Allende" (an identification which is in some dispute, as the same correspondent also signed his name on other letters to Jessup as "Carl M. Allen"), the experiment had taken place sometime in 1943, when Allende was a seaman, and had caused the U.S.S. *Eldridge*, a destroyer escort, to disappear, then to reappear in Norfolk, Virginia, only to disappear and reappear back at the Philadelphia Navy Yard. This incident, referred to as "the Philadelphia Experiment," allegedly was witnessed by Albert Einstein, whose work on the Unified Field Theory started the whole program in the first place. Supposedly, the crew of the *Eldridge* (those that survived, not all did) were discharged as being mentally unfit, and the entire experiment classified.

The Philadelphia Experiment is a favorite story among the credulous, and was made into a science fiction film a few years ago. (Notice the odd near-homonym at work between *Eldridge* and that word so favored by H.P. Lovecraft: "eldritch.") We would not even be addressing it here at all were it not for official US government interest in Jessup's correspondence with "Carlos Allende," and the mystery of the "annotated book."

While many—too many—of the supposed witnesses and participants to this "experiment" are off the record and unidentified in the book by William L. Moore and Charles Berlitz, *The Philadelphia Experiment: Project Invisibility,*[64] it nevertheless gives an otherwise detailed look at this controversy, and is virtually the only text available in print on the subject. Berlitz, of course, is the author of *The Bermuda Triangle*, the book that popularized that subject, and is of course *that* Berlitz, of the language schools. William L. Moore is identified as a schoolteacher from Minnesota who has been pursuing the subject of the Philadelphia Experiment relentlessly since hearing of it from people who claimed to have been there. While Moore is credited with authoring the book, it was done so "in consultation with Charles Berlitz," and bears the latter's Introduction.

Central to this story is the idea that, running parallel to the Manhattan Project which was, of course, the development of the atomic bomb, the US military was involved in other secret weapons research. Albert Einstein is known to have worked as a consultant to the US Navy in 1943 for unspecified research, as well, which adds more fuel to the fire. In addition, many of the various officers and ships mentioned in the rambling, near-hysterical Allende Letters were later proven to have existed and, indeed, Allende/Allen could only have known about these details if he had, in fact, been a seaman in the same theater at the time of the alleged incident, which was later shown to be the case, when a copy of his US Department of Commerce certificate was published in Moore's book. In fact, the Allende Letters evidence a knowledge of the details of the Navy yards where the "Experiment" was said to have taken place on the one hand, and of the involvement in secret projects by both Albert Einstein and Bertrand Russell, however murky or ambiguous this involvement was.

The rest of the Letters, however, are strictly Fantasyland. Ships disappearing at sea, sailors "frozen" half in and half out of this dimension, etc. Yet the letters were convincing enough that Dr. Jessup asked for further proof. Allende/Allen obliged by giving more names, dates and places and even offered to go under hypnosis and "truth serum" sessions in order to retrieve phone numbers, addresses, etc. He also brought up the idea that the Navy had used some of this science as a means of developing a propulsion system … for the UFOs. At the same time, his letters were virtually written in crayon: different colored inks, inappropriate capitalizations, underlinings … in short, the typical sort of communication one receives from people suffering from a mental disorder. Then, again, that also goes to evidence: according to the Letters, many of the sailors involved in the Philadelphia Experiment wound up being discharged as "mentally unfit."

Then, in the summer of 1955, a copy of Morris Jessup's book, *The Case for the UFO*, was sent to the Navy's Office of Naval Research. It was heavily annotated by the anonymous correspondent, and the nature of the remarks startled the naval officers who received it; so much so, that they contacted Jessup and asked to see him.

When Jessup arrived in Washington, he was shown the copy of his book with the plentiful notations and remarks, and the experience seems to have been unsettling. He recognized the handwriting as that of his crazed correspondent, Allende, and told the officers that he had two letters from the same man in his files. The officers insisted that they needed to see them as soon as possible. In return, they would give Jessup a copy of the annotated book in order to get his input.

What were the annotations like? They discussed everything from the UFOs, their propulsion systems, "magnetic fields, gravity fields, sheets of diamond, cosmic rays, force cutters, inlay work …" etc., etc.[65] The annotator knew of a great many details that were known only to Jessup or to a handful of specialists in the field of UFOs, and "many other matters usually of concern mainly to psychics, cultists and mystics. That these were true or not was not the point. The fact that they should be so precisely known to an unknown was."[66] This bothered the scientist more than anything else, this and the fact that the Navy was actually taking the ravings of this mysterious individual seriously. And, of course, the Philadelphia Experiment was also mentioned in the notes.

Demonstrating the extent to which the Navy took this matter to heart is the method by which they made copies of the book. There was no photocopy machine in 1955, so the book had to be retyped by hand on mimeograph stencils! This edition is referred to as the Varo edition, because the work of typing and mimeographing the entire work (in two colors, black for the original text and red for the annotations) was evidently undertaken by a temporary secretary hired by that company for that purpose.[67] Jessup was presented with three copies of his own, and he took to reading and re-reading the notes and eventually annotating the annotations.

This development contributed to a gradual deterioration of Jessup's mental and financial state. Various projects he had proposed for a return to the Central American jungles to research ancient civilizations had come to nought, and this brilliant scientist was reduced to writing for astrological journals and researching psychic phenomena … "reduced" may be too strong a word, for his sudden conversion to the purely paranormal may have been the result of his intense study of the annotated book and the realization that for some reason the Navy was taking it seriously. Like many who have come across the same or similar constellation of factors, he found the psychological stresses to be enormous—particularly for a man of science—and in 1958, at the end of his rope, he visited an old friend in New York. This was the naturalist Ivan T. Sanderson and it was, appropriately enough, "on or about Halloween evening." Jessup gave his friend his copy of the annotated book—this time containing his own annotations as well—and told him to hold it for safekeeping in case anything happened to him.

Sanderson later stated,

> At this our last meeting he was extremely distraught and admitted that due to an originally pure intellectual interest in natural phenomena, he found that he had been completely swept into a weird and insane world of unreality. He expressed outright terror at the endless stream of "coincidences" that had occurred in his work and in his private life …[68]

Again, the "coincidence stream" rears its head; it is a familiar phenomenon to artists, writers and especially researchers into the paranormal, the study of which seems to increase the number and frequency of coincidences to an almost alarming rate.

Jessup left New York shortly thereafter, and it was believed he was returning to his home in Indiana. However, he never made it there. Instead, he drove to a house he owned, unknown to anyone, in Coral Gables, Florida. His friends and publishers were frantically trying to locate him when they discovered he had been hurt in some type of automobile accident in December of 1958, but had recovered and was still in Florida, exhausted, struggling to revive his writing career and being rejected by his publishers.

Then, on April 20, 1959 Morris Jessup was found, barely alive, in his car in a park near his home. He had run a hose from his exhaust pipe into his vehicle. He was rushed to a hospital, but was pronounced dead on arrival.

Was it a suicide? Naturally, there are those who contest this verdict. Moore claims that he obtained access to medical examiner files on the Jessup suicide[69] showing that Jessup was quite drunk when he ran the hose into his car. The unsettling thing about this piece of evidence is that Jessup was known to be at that time on medication which, in combination with alcohol, would have either killed him immediately or at the very least rendered him incapable of driving a car and running the hose from his exhaust pipe in such a calculated manner. This means he would have had to start drinking after he arrived in the park and ran the hose. Was a bottle found in Jessup's car? Was Jessup still taking medication to save his life when he knew he wanted to end it? Unfortunately, we don't know any of this from Moore's book.

As mentioned, most of the more sensational claims in Moore's book come from unnamed informants, so it is virtually impossible to come to any conclusion about the Philadelphia Experiment. The facts that can be verified are those that relate to Morris Jessup himself, his work, his support of an aggressive research program on UFOs and on alternative forms of energy and propulsion, the "annotated book" episode and the Allende Letters, and his tragic end.

Two scientists, both fervent supporters of a more open and aggressive study of the UFO phenomenon, drive to secluded areas away from their homes and commit suicide. More recently, another scientist met a similar end: a UN weapons inspector, Dr. David Kelly, who went to an isolated location in the English countryside in July 2003 with a bottle of pain killers and a revolver. Dr. Kelly had leaked information to the British press that intelligence estimates of Iraq's weapons capability had been exaggerated, presumably in order to support Prime Minister Tony Blair's decision to join with the United States in the invasion of Iraq earlier that year. It led to a firestorm of controversy over the legitimacy of Blair's decision, with ramifications for President George W. Bush as well, similar claims having been leveled against his administration. (Clearly, terrorists have replaced UFOs as potential threats to national security.) We want our scientists to be priests of the truth, of scientific facts which we believe are the psalms of reality; but we don't want them to deviate from the line set down by our politicians and military leaders. We don't want them to tell *too much* truth. "For not all true things are to be said to all men."

The infamous Condon Report, published in 1968, is a case in point. Highly touted as an independent investigation to determine once and for all the reality behind the UFO phenomenon, it became obvious—through the "Low memorandum" that was leaked to the press—that the Condon committee had no intention of proving or disproving UFOs based on evidence, but was determined to put the controversy to rest no matter the damage to the cause of truth. The committee was formed in 1966 at the request of the United States Air Force, and was based at the University of Colorado under the stewardship of nuclear physicist Dr. Edward Condon, a scientist who had worked on the atomic bomb and on space technology. His attitude towards UFOs was biased from the beginning, and his introduction to the Report was grossly at odds with the actual report itself, which contained data on many unsolved cases that merited further study. What destroyed the credibility of the Condon Report—or *The Scientific Study of Unidentified Flying Objects* to give it its formal title—was the publication of the August 1966 Low Memorandum, written by Condon's second-in-command, Robert Low, which contained the following, damning paragraph:

> The trick would be, I think, to describe the project so that, to the public, it would appear a totally objective study but, to the scientific community, would present the image of a group of non-believers trying their best to be objective, but having an almost zero expectation of finding a saucer.

The Report was criticized long and loudly by many who had hoped for an unbiased approach to the problem (including its most vocal critic, Dr. James McDonald, as well as Dr. J. Allen Hynek who, in disgust with the Report, began his own organization to study UFOs), especially as the Air Force was about to cancel their own long-standing UFO program, Project Blue Book. Even Dr. Condon himself would eventually admit to the press that the Report was a waste of taxpayers' money, in this case $500,000 to cover two-years' worth of foot-dragging and obstructionism. In the end, even the files themselves (public property, after all, paid for with public funds) were never made public, and were eventually burned. It was said that Condon himself had been the victim of US government pressure to present a report that debunked UFOs, that he had been blackmailed concerning security investigations of his background that had taken place during the McCarthy era.[70]

This theory was documented rather convincingly in Major Donald E. Keyhoe's *Aliens From Space: The Real Story of Unidentified Flying Objects*,[71] which, despite its sensationalistic title, is one of the more sober and more revealing of the UFO books by insiders. Keyhoe—a retired US Marine Corps officer and a central figure in the UFO debates of the 1960s and 1970s—reveals the political machinations that went on behind the scenes of the Condon Report, and shows how the Air Force was desperate to use the Condon Report to discredit UFO sightings in general. The 1960s saw a huge increase in the number of UFO sightings around the world, and the Air Force was unable to respond to the problem in any way. It did not have the technology to engage the UFOs in either communication or combat, and the sightings by credible witnesses—including high-ranking military personnel—were rendering the swamp gas and weather balloon explanations laughable. Condon himself had been a target of the House Un-American Activities Committee investigation in the 1950s, and this presented the Air Force with another problem. The report was due out in the fall of 1968, around the time of the US presidential elections. Depending on who won the election, the Condon Report could be buried … or it could become a national (and international) cause célèbre. It was important to release the Report as the official word of scientists that there was nothing to the UFO reports, and that they were all the result of mistakes by untrained and non-credible witnesses, especially in view of the outcome of the presidential election of November 1968; for the man who won that election was the same man who had sat across from Dr. Condon during the HUAC investigation, a man who developed an intense dislike for the scientist: Richard M. Nixon.

Nixon would have been only too happy to attack Condon over the Report if the Report acknowledged the existence of extraterrestrial flying objects, if only to disgrace and humiliate Condon. The problem with this scenario is that it would put the Report front and center before the press and the public, and the Report was full of cases where the UFO sightings could *not* be explained away by the usual swamp gas and weather balloon scenarios. It was better if no one looked too closely at the Report. Hence, the public pronouncements by Condon, and his fabled introduction in which he claims that none of the cases studied by the Condon Committee were of otherworldly spacecraft, but could all be explained away.

In other words, the government once again told the scientists what to say to the world about the world, and about science itself.

In a related development, Rear Admiral Roscoe Hillenkoetter, first Director of the CIA and decorated war hero, quit his job at NICAP (National Investigative Committee of Aerial Phenomena, the most prestigious of all the UFO investigative groups) within days of a CIA investigation of his proposed role in opening the UFO investigation at the Congressional level with the support of Senators like Goldwater and Kefauver and many others. Although an ardent supporter of efforts to investigate UFOs and a harsh critic of US Air Force attempts to cover up and whitewash what were turning out to be hundreds of verified sightings (if not thousands), he inexplicably disappeared from the UFO scene in 1962 due, Keyhoe believes, to pressure from "a very high level" to block the proposed Capitol Hill investigation.[72]

Noting the presence of CIA officials at every level of this investigation (as reported by Keyhoe), and noting that this occurred only months after the firing of Allen Dulles as Director of the CIA over the Bay of Pigs affair and the ensuing hatred and distrust of President Kennedy by some of the remaining CIA hands, and noting that February of that year saw the first earth orbit by an American astronaut, we are left with an embarrassment of paranoid riches once again. The Capitol Hill investigation of the UFO phenomenon did not take place, Hillenkoetter retired from NICAP, John Glenn orbited the earth, and the world settled down to other matters: the Cuban Missile Crisis, the Kennedy assassination, a massive wave of UFO sightings in 1965 … the assassinations of Robert Kennedy and Martin Luther King in 1968, the election of Richard Nixon as president that same year, the Condon Report of January 1969 … the suicide of Dr. James E. McDonald.

It is a scene of awful beauty. A strange object is seen in the skies over Kentucky on January 7, 1948. It is a large, round metallic machine, and it is descending in the vicinity of Godman AFB, heading south towards Tennessee and witnessed by thousands of people including the base commander, Colonel Guy Hix, who authorizes a squadron of three P-51s to intercept the craft. All but one peel off and head back to base as it becomes obvious that the strange object has begun to climb at an alarming rate for a man-made device, and the World War II-era planes are not equipped with oxygen. But one pilot stays with the chase, oblivious to the danger to his life. A World War II veteran transport pilot, Captain Mantell climbs.

The object reaches an altitude of 20,000 feet and Mantell stays with it; man and machine, locked in ecstatic embrace, the light from the glowing object reflected in his eyes, his Mustang screaming with the effort of climbing to 30,000 feet, higher than ever a Mustang has climbed before.

His voice can be heard over the radio at Godman AFB.

"I've sighted the thing.... It looks metallic and it's tremendous in size.... Now it's starting to climb....I'm trying to close in for a better look."

His wingmen have given up the chase. Mantell is alone.

What happens next is the subject of tremendous controversy. Mantell, evidently due to lack of oxygen at the high altitude, has blacked out. His plane begins to descend in a sickening spiral, a power dive. There is a flash of brilliant white light, like an explosion, and then the Mustang belly-flops into a field. Mantell is dead. The Mustang, oddly enough, even though its wings and tail section have separated from the fuselage, shows no other signs that it has crash-landed. There is no damage to the fuselage. No scratching or any other indication that the plane had skidded or dived into the earth. No damage to surrounding trees or vegetation. The plane simply flopped down. Mantell is still strapped into his seat, having made no effort to eject, due to his unconscious or semi-conscious state by the time he reached 25,000 feet.[73]

Although initial reports in the newspapers claim that Mantell died chasing a UFO, the Air Force quickly acts to suppress that bit of information. Their story is that Mantell died chasing the planet Venus, which he had mistaken for a UFO. (This is the same story that would be given to future president Jimmy Carter when he reported a UFO sighting while he was still governor of Georgia.) The problem with this scenario is that the chase had occurred in broad daylight, at three o'clock in the afternoon, when Venus is hardly visible. The second problem is that the altitude of Venus at that time—even if visible—was close to the horizon and not straight up. The third problem is that Captain Mantell was an experienced combat pilot who would not have mistaken a planet for a bogie. The fourth problem is that thousands of other people saw the craft, including Mantell's base commander, who watched it through his binoculars. The story was then changed to a Navy "Skyhook" balloon, but that account was challenged by the military's own records: there were no Skyhook balloons anywhere near Kentucky at that time. Further, such a balloon would have had to have been at an extremely high altitude to account for all the eyewitnesses who reported it: more than 25 miles high, and closer to 50.

Also, the "balloon" seemed to take evasive action when pursued by Captain Mantell.

Only six months after Roswell and the Kenneth Arnold sighting, Captain Mantell gave chase to a UFO, determined once and for all to get to the bottom of the mystery since he alone had been given the opportunity. Suffused with the joy of flight, the excitement of the chase, and knowing that he was pushing himself and his plane (and, possibly, his government) to its limits, he locked on to his target and gave it everything he had, secure in the knowledge that whatever happened, his efforts would contribute to sure knowledge of the nature of the flying machines, the saucers, that were suddenly streaking across American skies. Was it a rictus of pain or a grin of boyish, joyful satisfaction on Mantell's face as he neared the 30,000 feet mark on his altimeter, the shining object tantalizingly out of reach, his fuselage rattling with the effort, his prop blades a blur … and then, blackness.

The debris of an aircraft that has plummeted to earth from 20,000 or 30,000 feet should spread over a wide area, not be found as relatively intact as Mantell's Mustang. The source of the flash of light as he neared the ground has never been identified. Eyewitnesses say it came just before the plane left its dive of mortal descent and "pancaked" to the ground … as if God had interceded at this last moment and decided to place the aircraft reverently on the ground rather than allow it to plunge into the earth, nose first. Whatever the case, Godman Base commander Colonel Hix transferred to San Antonio, Texas, where one day his son would play in the swimming pool with young Whitley Strieber.

A month after Mantell's death, the Air Force Director of Intelligence issued a Top Secret memo—dated February 12, 1948—requesting that all air bases have at least one plane equipped with camera equipment ready at all times to give chase to UFOs. The request was denied, due to the enormous cost it would entail in men and machines.

The Director of Intelligence was Charles P. Cabell, the man who would later become deputy director of the CIA under Allen Dulles, before they were both fired by President Kennedy over the Bay of Pigs—the man whose brother was mayor of Dallas, Texas the day Kennedy was assassinated in that city.

Reality is what has been defined by our political leaders and not by our priests *or* our scientists. The precedent established by our treatment of the UFO phenomenon—the manipulation of truth, the creation of reality through propaganda and psychological warfare and disinformation, the use of journalists and scientists and other men and women presumed to be dedicated to the truth—has worked its way into the Cold War, Vietnam, Chile, Watergate, Iran-Contra, and now the present situation in the Middle East. And people die: martyrs to a manufactured truth, to a cleverly-designed reality matrix, an invisible white rabbit pulled from a grinning black magician's black hat: a *pookah.*

"Harvey"… with guns.

Endnotes

[1] Julian Barnes, *Flaubert's Parrot*, McGraw Hill, NY 1985, p. 93-94

[2] Umberto Eco, "The Force of Falsity," *Serendipities*, Orion, London, 1998, p. 3

[3] Elaine Pagels, *The Gnostic Gospels*, Vintage Books, NY, 1981, p. 7

[4] Ibid., p. 32

[5] Ibid., p. 40

[6] Michael Baigent and Richard Leigh, *The Dead Sea Scroll Deception*, Corgi, London, 1991

[7] Cited in *The Secret Gospel* by Morton Smith and in *Bloodline of the Holy Grail* by Laurence Gardner,Element, Shaftesbury, Dorset, 1999, p. 92

[8] Whitley Strieber, *Communion*, Avon, New York, 1988, p. 57

[9] Ed Conroy, *Report On Communion*, William Morrow, NY, 1989, p. 113

[10] Strieber, op. cit., p. 11

[11] Ibid.

[12] Ibid., p. 16

[13] Ibid., p. 37

[14] Ibid., p. 38

[15] Ibid., p. 38-40

[16] John E. Mack, M.D., *Abduction*, Ballantine Books, New York, 1994

[17] Conroy, op. cit., p. 39-42

[18] Ibid., p. 43

[19] Octavio Paz, *El signo y el garabato*, Biblioteca de Bolsillo, Barcelona, 1991, p. 12-13 "If the Bomb had not destroyed the world, it destroyed our idea of the world.… We rediscover a feeling that was familiar to the Aztecs, to the Hindus and to the

Christians of the year 1000. Technology begins by being a negation of the image of the world and ends by being an image of the destruction of the world."

[20] Michel Foucault, *Madness and Civilization*, Vintage, NY, 1988, p. 202

[21] Peter Levenda, *Unholy Alliance*, Continuum, NY, 2003, Chapter 11, "Aftermath"

[22] This is from the Sarfatti Web site.

[23] Sarfatti email exchange with David Gladstone dated June 29, 2001.

[24] Jim Schnabel, *Remote Viewers: The Secret History of America's Psychic Spies*, Dell, NY, 1997, p. 165

[25] Ibid., p. 167

[26] Ibid., p. 168

[27] See http://www.Stardrive.org/Sarmail7-2-02.shtml

[28] http://groups.yahoo.com/group/SarfattiScienceSeminar/message/3079

[29] Conroy, op. cit., p. 87

[30] Ibid.

[31] 1996 interview with Mac Tonnies on www.beyondcommunion.com/breakthrough/96tonnie.html

[32] The Bell Witch story may also be found in *Witches, Wraiths and Warlocks*, edited by Ronald Curran, Fawcett Books, NY, 1971, p. 25-28.

[33] Graham Hancock, *The Mars Mystery*, Seal Books, Toronto, 1998, p. 169

[34] Lynn Picknett and Clive Prince, *The Stargate Conspiracy*, Warner Books, NY, 2000

[35] Robert Bauval and Adrian Gilbert, *The Orion Mystery: Unlocking the Secrets of the Pyramids*, Mandarin, London, 1995

[36] Giorgio de Santillana and Hertha von Dechend, *Hamlet's Mill*, Gambit, Boston, 1969

[37] CIC Foreign Documents Unit, dated 30.5.45, Title PWI reports dealing with HORTEN tail-less aircraft

[38] Statement of Bernardy dated August 5, 1947 in CIC files

[39] Memorandum for the Officer in Charge, 7 August 1947, Subject: BERNARDY, Guido, Helmut, Julius, "Flying Saucers"

[40] Hancock, op. cit., p. 169

[41] Strieber, op. cit., p. 95

[42] Aleister Crowley, *Magick In Theory and Practice*, Dover, NY, 1976 edition, p. 84

[43] Israel Regardie, *The Golden Dawn*, Llewellyn, St. Paul, 1986 edition, p. 347

[44] Kenneth Grant, *Outside the Circles of Time*, Frederick Muller, London, 1980, p. 225

[45] Kenneth Grant, *Hecate's Fountain*, Skoob, London, 1992, p. 221

[46] Kenneth Grant, *Cults of the Shadow*, Skoob, London, 1994, p. 167

[47] Kenneth Grant, *Aleister Crowley and the Hidden God*, Skoob, London, 1992, p. 202

[48] Conroy, op. cit., p. 279-282

[49] Whitley Strieber, *Breakthrough: The Next Step*, Harper, NY 1995, p. 14-15

[50] Regardie, op. cit., p. 92

[51] Strieber, 1988, p. 117

[52] Ibid., p. 134-136

[53] Ibid., p. 136

[54] Conroy, op. cit., p. 268

[55] C.G. Jung, *Flying Saucers*, Routledge, London, n.d., p. 79

[56] Ibid., p. 79

[57] Ibid., p. 121-122

[58] Strieber, 1988, p. 96

[59] *Symposium on Unidentified Flying Objects, Hearings Before The Committee on Science and Astronautics, US House of Representatives*, Ninetieth Congress, Second Session, July 29, 1968, USGPO, Washington, DC, p. 21

[60] Dr. J. Allen Hynek, *The Hynek UFO Report*, Dell Publishing, NY, 1977, p. 112

[61] *Symposium*, op. cit. p. 26

[62] Ibid.

[63] Ibid., p. 27

[64] William L. Moore and Charles Berlitz, *The Philadelphia Experiment: Project Invisibility*, Ballantine Books, NY, 1984

[65] Ibid., p. 66

[66] Ibid., p. 68

[67] Ibid., p. 70

[68] Ibid., p. 76, citing from Sanderson, *Pursuit* magazine, No. 4, September 1968

[69] Ibid., p. 253-54

[70] Jim Marrs, *Alien Agenda*, HarperCollins, NY, 1997, p. 154

[71] Donald E. Keyhoe, *Aliens From Space: The Real Story of Unidentified Flying Objects*, New American Library, NY, 1974

[72] Ibid., p. 86

[73] Marrs, op. cit., p. 102-104

Chapter Twenty-One

The Machineries of Joy

To be perfectly honest, we will always have a lingering suspicion that there could be something dark and dreadful going on behind the scenes, something much bigger, and much more awful, than a mere conspiracy. The universe is mysterious. Reality itself is mysterious. No human has any true idea whether life has any transcendent purpose or not, whether there is life after death, whether there are such entities as absolute good and absolute evil.
—Graham Hancock[1]

Mystery is an occult force or efficacy that does not obey us, and we never know how or when it will manifest itself.
—Octavio Paz[2]

Human force cannot be other than spiritual; surely earth does not need man's feeble stirrings.
—Kenneth Patchen[3]

He expressed outright terror at the endless stream of "coincidences" that had occurred in his work and in his private life …
—William L. Moore[4]

I knew by now that when a group of individuals gravitated toward one another for no apparent reason, or a group of individuals inexplicably headed in the same direction as if drawn by a magnetic field, or coincidence piled on coincidence too many times, as often as not the shadowy outlines of a covert intelligence operation were somehow becoming visible.
— Jim Garrison[5]

The complex theory of 'synchronism', partly based on the observation of such coincidences as these, might perhaps lead to an entirely new conception of history.
—Pauwels and Bergier[6]

The French team of Jacques Pauwels and Louis Bergier published one of the most explosive books of its decade, *The Morning of the Magicians* (*Le matin des magiciens*) in 1960. According to the accepted mythology, Pauwels and Bergier had served in the Resistance during World War II and since the end of the war had become interested in the paranormal, both from their reading of literature and history and what they observed among the Nazi elite, who were, in some cases, deeply involved in the subject. There are very few footnotes in *The Morning of the Magicians*, and very little in the way of primary source material, making confirmation of some their claims nearly impossible; yet, recourse to the National Archives in Washington, D.C. and the Library of Congress—as well as the former Berlin Documentation Center—has made it possible to verify some of their assertions, and to come up with quite a number more. These were covered in some detail in this author's *Unholy Alliance*, which has been cited before in this study, and we won't go into more detail here except to say that the basic premise of *Unholy Alliance* is that the Nazi Party was not a political party as we commonly understand it, but a cult. For confirmation of this, we only need to look at the modern manifestations of the Nazi Party to see how thoroughly they have become combined with cultic principles.

The Silver Shirts—an American pro-Nazi political party started by William Dudley Pelley in the 1930s—is a prime example of this. Pelley's organization was suffused with mystical concepts (including a great deal of UFO lore after the War), and Pelley himself was interned by the American government during World War II as a subversive and possible enemy agent. The National Renaissance Party of the 1950s through 1980s, run by James Madole, is another example of a pro-Nazi "cult" that quoted extensively from Madame Blavatsky and Alice Bailey's works as justification for anti-Semitism and genocide. Today, the pro-Manson Universal Order founded by neo-Nazi James Mason is another case in point, and we only have to see the swastika Charles Manson etched into his own forehead to understand how deeply elements of American society idolize the Nazis and the force it represents...and how dangerous these beliefs are to the rest of us. From the occult side, the enthusiasm shown by Michael Aquino and the Temple of Set for the SS castle at Wewelsburg is another indication that there is something more going on with the Nazi Party and its followers—even today—than what Americans read about in their newspapers in the 1930s and 1940s.

It is perhaps not going overboard to say that the Third Reich caused a massive shift of consciousness in the planet, a "paradigm shift" one might call it.

Although occultism and politics had long been bedfellows, since the days of Joseph interpreting dreams for Pharaoh, or King Saul consulting the Witch of Endor, or even earlier in the astral temples at Nineveh and Babylon, the world came very close to enduring a massive and industrialized "cult-ocracy" in the form of the Third Reich and the proposed division of Europe into states run by the fanatically esoteric SS of Heinrich Himmler. That millions of innocent people died because of this twisted dream is one of the tragedies of the twentieth century that has been visited upon the twenty-first, in the form of the Middle Eastern conflicts, the wars in the Baltic states, and so much else. Forces are at war in the world, causing immeasurable horror and suffering, and we do not know what they are. We do not understand how we could have become so thoroughly manipulated by these forces that we can no longer call a halt to the slaughter but have to watch, impotently, from the sidelines as the blood and the smoke of a thousand separate Holocausts drifts closer and closer to our own shores.

In *Morning of the Magicians*, the authors identified these forces in paranormal terms, but always linking them back to the fascist fantasies of Hitler, Himmler, Rosenberg, Darre, and Hess: blatantly occult fantasies that became government policy and which led to the Holocaust and World War II. But the authors insisted that there was something there, below the surface, of the Third Reich: a sinister force that had been successfully, for a time, evoked by the Nazi magicians of the SS. The phenomenon of "coincidence," or what Jung called "synchronicity" and Pauwels and Bergier call "synchronism," was the most obvious evidence of the operation of this force and one which the authors suggested could be the basis for a whole "new conception of history."

Indeed, this author himself has pointed out from time to time how often coincidence appears in the telling of everything from assassination conspiracies to UFO research; and he has suggested that either we agree with Jim Garrison that such coincidences are evidence of an intelligence operation (and, by extension, that some of our conspiracy theories may, after all, be correct), or that the coincidences represent something else: an "acausal connecting principle" perhaps (to use the phrase invented by Jung) that nevertheless demonstrates important linkages or "correspondences" between events in the world. To understand how this might be possible, we will have to examine the field of quantum physics for a short time, as we come across some amazing correspondence between Carl Jung and Wolfang Pauli, the former the father of the "archetype" and depth analysis, and the latter a Nobel Prize-winning physicist. While the primary sources for much of this information are quite dense, the basic outlines of the science will be presented in as intelligible a fashion as possible. As always, source material is noted in the text for those who wish to understand what is happening in the world of the physics of consciousness today, and why it is vitally important that we, as citizens of a shrinking world, remain current with these new discoveries.

Darkness at Noon

Goebbels: *You wanted to see me, Dr. Jung.*
Jung: *No, you wanted to see me.*
Goebbels: *No, you wanted to see me.*

Jung turned around and left Goebbels' office—and vomited ...

—Account of a visit by Carl Jung to Berlin during May 1933 upon being invited to a meeting by Nazi Propaganda Minister Josef Goebbels[7]

By all accounts, Wolfgang Pauli should have been the most satisfied man in Europe. In 1932, he was already world-famous as a physicist, a scientist of brilliance and possessed of an uncanny, creative insight. He was doing the work he loved, and recognized by his peers for his accomplishments. He was on the way to winning the Nobel Prize in physics in 1945.

Yet, his emotional life was in utter turmoil.

His mother, discovering that his father had been having an affair, committed suicide by poisoning herself. Pauli then became involved in a disastrous marriage with a cabaret singer which lasted less than a year. He turned to drink, got involved in bar brawls, fought constantly with his colleagues, and sank into a morbid state of what they used to call "melancholia." Wolfgang Pauli was on the verge of a nervous breakdown.

He also complained of very strange, very disturbing dreams, and it was possibly this problem among all others that led him to consult one of the world's most famous psychoanalysts, the St. Paul to Freud's Jesus, Swiss psychiatrist Carl Gustav Jung. At first, Jung gave him over to the care of a newly-trained assistant, a woman, as Jung felt Pauli's problems stemmed from relationships with women (his mother's suicide, his failed marriage), but as the sessions brought forth a mine of greater and greater symbolic material, Jung took over from Erna Rossenbaum and began to analyze Pauli personally.

In a state of profound personal misery, Pauli began his sessions with Jung every Monday at noon.

What resulted from this relationship, which lasted some twenty-six years (1932-1958), is a fascinating collection of letters the two men exchanged discussing Pauli's dreams and his scientific approach to Jung's deep and heavily symbolic psychoanalytic system. Although the actual psychoanalysis only lasted two years, Pauli continued to send reports of his dreams to Jung, and they discussed both the dream imagery as well as Pauli's concepts of physics and "symmetry," concepts that eventually won Pauli the Nobel Prize for his discovery of the "exclusion principle," which also bears his name as the "Pauli principle." The relationship between Jung and Pauli was probably the first real interface between modern physics and psychoanalysis, and paved the way for the development of what is now known as the field of quantum consciousness, a controversial and extreme form of physics in which it sometimes seems as if the slide rule has been applied to the soul.

The search for the basic "building blocks" of life, of reality, of the mind, has been going on for thousands of years. In the West, during the golden era of the Greek philosophers, all of reality was believed to be reducible to four elements: earth, air, fire and water. In the East, a similar impulse led to the identification of five elements: wind, water, fire, metal, earth. The intention was the same: to find common denominators for the bewildering profligacy of creation, a creation that included the palm tree and the platypus, the horse and the canyon, gold and lead, coal and diamonds. It was believed by both Western and Eastern philosophers that the elements—whether four or five—worked with each other in combination to produce all that the senses perceived. This understanding led to everything from the Periodic Table of the Elements to the nature of the DNA molecule, as science looked deeper and deeper behind what was visible to the naked eye to what was invisible: atoms, chromosomes, quarks. This effort was matched by the work of the scientists of the mind, the psychologists who sought to discover what hidden, invisible forces were at work behind the crazy-quilt veneer of consciousness.

Carl G. Jung (1875-1961) was of Protestant German Swiss parentage, and was for a time an important disciple of Sigmund Freud (1856-1939). It was Jung who understood the relationship that exists between mythology and unconscious psychological states, and the relevance of myths, fairy tales, and religious and mystical imagery to psychoanalysis and the interpretation of dreams, as well as the interpretation of cultural events and icons through an analysis of their symbolism. He also popularized the theory of the "archetype": images buried deep within our "collective unconscious" (another Jungian concept) that are carriers of a constellation of associations, and which are universal in nature, such as the Great Mother or the Wise Old Man or the Serpent. His analysis of alchemical literature is, itself, literature, much in the same way that Freud's writings are more than scientific articles and closer to philosophical essays, which, to some of his followers, are virtual scripture.

To Jung and his followers, there is a deep substratum of consciousness that lies beneath the layers of mechanical instincts and the measurable phenomena of clinical psychology, even below Freud's layer where the "pleasure principle" resides. This layer—called by Jung the "collective unconscious"—is a well of images and associations, myths and icons that all humans share. These images become visible under certain circumstances, such as in political rallies or religious rituals or on the movie screen or in advertising and propaganda, and we take them for granted without realizing the power they represent or the extent to which they may be manipulating our consciousness. One of Jung's most accessible and popular works—*Man and His Symbols*—usually appears as a large, coffee-table book replete with these images and explanations of what they represent, and why we react to them the way that we do.

Traffic with the collective unconscious is not all one-way, however. Like a living being, it can be influenced by consciousness and modified. Thousands of years of human civilization have modified the symbol stream and the structure of the collective unconscious, and there are regional differences in how these symbols manifest from culture to culture, although the basic elements of the collective unconscious—the archetypes—are the same for everyone. This is what Jung's patient and occasional collaborator, Wolfgang Pauli, found so fascinating, and what led the two of them to equate this process with those of quantum mechanics.

Jung's fascination with mystical and occult texts and themes—although not with occult practices *per se*—led him to write admiringly of the phenomenon of National Socialism in Germany, interpreting the Nazi pagan mythos in his *Wotan.* It was this, as well as his anti-Semitism, which has led many in recent years to question Jung's personality and motives, although it is clear from his later writings that he did not idolize the Nazis or defend their hideous excesses. That Jung was an anti-Semite is something that not even his own followers try to deny, as evidenced by the "Lingering Shadows" conference held at the C. G. Jung Foundation in New York City in 1989.[8] At the same time, Jung's anti-Semitism is virtually indistinguishable from that of, say, Aleister Crowley. Both men held contemporary views of Jews that were common for their time and place, and yet both men also studied Judaism and Jewish mysticism. While we expect more from both—since Jung was widely regarded as a deep and serious thinker, a man whose genius made an enormous contribution to psychology and philosophy, and in the case of Crowley we have a man who declared himself to be a god (!)—we are left with the realization that these idols have clay feet, as do all idols in every era. One tends to think that Jung's early fascination with Nazism had more in common with many a scientific observer at an atomic bomb test: in one's heart, one realizes that this is a horrible development, but at the same time one is awed by the sound and the light, amazed that the human race is capable of such elaborate and dramatic destruction.

(Of course, the focus on Jung as an anti-Semite is something of a smokescreen as well. One cannot compare Jung's admitted anti-Semitism with that of Henry Ford's rabid anti-Semitic tract, *The International Jew*, for instance, or the actions of a generation of American politicians and businessmen such as Herbert Walker, Prescott Bush or the Dulles brothers, who actively supported Nazism before and after the war.)

As the years went by, Jung became something of an ethnologist, and traveled to Africa in search of primitive cultures. He wrote extensively on alchemy both European and Asian, and studied the UFO phenomenon. He analyzed Christianity in light of his discoveries in psychology and mythology, and gave us terms we use today without realizing Jung's contribution: anima, collective unconscious, archetype, individuation. The goal of Jung's approach to psychoanalysis was the integration of the various elements of the personality to form a seamless whole, the process he called "individuation." The emblem of the successful conclusion of this process was the mandala, the famous Eastern symbol of the sum of creation, a symbol in which opposites are balanced with each other: north with south, east with west; fire with water, air with earth; male with female. Jung did not simply borrow the idea of the mandala from Hindu or Buddhist iconography; he believed the mandala was used by the Eastern mystics to mean the same thing, to represent the same process, as that described in his own work. To Jung, the world was full of symbols: from advertising logos and slogans to political speeches to arcane occult texts. In this, he was walking in the footsteps of Giordano Bruno, and, close behind them both was Ioan Coulianu.

Jung's collected works are available through the Bollingen imprint of Princeton University, and they are a tremendous resource not only as a guide to Jungian thought but also as a veritable Baedecker through religious and mystical thought and textual and iconographic references from around the world. The works of Wolfgang Pauli—those that are accessible to a non-scientific audience—are equally valuable, such as "The Influence of Archetypal Ideas on the Scientific Theories of Kepler" which was included in *The Interpretation of Nature and the Psyche* by Jung and Pauli. In this essay, Pauli analyzed Kepler's theories of astrology in the light of both physics and Jungian psychology.

But it is perhaps in the area of "synchronicity" that we will find the views of Jung and Pauli most valuable here, for it gives us a context for understanding the action (and, perhaps, the nature) of the sinister forces of which we speak.

> ... it is impossible, with our present resources, to explain ESP, or the fact of meaningful coincidence, as a phenomenon of energy. This makes an end of the causal explanation as well, for "effect" cannot be understood as anything except a phenomenon of energy. Therefore it cannot be a question of cause and effect, but of a falling together in time, a kind of simultaneity. Because of this quality of simultaneity, I have picked on the term "synchronicity" to designate a hypothetical factor equal in rank to causality as a principle of explanation.[9]

Jung's idea of an "acausal connecting principle" actually goes to the heart of physics; it is an attack on the most sacred of scientific sacred cows: cause and effect, something which Isaac Newton had enshrined in his work. In the traditional view, every effect has a cause, much like those swinging ball sets one sees on executive desks, where one ball knocks into another, which knocks into another, etc., in a straight line down from the first "knock." To this type of scientist, every effect can be traced back to an "ultimate cause," all the way back to the Big Bang that started the universe on its ancient path. But isn't that the problem?

An endlessly receding, linear chain of cause-and-effect eventually leads us back to a First Cause, and that implies a beginning without cause. Some have called it God. There is no room in traditional science for God, because the existence of a God would (presumably) render scientific theory *relative* to God, an unknown and undefined principle. Science has generally avoided facing this issue in any sort of intelligible way. The universe may simply be eternal, outside normal definitions of time since it contains all time (and all space); but then what does that do to cause-and-effect, which is conceived of as linear as opposed to … what, circular?

Arthur Young (one of the original "Nine") proposed the existence of the "quantum of action," what he identified as "first cause," and called it the "missing parameter of science." In his view, it would go a long way to accommodating the paradoxes one encounters in quantum physics, such as Heisenberg's "Uncertainty Principle." According to Heisenberg (a friend and classmate of Wolfgang Pauli at the University of Munich), one cannot precisely predict the position of an electron at any given time; its position will always remain "uncertain." This is because an electron has an inherent motion that is not the result of it being acted upon by other forces, and thus its motion seems to lie outside the realm of cause-and-effect. A molecule, on the other hand, is a static sort of thing: composed of atoms in a particular alignment and creating, for instance, water (two atoms of hydrogen, one of oxygen); it is a blunt fact and Newtonian laws work on water and on the rest of the molecules at that level of reality. Electrons, though, operate in a world where Newtonian physics no longer applies.

To go one step further, a photon—a particle of light—operates in a still more rarefied world. One of the mysteries of light, and that which prompted the discovery of the quantum by Max Planck around the year 1900, is that it does not lose energy in its travels through space. A light particle having left a distant star arrives on earth with the same energy it had when it left. This did not seem to be playing by the Newtonian rules. Heisenberg realized that in order to study a photon one of necessity has to "disturb" it; i.e., a relationship develops between the particle studied and the one doing the studying which changes the state of the particle (and, of course, of the observer). Thus, there is no such thing as a truly uninvolved, outside observer. The observer is a participant. The observer changes the object being observed by the very fact of observation, and this is not merely a semantic game: it is the reality of quantum physics and the laboratory observation of sub-atomic particles.

At the sub-atomic level, where light can be either a particle *or* a wave but not both (whimsically referred to as a "wavicle"), one can only study it as one *or* the other, thus making a judgment before one even begins. In a sense, then, the observer and the object observed are connected in some mysterious, acausal way; and if the observer and observed are connected, then the universe is a place of interconnectedness that transcends mechanistic Newtonian causality. And if this is true—and quantum physicists insist that it is—then the UFO phenomenon (as an example) is a function of that universe, and it is quite possible that if there are actual "aliens" piloting the craft, they may have been aware of this principle for a long time, which would account for their actions in ways that we are not prepared to accept. They would be aware, for instance, that their observation of us changes *them* in some profound way, and that our experience of them changes us; which could account for their strange appearance, such as the various beings experienced by Whitley Strieber in his published accounts: possibly an attempt to modulate our experience of them in ways that will not cause some kind of existential blowback.

In Newton's world of linear cause-and-effect, the possibility of free will is discounted. In the world of Arthur Young and the "quantum of action," free will is reinstated as a function of "action" and thus is given essentially its own existence as a separate quantum. How does this quantum unite and modulate the other quanta?

Meaning is the bridge between consciousness and matter.
—Physicist David Bohm, *Omni* magazine, January 1987

What Jung proposed was that another principle, a connecting principle, exists in the universe outside of cause and effect, linking "unrelated" elements at the level of *meaning*, creating what are called "meaningful coincidences." Since we are accustomed to interpreting events as cause-and-effect related, the appearance of coincidence has been variously understood as either "magic" or as something totally without meaning, a kind of accident that has no place in scientific discourse (as if any event could be considered to be "outside science"). Once again, we have drawn a line between an event observed and the observer, ignoring the importance of the coincidence as a carrier of information. Yet, as physics has progressed to the point where the old standby of an "outside observer" to an experiment is no longer to be taken for granted, but that "observer" has now become a "participant," it has become harder and harder to define a pure science that is not the result of human intervention and participation … with all that implies. (What is perhaps comforting to some to contemplate is that if creation itself is a kind of experiment, then, according to Heisenberg, God is not only an observer but is also a participant.)

Jung noted that the basis of modern science is statistical in nature: that is, scientific laws are really statements about probability. That is why it is thus far impossible, for instance, to predict the weather with any degree of accuracy, or the outcome of a sporting event in advance, or to give an absolutely certain medical prognosis; that is why it is impossible to predict where a given sub-atomic particle will be at any given time. We can make statements about probable results, but still cannot be one hundred percent certain about predicting specific events. When events occur which defy the laws of probability, science generally lumps them into a separate category, the one or two (or ten or twenty) percent not accounted for in their statistical calculations. Likewise, religion generally lumps them into a separate category, and calls them "miracles": spontaneous remission of a cancer, for instance, or the patient pronounced dead who comes back to life on the operating table. Or a shower of frogs. For the mystically-inclined, the occurrence of these "non-statistically predictable results" indicates the presence of God. For the scientifically-inclined, they may be thought of as accidents, or the result of inadequate data or a defective instrument, or as mere coincidences.

Sometimes, however, there are just too many coincidences, and their sheer number or frequency suggests the operation of another factor in the universe.

Jung posited that there are relationships among events that are not part of the cause-and-effect nexus, and that these relationships come to our attention when a large number of coincidences take place. While he had been aware of this phenomenon for quite some time and witnessed it in his own life and in the lives of his patients, development of a formal theory awaited his relationship with the Austrian scientist Wolfgang Pauli. It was Pauli who actually "proved" Heisenberg correct, and made a substantial contribution to quantum mechanics by his own "exclusion principle" or what is known as the "Pauli principle." The math behind this principle is daunting, as is any attempt to describe it without recourse to advanced physics, but suffice it to say that it involves principles of symmetry and asymmetry and explains the wonderful diversity of nature as a kind of cosmic "dance."

Theoretical physicist Dr. F. David Peat, who worked with renegade physicist David Bohm and who once interviewed Werner Heisenberg, Pauli's friend and classmate, has expressed the Pauli Principle this way:

> Electrons, protons, neutrons, and neutrinos, along with other particles, form one group (and engage in an *antisymmetric* dance) while the other group includes mesons and photons of light (and forms a *symmetric* dance). It turns out that, in the former case, the nature of this abstract movement or dance has the effect of keeping particles with the same energy always apart from each other. However, this *exclusion* of particles from each other's energy space is not the result of any force which operates between them nor indeed is an act of causality in the normal sense, rather it arises out of the *antisymmetry of abstract movement* of the particles as a whole. Hence the underlying pattern of the *whole dance* has a profound effect on the behavior of each individual particle. (emphasis in original)[10]

Thus we are talking about a pattern or matrix underlying the observed universe, a kind of grid of connections linking events according to a system we can only barely perceive, a pattern that is *in motion* if we take Pauli's symmetric and asymmetric dances literally. It is this pattern that differentiates one element from another, and which contributes to everything from, as Peat explains, "the intense coherent light of the laser as well as superfluids and superconduction" on the one hand to "the collapse of a star through the white dwarf, neutron star, and black hole stages" on the other.[11] In other words, all of physical creation. Peat sees this as a basis for a coherent theory of synchronicity, as the relation between the particles in Pauli's exclusion principle "is not the result of any force which operates between them nor indeed is an act of causality." Thus, we have links between particles that defy normal cause-and-effect calculations. And these are the particles that make up the universe as we know it, and everything in it.

Physicists normally do not appreciate it when non-physicists make statements about their science irresponsibly and make theoretical leaps not supported by mathematical proofs (and why should they?), so it is incumbent upon me to add a further caveat of clarification:

Modern theories of quantum physics do not invalidate traditional Newtonian physics when it comes to the tangible world we live in. What goes up must still come down; and for every action there is still an equal and opposite reaction. None of that has changed. The laws of physics that we learned in school are useful ways of interpreting the world we live in and its phenomena. The laws do not exist outside our perceptions, however. They are laws that man has made, not laws that exist in nature; they are ways of understanding and measuring nature and its processes. As such, however, they do not provide a definitive cosmology; they do not explain everything that we experience.

If we look at "reality" (what a concept!) as having layers, much like Jung's concept of consciousness, then the Newtonian world is the "top" layer, the layer we deal with every day. It is the layer of molecular structures, of mass and energy and dimension. It is our conscious level, if you will.

If we go a level down, we enter the atomic world which has a slightly different "reality" and set of laws that govern its processes.

Still further down, we have the world of nuclear particles, like the "uncertain" electrons. And, further down still, we have the world that light lives in: a mysterious realm of photons that defies Newtonian concepts of time and space.

Arthur Young described this as an "arc," illustrating the descent of light through the nuclear particles to atoms to molecules, and then up from molecular structures to plants, animals, and eventually man, in a glyph that is strangely reminiscent of ancient Gnostic and Manichean theories of the descent of spirit into matter,[12] and for a reason: these lower levels of reality are those frequented by the magician and the mystic, the psy-war expert and the advertising man. These are the levels upon which it is possible to exert some influence (all those spinning electrons, all those packets of light, that dizzying dance of symmetry and asymmetry in the dark and dirty basement beneath the nice clean house of consensus reality, the subtle connectivities like the invisible wiring in the walls, pipes of hot and cold running fractals, all Fast Fourier and fragile beauty) and thereby—according to the *Lesser Key of Solomon*, a medieval sorcerer's workbook that looks like notes on an advanced form of calculus by a demented or visionary Pauli or Heisenberg—"anticipate an effect, the which to the vulgar shall seem to be a miracle."[13]

While the system of levels posited by both Jung and Young (!) are intellectually satisfying to some degree—it seems to be "orderly" and capable of representing processes that are quantum mechanical as well as Newtonian depending on the level or layer of reality under discussion—there are other phenomena in the world of quantum physics that are counter-intuitive. For instance, time.

As Oxford mathematics Professor Sir Roger Penrose puts it,

> All the successful equations of physics are symmetrical in time. They can be used equally well in one direction in time as in the other. The future and the past seem physically to be on a completely equal footing. Newton's laws, Hamilton's equations, Maxwell's equations, Einstein's general relativity, Dirac's equation, the Schroedinger equation—all remain effectively unaltered if we reverse the direction of time.[14]

This means that, to use Penrose's example later on in the same book that a glass full of water falling off a table and breaking on the floor could—according to the above-mentioned laws of physics—just as easily assemble itself from the broken pieces of glass and spilled water and jump up onto the table: the entire episode but in "reverse" order.[15] Since that is not the way we perceive the universe to operate, there must be another factor—a factor in consciousness—that experiences the passage of time in a single direction: past-present-future. The future, then, is dependent on actions and processes that have taken place "before" it in time, which seems to indicate a degree of choice—of decisions made, directions taken—otherwise the future would be absolutely predictable in every aspect.

Penrose has attacked the contemporary discipline of Artificial Intelligence as being basically unscientific in its approach to consciousness and physics. He does not believe that the brain is nothing more than a glorified computer, or that eventually computers will develop to the point that they attain consciousness, as consciousness is obviously much more than mere computation. Penrose is part of a new movement in science and consciousness which has attracted a number of maverick thinkers with a variety of heavy credentials. F. David Peat—mentioned above—studied with Penrose at Oxford, as well as with David Bohm, and his integration of Jungian psychology with quantum physics is representative of the direction in which the movement as a whole is going.

Penrose has worked with microbiologists to come up with a novel and, if correct, profound theory of quantum consciousness, which is based on the examination of microtubules in the brain. As noted earlier, science has been occupied with discovering the smallest, most irreducible elements of matter and energy in order to understand how the universe is put together; as atoms were broken down into sub-atomic particles and quarks, fermions, bosons, mesons and a host of other strange and tricky entities made their appearance (either virtually, through mathematical calculation and prediction, or in the particle accelerator), so too did the biologists break down the human body into its constituent "particles": the genetic code, and its holy grail, the human genome. Still, none of these discoveries answered the basic questions of the human condition, such as the mystery of consciousness: of a mind that could conceive of realities that were not "real," of time that could flow backwards, of being in two places at the same "time," of life after death and reincarnation and the evil eye. Or, more prosaically, of communicating over vast distances and traveling in the air and watching images move before your eyes and hearing voices come out of a machine. All of these ideas were once thought to be the powers of sorcerers and magicians and fakirs, and are represented in the grimoires and other spellbooks of the occultist; they are now within the reach of everyone on the planet, no matter how spiritually undeveloped, how illiterate, how rational or irrational. They were the inventions of conscious minds working in ways that could not be explained by instinct or some other mechanical description of the brain and its nervous system. They were the inventions of men and women who dreamed the impossible, and who were haunted by the chants of the shamans lodged deep within their "collective unconscious," the prayers of human beings who longed to fly.

Is there a physical basis for consciousness? Or are body and mind functions of each other?

What Penrose and his colleagues have discovered is that—on what could be called the "sub-atomic" level of the human brain and nervous system—there exists an interface between mind and matter that has important implications for our study.

The Roots of Coincidence

The ... dilemma confronts us as we turn to a type of phenomenon which has puzzled man since the dawn of mythology: the disruption of the humdrum chains of causal events by coincidences of an improbable nature, which are not causally related yet appear highly significant. Any theory which attempts to take such phenomena seriously must necessarily involve an even more radical break with our traditional categories of thought than the pronunciamentos of Heisenberg, Dirac or Feynman.

—Arthur Koestler, *The Roots of Coincidence*[16]

Zombies are a useful philosophical concept.
—Stuart Hameroff in "A Sonoran Afternoon"

In 1996, Roger Penrose and Stuart Hameroff—in a paper entitled "Orchestrated Reduction of Quantum Coherence in Brain Microtubules: A Model for Consciousness"[17]—presented a theory of consciousness that stemmed from Penrose's concept of "objective reduction" or "OR," first promulgated in 1994's *Shadows of the Mind.* Objective reduction is, as the paper defines, "a newly proposed physical phenomenon of quantum wave function" which is "essential for consciousness, and occurs in cytoskeletal microtubules and other structures within each of the brain's neurons."[18] In other words, a professor of the mathematics of physics (Penrose) and a professor of anaesthesiology and psychology (Hameroff) teamed up to unlock the mysteries of quantum and consciousness and apparently found them hiding discretely within the very neural pathways of the human brain.

The exposition is very tough going for the non-initiate, especially as two very distinct disciplines are involved: quantum mechanics and neurobiology. An attempt will be made to "objectively reduce" the main thrust of the argument.

Penrose and Hameroff begin by describing some basic elements of quantum physics.

> At the base of quantum theory is the wave/particle duality of atoms and their components. As long as a quantum system such as an atom or sub-atomic particle remains isolated from its environment, it behaves as a "wave of possibilities" and exists in coherent "superposition" (with complex number coefficients) of many possible states.[19]

How, then, does the phenomenon move from this ambiguous "wave of possibilities" to become an actual particle or wave? What causes its "collapse"? Several theories are advanced, but Penrose prefers a "self-collapsing" model "growing and persisting to reach a critical mass/time/energy threshold related to quantum gravity."[20] This self-collapsing model is referred to as OR or "objective reduction," as opposed to the SR or "subjective reduction" model wherein the collapse is attributed to measurement or conscious observation.

The authors go on to describe another fact of quantum physics, one that seems extremely bizarre to those brought up on a healthy diet of Newtonian physics:

> Another feature of quantum systems is quantum inseparability, or non-locality, which implies that all quantum objects that have once interacted are in some sense still connected! When two quantum systems have interacted, their wave functions become "phase entangled" so that when one system's

> wave function is collapsed, the other system's wave function, no matter how far away, instantly collapses as well. The non-local connection ("quantum entanglement") is instantaneous, independent of distance and implies that the quantum entities, by sharing a wave function, are indivisible.[21]

Non-locality is one of the more attractive characteristics of quantum physics for the romantically-inclined, as it implies that a kind of communication is possible across vast distances, and that once two "wave functions" meet, they are always in instant communication and are, in fact, "indivisible." While this in itself is not a validation for extrasensory perception or telepathic communication, etc., it does present scientists with an uncomfortable premise. If such a phenomenon is possible—even at the sub-atomic level—then somehow it might be possible at a more macro level, the level of waking consciousness.

Penrose and Hameroff then go on to describe the research of various other scientists who have identified "apparently random quantum effects acting on neurotransmitter release at the pre-synaptic grid within each neural axon," and that one researcher, H.P. Stapp, "has suggested that (SR) wave function collapse in neurons is closely related to consciousness in the brain." The quest of Penrose and Hameroff for a physical structure wherein these effects take place brought them to the microtubule.

Microtubules are components of the neuron or, more specifically, of the cytoskeleton structure within the neuron which "establishes neuronal form, maintains synaptic connections, and performs other essential tasks." The microtubules themselves are "hollow cylindrical polymers of individual proteins known as tubulin" which are "interconnected by linking proteins (microtubule-associated proteins: MAPs) to other microtubules" which then form the "lattice networks" of the cytoskeletons. In the view of the authors, the MAPs are responsible for—"orchestrate"—the collapse of wave functions in the neurons; thus, "Orch OR." The wave function collapse is non-reversible in time, and it is the successive collapse of wave functions at the microtubule level that gives rise, in effect, to the passage of time (its seeming unidirectional nature: past-present-future) and thus to consciousness itself. (This would solve the conundrum posed by Penrose earlier (1994) and mentioned above: that the laws of physics are the same whether time "flows" forward or backward, and that the sensation of time going in one direction only is therefore a function of consciousness, since there are no physical laws to account for it.)

The reader will forgive me if I skip the proofs and formulae that are offered in support of this theory, and those interested are encouraged to seek out this information for themselves on the Internet or in an up-to-date science library. There are, however, some slightly more accessible accounts of this fascinating and ultimately quite revealing theory, and Penrose's partner Stuart Hameroff is responsible for a few of them.

In *Trends in Cognitive Sciences*, Hameroff's article "'Funda-Mentality' Is the Conscious Mind Subtly Linked to a Basic Level of the Universe?" sets out the parameters of the discussion in a style that is a bit easier to understand for those who do not have the math.[22]

Hameroff begins by discussing various attempts to come to a physics of consciousness, all of which are lacking in either scientific rigor or fall apart on close inspection. The main target of the Penrose-Hameroff approach is the "mind as computer" theory. The "physicalists"—those who believe that a purely physical solution will one day appear to explain consciousness as a kind of super-computability, a more sophisticated version of the desktop PC—see consciousness as the inevitable result of more complex neural circuitry, circuitry which could one day be duplicated in the laboratory and the test bench. Penrose and Hameroff, however, believe that consciousness is not purely physical in the traditional sense. It is certainly not a function of "computability":

> Regarding transition from pre-conscious or implicit processing to consciousness itself, the physicalist view is that consciousness emerges at a critical level of complexity. But no threshold is apparent, nor is there a reasonable suggestion why such an emergent property should have conscious experience. As physicalism is based on deterministic computation, it is also unable to account for free will or Penrose's proposed non-computability. But the major problem remains experience, for which physicalism offers no testable predictions. Something is missing.[23]

Hameroff then asks the question that is central to an understanding of how the sub-atomic phenomena—equally wave or particle, obeying the exclusion principle and the uncertainty principle, exhibiting features of non-locality—so bizarre in terms of Newtonian physics and the "real world," ever manage to organize themselves into the tangible, touchable, breakable, objects around us:

> The problem is the transition: why and how do microscopic quantum superposed states become classical and definite in the macro-world? This problem is called quantum state reduction, or collapse of the wave function, and it may be the key to both consciousness and reality.[24]

This, of course, is where "Orch OR" comes into the discussion and the magical microtubules make their appearance. The idea, basically, is this:

At the most microscopic level of "reality," the sub-atomic particles behave strangely, as if they are not really part of classical reality. Yet, they make up everything that we see, everything that our senses perceive. This means that, at some point, these sub-atomic particles (and waves) become organized in a fashion that permits physical reality as we know it. There is a threshold somewhere, a level of complexity is reached and—due to some type of combination of particles, waves, mass and energy that we do not yet understand—the wave function, the quantum state of the particles, collapses, becomes "reduced" to perceived and perceivable reality (OR or "objective reduction"). The ambiguous nature of an individual particle is "reduced" to one state only: either particle or wave. What Penrose and Hameroff are saying is that this process can take place not only within the external world of physics, but also within the brain, at the microscopic level of the microtubules which are components of the cystoskeleton of the neuron, and that this process is taking place constantly:

> OR in the brain would likely be linked to neural processes occurring over time scales in the range of tens to hundreds of milliseconds, for example 25 millisecond intervals in coherent 40 Hz.[25]

Naturally, then, the brain contains not only neurons and synapses and the entire wet machinery of cognition, but is also acting on—and being acted upon by—the quanta. Consciousness itself, according to this theory, is the result of this type of objective reduction, indeed a self-orchestrating objective reduction. The brain is plugged into the quantum world in a very dynamic way, and consciousness is the result.

The authors do not discount the possibility of consciousness in beings other than human. According to their model, as long as sufficient numbers of microtubules are present in the brain or nervous system of the creature under consideration, this phenomenon will obtain. The degree of sophistication is possibly a result of the complexity of the brain and nervous system itself: the sheer number of collapsing wave forms at any given "time" (and their relationship to each other across a complex matrix of neurons) indicating a corresponding degree of consciousness.

Hameroff, in another article in the same issue of the journal explains more fully:

> Regarding free will, the problem is that our actions seem neither totally deterministic nor random (probabilistic). The only other apparent choice is Penrose's non-computability. In the Orch OR model microtubule quantum superpositions compute and evolve linearly … during pre-conscious processing, but are influenced at the instant of OR collapse by hidden (Platonic) non-computable logic inherent in spacetime geometry. The precise outcome—our free will actions—result from effects of the hidden logic on the quantum system poised at the edge of objective reduction.[26]

Elsewhere in the same article, Hameroff describes this hidden logic as "some influence which is neither random nor completely deterministic, but due to hidden propensities embedded in fundamental spacetime." It's these "hidden propensities" and "hidden (Platonic) non-computable logic inherent in spacetime geometry" that are the catch. While the Orch OR model may explain the *mechanics* of consciousness—and it is still early days on that due to the amount of funding it would require to test the theory—there is still the mystery of consciousness itself. What Penrose and Hameroff have done is state the problem in terms that are clear and compelling, if not always convincing to their peers. The idea that consciousness is not merely the result of a kind of super-computation capacity of the brain, but of actions that take place on a sub-microscopic level within that brain that are identical to processes familiar to quantum physicists is significant, if only because it helps to answer another question, that of synchronicity and coincidence.

In case the reader is thinking that perhaps all this theorizing is quite abstract and is not useful in any pragmatic sense of the term, it should be noted that Penrose and Hameroff were invited to lead a group meeting at the RAND Corporation on October 22, 1998—one of a series of meetings that were sponsored by the Defense Advanced Research Projects Agency (DARPA), a US government agency that is the godchild of the Pentagon, and target of much speculation by conspiracy theorists. The series "focused on social and political governance questions arising from the impacts of the information and biological revolutions." Thus, the findings of Penrose and Hameroff were being examined for the possible application of their research in the "social and political governance" sphere by the military.

Before we leap from Orch OR to synchronicity, it is perhaps useful to look at what Penrose and Hameroff had to say during that study group concerning different mental states and their relationship to the collapse of quantum wave function. By the time of this meeting in October of 1998 the theory seems to have advanced somewhat and become even more compelling.

A chart that was included as part of the report on the RAND meeting is entitled "Quantum Superposition Entanglement in Microtubules for Five States Related to Consciousness." The first state is the normal waking state. The second shows the mental state during anaesthesia. The third is called "heightened experience." The fourth is called "altered state," and this one is the most interesting. The legend appended to this diagram states,

> D. Altered State: even greater rate of emergence of quantum superposition due to sensory input and other factors promoting quantum state (e.g. meditation, psychedelic drug). Predisposition to quantum state results in baseline shift and collapse so that conscious experience merges with normally subconscious computing mode.

In other words, the altered mental state brought about by meditation, psychedelics, or—we may assume—other mystical and occult practices, is actually *promoting* the quantum state posited by Penrose and Hameroff. These practices cause profound changes not only in the neural firing of the brain but also at the deepest level of matter and energy, at the level of waves and particles. It is not only a chemical change we are witnessing but changes at the sub-atomic level, the level where "uncertainty" and "non-locality" and "symmetry" … dance. And if this is causing a change in consciousness, it is also fair to say that consciousness is capable of causing a change in the operations of not only the neurons on the level of neurophysiology, but also on the sub-atomic processes represented by the microtubules on the level of the quanta. It is a conscious decision to perform meditation or the other "mind altering" (literally!) exercises—including taking psychedelic drugs—and this decision then causes changes to occur in one's own brain, altering its state and to some degree its structure. What kind of changes take place? What purpose do these changes serve? And more importantly, are we competent enough to take responsibility for creating these changes?

If we look at the legend for "Heightened Experience" on the same chart, we read:

> C. Heightened Experience: increased sensory experience input increases rate of emergence of quantum superposition. Orch OR threshold is reached faster and Orch OR frequency increases.

Only the next state in the chart, "Altered State," demonstrates a faster rate of quantum superposition with its proportional increase in Orch OR frequency. It is not stated exactly what a "heightened experience" might be, other than the result of "increased sensory input." One wonders. Could this include sex? Watching a film or television show? Listening to music? Could this state be achieved on a wide scale through clever use of the media? Through public performance of religious ritual? Propaganda?

This level of discussion is generally and noticeably absent from Penrose's public appearances before mathematicians and physicists, during which he usually focuses on the general outlines of his OR theory and presents evidence for non-computability as an important characteristic of consciousness; Hameroff—as an anesthesiologist and psychologist—is apt to concentrate on various aspects of consciousness, but the chart in the RAND discussion is much more to the point. It identifies those areas of the Orch OR model that would be of most interest to those responsible for military and political matters and, in light of our previous discussions of Puharich, MK-ULTRA, psychological warfare, etc., it's rather like a "blast from the past": can science be used in any way to modify the consciousness of individual human beings, of groups (or nations) of human beings, and can the consciousness of individuals or groups be used to modify or manipulate "reality"? When the most powerful weapon of a terrorist is the willingness to commit suicide in order to bring down an airplane, a bus, or a building full of people, or an entire city itself, suddenly consciousness becomes a central issue of national defense. We are a long way from using the science revealed by quantum mechanics to effect changes in consciousness, but the scientific theories presented by the quantum consciousness crowd permit the possibility of *thinking about* these strategies, and allows an environment in which the discussion goes up a level, from that of the crank and the schizophrenic with an aluminum foil hat to protect against "rays," to the level of scientific advisors to military theorists.

Is quantum mechanics a way of introducing into scientific discourse such concepts as ESP, or psychokinetics, or remote viewing? Will the research by Penrose, Hameroff, et al. lead to the development of devices that could be used to increase the abilities of the brain to encompass mental powers that used to be the stuff of either science fiction … or the oral traditions of shamanism and the encoded texts of alchemists and magicians?

We are perhaps a level "too deep" when we use quantum mechanics as a means of having this discussion, and the rules that apply in quantum physics do not apply in the world of classical, Newtonian physics in which we run our machines, drive our cars, watch television, and play baseball. But that's just the point. The powers and abilities of the shamans—and, now, of the remote viewers and the psychological warfare experts and the advertising men—are not demonstrable by Newtonian physics. They lie outside the realm of the classical scientific systems and are much more comfortable in the quantum world. And the interface between quantum physics and classical physics is our own nervous system; our brain is a site where quantum events are taking place, with all that implies, from "uncertainty" to "non-locality," albeit at a very sub-atomic level. The possibility that human beings may be able to consciously use this interface to defy normal, Newtonian physics by being in two places at once, or by leaping forward or backward in time, is something that has been tested under laboratory conditions in the United States under military and intelligence contracts. It was not only tested. It was used. And was successful.

Although contemporary science may scoff at the concept of "remote viewing," it became part of the American arsenal during the Cold War. In addition, the abilities of the remote viewers clearly demonstrate the mind's ability to duplicate—on a macro level—what quantum states do on a micro level, particularly in the area of "non locality." If the rules of quantum mechanics only apply on a deep, sub-microscopic level and the laws of classical Newtonian physics apply on our day-to-day level of reality, then there is another level of human experience entirely, in which it would appear that both worlds—quantum physical and classically physical—operate as one, in which a human being (a complex Newtonian structure if ever there was one) is able, through consciousness, to see into the future or the past, or to travel long distances and witness events taking place thousands of miles away, or even affect physical objects at that distance, using nothing more than the brain. In other words, to behave like a photon.

In 1982, the famous experiments of French physicist Alain Aspect demonstrated the reality of non-locality and, even more so, opened the door to this idea of consciousness affecting quantum states. Prior to these experiments, otherwise visionary scientists and mathematicians such as Albert Einstein, Boris Podolsky and Nathan Rosen considered non-locality as "spooky" or "ghostly"—appropriately enough—and Einstein in particular resisted this concept all his life. However, Aspect was able to arrange an experiment that vindicated (at least for some) the idea that two particles somehow "communicated" over vast distances instantaneously, thus violating Einstein's law that nothing could travel faster than the speed of light.

Basically, the experiment involved two photons whose "spins"—the direction and momentum of the particle's spin around its axis—were "entangled," or "mixed." In other words, they shared the same physical characteristics or properties. These photons were emitted at the same moment, and were thus "related." (I am simplifying this concept, of course, and the mathematicians and physicists in the audience may forgive me for taking shortcuts through the math in order to present the experiment in an intelligible manner.)

Once these photons were emitted, one was sent through a set of filters, let's call them filter A and filter B: the "external agents." A switch was employed to move the photon through either A or B, randomly. Through filter A, the photon would spin in one direction; through filter B, a different direction. What transpired, however, was earth-shaking in its implications, for when the first was affected by its "external agent"—passing through either filter A or filter B, and altering its spin respectively—its unfiltered twin responded *immediately* assumed the identical state, no matter how far away it was or in what direction it was traveling. There was no observable means of communication between the two particles, and the information was, necessarily, transmitted faster than the speed of light.

Further experimentation showed that the particles would remain in constant, immediate contact no matter how far apart they were, even if they were billions of miles distant. This implied that there is another fabric or web of interconnectedness underlying the physical universe that does not obey the laws of either Newtonian or Einsteinian physics. It also suggested that the human mind, by controlling the action of a particle in one place, could also control the action of a particle at a distance. It's a little like the notion that sticking a pin into a voodoo doll in Detroit could cause a pain in Dar-es-Salaam, with the caveat that the voodoo doll in Detroit must be made with the "particles" of the target in Dar-es-Salaam (the hair, fingernail clippings, etc.).

THE SHADOW OUT OF TIME

Recent experiments in remote viewing and other studies in parapsychology suggest that there is an 'interconnectedness' of the human mind with other minds and with matter...

—Survey of Science and Technology Issues, Committee on Science and Technology, US House of Representatives, 97th Congress, June 1981

My conception of time—my ability to distinguish between consecutiveness and simultaneousness—seemed subtly disordered, so that I formed chimerical notions about living in one age and casting one's mind all over eternity for knowledge of past and future ages.

— H.P. Lovecraft, "The Shadow Out Of Time"[27]

One of the strangest—and, at the same time, most documented and revealing of military and government appreciation of the paranormal—was the series of "remote viewing" experiments that were variously part of the Pentagon's own programs as well as sub-contracted by the military and the intelligence community to private contractors. As mentioned briefly in Book I, this program was known under a variety of rubrics, but the most dramatic and best known of these was STAR GATE, but it also included GRILL FLAME, CENTER LANE and SUN STREAK. Oddly enough, the most celebrated participants of the remote viewing endeavor were Scientologists.

Once again, and as so many times previously in our story, we find the influence of Aleister Crowley and Jack Parsons spreading through the political, military and cultic elements of American culture. Although this particular development was not as overt as the Manson Family, the Process, the Son of Sam, etc., it was as much a part of the establishment wing of the Crowley phenomenon as the former groups were part of the counter-culture or "anti-establishment" wing. We can credit Jack Parsons' contribution to the American war effort during World War II as well as to the American space program in general; when it comes to Hal Puthoff, Pat Price and Ingo Swann, however, we can credit Parsons' partner, L. Ron Hubbard, and his indirect contribution to the Cold War and anti-terrorism efforts, since Puthoff, Price and Swann were members of Scientology at the time they formed the nucleus of the remote viewing project in 1972 at the Stanford Research Institute in Menlo Park, California, an important scientific think-tank on the level of the RAND Corporation.

This sounds like the stuff of fantasy fiction, but it has been documented quite thoroughly by science writer Jim Schnabel in *Remote Viewers: The Secret History of America's Psychic Spies,*[28] and has also been ably presented on a number of Web sites, one of which has published a remote viewing manual compiled by the US Army. Schnabel's account brings us back to some of our old friends from Book I—Andrija Puharich, Uri Geller, "Spectra," and "Hoova"—and also introduces us to some new ones, including officers and enlisted men of the US Army, former NSA employees, the CIA, the National

Security Council, and a coven of US senators bent on protecting the psi-war program from federal budget cuts. In addition, two of the participants of that program—Russell Targ and remote viewer Keith Harary, both of SRI—have written their own book, *The Mind Race: Understanding and Using Psychic Powers*,[29] as has another participant, David Morehouse: *Psychic Warrior: Inside the CIA's Stargate Program*.[30] Thus, we have no lack of documentation provided by actual members of the remote viewing program as well as by Schnabel, who interviewed many of the program's participants.

The discussion of the modern technique of "remote viewing"—which was a scientific-sounding name invented by the SRI team to distance their practices from those of spiritualist mediums and Gypsy fortune-tellers—begins, according to Schnabel, in February of 1960 with the publication (in a French periodical, *Science et Vie*) of an article claiming that the US Navy had been able to communicate with the nuclear submarine *Nautilus* while it was submerged under the Arctic ice, using only telepathy. The article named names, but a volcano of controversy erupted, and everyone mentioned by name in the article condemned it as nonsense. But the damage had been done. The Soviets were worried that the US had found a way to harness psychic powers for military purposes, and the US was convinced that the Soviets were doing the same.

In fact, there was a great deal of similarity between the piece in *Science et Vie* and the Fred Crisman flying saucer affair in Ray Palmer's *Amazing Stories* magazine. These may have been two examples of disinformation specialists at work, stirring the pot for reasons known only to their case officers; for Fred Crisman was an intelligence officer specializing in disinformation, and on the French side, the consulting editor of *Science et Vie* who had planted the *Nautilus* story with a hapless staff writer was none other than Jacques Bergier, one of the co-authors of *Morning of the Magicians*, and a former intelligence officer himself with strong connections in the French intelligence community. The *Nautilus* story appeared in the French papers the same year that Pauwels and Bergier's *Morning of the Magicians* was published

We could take issue with Schnabel's timeline, though, since we have already learned that Andrija Puharich was performing telepathy experiments for the US military as early as 1955. That there was an American military interest in psychic abilities long before the *Nautilus* episode is documented, so it is not really very far-fetched to assume that some kind of psychic experiment might have been underway with the nuclear submarine. After all, there was no other way to contact the submarine once it had disappeared under the ice. A submarine in 1960 had to rise to periscope depth to send or receive radio transmissions. Thus, psychic communication—which is not, as demonstrated by the SRI team, dependent upon the same physical restrictions as radio waves—would have been an ideal medium, if it worked. Alas, in the case of the *Nautilus* we may never know; but in many other cases, however, the facts are quite clear and incontrovertible: the American military and intelligence organizations did use psychics for a variety of tasks, many of which were highly classified.

The year 1972 saw some amazing political developments, some of which were secret at the time and not revealed until much later, and some of which became obvious almost overnight. Howard Hughes declared the Clifford Irving book to be a hoax in January; the Zodiac killings were by then in full swing in California; J. Edgar Hoover died in May, and George Wallace almost died a few weeks later, victim of an assassination attempt by Arthur Bremer. In late May to mid-June the Watergate break-ins were taking place, to be discovered by a security guard on June 17, 1972, and subsequently broken as a national news story by the investigative team of Woodward and Bernstein of the *Washington Post* in the following months.

Quietly, however, another development was taking place. This time, the venue was a scientific laboratory in Menlo Park, California. On June 6, 1972, the artist and sometime astrologer Ingo Swann used his mental powers to disturb the operation of a magnetometer buried in a concrete well at the Stanford Research Institute.

Four months later, the CIA would fund SRI to the tune of fifty thousand dollars to continue that research, after intermediate testing had demonstrated the uncanny abilities of Swann and other psychics to penetrate top-secret military installations using only their minds.

If this information had appeared between the covers of *Amazing Stories* there would have been no need to consider it as anything more than either a hoax or a fantasy. Schnabel is a respected science writer, however, and the information revealed in Schnabel's book is reinforced by documentation readily available from a variety of sources. Even the no-nonsense *Journal of Defense & Diplomacy*, in their September 1985 issue, contained an article entitled "The Science of Psychic Warfare" by their science editor, Charles Wallace, which mentions the SRI research among other items of interest, such as the "Emotic Theory" of psychic phenomena that identifies the "five pairs of cranial sinus cavities as the sensors—mastoid, ethmoid, sphenoid, maxillary and frontal—of which the last two become the most important" as instruments of psychic abilities. This, between pages showing ads for submarines, small arms, and Harrier aircraft. Wallace goes on to mention a case that is discussed in more detail in Schnabel's work, and that is the successful use of psychics to locate a downed Soviet bomber in Africa, a story that was carried by Jack Anderson in his syndicated newspaper column.

Before we approach the Soviet bomber story, however, let's look at the SRI remote viewing program, since it stands out as the best-documented case thus far of the American government's interest in, and support of, psychic abilities as military weapons. Regardless of what scientists may have to say about the "reality" of psychic phenomena or the quantum consciousness debate, the evidence is conclusive that individual human beings are able to infiltrate secure locations at a distance using only their minds. The welter of evidence in Schnabel's book alone should be enough to cause scientists to re-evaluate their stand on ESP, telepathy, and other rejected paranormal abilities regardless of their "non-computability," if only because the world has become a much more dangerous place than ever before, and abilities of this nature are necessary to augment a national defense policy that relies overmuch on machinery, electronics, the suspension of civil liberties, and duct tape against enemies whose only resources are those of their own fanatic convictions.

The scientific approach to extrasensory perception (ESP) began with the statistical method of J.B. Rhine at Duke University in 1927, an approach characterized by thousands of tests of subjects using a special deck of cards consisting of twenty-five cards divided into five sets of five symbols: star, square, circle, cross, and wavy lines. People being tested are asked to guess at the sequence of symbols in a freshly-shuffled deck, or to predict the sequence before the deck is shuffled, etc., in a variety of experiments designed to evaluate different forms of ESP. Chance will account for a certain percentage of right answers. Any percentage above the chance calculation would suggest the presence of a psychic power of some description. Collating the results in a statistical format, Rhine hoped to prove the existence of psychic abilities by emphasizing those results that were statistically higher than chance would have predicted.

Rhine's experiments were never fully embraced by the scientific community, and in many cases the results were mediocre at best, and certainly not enough to encourage a full-scale investigation of the paranormal. However, the Rhine approach of using statistical methods to evaluate something as tenuous as psychic abilities did encourage others interested in researching the phenomena, by handing them a scientific precedent. Rhine's sterile laboratory environment for testing ESP, or "psi" as the phenomenon was eventually known, was a far cry from the séance table and the shaman's hut, and won some respectability for the pursuit.

In the 1950s, of course, paranormal abilities were the target of several US government projects, including those of Andrija Puharich for the military as well as the CIA's own efforts along the same lines. The Korean War had brought tales of brainwashing and mind control to the American public in the form of articles, books and movies (such as *The Manchurian Candidate*), and warned the population that it was possible for an enemy to exert control over a person's consciousness.

In the 1960s came the famous *Nautilus* incident—or non-incident—and the period also saw a heightened interest in UFOs and mystical and occult phenomena. Where the mysterious East was considered the source of brainwashing techniques in the 1950s, it became the source for spiritual enlightenment in the 1960s. Brainwashing is about conversion—as William Sargant and others have pointed out—so it could come as no surprise that many Americans and other westerners were joining Asian religions and cults, such as the Hare Krishnas, the Japanese Nichiren Shoshu sect, the Maharishi Mahesh Yogi's Transcendental Meditation, and various Tantric and other Eastern spiritual methodologies. Tales of the paranormal powers of Hindu yogis and fakirs as well as of Chinese magicians and sorcerers were commonplace in the literature (such as the excellent books on Asian mysticism by John Blofeld, and the more metaphysical approach of Alan Watts) as well as in the rumor mills surrounding the various disciplines.

California, of course, was the scene of much of this activity. As political counter-culturalism (the Hippies, the Yippies, the Weathermen) eventually gave way to spiritual counter-culturalism, California retained its position as the nerve center for American alternative religions.

But California was also the Jet Propulsion Laboratory, Stanford University, Lawrence Livermore Laboratories, and so much else associated with rocket science and nuclear weaponry. In the midst of this high-technology atmosphere one found the Stanford Research Institute or SRI, a think-tank that was connected with Stanford University, but which in actuality derived much of its income from government and military grants and contracts.

Professor Hal Puthoff was as much the product of his generation as anyone else. Although he had a stint with the National Security Agency (NSA), he was primarily a laser physicist and contributed heavily to the development of laser technology. His associate, Russell Targ, was another laser physicist, and the two formed an unforgettable partnership at SRI during this period. Laser technology owes a great deal to quantum mechanics, of which Puthoff was of course quite aware. It was perhaps this background in the strange science of lasers and the quanta that led Puthoff to examine alternative religions and mystical groups and individuals, and to his becoming a Scientologist. He eventually wrote a grant proposal, asking that he be allowed to conduct some preliminary tests of psychic abilities.

Somehow, the proposal came to the attention of Ingo Swann, who was himself a Scientologist and being tested for psychic abilities in New York City, where he lived. He contacted Puthoff, and it was agreed that he fly out to California in June 1972 to undertake some informal testing. Puthoff was interested to see whether or not Swann had the ability to move physical objects from a distance, using only his mind (an ability known as "psychokinesis," or simply "PK"). Swann managed to cause the needle in a buried magnetometer to move. This was a heavily-shielded device, buried in concrete, which was eventually used to prove the existence of the sub-atomic entities known as "quarks." Puthoff wrote a report of this experiment, and sent it on to various organizations in an effort to secure financing for the project. It was on the basis of that experiment that the CIA decided to start funding Puthoff's team at SRI, in an effort develop a means of using psychic abilities to supplement the American defense and intelligence effort, sending in CIA official Ken Kress with $50,000 for SRI.[31]

Testing began in earnest later that year (1972). It was a bit rocky at first, until Ingo Swann came up with a remarkable idea. He suggested that geographic coordinates be used by the tester as a target location. Telling the psychic no more than the coordinates, the psychic would have to mentally travel to that precise spot and report back on what he "saw" there. This method became known as "scanate" for "scanning coordinates," and the project informally known as Project Scanate.

This method was successful beyond expectations, and in worrisome ways. The CIA began to collaborate on the testing, giving the geographic coordinates of various locations to SRI, and Swann—and eventually a newcomer to the project, Pat Price—would mentally "go" to those coordinates and write down what they saw. This testing was done mostly through the CIA's Technical Services division, and involved CIA officers Ken Kress and the pseudonymous "Richard Kennett" and many others. In one case, in June of 1973, a CIA officer with a skeptical attitude towards the project gave a set of coordinates to his mountain cabin in West Virginia. Both Swann and Price came back with detailed information concerning what appeared to be a military base, replete with file drawers marked with operational code names. The CIA official scoffed, telling his associates that there was nothing to this SRI program after all.

A while later, one of the other CIA officials involved with the SRI program decided to take a look himself. After all, how could both of the psychics be wrong in exactly the same way, with the same details? Driving around near the mountain cabin, he stumbled upon a top-secret Pentagon installation.

Putting the details of the experiment in his report, and making mention of the location of the Army's facility, he inadvertently raised a hornet's nest of concern in intelligence circles. The details of the facility, and in particular the code names of secret projects, were known only to a few. How, Pentagon security officials wanted to know, had agents penetrated the facility? When apprised of the supernatural means used by SRI to do just that, the stern-faced men were not amused. They went to Menlo Park and interrogated all concerned until they were satisfied that there was no actual security leak and no enemy penetration of their facility.

The psychic prowess of the SRI "scanate" team was proven, unequivocally.

As more and more testing took place, Puthoff and Targ used different methods to shield their targets so thoroughly that even they did not know in advance what they would be. For instance, they used random number generators to come up with geographic coordinates to ensure that they were not somehow inadvertently and unconsciously signaling the coordinates to the psychics. They would try an "outbound" scanning experiment, in which a subject would drive to a location and sit there at a specific time while the psychic would try to "see" where the subject was located, essentially looking at the surroundings through the subject's eyes. These tests were also enormously successful, and in ways no one expected. In one case, involving psychic (and Scientologist) Pat Price, the random number generator gave a certain set of coordinates for a marina not far from the SRI facility. (The envelopes containing the coordinates were numbered, and the random number generator would produce a number corresponding to one of the envelopes, thus removing any human agency from the selection process.) A suspicious and skeptical SRI staffer, however, decided to change the location at the last minute without regard to the coordinates printed on a paper inside the envelope given to him before he set out. Instead, he drove around aimlessly for a while and then picked a completely different location.

Price not only identified the exact location where the wandering subject wound up, but gave the answer five minutes *before* the subject arrived on-site, thus predicting the future.[32]

As the testing programs continued, Pat Price wound up moving for a while to West Virginia, where he used his talents to locate veins of coal for a mining company; at the same time (and unknown to SRI), he was working directly for the CIA.

The CIA at this time was concerned with penetrating a number of Chinese and Soviet embassies abroad. This Price was able to do, with relative ease, using only his mind. He accurately described a number of Chinese embassies and in detail. (The only occasional hiccup occurred when he described a building the way it had looked in the past.) He was even able to look at a photograph of a building and tell the CIA where the building was located—with incredible precision—and in one case remind the CIA handler of exactly where the photograph had been developed!

Price had been a heavy drinker and smoker, and was fond of food as well. Therefore it came as no surprise when he developed symptoms of angina. Although his friends did what they could to try to convince him to cut down, he generally ignored this advice and continued his energetic lifestyle.

Then, one evening in Washington in mid-July of 1975, he had dinner with friends. The next day in Las Vegas, not feeling very well at dinner, Price mentioned to his friends that someone had slipped something into his coffee the night before. This did not sound like paranoia on his part; he seemed certain of it. Later that night he went to his room. His friends found him afterward in a state of cardiac arrest. He was pronounced dead in the hospital.

Perhaps no one would have thought much of Price's insistence that he had been poisoned or drugged the previous evening, but when CIA official "Richard Kennett" tried to find out more, he was told that no autopsy had been performed. This was indeed unusual, as the death had occurred to a non-resident outside the hospital and would have ordinarily required an autopsy. Further, the hospital staff reported that a man had arrived at the hospital within hours of his death with a briefcase full of Price's medical records and managed to convince the staff not to perform an autopsy based on this evidence of Price's poor physical condition. This gentleman has never been identified, not even by the CIA. The assumption among some of Price's associates was that he had been deliberately poisoned by the KGB or possibly the Chinese. There was never any evidence of this, of course, and Price's lifestyle certainly could have contributed to a heart attack; the anomaly in this affair is the lack of an autopsy and the mysterious man with the briefcase.[33]

Price was the SRI psychic who was the most stunningly successful and consistent. If news of his exploits percolated outside the small circle of SRI and the CIA's Technical Services Staff, he could have become a target of hostile forces. The same month as Price's death, Andrija Puharich was hosting a visit by Ira Einhorn and Holly Maddux at his "Turkey Farm" in Ossining, New York, where they witnessed a fourteen-year-old child in a remote viewing session "visit" the Pentagon, the White House, and the Kremlin. It is perhaps not outside the realm of feasibility to imagine that the Soviets were aware of this "psychic spying" and simply decided to remove the most powerful psychics from America's arsenal. Puharich's role was well-known by this time. He had been the man to introduce Uri Geller to the world, to bring him to SRI to be tested and thus come to the attention of American intelligence (which was, after all, funding the psychic research at SRI), and to place Geller within a very special context. In 1973, Puharich was still promoting the idea of The Nine, fully twenty years after the first session with the Indian medium Dr. Vinod. He brought Geller to a meeting with Arthur Young on February 27, 1973 at Young's home; again this is twenty years after the first communication with The Nine that involved both Puharich and Young.

Under hypnosis by Puharich, Geller admitted being the recipient of powers from The Nine (a claim he has denied in later years). Puharich's book *Uri: A Journal of the Mystery of Uri Geller*, is a good source for names, dates and places in the Geller timeline. It also contains the text of the film SRI made of Geller, and the text of the original statement by The Nine. Much of what was going on at SRI in the 1970s is covered by Puharich from his own perspective, which is almost completely related to Uri Geller.

And, according to Geller, Puharich was his CIA handler. This doesn't seem too outlandish a claim to make under the circumstances. After all, Puharich did have extensive ties to the military and intelligence communities dating back to the Korean War. And Puharich did bring Geller to SRI, a place that was testing psychic abilities under contract to the CIA. Whether or not Puharich was actually on contract to the CIA himself is moot under the circumstances; his mentorship of the young Israeli psychic brought them both into contact with officials from the CIA, the Pentagon, and the American government on an almost continual basis. For all practical intents and purposes, Geller was being observed by the CIA, and Puharich was the point of contact. The Uri Geller–Andrija Puharich relationship has already been covered in Books I and II. What is important to focus on now is the "extended family" around the SRI remote viewing program, including the quantum physicists and the military and intelligence operations that continued the psychic espionage project, bringing us into strange realms indeed.

At the time that SRI was experimenting with psychic abilities in a relatively benign fashion, the Soviet Union was engaged in its own psychic research. There were theoretical problems with psychic research in the Communist state, however; as long as ESP and other paranormal abilities were linked with superstition, magic and religion, no one in the Communist Party could become involved. Marx and Engels were quite clear about the position of religion in a Communist society. Religion, after all, was "the opiate of the people," and psychic phenomena were relegated to the fringe of religion. But with the publication of the presumably fictitious *Nautilus* story in 1960, it seemed necessary for the Soviets to counter the presumed Allied threat in mental telepathy and other powers, in the name of "national security."

There were several famous Soviet psychics, and some of this research was covered in *Psychic Discoveries Behind the Iron Curtain*, a 1970 bestseller by Sheila Ostrander and Lynn Schroeder, published two years before the experiments at SRI would begin. According to Schnabel, who bases his information on intelligence documents and sources, the Soviets "scoured the mystical eastern vastnesses of the Soviet Union in order to find the toughest Siberian shamans, the best-trained Tibetan priests, the most powerful Mongolian *chi gong* masters."[34] This effort yielded some fruit, for "a group of Tibetans succeeded in breaking a human skull a few yards away, just by concentrating on it."[35] All of this was undertaken by the Institute for the Problems of Information Transmission (known by its Russian acronym IPPI) in Moscow. This same Institute was responsible for a state-sponsored experiment in the blackest of black arts: the cursing of souvenirs by shamans so that the (foreign) recipients of these gifts would "suffer neuralgia, depression, and even nervous breakdown."[36] What is astonishing about these experiments is that they were undertaken by a state that considered itself the only truly scientific government on earth: one purged of religion, fantasy, and superstition and devoted to the liberation of the minds of humanity from the shackles of false religious sentimentality.

In *Nexus* magazine, an Australian journal that reports on psychic phenomena, UFOs, etc., former scientist and now the head of something called Paranormal Management Systems in the UK, Turan Rifat, makes an observation about Soviet parapsychological research which echoes that made by Kenneth Grant with regard to Jack Parsons and the Babalon

Working, i.e., that Soviet "research in the biophysical domain became so advanced that they opened doorways to other continuums and themselves fell prey to malevolent forces."[37] While this sounds far-fetched and the kind of thing one would expect of a popular magazine dealing with paranormal conspiracy theories, one must admit that if this were possible, then it is, of course, equally possible with regard to American military and intelligence mind-control and psychological warfare operations. The Soviets would have been using the very people who specialize in developing paranormal abilities through the "derangement of the senses" and the other techniques already described herein. These are individuals who would have attained some degree of spiritual enlightenment and psychological integration. Would they have willingly or enthusiastically supported their government's plan to utilize these abilities in the service of the state, for the assassination and control of foreign citizens? If one believes in the existence of "malevolent forces," then the Siberian and Mongolian shamans and Tibetan priests would be the likely contacts for these forces, as they had devoted their entire lives to the pursuit of otherworldly experience in the form of gods, demons, and disembodied souls. With the virtual destruction of the Russian Orthodox Church and the suppression of all religious organizations, the shamans would have been the only ones left in the Soviet Union still practicing spiritual techniques. Romanian émigré philosopher Mircea Eliade had written extensively concerning shamanism in the 1960s, and his insights into shamanism as a form of psychological conditioning could not have failed to come to the attention of the Soviets.

Back in the United States, the CIA and other government organizations were taking a good, hard look at the success ratio of the SRI program. A temporary blocking of federal funds for psi research took place in the mid-1970s, due to unfavorable publicity generated by reports of the CIA's own prior MK-ULTRA mind-control programs (the psi research of SRI and the CIA seeming a little too alike for comfort, as both involved experimentation on human subjects, and many in government were opposed to this type of research anyway as smacking too much of witchcraft or just plain nonsense), but the coffers slowly opened again during the Carter administration, and this time the military was taking a more central role.

The Pentagon's remote viewing programs eventually (in early 1979) came under the authority of the Defence Intelligence Agency, or DIA. The DIA set up its own remote viewing operation at an abandoned building at Fort Meade, code-named GRILL FLAME, but their remote viewers were generally still being trained at SRI in California, by the team of Puthoff, Swann and others. Swann helped to codify the remote viewing protocols, making it an easily-defined system, and it is Swann's contribution that comes through most clearly in the Internet-published DIA manual on CRV or "Coordinate Remote Viewing."

GRILL FLAME was under the authority of one Jack Vorona, a nuclear physicist who was a DIA officer, and who controlled other "alternative" projects, such as one that was designed to study mind-control using microwave technology.[38] This technique was thought to be a focus of Soviet research at the time, but there has also been a lot of research in the United States on not only the use of microwaves but also low-frequency radio waves, and on all sorts of electronic and mechanical approaches to mind control.

These days, the Internet is full of information (much of it suspect) on this type of technology, but a strange book published in 1998 and authored by Richard Sauder includes over one hundred pages of U.S. patent information for a variety of electronic devices for mind-control applications, including US Patent 3,951,139: *Apparatus and Method for remotely Monitoring and Altering Brain Waves* and US Patent 5,213,562: *Method of Inducing Mental, Emotional and Physical States of Consciousness, Including Specific Mental Activity, In Human Beings.* The inventor of the latter was Robert A. Monroe, and thereby hangs a tale.

Robert Monroe, a radio producer, began suffering from insomnia in 1958. It was a severe case that doctors could not do anything about, believing Monroe to be suffering from a nervous breakdown, especially when he began reporting that he was leaving his body at night. Of course, most mental health professionals when faced with a statement like that would diagnose some form of schizophrenia; depending on other presenting symptoms one could also be looking at dissociation. Monroe, however, was fascinated by his own "disorder," and began building a room where these episodes—known to psychic researchers as OOBEs or "out of body experiences"—could be monitored more closely. Eventually, this hobby turned into a full-scale methodology for initiating the OOBE using sound-waves which, when broadcast through a set of headphones, would mimic brain-waves of the same frequencies that he was targeting.

Soon, the Monroe Institute was established for the study of this (and related) phenomena and became a part of the overall US government's psychic warfare program. Located in Virginia, it was convenient to the Fort Meade contingent, and the devices that Monroe developed at his Institute appear to have been quite successful and popular among the remote viewers. Monroe authored several books on the out-of-body-experience (such as *Journeys Out Of The Body*, Doubleday, NY, 1971), and Richard Sauder became interested, and visited the Monroe Institute to go through the training. He would later claim that since then he had been in sporadic telepathic communication with Monroe himself.[34]

As bizarre as that sounds, the reactions of SRI and GRILL FLAME staffers when faced with the Monroe techniques were just as startling. Army Captain Skip Atwater was the intelligence officer who, in 1977, founded the Army's version of the SRI team at Fort Meade and ran it until 1987. Atwater visited the Monroe Institute in 1977 and tried out the equipment, which consisted of a set of headphones that broadcast a pre-recorded tape with Monroe's voice and special effects. According to Schnabel's account, Atwater experienced a sense of levitation on the very first attempt![40] Astonished by this result, Atwater became a fixture at the Monroe Institute, and eventually became director of research there after retiring from the Army.

Other military remote viewers at the Monroe Institute experienced everything from spirit possession to a sense that they were being remotely-viewed by the Soviet opposition; but by far the strangest and most compelling case for the dangers of meddling in the paranormal for those who have not undergone rigorous spiritual training beforehand is the Lawrence Livermore episode.

This is recounted in very few places. Uri Geller mentions being at Lawrence Livermore in passing in *The Geller Effect*—co-authored with Guy Lyon Playfair (the AID worker from Brazil who became very involved in occultism and the paranormal)—but it is not mentioned at all in Puharich's *Uri* or in the book co-authored by SRI scientist Russell Targ and SRI remote viewer Keith Harary, *The Mind Race.* It appears in various places on the Internet, and in some detail in Schnabel's work on remote viewers and in *Mind Reach* by Puthoff and Targ. It is worth repeating here in brief, as the individuals concerned were all scientists at Lawrence Livermore, and not psychics or mediums or anyone traditionally connected with the occult.

Uri Geller had been invited to SRI for some informal tests of his abilities in 1972. By 1974, word of his prowess had leaked out around the world, and the nuclear weapons specialists at Lawrence Livermore were concerned that someone with psychic abilities—particularly psychokinesis, an ability Geller demonstrated by bending metal spoons, rings, and other objects with his mind—could detonate a nuclear weapon using only mental energy or could scramble the nation's military computer systems, thus disabling the country's missile defences. Therefore, in late 1974 and 1975 a select group of scientists and security officers began testing Geller at an off-site location.

The tests showed that Geller could only affect metal objects, computer systems, and computer disks if he was in physical contact with them. Therefore, it was a reasonable assumption that PK was not a threat to the nation's missile systems. However, other developments took place that caused not only concern but hysteria among the Lawrence Livermore staff

While technicians were listening to the audiotapes routinely made during the Geller PK sessions, they noticed a voice on the tape that had not been there during the tests. It was a "metallic voice" and was largely unintelligible, although the few words that were understood turned out to be top-secret codenames for intelligence operations, names that were unknown to the scientists at Lawrence Livermore. In addition, an infrared camera that had been used during the sessions showed patches of radiation on the laboratory walls where no such radiation should have been present.

These were more than merely scientific anomalies. They were captured on tape and film under controlled circumstances. However, this would have been worth a few paragraphs in a report and not much more, were it not for the fact that personnel involved in the Geller experiments began to experience exceedingly strange phenomena. One of the recurring motifs was the appearance of a flying saucer in the laboratory: a hovering, hologram-like image that would float around and then disappear. And this "saucer" appearance was not restricted to the laboratory. Some of the scientists witnessed the phenomenon when they were at home with their families. There was no conceivable explanation for this, no way such a hologram could have been projected inside the secure laboratory environment without a lot of equipment and expensive electronics that could have easily been discovered. Since Geller was known to put out the story that he was in communication with extraterrestrial agencies aboard a spacecraft that hovered over the earth, the connection was obvious, but the reason or motivation behind the apparitions was not.

In addition to the saucer, there were reports of appearances of strange and fantastic animals to the Lawrence Livermore personnel and their families, including very large black birds, ravens, that would appear from nowhere and wander across their lawns ... or suddenly appear in the morning standing over their beds. This association of birds with Geller was something that the laboratory staff may have not recognized, for Geller's supernatural experiences included that of a bird of prey, usually a hawk (symbol for the Egyptian god, Horus). The appearance of fantastic animals is common in the literature of shamanism, and their purpose is usually totemic in nature; but what was happening to the scientists?

As the personnel began to break down and exhibit signs of intense mental distress, the security officer in charge of the group broke down and contacted "Richard Kennett" of the CIA. As Kennett not only had security clearances but was also aware of the psychic research programs and had a doctorate in neurophysiology, he was the logical choice.

Kennett listened to the men—some of whom broke down and wept in his presence—describe their symptoms. He was not convinced that this was simply a textbook case of hysteria. These men were scientists with no occult leanings; furthermore, they had all been psychologically vetted, as they were involved with classified government and military projects. It didn't make sense.

And then he listened to the audiotapes, and heard the secret codewords mentioned that none of the Lawrence Livermore staff could have known.

This was not the end of the story, however. One of the scientists received a phone call and heard the "metallic voice" that so often pursues researchers in this field, man and boy, and this time the voice told him to drop the Geller experimentation completely. The team was only too happy to do so, and the "hauntings" gradually stopped.

(I hesitate to mention another incident among these many strange occurrences at America's most important nuclear weapons research facility after that at Los Alamos. Although the incident has been documented, I feel I am so straining credulity as it is, with these stories of paranormal powers, government agencies, military remote viewing and the rest, that to bring up the denouement of the Lawrence Livermore episode might be to lose my audience completely after we have come so far. I have made it a core element of my approach that everything I claim in this book is thoroughly documented and with as much reliance on primary sources as is practicable, considering the subject matter. I have, indeed, omitted many anecdotes and other material that I considered too questionable, or for which evidence was not sufficient to overwhelm any reasonable objections. So ...)

Apparently, one of the Livermore scientists was at home one evening speaking with his wife when another of the apparitions occurred in their living room. This time it was of a man's arm, clad in a grey suit jacket, that hovered and twisted in the air between them. The end of the arm consisted not of a hand, but of a hook. It appeared, and then just as mysteriously disappeared.

When this account was related to "Richard Kennett," he must have wondered whether or not Puthoff and Targ had been playing games with lasers and holograms. When he met with them, he repeated what he had heard from the Livermore scientists, ending with the story about the arm. At that precise moment, there came a loud, insistent pounding on the door of their motel room. The door was opened to reveal a man dressed in a grey suit. He walked into the center of the room and said in an odd voice, "I guess I must be in the wrong room," and turned and left. They had enough time to see that he had one sleeve pinned to his shoulder. The man in the grey suit was missing an arm.

Schnabel, in whose book this account also occurs, gives it the benefit of a doubt.[41] Some of the Lawrence Livermore staff refused to go into details about these experiences with him; one of them was writing his own book about the Geller affair and wanted to keep the details to himself, understandably. Others were not directly involved in the day-to-day proceedings and could not offer much corroboration. Schnabel has wondered if the "man in the grey suit" episode was invented as a fictional device by Puthoff and Targ, if not the first apparition then perhaps the melodramatic, *Weird Tales* ending. There is no particular reason to believe that Puthoff and Targ would have invented such an ending, however, considering all the problems they have had in getting scientists to take their paranormal research seriously. To invent such a Hollywood ending would be to jeopardize whatever ground they had won, painfully and at great cost. At this time, we simply have to take the story at face value. It is certainly no stranger than other episodes in the literature, and finds resonance with mysterious and "synchronistic" events recounted by Strieber, Sarfatti, and so many others. Even more incredible, all of this was taking place in the heart of the American defense industry, in the core of the "military-industrial complex" President Eisenhower warned us all about in 1960.

During the Carter Administration, remote viewers were involved in everything from looking for the Iranian hostages to locating a downed Soviet spyplane. In May of 1978, Hal Puthoff received an urgent fax from the Army tasking his remote viewer team to locate a Tu-22 bomber that had disappeared somewhere over the African nation of Zaire. The man who gave Puthoff this mission was General Ed Thompson of the Pentagon's intelligence agency, responsible for the Army's remote viewing projects among other duties. Thompson was a strong supporter of remote viewing, as was General Albert Stubblebine of the Pentagon's INSCOM (Intelligence and Security Command) division, under whose wing GRILL FLAME, CENTER LANE, and the other codenames for the remote viewing operations would find themselves in the 1980s. (INSCOM would also develop a close working relationship with the Monroe Institute.)

The Soviets and the American CIA were hot in pursuit of the downed bomber. If the CIA could get there first, they would uncover a treasure trove of Soviet secrets, since the Tu-22 had been on an intelligence-gathering mission over Africa. The CIA had its own ideas about where to find the plane, but the SRI remote viewer came through with flying colors. He was corroborated by another remote viewer, this time working out of Wright-Patterson Air Force Base. Between the two of them—and unknown to each other—they developed a detailed map and description of where the plane would be found, tail-up in a jungle river. The CIA recovery team—on their way to the site where they estimated the plane would be—came across the site identified by the remote viewers first: there was the plane.

This story eventually made Jack Anderson's syndicated newspaper column and became a world-wide sensation. Other spectacular results would follow from time to time, involving terrorists, hostages, nuclear weapons testing, and other areas of intense concern to military and intelligence chiefs. And the experiments continued as Puthoff and others sought ways to fine-tune the results of their most talented remote viewers as well as to develop methods by which virtually anyone can be trained in the process.

There was considerable opposition to these programs both within and outside the military, however. Some among the general staff could not understand the value of having "tea leaf readers" work for the Pentagon; others felt that the mystique of the remote viewers detracted from the real work of intelligence gathering, which involved either satellites in the sky or assets on the ground. Many were dismayed by the cozy relationship that developed between INSCOM and the Monroe Institute. Also, remote viewing reached a kind of crescendo during the Democratic Carter administration, and after the Republican Ronald Reagan was elected President in 1980 there was a mad dash to distance the new administration from the perceived weaknesses of the old. The CIA's Robert Gates as well as Defense Secretary Frank Carlucci both opposed the remote viewing programs, which is amusing considering that their president was a man who consulted astrologers, and had been doing so since at least the time he was Governor of California.

Although Gates and Carlucci did their best to destroy the remote viewing program, the psychics had champions in the persons of Senator Robert Byrd (D) of West Virginia, Senator Daniel Inouye (D) of Hawaii, Senator and former astronaut John Glenn (D) of Ohio, and two Republican senators, William Cohen of Maine and Ted Stevens of Alaska. (It should also be mentioned that one of the most vocal supporters of the SRI and military psi-war programs was former astronaut Edgar Mitchell, who had been on hand to welcome Uri Geller to SRI back in 1972. Mitchell—a member of the Masonic society—has been intimately involved with paranormal research since his retirement from NASA. Astronaut Buzz Aldrin, another Mason, brought a Masonic flag with him on his Apollo 11 flight to the Moon on July 20, 1969, an event he commemorated in a letter to the Masonic Grand Commander on NASA stationery, dated September 19, 1969. That quite a number of astronauts have been Masons, and that the Grand Secretary General of the Society at the time of the lunar landing in 1969 was the brother of an important NASA official is noted in Richard Sauder's book.)[42]

The senators managed to protect the remote viewing program for quite a while, but the psychics still wound up as moving targets, working now for INSCOM, now for the DIA, fighting for funding all over Capitol Hill. Puthoff managed to win a ten-year contract from an unidentified government agency that saved the SRI program, but he had tired of the politics—both internal and external—at SRI and retired from the Institute in 1985. Major General Stubblebine was forced to retire from the Army—and thus as protector of the remote viewing apparatus—in 1984. Oddly enough, Stubblebine would wind up in New York, having divorced his first wife, living with a psychiatrist who specialized in alien abduction cases. Many of the remote viewers and support personnel became UFO "believers"—if that is the correct term—including Ingo Swann, who eventually returned to New York City after dealing with numerous internal political squabbles himself, most notably with Russell Targ. Swann has written and self-published a book about his UFO beliefs, *Penetration: The Question of Extraterrestrial and Human Telepathy*, which does not add much to our knowledge of the SRI remote viewing program, but which does expand considerably on the theme that remote viewers were occasionally tasked with UFO research—including attempting to learn the truth behind the flying saucer phenomenon—as well as viewing other planets. Stubblebine himself became a UFO enthusiast and is on the record as stating that there are "structures underneath the surface of Mars" as well as machinery, and that all of this information was obtained through remote viewing.[43]

In light of the fact that that so many military men, from enlisted personnel to generals like MacArthur and Stubblebine, have gone on the record as supporting the idea that UFOs are extraterrestrial craft visiting the earth, the constant ridiculing of this hypothesis from all corners of both the military and the scientific communities seems highly suspect. We are constantly being told that the eyewitnesses to UFO sightings are not credible, not trained observers, and have mistaken natural objects for spacecraft; then we have a wide cross-section of military and scientific personnel who insist that the phenomenon is genuine and not the result of swamp gas or the planet Venus. What is the citizenry to make of this apparent dichotomy? We may accept—reluctantly—that a farmer in Iowa who has lived there all his life has mistaken a common natural event for a flying saucer landing; we find it difficult to accept that a major general would have made a similar mistake.

Indeed, the reactions of men like Stubblebine and MacArthur are based on military records rather than personal, eyewitness accounts or—like Stubblebine—are the result of paranormal "scrying" (a method which was, of course, supported by the military and proved useful in a number of occasions, such as locating SCUD missiles during the Gulf War with Iraq); but then, are we not to trust the analyses of this data by generals and other officers, especially those—like Stubblebine—who were in charge of intelligence and security? If not, if we can't trust the observations and conclusions of the men who are effectively in charge of our national security, and who have been for the past fifty years at least, then certainly that security is in serious disrepair!

One of SRI's remote viewers—Keith Harary—co-authored a popular book on remote viewing and psychic phenomena in general with Russell Targ, entitled *The Mind Race*. Harary joined SRI in 1980, and has since become a psychologist, but in 1979 he found himself counseling former members of the Peoples Temple and working closely with Al and Jeannie Mills, the Temple whistle-blowers who would soon be murdered in their home. Targ and Harary teamed up after leaving SRI in the early 1980s, and traveled frequently to Eastern bloc countries, which was a concern to the American intelligence establishment, particularly the DIA. Targ claimed they were working with their Russian counterparts in a "pure science" and non-military environment, but it is not certain that statement satisfied the DIA.

Eventually, the two men began playing the silver-futures market using Harary's psychic abilities and Targ's analysis of the results, and making considerable progress, attracting an investor. After a few misses, however, the men began blaming each other for the losses—and in public, during a lecture at Esalen—and the lawsuits started to fly. The men are still at loggerheads.

The remote viewing program lasted well into the 1990s, due to the $10 million contract won by Hal Puthoff in the last days of his administration at SRI, but as early as 1988 the Pentagon Inspector General had recommended that the Fort Meade operation be shut down. The days of the remote viewers were numbered. By 1995 and at the end of the SRI contract, word of the "psychic spies" had leaked once again to the press, and CIA directors and military men and former remote viewers were appearing on television and in the print media, answering questions and trying to put a better appearance on the revelations than the image of a spy with crystal balls. Ingo Swann went on the record to state that the original purpose behind SRI's remote viewing program was to discover what the Soviets had accomplished in the field, in order that American military and intelligence personnel could be kept informed.

Much of the methodology of the SRI remote viewing teams leaked out, including Swann's elegant (and often criticized) terminology. One of these was the "Matrix": a description of the underlying interconnectivity of the universe that a remote viewer would enter in a trance state. Without putting too fine a point on it, what Swann proposed was that psychics could enter what was essentially a kind of quantum state; within the Matrix, a remote viewer could theoretically go anywhere and see anything, regardless of normal limitations of space and time. That a popular film series would be made based on this very premise within a few years of the press revelations about GRILL FLAME, STAR GATE and Ingo Swann's "Matrix" should, perhaps, no longer surprise us.

The films' treatment of normal human consciousness as the creation of an enormous computer-like grid run by alien forces is probably as close as we will get to seeing the theories and doctrines of The Nine, Spectra, Hoova and all the rest portrayed cinematically, albeit from a very negative standpoint. It should also be mentioned that central to the screenplay of the the *Matrix* films are the "Men in Black"; this time they are assassins bent on stopping characters Morpheus, Neo and their cohorts from taking back the planet and waking up the world.

How could people respond to these images if images didn't secretly enjoy the same status as real things? Not that images were so powerful, but that the world was so weak.

—Jonathan Franzen[44]

The remote viewing programs of the military and intelligence communities—under the general rubric of GRILL FLAME and the other, later, modifications of the same—were extremely cheap by Pentagon standards. Hal Puthoff had secured a ten million dollar, ten year contract to support that research. By comparison, some of the Pentagon's frivolous spending on toilet seats and screwdrivers seems insane. It was not remote viewing in and of itself that threatened the American military establishment, however; it was the fact that the very nature of the program threatened its comfortable, Newtonian worldview. Officers were nervous about the "giggle factor"—when talk of the psychic spies and their exploits would elicit giggles and outright guffaws from their peers—and probably this more than anything else caused the remote viewing programs to be sidelined and eventually cancelled altogether. This is a pity, for several reasons.

In the first place, SRI and Hal Puthoff and the others were unable to publish much of their research due to security restrictions and the highly classified nature of some of their taskings. That means that an area of science in which we desperately need to know more has been effectively shut off from peer review, with the result that few individuals and organizations in the scientific establishment take the program—and all it implies for science—seriously.

In the second place, America (and the West in general) is now engaged in a serious struggle for survival against forces that are not technologically or economically superior. These forces succeed on the basis of power derived from the very mental states studied by the mind-control experts of the past fifty years: conversion, dissociation, and the whole eros-driven "derangement of the senses" that contributes not only to art and the manufacture of images, but to the conscious and willful use of those images to effect political change: the science of the shaman, the magician, the psychological warfare expert. The leaders of these assaults cynically manipulate the minds of their followers to the extent that suicide missions become glorious ... particularly those in which large numbers of civilians are murdered, as hideously and as brutally as possible for maximum effect. This is not a new development, of course. The Japanese in World War II gave us a foretaste of the "kamikaze" impulse. The black magicians behind these and other acts of desperate courage committed by the credulous and the lonely and the pious never lead these doomed individuals in the suicide runs, but pull the strings from a safe base in a friendly country, moving huge funds across borders with alacrity, and ordering mayhem by email and mobile phone. To find these sorcerers we need more than satellites and smirking condescension. We need more than SIGINT and HUMINT. We need a "backdoor" into their psyches.

This was begun during the Carter administration when remote viewers were tasked with locating hostages taken by terrorists, including CIA agent William Buckley, whose exploits and murder were detailed in Books I and II; it was reinforced when remote viewers were tasked with finding SCUD missile launchers during the Gulf War. At this time, remote viewing cannot be considered a replacement for normal intelligence gathering operations and probably will never be; but it is a valuable supplement to those endeavors and has the additional virtue of being inexpensive and seemingly undetectable. There is no earthly reason why these programs cannot be reinstated and the methodology perfected. There is, in fact, no reason why private individuals or private organizations cannot practice these techniques on their own, independent of government supervision or involvement. Shamans and magicians have been doing so for thousands of years. And the training manuals exist: either the grimoires of the sorcerers or the official manuals of the remote viewers. Terrorist organizations have been using methods very similar to these for indoctrination and training of assassins, and the Soviet Union has experimented to an unsettling degree with the ability to cause heart attacks and other ailments from a distance using the powers of the mind. The powers of consciousness.

THE GHOST IN THE MACHINE

Art is a school of self-transcendence. So is a voodoo session or a Nazi rally.
—Arthur Koestler[45]

Arthur Koestler, himself fascinated for many years by the phenomenon of coincidence (and author of the influential essay *The Roots of Coincidence*), traces modern preoccupation with it to Schoepenhauer, and from Schoepenhauer to Paul Kammerer and from there to Jung and Pauli. What all of these gentlemen had in common was an understanding that coincidence represents an acausal "force" or "principle" in the world, operating outside traditionally-understood science, but nevertheless a part of our experience. Koestler actually goes much further and much deeper into the study of this phenomenon than even Jung and Pauli, who seemed to stop short: Jung not enough of a physicist and Pauli not enough of a psychologist, perhaps.

In *Janus*, a book published towards the end of his life, before this accomplished philosopher, sometime Marxist, and historian of science committed suicide with his wife of many years after he learned he was stricken with a debilitating terminal sickness, Koestler laid out the parameters for an educated debate over the issue of coincidence and its role in both physics and in consciousness. As it transcends the initial attempts by Jung and Pauli to identify coincidence beyond the tag "acausal connecting principle" and goes right to the heart of the matter by identifying coincidence with paranormal abilities as well as with events in the "real world," his ideas bear some review. One should remember that Koestler did begin his professional life as an admirer of Communism, later abandoning this political creed and defecting to the West; his political life and background are therefore valuable to us, for they give Koestler a unique perspective on the historical and scientific problems we face when we consider coincidence as more than just a curiosity.

Koestler begins his argument by pointing out that a human being's brain is actually two brains: a reptilian brain, responsible for our instinctual behavior, and a neocortex, a "new brain," that lies atop the old brain and is responsible for our intellectual superiority to other creatures on the earth. Koestler believes that it is the imperfect control of the reptilian brain by the neocortex that has led to humanity's predicament. He points to an explosive growth in technology from the time of the ancient Greeks to modern space exploration in only 2500 years, and the parallel decline in human ethics and morality, which began with Taoism, Buddhism and Confucianism and which led to Hitler, Stalin, and the spiritual poverty of modern psychology.

He emphasizes that only human beings feel no compunction about killing members of their own species and, indeed, are capable of such obscenities as human sacrifice to appease some invented deity. He does not believe that humanity wages war and commits genocide because of aggression; instead, he blames humanity's ills on an excess of devotion. It is loyalty to a king or to a cause or to a religion (quite often, all three) that motivates a man to leave his home and put on a uniform and endure months or years of self-sacrifice, boredom, hunger and deprivation. Soldiers, as Koestler points out, are rarely aggressive and certainly not territorial. They have subsumed their individuality in the group, the tribe, the cult. They follow orders. They kill, not out of conviction or aggression, but on command, out of loyalty to an authority figure and identity with a group.

For Koestler, the most powerful weapon in the arsenal of humanity is language.[46] The Word. For it is language that both unites groups and divides humanity among those very groups, and gives it the rationale for killing fellow humans. It is language as it is understood by the psychological warriors and the advertising executives. It is language as understood by the ancient Greeks as well as by Bruno the Renaissance magician.

Thus, Koestler attacks the reductionism of scientists and philosophers from Pavlov to Skinner, from Freud to Desmond Morris, which blames the evils of history on instincts and natural aggression. In fact, he goes even further to suggest that this loyalty to authority begins as a form of brainwashing in the human infant, which remains helpless and in parental control for a much longer period than the infant offspring of other mammals. "Brainwashing," he writes, "starts in the cradle."[47] Children drink in religious fanaticism and tribal identification along with their mother's milk. In this, Koestler and psychiatrist R.D. Laing (and Ignatius Loyola) are in perfect agreement. It was the malleability of the brain of the human child that encouraged a generation of behaviorists and determinists to devote special attention to the establishment of those "secret schools" for the indoctrination of the young and their molding into the Cold Warriors of the future. Whether we believe the Whitley Strieber model of the secret school, or the Jack Sarfatti model, it is clear that this type of environment did exist, and not only in the United States but most especially in other countries, such as in China under Mao, in the Soviet Union under Stalin, in Germany under Hitler, and in those African and Asian nations of today which train boys and girls of nine and ten years old in the arts of assassination and soldiering.

Koestler's interest is obviously political in much of what he writes, but he has abandoned the jingoistic politics of the political party, the slogan, the mass rally, for a scientific view of the human being that transcends social organizations. (He was imprisoned as a suspected spy during the Spanish Civil War and narrowly escaped execution.) Like Jung and like historian of religion Mircea Eliade, who both had a flirtation with Nazism, Koestler's brief involvement with Communism was salutary in the long run: they all abandoned the dream of equality and freedom from want promised by social organizations and turned towards a pursuit of spiritual (or, perhaps, psychological) freedom as the means to cure humanity's ills. Marxism—as self-consciously more "scientific" than its competitors—was in a sense the perfect laboratory environment for the development of these ideas, for Marx looked at history as inevitability: human society progressed from a feudal state to an industrialized state to a socialist state and then to a communist state (I am summarizing mightily here) according to the Marxist dialectic. The world would eventually evolve into communism and workers would live in a paradise on earth as there was no paradise anywhere else. When the "inevitability" of this process was called into question—when the workers' states of the Soviet Union and China did not automatically induce working class ecstasy—then history as evolution was called into question, as well. As Koestler understands, the history of science and technology is one thing; the history of human civilization is quite another.

In an effort to come to terms with this schizophrenic aspect of humanity, Koestler considers human beings to have two (at times mutually contradictory) impulses: that of self-transcendence and that of self-assertion. Self-assertion may be thought to be analogous to the instinct of individual survival and expression at the cost of society; self-transcendence—to which he also refers as the *integrative* faculty—is the impulse to go beyond one's personal comfort and satisfaction to meld with the common good, to sign the social contract. These two impulses, to Koestler, represent a continuum of two extremes, with much of human behavior occupying a kind of middle ground, as humans attempt to satisfy both at once. This leads to Koestler's concept of "bisociation," by which he means "a distinction between the routines of disciplined thinking within a single universe of discourse—on a single plane, as it were—and the creative types of mental activity which always operates on more than one plane."[48] Koestler uses this concept to explain both humor and tragedy, and the creative arts (which includes every creative act, including those that occur within science and mathematics) and then inevitably turns to the subject of coincidence:

> *Coincidence* may be described as the chance encounter of two unrelated causal chains which—miraculously it seems—merge into a significant event. It provides the neatest paradigm of the bisociation of previously separate contexts, engineered by fate. Coincidences are puns of destiny. (emphasis in original) [49]

Koestler goes on to talk about the "law of large numbers" or "law of probability" that Jung identifies with Newtonian science in general. When observing, for instance, that dogs were biting people according to an average of about seventy-five incidents per day in the 1950s in New York City, Koestler asks a question: "How do the dogs of New York know when to stop biting and when to make up the daily quota?"[50] He reprises the sentiments of mathematician Von Neumann who looked at probability as "black magic," in which "we are faced with *a large number of uncertainties producing a certainty*, a large number of random events creating a lawful total outcome" (emphasis in original).[51] This, of course, is also the case with quantum physics, in which the uncertainty of life at the quantum level produces the relative stability and certainty of the perceived universe.

Koestler realizes the implications of what he is writing, of course, and draws the same comparison between paranormal abilities and coincidence that are drawn by Jung and many others. He begins by speaking about the "integrative tendency"—which he also refers to as the "self-transcendent tendency"—as the impulse to create order out of disorder: i.e., *transcending* the individualistic instincts of survival to attain a high degree of *integration* of the individual with society. He then draws a parallel between the self-transcendent tendency and psychic phenomena:

> The present theory is even more hazardous by explicitly suggesting that the integrative tendency operates in *both causal and acausal* ways, the two standing in a complementary relationship analogous to the particle-wave complementarity in physics. It is accordingly supposed to embrace not only the acausal agencies operating on the sub-atomic level, but also the phenomena of parapsychology and 'confluential events'. We have seen that ESP and 'synchronicity' often overlap, so that a supposedly paranormal event can be interpreted either as a result of ESP or as a case of 'synchronicity'.... The present theory suggests that in a similar way telepathy, clairvoyance, precognition, psychokinesis and synchronicity are merely *different manifestations under different conditions of the same universal principle*—i.e., the integrative tendency operating through both causal and acausal agencies. (emphases in original)[52]

This connection between the paranormal and the synchronistic is at the heart of this entire three-volume study. We have examined the coincidences of history, such as those that surround the various political assassinations in America in the last half of the twentieth century. We have also studied some paranormal phenomena. We have explored theories regarding the practices of shamanism, the techniques of mind control, the manifestos of the surrealists, the espionage of the remote viewers, and the visions of the UFOlogists. The Frenchmen, Pauwels and Bergier, have suggested that coincidence may offer us a new way of looking at history; Jung and Pauli have suggested that coincidence may offer us a new way of looking at reality. The theories presented in this chapter—to which an increasing number of physicists and other scientists subscribe—may offer not only a way of looking at history, but a way of taking an active part in its creation.

THE RED TINCTURE

Consciousness is basically a device for registering meaning ...
—Colin Wilson, *Order of Assassins: The Psychology of Murder*[53]

There is a tool with which we are theoretically able to cause change to occur at what we may call the quantum level (and, correspondingly, on the higher levels as well, once the fundamental change has taken place at the root level of the quantum). That tool is *meaning*. And the phenomenon of synchronicity as understood by Pauli and Jung reveals this meaning in action.

Those new to quantum physics will probably find it strange that one of the pioneers of this discipline was intimately familiar with alchemy, psychology, and even the *I Ching*, and could carry on a correspondence (and hold his own) with the likes of a Carl Gustav Jung. One comes away from the correspondence between Jung and Pauli with a sense that the physicist Pauli understood that the Jungian idea of the unconscious and its structures was essential to a complete grasp of not only psychology but also physics. Pauli's letters are full of reference to Kepler, whom he studied not so much for his contribution to science but rather for his alchemical work, in which Pauli saw the germ of quantum physics.

Pauli was a consistent and dedicated recorder of his dreams, and he would analyze them in concert with Jung, not only during the two years of Pauli's therapy with Jung, but long after that therapy had ended and the two had developed a kind of professional relationship based on the exchange of ideas, principally those concerning synchronicity.

Pauli's dreams were remarkable in that their symbolism seemed to mirror his philosophical preoccupations. As someone who was familiar with alchemical authors such as Robert Fludd, he was able to communicate with Jung on a shared deep level. Pauli understandably felt a certain kinship with the alchemists, since they were—at least in Jung's view—attempting to harmonize physics with consciousness, with spirituality, and this was obviously a concern of Pauli's, as is evident from the correspondence. While Pauli was certainly interested in how his dreams were relevant to his personal growth, he also had the desire to learn how they contributed to understanding the broader picture of quantum physics and consciousness.

These letters are a valuable resource, for they demonstrate an approach toward psychology by a physicist, while Jung is approaching physics through psychology. There are occasions when Pauli will correct a malapropism of Jung's indicating a too hasty-analogy between some element of physics and that of psychology, and these are valuable as well, for they show how deeply Pauli was reading Jung.

They also discuss astrology and other "occult" practices, as well as some of the experiments in parapsychology of the day, such as those by Duke University professor J.B. Rhine. It should be remembered that this correspondence lasted from the 1930s to the 1950s; that is, it spanned the years of the rise of Nazism, World War II, the first atomic bombs, and the Cold War. Pauli was Austrian, and Jung was Swiss. They were both German-speaking Europeans caught up in the madness that science, occultism, and politics had unleashed on the world. Taken in this light, their letters have a certain poignancy.

It is on the subject of synchronicity and the "meaningful coincidence" however that the two men are most fascinating. Rather than dismiss coincidence as scientifically irrelevant or trivial, they approach it as evidence of the operation of a deeper physical process, and quite possibly as the crossroads of physics and consciousness.

In a letter to Jung dated June 28, 1949, Pauli—discussing a little-known essay of Schoepenhauer's on "the ultimate union of necessity and chance"—writes,

> ... whereas [Schoepenhauer] wanted at all costs to cling to rigid determinism along the lines of the classical physics of his day, we have now acknowledged that in the nuclear world, physical events cannot be followed in causal chains through time and space. Thus, the readiness to adopt the idea on which your work is based, that of the "meaning as an ordering factor," is probably considerably greater among physicists that it was in Schoepenhauer's day.[54]

Jung and Pauli were discussing "meaning as an ordering factor" in the context of consciousness—in the perception of meaningful coincidences by the conscious mind—as well as in the nuclear world. The assumption being made by both Jung and Pauli is that somehow the rules of the quantum or nuclear world also obtained in consciousness, if not in the Newtonian world of linear cause-and-effect. What the modern theories of "quantum consciousness" propose is that there exists a mechanism in the brain that may be in control of consciousness and that this mechanism functions at the quantum level where non-locality is a feature: a level where the Newtonian concepts of time and space do not apply. Pauli goes a step further by associating Jung's idea of synchronicity with an alchemical process that Jung refers to as the *conjunction process* and what the alchemists referred to in the Latin as *coniunctio.* The conjunction process is the union of opposites that leads to wholeness, to healing, for which normal human sexual relations (or "Eros") may be considered emblematic. And one of the alchemical symbols of the successful completion of this process is the "red tincture":

> ... what strikes me first from the psychological angle is that a far-reaching parallel exists with what the alchemists referred to as the "production of

> the red tincture." Experience has shown me that what you call a "*conjunction process*" is generally conducive to the appearance of the "synchronistic" phenomenon.... And it is more likely to make its appearance *when the pairs of opposites keep in balance as much as possible.* (emphasis in original)[55]

Pauli goes on to compare the concept of radioactivity to synchronicity:

> ... Just as in physics, a radioactive substance (through "active precipitation" from developing gaslike substances) radioactively "contaminates" a whole laboratory, so the synchronistic phenomenon seems to have the tendency to *spread* into the consciousness of several people. (emphasis in original)[56]

And:

> ... The physical phenomenon of radioactivity consists in the transition of the atomic nucleus of the active substance from an unstable early state to its stable final state ... in the course of which the radioactivity finally stops. Similarly, the synchronistic phenomenon ... accompanies the transition from an unstable state of consciousness into a new stable position, in balance with the unconscious, a position in which the synchronistic borderline phenomenon has vanished again.[57]

This is quite clearly a workable hypothesis for the operation of synchronicity as a phenomenon which moves from an unstable state of consciousness to a stable one, at which point it disappears.

Pauli goes a bit further in a letter written to Jung on June 4, 1950 (at the outbreak of the Korean War), in which he relates more dream material, and then writes of his experiences at Princeton University, where he discussed synchronicity "on several occasions." He then makes an interesting comment which is very much in line with Jung's own published writing on synchronicity:

> ... I made a point of stressing the difference between the *spontaneous* appearance of the phenomenon ... and the *induced* phenomenon (by means of a preliminary treatment or a rite), as is the case with mantic practices (*I Ching* or *ars geomantica*). (emphasis in original)[58]

Spontaneous synchronicity and *induced* synchronicity. Here we come to the very heart of the power behind the sinister forces. Even Pauli seems somehow aware of the larger implications of this theory when he writes to Jung on November 28, 1936:

> I would like to hear sometime what you think about the collection of dreams ... in which the dark anima asserts with a certain persistence that there is

a "magical" connection between sexuality and eroticism on the one hand, and political or historical events on the other.[59]

In all the writings of the physicists and the quantum consciousness theorists we have encountered thus far, there has been avoidance of the core question at the heart of their identification of synchronicity ("meaningful coincidence" and "acausal connecting principle") with quantum mechanics: the political ramifications of a consciousness that can be manipulated as much as subatomic particles can be manipulated, but using as the "energy source" what Pauli's "dark anima" calls "sexuality" and what Ioan Coulianu's Giordano Bruno calls "eros," resulting in the phenomenon of *induced* synchronicity

Are the many, many coincidences that surround some of America's most critical "political or historical events" representative of this type of *induced* synchronicity? Were Pauwels and Bergier correct in postulating that the phenomenon of synchronicity and meaningful-coincidence could lead to "an entirely new conception of history"? Were these scientists-intelligence officers-occultists, godfathering the birth of modern remote viewing with their disinformation article on the *Nautilus* experiments in telepathy, telling us something they already knew?

It would seem at first glance that an induced synchronicity is one in which there is an element of cause-and-effect, and thus negates the entire concept of an "acausal connecting principle"; but what Pauli references is not a means to *cause* a synchronicity to occur, but a means of *observing* synchronicity by creating an environment conducive to its observation—such as the Chinese system of divination known as the *I Ching*—or by creating an event through a normal cause-and-effect mechanism in the narrow, determinist sense which "throws off" synchronicities the way radium throws off radiation. There are occasions in which synchronicities seem to multiply; it is not known whether this is the result of conscious observation (in which naturally occurring synchronicities normally ignored are singled out for study, and thus *seem* to be multiplying) or of some other factor.

While the entire Jungian theory of synchronicity is based on its acausality, are there circumstances that are more conducive to synchronicity than others? Synchronicity is a connecting principle, connecting events that are otherwise not related by cause-and-effect, and it involves *meaning*. Meaning, as we have seen, is the bedrock of consciousness.

As Pauli pointed out above, synchronicity seems to accompany the transition from an unstable state of consciousness to a stable one. Perhaps, then, the appearance of synchronicity is an indication that an unstable state in the unconscious mind is reaching stability in full consciousness. This is in accord with Jung, who gives the phenomenon of synchronicity a grounding in the archetypes, those structures in the unconscious mind that are sources of psychic energy and which manifest themselves in dreams, visions, and art. It is the search for meaning in these phenomena that has given rise to religion and philosophy, reaching a kind of apotheosis in alchemy, which celebrated the image as repository of meaning—something which the surrealists understood at once.

Jung drew a strong comparison between ESP and synchronicity in his one published essay on synchronicity, because both phenomena seemed to violate the laws of classical physics in the same way: they ignore the limitations of space and time. The experiments in remote viewing, therefore, would be related—in Jung's view—to the phenomenon of synchronicity. One of the remarkable facts about psychic phenomena that attracted Jung's attention was the degree to which enthusiasm or strong emotional excitement affected the results of ESP tests conducted under laboratory conditions: the results were actually better if the subjects were enthusiastic about ESP, believed in ESP, or were otherwise emotionally stimulated by the testing procedure. Famous psychics, when presented with the sterile laboratory environment, often tested badly. The English trance medium Eileen J. Garrett attributed her own poor performance to the fact that "she was unable to summon up any feeling."[60] This close association of feeling and paranormal abilities (on the one hand) and feeling and synchronicity (on the other) would have been familiar to Renaissance magicians like Bruno, who considered such feelings an aspect of "eros." Given a workable set of correspondences—i.e., the magical "links" determined by the structure of the "Matrix" (to use Swann's terminology)—and sufficient "eros" in whatever form, the magician would be able to cause paranormal phenomena to occur.

In the case of Eileen Garrett, the ESP test cards used were "soulless"; she would have had better results (in her view) with something more akin to a Tarot deck. In other words, with images drawn from the pool of archetypes in the collective unconscious: the spring of synchronicity as well as of paranormal abilities.

We may recall the presentation of Penrose and Hameroff to the RAND Corporation, during which they said that the "heightened experience" was conducive to achieving the quantum state in the human brain. Psychology, medicine, and physics seem to agree with the Renaissance sorcerers in this regard.

Jung ends his 1973 monograph on synchronicity with the following sentiments:

> Synchronicity is no more baffling or mysterious than the discontinuities of physics. It is only the ingrained belief in the sovereign power of causality that creates intellectual difficulties and makes it appear unthinkable that causeless events exist or could ever occur. But if they do, then we must regard them as *creative acts*, as the continuous creation of a pattern that

> exists from all eternity, repeats itself sporadically, and is not derivable from any known antecedents.... For these reasons it seems to me necessary to introduce, alongside space, time, and causality, a category which not only enables us to understand synchronistic phenomena as a special class of natural events, but also takes the contingent partly as a universal factor existing from all eternity, and partly as the sum of countless individual acts of creation occurring in time. (emphasis in original)[61]

Creative acts. A pattern, like Swann's "Matrix," that exists from all eternity. The sum of countless individual acts of creation. The creative acts not only of art and music and literature in the normal sense of creation but also the creative acts of politicians, generals, bishops, and popes. The creative act of ritual magic, the shamanistic séance, the Nuremberg rally, the assassination of a president, the coronation of a king.

History, then, can be understood as a function of the operation of this principle in a higher sense as surely as—in a grosser sense—the cause-and-effect mechanism of Newtonian physics is a useful way of looking at wars and elections and assassinations: accumulations of dates and places and names that are quantifiable and identifiable, like the chemical formulae we learn in high school science classes. In this "higher sense," historical events are linked *sub rosa* or *sub mensa* by connections and "correspondences" that only come to our attention as intriguing little coincidences or ironic commentaries, the stuff of "deep politics," not admissible as evidence in a court of law but nonetheless demonstrating motive in a more profound way: the motive of another, occult participant in the crime; for the pattern of connections understood by Pauli, when acted upon by Arthur Young's "quantum of action," can produce effects in unforeseen ways and lead us back to "first causes" we would never have expected.

To students of Renaissance magician Giordano Bruno, such as the late Professor Ioan Culianu, the links between persons, objects, and events can be activated through "eros." As Aleister Crowley would say, centuries after Bruno, "Love is the law, love under Will." Will is Arthur Young's "quantum of action," and "love" or "eros" is the energy expended by that Will. Will may be thought of as intention, an intellectual decision made by a human being to effect some change; love or *eros* is the power of that intention when linked to the object of the will. If the energy is powerful enough, and the link substantial enough, then change can be effected *at a distance, instantaneously* and with *no loss of energy.*

This idea of unmediated change at a distance is central to the idea of occultism, but anathema to most modern models of science beginning with Newton, though Newton himself was a practicing astrologer and occultist. In the kind of physics one learns in school, objects must act upon each other to effect change. A billiard ball must strike another billiard bill, or a gust of wind toss dried leaves along the ground, or radio waves be picked up by an antenna and modulated into sound. In other words, all change is mediated locally. The idea of a kind of mental ray that emanates from our brain or our eyes and charges across space in an instant to move a solid object, or "see" events at a distance, is the stuff of comic books and science fiction; yet that is just what the modern theories of quantum consciousness suggest *might* be possible.

To Jung, the link that exists between these events is entirely psychological; i.e., there is no physical basis for the link, otherwise we are back at the cause-and-effect Newtonian school of physics, and synchronicity operates outside those parameters. The links are connections of *meaning*, and it is still doubtful whether physics can demonstrate a scientific basis for meaning. However, can consciousness act upon matter and change it?

Of course, every time we make a conscious decision to do something—to lift a book or throw a ball—we are demonstrating the action of consciousness upon matter. A traditional scientist could disagree, however, by saying that a complex series of physical actions involving human musculature and the firing of neurons in the nervous system is what "caused" the book to be lifted or the ball to be thrown. To Arthur Young, the decision to lift the book or throw the ball is a demonstration of another type of law, but just how "physical" is decision-making? Is it the result of an eventually-predictable set of natural steps in a linear chain of cause and effect? If so, then human beings have no will and cannot be judged for their actions. This was the problem facing Arthur Young, and it contributes to the discussion about synchronicity.

Manson's situation is, however, infinitely worse. From the very beginning, his experiences seemed to inform him that what we all secretly know about our existential condition might very well be wrong!

—R.C. Scharff, "Understanding Charles Manson," in *The Manson Murders: A Philosophical Inquiry* (emphasis in original)[62]

The issues of good luck versus bad luck are familiar to the general public, but these matters scientists consider to be sheer chimeras of superstition, without any basis in reality. The Communists, of course, considered luck—and all its ancillary charms, talismans, potions, spells—to be part of the opiate of the people for the very same reason: it was unscientific, and adoption of practices like these only enslaved the people and kept them from participating in the real power of the oligarchy, where it was believed luck (good or bad) did not exist. Likewise, any belief in miracles and psychic healing, etc. was derided in favor of confidence in the science of medicine. If only everyone abandoned these silly beliefs and instead adopted a purely scientific outlook with its faith in the miracles of modern medicine, then everyone would be better off.

Except that people still die in hospital beds. People are still hit by cars, drown at sea, and have jetliners crash into their office buildings. While science can account for *how* so much evil happens in the world, it cannot offer any reason *why*. It has abandoned that aspect of chemical and physical reactions to the moralists, but at the same time it has cut the moralists off at the knees with its insistence that everything that happens in the universe happens as a result of mechanistic laws. Thus, the people—for whom their own individual lives are perhaps more important than the big picture of scientific advancement and statistical probabilities of survival—fall back upon charms, talismans, prayers, shamans, psychic healing and all the rest. While science insists that none of this works, it is incapable of ensuring any individual that he or she will not be stricken by disease, or die as the result of a car accident, a terrorist strike, a falling brick.

These things are the result of a confluence of events in the Matrix, and the person who is victimized by them is occupying a particular spot—not only in space and time but also in another dimension, the quantum dimension perhaps where considerations of space and time are not so ironclad as they are in the perceivable world—where the scarlet threads of murder, sickness, and natural disaster may run through him and annihilate him. The use of charms, talismans, prayers, etc. is intended to readjust an individual's position in the Matrix so that these threads do not strangle him; this conscious focus on avoiding pain and misery may cause neural firings affecting the quantum level, where the microtubules make minute adjustments to the parameters of time and space, and the individual narrowly misses being beaten, eaten, or otherwise incapacitated in an event we refer to as "coincidence."

Science is also unable to explain the basis for the profound sense of loss we can feel at the death of a loved one; or the guilt in recognizing the evil of our own past actions. These are the emotions, after all, that prompt the survivors to pick up a gun or blow up a bus. Psychology (surely an inferior science by any method of calculation) only admits that these feelings exist, and that one must come to terms with them … but these are ideas that are the product of a worldview that has been formed by scientific thought, which is, itself, weak on questions of moral responsibility and spirituality. The idea that negative feelings should be exorcised—by psychotherapy or drugs—is the mechanistic scientific worldview taken to its logical conclusion. As R.D. Laing and others have pointed out, it may be wrong to consider anti-social behavior (such as that of the schizophrenic) as something that must be suppressed with anti-psychotic drugs and leather restraints. There may be another dimension to the human experience—to consciousness—that science does not understand, because it refuses to acknowledge that there is any importance to events outside the parameters of its measurements. It is, once again, the case of the drunk looking for his keys under a streetlight because the light is better there. The keys are in the darkness. And in the darkness is superstition, mysticism, art, music, madness, and death. The hungry ghosts.

Endnotes

[1] Graham Hancock, *The Mars Mystery*, Seal Books, Toronto, 1998, p. 380

[2] Octavio Paz, *The Labyrinth of Solitude*, Grove Press, NY, 1978, p. 69

[3] Kenneth Patchen, *The Journal of Albion Moonlight*, New Directions, NY, 1961, p. 152

[4] William L. Moore, *The Philadelphia Experiment*, Fawcett Crest, NY, 1984, p. 76

[5] Jim Garrison, *On The Trail of the Assassins*, Warner Books, NY, 1991, p. 135

[6] Louis Pauwels and Jacques Bergier, *The Morning of the Magicians*, Mayflower, St Albans, 1973, p. 135

[7] James Kirsch, "Carl Gustav Jung and the Jews: The Real Story," *Journal of Psychology and Judaism* 6, No. 2 (Spring-Summer 1982), p. 113-43

[8] *Lingering Shadows: Jungians, Freudians, and Anti-Semitism*, Aryeh Maidebaum and Stephen A. Martin eds., Shambhala, Boston and London, 1991

[9] C.G. Jung, *Synchronicity: An Acausal Connecting Principle*, Bollingen, Princeton University Press, Princeton, 1973, p. 19

[10] F. David Peat, *Synchronicity: The Bridge Between Matter and Mind*, Bantam Books, NY, 1987, p. 16

[11] Ibid., p. 16

[12] Arthur Young, *The Foundations of Science: The Missing Parameter*, Broadside Editions, San Francisco, 1985, p. 6

[13] Aleister Crowley, *Goetia*, Magickal Childe Publishing, NY, 1989, p. 6

[14] Roger Penrose, *The Emperor's New Mind*, Oxford University Press, Oxford, 1989, p. 302

[15] Ibid., p. 304-5

[16] Arthur Koestler, *The Roots of Coincidence*, Hutchinson & Co., London, 1972

[17] S.R. Hameroff, A. Kaszniak, and A.C. Scott (eds.,), *Toward a Science of Consciousness—The First Tucson Discussions and Debates*, MIT Press, Cambridge, MA, 1996, p. 507-540

[18] Ibid.

[19] Ibid., p. 507

[20] Ibid., p. 507-8

[21] Ibid., p. 508

[22] S. R. Hameroff, "'Funda-Mentality' Is the Conscious Mind Subtly Linked to a Basic Level of the Universe?" *Trends in Cognitive Sciences,* 1998, vol.2, p. 119-24

[23] Ibid

[24] Ibid.

[25] Ibid.

[26] S. R. Hameroff, "Quenching qualms about quantum consciousness: Reply to Spier and Thomas," p. 125-127

[27] H.P. Lovecraft, *The Best of H.P. Lovecraft*, Ballantine, New York, 1982, p. 356

[28] Jim Schnabel, *Remote Viewers: The Secret History of America's Psychic Spies,* Dell, NY, 1997

[29] Russell Targ and Keith Harary, *The Mind Race: Understanding and Using Psychic Powers* New English Library, London, 1986,
[30] David Morehouse, *Psychic Warrior: Inside the CIA's Stargate Program*, St Martin's Press, NY, 1996
[31] Schnabel, op. cit., p. 89
[32] Ibid., p. 151
[33] Ibid., p. 182-183
[34] Ibid., p. 188
[35] Ibid., p. 188
[36] Ibid., p. 188-189
[37] Turan Rifat, "Military Development of Remote Mind-Control Technology," *Nexus*, Volume 3, #6, Oct-Nov 1996
[38] Schnabel, op. cit., p. 220
[39] Richard Sauder, *Kundalini Tales*, Adventures Unlimited Press, Kempton, Illinois, 1998
[40] Schnabel, op. cit., p. 296
[41] Ibid., p. 168-169
[42] Sauder, op. cit., p. 14
[43] Schnabel, op. cit., p. 213
[44] Jonathan Franzen, *The Corrections*, Picador USA, NY, 2002, p. 322
[45] Arthur Koestler, *Janus*, Vintage Books, NY, 1979, p. 76
[46] Ibid., p. 15
[47] Ibid., p. 13
[48] Ibid., p. 113
[49] Ibid., p. 144
[50] Ibid., p. 267
[51] Ibid., p. 266
[52] Ibid., p. 270
[53] Colin Wilson, *Order of Assassins: The Psychology of Murder*, Panther Books, St Albans, 1975, p. 167
[54] *Atom and Archetype: The Pauli/Jung Letters 1932-1958*, edited by C.A. Meier, Princeton University Press, Princeton, 2001, p. 38
[55] Ibid., p. 40
[56] Ibid., p. 41
[57] Ibid., p. 41
[58] Ibid., p. 44
[59] Ibid., p. 16
[60] Jung, op. cit., p. 18
[61] Ibid, p. 102-103
[62] R.C. Scharff, "Understanding Charles Manson," in *The Manson Murders: A Philosophical Inquiry*, David E. Cooper, Editor, Schenkrian Publishing Co., Cambridge, 1974

INFORMATION AWARENE
ICE
DARPA
SCIENTIA EST POTENTIA

SECTION SIX: HUNGRY GHOSTS

Buddhism teaches the existence of hungry ghosts.... The Chinese call these ghosts 'kwei' and believe that it is they who give an enormous amount of trouble to human beings such as making them sick, taking possession of them, haunting their houses, and so on. Those 'kwei' or evil dissatisfied spirits whose families have neglected them by not making ritualistic offerings to them or those who died suddenly and violently, become hungry ghosts, out to seek vengeance against human beings.

—Tan Teik Beng, *Beliefs and Practices Among Malaysian Chinese Buddhists*[1]

I am wearing the talisman of invisibility so that now even my shadow is gone, shrink-wrapped around my invisible flesh, tight to the invisible bone. I wander abroad, among the nomads, stepping carefully over the moving bundles of rags that clot the landscape like sores on diseased flesh. These are the Arabs that haunt my dreams, the wanderers of the waste I know as Queens.

Some of them will die tonight, of exposure to the harsh winds and the cancerous dampness that creeps up from the pavement and down from the walls. Their minds feast on their bodies, devouring their anatomies by inches, and when a homeless street person dies the mind lives on as a hungry ghost, haunting the Underground stations, the crumbling concrete platforms, the rusted rails....

Lee Harvey Oswald once lived in Russia. Like Gogol. Like Dostoevsky. He spoke Russian, and had a Russian wife. That is why Gogol never finished Dead Souls, *for Lee had not yet been born.*

But Gogol, a voice crying in the wilderness, was his John the Baptist, and Dostoevsky was his St. Paul.

I passed by Jesus on the street today, but he pretended not to know me.

—Peter Levenda, *The Black Pullet*, unpublished ms.

Are you being sinister or is this some form of practical joke?

—Allen Ginsberg, "America," January 17, 1956

Chapter Twenty-Two

Haunted House

Without absolutely expressing a doubt whether the stalwart Puritan had acted as a man of conscience and integrity throughout the proceedings which have been sketched, they, nevertheless, hinted that he was about to build his house over an unquiet grave. His home would include the home of the dead and buried wizard, and would thus afford the ghost of the latter a kind of privilege to haunt its new apartments, and the chambers into which future bridegrooms were to lead their brides, and where children of the Pyncheon blood were to be born.

—Nathaniel Hawthorne, *The House of the Seven Gables*

... agents from the federal intelligence community have entered private practice by the tens of thousands, impinging invisibly, but profoundly, on current events and our perception of them. The specter they raise is one of a country "haunted" by its wandering spooks ... light has always been the most dependable means of exorcism. So it is that the haunting of America will end only when our secret history becomes public knowledge.

—Jim Hougan, *Spooks*[2]

I have been asked if it is possible to strike an entire community through magic. My answer must be yes.... It is possible for the demon to use one person to strike even a very large group—these groups can even take over or influence one or more nations.

—Fr. Gabriele Amorth, Chief Exorcist of Rome[3]

As we have seen, not only do private intelligence agents haunt America, but the entire secret history of the nation is replete with covert action by a variety of individuals and official and quasi-official government organizations that have penetrated not only domestic political parties, terrorist groups, revolutionary cabals, and cults, but have also penetrated the inner senses of the human mind. Like the ghost-story spooks of children's fairy tales, they have invaded our dreams, our waking thoughts, and our sleeping unconscious to an extent no one would have believed possible one hundred years ago, using a variety of techniques: from the hypnosis and automatic writing of the shell-shock therapists and surrealist artists of the first half of the twentieth century, to the drugs, psychic driving, psychological warfare, and remote viewing of the last half, governments have been intent on delving into the powers—and understanding the weaknesses—of the human mind. But by limiting our collective attention to questions of the mind only, we have ignored what may be a larger issue, a more dangerous threat; when we use the word "mind" we are making a value judgment where psychological, parapsychological, and paraphysical phenomena are concerned. We have successfully robbed "mind" of spirit. That may have been a mistake.

While medical men like Dr. Cameron hammered at the neurological functions of the human brain with drugs and sensory deprivation in an effort to erase memory and recreate personality from the ground up, other scientists and intelligence officers approached the mind directly through the manipulation of images. In this, they were following in the footsteps of the ancient Greek philosophers, who understood that phantasms were the only means through which the real world was perceivable to the soul. The Greek word from which we get "fantasy"—*fantasia*—is translated as "imagination, the power by which an object is presented to the mind (the object presented being *fantasma*),"[4] and was common usage in the age of Plato and Aristotle. It represents a surprisingly prescient understanding of how the brain "sees": an object is presented to the brain as a *phantom*, as an image. In other words, there is an intermediate step between the perception of an object and its appearance in the brain: the image. The ancient Greeks understood this and, later, the Renaissance philosopher-magicians who realized that in this image-making faculty of the brain there resides great power, for the brain relies on images exclusively, and treats everything it "sees"—trees, sky, people, artifacts—as images. It is not dissuasive that the images thus perceived also bring with them sounds, and smells, and tactile sensations. These are all part of the complex "image" created by the brain in order to contemplate "reality." To the Renaissance magician, this entire construct could be fabricated in order to cause change to occur in the world: focus on the image itself, on the "technology" of the image, and one could obtain tremendous power, for the language of the brain is image. Image *is* reality, and reality is nothing more than one long propaganda film.

When one speaks or writes of "mind control," a presumption is often made that one is a conspiracy theorist reveling in the most outlandish tales of sinister government plots to brainwash the masses. Unfortunately, the historical record is clear. Intelligence organs—including those of the military—have been involved in precisely that sort of research in many countries for at least the past sixty years, if not longer. What has been generally ignored in the books and papers published thus far on the subject is the extent to which real knowledge about the functions and processes of human consciousness has been obtained in this manner; what has also been ignored is the blowback from these programs. Scientists were not allowed to publish the most exciting results of their research, as they came under security classification. Men like Hal Puthoff and Russell Targ, Ewen Cameron and Frank Olson and William Sargant were prohibited from sharing their work with their peers. Always listening was the enemy—the Soviet Union and the People's Republic of China, countries devoted to atheism and credited with the first applications of what would become known as "brainwashing," itself a spiritual technology stripped of its religious context.

Most writings on the technology of the religious experience—whether it be yoga, or meditation, or shamanistic ritual, or the taking of peyote or magic mushrooms—stress the dangers of unguided spiritual "experimentation." In the days most of these texts were written, there was no science of psychology, no practice of neurology or understanding of neuropathy. Madness was often considered in purely theological terms. Even so, the warnings were explicit: disaster would be the outcome of any attempt to reach nirvana through crude, artificial means, or without the guidance of an experienced guru, or by an unclean and untrained ascetic. In the case of government investigation of the paranormal, and of the human mind, none of these precautions were heeded. Psychiatrists like Ewen Cameron ran roughshod over their patients' psyches, doing permanent damage to the consciousness of innocents. Bureaucrats like Sidney Gottlieb authorized government expenditures for covert research that was responsible for massively dosing prisoners, psychopaths, and children with hallucinogens and other drugs ... human beings whose identities are no longer known to us or to anyone. Alive? Or dead? Serial killers ... or ghosts?

Others have died in the attempt to discover the truth about reality, truth that was protected by men in white jackets or blue uniforms or grey flannel suits. Captain Mantell, Morris Jessup, James McDonald ... all died in pursuit of that truth, the first man in actual pursuit of a UFO, and the last two suicides from the stress and humiliation that dogs every genuine researcher into this extremely sensitive subject.

These are the hungry ghosts that haunt America. These, and so many others. As we have seen in various statements by a wide range of experts, it has become increasingly difficult to separate an intelligence operation from the operation of another force in the world: two phenomena, both secret and "occult," linked by a common thread of coincidence and synchronicity. Where did this "other" force come from? How do we cope with its effects? How do we exorcise the hungry ghosts of America?

As frivolous as these questions may seem to a traditional historian, they actually go to the heart of what it means to be human, and as well to the heart of what we have come to call "reality." Questions of good and evil, life after death, punishment and revenge, God and demons ... for all of these ideas, which are central to the life of every human being, we normally rely upon priests or ministers or other religious leaders, or, if we are atheists, upon philosophers, artists and even scientists. It would never occur to us to question history itself, which we see largely as a stage on which these ideas are played out in a kind of cosmic drama, the end of which we cannot predict but which we hope will mean that the guilty will be punished and the sufferings of the innocent redeemed; but the answers to our perpetual questions about life and existence may be encoded in our history—not the "Disneyland" version, to use Jim Hougan's phrase for the type of canned history one is taught in schools and universities, but—our secret history, our forgotten history for which our classical, schoolroom-style history is but the outward sign and symbol.

The historical model I am proposing in these volumes should be obvious by now. By tracing the darker elements of the American experience from the earliest days of the Adena and Hopewell cultures through the discovery by Columbus, the English settlers in Massachusetts and the Salem witchcraft episode, the rise of Joseph Smith, Jr. and the Mormons via ceremonial magic and Freemasonry, up to the twentieth century and the support of Nazism by American financiers and politicians before, during, and after World War II, and the UFO phenomenon coming on the heels of that war, we can see the outlines of a kind of political ectoplasm taking shape in this historical séance: politics as a continuation of religion by other means. The ancillary events of the Charles Manson murders, the serial killer phenomenon, Jonestown, and the assassinations of Jack Kennedy, Bobby Kennedy, Martin Luther King, and Marilyn Monroe are all the result of the demonic possession of the American psyche, like the obscenities spat out by little Regan, tied to her bed and shrieking at the exorcists. It is said that demonic possession is both a way of testing us, and of making us aware of the real conflict taking place within us every day.

The fact that so many American men and women in positions of power and authority have been specifically involved with occult practices is something that not even I had anticipated before I began the research for this work. Initially, I treated the one or two politicians who "dabbled" as a kind of anomaly; my original focus had been the unhealthy, almost incestuous relationship between Church and State, in America specifically and in the world in general: religious beliefs as the motivation for dangerous policy decisions and strategic maneuvers (such as Ronald Reagan's apocalyptic Christianity, and Nancy Reagan's devotion to agenda by astrology, and George W. Bush's devotion to evangelical Christianity). The more I looked, however, the more I found men with bizarre beliefs and involved in questionable, occult practices at the highest levels of the American government, and buried deep within government agencies. I also discovered that occultism was embraced by the American military and intelligence establishments as a weapon to be used in the Cold War; and as they did so, they unleashed forces upon the American populace that cannot be called back.

Those that were not involved in occultism *per se* were involved with Nazism in one form or another, and thus were aiding and abetting not only an enemy of America and an enemy of humanity in general, but what was most certainly and by any definition a cult: the most powerful and most dangerous cult the modern world has seen so far. The moral imbecility of those engaging these men as scientists, spies, and agents of American foreign policy—and then defending them against those who begged for justice, hiding them on American soil—is beyond comprehension. The guilty include the Dulles brothers, Walkers and Bushes, Henry Ford, Richard Nixon, and so many other household names in American politics. We can try to make excuses for them, try to rationalize away their actions in the light of *realpolitik*, but then we become as bad as the Germans who claimed they were only following orders.

Watergate revealed the existence of "sinister forces" to me in many ways. The scandal opened the floodgates of conspiracy theories going back to the Kennedy assassination and beyond. It tied together so many loose ends, yet posited more questions than it offered answers, revealing a secret political struggle that had been going on for decades, ripping apart the very fabric of America with a populace oblivious to it all. One inevitably was forced back to the CIA and the mind-control experiments that began in the late 1940s and extended nearly to the present day. Coincidence piled on coincidence, indicating the existence of a powerful, subliminal force working at the level of chaos—at the quantum level—and struggling to manifest itself in our reality, our consciousness, our political agenda. This dynamic was uncovered by a Swiss psychologist and an Austrian physicist, but it capably describes a force working within the context of American history and American politics that is suppurating below the consciousness of the people but able to erupt without notice. A sinister force.

Fascism.

When the science editor of *Time* magazine—Leon Jaroff—became aware of the remote-viewing experiments taking place at SRI under Puthoff and Targ, he was alarmed. To Jaroff, the paranormal research at SRI was akin to the occultism that, in his view, gave rise to fascism in Germany, and he felt that *their research should be destroyed.*[5] Theodore Adorno (1903-69), the German philosopher whose "F-scale" or "fascism scale" became a controversial subject in psychological circles after his expulsion from Germany in 1934, attacked the "irrational" for the very same reason: his belief that the irrational (to Adorno, everything from astrology to occultism) in mass culture inevitably leads to fascism.[6] One is almost forced to ask the obvious question, the one not asked in polite company: does the "irrational" include religion? Of course, it does, but science prefers religion to be a vehicle for instruction in ethical culture, and not supernaturalism; yet it is humanity's confrontation with the supernatural that lead to the development of religion and, eventually, ethics and moral values.

Therefore, it is perhaps not the belief in the irrational that leads to fascism, however, but the *marginalization* of the irrational that does so, for it encourages a parallel belief in conspiracy. Since people in general have direct experience of the paranormal in their lives—from events as trivial as coincidence to as traumatic as poltergeist activity, incidents of ESP, UFO sightings, or even remote-viewing—to find their experience ridiculed by the established authority is insupportable. They confront this "disconnect" coming to them from authority, and thus begin to question authority—its wisdom, or its motives—itself. They become prey to those who would encourage their "irrational" beliefs and point an accusing finger at the very authorities—scientific or political—who would deny them the secret power or arcane knowledge they could otherwise possess. The debasement of the paranormal in culture only serves to increase its value among the population, who treasure their unusual experiences in secret, and who build up entire cosmologies around them, since they have no other context in which to understand what they *know* to have occurred. Thus, for me, fascism is the result not of irrational beliefs but of *the monopolization of those beliefs by others*: men and women who exploit the divide between the direct experience of the masses and the intellectualist denial of their experiences by a privileged, powerful elite.

The shaman in primitive cultures is a person who has managed to integrate the irrational into his own personality and, by extension, into the life of his society. His act of personal self-transcendence—to use Koestler's terminology—is an act of social integration which also successfully integrates the irrational into the life of society through his social role as healer, therapist, and seer. The serial killer is a shaman who has not managed to integrate the irrational with the life of his society, as society no longer has a place for it or a context within which to understand what is happening to him. The irrational in modern society is consigned to the dustheap of psychoanalysis, if not of history itself. The same is true of the fascist.

The fascist embraces the irrational because it is transcendental, and the fascist yearns to transcend his natural state, to become more than human, to become—as Hitler said—a "new man." Since the fascist becomes the only political person who tolerates the irrational, he becomes the figurehead of the people who have encountered the irrational in their own lives. The fascist is a shaman who has not managed to integrate the irrational in his own life, but who still needs the approval and support—and, if possible, the adulation—of society in order to act out his fantasies. The serial killer differs only in that he has no need of society's approval: he gave that up a long time ago, and regards society with hatred and suspicion. The fascist and the serial killer share this in common: they both feel a tremendous need for self-transcendence but fail to integrate the irrational needs and experiences of their psyches with either themselves (the fascist) or with society (the serial killer). The successful shaman has done both: he has interiorized the essential conflicts of the irrational experience in the "rational" world, and has also integrated both the elements of his own personality as well as his own personality (with all of its irrational experiences) with society in general. However, had society in general not welcomed his achievements, there is every possibility that he would have become a social pariah and, from there, a dangerous individual, fueled by the dangerous component of shamanism: sexuality.

Our society has no place for the shaman, so we marginalize both him and his experiences. The shaman comes back, then, to haunt us in other ways: either as the iconic serial killer or as the dreary fascist. Both are evil, either evil "in and of themselves" to borrow the clanking terminology of the existentialists, or as channels for an evil force that is older than history, but of whose machinations history is the unhappy result.

THE ORIGINS OF EVIL

Myth is a two-way mirror in which ritual and philosophy may regard one another. It is the moment when people normally caught up in everyday banalities are suddenly (perhaps because of some personal upheaval) confronted with problems that they have hitherto left to the bickerings of the philosophers; and it is the moment when philosophers, too, come to terms with the darker, flesh-and-blood aspects of their abstract inquiries.

—Wendy Doniger O'Flaherty[7]

The problem of evil is one that has bothered theologians and philosophers for thousands of years. The problem can be expressed simply: Why does God permit evil to exist in the world? If God is all-powerful, then God must be permitting evil to exist; if so, then God is evil, or blind to the sufferings caused by evil (which cannot be so, because one of the definitions of God is that he/she is all-powerful and all-knowing). The only logical conclusions to draw are that either God is not all-powerful, or not all-knowing, or … that God is evil.

This problem did not exist in ancient times, when there were a multiplicity of gods all in conflict with each other. Human beings would cast their lot with one side or the other; the opposing side was the enemy, but not necessarily evil in the moral sense. The disasters that befell human beings—sickness, death, famine, drought, etc.—were caused by demons, the foot-soldiers of the "bad" gods. One could appease them, or exorcise them.

As the pantheism of our ancestors became the monotheism of the Jews, Christians and Muslims, God became One: the Creator and the Redeemer, the

Preserver and the Destroyer. Yet, somehow God was "all good." The Christian New Testament offered us a God who was loving and merciful, holding out expectations of reward in an afterlife (obviously, it would have to be an afterlife; the good and the innocent are cannon-fodder in *this* world). The God of the monotheists demands loyalty above all else. He will test that loyalty with severe trials, such as experienced by Job in the Old Testament, when Satan persuaded God to let him push Job to the limit with every imaginable suffering: essentially laying a wager with God that Job would give up His worship and turn apostate. Somehow that scenario became the operative one in the monotheistic cults: evil existed because it was God's way of testing our loyalty to Him.

Of course, that gave rise to a host of other logical inconsistencies. If God is, indeed, all-knowing, then God would have known in advance how Job would have reacted. There would have been no need of any test, not for Job and not for the rest of us. Why, then, are we tested?

We are then given the argument that God is demonstrating that we have free will, and can choose to be loyal to Him or not. Again, that begs the question. If God is all-knowing, then He already knows what choices we will make. And so on.

Another argument, and one that has never garnered much support, is that what we consider to be evil—pain, suffering, death—is not evil at all. It is only our perception of these things that makes them evil. "It's all good." Unfortunately, we can easily think of dozens of cases where that argument is unacceptable: the suffering of children, for instance—beings so small and vulnerable that their suffering cannot be the result of any choice they have made. The Asians, confronted with this obvious fact, came back with the elegant concept of reincarnation. Thus, an infant who suffers in this life is paying for a sin committed in a previous incarnation. This also provides the satisfying corollary that there is a continuity of identity of some kind after death and through a long succession of rebirths. There have even been fully documented cases of small children spontaneously exhibiting knowledge of other lives in other places that they could not have garnered in their short lives but must have "remembered" from a previous existence (e.g. in *Twenty Cases Suggestive of Reincarnation*). The fact that many of these cases take place in countries and amid cultures where reincarnation is an accepted phenomenon may skew the statistics in an unsatisfactory way, and raises the suggestion that these experiences may be the result of some other kind of paranormal event, such as telepathy.

Reincarnation (with its concomitant ideal of *karma*, the burden of one's actions—good and bad—that one carries from lifetime to lifetime) *is* an elegant solution, but—like the heaven and hell of the monotheists—it admits of no real proof beyond the anecdotal. If evil is not the result of a linear chain of cause and effect—a chain over which we have control—then where did it come from? What is its purpose? Whom does it serve? And why does God not protect us from it?

The answers to these questions may not be palatable. They bring us to a mythology that is at once quite old and at the same time the stuff of science fiction and fantasy. It is as much part of the ancient Sanskrit texts as it is of the Middle Eastern Gnostic documents. It is also a recurring theme in UFO lore as well as in pulp fiction. Because it comes up so often in the human psyche, it is worth examining here, even as it has been abandoned as a workable hypothesis by the monotheists who have given us thousands of years of refinement and civilization, art and music and literature ... and Inquisitions, Crusades, Holy wars, and genocide. It is an explanation for the schizophrenia that characterizes the human experience.

Wendy Doniger O'Flaherty—a colleague of the slain Ioan Culianu at the University of Chicago—has studied the problem of evil as it appears in Hinduism, one of humanity's oldest religions, based on one of its oldest languages: Sanskrit, a language so ancient and so complex that even today it is extremely difficult to give satisfactory translations of Sanskrit texts (as the ongoing and still uncompleted project to create a comprehensive Sanskrit dictionary has shown). What she has to say about Hindu concepts of evil is universal in application, and has resonance with early Christian and gnostic belief systems, as well as with mythologies as remote from each other as the Aztec and the Daoist. She writes,

> The belief that the gods create evil for man in order that man should depend on the gods—and the priests—recurs in Sanskrit texts. The gods find evil necessary for their very existence; they allow the demons to thrive in order that they themselves may thrive as gods, to force men to worship them.[8]

This is, of course, an exceedingly cynical appraisal of the problem, but one that is familiar to students of Hinduism. It depicts the gods as venal entities who desire worship and sacrifice, and use men—and their fear of demons—the way governments use their populations. If it is true that "the organizing principle of nations is war" then it is equally true of the cosmos, according to this view.

> The one invariable characteristic of the gods is that they are the enemies of the demons, and the one invariable characteristic of the demons is that they are opposed to the gods. For this reason, when the later myths began to apply new moral codes to the characters of individual gods and demons in myths, a number of inconsistencies arise, for the two groups, as groups, are not fundamentally *morally* opposed. (emphasis in original) [9]

This important point speaks to the problem we face in dealing with spiritual evil. Although gods and demons are at war with each other and—as Wendy

Doniger O'Flaherty says elsewhere—"mankind is caught in the crossfire,"[10] there is no moral difference between the two. Each is equally good or equally bad, depending on whose propaganda you believe. It also posits an ongoing struggle for supremacy between the two groups, something that would be familiar to anyone who has studied Manichaeism and Gnostic dualism, which considers humanity the battleground between the opposing forces of light and darkness. Yet, even this concept is "reductionist":

> ... in most Hindu texts, even when life is clearly desired and death feared, death is not the key to the struggle between gods and demons. For although they fight for the elixir of immortality, and the gods are said to win it ultimately, gods and demons are equally mortal and equally murderous to mankind. Finally, though the gods and demons are sometimes identified with light and darkness, these are merely symbolic expressions of contrast rather than true opposition.[11]

"Equally murderous to mankind." A sobering thought, and one which the monotheists reject, even as their texts are replete with instances of an angry God destroying entire cities in his wrath. The monotheists struggle to explain why God would take vengeance on living beings in one instant, but threaten eternal punishment for evildoers in hell after death in the next. Which is it? Punishment here and now, or punishment later? Or both? If we understand the existence of evil in the context of a war between opposing "gods" then evil becomes, in a sense, more palatable. The innocent always suffer in a war; civilian targets and "collateral damage" are inevitable. If we, as human beings, can assist one side or the other in this conflict and thereby ensure that one side wins, then evil—as we understand it, as the "collateral damage" of the conflict—should come to an end. This is not as sophisticated an approach as that of, say, Thomas Aquinas or St. Augustine, but it has the advantage of being logical and clear, and of not requiring the mental gymnastics necessary to place evil within a framework of the divine testing of free will and human choice.

But if the gods and demons—merely opponents in a cosmic war, after all—are in combat with each other, and if humanity has become a kind of spiritual battlefield, then where did the gods and demons come from in the first place, and why is humanity "caught in the crossfire"?

> The belief is often expressed that the demons were not only the equals of the gods but their superiors—the older brothers, the original gods from whom the gods stole the throne of heaven.[12]

This, of course, is pure Lovecraft. It is also purely Sumerian, which is probably the most ancient of all recorded religious cultures. The idea that there once existed an ancient race of gods that was overthrown by another group of deities goes back to the Sumerian creation epics. It is even reflected in the Talmudic idea of the *nephilim.* It is resurgent in the gothic horror of H.P. Lovecraft, and it makes an appearance in some of the theories of alien abduction and the Erich von Danniken "chariots of the gods" books. It is such a common and universal theme, that it is amazing the monotheistic religions have not managed to incorporate it into their theologies in such a way that this is no longer a controversial issue; instead it is a persistent "rumor" in literary circles as well as in alternative spiritual beliefs.

The identity of a class of Hindu gods known as the *asuras* has been the subject of a great deal of controversy in this regard. They are among the oldest of spiritual forces recognized in the Sanskrit literature, and even the name *asura* is quite controversial itself. Religious historian Wash Edward Hale (recipient of a Ph.D. in Comparative Religion from Harvard University's Divinity School in 1980) has written an entire book on the subject, demonstrating how little we actually know about the origins of Sanskrit terminology.[13] *Asura* has been linked etymologically to everything from the Zoroastrian god Ahura Mazda to a hypothetical Assyrian cult; the term *asura* itself seems to mean "lord," on that there is no disagreement, and has been applied to both humans and gods. With the passage of time, however, it seems that these beings were devalued in comparison with the *devas* who were considered the "good" gods, the *asuras* gradually taking on the characteristics of demons.

Professor of Comparative Religion at the University of Manchester, Trevor O. Ling has made a study of evil in Buddhist thought, and begins with an overview of the Hindu beliefs from which Buddhism developed. What he has to say about the *asuras* is relevant to our theme:

> According to the Udana and the Anguttara Nikaya they are said to be *ocean-dwellers,* together with various sea-monsters, nagas and gandhabbas. On the other hand they are said in the Samyutta and Anguttara Nikayas to be *dwellers in a city.* (emphasis in original)[14]

This idea of the asuras as ocean-dwellers as well as dwellers in a city, and their association with sea monsters is, of course, pure Lovecraft. His "Cthulhu" is a type of sea monster who "lies dead, but dreaming" in a lost city at the bottom of the abyss, but who is worshipped in secret by strange cults who dream of the day when his rulership will be reinstated on earth.

This concept appears also in the Sumerian creation cycles in which the ancient goddess of the abyss Tiamat—who reappears in the Biblical Hebrew term *tehom* for a kind of sea monster—is slain by a race of younger gods, children of Tiamat, who create the known world from her body ripped asunder, and from her blood and their own breath, the young gods create human beings. This is an ancient story, which nonetheless is echoed in Arthur Koestler's idea of the two human brains, one reptilian and ancient and one newer and more intellectual and calculating: humans partaking of the characteristics of both "gods."

In Biblical times, the existence of this sea-monster/demon was recognized in the term *Leviathan*, and the existence of a cult that worshipped Leviathan:

> Let them curse it that curse the day, who are ready to rouse Leviathan. (Job, iii:8)

And:

> In that day the Lord will punish with his sword, his fierce, great and powerful sword, Leviathan the gliding serpent, Leviathan the coiling serpent, he will slay the monster of the sea. (Isaiah, xxvii:1)

Certainly a strange preoccupation for a tribe who lived in the desert lands of Palestine; it is possibly a survival of Babylonian mythology, although some (such as William Smith in *Smith's Bible Dictionary*) have claimed that the Leviathan mentioned in the Bible is either a whale or a crocodile, and some translations of the Hebrew have used "dragon" in place of "monster" or "Leviathan."

Buddhism differs from Hinduism in several important respects, but germane to our study is its concept of evil. In Buddhism, evil is personified as Mara, a god (or demon) of death and evil. It is Mara's project to tempt the Buddha away from his meditations. Buddha, however, conquered Mara and at the same time conquered death itself.[15] In this, perhaps, he is a precursor to the Jesus who also conquered death, albeit in a different fashion. In Buddhism, we have a single powerful god-man, the Buddha, in conflict with a single, powerful demon, Mara. Buddha becomes superhuman during his life; Jesus—according to the predominant theology of the twenty-first century—was born a God, although there were heresies that insisted that Jesus became God while on earth.

But Mara shares a great deal in common with the Christian Satan, for Mara is an adversary and represents the created world, *Samsara*, the world of illusion and *Maya*,[16] just as Satan is said to be "Lord of this world" and is capable of taking Jesus to the mountaintop and offering him everything in sight if only he will fall down and worship the demon. Indeed, it has been alleged in various places that Buddhism—which began in India during the sixth century B.C.—came to influence Christianity through Buddhist missionaries that were said to have traveled as far as Palestine by the first century A.D. Buddhism comes as close as possible to a kind of monotheism while still retaining much of its polytheist, Hindu roots and terminology.

The danger in this approach is that one elevates evil to the level of a god, a force balancing that of good and threatening to conquer goodness, or at the very least to thwart its plans. Even Aleister Crowley, no stranger to the demonic, asserted that the Devil *per se* does not exist, that evil had been elevated by the ignorant to a monad equal in power to that of any God:

> The Devil does not exist. It is a false name invented by the Black Brothers to imply a Unity in their ignorant muddle of dispersions. A devil who had unity would be a God.[17]

Crowley accused those who worshipped evil (the "Black Brothers") of having created the Devil, which is quite a difference from the evidence of historical and scriptural texts, of course, and may reflect more of Crowley's own personal philosophy than it does years of philological and theological study. However, as the world progressed from wars fought with rocks, to bows and arrows, swords and shotguns, it still seemed as if evil was the stuff of smaller demons: the spent cartridge, the torched hut, the thrown spear. Then, the Bomb was dropped on Hiroshima and Nagasaki in August 1945. It suddenly became possible to start thinking about a *force* of evil, something unitary and powerful beyond all previous imagining. It suddenly began to look like there *was* a Devil, and weapons of mass destruction became his calling card. To concern oneself with individual demons seemed almost quaint, missing the point.

Like the Christian (and Manichaen) concept of an eternal conflict between good and evil, Buddhism acknowledges the ongoing struggle against Mara but—again, like Christianity—also maintains that the Buddha was the first to overcome Mara, and therefore opened the road to Enlightenment for everyman. Jesus is said to have suffered and died "for our sins" and to redeem humanity; he descended into hell after his crucifixion and then ascended into heaven after his resurrection on earth, thus demonstrating his power over death. Thus, both Jesus and Buddha overcame death and became immortal; whether Jesus was born superhuman or became so during his trials in the desert and his other mortal struggles against evil and death is a purely theological issue. (Of course, one could always say that since the conquest of death by Jesus was foreordained, that he was certainly "born a God," in a kind of exegetical Monday-morning quarterbacking.) And, just as demons possess the innocent in the Christian (and Jewish) traditions explored by Oesterreich and others, so too does Mara possess innocent villagers, requiring the application of exorcisms.[18]

Although no case can be made that the Christian mythos is merely Buddhism in fancy dress, there are important similarities between Jesus' confrontation with Satan and the Buddha's confrontation with Mara. As Ling points out in his analysis of some of the literature on comparative religion which focuses on Satan and Mara,

> In each case the symbol came into being as the result of the experience and insight of a great personality. In each case it appears to have reflected the

> experience of critical encounter with *a spiritual force which was hostile to holiness.* (emphasis added)[19]

Of course, it is this very spiritual force that concerns us in this study.

What is fascinating about Mara is that he is the lord of the five senses, of physical reality, and *of consciousness as well.*[20] Mara is, in fact, the lord of the Matrix, for Mara's domain (*Maradheyya*) represents—in the Pali scripture known as the Sutta-Nipata—an "entanglement, strongly stretched out and very deceptive. Sometimes this is called Mara's stream."[21] The goal of Buddhism is to transcend not only physical reality (with all its limitations, passions, and other emotions) but consciousness as well, in order to attain Nirvana. This entails gradually reducing one's attachment to physical objects, then to physical sensations, entering a state of sensory deprivation in which even thoughts and ideas are "objects" to be avoided and one's individual consciousness disappears, subsumed into the collective "cosmic consciousness" that is Enlightenment. It is easy to see how attaining this state would be tantamount to conquering death, for death is an event that occurs to the physical body; in the perfect state of meditation envisaged by the Buddhists, the reliance on the body as a means of survival is abandoned. It is, perhaps, the ultimate "self-transcendence," just as Mara represents the ultimate in "self-assertion." Mara is, quite simply, the source of all problems, the pulsating core of evil.

Trevor Ling uses the analogy of a man fighting mosquitoes; one can take measures to fight against each individual mosquito, or one can take measures to defeat all mosquitoes. The same with a man being shot at: does he dodge each bullet individually, or does he take measures against the man with the gun?[22] In polytheist traditions with a multiplicity of demons, man has fought each one individually. With the coming of the Buddha, according to Ling, there was a revelation: namely, that the source of all demons was, in essence, one demon; the source of all ills was one Father of Sickness. It reoriented the focus of humanity from the day-to-day battle against hordes of individual demons/sicknesses/cruelties/horrors to the identification of a single, monist fountain of all suffering. In the Pali Canon, this is Mara.

Unfortunately, knowing this and doing something about it are two different things! We still have to dodge bullets, and mosquitoes, and evil people, one by one. It takes a certain type of individual—a Buddha, or a Buddha in the making—to focus his or her attention on the source of all evil and take careful aim. For the rest of us, there is Kevlar, and pesticides, and exorcism.

> The essence of the animistic attitude to life is that the ills which man experiences are attributed to wholly external forces. These forces, conceived as having an existence separate from his own, he regards as hostile. They must be avoided if possible … or they may be manipulated to advantage by one who possesses the means or the skill to do so. This last kind of response,

> the manipulation of hostile forces, is the one characteristic of animistic and other forms of magic. It was in this direction that animism shaded into Brahmanism in a way that is in striking contrast to the Buddhist attitude to what are called the 'low arts'. The object of the Brahmanic sacrifices was ostensibly to chain the demons; the real object was an extension of this attitude at a more profound level, namely the manipulation for men's advantage of what were believed to be certain hidden natural forces.[23]

We have already studied this "manipulation of hostile forces" as put into practice by everyone from Siberian shamans to remote viewers. It is a mainstay of Hinduism today, and the practices of Hinduism which verge on the paranormal are evidence that the knowledge of the manipulation of these forces has been cultivated and preserved through thousands of years, even as the monist traditions of Judaism, Christianity, Islam and Buddhism decry their use.

The last twenty years or so has shown a marked interest in, and popularity of, the subject of Evil. There have been cultural studies of Evil, from Howard Bloom's *The Lucifer Principle* and Paul Oppenheimer's *Evil and the Demonic*, to sociological and historical overviews such as Jeffrey Burton Russell's *The Devil: Perceptions of Evil from Antiquity to Primitive Christianity* and Ervin Straub's *The Roots of Evil: The Origins of Genocide and Other Group Violence.* Even Elaine Pagels has published *The Origins of Satan*, a study of how Satan came to be identified in early Christianity. In this age of holocaust and genocide, of Kosovo and Croatia and Cambodia, nuclear, chemical and biological weapons, the subject of Evil has become fashionable again and no historian of religion is able to ignore its appeal.

Howard Bloom, who trained as a scientist and then left science to run a public relations company for musicians such as Prince, Billy Joel, Billy Idol, Bob Marley and Bette Midler (among many others), is an example of someone who (like Koestler) has functioned in two separate worlds and has the benefit of a larger perspective. Bloom blames Evil on the necessities of evolution, and—like a first century Gnostic—places the onus directly on Nature itself. Anyone who watches the Discovery Channel is likely to be confronted with dramatic evidence of the cruelty of Nature, of course, whether it is a hurricane, earthquake, flood or simply one animal devouring another. Of course, Bloom's thesis is not so narrow as that. He borrows from Koestler even as Koestler is not identified in the text, by recapitulating Koestler's theory of the *holon,* except that the holon in this instance Bloom calls the "superorganism."

Koestler viewed everything in nature as inferior to the level above it in terms of complexity, and superior to the level below it. Essentially, what Arthur Young described in his "arc" that led down from light to nuclear particles, atoms and then molecules and from there up through plants, animals and finally man, Koestler was describing in terms of a hierarchy leading down from organisms at the top to sub-atomic particles at the bottom. Each level of Koestler's hierarchy is a subset of the level above it; conversely, each level of the hierarchy contains within it complex arrangements of the level (cells, molecules, atoms, etc.) below it. Koestler understood each "sub-assembly" of this hierarchy—whether the cells of the human heart, or the atoms that make up a molecule of water—as functioning as a "quasi-independent whole, even though isolated from the organism or transplanted into another organism."[24] To Koestler, each of these "sub-assemblies" was "Janus-faced," i.e., one face looked to the level above it and was a sub-assembly of that level, and one face looked at the level below it which contained its own sub-assemblies. This Janus-faced object Koestler calls a *holon* and emphasizes that the holon is more than the sum of its parts (in reference to its quasi-autonomous features, but also in consideration that a human being for example is more, obviously, than simply a collection of its component elements).

As noted, Bloom characterizes human beings as parts of what he calls a "superorganism,"[25] "disposable parts of a being much larger than ourselves." This is one of his "five ideas," which—he writes—"illuminates a mystery that has eternally eluded man: the root of the evil that haunts our lives. For within these five small ideas we will pursue, there lurks a force that rules us."[26] The other ideas include the principle of the self-organizing system (which is similar, again, to Koestler's concept of a "self-regulating open hierarchic order,"[27]) the meme (a "self-replicating order of ideas" which is the root of the images and visions that provide both coherence to society and which encourage it to go to war), the neural net or "group mind," and the "pecking order."

To Bloom, humanity's contribution to the violent way of life it has inherited from the apes, from Nature itself, is the "dream of peace. But to achieve that dream he will have to overcome what nature has built into him."[28] It is interesting that a writer with a scientific background as well as a political background (who wrote position papers for congressional candidates) and a business background in the media should arrive at the conclusion that evil is hard-wired in us by Nature itself, and that only by overcoming this programming can we achieve our "dream of peace." This is something that no church-going Roman Catholic would disagree with, as it is a modern explanation for what is known in the Church as "original sin": the dogma that every human being is born with the taint of sin which only a decent life of holiness can neutralize. In other words, every person born of woman is born defective in the eyes of the Church. Only becoming baptized into the Church and following its regulations will free one of this defect. (It is a great marketing gimmick, of course: *"What? I have original sin? Get it off me! Get it off me! What's it going to cost?"*)

As mentioned, this concept was well-known to the Gnostics, that disparate group of syncretist mystics who wielded tremendous influence in the first few centuries of the Christian era. By blending eastern and western, Jewish and Christian concepts into a single coherent whole, they cast a long shadow over everything from the Dead Sea Scrolls of Qumran to the Nag Hammadi texts of Egypt … to the Cathars and Manichaeans, and eventually to modern ceremonial magic, the rise of the secret societies, and the occult revival of the twentieth century. While there were many different versions of Gnostic belief, they agreed on some basic issues. First and foremost was the idea that matter was inherently evil, and had been created by the "demiurge," a being that opposes God and who fashioned the world from chaos, the abyss, one of whose terms is the Latin *matrix*. According to some Gnostic texts, the God in the Garden of Eden who created Adam and Eve and warned them against eating of the Tree of Knowledge was the Demiurge and *not* the benevolent Deity; God's presence in the Garden was actually that of the Serpent, who pointed the way of freedom to Eve.

The Gnostic texts—as well as traditional Biblical scripture—refer to the demonic rulers who assist the Demiurge as *archons*, a term that means "chief" or "ruler" or "prince." The archons are invariably evil, and represent forces that oppose God. In this, they are virtually identical to the Hindu *asuras*, a Sanskrit word with the same meaning as *archons*.

In Gnosticism, there are two main schools of thought concerning the true nature of evil. The "Eastern" view—which has its origins in Zoroastrianism and Manichaeanism, and thus demonstrates a possible link to Aryan Hinduism—states that good and evil are two supreme powers struggling for control of the world, and will continue to struggle forever. The "Western" view—which has its origins in Egypt and the Middle East—defines evil as a *result*, rather than something with an autonomous existence. This theory describes the creation of matter as a series of emanations of light, of spirit, leading from the divine Source and becoming grosser with each rung of descent until spirit is buried as a dim spark within matter. (This is virtually identical to the way Arthur Young explains creation.) Benjamin Walker, who writes on culture, history, and religion, has offered a concise introduction to this Gnostic belief:

> … evil is the natural consequence of the descent of the emanations, so that as the emanations recede from the primary divine source there is a progressive diminution in their goodness and light. Again, when God withdrew his presence to make room for the world, Satan was free to exercise his will in opposition to the divine, as a consequence of which evil arose.… Evil is not an abstraction or a passive condition, but a positive and violent force arising from the active operation of Satan and his archons.[29]

Of course, this is so similar to the Indian concept of Mara, the Lord of Evil, as the ruler of physical creation, the five senses, matter and even consciousness itself, that it could have been devised by a Pali scholar rather than a Syrian Gnostic.

From India to Egypt and Palestine, evil is perceived as a force under the direction of what can only be called politicians. "Lords," "chiefs," "rulers," "magistrates," or "princes," *archons* or *asuras*, the implication is the same: evil is somehow under political control. Further, matter is seen as evil, the result of an entrapment or degradation of *light*. Thus, we have two disciplines in which evil is being described: one, a scientific approach, shows evil to be the result of light "descending" and becoming matter, much like Arthur Young's famous diagram of the "arc"; the other, a political approach, shows that this matter—creation itself—is under political control by a Demiurge and his team of archons, or "rulers." God, in this context, was the Serpent in the Garden of Eden: a kind of rabble-rouser who urged Adam and Eve in their rebellion. "God," as Nik Aziz said in Malaysia, may truly be "a gangster."

Evil as matter, evil as a blind force. There is no contradiction necessary between the two, since the discoveries of quantum physics illustrate that the heart of all matter *is* force.

Ancient Egyptian religion was no exception to this rule of evil as blind force, and as an eternal opponent to the forces of light. Osiris and Set were brothers, Osiris representing Light and Set, Darkness. There are several versions of the story of the murder of Osiris by Set, but it is certain that Set did, indeed, kill his brother (the first murder in Egyptian religion is fratricide, as it is in Genesis) and dismembered his body. Again, we face dismemberment in a religious or spiritual context that is far removed from the dismemberment visions of the Siberian shamans, but which shares essential characteristics. In both the case of Osiris and the case of the shamans, dismemberment precedes illumination.

Isis, the wife (and sister) of Osiris collects the various pieces of Osiris' body after they had been scattered throughout Egypt and the Nile by Set. She puts the pieces together and becomes impregnated by the momentarily reanimated corpse. She gives birth to Horus, the Hawk-headed God, who then goes to battle with Set. Osiris, meanwhile, is reborn and takes his place among the constellations of the heavens, becoming the prototype for the resurrection of humans. The mummification ceremonies typical of ancient Egypt were designed around the premise that the deceased would become an "Osiris" and experience rebirth just as the original Osiris did.

The parallels with Christianity are interesting, of course. The betrayal of Osiris by his brother, Set, is analogous to the betrayal of Jesus by Judas. In some accounts, Set manages to convince Osiris to try out a sarcophagus which has been built specifically for his size. This occurs during a party at which the friends of Osiris and Set are in attendance. Osiris lays down in the coffin, and Set nails the cover shut, killing his brother. In the Christian account, Jesus is at a Passover seder with his disciples, and Judas leaves early to report his presence to the Roman authorities. In both cases, there is a gathering of friends and colleagues and the betrayal of a "brother."

And in both cases, the manner of death is not a simple one. In the case of Osiris, he is either shut up in a coffin to die a slow death of suffocation or, in the more generally accepted form, he is dismembered and the pieces of his body (fourteen in number) are scattered throughout Egypt. In the case of Jesus, he is first beaten and tortured, and then crucified, with nails driven into his wrists and ankles; but even crucifixion is not enough, for his side is pierced with a lance. In a Christian hymn, it is written, "They have pierced my hands and my feet; they have numbered all my bones," which is about as close to a description of dismemberment as one would wish, the total violation of the human body.

And, of course, both Osiris and Jesus are "reborn."

The number fourteen is of interest, as well. Osiris was chopped into fourteen pieces. In every Catholic church, one will see a commemoration of the suffering, crucifixion and burial of Jesus in a series of plaques—called the Stations of the Cross—which are invariably fourteen in number. (Oddly, to the Chinese, fourteen is an unlucky number (not thirteen), because the pronunciation of "fourteen" in Mandarin and other dialects is a homonym for "is dead": *shi si.*)

In the revisionist Christianity of the secret societies, the Priory of Sion, the books of Baigent, Lincoln and Leigh, Jesus does not die on the cross but is secreted out of Palestine and flees to France in company with Mary Magdalen, who bears him children … a bloodline that is said to exist to this day. (Naturally, the French believe that the heirs of Christ are French, a belief that explains a great deal!) Mary Magdalen could be seen as an analogue of Isis, of course, hiding with Jesus and becoming pregnant by him. In the *exoteric* Christianity with which we are familiar, however, the Virgin Mother of Jesus is iconographically identical with images of Isis. The same blue robes covered with stars. The images of the Virgin Mother holding the Baby Jesus are identical to statues and drawings of Isis holding the Baby Horus, son of Osiris.

Either this is the result of deliberate borrowing by Christianity of Egyptian religious concepts—which has not yet been proved beyond reasonable doubt—or another force is at work, like Jung's archetypes, manifesting in the unconscious minds of various races at various times across the globe. Gnosticism comes closest to weaving the various occult strands of Egyptian mysticism, Jewish mysticism, and Christian theology, as well as concepts from the Persian cult of Mithra and the Phrygian cult of Attis (both of which eventually became Roman cults) as well as other cults of west Asia, into a coherent whole representing the consistent features of each of these beliefs and practices, and finding common ground among them. Of course, in the process Gnosticism has overturned some traditional beliefs, as they sought the *esoteric* meanings behind the accepted scriptural texts. Thus, to the Gnostics, the Creator of the Old Testament is the Demiurge and not the benevolent God represented by Jesus. A close reading of the Old Testament would tend to support this view: Jehovah is forever destroying cities and smashing armies, laying waste to huge tracts of the Middle East, sometimes for the merest of slights. He certainly seems to act in the role of a fantastically powerful demon rather than a Prince of Peace of the "God is Love" variety.

The Gnostics were not the only ones pulling together a religion out of several disparate cultic elements; what we know today as modern Christianity owes much of its character to St. Paul, a convert to the new faith who decided that the religion would have broader appeal to the Gentiles if it incorporated some pagan elements. In this, he was like a modern takeover baron, buying a small, successful corporation and changing its identity to fit a larger market strategy, thus stripping the original company of its character and firing its most loyal employees to make the new shareholders happy, at least for the first fiscal quarter or two. St. Paul as the Gordon Gecko of Christianity? Perhaps.

What happened to the original Christian message has virtually disappeared under the heavy furniture of the Church; the cults who were the closest in mission and theology to the early Church were dissipated throughout the Middle East and as far as Afghanistan and, some say, Kashmir: small groups of Jewish mystics considered heretics by both Jews and the new, Pauline Christians. Another branch wound up in Africa, in Ethiopia, in possession of a Gospel of St. Thomas, unaware that the New Testament canon would be decided by the emissaries of Constantinople and that their Gospel had no place in it. It is not only modern American history that has to be revisited; as we have seen, the history of the Church is now under heavy attack from the revisionists, experts in Biblical exegesis and analysis, archaeology and philology, who are piecing together the events of the time of Jesus from the Dead Sea Scrolls, the Nag Hammadi texts, and new scholarship. Writers such as Elaine Pagels, Robert Eisenman, and Hugh Schonfield have made tremendous contributions to our understanding of this pivotal period in Western history; popularizers such as the team of Lincoln, Baigent and Leigh (*Holy Blood, Holy Grail*) have brought the results of this research to the mainstream media. Through all of this, the Church has remained silent, preferring to offer no answer than to trap itself in responses that it knows will be undermined by the next discovered parchment, the next jar of scrolls.

A new approach to Jesus and to God; and, with all of this, a new approach to the idea of divinity, and a new concept of the problem of evil.

Trevor Ling reminds us, in his book on the Buddhist mythology of evil, that there is consternation in our hearts when we confront the otherworldly. He refers to the work of Rudolf Otto who, in his influential *Idea of the Holy*, argued that our experience of the divine and the demonic may be confused, a feeling he called "daemonic dread":

> This daemonic dread, [Otto] claims, 'first begins to stir in the feeling of "something uncanny," "eerie" or "weird." It is this feeling which, emerg-

> ing in the mind of primeval man, forms the starting point for the entire religious development in history. "Daemons" and "gods" alike spring from this root ...[30]

In this, Otto agrees with Jungian psychoanalyst Adolf Guggenbuehl-Craig, who identifies the sinister with the divine:

> The sinister is always the unintelligible, the impressive, the numinous. Wherever something divine appears, we begin to experience fear.[31]

And:

> Everything that has to do with salvation possesses ... a sinister, unfamiliar character ... [32]

Even Elaine Pagels, Professor of Religion at Princeton University, was unable to avoid the implications of the experience of the paranormal for the idea of evil: "Evil, then, at its worst, seems to involve the supernatural ..."[33]

The emphasis in these writers is on the personal experience of evil as something of an otherworldly, paranormal or supernatural nature, evil "at its worst." Further, it is possible to confound the experience of the divine with the experience of the satanic, as both Otto and Guggenbuehl-Craig point out. These sinister forces are also numinous; the sinister may also be ... divine.

This is clear in the mystery religions, of course. Initiation into these cults always involves a preliminary period of tremendous fear and horror, the initiate blindfolded and bound, brought into the sacred precincts on the point of a sword, and made to swear terrible oaths which involve—in Freemasonry, for instance—threats of death and dismemberment should the initiate reveal anything that is to be shown to him. Our problem, as human beings, is that we are unable to differentiate between the divine and the demonic: our psychological reactions—fear the experience of the sinister, dread—are the same for both. Certainly, the stars of the Old Testament felt this way when coming face to face with Jehovah. God is not only stern and just in the Old Testament, he is positively homicidal. He demands absolute loyalty on the pain of death. He tells Abraham to kill his own son, and then changes his mind a little later on. He submits Job to unimaginable torment, just to win an argument with Satan. He comes up with circumcision as a means of identifying the Chosen People (a simple tattoo would have been nice, or an identification card). He destroys Sodom and Gomorrah, tears down the walls of Jericho, floods the earth to destroy every living thing except whatever Noah could fit on his ark. Speaking of arks, the Ark of the Covenant was so dangerous that merely to touch it was enough to cause death, so it was paraded before the enemies of Israel, who promptly fell down with hemorrhoids.(I Samuel, V) So, yes, our experience of the divine has been ... sinister. It has been frought with danger, with threat of destruction both physical and spiritual. And, at the same time, we have seemed to have been pawns in some larger game.

Why did Jehovah permit the enslavement of the Jews under the Pharaoh, for instance? Why the seven plagues of Egypt? Why didn't Jehovah simply appear to the Pharaoh—as he had with Moses—and *tell* him to let his people go? Since Jehovah was so capable of destroying entire cities on a whim, why did he allow the Egyptian cities to survive undamaged? Why the elaborate miracle of the parting of the Red Sea, and then luring the Pharaoh's troops into a trap, drowning them in the suddenly "unparted" waves? If we are to take these stories at face value—and many, many do—then Jehovah was a god to be feared, yes, a god capable of supernatural abilities, but not a god one could love. Jehovah appears in the Old Testament as a kind of military dictator with psychic powers. How, then, to tell the difference between god and demon? When Jehovah himself is capable of so much bloodshed, so much vast destruction, what then is evil?

SEX, DRUGS AND ROCK 'N' ROLL

The philosophers have struggled with the concept of evil only because the existence of evil in the world seems to laugh at any pious descriptions of the nature of God. All of the religious and metaphysical texts of the world rationalize the existence of evil: it is either God's means of testing us (a ridiculous assertion on the face of it, and especially when we confront the suffering of children and infants), or it is the result of humanity's abandonment of God's laws (also ridiculous, and for the same reasons), or it is the result of a war taking place between the forces of light and darkness (somewhat better, but substitute "light" and "darkness" for virtually any pair of opposites you like, and then degrade the image of God somewhat to that of a combatant of roughly equal powers as the Devil). What most religions agree upon, however, are the *effects* of that evil: murder, war, rape, sickness, human suffering in general, and particularly that of the innocent.

Evil only describes the suffering of human beings, the beings uniquely—it is believed—conscious of their own mortality, aware of the linear passage of time, capable of falling in love ... in short, those things that depend upon a certain perspective about reality that is unique to us. Religion attempts to transcend those basic assumptions, especially the Asian religions in which even the passage of time is dismissed as a kind of illusion (something with which our quantum scientists would agree). If we are able to disown fears about mortality, ignore time as the dance of Maya, and renounce the love of one person and translate that into love for all of humanity, and then abandon even *that* love, then we are able to destroy Evil. Evil comes from attachment, say the Buddhist scriptures. Dissolve all attachments, and absolute freedom is the logical conclusion.

I fear nothing; I hope for nothing.
—Blaise Pascal, *Pensees*

What is compelling about the shamanistic approach to spiritual freedom is that the very practices which the Buddhists believe tie one down to attachments on the material plane are the same practices the shamans use to attain supernatural powers. Yes. Sex, drugs and ... well, drumming. Tools that had been used by occultists, artists and shamans for millenia gradually became part of the culture, and in so doing were robbed of their transcendent influence. Just as the scientists would have us worship technology in place of religion, we find ourselves using the technology of religion as entertainment. Yet, even then, there is some "redeeming social value."

Susan Sontag brought to our attention earlier the link between creativity and madness, especially with reference to the case of French playwright Antonin Artaud. In another essay, this one on pornography, she brings to our attention the similarities between pornography on the one hand, and science fiction on the other.[34] By doing so, she makes some very compelling points about spiritual transcendence and the appropriateness of marketing this transcendence to the masses.

> Pornography is one of the branches of literature—science fiction is another—aiming at disorientation, at psychic dislocation.[35]

This idea of disorientation and psychic dislocation is familiar to us by now from our study of Rimbaud, as well as from our treatment of shamanism and occultism, as well as our foray into the mind-control projects of the American (and Soviet) governments. Sontag takes these ideas further in her idea that pornography fits the criteria of psychic dislocation as easily as do the various religious technologies themselves. Many people will be offended by what seems to be a defense of pornography, when what Sontag is doing is explaining its power rather than moralizing about its role in society. Both pornography and science fiction depend heavily on fantastic elements which bring the reader out of the normal, everyday world and into a sacred space of tabu. In the case of science fiction, the tabus are largely scientific: one bends the rules of Newtonian physics using words instead of mathematical formulae. One is expected to suspend disbelief, to permit one's mind to wander outside the limits of consensus reality. Pornography operates on similar principles. It removes the experience of sexuality from social norms, social limits, and places it in another sacred space of tabu: one in which every conceivable type of sexual coupling and sexual act is not only permitted but encouraged. Both forms of literature excite the imagination and encourage a kind of mental daring. Both are heavily oriented towards manipulation of the *image.* And, in this, they share a great deal with religion and the technologies of the religious experience.

> In some respects, the use of sexual obsessions as a subject for literature resembles the use of a literary subject whose validity far fewer people would contest: religious obsessions. So compared, the familiar act of pornography's definite, aggressive impact upon its readers looks somewhat different. Its celebrated intention of sexually stimulating readers is really a species of proselytizing. Pornography that is serious literature aims to "excite" in the same way that books which render an extreme form of religious experience aim to "convert."[36]

This comparison of the influence of pornographic literature to the conversion phenomenon studied by Sargant, Lifton and others may clarify somewhat the idea behind the sinister forces of this work's title, for sex has always been a major focus of the world's religions, and control of the sexual impulse—either through celibacy or strict regulations concerning matrimony, homosexuality, pedophilia, bestiality, etc.—is a hallmark of virtually every religion in the world. Even the curse of the serial killer is linked inextricably to sexual impulses (after all, the serial killer was first known as a "lust killer"), and avant-garde philosophers such as Wilhelm Reich could postulate that sexual function and dysfunction were behind everything from mental illness and physical illness to totalitarianism and even the UFO phenomenon.

The virtual impossibility of regulating the sexual impulse, however, has given rise to the tremendous degree of inconsistency and hypocrisy in our world, and this is not only a matter of Western decadence but a problem in virtually every corner of the globe. We have the spectacle of Catholic priests being brought to trial for sexually abusing children. We have women in Africa, as well as in Pakistan and some other Muslim nations, being subjected to corporal punishment—including, incredibly, rape—for being the victims of rape. We have entire villages in Southeast Asia dedicated to supplying the "sex tourist," offering children of both sexes for the pleasure of middle-aged European and American travelers. All of this makes the secret practices of Hindu Tantrism seem tame and decorous by comparison, and elevates even so venal a character as Aleister Crowley to the status of a true Victorian gentleman.

Predictably, everything from rape to serial murder to pedophilia is blamed on access to pornography. In other words, and according to this theory (which is very popular among the Christian Right), the minds of otherwise innocent men and women are being manipulated by images (in pornography and in mainstream television and cinema programs with violence and/or sex as the subject matter) to commit atrocious acts against individuals and society. In the

East, modern Western movies and music videos are routinely blamed for the decadence of Asian youth. While this argument seems puerile to anyone with an ounce of common sense (from "the Devil made me do it" to "Madonna made me do it"), it does reveal an unconscious understanding of the function and power of the image, something that is *not* discussed openly in any of these societies, since elites in every society wish to manipulate images in their own way and not have their agenda (and methodology) revealed to the public at large. To open up this discussion to general public dialogue on the power of the image and how it is used by political parties, religions, intelligence agencies, and advertising companies would be to invoke doubt as to the relevance or justification of using *any* images. It would most certainly instigate a serious conflict over the role of censorship, and probably place authority for media and image manipulation right back in the hands of governments.

Pornography occupies a special place in this discussion, since it is a form of manipulation that is almost universally proscribed in all places yet still enjoys a strong and resilient popularity despite its official status as an illegal, or at the very least immoral, medium. It is difficult to understand the undeniable power of pornography if it is regarded simply as another form of literary or artistic expression. Although it does address one of the most basic of human appetites, one has the feeling that cookbooks—which, after all, address the most basic human appetite—do not enjoy quite the same cachet. There is another dimension to pornography that transcends that of all other literary and artistic forms. Even today, the number of Web sites devoted to pornography outstrips by far every other genre of site. Pornographic sites on the Internet actually finance the Internet and are a source of tremendous wealth for their owners. The ease of downloading pornographic images, stories, and even entire movies, has made the Internet the method of accessing pornography favored over retail outlets in the strip malls and on the back roads of America. Pornographic Web sites have even been used by Islamic terrorist organizations as a means of communicating, by encoding information in graphics files.

Sontag's remarks on pornography vis-à-vis the expression of religious sentiments, and in comparison to science fiction, are worth recalling today. The essay was written in 1967 in response to an erotic novella by Bataille, and it contains virtually an entire precis of Hermetic thought as it pertains to the initiatory process. It is an extraordinary document, and one that perhaps could only have been written in the Sixties. So much of what was written—indeed, discovered—in the Sixties has since been devalued in a kind of scientific backlash, yet will one day form the core of another discipline, something akin to art and yet more like magic; or perhaps it will be magic, the Western Tantra that Francis King thinks magic really is.

Sontag's writings of this period can be taken together with those of R.D. Laing, Michel Foucault, Wilhelm Reich, Antonin Artaud, even Noam Chomsky and other legends of the time. Laing's breathtaking and ground-breaking works on psychology and psychiatry—especially concerning schizophrenia—have been devalued by a mechanical approach to mental illness which insists that the origins are organic and that schizophrenia can be treated with drugs. Thus, it is assumed, Laing's work has no merit and can be safely ignored. By stripping meaning from the experience of mental illness, science has merely shoveled the dirt under the carpet. Would Artaud have been happier if he were sane? Van Gogh? Strindberg? Nietzsche? Is their art the result of mental illness, or was mental illness merely a means to an end, a necessary approach to that level of truth? With the right drugs, the schizophrenic is now a functioning human being, more or less acceptable in society, and science is happy with the result. What if this approach had been taken towards the schizophrenia of the Siberian shaman? Obviously, the response of science would be to rejoice in the "cure" of the shaman, because who needs shamans, anyway? And isn't that the point, after all?

The war of science on superstition is a front for another war, the war on meaning. Science manifestly does not provide meaning for scientific events, and in fact is unequivocal about the lack of meaning in scientific phenomena (as opposed to the last five thousand years of recorded history in which every event is accorded some degree of meaning). Meaning is the enemy; there is only the fact of science, the raw data. At the heart of science's war on superstition is the war on religion, and on mysticism and the possibility of spiritual enlightenment. To an extent, one can sympathize with science's point of view that religion has brought nothing but trouble to humanity (as if science has brought nothing but goodness). One can point to the Inquisition, to the Crusades. One can also point to the glories of the Renaissance, of the Gothic cathedrals, of religious music and art. Both religion and science have given, and have taken away.

Sontag is right to link the literature of sex with the literature of religion and, even, to science fiction. That is a perceptive and illuminating conclusion. In the East, the literature of sex is quite often the literature of religion, as in the Hindu Tantras for instance. And both sex and religion have as their goal in these literatures the quest for fabulous powers, mystical cities, and alternate realities ... i.e., have something in common with the literature of science fiction.

And the linkage of madness with art, with religion, with pornography is a valid one, as we have been at pains to demonstrate in these pages. The sexual powers are demonic, and they live at the juncture—perhaps, the tangent—of the real and the ideal, of this world and another. Demonic forces can be summoned by the sexual act; demonic forces perhaps do the summoning themselves at times (the incubus and sucubus of medieval legend). In India, the forces are more divine than demonic, but to a Western observer gazing on the frightening image of Kali, an important Tantric goddess, the distinction may seem moot. These forces are making themselves known in alien abduction experiences and in satantic cult survivor experiences. The perverse, the obscene … these are the elements of pornography that point to a transcendental state of mind, one that is not accessible to everyone and, in fact, shouldn't be.

The experiences of Whitley Strieber and other self-confessed "abductees" almost invariably contain a sexual element. It would seem that the alien forces that abduct our citizens are inordinately concerned with human reproduction, and remove ovae and sperm from healthy individuals for further study or experimentation (according to the published accounts). The witches' sabbats as reported in the medieval press reveal the same sort of link between paranormal contact and sexuality. The Hindu Tantras are themselves a technology for achieving this type of contact through the manipulation of sexual imagery and energy. The Renaissance magician Giordano Bruno set out the parameters for this technology in his own work, principally in *De Vinculis*, the text analyzed so thoroughly by Ioan Culianu. The implications are obvious: the manipulation of the image, and especially of the sexual image or image of sexual potency or reference, need not be the sole domain of the intelligence agency or the secret society; it can become the practice of the individual, the mystic, the artist, the magician.

On a biological level, we may characterize this as the conscious control of unconscious forces: as the deliberate control of the autonomic nervous system, such as is revealed in the alchemical documents of, for instance, Thomas Vaughan. This control of previously automatic nervous system functions has as its corollary the conscious reorganization of the firing of the synapses in the human brain in an attempt to exert some influence over the quantum level of consciousness. As such, this technology is extremely dangerous. As poet and philosopher Kenneth Rexroth pointed out in his introduction to the work of Thomas Vaughan, it was this very technology—in an unsupervised environment—that killed the Welsh alchemist and his wife.

Sexuality may seem like a jarring note in a political history, except that the case of Bill Clinton has brought the connection between sex and politics to international prominence, even as there has been no real attempt to understand what significance the combination of political leaders and sexual activity has for the electorate. There have been other politicians whose careers were marred by sexual exploits, of course, such as Wilbur Mills, the Democratic chairman of the House Ways and Means Committee back in the 1970s (a Thirty-Third Degree Mason, incidentally), who got in trouble with an Argentine stripper; former Indiana Senator Gary Hart, whose presidential campaign imploded with the revelation of *Monkey Business*; or even President Jack Kennedy, tarred in revisionist histories with a succession of mistresses that included everyone from Mary Pinchot Meyer and Judith Exner to Marilyn Monroe. The fact that Republican campaign strategists routinely search for sexual gossip regarding their Democrat opponents is ignored by most commentators; no one looks any deeper into the sexual obsessions of career Republican politicians, perhaps fearful of what might be found there.

Fascism is another area in which sexuality plays an important role, and it was this close relationship between sex, mysticism and politics that caught the attention of Susan Sontag, whose insights into the functions of creativity, madness, pornography and fantasy have helped us thus far already. Her essay "Fascinating Fascism" clearly shows how the culture of Nazism rang hidden bells deep within the Western psyche, and continues to do so today. That Nazism is a cult similarly obsessed with sex is no revelation; it begins with a faulty theory of genetics (eugenics) which attempts to justify a "purity of blood" program in which, for example, only Germans who could demonstrate an unbroken line of Aryan ancestry going back to the year 1750 were permitted to join the SS. Sexual relations with Jews were believed to cause a pollution of the bloodstream, even if no children were conceived as a result. The mere fact that one had slept with a Jew was enough to convince the Nazis that one's spirit was now impure.

At the same time, the Nazis set up the infamous Lebensborn project in which SS officers (and thus of proven purity of blood) were encouraged to mate with as many pure Aryan women as possible in order to increase the number of Aryans on the planet. These children were brought up in Nazi orphanages, "baptized" according to Nazi ritual, and indoctrinated with the Nazi beliefs on the superiority of their race and the divine nature of the Fuehrer. Homosexuality was believed to be an illness of which one could become cured; alternatively, it was viewed as a crime against nature, and homosexuals were sent to the concentration camps along with the Jews, the Communists, and anyone else believed to be "deviant" politically, racially, or sexually. When it came to sex, the Nazis were as relentless in their own way as the Vatican. The newsletters and broadsides published in Germany in the early years of this century, showing blonde Aryan women being violated by crazed, hairy, Semitic monsters was a clear expression of German sexual insecurity, a major motivating force behind the creation and success of the Nazi Party.

The German occult organizations that existed until their suppression by the Nazis in the 1930s were openly concerned with sexuality and the mystical or magical attributes of sexual relations. As described in more detail in *Unholy Alliance*, organizations such as the Ordo Templi Orientis, the Brotherhood of Saturn, and so many others believed that there was a sexual secret at the heart of occult literature, concealed behind symbols and archaic references to the Rose and the Cross, the Dew, the Red Tincture, etc. Biological functions from menstruation to ejaculation were examined carefully and compared to steps in the alchemical process. When Aleister Crowley was initiated into the Ordo Templi Orientis, he rewrote many of their basic rituals to reflect more brazenly the sexual component of the "mysteries." The "sacrament" of the Gnostic Mass, for instance, was (and possibly still is) composed of both semen and menstrual fluid, mixed with flour and fashioned into "cakes of light" ... certainly a dangerous substance to consume in these days of AIDS and other sexually-transmitted diseases. The rubric of the Gnostic Mass which requires the Priestess to stroke the Lance of the Priest in a prescribed fashion comes as close as one would wish to a *Grand Guignol* approach to organized occultism, something which the late Italian director Federico Fellini would have appreciated.

It is not for nothing that Sontag calls sexuality one of the "demonic forces" in human consciousness:

> Human sexuality is ... a highly questionable phenomenon, and belongs, at least potentially, among the extreme rather than the ordinary experiences of humanity. Tamed as it may be, sexuality remains one of the demonic forces in human consciousness—pushing us at intervals close to taboo and dangerous desires, which range from the impulse to commit sudden arbitrary violence upon another person to the voluptuous yearning for the extinction of one's consciousness, for death itself.[37]

This demonic force *can* be tamed, however, and made subject to conscious control. It is probably this ancient idea that informs modern Church requirements of celibacy for its priests, while at the same time it forgets to train its clergy in the transcendental nature of celibacy as a means for controlling the sexual impulse and, by extension, deeper, autonomic nervous system responses. The ecstatic sexual union so prized and so sought after by romance novelists and pornographers alike is only a preview, a kind of demonstration, of the potential of the human nervous system. Like the visions that come from ingesting a hallucinogenic drug, the transcendental moment that can be obtained from a powerful orgasm in the normal course of events is only advertising. The main event takes place at the point one is able to control these visions (or these orgasms) consciously, for it is then that the "heightened state" of Sir Roger Penrose's quantum consciousness can be initiated, manipulated, and made to serve a higher purpose, but only in those who have been prepared—through a system of initiatic instruction—for this experience, for this power:

> What's really at stake? A concern about the uses of knowledge itself. There's a sense in which all knowledge is dangerous, the reason being that not everyone is in the same condition as knowers or potential knowers. Perhaps most people don't need "a wider scale of experience." It may be that, without subtle and extensive psychic preparation, any widening of experience and consciousness is destructive for most people.[38]

To have initiated this process in oneself without proper preparation or guidance is dangerous, and possibly suicidal. To initiate it in others without their conscious understanding of the dangers involved, or even—as in the case of

Ewen Cameron and other scientists and doctors under the intelligence agency programs—in unwitting and involuntary subjects, is not only unethical, it is homicidal. The case of Frank Olson is just one case among many hundreds, if not thousands, that took place in the United States alone. It was as if a cult began initiating members without their knowledge, and without their psychological preparation: members who would not have been accepted as novices under normal circumstances and who were then subject to extreme spiritual and psychological pressures all at once. Some would have survived; most would have become victims, Children in the Land of Memory who can never find their way home.

In case this assertion seems unduly hyperbolic, one only has to refer to the work of one of the early LSD researchers from the days of Timothy Leary and Richard Alpert and the Esalen Institute: the Czech defector Dr. Stanislav Grof.

The Soviets seem to make a habit of exploring coincidences.
—Ostrander & Schroeder, *Psychic Discoveries Behind the Iron Curtain* [39]

Grof is perhaps best known as one of the founders (along with psychologist Abraham Maslow) of the field of Transpersonal Psychology, a system of psychology that maintains that individual consciousness is part of a larger, "cosmic" or "transpersonal" consciousness, and that we share many psychological features in common with everyone else. This is a form of Jungian psychology, which itself asserts the existence of an "ancient racial memory" that is common to all peoples, and which is populated—as we have seen—by the archetypes. But Grof did not arrive at these conclusions through a normal academic path.

A native of what was then known as Czechoslovakia, Dr. Grof had begun his career as a Freudian analyst in the 1950s, earning an M.D. from the Charles University School of Medicine and then his Ph.D. from the Czechoslovakian Academy of Sciences. (This after Grof, a hardcore Walt Disney fan, first seriously considered a career in animated movies!) Before obtaining his degrees, he worked as a medical student at the School of Medicine, Department of Psychiatry, during the 1950s. Without going into too much detail concerning his duties under what was a Communist—if eventually a somewhat dangerously liberal Communist—regime, he states in many places that the Sandoz Pharmaceutical firm had sent his institute a quantity of LSD-25 for testing and evaluation in 1954. He participated in that testing regimen. From 1960-1967, he worked as the Principal Investigator of the psychedelic research program at the Psychiatric Research Institute of Prague. All in all, he studied the effect of hallucinogens—principally LSD—on thousands of hospital patients for ten years in Czechoslovakia before finding himself in the United States at the time of the Soviet invasion and the end of the Prague Spring of 1968.

Czechoslovakia at that time was a hotbed of paranormal research and scientific studies at the cutting edge of consciousness technology, as the Ostrander and Schroeder book—published in 1970—so amply documents. Dr. Karl Pribram—whose holographic theory of the universe is one of the most important meta-physical systems to be unveiled in the last 30 years—also hails from Prague, the capitol of Czechoslovakia; David Bohm, the physicist who has had such an impact on the "quantum consciousness" field, is of Czech ancestry and was a good friend of Pribram. ESP research in Czechoslovakia was highlighted in *Psychic Discoveries Behind the Iron Curtain*, and the application of astrological methods to the field of conception and fertility also has its roots in Communist Czechoslovakia.

While it is generally known that the Soviets abused psychiatry for their own ends, and hospitalized many a political prisoner, using electroconvulsive therapy (ECT or electro-shock) on healthy individuals as a means of torture and interrogation, and applied various other types of "alternative therapies" as well, such as the use of narcotics and hallucinogens, it is not known to what extent these methods were used in what was, after all, a Soviet satellite state. In the 1950s, at the very height of the Cold War, the pressure on the staff at the various psychiatric clinics to make every use of new technologies must have been enormous—either as genuine therapies, as experimental programs on unwitting or unwilling subjects, or as out-and-out torture, interrogation and "brainwashing" techniques. As LSD was introduced into the Iron Curtain countries in 1954, and Grof eagerly accepted any opportunity to test it (on himself, and later on others) the CIA was experimenting with LSD in the United States—on both unwitting *and* voluntary subjects, and not with the slightest interest in using LSD as a "therapy" of any kind. Grof became the lead or principle investigator in the use of LSD in Czechoslovakia, and tested or reviewed the testing of thousands of subjects there before he accepted a position at Johns Hopkins University as a Clinical and Research Fellow in 1967.

Prior to this, however, we find Grof among interesting company. In the period May 8–10, 1965 we find him listed as one of the registered participants at the Second International Conference on the Use of LSD in Psychotherapy. Among his fellow participants we find Harold Abramson, Humphrey Osmond, Walter Pahnke, and others familiar to us from Operation BLUEBIRD and MK-ULTRA documentation. At this time, Grof was still living in Czechoslovakia, but it would not be long before he found himself in the enviable position of holding an important position at Johns Hopkins in the United States … one that would leapfrog him to the Maryland Psychiatric Research Center in Catonsville, Maryland—where he became the Chief of Psychiatric Research, remaining there until 1973 in charge of the "last surviving government-sponsored psychedelic research project in the United States."[40] Czechoslovakia was invaded by the Russians in 1968, to put down what was seen as a trend towards liberalization, as the Czech satellite began to wobble off course. Fortunately, Grof was in the United States and decided to stay. In other words, defected; a defection made easier by the public acknowledgement of his contribution to the field of psychedelic research in the form of his fellowship at Johns Hopkins; a contribution that was obviously noticed by those in the CIA responsible for LSD testing and other mind-control technologies.

I am not trying to make any kind of judgment on Grof's motives, or to impugn his history as a therapist, either in Czechoslovakia or in the United States. There is no evidence that he worked for the CIA, either wittingly or unwittingly, either voluntarily or through some kind of coercion. It is just a question of being in the right place at the right time. Absent a *Russian* specialist in LSD research, though, a Czech specialist would have been a godsend to the Agency. Grof would have had up-to-the-minute knowledge of the state of the art of LSD applications in psychotherapy and thus could have given the Agency a window onto the Soviet capabilities in that regard. This would have been of great importance and interest to Sidney Gottlieb and the other MK-ULTRA staffers, since it was largely due to the perceived threat of a Soviet mind-control program that the American version was begun. In addition, the CIA would have been crazy to ignore the fruits of Grof's data on thousands of LSD treatments in Czech hospitals. However, that he is a respected and honored psychiatrist with a string of accomplishments to his credit is not to be denied. That he abandoned the proforma atheism of his Communist youth is obvious from the work he has done since then, and from his wholehearted embrace of spirituality as a necessary factor in human growth and development. It is to this work that we now turn for reasons that will become obvious.

Grof's interest in the psychedelic experience can be gleaned from his many writings, in books, articles and interviews over the years. His focus has been on the death and rebirth experience of those who have taken LSD, and his remarks on the use of the drug by unprepared individuals are worth study. He also realizes that insights obtained during the "non-ordinary states of consciousness," or "NOSC," as he calls them, bear striking similarities to the theories of quantum physics on the one hand (he mentions David Bohm, Karl Pribram, Rupert Sheldrake and Gregory Bateson in this context[41]) and the many anthropological reports of shamanistic experiences on the other. Grof realized that there was a connecting thread between the state of consciousness obtained by taking hallucinogens and that spoken of as quantum consciousness, much as Penrose and Hameroff themselves were implying in their Defense Department lecture. He also understood the relationship that exists between these states and the occult trances of the shaman and the mystic. What is astonishing to someone who is coming to all of this material "fresh" is that no one took this argument to its logical conclusion. We shall do so shortly.

After leaving his position at the Maryland Psychiatric Research Center, Gof took up a post at the Esalen Institute—stomping ground of Jack Sarfatti, Saul-Paul Sirag, Alan Watts, John Lilly, Timothy Leary, and so many others who figure in our story, including a side-trip by Charles Manson—where he stayed for many years.

The Esalen Institute was founded in 1962 by Richard Price and Michael Murphy, and takes its name from a Native American tribe who once lived in the region. It was the first of the "human potential movement" centers, and attracted a diverse group of spiritual leaders, psychotherapists, physicists, philosophers, martial-arts experts, painters, writers, filmmakers, etc. For many Americans, the Esalen Institute would probably typify everything they hate about California, but the influence of Esalen on the fields of medicine, psychotherapy, and international relations cannot be denied. Their establishment of a group designed to reduce conflict through peaceful resolution brought them to the attention of American political and intelligence careerists, as well as the Soviets. (It was the Esalen Institute that brought Boris Yeltsin to the United States for the first time, to visit President George H.W. Bush as well as former President Ronald Reagan.)

The same year that Esalen was founded, Abraham Maslow (who developed the concept of the "peak experience") appeared on the scene and—according to the Esalen Web site—"came to play an important role in its development, leading several workshops and guiding the founders. Esalen workshop leaders eventually played a pivotal role in the growing discipline of humanistic psychology." These would include, of course, Stanislav Grof who—with Maslow—would found Transpersonal Psychology.

Before Grof arrived at Esalen, however, Esalen members would play a pivotal role in the founding of Arica, the mystical school established in Chile by Oscar Ichazo. (One of the Esalen members who traveled to Chile to work with Ichazo included John Lilly, he of the dolphin studies.) Ichazo, the son of a Bolivian military officer, joined a mysterious occult group in Buenos Aires in the 1950s when he was a young man. Based largely on this experience, he wound up in Chile training people in his system of mysticism and psychotherapy formed around the Enneagram, a nine-pointed symbol that is familiar to students of Gurdjieff. In the arid, northern Chilean city of Arica he attracted the attention of a Chilean psychiatrist, Claudio Naranjo, who then spoke about him and his technique to the Esalen crowd back in California. A group of about fifty Esalen participants flew to Arica in 1970 to undergo a rigorous training program under Ichazo, including one Jan Brewer. Brewer would tell Jack Sarfatti that Arica had "been started in Chile by high-ranking fugitives from the Third Reich who were masters of the occult."[42]

This may seem an outlandish claim at first, except that it was made by one of the first Esalen trainees to study in Arica, and my own direct experience in Chile with occultists who had Third Reich connections tends to make me less incredulous than I otherwise would be.[43] Ichazo's background as the son of a Bolivian army officer—at a time when Bolivia was riddled with Nazi fugitives, one of whom (Klaus Barbie) would become head of Bolivian Intelligence—is also suggestive of a deeper military and fascist connection to the Arica movement in Chile.

One has to put oneself back in the context of the time: Chile had been a supporter of Nazism during the war, and was in the midst of political upheaval at the time Esalen visited Chile in the period 1970-71. Salvador Allende had become the first democratically-elected Socialist president in Latin America, and efforts were underway by President Nixon and Henry Kissinger to have him ousted militarily, a program that culminated in his assassination and the military coup of September 11, 1973 that put General Augusto Pinochet in power. Chile's own self-proclaimed Nazi occultist, Miguel Serrano (a former Chilean ambassador and intimate of Hermann Hesse and Carl Jung), was applauding the overthrow even as Nobel Prize-winning poet Pablo Neruda was dying, surrounded by Chilean troops who did not permit him to get the medicine he needed to save his life. Whithin this suppurating political morass we find forty of America's best and brightest sitting at the feet of a Bolivian mystic, characterized by Claudio Naranjo as a kind of control freak who was not to be trusted.

Nevertheless, Esalen embraced the Arica work and helped to establish Ichazo as a New Age guru in North America. This is something that Sarfatti finds disturbing, going so far as to wonder if Michael Murphy—one of the co-founders of Arica and the most visible spokesman for the Institute—was a kind of "Puppet Master," or possibly an innocent dupe of the intelligence community, citing the involvement of one George Koopman who was an employee of the Defense Intelligence Agency with the Institute and with Sarfatti himself, as well as of Harold Chipman, a former CIA officer with heavy involvement in Asia for the Agency and then in California overseeing the remote viewing research of Puthoff and Targ at SRI on the Agency's behalf. This was the Institute in 1973 when Stanislav Grof joined the faculty, fresh from his stint researching LSD on the government payroll.

I do not want to appear as someone who sees a fascist or a satanist hiding in every corner. My intention is somewhat more specific. The political consciousness of those who have been leaders of some of the manifestations we know as the human potential movement has been somewhat shallow, or non-existent. Their writings, speeches and interviews reveal no interest or understanding of political responsibility; indeed, their view of life as "bliss," and that the world would be a happier place if everyone practiced a more spiritual approach to life, ignores the immediate problems of hunger, disease, and genocide. In many ways, the quest for personal fulfillment that is the hallmark of the human potential movement is possible only in a safe, healthy and relatively affluent environment, such as obtains in the United States and in other Western countries.

This is a dilemma that has concerned me for much of my life: the desire to pursue a spiritual path and lifestyle against the responsibility to act in a socially accountable way to aid those oppressed by political regimes, epidemics, famine, war. There are those who say that the individual pursuit of one's spiritual goals can go a long way towards helping rid the world of evil, but to those on the front lines it seems a vain and self-serving fantasy, especially in light of the terrible suffering visited upon the innocent by religious fanatics the world over.

It is probably this basic dichotomy between these two approaches to life that leads to the attraction between fascism and occultism on the one hand, and atheism and communism on the other, each missing an essential element only to be found in its opposite; for it is the fascist who despises humanity in general and the common good, and the communist who despises spirituality and the higher good. Both are interested in the technologies of consciousness, however, if only as weapons to be used in their continuing struggle ... with each other. Yet, none of those involved with the human potential movement of the 1960s and 1970s—amid the assassinations, the Vietnam War, the military coup in Chile, Watergate, etc.—seemed to understand the political ramifications of what they were studying and doing, and how this "technology" could be used, and was being used, for political and military purposes both overt and covert by forces on both sides of the great Cold War political divide.

Grof in his writings about this time (1973, when he joined Esalen) is extremely prescient about the psychological and spiritual value of the LSD experience. Like Koestler, he is a European Communist who has defected to the decadent West and discovered the Soul in the process. What is more important, he bases his conclusions on more than 4,000 LSD experiments, a huge database that surrenders some interesting data.

In 1973, he published an article entitled "LSD and the Cosmic Game: Outline of Psychedelic Cosmology and Ontology" in the *Journal for the Study of Consciousness*. In this article, he states that he had "personally conducted over 3000 psychedelic sessions" since 1954, when the first shipment of LSD arrived in Prague from Sandoz Pharmaceutical. He also had "access to records from over 1800 sessions run by several of my colleagues in Europe and in the United States." More importantly, he goes on to state,

> The majority of subjects in these sessions were patients with a wide variety of emotional disorders, such as severe psychoneuroses, psychosomatic diseases, borderline psychoses and various forms of schizophrenia, sexual deviations, alcoholism and narcotic drug addiction.

This is in parallel with the US government's own practice in the 1950s of testing LSD on prisoners—usually violent offenders and sexual psychopaths—and patients in mental institutions. Dosages ranged from 10 to 250 micrograms of LSD (in Prague) and from 300 to 500 micrograms at the Maryland Psychiatric Research Center; in the latter case, Grof was using the LSD in an atmosphere conducive to "healthy" spiritual and psychological states, the "set and setting" approach. In Prague, however, the approach was rather more clinical. His report is based on both the Prague and the Maryland research.

He talks about the current (1973) state of LSD use in the United States, when it was largely a phenomenon of the young, anti-war crowd so perfectly exemplified by Leary and others:

> Many hundreds of thousands of persons in the United States alone have been involved in unsupervised experimentation with psychedelic substances … many of them are repeatedly confronted with the experiences and insights described in this paper. Experiential sequences of this kind can have an enduring effect on the world-view of the psychedelic drug users, their life philosophy, and basic system of values.

This is an interesting and ambiguous statement. He begins by speaking about unsupervised experimentation (which he clearly dislikes) and then ends by linking that to an "enduring effect" on the world-view, philosophy and values of the users. One wonders if the effect is to be understood as positive, or negative? One also wonders if the LSD experimentation undertaken by the military and the CIA falls under the category of "supervised" or "unsupervised," since the military and intelligence applications would not have been designed to elevate the mind or spirit of the subject, but to break down his or her psyche and make it more malleable to the controllers.

Grof continues by linking the insights obtained by LSD users to the sacred scriptures of the Hindus, the Vedas, which—as we have seen—had some very interesting things to say about the nature of Evil, God and the Devil. He then goes further to associate LSD insights with the new, post-Newtonian physics of Einstein, Heisenberg, Schroedinger and Niels Bohr, eventually culminating in a brief overview of the work of David Bohm and Karl Pribram, the "holonomic" model of the universe.

Since his article addresses cosmology and ontology, he finds himself considering the problem of Evil. He speaks of his LSD subjects having visions of gods and demons from every culture, even cultures with which they were not familiar (and thus reinforcing Grof's idea that there does exist a kind of "ancient racial memory" or "collective unconscious" à la Jung, common to all humans regardless of their ethnic origins). Subjects would see ancient Egyptian gods as well as Christ, Buddha, etc. In addition, visions of "Satan, Lucifer, Kali, Lilith, Moloch, Hekate, Pluto, and Coatlicue" were not uncommon.

According to Grof, his subjects revealed a sense that Creation had taken place as a kind of outpouring of consciousness from the unitary Universal

Mind, which "initiates a creative play that involves complicated sequences of divisions, fragmentations, and differentiations" that eventually leads to "an infinite number of derived entities that are endowed with specific separate forms of consciousness and selective self-awareness." These "derived entities" or "filial conscious entities" then gradually lose contact with the Universal Mind, building screens that divide them from each other and from the Universal Mind. That is, they gradually "forget" their origins, and their interconnectedness with each other.

This is nothing less than Gnosticism, of course. The descent of spirit into matter is discussed from a psychedelic, twentieth century perspective but it is the descent of spirit into matter nonetheless. It is also reminiscent of Arthur Young's "arc" and Arthur Koestler's Janus-faced holon system. (Later in the same article, Grof actually refers to the "derived entities" as Janus-faced, but with no reference to Koestler, as Koestler had not yet published *Janus.*) Under the influence of LSD, the subjects experience this "screening" process and gradually break down these barriers and eventually enter into the Presence of the Universal Mind. This, again, is Gnosticism and shares a great deal in common with the shamanistic experiences described by Eliade and others. Grof links them to Jain philosophy, as well as to "the monadology of G.W. Leibnitz, and to the holonomic theory of David Bohm and Karl Pribram." He goes further, linking them to Sri Aurobindo and "the system of Kashmir Shaivism," and again illustrating the Asian focus of many consciousness pioneers of the 1950s, '60s and '70s. (A popular and amiable authority on Zen Buddhism, Alan Watts, gave the very first Esalen seminar.[44])

Thus, it should probably come as no surprise that the conclusions of Grof when it comes to the nature of Evil are typically Asian, and specifically Hindu or Vedic. As Alan Watts says in his autobiography, "Somehow the atmosphere of Hindu mythology and imagery slid into [LSD experiences], suggesting at the same time that Hindu philosophy was a local form of a sort of undercover wisdom, inconceivably ancient, which everyone knows in the back of his mind but will not admit" (Watts, p. 344).

LSD subjects, Grof reports, describe Evil as "an indispensable instrument in the cosmic process."

> The recognition that evil is the price that has to be paid for the creation of the existing experiential realities and that it is not only a useful, but necessary ploy in the universal drama tends to bring forgiving and reconciliation.
>
> According to the insights of LSD subjects, the Universal Mind has to negate itself and create its polar counterpart in order to enter the process of creation.

This could have been extracted from the work of a Wendy Doniger or a Trevor Ling, or one of the first or second century Gnostic writers. To Grof, working from his LSD database, this negative principle of creation "permeates in increasingly concrete forms all the levels of the process of creation" including being responsible for the splits and "screening" that prevent the individual "derived entities" from contact with each other, and with the Universal Mind.

> Since the divine play, the cosmic drama, is unimaginable without separate entities, without distinct protagonists, evil is thus absolutely essential for the creation of the universe ... the experience of unification and consciousness expansion is typically preceded in the LSD process by an encounter with the forces of darkness, confrontation with evil appearances, or passing through demonic screens; this is typically associated with extreme physical and emotional suffering.

Again, we are on familiar ground. The hideous visions and experiences of the shaman—externalized in the case of the serial killer—are once again before us. LSD provides an opportunity to undergo this experience, but in a socially acceptable "set and setting," under the comfortable supervision of a therapist who may or may not have undergone the complete spiritual transformation personally. There are those who might complain—reasonably enough—that the drug-induced spiritual experience is to the real spiritual experience as the travelogue is to the place visited. Alan Watts mentions that many people who have had a positive experience with LSD then abandon the drug and go on to more spiritual work.[45] The implication is that the LSD experience (or any experience with a hallucinogen, such as psychedelic mushrooms or peyote) is initiatory: it starts one on a spiritual path, like the drugs taken at the Rites of Eleusis, but is not the path itself. That is why it is dangerous to take the drug under any circumstances other than under the careful tutelage of an experienced user and in a setting of spiritual (psychological) protection. That is why the BLUEBIRD and MK-ULTRA experiments were so wrong, not only from a moral or ethical standpoint, but from a deeper, more profound point of view.

Grof reiterates that evil "is inextricably woven into the cosmic fabric and indispensable for the existence of experiential worlds" and thus that "it cannot be defeated and eradicated in the world of phenomena." The parallels with Gnostic thought and ancient Hindu theology could not be more emphatic. The world, then, is under the control of the Demiurge, or Lord Mara, or Satan. The phenomenal world *is* evil, and since it cannot be defeated there is only ... escape.

> Thus the polarity between good and evil is usually transcended simultaneously with the sense of alienation and individual separateness, with the distinction between inactivity and action, and with the illusion of the objective reality of the phenomenal world.

While all of this may be perfectly valid, and is certainly in line with some of the more advanced spiritual disciplines throughout the world and throughout the ages, it can also be understood as a way of avoiding political commitment and social involvement. We can comfort ourselves with the consideration that the phenomenal world is an illusion of which Evil is a necessary component; but when a little girl dies from a sniper's bullet, or an old lady collapses from hunger on a city street, or one million Cambodians are slaughtered in the killing fields, or six million Jews are turned into smoke and ash in the concentration camps, then these theological, cosmological, and ontological speculations are of very little use.

But does that mean that we must abandon the technology of the spirit, the "machineries of joy" as I have called them, after Bradbury, in order to do "good works"? When spiritual growth virtually requires isolation from the world at large, how to look out for our fellow human beings? How to contribute in a meaningful way to the world and its relentless struggle with the very real, if also very illusory, forces of evil? Perhaps the example of the shaman—a person who has undergone all the enormous psychological pressures and spiritual stresses of which Grof, Eliade, and so many others write—is the example to follow, for the shaman returns to his village and becomes a healer, a seer, a therapist, and a spiritual force to be reckoned with. The shaman is not a luxury in his village; he is not reading tea leaves or bending spoons or checking your aura. The shaman is a necessity, a requirement for the life of the village. For all of his or her strangeness and other-worldliness, the shaman is a committed member of the community and performs valuable (and life-saving) services. The shaman can also, however, attack villagers, attack other shamans, and kill from a distance. The interest of governments in these latter powers at the expense of the former is what has damned them, and led to the present state of affairs in which the Pandora's box of consciousness—what is commonly known as the "black box"—has been recklessly opened, and the demons and evil spirits of the Other Side let loose upon the world.

And the opening of that box was quite easy, once the right tools had been obtained and a general understanding of the problem was at hand. As Grof explains later in the same article:

> There exists a wide spectrum of mind-altering techniques that can facilitate the occurrence of such unusual states. ... They involve the use of psychedelic substances or a combination of various extreme situations, such as prolonged stay in the desert, exposure to unusual temperatures, sleep deprivation, fasting, social isolation, sensory overload, physical pain, difficult body postures, and respiratory maneuvers combining hyperventilation and withholding of breath.
>
> Similar changes of consciousness can also be produced by various laboratory and clinical techniques. We can mention in this context sensory

> deprivation and overload, electric stimulation of the brain, kinaesthetic devices, variations of hypnotic induction …

Paging Dr. Cameron. Will Dr. Mengele please pick up the white courtesy phone?

I don't want to make light of the above, and I don't want to over-react. In fact, what Grof is saying is quite correct: non-ordinary states of consciousness can be reached by any and all of these methods, and many more besides. This is obvious from the vast literature on the subject, from the lives of the Christian saints, from the examples of Hindu ascetics and Siberian shamans. What is missing is the context under which these technologies should be used. The non-denominational methods advanced by Grof and others in the field may not be sufficient; cultural loading may actually be a requirement in this case, rather than an obstacle. Yet, Grof is understandably reluctant to call in the priests.

Further along in this seminal essay on LSD and the "cosmic game," Grof complains that most existing religious systems are replete with "inconsistencies and paradoxes," and says,

> Many of them are unable to reconcile such fundamental contradictions as the assumption of a benevolent, omnipotent and omniscient creator and the existence of evil and suffering in the world; omnipotence of God and the concept of sin, as well as man's responsibility for his actions; or the supreme justice of God and the inequities existing among people.

He then notes that many religions are in conflict with each other, each cult claiming a "monopoly on God and infallibility of their creed; they hate, reject and persecute the members of the competing religions." Then he goes on to explain this gross inconsistency by falling back on the game scenario of the Universal Mind:

> According to the metaphysical system described above, the inconsistencies and paradoxes existing within the individual religious frameworks, as well as the conflicts between them, have been deliberately created by the Universal Mind and built into the scheme of things as important elements in the cosmic game.

In other words, we are back to the Gnostic Demiurge, a God who created the phenomenal world as a place of evil, a matrix of matter in which to entrap spirit.

The only religions exempt from this problem are those that are "characterized by their universality and all-encompassing understanding, compassion and tolerance. They have a definite pantheistic emphasis and believe in ultimate unity of all creation." The spiritual path, according to Grof, is one in which the individual gradually rises from self-awareness, to awareness of the connections that connect him or her to everything else in creation, and then eventually back to the Universal Mind itself. This is a basic blueprint for the initiatory systems of most of the world's secret societies. The identification of a matrix underlying all of creation and the interconnectedness (as detailed in the doctrine of signatures, or correspondences, of the medieval magicians and alchemists) of all "things," all phenomena, used as a machine to elevate consciousness to higher levels, is familiar to all students of hermeticism and of the hierarchical structure of occult lodges or orders, from the Freemasons to the Rosicrucians and the Golden Dawn, the OTO, etc. These disciplines provided a framework, an intellectual context, within which the non-ordinary states of consciousness described by Grof could be integrated into the psyches of the initiates, while at the same time surrounding the initiate with a social support apparatus so that the intense preliminary stages of psychological disintegration would not be summarily dismissed as psychosis or mental disease.

Like Eliade and R.D. Laing, Grof understands that the mental states accompanying the various stages of "illumination" are construed as mental illness, "particularly schizophrenia," by mainstream science. He claims that the work of his colleague, Abraham Maslow, has begun to change all of that, with Maslow's discovery of the "peak experience" and its identification as a "supernormal" state rather than a pathological one. Grof was probably being optimistic in this regard, since mainstream psychiatry and psychotherapy at this time are still resistant to the idea of these states as anything other than mental disorders. With new drugs to combat some forms of schizophrenia, Laing's insistence that "mental breakdown may also be mental breakthrough" has been devalued, even though one could argue that suppressing a mental state through chemical means is not the same as curing it, and does not mean that the existential nature of the schizophrenic state has been somehow explained away by describing it as a chemical imbalance. One could reasonably wonder if the state preceded the imbalance, or the imbalance the state; and then ask if the cause-and-effect relationship between chemical "imbalance" and mental state was a valid perspective in the era of quantum consciousness.

At least Grof realizes that not all "peak experiences" may be blissful, and once again touches the edge of our argument by stating,

> However, the peak experiences can also occur under circumstances which are unfavorable and critical for the individual; in this case, the ego consciousness is shattered and destroyed rather than dissolved and transcended.
>
> This is true for situations of severe acute or chronic physical and emotional stress, as well as circumstances in which body integrity or survival are severely threatened. Many people have experienced fundamental spiritual opening at the time of accidents, injuries, dangerous diseases or operations.

And, we may add, during torture, interrogation, "brainwashing," "psychic driving" and "depatterning." Remember that Grof is coming from a background in which he performed LSD research—since 1954—on the behalf of first the Czech government and then the US government at the same time that these governments were experimenting with LSD for military and intelligence applications. The above remarks by Grof would have been quite interesting to the project leaders of these agencies, as they point the way towards alternate methods of interrogation and "brainwashing," using techniques already in their arsenal but applying them towards different goals. Although the agendas of the intelligence agencies would have been unique to them, the resultant effects on the psyches of their subjects would have been to open them up to spiritual forces for which they were not prepared (neither the subject nor the controller), and for psychological (and spiritual) blowback that could not be predicted.

Grof then makes reference to the works of Arthur Young (of the original Nine) as representative of the "convergence between mysticism, modern consciousness research, and quantum-relativistic physics," before proceeding to a discussion of the holonomic model of the universe proposed by David Bohm and Karl Pribram. He mentions in passing that "Karl Pribram formulated then a neurophysiological theory that connects the holonomic concept of the Universe to brain anatomy and physiology." From there, he goes on once more to associate these ideas with the Hindu Vedas.

That Arthur Young should appear in this article is not surprising, but what may be more astonishing is the fact—related by Jack Sarfatti—that The Nine actually lectured at Esalen! Twenty years after the first appearance of The Nine to the circle around Andrija Puharich, they again manifested in the person of one Jenny O'Connor. Ms. O'Connor was "channeling" The Nine and came to the attention of Werner Erhard, the neo-fascist creator of a school of self-development known as "est," for "Erhard Seminar Training," and always printed in lower-case letters. (Erhard had famously changed his name from Jack Rosenberg to "give up Jewish weakness for German strength.") Sarfatti himself had been a visitor to Arthur Young in the company of Puharich and Ira Einhorn, and had worked sporadically with Arthur Young's Institute in Berkeley, California. Oddly enough, he seems not to have been aware of Young's involvement with The Nine in its earliest incarnation. In the late 1970s, Jenny O'Connor was referred to Sarfatti by one of the est people, and Sarfatti was not impressed. Nonetheless, O'Connor became ensconced at Esalen, channeling messages from The Nine and having influence over some management decisions and organizational structuring at the Institute, at the same time that Esalen was being visited by Soviet officials as well as by Einhorn, various physicists, Stanislav Grof (who was "Scholar-in-Residence" from 1973 to 1987), and many, many others.

Grof does not ignore the psychic abilities and coincidences that sometimes attend the spiritual awakening. In a 1996 interview with Russell E. DiCarlo, he states,

> ... karmic experiences are often associated with meaningful synchronicities. For example, a person has a difficult relationship with another person and

> has a past life experience that shows the two of them engaged in some sort of violent conflict. One of them is the victim and the other the aggressor. If this person completes reliving that incident and reaches a sense of forgiveness, his or her attitude towards the other protagonist changes in the positive direction.... What is quite extraordinary is that at exactly the same time a significant change in the same direction often occurs in the other person.... This can happen even if there was not a conventional communication or connection of any kind between these two persons.[46]

In other words, a "non-local" relationship develops of which quantum physics has given us the exemplar. Grof believes that reincarnation is a "pragmatic concept, reflecting an effort to understand the complexity of these experiences that spontaneously emerge in non-ordinary states."

In his work *Books of the Dead: Manuals for Living and Dying*,[47] Grof provides us with illustrations of some of the visions seen by his LSD patients, those who had taken high doses of the drug and experienced death and rebirth scenarios. On page 29, for instance, we see a drawing of a "Moloch-like deity with a furnace-belly and tearing claws" which "immediately preceded psychological rebirth and the opening into light." One wonders what would have happened had the individual been given the same dose of the drug but under conditions less than ideal: a government laboratory, for instance, or a CIA safe house? Would they have been classed as psychotic, and would they have been programmed—inadvertently to be sure—to regard the experience as a negative one, thus blocking their psychological or spiritual growth? And would anyone have cared? Would this person's rather ambiguous mental and emotional state have affected his or her performance in the outside world, as a teacher, or scientist, or criminal, or spy, or soldier?

Or would the weight of what they had experienced—and the lack of a competent social structure to explain it and support it—have led that person to leap from a hotel room window on a cold night in the City of New York?

Probably this chronic mutual suspicion of our neighbor's capacities ... will never be settled to everyone's satisfaction.... It doesn't seem inaccurate to say most people in this society who aren't actively mad are, at best, reformed or potential lunatics. But is anyone supposed to act on this knowledge, even genuinely live with it? If so many are teetering on the verge of murder, de-humanization, sexual deformity and despair ... all forms of serious art and knowledge—in other words, all forms of truth—are suspect and dangerous.

—Susan Sontag[48]

This last refuge—the statement that evil is the work of a madman—is occasionally applied to God, as well as to demons; thus Siva is often said to be a madman.

—Wendy Doniger O'Flaherty[49]

Endnotes

[1] Tan Teik Beng, *Beliefs and Practices Among Malaysian Chinese Buddhists*, Buddhist Missionary Society, Kuala Lumpur, 1988, p. 67

[2] Jim Hougan, *Spooks*, William Morrow and Company, NY, 1978, p. 9-10

[3] Fr. Gabriele Amorth, *An Exorcist Tells His Story*, Ignatius Press, San Francisco, 1999, p. 150

[4] Liddell and Scott's *Greek-English Lexicon*, Oxford University Press, 1896

[5] Jim Schnabel, *Remote Viewers*, Dell, NY, 1997, p. 197

[6] Theodore Adorno, *The Stars Down to Earth*, Routledge, London, 1994

[7] Wendy Doniger O'Flaherty, *The Origins of Evil in Hindu Mythology*, Motilal Banarsidass, Delhi, 1976, p. 9

[8] Ibid., p. 55

[9] Ibid., p. 58

[10] Ibid., p. 75

[11] Ibid., p. 63-64

[12] Ibid., p. 66

[13] Wash Edward Hale, *Asura in Early Vedic Religion*, Motilal Banarsidass, Delhi, 1986

[14] Trevor O. Ling, *Buddhism and the Mythology of Evil: A Study in Theravada Buddhism*, Oneworld Publications, Oxford, 1997, (originally published 1962), p. 23

[15] Ibid., p. 47

[16] Ibid., p. 58

[17] Aleister Crowley, *Magick In Theory and Practice*, Dover, NY, p. 193

[18] Ling, op. cit., p. 75

[19] Ibid., p. 87

[20] Ibid., p. 58

[21] Ibid., p. 59

[22] Ibid., p. 66-67

[23] Ibid., p. 26-27

[24] Arthur Koestler, *Janus*, Vintage, NY, 1979, p. 292

[25] Howard Bloom, *The Lucifer Principle: A Scientific Expedition Into the Forces of History*, Atlantic Monthly Press, NY, 1997, p. 10

[26] Ibid., p. 11

[27] Koestler, op. cit., p. 289

[28] Bloom, op. cit., p. 29

[29] Benjamin Walker, *Gnosticism: Its History and Influence*, The Aquarian Press, Wellingborough, 1983, p. 46-47

[30] Ling, op. cit., p. 87

[31] Cited in Daniel Hecht, *Skull Session*, Signet, NY 1998, epigraph

[32] Ibid.

[33] Elaine Pagels, *The Origin of Satan*, Penguin Books, London, 1997, p. xviii

[34] Susan Sontag, "The Pornographic Imagination" in Bataille's *Story of the Eye*, Penguin, London, 2001, originally published in 1967

[35] Ibid., p. 94

[36] Ibid., p. 94-95
[37] Ibid., p. 103
[38] Ibid., p. 116-117
[39] Sheila Ostrander & Lynn Schroeder, *Psychic Discoveries Behind The Iron Curtain*, Bantam, NY, 1971, p. 139
[40] "The Multi-Dimensional Psyche," interview with Stanislav Grof by Russell E. DiCarlo, Health World Online, http://www.healthy.net
[41] Stanislav Grof, *Books of the Dead: Manuals for Living and Dying*,Thames & Hudson, London, 1994, p. 27
[42] Jack Sarfatti, "Illuminati, In The Thick Of It!," http://www.qedcorp.com/pcr/pcr/si03.html
[43] Peter Levenda, *Unholy Alliance*, Continuum, NY, 2003
[44] Alan Watts, *In My Own Way*, Pantheon, NY, 1972, p. 298
[45] Ibid., p. 347
[46] Russell E. DiCarlo, *Towards A New World View: Conversations At The Leading Edge*, Epic, 1996
[47] Grof, op, cit., p.
[48] Sontag, op. cit., p. 117-118
[49] Doniger O'Flaherty, op. cit., p. 65

STAY
VIETNAM
WIN
VIET NAM
NO!
KENNEDY
The New York Times
KENNEDY IS DEAD, VICTIM OF ASSASSIN;
SUSPECT, ARAB IMMIGRANT, ARRAIGNED;
JOHNSON APPOINTS PANEL ON VIOLENC
LIFE
The Love
and Terror Cult
CALIF PRISON
B 21014
B S SIRHAN
5 23 69
54018

Chapter Twenty-Three

The Manson Secret

Chinese alchemists are said to have told their pupils that not even a fly on the wall should be allowed to witness an operation. 'Woe unto the world,' they said, 'if the military ever learn the Great Secret.'

—Walter Lang, in his Introduction to Fulcanelli's *Le Mystere des Cathedrales*[1]

If the Pentagon ever formulates the Manson Secret, the world's in trouble.

—Ed Sanders, *The Family*, first edition

If the Kremlin, or the Pentagon ever formulates the robopathic secret of M, the world's in trouble.

—Ed Sanders, *The Family*, 1989 edition

An article in the *Village Voice* thirty years ago set me on a quest to learn once and for all the arcana that lurk behind American politics. It was an attempt whose ambition was exceeded only by my general ignorance. I did not belong to any political party. I did not study political science, or have a degree in American history. I was, however, an American born and raised. My father had been politically active, and the FBI had taken notice of him, however slight it might be. I had been politically active in New York City to an extent during the Sixties. And during all that time I was surrounded by the converging elements of radical, alternative politics and radical, alternative religions. They seemed to belong together, as if resistance to one form of authority demanded resistance to all others: religion, art, music, literature, psychotherapies, sex. In 1967, anti-Vietnam War protesters—led by Crowley-follower Kenneth Anger—had linked arms at the Pentagon and tried to levitate it, chanting prayers of exorcism. Exorcism! And the Pentagon, after all, is a five-sided figure that would have been familiar to medieval sorcerers as an emblem of Mars, and of protection against sinister forces.

I suspected that the secrets I sought involved some equivalent convergence of religion and politics; after all, religion has influenced politics and politics, religion for thousands of years. In many cultures, political leaders are also religious leaders, such as the Dalai Lama of Tibet, the Emperor of Japan, the Pharaohs of Egypt, etc. Did we, as Americans, leave all of that behind? The "divine right of kings," the sanctity of the royal blood, and "whom does the Grail serve?" Did we break so thoroughly and so completely with our European inheritance? Is the American miracle a result of "independent inventionism" or the more logical and aesthetically appealing "diffusionism"? Is America the result of European culture taken to its logical conclusion? Or is it truly an alien force in the world, a magnet for the dispossessed, the greedy, the criminal, the apostate, the heretic, the eros-driven immigrants of four centuries?

More generally, what is the role of coincidence in history, particularly in American history? Is coincidence an actual force in and of itself, or evidence of the action of another force, something working outside linear, Newtonian, Cartesian consensus reality? Is there a scientific basis for this force? If there is, then how do we explain its role in our own history? How can we ignore it, when so many commentators on history and science have spoken of its insidious power, from District Attorney Jim Garrison to nuclear physicist Wolfgang Pauli? Indeed, coincidence piled on coincidence during my own research for this work, defeating logical explanation. How else to explain the appearance of books I specifically needed—little-known works on particular events in US history—turning up with eerie regularity in second-hand book stalls on side streets in Kuala Lumpur? Even a privately-published monograph by remote viewer Ingo Swann? And a series of academic works on Salem witchcraft, etc.?

The *Voice* article linked such disparate elements as the Charles Manson murders, Richard Nixon and Watergate, E. Howard Hunt and occultism, Howard Hughes, and even Disneyland. It may have been intended as whimsical, but the links—as I would later learn from the work of Professor Culianu—are themselves evidence of one of the strongest forces in history. For the sin of revealing these forces, Giordano Bruno was put to the stake during the Inquisition. For the sin of revealing these same forces, Professor Culianu was murdered in 1991.

Where should I start?

I began Book I with the assumption that the phenomenon of Charles Manson and his "family" was a case study in the manipulation of these forces, whether consciously or unconsciously or, what is more likely, *intuitively*: a combination of both. Village Voice reporter Craig Karpel saw a link there, and his association of Manson with Richard Nixon was enough to start a whole train of thought going in a bizarre direction. Like most people in the mid-1970s, I knew a little about the idea of the "Manchurian Candidate," and the suspicion that our government had been involved in projects of that nature. It would be a few years before the story was generally known, due to the revelations that came out of the Watergate and associated hearings, but the theme was an ever-present one in the media, from the British television series *The Prisoner* to Anthony Burgess' *A Clockwork Orange* to the culturally-distorted mind-control scene in *Casino Royale*, starring "War of the Worlds" broadcaster Orson Welles as a crypto-Aleister Crowley.

There was an assumption on the part of many Americans that Nixon and Manson represented an evil force in their country, Robin Williams' famous "Manson-Nixon Line." Many readers will be appalled at the association, however glib, of one of their Presidents with a murderer like Charles Manson, but it is nevertheless true that many Americans did feel this way, and that from their point of view Nixon's body-count was much higher than Manson's. Although I was one of those Americans who disliked Nixon and who opposed our involvement in the Vietnam conflict, I did not suspect—at the time I began this work—that Nixon's perfidy extended beyond the Watergate break-in to include collusion with the Dulles brothers to protect Nazi war criminals and the attempt to keep the Vietnam War going on long enough to ensure his election in 1968.

But it was Manson himself that beckoned from the American heartland. We are accustomed to a certain belief that our politicians say and do unpleasant things in order to win elections or stay in power; although Nixon's crimes are a matter of public record and will be distilled many times by historians in the decades and centuries to come in the context of twentieth century American politics, Manson's crimes represent something far darker and more mysterious than simple greed or cupidity. Manson became an icon of evil in its pure form, an icon rivaling Nixon's own. Manson was not a politician, not supported by wealthy businessmen and neo-fascist bankers. He was "poor white trash," the type of man we associate with trailer parks, reformatories, and biker gangs. He carved a swastika into his forehead. He compared himself, favorably, with Jesus. He spent most of his life in prison, and most of the rest of his life trying to get back inside. He ordered murders to be committed. He had sex with minors. He stockpiled weapons and stole cars. He may be thought of as the opposite end of the spectrum from Nixon, but it is a spectrum of evil nonetheless.

If I wanted to understand political witchcraft, I would have to begin with Manson, and if I began with Manson I would have to begin with the town where Manson was raised. That led me to the Indian mounds of Ashland, and from the mounds I began to wonder if these ancient Adena structures in the very center of Manson's home town worked a weird kind of sorcery over its citizens. To understand that, I would have to understand Indian mounds in general and from there try to put the entire concept of sacred structures into some kind of context. This led me, inexorably, to early American history and prehistory, and I found myself reading Hawthorne and Lovecraft, New England's native sons and spiritual heirs of the Salem witchcraft tradition.

Slowly, an entire secret history of America was making itself known, through obscure academic journals, narratives both fictional and non-fictional, epigraphic remains, archaeological digs, and fragmentary documentation of all sorts. It was a detective story, and at the heart of this story is a mystery deep and profound: the hungry ghost that haunts the American landscape.

Manson would lead me to the Scientologists and occultists who supervised his psychological and spiritual training while in prison; to more Indian mounds, this time at Chillicothe where he underwent his spectacular "conversion" experience in 1954 and "stopped thinking"; to his alleged murder of Marina Habe in Los Angeles; and from there to her father, Hans Habe, the Nazis and Operation Paperclip.

Operation Paperclip would lead to Nazi General Walter Dornberger and Bell Aerospace, and from there to Michael and Ruth Paine and the Kennedy assassination; it would also lead to Nazi General Hubertus Strughold and Randolph Air Base, Nazi medical experimentation, and Whitley Strieber and alien abductions.

The Kennedy assassination would lead me to David Ferrie and the American Orthodox Catholic Church, to Fred Crisman and Guy Bannister and the UFOs over Washington State, and before I knew it to Andrija Puharich, Arthur Young, "The Nine," and the New Age movement, even including Jim Jones and the massacre in Guyana.

Manson would also lead me to Hollywood, for it was here in Southern California that he worked his black magic, convincing *even the Beach Boys* of his *bona fides* as a spiritual leader, and becoming de facto guardian of DiDi Lansbury, the daughter of the woman who portrayed the control agent of the Manchurian Candidate in the film. It was in the Tate/Polanski home that Jane Fonda—who portrayed Night in the film version of *The Blue Bird*, filmed in Moscow where the original stage play had its Stanislavski-directed premiere—had a party for her husband director Roger Vadim only hours before the Manson killings were to begin. Manson Family victim Sharon Tate, of course, had been one of the last persons to dine with Robert F. Kennedy the night of *his* assassination, at a small gathering hosted by *Manchurian Candidate* director John Frankenheimer.

Through all of this, the rhythm of coincidence and synchronicity beat softly but persistently. It seemed as if everyone were aware of the pattern of coincidence underlying historical events, despite the fact that no one looked any deeper at the phenomenon; so this prompted me to investigate coincidence from a scientific perspective which meant, of course, quantum physics and the newly-emerging concept of quantum consciousness. With this, we were investigating not only American history but the very nature and composition of reality itself.

The physical territory of the Americas in terms of ancient prehistory gave us the "deep background" that we needed to place this Secret in some kind of physical context: the Adena and Hopewell cultures that predated what we know of the Native American civilizations. In Book I, we looked at the "Indian burial mounds" and marveled at their astronomical alignments, in some cases the equal of anything to be found in Egypt among the pyramids: a science that was not maintained by their putative descendants, the Native American Indian tribes. We examined some of the evidence supporting a Diffusionist theory of the population of the Americas by races from Europe, Africa and Asia, and looked at epigraphical evidence for a Phoenician and Celtic migration to the Americas before the arrival of Columbus: pagans from the East setting up altars in the West.

We also looked at the voyages of Columbus and realized that the motivation for these journeys was religious and political: to find a way to raise money for a new Crusade against the Muslim rulers in Jerusalem, and to find a way to attack the Muslim nations from the eastern side rather than from the Mediterranean. In so doing, we came across the story of the Arawak Indians encountered by Columbus, a member of whose race would eventually wind up in Salem, Massachusetts, accused of igniting the witchcraft hysteria of 1692.

From there, we saw how Joseph Smith, Jr.—the founder of the Mormon religion, and descendant of one of the Salem accusers—began his career as a ceremonial magician in the woods of upstate New York, an American Dr. Dee or Faustus conjuring spirits at a burial mound in an attempt to find gold and buried treasure. We watched as he became a Freemason, and was soon thereafter murdered by an angry mob, even as he was clutching an imperfectly-made talisman for protection.

The first people who lived in the Americas; the discovery of America by Columbus; the Salem (and many other) witchcraft trials (with notes on the practice of occultism, alchemy, astrology and magic by both political leaders in high positions as well as impoverished Joseph Smith, founder of Mormonism) ... all of these important episodes of American history—many familiar to schoolchildren—had at their root religious and occult motivations and agendas that are not discussed in the classroom. Cotton Mather himself viewed America as a land possessed by the Devil, even as it was destined to become a New Jerusalem.

That was our "deep background," a preparation for what was to come.

For it was an investigation of Charles Manson that led us to Ashland, Kentucky and the burial mounds that are the heart of the town, and to a horrible crime on Christmas Eve in which three children were killed and their house burned down, after two of the children—young girls—were raped in the sight of a handicapped boy who could do nothing to defend them, or himself. The alleged perpetrators of this crime were caught, amid much controversy, and caused the Ashland Massacre, in which troops and civilians fired on each other in an effort to retain custody of the three killers. So much death and violence for such a small town, in an area that gave us Manson, Bobby Joe Long, and other murderers, as well as the deadly Hatfield and McCoy feud. And, in the midst of all of this, the mounds quietly at rest, dead but dreaming.

Manson's childhood in Ashland progresses to his incarceration at Chillicothe, Ohio, at the site of another, more elaborate, complex of burial mounds. His lieutenant in the Manson Family, Squeaky Fromme, will do time at another prison situated at another set of burial mounds, this time in West Virginia, and now for the attempted assassination of President of the United States.

The mounds seem to be a silent element in this story, and it is odd how many prisons are built on or near a set of burial mounds. Do we unconsciously associate violent offenders with something ancient, pagan, and shamanistic? Indeed, these mounds are not all "burial" mounds, but *were* constructed according to the same astronomical principles as the monuments at Stonehenge and the Pyramids at Gizeh: alignments to the sun and the moon and the stars, an attempt to measure time and to channel mysterious forces. Certainly, these were the actions of uneducated, illiterate humans from the dawn of prehistory. It is all superstition, nothing more.

Odd, then, that Wright-Patterson Air Force Base is also built on the site of Indian burial mounds. It was to Wright-Patterson that the first Paperclip scientists were taken, in July of 1947 at the time of the purported Roswell crash of a flying saucer, and at the same time that debris from the crash was purportedly taken there. Odd, then, that the Atomic Energy Commission built a nuclear facility less than half a mile away from the "Seal mounds," a few miles south of the Chillicothe complex. The Seal mounds are virtually unique among the Hopewell mounds in that they are oriented (precisely) towards the four cardinal directions and the vernal and autumnal equinoxes, rather than towards the winter and summer solstices which is the more common mound orientation. More stuff to fuel a television mini-series, or an episode of *The X-Files.* But nothing there. No smoking gun. Just fantasy and science fiction, paranoia and superstition.

After all: Charles Manson, UFOs, burial mounds, serial killers, Nazi scientists, Indian shamans, astronomical alignments, nuclear energy … this is not the stuff of mainstream history, of academic scholarship. It's the raw material of adolescent daydreams and the slick, pre-packaged pablum that has replaced organized religion in the United States at a time of great moral, political and cultural upheaval. It's H.P. Lovecraft on steroids, nothing more.

But then we took apart these elements, piece by piece, to see what was ticking (like a bomb, if not a clock) behind them. We discovered that the FBI did indeed investigate UFOs in the late 1940s, and did indeed file these reports under the rubric "X"; but what we did not expect to find was that one of the principle players in this episode was a man who would later figure prominently in Jim Garrison's Kennedy assassination investigation: Fred Crisman, a man said to have worked for the OSS during World War II and later for the CIA, a man whose role was to create confusion and disinformation. We did not expect to find that one of the FBI agents responsible for investigating the series of UFO sightings in the Pacific Northwest in 1947—the "X" files—was Guy Banister, another player in the Kennedy assassination conspiracy who would wind up in New Orleans as an associate of Lee Harvey Oswald, running anti-Castro operations from his walk-up office on Camp Street, an address stamped on Oswald's "Fair Play For Cuba" flyers. Confusion and disinformation.

We looked at the claim of alien abductee Whitley Strieber who said that, as a child in the 1950s, he had been taken to a "secret school" with other small children. A claim with very little documentation to support it, until we come across other "secret schools" in operation at the same time, including one attended by theoretical physicist Jack Sarfatti and operated by the Sandia Corporation, a company that ran on Defense Department contracts. Then we come across a man who shared a bus ride into Mexico with Lee Harvey Oswald, a man who ran a "secret school" in that country and who had been a Nazi supporter during World War II, running a paramilitary camp for adolescents in Tennessee. Strieber claimed his "secret school" had two locations: one in San Antonio, at the Olmos Basin, and another in Monterrey, Mexico. Strieber had also been taken to Randolph Air Base, which was staffed with more than a hundred former Nazi scientists and medical officers under the Paperclip program, including General Hubertus Strughold: men responsible for experimentation on live human subjects at the death camps.

Then we came across the startling episode of the Finders, a group of cultic pretension and CIA protection, and with an international reach that specialized in children, shipping some of them to a "secret school" in Mexico. In 1987.

What did all of this mean?

We investigated the possibility that some of these events may have been related to an ongoing psychological warfare program of the Army and the intelligence agencies, which we have come to know as BLUEBIRD or as MK-ULTRA, but which had many names depending on the military or intelligence agency involved. Again, we discovered more than we expected to find.

We found what Ed Sanders referred to as the "Manson Secret."

The arcane doctrines and methods of a discarded science are at the heart of this study, because they reveal the mechanisms by which society in general, and individuals in particular, have been manipulated by forces beyond their comprehension. The modern adoration of the principles of Newtonian science—as best represented by commentators such as the late Carl Sagan, Martin Gardner, and the coven of professional skeptics around them—has served only to obscure the means by which more open-minded specialists have been able to work their magic with impunity, often to the detriment of entire populations.

If we review the manuals on psychological warfare as practiced in the Congo in the 1950s, or in Vietnam in the 1960s, we see the politically-correct ("wink, wink, nudge, nudge") approach to what is, after all, witchcraft and black magic. The same may be said for the manual on remote viewing that was used by the US military as late as the 1980s, and perhaps even more recently than that. The opposition to the remote viewing programs came not as a result of a cost-cutting consciousness or a desire to rid the Pentagon of an unprofitable boondoggle, but because it smacked of New Age, anti-Christian sorcery. Remote viewing was attacked by the *Time* magazine science editor because it was a form of occultism that could lead to fascism. In other words, opposition to this program was based on religious and political grounds, not on scientific ones.

While the agencies may have abandoned the remote viewing programs, they have not jettisoned psychological warfare, which is, after all, an essential weapon in their arsenal. All of these techniques, from psychological warfare to remote viewing, have their origins in occultism. Although we can confidently trace the beginnings of this art to Giordano Bruno and the magicians of the Renaissance, they go back much further in time than that, to the days when occultism, religion, science, art and politics were one, and the chief of state was worshipped as a god and reality determined by the limits of his kingdom; and works of theater were works of ritual; and magic was the context within which science evolved; and works of art were media to communicate directly with sinister forces.

We have suggested that much of this material can be learned through a careful study of the religions of the East: Hinduism, Taoism, Buddhism, etc., or through an examination of modern writings on shamanism. However, the most accessible technology for a Western mind would be the theory and practice of ceremonial magic. This, after all, was the method by which Joseph Smith, Jr. talked to angels and looked for buried treasure, founding a new religion in the process. It was also under study by governors, doctors, and clergymen in the early days of Colonial America and provided the atmosphere in which the Salem witchcraft trials took place. Miscellaneous tomes on magic can be found at the crime scenes of serial murder, and in the libraries of politicians. It was the means by which L. Ron Hubbard jump-started Scientology; and by which Jack Parsons made an important series of contributions to the defense and space programs. Magic was there when MK-ULTRA began its search for the secrets of the paranormal and interviewed witches and wizards in America and beyond. It is a fascination that has not died with the passage of time, or the passage of laws, whether civil or scientific. If, as Crowley has written, "magic is the science and art of causing change to occur in conformity with will," then it has obvious attractions for the politician and the general, type-A personalities whose will is surpassed only by their egos.

Ceremonial magic begins with a basic premise that is sometimes formulated as the Hermetic axiom, "As above, so below," a simple phrase with enormous implications. Magicians believe that connections or links exist between perceived phenomena, and that to operate on one side of the link is to cause change to occur on the other. To fashion a talisman of gold is to trap the power of the sun; to make love to a priestess is to invoke a god. The magician operates in a world of "non-locality," a world where a force may be an object, a wave may be a particle, and everything is in immediate communication with everything else, from the very basic sub-atomic particles that comprise matter and energy, to the couplings of Tantric deities in a cave on Mount Meru. The magician deals with multiple personalities as a matter of course: demons, angels, spirits of the dead, are all around him, all the time. Like the G-scale doctor in his white robes in a basement somewhere in the Virginia countryside, or the Canadian psychiatrist in his Mount Royal retreat, surrounded by tape recorders and hallucinogens, the magician also uses these multiple personalities as subjects to work his own will in the world: to gain wealth or knowledge, to penetrate mysteries and reveal secrets ... to assassinate from a distance.

The magician, to protect himself from the terrible forces he evokes, stands within a magic circle made of concentric rings and illuminated by candles and esoteric symbols. From within this position, he gives the orders that cause change to occur. (As William Burroughs once said, the magician in his circle is a like a Mafia don, insulated from the acts he orders to be committed by rings of spiritual "made-men.") The magician speaks with invisible beings and summons infernal powers. The demons he conjures all have titles like Prince and Duke, King and President. The demons are all politicians, with constituents of their own. And the magician pulls their strings, surrounded by an aura of deniability, an aura created by Newtonian science, since science states that what the magician does is impossible, the result of superstition and ignorance. "There is no such thing as the Mafia," stated J. Edgar Hoover, Director of the FBI. And the capos laughed.

In the texts of ceremonial magic we find the formulas for attaining that "*abaissement du niveau mental*," that "*dereglement de tous les sens*" so necessary for the first step of initiation, that toe-dip into chaos, that lifting of the Veil of the Temple, that courting of madness and ecstatic vision. More importantly, however, we also find the technology for keeping oneself sane, for putting order into chaos, a *system* and a systematized approach to controlling psychosis and for tripping across that *corpus callosum* between the right and left hemispheres of the brain, lowering and raising the threshhold of consciousness, the *niveau mental*, at will.

Like the texts of alchemy, the grimoires of magic appear on their face to be incomprehensible works of superstition and fraud. The promises of riches are no less frequent in the grimoires than they are in the alchemical works; but the grimoires are written in language plain enough to follow: cut a willow branch at dawn, or summon Jupiter on a Thursday. It is the accumulation of all of these actions, in the order prescribed, that elicits from the operator the sensation of incipient psychosis, a gradual descent into madness, which is the first sign of success. The magician dissociates, creates alternate identities for himself with their own names and abilities and personalities. As the magician travels through the various levels of his art, his costume changes (red for Mars, white for the Moon) and the incense burning on the brazier changes (sandalwood for Venus, myrrh for Saturn) as each stage in the process prompts the appropriate response from him, elicits a new personality with all the subterfuge of scent and sight and touch and taste and hearing, all manipulated according to the rubric, all designed to break the magician down into multiple personalities and rebuild him again like Osiris from his dismembered bones, fragments of identity scattered throughout the landscape.

During this process the magician learns the power of the symbol, of the image. He learns to manipulate these images, and to create ones of his own. He learns how to influence judges, sway kings, defeat armies, be worshipped, loved, adored … all through image, through what today we might call advertising, or psychological warfare, using a technology that existed before printing, before advertising, before psychoanalysis. Through auto-hypnosis, the magician learns to hypnotize. Through self-degradation, he learns how to degrade others. Through self-manipulation, he discovers how you can be manipulated. After gazing into the Abyss of his own soul, he has no fear of gazing into yours, of reaching down and pulling up the sludge of your sins, draping them around your shoulders like a cloak, and never getting dirty himself in the process.

In all the revivalism of pagan religions, shamanism, Wicca, Buddhism, Taoism, Hinduism and Tantra that has taken place alongside est, and neurolinguistic programming, and enneagrams, and the self-congratulatory seminars at Esalen, and the new psychologies of Maslow, Perls, Adler, Grof, and others, all that New Age California dreaming, the one medieval subject that has been studiously ignored has been ceremonial magic. Even alchemy has won its pride of place, due to volumes of alchemical analysis by Jung and his followers, gaining credibility and acceptance among the gentle, bearded, silently enraged men of the Pacific Northwest.

But ceremonial magic is the black sheep of this earnestly sincere family of "alternative" beliefs and practices. It is too literal, too "hands on," for an industry that is more comfortable with ambiguity and theory. It seems to have more demons than angels, and the Latin, Greek and Hebrew prayers and chants are fierce and aggressive and threatening, replete with curses and the waving of swords. Yet the technology hidden among the conjurations and exorcisms of the grimoires goes to the heart of psychology, alchemy and shamanism. The complex doctrine of signatures and correspondences that forms the infrastructure of ceremonial magic is the key to the good-natured, well-intended but confused therapies of the New Age gurus.

And, of course, it is also the key to the foul-natured, evil-intended programs of the military and intelligence organs of America and its allies and its enemies.

In order to understand fully what we mean by "the Manson Secret," we must examine the technology of consciousness as it has been revealed in the course of this entire work. The reader must also be thanked for persevering on a long road that may have seemed confusing or obscure at various turns. It is hoped that the following pages will put all of the previous chapters into sharper perspective.

SPACE: THE FINAL FRONTIER

The ancient cultures of the world have not left us much in the way of writing. The earliest forms of the written language—Sumerian cuneiform, Egyptian hieroglyphics, and Chinese characters—did not make their appearance until roughly five thousand years ago; but some of the world's most astonishing feats of architectural engineering were built by cultures that did not have a written word. Stonehenge in England is a prime example, a neolithic monument that is dated to about 2800 B.C., or about the same time writing developed in the Middle East. The menhirs of northern France, the pyramids of Peru and China, and the burial mounds of North America are further examples of this phenomenon. What is important about this is the fact that these stone and earth structures were aligned astronomically, as even the toughest of critics among the scientists are now forced to agree. More than that, however, is the actual location of many of these sites, for they occupy points on the surface of the earth that are mathematically significant or are built in dimensions that suggest a precise knowledge of the curvature of the earth and the exact distance from the earth to the sun. That such a perfect science could exist in the absence of a written language or symbol system is startling enough … but that the ancients demonstrated a knowledge of everything from the precession of the equinoxes to the circumference of the earth at different degrees of latitude indicates that they possessed a source of information unique to them, and which has been lost to history.

However, when one speaks of the pyramids, for instance, and their relationship to specific stars and then extrapolates from there to a presumption of the historical basis of ancient religions, one is apt to sound like a crank or at best extremely credulous. Some of the brightest minds of the past hundred years have been castigated for holding theories in contradiction to those of organized academia, even though those theories were based on the same evidence available to the professional historians, archaeologists and anthropologists of their generation. What is usually lost in this bitter exchange is the acknowledgment that previous cultures held some of the same, "exploded," theories and built their civilizations around them. This is the point that interests us here. As I pointed out in *Unholy Alliance*, it is not necessary to believe in astrology to believe that the Nazis believed in it. In the case of sacred geometry and what the modern New Age movement calls "geomancy," we have a case in point.

Spaces can be considered sacred or demonic, and structures can be built in those spaces to take advantage of the former or protect against the latter. We have the examples in our own culture of the church and the haunted house: two buildings at the opposite ends of the spiritual spectrum. In the case of the church, it is interesting to realize that many of the Gothic cathedrals of France—for instance—were built on sites sacred to the pagans who had worshipped there previously. Even St. Peter's Basilica in Rome was built on the site of the Mithraic tauroboleum, where bulls were sacrificed and initiates bathed in their blood. The Cathedral of Chartres is a famous example of a Gothic structure built over a pagan shrine, complete with a spring and a "black Madonna." It is said that the Cathedral of St. John the Divine in New York City is another such example.

The orientation of sacred structures always follows strict guidelines, no matter what the religion or the country. In the Catholic Church, the altar is always in the East, the place of the rising Sun. Worshippers enter from the West, the place where the Sun "dies." There are similar requirements in India—the system of sacred architecture known as *Vaastu*—and in China, the now-popular system known as *Feng Shui* or "Wind and Water." Many volumes have been written about the orientation of the pyramids of Egypt, some more credible than others; no matter how one feels about some of the theories advanced for their design, no one can deny that the pyramids do follow a strict layout and orientation according to the four cardinal points. The great stone circle at Stonehenge is acknowledged to be a kind of astronomical calendar, as are many of the mound systems in North America.

This insistence on the precise design and placement of sacred structures is a means of creating a microcosm, a perfect image of the entire world. To the European initiates of the secret schools—such as the mysterious Fulcanelli, whose book on the Gothic cathedrals was seminal, and Schwaller de Lubicz, whose work "deciphering" the Egyptian temples is famous among a certain class of Egyptologist—these buildings are books, meant to be read by those who have been schooled in their "language." From the perspective of the occultist of the last hundred years or so, we are just beginning to understand sacred architecture now; it would be a mistake to ignore its message only because we feel that such edifices were the work of the scientifically naïve or of ignorant savages mindlessly baying at the sight of the moon. The investment of time and resources in the creation of these monuments was enormous, stressing their respective cultures to their limits. It was important for these peoples to do what they did, to build the structures they did, and to orient them as precisely as they did. To look at them as mere curiosities only demonstrates our ignorance, not theirs.

This is not to say that American architects have been totally ignorant of the idea of sacred geometry. As many authors have pointed out in the past—usually in those volumes of discarded science to which I have frequently referred—even Washington, D.C. was designed according to arcane principles for the manipulation of secret forces. The same author whom we mentioned in the context of the "green language"—the erudite David Ovason, also the author of the New Age bestseller *The Zelator: The Secret History Behind History*—has written *The Secret Architecture of Our Nation's Capital.* The Masonic and Rosicrucian (read "Templar") influences are all there to be examined.

Unfortunately, with all the recent volumes that have been written on the subject of arcane geometry and sacred architecture, there seems to be very little in the way of explanation regarding just how these vast machines of stone and earthwork were to be "used." Some scholars have risked their reputations in support of the idea of a kind of sophisticated paleo-astronomy which was linked to architecture and the erection of huge buildings in accordance with a secret tradition—the Pyramids of Gizeh arranged like the constellation Orion, for instance, with openings in their faces placed in order to capture the rays of distant stars. Yet the fact that these buildings are bare of written explication means that we can only guess at their true purpose. It's a bit like looking at an elevator for the first time: we can see it's a small room with a door that closes, and a set of numbers on a kind of magic plate next to the door, but unless we can associate that little room with the number of floors in the building, and from there to finding the machinery of cables and pulleys that would levitate the room, floor by floor, and the openings at each floor that would allow the room to access them, we will be at a loss to describe its function. In the case of the Pyramids at Gizeh, we have the small room and we have the dimensions of the Pyramid, the various shafts, the mathematical relationship of the Pyramid to the circumference of the earth at that latitude, and the relationship of the size of the Pyramid to the distance between the sun and the earth … but we have no idea of its function. We have not seen the elevator "move."

In the case of the Gothic cathedrals, we have at least some very suggestive statues and stone carvings that, albeit obscurely, can point us in some direction and give us some hint as to their function. To Fulcanelli (and, later, Louis Charpentier), the message of the cathedrals was alchemical in nature, an allegory describing the steps to be taken in the Great Work: the perfection of the soul, the refinement of its grosser elements, and its alignment—like a pyramid—to a distant Star. Jung understood alchemy to be a form of psychoanalysis, a means of achieving psychic integration through the use of a symbol system incorporating many of the archetypal elements he had discovered in his own work. Thus, we can jump from the alchemical allegory of Fulcanelli to the psychological allegory of Jung to get at least the beginning of an answer to the mysteries of the Gothic cathedrals.

But can a "sacred space" also be dangerous? Can it be sinister?

When I studied the life of Charles Manson and found several links to Indian mounds—from Ashland, Kentucky to Chillicothe, Ohio and Moundsville, West Virginia—it occurred to me that burial mounds are the haunted houses of American prehistory. While they were sacred to the Adena and Hopewell cultures that built them—places of burial and of astronomical orientation and ritual observances—they might very well be inimical to outsiders. In addition, some of the ancient sites were possibly erected by outsiders to the American shores: Phoenicians, according to Barry Fell, or Celts; Druids, perhaps, or Irish monks. (That there was a large "Mound Culture" in neolithic Europe is by now accepted by most archaeologists and historians; the mounds of Asia and South America are now coming to light, as well.) There is no way to know for sure how their rituals were conducted, or to what gods or goddesses. It is a distinct possibility that some of these practices may have migrated to America on forgotten waves of tentative immigration centuries—if not millennia—before Columbus, even though this transports us back to the disturbing fictions of H.P. Lovecraft.

But how to connect the burial—and other—mounds of America to something as contemporary as serial murder and the Manson Family? That does seem to be quite a stretch. Oddly enough, it is a theme that has begun to influence American literature, particularly of the horror variety, although it is nowhere articulated to the extent it has been here.

Stephen King, in *The Shining*, describes the Overlook Hotel which is the scene of murder and mayhem in his novel as built over an Indian burial mound. In the film *Poltergeist*, a housing development is found to be erected over another Indian burial mound, with ensuing supernatural events including hauntings, possession, and poltergeist activity. In 2003's *Identity*, starring John Cusak, a motel which is a scene of murder and mayhem and also a platform for working out a complicated plot involving multiple personality disorder is likewise built on the site of Indian burial mounds. A hotel, a housing development, and a motel. Possession, hauntings and MPD. Burial mounds in all three. It would seem that awareness of a link between these phenomena is moving just beneath the conscious threshhold of American culture, looking for a way to make itself better known and understood. It may be nothing more than a kind of repressed guilt over the treatment of the Native Americans, manifesting as an evil force that threatens our lives and our sanity. Or it may be something else.

Another early 21st century production, the 2002 European film *Darkness*, starring Lena Olin and Anna Paquin, treats this subject in even deeper terms: set in a house in Spain that was built according to occult specifications to evoke the god of Evil, a house haunted by the ghosts of six slain children, and a ritual that can only be performed during a particular solar eclipse that occurs only once every forty years; the slain children laid in a circle, their heads towards the center and their legs extending outside, like the burials in the Indian mounds of America, the Cathar burials, the bodies found at Waco. This film is fictional, of course, but the occult details are remarkably coherent: artists, as in the Lovecraft tale, sensing the forces at work before the rest of us.

The old Clovis migration theory that has dominated American archaeology for so long is now on the verge of being exploded. Archaeological finds in South America have gone a long way to disproving the dates used for the Clovis peoples, wreaking havoc with the timeline. Something was going on in America long before the arrival of Columbus. Successive waves of European migration after 1492 trampled on the sacred sites of unknown civilizations. Early pioneers remarked on the appearance of "Indians" with blue eyes and blonde hair, or "Indians" speaking, incredibly, Welsh.

Adena and Hopewell artifacts show raptorial birds, objects found in the same areas as modern sightings of the Mothman and other creatures of dubious origin. Our early forefathers in New England were obsessed with religion and occultism to an alarming degree. They brought slaves and indentured servants from Africa and South America, people who brought their own religious sensitivities with them and who would have looked at the mounds and other prehistoric evidence from a perspective different from their white owners'. The founder of the Mormon religion was himself a ceremonial magician, using the same grimoires that generations of European occultists had used before him to conjure spirits and command demons. He used this magic at the site of another mound, and thereby "discovered" the plates on which he claimed the Book of Mormon was written.

There is something about the American landscape that elicits a superstitious response in its inhabitants. Writers like Nathaniel Hawthorne, Edgar Allan Poe, and H.P. Lovecraft created bodies of work that are appreciated more in Europe than in America: stories of early American witchcraft and superstition, linked with flamboyant deaths, murders, and mysteries, ancient cultures, and visitors from the stars. It is startling, and a little unnerving, to see the extent to which these gothic horrors have found expression in modern American historical and political events. America itself is a housing development built over a series of "Indian" burial mounds, a development erected largely with the aid of African slaves, so it should come as no surprise when our children become deranged, violent, and possessed. An alien past has come to haunt us, so it should come as no surprise when we confront demons we do not recognize, demanding sacrifice we do not understand.

The medieval grimoires have told us that the best places for an operation of ceremonial magic is the abandoned building or ruined church, the cemetery, or a crossroads at midnight. In other words, a place of ghosts and hauntings, of tabu and desecration, or a place of fateful decision. In pagan Europe, Hecate—the goddess of witchcraft—was the goddess of the crossroads. In Haitian *voudoun*, the crossroads are sacred to Baron Samedi, he who guides one into the Underworld. A crossroads, à la Lovecraft, is a place "between," an intersection point of the ley lines that are said to run through the earth, channeling its telluric energy at those very sites where the sacred monuments were erected: Stonehenge and Newgrange, the Pyramids and the ziggurats, the Gothic cathedrals and the burial mounds. Asian culture is similarly concerned with the flow of this putative energy, as demonstrated by their adherence to frankly mystical practices such as *vaastu* and *feng shui*. America, ignoring these ideas, has seen fit to build prisons and military bases at the sites of the burial mounds: Chillicothe, Moundsville, Wright-Patterson … In other places, the burial mounds have sat in the center of horrible events, such as the mounds at Ashland, Kentucky; no attempt was ever made to placate or pacify whatever spiritual forces may exist in those places, if only to appease the consciences of the European settlers who had evicted the previous inhabitants to build their farms, their houses, their saloons and banks. And prisons.

If America was truly settled by Asians who had walked across the land-bridge joining Siberia with Alaska—the Clovis argument—then it stands to reason they would have brought their religion and their magic with them. It would have offered them a sense of identity and cohesiveness as they trekked thousands of miles in an inhospitable climate into unknown territory. As they walked in the direction of the rising sun, they might have been seeking the source of light and life itself. We know very little of what they practiced, and can only refer to the shamanism of Siberia and the Taoism of China for clues. Both of these cults were (and are) stellar-oriented, with myths containing the element of a ladder leading up a central pole into the heavens, a pole that linked the world above and the world below with this world; if nothing else, it was the leitmotif of the pyramids and the ziggurats.

If, on the other hand, America was also settled by refugees or explorers or traders from Europe and North Africa, then we have a better idea of the faiths they brought with them, which would have included the unknown astronomical beliefs of the builders of Stonehenge or the astrology cults of the Middle East. In either case, an awareness of astronomy and its association with architecture and sacred buildings and sites would have been an essential part of their cosmology, as well as provided the technology of spiritual transformation (either of the individual or of the whole tribe), and would have included a belief in magic and the cultivation—in their shamans—of the "heightened states" mentioned by Penrose and Hameroff thousands of years later in their presentation before the Defense Department, states that are capable of exerting an influence over reality itself.

The academically-neglected rituals of European ceremonial magic are clear about the importance of the ritual site, and its careful preparation. They are clear about what the LSD prophets would later refer to as "set and setting": the creation of a specific environment to elicit a specific psychological response. The experiments of Ewen Cameron in Montreal also included the careful manipulation of the environment of his subjects. What these latter-day shamans ignored was the second integral part of the technology of consciousness: time.

TIME: OUT OF MIND

As may be expected of cultures that placed a tremendous value on the astronomical orientation of their sacred structures, the notion of time and periodicity was inextricably linked to notions of sacred space, and both were essential to their religions. Early on, the ancients demonstrated a sure knowledge of the solstices and equinoxes. The pre-literate culture that created Stonehenge was able to arrange that massive stone circle in such a way that it could be used to calculate the solstice sunrise. This was important to a civilization that depended on agriculture, for they could compute the seasons of planting and harvesting according to the length of the solar year, although we do not know for sure if that was the use to which Stonehenge was put. Admittedly, we can think of no other use unless the calendar was important for other reasons, such as for some unknown ritual calculations.

In the case of the Great Pyramid at Gizeh, however, the precise astronomical and geophysical design and placement of that structure cannot have had anything to do with seasons of planting and harvesting, which were determined by the inundations of the Nile. There was obviously something much more profound taking place in the minds of the Pyramid architects, something that was also responsible for the spate of pyramid-manufacture throughout the world at roughly the same time, as discussed by Dr. Robert M. Schoch of Boston University in *Voyages of the Pyramid Builders: The True Origins of the Pyramids from Lost Egypt to Ancient America,*[2] and by anthropologist William F. Romain in *Mysteries of the Hopewell: Astronomers, Geometers, and Magicians of the Eastern Woodlands.*[3]

The astronomical alignments of these monuments and the prevalence of tombs in or near them indicates an association of sacred spaces with the "travels" of the dead into the heavens, what Romain calls the "azimuths of the underworld." Romain identifies three different types of sacred geometry in use by the Hopewell peoples: the square, the circle, and the octagon. The square he believes was used by the builders of the mounds to indicate the heavens, the circle for the earth, and the octagon for the phases of the moon. While there is not enough space to go into all of Romain's calculations and other evidence, it is enough to say that he provides a compelling argument for the orientation of the various Hopewell mounds as a means of facilitating the transport of the souls of the dead to the Afterlife, which, in this case as in the case of ancient China, ancient Egypt, etc., meant outer space. In other words, the Hopewell mounds (and, perhaps the Adena mounds as well) were a type of machine, a technology for extraterrestrial travel. And the travel could go both ways.

The alignments of the mounds—and, again, of the pyramids of various civilizations including the Egyptian, the Sumerian, the Aztec, the Chinese, the Peruvian, etc.—are all to very specific points on the horizon. In some cases—perhaps most cases—these alignments are to the rising and setting sun at the winter and summer solstices. In other cases, they may be to the rising and setting sun at the spring and fall equinoxes. In still other cases, they are to the maximum and minimum rising and setting of the moon. In one or two special cases, we even have instances of the orientation of some of these monuments to the cross-quarter days, the days midway *between* the solstices and equinoxes. Always, however, the orientation of these structures is in a sacred space and oriented to a sacred time.

In the case of the American mounds, we know very little about the religion and cosmology of their creators, except where revealed by the very structures themselves, which are huge and represent the investment of tremendous resources in their design and erection. Found within the Hopewell mounds in various sites across the American midwest—in Ohio, Kentucky, Indiana—are artifacts that are compelling in their design, which seem to be focused on the square and on variations of the theme of four corners or four directions. Among these is the swastika.

Although commonly associated with the Nazis, the swastika is an ancient symbol that was known in India, China, northern Europe, the Caucasus, and in North and South America as well. Pieces of copper cut into swastika shapes have been found in various mound sites. It was one of the "proofs" that the crank anthropologists of the SS-Ahnenerbe used to justify their claim that at one time the Aryan race was in control of the entire globe and had penetrated to its furthest reaches. Discoveries of swastika-decorated pottery and potsherds have been found in the Taklimakan desert of western China as well as in Tibet, and in the burial mounds of America.

When Charles Manson carved a swastika into his forehead, was he invoking the horrors of the Third Reich, or was he evoking an ancient Adena or Hopewell deity, something from beneath the burial mounds in his home town of Ashland, Kentucky; something that may have possessed his spirit one evil night when his mother was at the bar, picking up another "uncle" while she left little Charlie outside, alone, prey to the demons of hunter-gatherers, worshippers of the raptorial bird?

While it is fashionable to speak of the people of these civilizations as peaceful agrarians, that is not necessarily the complete picture. Burial evidence in some of these mounds raises suspicions that the bodies interred were not always the result of death from old age, sickness, or accident. Further, the orientation of charnel houses to specific points on the horizon which would only become "activated" by the passage of a celestial body once in a year or, in the case of some of the lunar placements, once in every nine years, suggests another line of questioning: were human beings killed, sacrificed, at specific times to coincide with the rising or setting of the sun, the moon, or a star?

We have seen that many of the serial murders carried out by the Son of Sam cult, the Zodiac killer, etc. took place on days special to the calendar used by these ancient Americans (as well as by European pagans and occultists). This may have been accidental—"coincidental"—but their number suggests otherwise. We have also seen how often the mounds themselves appear in our narrative of the cases of Charles Manson, Squeaky Fromme, and others. Chillicothe itself, one of the foremost mound sites in America, is the site of a federal prison which has boasted not only Charles Manson among its guests but also serial killer Henry Lee Lucas (and who knows how many others?). Another mound site, of possibly less importance, lies in Beaumont, Texas—a site that shows up in both the Son of Sam case as well as in the Henry Lee Lucas case. According to Lucas, the "Hand of Death" cult that he insisted existed in Texas, and was responsible for murders throughout the United States, was based in or around Beaumont at one point, and was responsible for the murder of a lawyer there. Beaumont is a suburb of Houston, and is where Sam cultist John Carr's ex-wife lived with their daughter. Berkowitz visited Beaumont when he obtained the famous .44 Charter Arms Bulldog revolver that was used in the Sam killings. Houston has been identified in the Sam literature as a cult center for the group rivalling Los Angeles; Minot, North Dakota; and New York City.

According to *Beaumont: A Guide to the City and Its Environs* "compiled and written by the Federal Writers' Project of the Work Projects Administration in the State of Texas" and published circa 1939, the area had been home to a tribe of Native Americans known as the Attacapas. This name, we are informed, comes from the Choctaw words *hatak* (man) and *apa* (eats). In other words, they were cannibals. On page 25, the anonymous but federally-funded writers go on to state,

> They told of a deluge that once destroyed the world except for those people who lived on high land. The women of the tribe, using the shoulder blades of buffalo for spades, were made to build great earthern [*sic*] mounds with their hands, and atop these mounds the big chiefs had their lodges.

Some of these mounds still exist in the Beaumont area, or did at the time the book was compiled.

Thus, we have cannibals and mound-builders in the same breath. We are told that the Attacapas (like the ancient Sumerians) believed their origin was in the sea, so they tended to stay near the water as much as possible, building their mounds on the banks of the Neches River that winds through Beaumont like gentle persuasion. In fact, the Attacapas mounds are the *only* evidence of a mound-building culture in the entire State of Texas, aside from a set of mounds on a farm near Nagodoches.

Beaumont is probably not so well-known today as it was in the 1930s when the book was written. On January 10, 1901, oil was discovered at Beaumont—at the now famous Spindletop oil fields—and history was made: Texas became an oil state, and the fortunes of George DeMohrenschildt, the Hunt brothers, the Bush family, and so many others were in the process of being made. "Spindletop" became anonymous with wealth and prosperity and conspicuous consumption, as any of us who may remember the old Spindletop restaurant in Manhattan can safely attest. Strange, then, that the place that gave America its oil wealth and oil barons should also be the place where cannibals and mound-builders, satanists and serial killers would have come calling; for in the age of the Attacapas (or "Attakapas") Indians there was no wealth to be had in oil, and in the days of Henry Lee Lucas and the Son of Sam, Beaumont had fallen from its old glory days: the fields were dry, and the mounds had all but disappeared.

The Chinese word for "coincidence" is composed of two characters, *fu* and *he*. The first character, *fu*, means "symbol" and is the same character used to represent *fuzhou*, or the name given to Taoist magic symbols and occult incantations. The second character, *he*, is familiar to me from my work abroad, as it appears in the ever-present *hetong* or "contract": it means "to join" or "to combine" even "to agree" or "to be equal to." Thus, the Chinese term for "coincidence" actually means "symbols joined together" or "combined symbols" or even, perhaps, "symbols that agree with each other."

Thus, we see the theme of Giordano Bruno and the other Renaissance occultists reprised in this simple combination of characters from half a world away: coincidence as symbols combined. Coincidence as evidence of magical forces, or even as a kind of agreement or contract: a covenant. The Latin word for *sacrament*—used these days in its ecclesiastical sense to refer to specific rituals such as communion, confirmation, and penance—originally meant a "contract," or an "oath taken by soldiers." The "Holy Sacrament" in Catholic terminology refers specifically to the consecrated Host of the Mass, the white wafer that represents, that *is*, the Body of Christ, and which represents a New Covenant between God and humanity.

I only point this out to show how pervasive certain concepts are, regardless of culture, race or religion: that the rituals performed by Chinese sorcerers and

Catholic priests have at their heart an understanding that there is an agreement, a contract, between human beings and spiritual forces, and that the rituals themselves are representative of this. To take this one step further, may we suggest that the phenomenon of coincidence is an indication that just such a "contract" is in effect? We have already seen that there is a clear relationship between ritual (the "heightened states" of Penrose and Hameroff) and coincidence, a dynamic that works at the sub-atomic, quantum level. We have also seen that the doctrine of signatures or correspondences is an integral part of all magic ritual. Is this Hermetic concept what is understood by the term "contract" or "covenant"? After all, in a Christian context, Jesus promised St. Peter, "What you seal on earth shall be sealed in heaven, what you loose on earth shall be loosed in heaven." Is this the New Testament version of "as above, so below"?

The Chinese also believed in sacred space and sacred time, and more elaborately created entire technologies for traveling in "heightened states" to the stars. At the time the CIA was investigating these same methods, R. Gordon Wasson had already sampled the "magic mushroom" (known as "God's flesh") in a small village in Mexico and written about his experience in *Life* magazine, prompting a scientist on a CIA contract to accompany Wasson on his next trip. This fascination with psychotropic substances was to prompt Wasson's study of the hallucinogenic mushroom's influence over religious and mystical experience the world over, a perspective that was adopted by Allegro in *The Sacred Mushroom and the Cross*, and by Timothy Leary in his experiments with LSD-25. What was not well known at the time—but has become better understood now with the renewed interest among archaeologists in American prehistory—is that these same mushrooms (versions of *Amanita muscaria*) were in use among the mound builder cultures, where carved effigies of the mushroom have been found in the burial sites.

This association of the hallucinogenic mushroom with the sacred sites indicates a reverence for the psychedelic experience and a context of sacred space and sacred time surrounding its use. To researchers like William F. Romain, it is an indication of the beliefs of the prehistoric peoples of America in the creation and use of the mound structures as a gateway to other worlds, a gateway that could be used in both directions. The conjunction of lunar, solar and stellar earthworks in early America with the use of psychotropics and ritual lead us to the conclusion that the early Americans—possibly, but not definitively, the ancestors of the present-day Native Americans—had a technology for otherworldly "travel" (such as remote viewing) of a type which eventually came to the attention of our military and intelligence agencies, and which would have led to social organization and control of these early peoples such as the Adena and the Hopewell in line with extraterrestrial forces (as the design and orientation of their sacred structures to the stars instructs us).

This ancient American preoccupation with the stars—a consuming interest that is paralleled in virtually every other ancient civilization—found its apotheosis in the Postwar appearance of The Nine. We would not be talking about this event at all, had it not been for the participation of some of America's most notable families in this series of séances taking place in Glen Cove, Maine. We would not be talking about this event at all had it not been for the organization of these séances under an Army captain who was responsible for paranormal, chemical and biological research during the Korean War. A man who worked for Dr. Laurence Layton, the father of the only convicted Jonestown murderer.

The message of The Nine—that it was an extraterrestrial force hovering over the earth in a flying saucer of some kind and that it intended to guide a generation of human beings in expanded consciousness—was something that Andrija Puharich took very much to heart, so much so that twenty years later he was *still* talking about it, this time to Uri Geller and the people at SRI who worked on Defense Department contracts in remote viewing. As we recall, one of the original members of the séance that contacted The Nine was Arthur Young, the father-in-law of one of the Kennedy assassination personalities, Ruth Paine. (It was to Arthur Young that Puharich would take Geller, Einhorn and Sarfatti twenty years after the original seance.)

One wonders: was the assassination of John F. Kennedy something in line with the agenda of The Nine? After all the discussion we have entertained here on the subject of coincidence and synchronicity, it would be foolish to ignore the relationship between a charter member of The Nine and the family of the alleged assassin of the President of the United States. It strains credulity to the breaking-point to simply assert that the fact that Lee and Marina Oswald lived with Arthur Young's daughter-in-law, a woman who visited Young only two months before the assassination, is pure "coincidence," a mere accident of history with no meaning. Yet, we are puzzled by the eminence of Arthur Young and his wife, Ruth Forbes Paine Young, among the New Age philosophers of the American Postwar era. There is no mystery about Arthur Young's contribution to the defense establishment; his invention of what would become the Bell Helicopter would have far-reaching effects, through the Vietnam War and beyond. To his credit, he abandoned the military-industrial establishment shortly after the end of World War II to devote himself to the philosophical questions that haunted his waking hours.

Yet, he managed to obtain for his son-in-law—Michael Paine—a position with Bell Aerospace, a company that was being run by the former Nazi General Dornberger. All of this leads us to wonder if we have been mistaken in our belief that the field of alternative religion, mysticism, and the paranormal was solely the domain of the Beats, the hippies, yippies, and other counterculture types that proliferated during the 1960s on a wave of acid and angst. The Christian Fundamentalists would have us believe that the New Age is a work of Satan, and that it represents the Left in America. But mysticism has rarely been the focus of the Left anywhere.

As we have seen, the Nazis (at least, in the form of their most rabid devotees, the SS) were ardent occultists and mystics. These were the same people who were wooed by the American Right after the war, brought to the United States and protected by prominent Republicans even as prominent Democrats—like Helen Gahagan Douglas and Eleanor Roosevelt—were arguing for their arrest and prosecution. Many of the individuals who claim to have been approached by The Nine or by their representatives—men like Jack Sarfatti, Andrija Puharich, Arthur Young, Walter Breen, etc.—worked for the military-industrial complex at some point in their lives, if not for long periods at a time. Whether they did this as convinced members of the Right, or simply because that is where the jobs were, is actually not relevant to our case. What is relevant is that this is where they wound up, deliberately or not, intersecting with some of the most important and pivotal events and personalities of the Postwar era. Men who attended séances with The Nine, who heard metallic voices on the phone, knocks on the walls, and who spent murky months or years of their childhoods at "secret schools."

The Technology of Sociopaths

These were not the men, however, who found their personalities splitting, a gun or knife in their hands, blood on their clothes. These men went on to lead lives of privileged sanity. It was the other group of individuals who came to the forefront of America's attention: the sociopaths who formed cults and sought the massive initiation of the planet in their own perverse secret societies, the men who used the tools of the magician like the famous Sorcerer's Apprentice and wrought chaos and destruction all around, to the edification of the men in the lab suits and government grants who were busy refining the very same techniques.

The use of hallucinogens by Charles Manson and those around him leads us to view what he was doing with his "Family" in a more specific way. Previously, it was thought that Manson and his "hippie" followers were simply following the general trend inspired by Leary of "turning on, tuning in, and dropping out," and were using psychedelics as an escape, or a crutch, or as a source of cheap mystical experience. But the combination of Manson's Scientology and occult training in prison (including his contact with the Process and possibly the OTO), his horrific childhood experiences, his compulsive sexuality, and the use of LSD and other hallucinogens *in specifically ritual circumstances* suggests another agenda entirely. He was conscious of the uses to which hallucinogens could be put, and he himself underwent an LSD-assisted "crucifixion" in the California desert, as we have seen. The breakdown of the psyches of his followers through indoctrination, sex, and drugs, coupled with the creation of alternate personalities, the removal of his followers to isolated encampments far from city centers, his insistence that they commit criminal acts like stealing, fraud, etc. to further isolate them psychologically from society, and the manipulation of their memories so that they began to view their childhoods as something evil and "programmed," all contributed to their creation as murderous robots who would do anything to please "Charlie."

Manson's doctrine of an imminent race war in which whites and blacks would be at each others' throats was merely a reprise of the Gnostic doctrine of the war of Light and Darkness, made vulgar and devalued by identifying the races as the warring factors but, ironically, more accessible to his innocent listeners by using racial color as an indicator of spiritual worth. After all, skin color is a uniform you cannot change; there is no defection possible from race, which is why racism has been kept alive for so long and with such hideous consequences.

Mansonism is a peculiarly American form of Nazism, of fascism. It was born in the streets of Ashland, Kentucky and reared in the reformatories and prisons of the heartland among the poor, dispossessed class we cavalierly categorize as "poor white trash," but which contains in its bloodlines the heritage of the first English settlers: religious refugees and criminals fleeing persecution who carved a hardscrabble life in the hollers and later the coal mines of West Virginia and Kentucky. Like many a Skinhead of Europe and America, Manson was a white man who felt he had been cheated of his birthright, and who was prepared to take matters into his own hands in order to achieve some kind of parity, if not superiority. The fact that he was short in stature, of limited education and bizarre appearance, was both an obstacle to his becoming even more powerful than he was, and an asset among the young women who were drawn to him and who felt unthreaten by his demeanor and attitude. In addition, he understood instinctively the value of associating with Hollywood celebrities, for there are no better manipulators of images than Hollywood directors, producers, screenwriters and actors. Hollywood has a power that has still not been thoroughly appreciated and dissected by social critics, because to fully understand Hollywood one must understand the discarded sciences.

Manson did, to a large extent, understand these sciences and what they could offer the man who could use the technology to create a New World Order out of the flotsam and jetsam of America's youth. Everything we have seen in print about Manson's philosophy has shown it to be derivative and weak, a hodge-podge of jargon from various disciplines half-learned and half-invented. It didn't have to be sophisticated; it only had to be immediate, forceful and raw. What could seem more real, more edgy and avant-garde, than a lifelong prisoner turned mystic and revolutionary? A sort of poor man's Jean Genet? What was there, after all, that made Manson different from Jim Jones, for instance? They both espoused a philosophy that was part alternative religion, part revolutionary politics, and used the force of their cults of personality to convince others that they were reincarnations of gods, meanwhile focusing attention on racial issues; they drew their followers from the streets, literally, preaching an amalgam of Marxism and Manichaenism, and both would eventually instigate mass slaughters while fueled by apocalyptic visions.

It was important to both Manson and Jones to keep their followers off balance, through poor diet, erratic schedules (disruption of the body's circadian rhythms), the breakdown of sexual identity through forced sex acts with members of the opposite sex, the same sex, and with Manson and Jones themselves. Manson incorporated drugs into this repertoire for a more complete *dereglement de tous le sens*, and both men created a bunker-like mentality among their followers by insisting that outside forces were bent on their destruction and could not be trusted. Both men created a very specific spiritual context for all of this through their diatribes on religious and mystical themes laced liberally with sexual and political references.

At the same time that Manson cultivated Hollywood celebrities, Jones cultivated political leaders on a local and national scale. Had Jones and Manson managed to link up, they would have made a formidable pair, covering all the social and political bases. But sociopaths rarely work together.

The "technology" of sociopaths, however, was found to be amenable to conscious control and emulation. What Manson and Jones were doing was nothing that was not already understood by the experimental psychology programs of the CIA and its sub-contractors. They had been performing such operations for quite some time. We have the hypnosis experiments as recounted by Estabrooks and others; the LSD experiments that had taken place in prisons and mental hospitals and military bases; and, of course, the whole panoply of psychological warfare operations through the past decades. The Army had experimented with a psychotropic drug known as BZ (a "phenylglycollate ester of 3-quinuclidinol" which was termed a "hallucinogenic chemical warfare agent") in Vietnam, at Bong-san in March of 1966,[4] an event that was fictionalized in the film *Jacob's Ladder*.

The "contribution" of people like Manson and Jones was the revelation that masses of people could be made to do almost anything if their psyches had been manipulated through the use of image and emotion: the technology of magic and eros. The sexual component of the Manson Secret is very important: it provides the energy by means of which the links—the interconnectedness between events, people, objects, ideas—may be "activated." This is very old, very standard occult practice even if it is not always explained as such in the grimoires. After all, in many cases the magician uses eros to forge links with objects and ideas in his *own* unconscious, without the intermediary of other people. This was considered to be a grave secret, for it would enable virtually anyone to contact the "sinister forces" independently. Such a person would be virtually invulnerable to surveillance, unlike a group of people meeting for rituals, training, etc., a group that could be penetrated by a government agent or an Inquisitor.

But men like Manson and Jones need an audience; they need a group, for they need the power of the group. Their psychology is messianic; it's no fun being God if no one knows it but you. Their purpose was to replace the existing power structures with one of their own, and for that reason their doctrines were almost always self-defeating. Their philosophy was impure: their goal was not the spiritual liberation of individuals or even the emancipation of the proletariat, but the creation of a theocracy based on their own, personal revelation. These were cynical men, beholden to another force from which they took their orders. In Jones' case, it seems he was working for the CIA; the information in Book II demonstrates that. His relationship with Dan Mitrione demonstrates that.

In Manson's case, the votes aren't in yet, but the details of the Tate and LaBianca killings strongly suggest specific motives for those crimes that may have had little to do with Manson personally, being contract hits. These were men who could use the Manson Secret effortlessly, pragmatically, and cynically: a new brand of covert operative who hides in plain sight, committing assassinations thick with plausible deniability. The individuals who followed them were only a means to an end. In this, they are what other magicians like Crowley would have termed "black brothers": magicians who have confused their own illumination (and, it must be insisted, a *genuine* spiritual illumination) with the Ultimate Truth, and their own egos with divinity. They were not prepared to sacrifice their egos completely, to "take the oath of the Abyss" and renounce everything in the Long, Dark Night of the Soul. Instead, their powers turned inward and rancid. They became demons that feasted on human blood: spiritual entities, to be sure, and powerful, but of such an evil nature that they are not exactly poster-boys for the New Age.

The American intelligence and defense establishments were not concerned with that, however. They only wanted to know how all of this was done.

They wanted to understand—and employ—the Manson Secret.

The secret, as employed by Manson, seems simple:

First, the removal of subjects to a "sacred space" in the desert, with attending isolation from society; breakdown of personality through drugs and sex and "mind games"; bestowal of alternate personality or personalities (new names like "Squeaky," "Sadie," etc.) operative only in relation to Manson, thus becoming Manson's "alternates," like multiple personalities of Manson himself; identification of an external evil—the police, the blacks, etc.—as a threat to the group. And *fear* is the key element of the Manson Secret that makes it different from other initiatory or shamanistic practices. "Get the fear," Manson is known to have encouraged more than once. There is life only within the Family; outside is death and loss of identity. Identity is race, and gender, and devotion to the leader, the *Führerprinzip*. Family is reinforced through crimes committed together, through mutual sex, and through paranormal experiences. Leadership is tantamount to divinity: Manson is a son of God.

The paranoia of the occultist becomes the paranoia of the social outcast, the prisoner, the criminal, the junkie, the murderer. Murder is a form of human sacrifice in Manson's gestalt, and commission of the murder makes a Family member "made," as in the Mafia, as in the Son of Sam cult.

Manson has thus brought together elements of Scientology and the Process, along with the Crowleyan "Do what thou wilt," and crystallized them in the persona of an outlaw. The development of "heightened states" among his followers caused them to experience the world and reality so differently that the cohesiveness of the original Family members still exists: those that have abandoned the Family have become born-again Christians or some type of mystic, i.e., they have not really abandoned the path that Manson set them on. While serial killers are shamans who have not made it back, Manson Family members are a programmed shaman: i.e., people chosen from society at random and forced to go through the shamanistic experience even though they were not ready and their guru was not prepared for the responsibility; thus, the CIA's mind-control experiments were mirror images of what Manson was doing to his followers in the desert. They were both forcing individuals to go through an initiatory experience, the difference being that with Manson there was at least the context of a religious or mystical nature—however eclectic or wrong-headed and undeveloped—which the CIA experiments lacked.

With the Manson Family you had a tribe of shamans who were willing participants, and that made them stronger. With the CIA, you had unwitting guinea pigs who were only useful to the extent that the programming was effective and focused on a single target or targets, such as assassination. Sirhan Sirhan might have made a good Family member: he had already tried Rosicrucianism and Theosophy in Southern California and was walking in Manson's footsteps, but he had no social group for reinforcement; instead, he most likely had a controller and a single target. Sirhan was as much an outsider as Manson, due to his Palestinian background and his thwarted dreams of becoming a jockey, etc. Like Manson, he turned to occultism and mysticism for answers. Like Manson, he became a murderer, except that in Sirhan's case he was likely programmed to kill by someone who saw in him the same elements as a Mansonoid, and knew that Sirhan would do as instructed.

How can we draw such a strong comparison? The dates for Manson and Sirhan are only one year apart, in the same city, and they shared the same cell (albeit a year apart), built especially for Sirhan and occupied later by Manson. Manson's victims included the actress Sharon Tate; Sharon Tate had dinner with Robert Kennedy the night he was assassinated by Sirhan. The coincidences link the two murderers as they do the two victims. The alchemical/hermetic path of initiatory death and transformation was consciously applied by Manson, even to the extent of an LSD-assisted crucifixion in the desert; one of his members had participated in rituals with the Church of Satan, and Sharon Tate's husband had filmed *Rosemary's Baby* while Sharon herself was rumored to have been initiated into witchcraft by Alex Saunders. Manson had been audited in prison by a Scientologist who later turned up around Squeaky Fromme. The initiatic elements behind Manson are many; they are reprised in the Son of Sam case, and in many others (such as Matamoros, the Zodiac Killers, etc.).

This is the Manson Secret: the use and abuse of hermetic and initiatic (shamanic) processes as a means of manipulation of individuals and groups; the recognition that within the initiatic process is a wealth of psychological knowledge and technique that can be used for evil as well as for good; the incorporation of Fear as a substitute for Faith.

The Manson Secret is black magic, and it was black magic that informed the CIA's mind-control programs as well. These same processes are being used—virtually without change—among terrorist organizations and revolutionary cells throughout the world, who have realized that the most effective tool for violent action is the properly initiated cult member. Ecstasy is just another face of fanaticism; eros is another face of magic. Fascism is the natural environment for both, for it speaks directly to the passions and the unconscious mind, through the use of symbols, repetitive slogans, and group ritual; i.e., magic. Socialism, being more cerebral, lacks the erotic element so necessary for mass appeal. Mao changed that for a while by ignoring Marx's dictum against creating a "cult of personality" and turned himself into an image, a magical link to the eternal. Transmute the ecstasy or the eros to a high pitch of passionate dedication to a cause, and use the theory of the magical link competently, and you have created an assassin, or a priest, a lover, an actor; or a politician who cannot be stopped except by a bullet.

Many of our most infamous cults have been apocalyptic: that is, they fueled the passion and the anxiety of their followers through identification with a given date, a point in *time*. This point was to be the end of time, the end of history, the end of the world. This apocalypse point was central to the thinking of both Manson and Jim Jones, as well as so many other cults, including some of the Christian Fundamentalist sects that have been predicting the end times for so many years it has lost its allure. The Jehovah's Witnesses have been making specific predictions, as have many others. As pointed out by Picknett and Prince, even The Nine have not been averse to millennial fevers, scheduling an event at the Great Pyramid of Gizeh for the turn of the millennium that was somehow called off at the last moment due to machinations behind the scenes involving the Egyptian Museum.

The point is that while the cults have identified their sacred space—their temple, ashram, cave in the mountains or shack in the desert—they also needed a sense of urgency, an idea that revolution was around the corner, a sense of fear. They sought to transcend the kind of sacred time represented by the pyramids, Stonehenge, the Indian mounds: a time that is cyclical, reliable, permanent. They needed to extend their boundaries beyond sacred time to a profane time, a demonic time. For the Son of Sam cult and others like it, it was enough to adopt the pagan calendar of quarter and cross-quarter days because it was an anti-calendar, a calendar valued by the underdogs, the satanists, the pagans, the occultists, a calendar that speaks of ancient mysteries and supernatural power and which is in tune with the actual movements of the sun and moon; but for the modern apocalyptic cults, cults shorn of mystery and individual possibility and initiation, an end-point was needed, since in an apocalyptic cult there can only be one leader, one initiate, one *Führer.*

These cults are full of people who lack the imagination to look beyond what they see as the general decay and decadence of our society, of our entire world. They feel history winding down, coming to a stop, and pray that all the evil in the world will be destroyed by an avenging angel they like to think is on their side. Those who follow a sacred calendar know that time does not flow in a linear direction, but in cycles and epicycles, spirals and holograms. They knew this before our scientists did, and they memorialized this information in their standing stones and mounds of earth. There is a pattern to time, as there is a pattern to space, a pattern to our nervous systems, a pattern to consciousness.

What goes around, comes around.

This idea of a sacred calendar—dates associated with meaning—provides a platform for the operation of coincidence and "synchronicity." Sacred calendars program the mind, the unconscious, so that it vibrates in accordance with an ancient pattern. Coincidence can best be understood within the context of time, the timeline, the calendar personal and general. There is the grand calendar of the masses, of society: the quarter and cross-quarter days, or the Christian ecclesiastical calendar, the Jewish calendar, the Islamic calendar with its fasting month and pilgrimage month, the Asian lunar calendars with their colorful gods and goddesses, etc. Then there is the microcosmic, individual calendar of family deaths and births, moves and changes. The synchronization of these two calendars gives rise to dates of meaning, of importance. To perform an act of acknowledgment on one of these dates is to give it added power, added meaning, a more profound sense of importance which then forges further links deep within the matrix of correspondences, giving the consciousness of the individual a rare power and more penetrating insight into not only society but the individual's own role and relationship to society. One begins to experience a flow: of time, of awareness, of meaning, even of power.

Christianity adopted the pagan calendar because of this very phenomenon. Jesus was not born on December 25; but it was an important Roman festival. Halloween was scheduled to occur on the same day that the European pagans believed the door between the worlds of the living and the dead were open, October 31, a cross-quarter day. The feast of the Virgin Mother was scheduled for May 1, another cross-quarter day of tremendous importance to pagans. Just as Christianity adopted the sacred *places* of the pagans—the sites of pagan worship that became Christian shrines, even including St. Peter's Basilica itself—so they adopted the sacred *time* of the pagans, performing a coordination of astronomy and geography that would provide their leaders and their saints with an enormous reservoir of meaning, a matrix of secret power. It was a platform that enabled their faithful to soar. Is it any wonder the Muslims wish to deny both Jews and Christians complete access to the Dome of the Rock in Jerusalem, the site of Solomon's Temple, knowing how the apocalyptically-minded of both religions view the building of a third Temple on the site as a signal to usher in the End of Days?

By focusing on apocalyptic time—the end of time, the end of history—one robs oneself and one's co-religionists of power. Everything is drained towards that single end, that omega point of destruction. Life begins to loose its beauty, its meaning, its relevance. The time for redemption runs out. Grace is in short supply. Careers are denied; love is postponed.

But the apocalyptic cults function within the other calendars, like it or not. There are points of tangence, of convergence, with calendars they do not recognize and they can be interpreted thereby. Thus the rise and fall of a Manson, or a Jim Jones, can be predicted; the graves of their followers and their victims can be visited on special days, days made sacred by the blood of human sacrifice. And the cycles start again.

I like to think that most people, if given a clear choice, would select good over evil. The problem is that good and evil are often only relative terms; the absolute nature of either one is difficult to confront, face to face. The experience of the divine may often be confused with an experience of evil; that is what is meant by "sinister": a threat of something dangerous, of something nefarious, an attitude of secret knowledge and secret strength. As many quoted passages have already noted in the preceding chapters, we often see the divine as "sinister." The other reflex is to see the demonic as divine. After all, in the Western tradition, Lucifer was a fallen angel, the most beautiful of God's creation. It is natural that our experience of Lucifer would be a positive one.

That is why the image is so powerful, much more so than the written word, which requires some level of thought and conscious participation. The image acts directly on the unconscious mind, conveying whole libraries of information in a single moment, setting up connecting links with other images, other ideas. That is why, frankly, the image is not to be trusted. One needs a powerful internal editor, one that questions each image to understand its purpose, its target, its origins. This is what the Christian Fundamentalists call the "power of discernment": the ability to tell if a spirit is truly good or evil. One cannot rely on pure image alone. One needs another source of information. One needs a context.

Unfortunately, as in the case of the UFO phenomenon and many paranormal experiences, we have very little in the way of context. Our religious training has been largely abandoned in the last fifty years, or has been abused by venal leaders and prophets who see a way to make a fast dollar and an easy reputation. Our scientific training has been outdated and monopolized by a scientific elite. Our political awareness has been virtually useless, manipulated by clever pitchmen, campaign managers and spin doctors, to the point where we don't know what we value anymore, or what the American experiment is all about. We need to start relying on ourselves, and that means thinking for ourselves (as painful a process as that may be, and I do not say that lightly).

It means going back to our museums and art galleries, concert halls and libraries, to get a better understanding of our own culture and the sacrifices made by individual artists, musicians, and writers to bring eternal truths to our attention. It means turning off the television set. Now, at a time when Western—and particularly American—culture is under attack as "decadent" or "worthless" or "non-existent" or "shallow," it is important for us to re-evaluate our culture, for it contains some surprises. We have listened for a long time to the Europeans tell the Americans that they have no culture; the problem is not that Americans have no culture, it is that they do not know what that culture is. American culture is far richer and far more powerful than our European relations would admit. We need to know what it is and to understand it, and to teach it in the schools, and to do that we need to have a context in which to understand it. And that means learning about the creative functions and their relation to psychology, to visionary experience, and to the frontiers of quantum physics.

It also means learning how to use our neglected "paranormal" abilities: those abilities so assiduously studied by our military and intelligence agencies for the past fifty years. These abilities only seem paranormal now; in future generations they will be realized for what they are: the application of consciousness to science, the continuation of politics by other means … means not dreamed of by Clausewitz.

The "sinister forces" of our title were identified as Nazism by Robert Jackson, and as extraterrestrials by General MacArthur. The Bible warns of spiritual evil in high places, and the scriptures of India speak of the dangers of a human being storming heaven using occult practices; the ancient Sumerians understood that evil dwells beyond the planets in the realm of the stars (*Igigi*); and Nazism was concerned with the creation of a new man and the worship of Lucifer. So what are the sinister forces? Are they simply the emanations of a deeper evil force, or do we confuse the sinister divine with the sinister satanic? For most of us, confrontation with any spiritual power is a matter of dread, awe, and fear (*vide* Guggenbuehl-Craig).

The Nazis took the bold—and insane—step of evoking these forces deliberately, by institutionalizing all sorts of occult ideas and theories and practices in the SS, the Ahnenerbe, and other places. The American political and economic machine emulated some of these practices in their support of Nazism, racism and eugenics; by supporting Nazism they were allowing a deep moral evil to enter the country at the highest levels of power: the CIA, NASA, the USAF, etc., and eventually US corporations, such as Bell Aerospace, ITT, etc. When the CIA scientists began their assault on human consciousness, without regard to psychological or spiritual fallout, they were following in the steps of the Nazi doctors, and in some cases using captured Nazi files and captured Nazi scientists as their guides. American politics and American science began to incorporate Nazi elements at the same time they were opening the American mind and consciousness, through drugs like LSD and through irresponsible mental programming experiments on prisoners, the mentally-ill, the unwitting, and the unsuspecting. As the remote-viewing program has shown, there is a possibility that "heightened states" of consciousness are capable of near-miraculous feats, including space exploration (*vide* Swann). The alien abductees speak of the sinister agenda of the aliens, the horrors to which they have been subjected. If these are truly alien beings, then they are adept at using the Manson Secret on their subjects; if they are not alien beings, but military or intelligence officers in the midst of an experimental program, then the Manson Secret is already in their hands, and MK-ULTRA was a decoy.

The only defense we have against the sinister forces is to develop our own mental capabilities—individually—as a firewall against psychological warfare, cultural colonialism, mind control, and the remote viewers and telepaths of the enemy. Our churches, our political parties, our schools, our media are all as suspect as our secret government agencies. The Republicans have shown a callous disregard for the hideous crimes perpetrated by the Nazis in order to allow them to fight the Communists. I do not believe it was simple pragmatism that led them to that position; they too often voice opinions and demonstrate actions that would be clearly in accordance with a Nazi agenda. Richard Nixon was the most obvious example of this, with his anti-Semitism and his sociopathic personality, as evidenced by his collaboration with Nazis and by his version of the October Surprise. This is not to exempt the Democrats from the same accusations, but in the case of the Democratic Party, the anti-Semitism or pro-Nazism of *individuals* is more the rule than is a wholesale collaboration with Nazism as a virtual party platform. Remember that "sinister forces" were accused of creating the eighteen-and-a-half minute gap in the Nixon Oval Office tapes. Haig was more right than he knew.

The involvement of Hollywood as the medium for the sinister forces is previewed in the Lovecraft story where artists are the first point of contact for upcoming events of a global nature: Hollywood represents the artist of America, at least in a gross and commercial way, fueled by the fantasies and dark dreams of the men and women who have prostituted themselves and their abilities to the engines of the major studios while struggling personally to put forward a more wholistic point of view, sometimes below the radar and sometimes unconsciously. Hollywood is the new religion of America and, to a certain extent, of the rest of the world as well. Hollywood brings the gods—the stars, "every man and every woman is a star"—down to earth, where they can be seen and heard and touched by the masses; not only Hollywood, of course, but also the music industry, and not only in California and New York but also in Bollywood and Europe and Mexico and Brazil and Venezuela and China and Hong Kong and so on. Americans emulate movie characters more than they do the saints of their religions: they dress like them, drive the same cars, have the same attitudes, talk like them, and eventually adopt the same cultural mores. Hollywood is a vast mind-control engine, which is why many independent films are ignored by the public: they do not want to think independently, they want to have their consciousness massaged by the old, familiar rituals. The tools of Hollywood are the tools of psychological warfare, of mind control and behavior control. Of advertising, in its most pernicious sense.

Ronald Brownstein, in *The Power and the Glitter: The Hollywood-Washington Connection*, makes this idea very clear with examples from the 1940s to the present day. He speaks of Hollywood's dismay when Ronald Reagan was embraced by the electorate:

> It was widely assumed that Reagan had mesmerized the public with cheap stagecraft.... Almost without exception, the Hollywood left was convinced that its own understanding of the actor's tools provided unique abilities to penetrate Reagan's façade and expose the shallowness it saw behind it.[5]

Hollywood seems most powerful when it is least conscious of what it is doing. The actor Mike Farrell—who portrayed B.J. Hunnicutt on the television series M*A*S*H—was stunned by the fact that he was recognized by refugees from the Khmer Rouge living in camps set up on the Thai-Cambodian border in the 1980s.[6] This is the phenomenon against which the developing nations—and particularly those nations dominated by religious fundamentalism—are now protesting, sometimes with violence. They have understood that media—all media—are a form of psychological warfare, "world-view warfare." All media contain elements of cultural assumptions and biases that may not be obvious, even to their creators, and which, to governments with a tenuous hold on the loyalty and confidence of their citizens, seem subversive and dangerous. America's experience during the Cold War instructed its leaders that the best wars are those which are never fought with guns and bombs, but with ideas. Colonialism in the old sense is expensive and unfashionable. Cultural colonialism, however, is much cheaper, uses fashionable media, and is plausibly deniable.

The same elements we have discovered used by Manson and Jones and many others can be found in the dissemination of media messages throughout the world. Television has replaced scripture in many households; certainly many people pay more attention to their television set than to their religion, even in religious states. Sitting around a television set in the comfort of their own homes, people are isolated from one another in a social context, but united with others thousands of miles away in a cultural context. They are massaged by images that carry subtle sexual intentions—attractive actors, singers, models, the sexual tensions of the soap opera and the movie—and are introduced to a world that encourages a value system somewhat at odds with their own, using powerful images, colors, music: a subliminal package that causes shifts in consciousness. The danger of this can only be sensed by those already attuned to a deeper spiritual state of mind, where the assault of these images can be seen for what it is: a form of psychological warfare, of brainwashing, of cultural imperialism.

By encoding this system in a vast media machine that incorporates television, cinema, and the music industry, Hollywood has developed tremendous power. This is not to say that this power is evil in and of itself; that would be naïve. The power of Hollywood should be respected for what it is, a kind of institutionalized—or industrialized—mind control. The more actors, writers, directors and producers are aware of this, the more powerful this system becomes. The Reagan phenomenon was the wake-up call for many in Hollywood, even if they had not understood that the Kennedy election, twenty years earlier, owed a great deal to the power of television, the first such election to do so. Now it is important to maintain the struggle in Hollywood among the factions that would seek to dominate this power for one agenda or another. Hollywood has already learned the Manson Secret; it would be a disaster if only one party or one set of fundamentalist beliefs were to monopolize its use.

Terrorism, by contrast, is the new witchcraft; terrorists are aligned against all states, and thus are rebels everywhere and despised everywhere. They attack culture, and not military targets, to maximize the fear factor. Terrorist cells are the modern equivalent of the witches' coven, and the Patriot Act is the equivalent of the Inquisition.

A favorite target of terrorist states is Hollywood, for all the obvious reasons. Yet, they have learned a great deal about the power of the image from Hollywood. Why else bomb a school bus? A hospital? The World Trade Center? Terrorism, as we have seen, is a form of psychological warfare, and as such owes a great deal to the same technologies in use by Hollywood and by our own intelligence agencies. Indeed, many of the important terrorist figures now arrayed against America got their training from the CIA during American support for the Taliban guerrillas fighting the Soviet invasion. One of the more infamous of terrorist "interrogators"—Dr. Aziz al-Abub of the Hezbollah in Lebanon—had received his training in mind control at Patrice Lumumba University in Moscow, and employed virtually the same methods as his American counterparts. The "brainwashing war" that began in 1950 with the Korean conflict, and which involved the United States versus China and the Soviet Union, has now percolated down to the popular level, the terrorist level: the technology of torture, pain, sensory deprivation, hypnosis, and drugs is available to everyone, and is much cheaper to employ than a Stinger rocket or a Kalashnikov.

In the case of the Islamic terrorist organizations, these heinous practices are carried out in the name of God by men who, "inflamed with prayer," do not question their application. Just as America viewed the Communist nations as atheistic and godless, and used that as one of their many justifications for the excesses of the Cold War, so do the Islamic terrorists view America as the Great Satan, a decadent society that is an affront to God and which must be destroyed. The real war may very well be that which is being played out in Jerusalem between fundamentalist Christians, messianic Jews, and determined Muslims over the site of the Temple of Solomon and the Dome of the Rock. In the Middle East we have catastrophic military technology in the hands of religious fanatics, true believers who will fight to the last drop of their blood—and ours—for God, manipulated by cynical men who know these robot warriors for what they really are: pawns in a game whose rules only they know, men who gleefully employ the Manson Secret.

Who, then, are the sinister forces? Demons? Or Gods? Aliens, or … us? We are in danger of losing our freedom because of this threat to our lives and culture, since our leaders know only one way to respond to terrorism/witchcraft, and that is the stake and the forced confession. Our leaders cannot talk to us about the real problem; they cannot admit their own failure of imagination.

We have been talking about the end-times endlessly, this begun by our fundamentalist Christian Coalition, whose most notable spokespersons have been Jerry Falwell, Pat Robertson, Ronald Reagan and, now, George W. Bush—and have been making films and writing books and articles about the apocalypse (by nuclear war, nuclear accident, asteroid strike, holes in the ozone, etc.) at such a furious pace, that we may infer that we are either predicting it through some unconscious means, some "heightened state" that has been activated in our quantum consciousness, or that we are calling it, summoning it in an act of desperation, so tired of the world the way it is and simply wanting it all to end.

We are all so tired of the epidemics, the urban violence, the danger of terrorism, of biochemical warfare, of nuclear war, of hunger and starvation, of grinding poverty and fear of unemployment, of the bankruptcy of both ourselves and of the private and public sectors, of the dwindling rain forests, the rapidly depleting water supply, the absence of anything like spiritual renewal or cultural values in our media (except, perhaps, in the art, concert music, opera, and literature that has become less and less accessible to the people, with the dwindling financial support of our respective governments for both the arts and for the education necessary to enjoy them), of sexism, racism, ethnophobia, anti-Semitism, of the sheer volume of noise being created by technology without content, without meaning, of air and earth and water pollution, of the toxic substances in our food, of the incapability of science and medicine to be consistent about what is good or bad for us to do, to consume, to behave, to believe.... And at the same time we are so terrified of some cosmic apocalyptic event that would wipe out the planet that we live under a cloud of danger and despair and try to smile through it all for the sake of our children. We have a love/hate relationship with life itself. We, as a society, have become sick; and that is actually the good news.

As we have noted in the above pages and at length, the sickness of an individual paves the way for spiritual enlightenment and psychological integration. The acute schizophrenia we are now experiencing as a society may be the necessary preliminary step to a shamanic-style rebirth. The hideous violence and degradation we see all around us—and on our television screens and computer monitors—may be the signal that the dismemberment of our society is at hand. The sinister forces have been evoked from within the magic circle of the Oval Office, the videocam, the seal on the floor of CIA headquarters at Langely, and in a million other places. These may be alien forces from another planet or another dimension; or they may be demons, battalions of demons as in a painting by Breughel, marching through our blasted landscape and meting out torture and death along the way. Our saving grace as Americans is the fact that we can recognize this, that we do not simply sit still and watch from the sidelines as our civilization crumbles around us.

We are not "good Germans." Hitler's Germany will forever remain our example of the sinister forces that we have come to despise, the complacency of a citizenry in which evil triumphs because good men do nothing. We are Americans, and we are biased, and bigoted, and provincial, and arrogant, and naïve, and stupid; all of this is true. But we are also dreamers; our worst citizens have been guilty of bad dreams, perhaps, but were dreamers nonetheless. We are a sentimental people who cry at Disney movies, for which the sophisticated European laughs at us. Europe, the heir to the Renaissance: clearly the last time there was anything remotely resembling grandeur on that continent. Bitter in their shameful history of genocide and holocaust and collaboration and cowardice, and eager for company in their spiritual deterioration, Europeans are the crowd that stands below a building and urges the potential suicide to jump. We will ignore them, for we are not standing on top of that building to jump, but to reach just a little higher.

We have committed some grave sins in our history; of this there can be no doubt. The slaughter of the Native American population is perhaps the first sin, and one of the most grave. The brutal, inescapable fact of slavery is another, with its sickening offspring, racism; also the way some of our wealthiest and most powerful families and leaders sponsored eugenics and genocide in everything from the murderous Tuskegee syphilis program to state laws banning interracial marriages. Our colonial attitude to the peoples of Latin America is another, an ugly legacy from the people we fought for our own independence, foisted on weaker neighbors to the south; thousands upon thousands of people have died in Latin America, and millions more suffered incredible hardships, due to American foreign policy in the region. Our support of military dictatorships around the world is another grave sin, from the Shah of Iran to Pinochet of Chile, from Marcos in the Philippines to Saddam Hussein in Iraq, and so many others. Hiroshima was a horrible crime, and Nagasaki even greater, for we did not need a Nagasaki after the holocaust of Hiroshima.

Many wonder why America is so violent; possibly it is an understandable reaction to a sense of enormous guilt, and the unfairness of this burden of guilt on the shoulders of decent men and women who would have had nothing to do with the above crimes, if they had been given a choice. Our gun-toting population is perhaps consumed with a kind of death wish, a suicidal need to purge the earth, and this may be due—I contend—to the necessity of confronting our collective history and not finding enough to rejoice and celebrate, not enough that is inclusive of all Americans. Since the assassination of President Kennedy, we have become a distrustful and cynical population; we watched our sons and daughters come back from Vietnam and wept for those who made it back alive as well as for those who did not. We began to doubt our goodness, and this has made us angry and hateful and paranoid; for it is of central importance to every American to believe in the American dream. Without that belief, we become lesser beings living in a lesser country: a crass, commercialized landscape of strip malls and fast food and electronic churches.

Thank God we have people in our country who bring these sins to our attention, and some of us listen, and some of us grow up to work against that mentality. When the rest of the world wishes to criticize us, they do so by referencing reports and data in *our own* newspapers, magazines, and news programs: they do not realize the irony of this, since in their countries it is illegal to use the media to criticize their governments. But while our elected officials may be guilty of cynicism and cowardice and evil intentions, our electorate is not. Our people still believe in the old dreams, the idea of what it means to be an American. That is why they were all so shocked by the events of September 11, 2001.

They could not understand why anybody would hate them. They have not been abroad. They don't speak the language. They haven't done the reading. They have not seen the handiwork of which our elected officials and our intelligence agencies and our corporate leaders are capable. And for that, we should be grateful. For if they did know all of this, and if they were not shocked by September 11, then the only conclusion we could draw is that they were accomplices in all of this and actually *were* the war-mongers and racists and neo-fascists the rest of the world thinks they are.

But their shock was the shock of the innocent, and perhaps of the stupid and of the ignorant ... but not of the evil.

We could sum up with a quotation from the late, lamented Walt Kelley's *Pogo* comic strip: "We have met the enemy and he is us." Once we realize this, we can begin to make America the place of greatness and beauty and transcendence that it was intended to be, intended to be by our founding fathers who were, after all, Freemasons and Rosicrucians and Templars and freethinkers and mystics, who believed in spiritual regeneration and psychological integration.

Instead, we will end with another quotation.

That first Sunday in June 1968, at the funeral for Robert F. Kennedy—the last, best hope for a renewed America for a long time to come—his brother, Senator Edward Kennedy, read the eulogy. It contained Bobby's favorite quotation, one that he would use to revive his flagging spirits or to raise the energy of his followers.

It is a beautiful sentiment, but how many listeners in St. Patrick's Cathedral in Manhattan that solemn spring day realized the original context? As Bobby's body lay in the center aisle of that Gothic pile, surrounded by those who loved and admired him, his "robopathic" assassin in jail in Los Angeles staring stupidly around him in confusion, the men who authorized that murder toasting themselves in comfort in the boardrooms and cloakrooms and living rooms and conference rooms and bedrooms of America, some of them even *there*, in the church watching the funeral service with cynical satisfaction, knowing that the last assassination had taken place and that America was ripe for the plunder, the words of their sinister god were being quoted as epitaph:

"You see things; and you say, "Why?" But I dream things that never were; and I say "Why not?"

The quote comes from George Bernard Shaw's *Back to Methuselah*, and they are the words of the Devil.

Brooklyn Heights, 1975—Kuala Lumpur, 2003—South Florida, 2006

Endnotes

[1] Walter Lang, in his Introduction to Fulcanelli's *Le Mystere des Cathedrales,* Brotherhood of Life, Las Vegas, 2000, p. 22

[2] Dr. Robert M. Schoch & Robert Aquinas McNally, *Voyages of the Pyramid Builders: The True Origins of the Pyramids from Lost Egypt to Ancient America,* Tarcher/Putnam, NY, 2003,

[3] William F. Romain, *Mysteries of the Hopewell: Astronomers, Geometers, and Magicians of*

the Eastern Woodlands, University of Akron Press, Akron, 2000
[4] *Harvest of Death: Chemical Warfare in Vietnam and Cambodia*, Neilands, et. al., The Free Press, NY, 1972, p. 18
[5] Ronald Brownstein, *The Power and the Glitter: The Hollywood-Washington Connection*, Pantheon, NY, 1990, p. 278
[6] Ibid., p. 282

ANNUIT
XVI
SEAL OF THE PRESIDENT OF THE UNITED STATES

Epilogue

January 2006
South Florida,

Friends of mine in Kuala Lumpur—otherwise intelligent, rational people with a love of business and the easy, good life of their tropical paradise—take it for granted that the world has targeted Muslim Malaysia out of jealousy for the strength of their economy; that Jewish bankers and financiers (like the demonized George Soros) were hell-bent on global domination; that there was simply no truth to the reports that Malaysia was a haven for terrorists, even as one of their political parties praised the bombers of Bali, of the World Trade Center, of the Marriott Hotel in Jakarta and met with Hamas and Hizbolleh leaders in Malaysia in May of 2002 …

No matter how long I argued that most Americans couldn't find Malaysia on the map if you paid them, and that the only nationality bankers understand (I, who had worked for an Israeli bank for four years) is the nationality of money, they refused to believe me. The Prime Minister was able to unite his people against a mysterious, common enemy: a foreign enemy, an infidel army, a colonial power preparing to invade Malaysia if not with troops (although, after the invasion of Iraq, that still looked like a possibility to many) then with bearer bonds. International Jews. Foreign bankers. The IMF.

Sinister forces.

Outside my window the mosques still rang with the amplified call of the muezzin. But down the street, the prayer hall on Jalan Damai was filled with idealistic, clear-eyed, sometimes hateful young men in sarongs and knit skull-caps, sitting cross-legged, listening to a sermon mixed with political speeches, and calls to *jihad.* Other Muslims could be seen getting into their cars. Mercedes. BMWs. Hondas. The more plebeian in Protons and Kancils. They have asked God for protection, but they are still paranoid. And why not?

So am I.

Dogs with broken legs are shot; men with broken souls write through the night.
—Kenneth Patchen' *The Journal of Albion Moonlight*

What has obsessed me in these pages is not the paranoia of the clerk, but of the congressman. Of the President, and the Pentagon. Of five-star generals and CIA directors and scientists and clergymen. Of police officers and FBI profilers. This is not the paranoia of the loser, of the victim—pathetic, understandable—but of the winner, the victor. The paranoia of the people in charge. People who should know better, and probably do. It is what they fear most that I fear most: what they do not want us to know. The paranoia of experts. *If you're not paranoid, you don't know all the facts.*

It is the paranoia of men who shred documents in the executive offices at CIA headquarters, like schoolboys hiding dirty magazines; of a sitting President, nervous about "the Bay of Pigs thing"; of an Attorney General, and his murdered brother.

There is blood, and there are documents. This is history. You can't have one without the other. Blood. Documents. Guilt. Innocence. Knowledge. Ignorance. Frustration. Fear. But you can't know history unless you know fear. You can't know history unless you feel the pulse of life under your fingers; unless you can stare the guns in the face. Unless you can stand in the prisons, and the death camps, and feel the gaze of informers and spies and soldiers on your back in foreign countries ... and on your own doorstep, your own driveway. The rest is only bookkeeping.

The world has always been like this, of course. It has always been run by people: superstitious, religious, fearful, paranoid, ugly, hateful, murderous people. That is nothing new. But at a specific point in the century we took this a step further. We opened Pandora's box, the black box of human consciousness. We flipped open the lid, and rummaged around inside. And we loosed monsters on the earth. Monsters who feed on human flesh, and who drink the nectar of human souls.

Churches harbor the danger as much as hospitals; there is nowhere to go, no one to trust. To come to that conclusion one would have to read all these books, mountains of references to be cross-checked and verified in virtually every discipline known to us: political science, history, archaeology, paleo-astronomy, comparative religion, occultism, psychology, philosophy, medicine, physics, chemistry, business, finance, geology, geophysics, mathematics, anthropology, Watergate, Wall Street, assassinations, intelligence programs, alien abductions, epigraphy, linguistics, Hollywood, communications science, military history. Thousands of books, piles of documents. Is it any wonder, after all, that the shots—the shots that changed the world, that martyred a President, that ended a reign of hope—were believed to have come from a place where books were stored?

Back in Kuala Lumpur, the phone would ring very late at night (or very early in the morning). I was in Asia, so twelve hours separated me from the people I know and love in the States. They, in the sunlight of yesterday, still dealing with a day that is already closed for me. I didn't want to answer. I didn't want to tell them how that day would turn out.

Back on the East Coast, the days are reversed, but the phone no less ominous.

I hate telephones. I hate being summoned to account for myself, my presence, my actions, when those who should be accountable never are. More to the point, I cannot talk now. Faced with this horrible reality, I have come to learn that I know as little about myself as about anything else. How can I speak on the phone? Who will do the talking, the listening? What truth can really be spoken, when we have been baptized with lies?

The phone continues to ring, then stops.

ACKNOWLEDGMENTS

The task of acknowledging the many hundreds of people who have contributed to my understanding of this subject is gratifying, but daunting. In the first place, research for this three volume work began in 1975 and continued at a more or less steady pace—interrupted by the vicissitudes of a quotidian existence (a day job)—and took place all over the United States as well as in many foreign countries. In addition, recourse was had to archives and libraries and, with the advent of the Internet, to on-line resources as well. That means that the number of individuals who had some input to my work increased exponentially with each passing decade.

I will try to identify those who most influenced my work and my point of view, therefore, with apologies to anyone I may have missed.

Pride of place must go to Norman Mailer, whose support of my earlier work— *Unholy Alliance*—provided a tremendous boost to my self-confidence at a time when I was ten thousand miles from the States and deeply immersed in the research for *Sinister Forces.* I will be forever grateful to the man who is arguably the best living American writer for so openly sharing his views and opinions on the massive undertaking I had set for myself.

Close behind are some of the other members of the Dynamite Club, such as Jim Hougan and Dick Russell, who not only provided forewords for Volumes 1 and 2 respectively, but who also contributed their advice and information. Jim Hougan, particularly, was extremely helpful when it came to the chapter on Jonestown, and his article on the subject in *Lobster*—cited in the text—is groundbreaking. Dick Russell's magisterial work, *The Man Who Knew Too Much*, was inspirational in its scope (and its size!), and his background on some of the other characters mentioned in these pages was valuable and enlightening.

Paul Krassner is a hero and an icon to many of us who remember and cherish the Sixties and the crusading journalism of *The Realist*, a tradition that has not faltered in lo, these many decades; I found myself referencing his work—particularly concerning John Lennon—long before he agreed to provide a foreword for Volume 3. Paul, I am not worthy!

Whitley Strieber was someone who believed in this effort from very early on, while I was still in foreign lands and struggling to put this initiated view of American history into some kind of perspective. His own works show how events can be seen and understood on more than one level, and even more than one dimension, and this idea helped me to formulate my own ideas concerning synchronicity, coincidence and conspiracy. We vacillate between a no-nonsense, empirical and near Positivist approach to the subject matter … and a mystical, transcendental illuminative vision of the same material.

I think we both realize that the truth lies somewhere in that twilight zone between the waking world and the sleeping, between consciousness and the unconscious, between occult revelation and scientific certainties. There are conspiracies, and there are coincidences; what we explore is the matrix that accommodates both and takes reality into another realm of connection and coherence altogether. As is shown in this work, one can be a conspirator and a mystic both; it will be up to history to decide which approach is the more ... reliable.

But this book would never have seen the light of day had it not been for Kris Millegan. As the publisher of TrineDay, a small house that dares to print uncomfortable facts and to "speak truth to power," Kris has weathered many a political storm over the books he has midwifed to press. Attacked by lawsuits from the Special Forces Association, among others, because he dares to expose the harsh realities of government conspiracy and corruption, he bravely accepted the onerous task of publishing a huge work—*Sinister Forces*—that ran to almost 2000 pages of manuscript, something no other agent or publisher wanted anything to do with; but that didn't stop Millegan, himself the son of a former CIA officer, and who spent some years of his early childhood in the same countries I would wind up living in decades later. Kris' work on Skull & Bones has already won him worldwide acclaim (there is a Japanese translation of his work). The work he has done will stand the test of time, and future generations will be amazed that our country was able to function for so long (while ignoring the vast corruption and injustice uncovered by Kris), like the man in the Malcolm Lowry novel who ignores the tiger chewing on his shoulder and pretends there is nothing wrong.

I'm proud to be part of the Kris Millegan tradition, and this necessarily includes Russell Becker, TrineDay's editor, who painstakingly walked me through this entire manuscript to clarify and correct, identify and determine, both my ideas and my language, which, at times, had resulted in sentences that were nearly gothic in construction. Many thanks to you both.

Between all these brave men of vision there is a woman of equal vision and strength of character, and that would be the late Judith McNally, who passed away prematurely just as this book was going to press. I'd known her for thirty-five years, from when I was a struggling writer in Brooklyn Heights to the present day, when I am a struggling writer in South Florida. The struggle goes on—*la lucha sigue*—but with staunch allies and friends like Judith McNally, it seemed more like choreography than chaos. Thankfully, she was also a person who spoke her mind without reservation and was an unforgiving critic; many is the writer whose work has been tested and refined in the heat of her *athanor*, the dross slowly transformed to the glitter of something redeemable. Thank you.

Other influence, information and support have come from a diverse group of friends, associates, and fellow-travelers, among whom must be mentioned

David Blackburst, for whose biography of David Ferrie we all await; and Tracy Twyman, whose late-lamented publication *Dagobert's Revenge* was a fascinating collection of all things Grail-ish, and who since has written persuasively on everything from the Merovingians to the American monetary system to the furor over the Danish cartoons of the Prophet (for which she has been "banned in Pakistan"). I wish to acknowledge the novelist Katherine Neville as well, for the long phone conversations that cleared up a lot of my thinking on some of the scientific personalities discussed herein; your fans (among whom I number myself) eagerly await your next novel.

In Europe, my old friends Gennaro Oliva and Patrizia Ronchetto deserve pride of place; there can be no more amiable guides to the life and culture of the Continent. *Grazie mille.*

In China, the same can be said of Peter Wong and Wang Lei, whom I have known for almost two decades. There is a book waiting to be written on Peter Wong's life, but who would believe it? *Xie-Xie Ninmen.*

In Malaysia, the trilingual Cecelia Ang was professional as well as patient and understanding with this ignorant *gwei-lo* during his long and sometimes frustrating sojourn in her native land. In business, as in culture, she helped me to see layers of meaning as well as of beauty in her country that the tourist or the foreign businessman could never discover. *M'goi* and *terimah kasih.*

In Singapore, Tham Yar Leong—businessman and geomancer—was my window to the world of Asian religion and mysticism. We spent many long hours discussing everything from the Knights Templar and the Freemasons to *feng shui* and Buddhist iconography. *O mi to fo.*

I have to give special thanks to the late Steve Orlando, of Longboat Key and Stonington, a man among men who understood that life was for living. His sense of what was valuable and important extended to his employees and his friends … and they were often the same people. A rare human being, he is missed.

And to Frank Diener, "Third World Man" and fellow-traveler in the dark realms of developing nations. This green beer is for you, Doctor!

To the Australians David Redfern and Larry O'Toole, the latter who told me to do the counter-intuitive and focus on my strengths instead of trying to correct my weaknesses. You were right.

And to the bishops, Walter Propheta, Colin Guthrie, and George Augustine Hyde among many others. Propheta introduced me to the arcane world of the Wandering Bishops when I was still only seventeen years old. Colin Guthrie and George Augustine Hyde helped to fill in some blanks since then.

To Anthony Chang, Zhang LiDe and Zhang Qiang, who introduced me to China trade and, more importantly, to China itself, in the process giving me some of my most unforgettable memories.

To Kurt Neustaedter, who started me on the trail to the East without knowing it.

To Ingrid Celms, who was there at the beginning.

To the 16th Gyalwa Karmapa, from whom I accepted an initiation many years ago in New York City.

To the occultists Herman Slater, Ray Buckland, Maurice Woodruff, Leo Martello, Ed Buczynski, Ed James, Jim Wasserman, Martin Mensch, Richard Capuro, and so many, many others known over the years, such as Allyn Brodsky and the late Jerry Birnbaum, Kris Dowling, Elizabeth Bick Dowling … the list goes on and on.

To CIA agent Arthur Hochberg, and to contract agent Antonino Rocca, and several others who do not wish to be named. I value your (both voluntary and inadvertent) confidences.

To Clark Stiles ("Sunken civ") able electronic forum administrator whose long-standing support of different ideas in archaeology and anthropology were stimulating and productive.

And of course to Rose and Vivica. Vivica was not yet born when I began this work, and she is now a beautiful and talented woman of 25 years. As for Rose, strangely she hasn't aged at all. She must have a portrait hiding somewhere; yet I am sure it would look just the same anyway.

To these, and to all the others not mentioned here, I offer my sincerest gratitude. I hope this work is worthy of your many and varied contributions and lives up to the expectations you have had of a project that has taken thirty years to complete.

Any errors, of course, remain my own.

PETER LEVENDA

BIBLIOGRAPHY FOR *SINISTER FORCES*

Not all the books, documents and other sources used as background for this trilogy are listed here, for the simple reason that such a Bibliography would be book-length itself. Instead, I have chosen those items that would give the reader an idea of where to begin to duplicate the research I have done. In addition, I have not divided the Bibliography simply into a "Primary Source" section and a "Secondary Source" section, since it was suggested that dividing the Bibliography by categories might be more valuable, as *Sinister Forces* covers a wide range of disciplines, cultures, and historical eras. Instead, I have identified primary and secondary source material within each category, where appropriate.

I hope that this decision was the right one.

That said, one can reasonably be assured that where documents are listed in the text—such as items from the JFK Collection at the National Archives or the MK-ULTRA documents released by the CIA—these are primary source material. I have taken pains to ensure that these documents are identified as clearly as possible, enabling future researchers to find them in their respective locations.

Naturally, over the past decades, research has also entailed not only documents, but flesh and blood human beings. I have spoken with literally hundreds of persons over the course of this historical investigation, many of whom would not be pleased to find themselves identified here. In the Acknowledgments section, therefore, some individuals have been mentioned but without revealing how they assisted me or what type of information they offered. In the case of Chinese military officials, former CIA and FBI officers, and others with links to their governments, this is understandable. In the case of religious leaders and cult members, this is perhaps less so but just as necessary in many cases. I interviewed all these on a "deep background" understanding, and I have not allowed these interviews to form the core of this research but have instead bolstered their statements with documentation and independent corroboration.

In the case of the wandering bishops, I was—as discussed in the Appendix to Book I—personally involved with this phenomenon and knew many of the primary players during the 1960s and 1970s, and have since interviewed others in the past ten years. My previous association with Walter Propheta and his colleagues enabled me to open dialogues with surviving members of his operation, as well as with various sects, denominations, and other splinter groups.

Further, my personal association with members of various "cults" and New Age denominations going back thirty years has made it easier for me to understand the relationship that exists between cults, crime, and political maneuvering, including intelligence-gathering. I hasten to point out that not all cults have criminal or intelligence agency connections or interests; many of these groups are composed of sincere seekers after spiritual realities. Yet, even then, they and their technologies can be manipulated by others less scrupulous.

But, isn't that the theme of this work?

Salem Witchcraft and Pre-Revolutionary America

BELL, Michael E., *Food for the Dead: On the Trail of New England's Vampires*, Carroll & Graf, New York, 2001

BOYER, Paul and NISSENBAUM, Stephen, *Salem Village Witchcraft*, Northeastern University Press, Boston, 1993

—*Salem Possessed: The Social Origins of Witchcraft*, Harvard University Press, Cambridge, 1994

BRADFORD, William, *History of Plymouth Plantation 1620-1647*, Boston, 1912

BRESHAW, Elaine G. *Tituba: Reluctant Witch of Salem*, New York University Press, New York, 1996

BURR, George Lincoln, *Narratives of the Witchcraft Cases 1648-1706*, Scribners, New York, 1914

CAHILL, Robert Ellis, *New England's Viking and Indian Wars*, Old Saltbox Publishing, Danvers, (no date), ISBN 0916787-11-7

DEMOS, John Putnam, *Entertaining Satan: Witchcraft and the Culture of Early New England*, Oxford University Press, Oxford, 1983

DUNN, Oliver and KELLEY, James E. Jr., *The* Diario *of Chrisopher Columbus's First Voyage to America 1492-1493*, University of Oklahoma Press, Norman, 1991

GODBEER, Richard, *The Devil's Dominion: Magic and Religion in Early New England*, Cambridge University Press, Cambridge, 1994, ISBN 0-521-46670-9

HANSEN. Chadwick, *Witchcraft at Salem*, George Braziller, New York, 1992

HART, Albert Bushnell, ed., *American History Told by Contemporaries*, New York, 1898

LeBEAU, Bryan F., *The Story of the Salem Witch Trials*, Prentice Hall, New York, 1998

MATHER, Cotton, *Wonders of the Invisible World*, 1693

MORTON, Thomas, *Revels in New Canaan 1637*, reprinted in Hart, q.v.

STARKEY, Marion L., *The Devil in Massachusetts*, Anchor, New York, 1989

Mormonism

BROOKE, John L., *The Refiner's Fire*, Cambridge University Press, Cambridge, 1994, ISBN 0-521-34545-6

LARSON, Stan, *Quest for the Gold Plates: Thomas Stuart Ferguson's Archaeological Search for the Book of Mormon*, Freethinker Press, Salt Lake City, 1996

NAIFEH, Steven and SMITH, Gregory White, *The Mormon Murders*, Penguin, New York, 1989

OSTLING, Richard N. and OSTLING, Joan K., *Mormon America: The Power and the Promise*, Harper San Francisco, 1999

PERSUITTE, David, *Joseph Smith and the Origins of the Book of Mormon*, McFarland & Co., Jefferson, 2000

QUINN, D. Michael, *Early Mormonism and the Magic World View*, Signature Books, Salt Lake City, 1998

SMITH, Joseph Jr., *The Book of Mormon: Another Testament of Jesus Christ*, The Church of Jesus Christ of Latter-Day Saints, Salt Lake City, 1991

TANNER, Jerald and Sandra, *Mormon Spies, Hughes and the CIA*, Utah Lighthouse Ministry, Salt Lake City, 1976

American Prehistory

BRINE, Lindesey, *The Ancient Earthworks and Temples of the American Indians*, Oracle Publishing, Royston, 1996

BROSE, David S., BROWN, James A., and PENNEY, David W., *Ancient Art of the American Woodland Indians*, Harry N. Abrams, New York, 1985

CERAM, C.W., *The First American: A Story of North American Archaeology*, Harcourt Brace Jovanovich, New York, 1971

—*Hands on the Past*, Alfred A. Knopf, New York, 1966

FELL, Barry, *America BC: Ancient Settlers in the New World*, Pocket Books, NY, 1989

HOLAND, Hjalmar R., *Norse Discoveries and Explorations in America 982-1362*, Dover, New York, 1968

JENNINGS, Jesse D., *Prehistory of North America*, McGraw-Hill, NY, 1968

KENNEDY, Roger G., *Hidden Cities: the Discovery and Loss of Ancient North American Civilization*, The Free Press, New York, 1994

STRUEVER, Stuart and HOLTON, Felicia Antonelli, *Koster: Americans in Search of Their Prehistoric Past*, Anchor Press, New York, 1979

ROMAIN, William F., *Mysteries of the Hopewell*, University of Akron Press, Akron, 2000

WOODWARD, Susan L., and McDONALD, Jerry N., *Indian Mounds of the Middle Ohio Valley*, McDonald and Woodward, Blacksburg, 2002

Native American History

ARIAS, Larreta, A., *Popul Vuh: The Sacred Book of the Ancient Quiche Mayas*, Editorial Verdad y Vida, Mexico City

CHILTOSKY, Mary Ulmer, *Cherokee Words with Pictures*, Cherokee Publications, Cherokee, 1972

HINTON, Leanne, *Flutes of Fire: Essays on California Indian Languages*, Heyday Books,

Berkeley, 1994
KELLEY, Klara Bonsack and FRANCIS, Harris, *Navajo Sacred Places*, Indiana University Press, Bloomington, 1994
LEON-PORTILLA, Miguel, *The Broken Spears: The Aztec Account of the Conquest of Mexico*, Beacon Press, Boston, 1992
NABOKOV, Peter, *Native American Testimony*, Penguin, New York, 1991

World Prehistory

BARBER, Elizabeth Wayland, *The Mummies of Urumchi*, Pan Books, London, 1999
CLAPP, Nicholas, *The Road to UBAR: Finding the Atlantis of the Sands*, Mariner Books, Boston, 1999
CONNAH, Graham, *African Civilizations*, Cambridge University Press, Cambridge, 1990
OPPENHEIMER, Stephen, *Eden in the East*, Weidenfeld & Nicolson, London, 1998
RUDGLEY, Richard, *Lost Civilizations of the Stone Age*, Arrow, London, 1999

Charles Manson and the Son of Sam

ANDERSEN, Christopher, *Citizen Jane*, Henry Holt, New York, 1990
BRAVIN, Jess, *Squeaky: The Life and Times of Lynette Alice Fromme*, St Martins Press, New York, 1997
BUGLIOSI, Vincent, *Helter Skelter*, Bantam Books, New York, 1988
—*Helter Skelter*, Bantam Books, New York, 1995
CAPOTE, Truman, *Music for Chameleons*, New American Library, New York, 1981
COOPER, David E., *The Manson Murders: A Philosophical Inquiry*, Schenkman Publishing, Cambridge, 1974
GILMORE, John, *Manson*, Amok, Los Angeles, 2000
GUILES, Fred Lawrence, *Jane Fonda*, Doubleday, New York, 1982
KING, Greg, *Sharon Tate and the Manson Murders*, Barricade Books, New York, 2000
PHILLIPS, John, *Papa John: An Autobiography*, Dell, New York, 1987
POLANSKI, Roman, *Roman*, William Morrow, New York, 1984
SANDERS, Ed, *The Family*, Dutton, New York, 1971
—*The Family*, Signet, New York, 1989
SCHRECK, Nikolas, *The Manson File*, Amok, San Francisco, 1988
TERRY, Maury, *The Ultimate Evil*, Bantam, New York, 1989, ISBN 0-553-27601-8
TERRY, Maury, *The Ultimate Evil*, Barnes & Noble, New York, 1999, ISBN 0-7607-1393-6
WICK, Steve, *Bad Company: Drugs, Hollywood, and the Cotton Club Murder*, Harcourt, Brace, Jovanovich, New York, 1990, ISBN 0-15-110445-X

Wandering Bishops

ANSON, Peter, *Bishops At Large*, October House, New York, 1965
BRANDRETH, Henry R.T., *Episcopi Vagantes and the Anglican Church*, Society For Promoting Christian Knowledge, London, 1947
BURGESS, Michael, *Lords Temporal and Lords Spiritual*, The Borgo Press, San Bernardino, 1995, ISBN 0-89370-426-1

MELTON, J. Gordon, *Encyclopedia of American Religions*, McGrath, Wilmington, 1978
SMITH, Charles Merrill, *How To Become A Bishop Without Being Religious*, Pocket Books, New York, 1966

Interviews and Personal Contacts:

ABRUGNEDO, Dom Lorenzo (Archbishop), personal communications 2004
BLACKBURST, David, personal communications regarding David Ferrie
BRENNAN, Andrei (Archbishop), personal communications 2004
CHIASSON, John "Christian", (Bishop), personal communications and interviews 1968-1969
DeVALITCH, Count Lorenzo Michel Pierre (Bishop) personal communications and interviews 1968-1969
DeWITOW, Theodosius (Archbishop), personal communications 1967
DOWLING, Kris (Bishop), personal communications 1977-2005
GUTHRIE, Colin (Archbishop), personal communications 2004-2005
HILL, Leonard G. (Bishop), personal communications and interviews 1968-1969
HYDE, George Augustine (Archbishop), personal communications and interviews 2004-2006
KONTAGEORGIOS, Eftimios (Bishop), personal communications 1971
MAKARIOS, (Bishop), personal communications and interviews 2004-2005
MARKUS, Mar (Archbishop), personal communications 2004
MOISEY, Archbishop-Metropolitan, personal communications 2004-2005
MYLES, Ivan (Archbishop), personal communications 2004
NUNEZ, John (Bishop), personal communications 2004
PENNACHIO, Andre (Bishop), personal communications and interviews 1968-1969
PERRY, David, personal communications regarding David Ferrie
PIERRE, Lawrence (Bishop), personal communications and interviews 1968-1969
PITT-KETHLEY, Fiona, personal communications 2005
PROPHETA, Walter (Archbishop Vladimir), personal communications and interviews 1968-1969
RICCIO, Dominic (Reverend), personal communications 2005
SCHILLEREFF, William (Reverend), personal communications 2004 – 2005
"SOROR M.A.," Societas Rosicruciana In America, personal communications 2004

Nazism and World War II

AARONS, Mark & LOFTUS, John, *Unholy Trinity: The Vatican, the Nazis, and Soviet Intelligence*, St Martin's Press, New York, 1991
BAIGENT, Michael & LEIGH, Richard, *Secret Gemany*, Penguin, London, 1994
BAR-ZOHAR, Michael, *Bitter Scent: the Case of L'Oreal, Nazis, and the Arab Boycott*, Dutton, New York, 1996
BIRD, Lt. Col. Eugene K., *Prisoner #7, Rudolf Hess*, Viking Press, New York, 1974
BLACK, Edwin, *IBM and the Holocaust*, Little Brown, Boston, 2001
BLUM, Howard, *Wanted! The Search for Nazis in America*, Quadrangle, New York, 1977
BOWER, Tom, *Blind Eye to Murder*, Warner Books, London, 1997

—*The Paperclip Conspiracy*, Michael Joseph, London, 1987
BREITMAN, Richard, *Official Secrets*, Penguin, London, 1998
CLAY, Catrine & Leapman, Michael, *Master Race: the Lebensborn Experiment in Nazi Germany*, Coronet Books, London, 1995
COHN, Norman, *Warrant for Genocide*, Harper & Row, New York, 1967
CORNWELL, John, *Il Papa di Hitler: La storia segreta di Pio XII*, Garzanti Libri, Italy, 2000
FARAGO, Ladislas, *Aftermath: Martin Bormann and the Fourth Reich*, Simon & Schuster, New York, 1974
—*The Last Days of Patton*, Berkley Books, New York, 1982
FORD, Henry, *The International Jew*, Global Publishers, Johannesburg, 1997
FRANZINELLI, Mimmo, *Delatori*, Mondadori, Milan, 2001
GODWIN, Jocelyn, *Arktos: The Polar Myth in Science, Symbolism and Nazi Survival*, Phanes Press, Grand Rapids, 1993
GOODRICK-CLARKE, Nicholas, *The Occult Roots of Nazism*, New York University Press, New York, 1992
GROUEFF, Stephane, *Manhattan Project*, Little Brown, Boston, 1967
HABE, Hans, *Agent of the Devil*, George S. Harrap, London, 1958
HAYMAN, Ronald, *Hitler and Geli*, Bloomsbury, London, 1998
HIGHAM, Charles, *American Swastika*, Doubleday, New York, 1985
HUNT, Linda, *L'affaire Paperclip*, Stock, Paris, 1995
INFIELD, Glenn B., *Secrets of the SS*, Jove Books, New York, 1990
JONES, R.V., *Most Secret War: British Scientific Intelligence 1939-1945*, Hamish Hamilton, London, 1978
HUTTON, J. Bernard, *Hess: The Man and His Mission*, Macmillan, New York, 1971
LANGER, Walter C., *The Mind of Adolf Hitler*, Basic Books, New York, 1972
LAPON, Lenny, *Mass Murderers in White Coats*, Psychiatric Genocide Research Institute, Springfield, 1986
LEVENDA, Peter, *Unholy Alliance*, Avon, New York, 1995
—*Unholy Alliance*, Continuum, New York, 2002
LIFTON, Robert Jay, *The Nazi Doctors*, Basic Books, New York, 2000
LOFTUS, John & AARONS, Mark, *The Secret War Against the Jews*, St Martin's Griffin, New York, 1997
McGOVERN, James, *Crossbow and Overcast*, William Morrow, New York, 1964
MEDAWAR, Jean & PYKE, David, *Hitler's Gift: Scientists Who Fled Nazi Germany*, Piatkus, London, 2000
MUELLER-HILL, Benno, *Murderous Science*, Oxford University Press, Oxford, 1988
POSNER, Gerald L. & WARE, John, *Mengele: The Complete Story*, Dell, New York, 1987
RAHN, Otto, *La Cour de Lucifer*, Tchou, Paris, 1974
SERRANO, Miguel, *La Resurreccion del Heroe*, Solar Editores, Bogota, 1987
—*NOS: Book of the Resurrection*, Routledge Kegan & Paul, London, 1984
—*El Cordon Dorado*, Editorial Solar, Bogota, 1992
SICHROVSKY, Peter, *Incurably German*, Swan Books, Pine Plains, 2001
SIMPSON, Christopher, *Blowback*, Weidenfeld & Nicolson, New York, 1988

—*The Splendid Blond Beast*, Grove Press, New York, 1993
SMITH, Richard Harris, *OSS: The Secret History of America's First Central Intelligence Agency*, University of California Press, Berkeley, 1981
THOMAS, Hugh, *The Murder of Adolf Hitler*, St Martins Press, New York, 1995
JOVIN, M.E., *Los Protocolos de los Sabios de Sion*, Editores Mexicanos Unidos, Mexico
VON LANG, Jochen (ed.), *Eichmann Interrogated: Transcripts from the Archives of the Israeli Police*, Vintage Books, New York, 1983

Ashland, Kentucky

AP, "War on Poverty Figure Accused of Murder," *New York Times*, April 26, 1992, p. 30
Bloomberg Business News, "Ashland Oil Settles Civil Suits Over Air Pollution," *New York Times*, Feb 23, 1993, p. D5
ANON, *A History of Ashland, Kentucky 1786-1954*, Ashland Centennial Committee, 1954
ANON, *Ashland Historical Tour*, Ashland/Boyd County Tourism Commission, Ashland, 1990
HANNERS, Arnold, *Ashland's Pictorial Past*, Ashland, 1986 WALD, Matthew L., "Ashland Oil Appoints Successor to President," *New York Times*, Nov. 8, 1991, p. D4

Bluebird, Multiplicity and Mind-Control

Diagnostic and Statistical Manual, Mental Disorders (first edition), American Psychiatric Association, Washington DC, 1965
BAIN, Donald, *The Control of Candy Jones*, Playboy Press, Chicago, 1976, ISBN 0-87223-457-6
—*Long John Nebel*, MacMillan, New York, 1974, ISBN 0-02-505950-5
COLLINS, Anne, *In The Sleep Room*, Key Porter Books, Toronto, 1997, ISBN 1-55013-932-0
DeBOLD, Richard C. & LEAF, Russell C., *LSD, Man & Society*, Wesleyan University Press, Middletown, 1968, LOC 67-24111
FLOURNOY, Theodore, *From India to the Planet Mars: A Case of Multiple Personality with Imaginary Languages*, Princeton University Press, Princeton, 1994, ISBN 0-691-00101-4
HUXLEY, Aldous, *The Doors of Perception and Heaven and Hell*, Flamingo, London, 1994, ISBN 0-00-654731-1
KEYES, Daniel, *The Minds of Billy Milligan*, Bantam, New York, 1995, ISBN 0-553-26381-1
LEE, Martin A., & SHLAIN, Bruce, *Acid Dreams: The Complete Social History of LSD: The CIA, the Sixties, and Beyond*, Grove Weidenfeld, New York, 1992, ISBN 0-8021-3062-3
LIFTON, Robert Jay, *Thought Reform and the Psychology of Totalism: A Study of 'Brainwashing' in China*, University of North Carolina Press, Chapel Hill, 1989, ISBN 0-8078-4253-2
LOFTUS, Elizabeth & KETCHAM, Katherine, *The Myth of Repressed Memory: False Memories and Allegations of Sexual Abuse*, St Martin's Griffin, New York, 1994, ISBN 0-312-14123-8
MARKS, John, *The Search for the "Manchurian Candidate": The CIA and Mind Control*, Times Books, New York, 1979, ISBN 0-8129-0773-6
—*The Search for the "Manchurian Candidate": The CIA and Mind Control*, WW Norton, New York, 1988 edition, ISBN 0-393-30794-4
MEDVEDEV, Zhores & MEDVEDEV, Roy, *A Question of Madness: Repression by Psychiatry in the Soviet Union*, Vintage, New York, 1972, ISBN 0-394-71816-X
ROSS, Colin, *Bluebird: Deliberate Creation of Multiple Personality by Psychiatrists*, Manitou

Communications, Richardson, 2000, ISBN 0-9704525-1-9
—*Dissociative Identity Disorder: Diagnosis, Clinical Features, and Treatment of Multiple Personality*, John Wiley & Sons, New York, 1997, ISBN 0-471-13265-9
SARGANT, William, *Battle for the Mind*, Malor, Cambridge, 1997, ISBN 188353606-5
SIMPSON, Christopher, *Science of Coercion: Communication Research & Psychological Warfare 1945-1960*, Oxford University Press, New York, 1996, ISBN 0-19-510292-4
SINASON, Valerie (ed.), *Attachment, Trauma and Multiplicity: Working with Dissociative Identity Disorder*, Brunner-Routledge, Hove, 2002, ISBN 0-415-19556-X
STEVENS, Jay, *Storming Heaven: LSD and the American Dream*, Atlantic Monthly Press, New York, 1987, ISBN 0-87113-076-9
THOMAS, Gordon, *Journey Into Madness*, Bantam Books, New York, 1990, ISBN 0-553-28413-4
WEINSTEIN, Harvey M., *Psychiatry and the CIA: Victims of Mind Control*, American Psychiatric Press, Washington DC, 1990, ISBN 0-88048-363-6
YATES, Frances A., *The Art of Memory*, University of Chicago Press, Chicago, 1966, SBN 0-226-95001-8

President John F. Kennedy Assassination

Report of the Warren Commission On The Assassination of President Kennedy EPSTEIN, Edward Jay, *Legend: The Secret World of Lee Harvey Oswald*, Hutchinson, London, 1978
FELTZER, James H. (ed.), *Assassination Science: Experts Speak Out on the Death of JFK*, Catfeet Press, Chicago, 2001
—*Murder in Dealey Plaza*, Catfeet Press, Chicago, 2001
GARRISON, Jim, *On The Trail of the Assassins*, Warner Books, New York, 1991
KANTOR, Seth, *The Ruby Cover-Up*, Zebra Books, New York, 1992
GIANCANA, Sam and Chuck, *Double Cross*, Warner Books, New York, 1992
HINCKLE, Warren and TURNER, William, *The Fish Is Red: the Story of the Secret War Against Castro*, Harper & Row, New York, 1981
KIRKWOOD, James, *American Grotesque*, Harper Perennial, New York, 1992
MAILER, Norman, *Oswald's Tale*, Ballantine, New York, 1996, ISBN 0-345-40437-8
MARRS, Jim, *Crossfire: the Plot that Killed Kennedy*, Carroll & Graf, New York, 1990
MORROW, Robert D., *First Hand Knowledge: How I Participated in the CIA-Mafia Murder of President Kennedy*, SPI Books, New York, 1992
PIPER, Michael Collins, *Final Judgment: The Missing Link in the JFK Assassination Conspiracy*, The Center for Historical Review, Washington, 1998
RUSSELL, Dick, *The Man Who Knew Too Much*, Carroll & Graf, New York, 2003
RUSSO, Gus, *Live By The Sword: the Secret War Against Castro and the Death of JFK*, Bancroft Press, Baltimore, 1998
SCOTT, Peter Dale, *Deep Politics and the Death of JFK*, University of California Press, Berkeley, 1996
SCOTT, William E., *November 22, 1963: A Reference Guide to the JFK Assassination*. University Press of America, Lanham, 1999
SUMMERS, Anthony, *The Kennedy Conspiracy*, Warner Books, New York, 1996
SZULC, Tad & MEYER, Karl E., *The Cuban Invasion: the Chronicle of a Disaster*, Ballantine

Books, New York, 1962
SZULC, Tad, *Fidel: A Critical Portrait*, William Morrow, New York, 1986
WYDEN, Peter, *Bay of Pigs: The Untold Story*, Simon & Schuster, New York, 1979

Senator Robert F. Kennedy Assassination

KLABER, William and MELANSON, Philip H., *Shadow Play: The Untold Story of the Robert F. Kennedy Assassination*, St Martin's Paperbacks, New York, 1998
MELANSON, Philip H., *The Robert F. Kennedy Assassination: New Revelations on the Conspiracy and Cover-Up 1968-1991*, SPI Books, New York, 1994
TURNER, William and CHRISTIAN, John, *The Assassination of Robert F. Kennedy: The Conspiracy and Cover-Up*, Thunder's Mouth Press, New York, 1993

John Lennon Assassination

BRESLER, Fenton, *Who Killed John Lennon?*, St Martin's Paperbacks, New York, 1990
JONES, Jack, *Let Me Take You Down*, Villard Books, New York, 1992

Marilyn Monroe Assassination

BROWN, Peter Harry & BARHAM, Patte B., *Marilyn: The Last Take*, Dutton, New York, 1992, ISBN 0-525-93485-5
SMITH, Matthew, *The Men Who Murdered Marilyn*, Bloomsbury, London, 1996
SUMMERS, Anthony, *Goddess: The Secret Lives of Marilyn Monroe*, Indigo, London, 1985
WOLFE, Donald H., *The Assassination of Marilyn Monroe*, Warner Books, New York, 1998

Serial Murder and True Crime

BRUSSEL, James A., *Casebook of a Crime Psychiatrist*, Dell, New York, 1970
COOK, Thomas H., *Early Graves*, Onyx, New York, 1992, ISBN 0-451-40296-0
COX, Mike, *The Confessions of Henry Lee Lucas*, Pocket Star, New York, 1991, ISBN 0-671-70665-9
CROWLEY, Kieran, *Sleep My Little Dead*, St Martin's, New York, 1997, ISBN 0-312-96339-4
DEAR, William, *The Dungeon Master*, Ballantine, New York, 1985, ISBN 0-345-32695-4
DENTON, Sally, *The Bluegrass Conspiracy*, Doubleday, New York, 1990, ISBN 0-385-26272-8
DOUGLAS, John & OLSHAKER, Mark, *Journey Into Darkness*, Pocket Books, New York, 1997, ISBN 0-671-00394-1
FLOWERS, Anna, *Blind Fury*, Pinnacle, New York, 1993, ISBN 1-55817-719-1
GANEY, Terry, *Innocent Blood*, St Martin's, New York, 1989, ISBN 0-312-92269-8
GRAYSMITH, Robert, *Zodiac*, Berkley, New York, 1987, ISBN 0-425-09808-7
—*Zodiac Unmasked*, Berkley, New York, 2003, ISBN 0-425-18943-0
KELLY, Susan, *The Boston Stranglers*, Kensington, New York, 2002, ISBN 0-7860-1466-0
KEPPEL, Robert D., *Signature Killers*, Pocket Books, New York, 1997, ISBN 0-671-00130-2
—*The Riverman: Ted Bundy and the Hunt for the Green River Killer*, Pocket Books, New York, 1995, ISBN 0-671-86763-6
KNOWLTON, Janice, *Daddy Was the Black Dahlia Killer*, Pocket Books, New York, 1995, ISBN 0-671-88084-5
LAVERGNE, Gary M., *A Sniper In The Tower: The Charles Whitman Murders*, Bantam Books,

New York, 1998, ISBN 0-553-57959-2
LEYTON, Elliott, *Sole Survivor: Children Who Murder Their Families*, Seal, Toronto, 1990, ISBN 0-7704-2408-2
MAAS, Peter, *In A Child's Name*, Pocket Books, New York, 1991, ISBN 0-671-74619-7
MARTINEZ, Thomas, *Brotherhood of Murder*, Pocket Books, New York, 1990, ISBN 0-6711-67858-2
McGINNISS, Joe, *Fatal Vision*, Signet, New York, 1984, ISBN 0-451-13098-7
MICHAUD, Stephen G., & AYNESWORTH, Hugh, *Ted Bundy: Conversations with a Killer*, Signet, New York, 1989, ISBN 0-451-16355-9
MOSS, Jason, *The Last Victim*, Warner Vision, New York, 2000, ISBN 0-446-60827-0
NEWTON, Michael, *Rope: The Twisted Life and Times of Harvey Glatman*, Pocket Books, New York, 1998, ISBN 0-671-01747-0
NOGUCHI, Thomas T., *Coroner At Large*, Simon & Schuster, New York, 1985, ISBN 0-671-54462-4
NORRIS, Joel, *Serial Killers*, Doubleday, New York, 1988, ISBN 0-385-26328-7
NORRIS, Joel, *Henry Lee Lucas: The Shocking True Story of America's Most Notorious Serial Killer*, Zebra Books, New York, 1991, ISBN 0-8217-3564-0
NORRIS, Joel, *Jeffrey Dahmer*, Pinnacle, New York, 1992, ISBN 1-55817-661-6
NORRIS, Joel, *Arthur Shawcross: The Genesee River Killer*, Pinnacle, New York, 1992, ISBN 1-55817-592-X
NORRIS, Joel, *Walking Time Bombs*, Bantam, New York, 1992, ISBN 0-553-28996-9
O'BRIEN, Darcy, *A Dark and Bloody Ground*, HarperCollins, New York, 1992, ISBN 0-06-017958-9
OLSEN, Jack, *The Misbegotten Son: A Serial Killer and His Victims, The True Story of Arthur Shawcross*, Island Books, New York, 1993, ISBN 0-440-21646-X
OLSEN, Jack, *Hastened to the Grave: The Gypsy Murder Investigation*, St Martin's, New York, 1998, ISBN 0-312-96699-7
PHILBIN, Tom, *Murder U.S.A.*, Warner, New York, 1992, ISBN 0-446-36091-0499
RESSLER, Robert K. & SHACHTMAN, Tom, *Whoever Fights Monsters*, St Martin's, New York, 1993, ISBN 0-312-95044-6
RESSLER, Robert K. & SHACHTMAN, Tom, *I Have Lived In the Monster: Inside the Minds of the World's Most Notorious Serial Killers*, St Martin's, New York, 1998, ISBN 0-312-96429-3
RHODES, Richard, *Why They Kill: The Discoveries of a Maverick Criminologist*, Vintage, New York, 2000, ISBN 0-375-70248-2
ROSEN, Fred, *Flesh Collectors*, Pinnacle, New York, 2003, ISBN 0-7860-1583-7
RULE, Ann, *The I-5 Killer*, Signet, New York, 1988, ISBN 0-451-16559-4
SCHECHTER, Harold, *Bestial: The Savage Trail of a True American Monster*, Pocket Books, New York, 1999, ISBN 0-671-73218-8
SCHREIBER, Flora Rheta, *The Shoemaker: The Anatomy of a Psychotic*, Signet, New York, 1984, ISBN 0-451-12855-9
SEXTON, David, *The Strange World of Thomas Harris*, Short Books, London, 2001, ISBN 0-571-20845-2
SINGULAR, Stephen, *Talked To Death: The Life and Murder of Alan Berg*, William Morrow,

New York, 1987, ISBN 0-688-06154-0
SMITH, Carlton & GUILLEN, Tomas, *The Search for the Green River Killer,* Onyx, New York, 1991, ISBN 0-451-40239-1
SULLIVAN, Terry, *Killer Clown: The John Wayne Gacy Murders,* Pinnacle, New York, 1993, ISBN 1-55817-476-1
THOMPSON, Thomas, *Serpentine,* Robinson, London, 2001, ISBN 1-84119-384-4
VORPAGEL, Russell, *Profiles In Murder: An FBI Legend Dissects Killers and Their Crimes,* Dell, New York, 2001, ISBN 0-440-23552-9
WAMBAUGH, Joseph, *Echoes In the Darkness,* Bantam, New York, 1987, ISBN 0-553-26932-1
WHITTLE, Brian & RITCHIE, Jean, *Prescription for Murder: The True Story of Mass Murderer Dr. Harold Frederick Shipman,* Warner, New York, 2000, ISBN 0-7515-2998-2

Jack the Ripper

CORNWELL, Patricia, *Portrait of a Killer: Jack The Ripper, Case Closed,* Little, Brown, Boston, 2000, ISBN 0-316-72508-0
EDWARDS, Ivor, *Jack the Ripper's Black Magic Rituals,* John Blake, London, 2003, ISBN 1-90403-487-X
EVANS, Stewart & GAINEY, Paul, *Jack The Ripper: First American Serial Killer,* Kodansha International, New York, 1998, ISBN 1-56836-257-9
GRAHAM, Anne E. & EMMAS, Carol, *The Last Victim: The extraordinary life of Florence Maybrick, the wife of Jack the Ripper,* Headline, London, 1999, ISBN 0-7472-6206-3
HARRIS, Melvin, *The True Face of Jack the Ripper,* Michael O'Mara, London,1995, ISBN 1-85479-726-3

Cult Crime

CLARKSON, Wensley, *In The Name of Satan,* St Martin's, New York, 1998, ISBN 0-312-96389-0
DUNNING, John, *Mystical Murders,* Arrow, London, 1989, ISBN 0-09-963530-5
HICKS, Robert D., *In Pursuit of Satan: The Police and the Occult,* Prometheus, Buffalo, 1991, ISBN 0-87975-604-7
HUBNER, John & GRUSON, Lindsey, *Monkey On A Stick: Murder, Madness, and the Hare Krishnas,* Onyx, New York, 1990, ISBN 0-451-40187-5
KAHANER, Larry, *Cults That Kill: Probing the Underworld of Occult Crime,* Warner, New York, 1989, ISBN 0-446-35637-9
LARSON, Bob, *Satanism: The Seduction of America's Youth,* Thomas Nelson, Nashville, 1989, ISBN 0-8047-3034-9
LINEDECKER, Clifford L., *The Vampire Killers,* St Martin's, New York, 1998, ISBN 0-312-96672-5
LYONS, Arthur, *Satan Wants You: The Cult of Devil Worship in America,* Mysterious Press, New York, 1989, ISBN 0-445-40822-7
MANDELSBERG, Rose G. (ed.), *Cult Killers,* Pinnacle, New York, 1991, ISBN 1-55817-528-8
MOORE, Carol, *The Davidian Massacre: Disturbing Questions About Waco Which Must Be Answered,* Legacy Communications, Franklin, 1995, ISBN 1-880692-22-8
NEWTON, Michael, *Raising Hell: An Encyclopedia of Devil Worship and Satanic Crime,* Avon,

New York, 1993, ISBN 0-380-76837-2
SCAMMELL, Henry, *Mortal Remains: A True Story of Ritual Murder*, Harper, New York, 1992, ISBN 0-06-109958-9
SPENCER, Judith, *Satan's High Priest: A True Story*, Pocket, New York, 1998, ISBN 0-671-00790-4
WILSON, Colin, *Order of Assassins: The Psychology of Murder*, Panther, London, 1972
WINCHESTER, Simon, *The Professor and the Madman*, Harper, New York, 1999, ISBN 0-06-103022-8

Matamoros

HUMES, Edward, *Buried Secrets: A True Story of Serial Murder*, Signet, New York, 1992, ISBN 0-451-17164-0
PROVOST, Gary, *Across The Border: The True Story of the Satanic Cult Killings in Matamoros, Mexico*, Pocket, New York, 1989, ISBN 0-671-69319-0
SCHUTZE, Jim, *Caulron of Blood: The Matamoros Cult Killings*, Avon, New York, 1989, ISBN 0-380-75997-7

Cathars, Templars, Freemasonry and the Assassin Cult

ALARCON H., Rafael, *A la sombra de los Templarios*, Martinez Roca, Barcelona, 1986
BAIGENT, Michael & LEIGH, Richard & LINCOLN, Henry, *Holy Blood, Holy Grail*, Dell, New York, 1983
—*The Messianic Legacy*, Dell, New York, 1989
BAIGENT, Michael & LEIGH, Richard, *The Temple and the Lodge*, Arcade, New York, 1989
—*The Elixir and the Stone*, Penguin, London, 1997
BAIGENT, Michael, *Ancient Traces*, Penguin, London, 1998
—*From the Omens of Babylon: Astrology and Ancient Mesopotamia*, Arkana, London, 1994
BARBER, Malcolm, *The Cathars*, Pearson Education, Harlow, 2000
BENITEZ, J.J., *Caballo de Troya*, Planeta, Barcelona, 1996
BINKS, Walter & GILBERT, R.A., *The Treasure of Montsegur*, Crucible, London, 1987
BOUTTIER, Michel, *Cathedrales: Comment elles sont construites*, Creation et Recherche, Le Mans, 1989
BULLOCK, Steven C., *Revolutionary Brotherhood: Freemasonry and the Transformation of the American Social Order 1730-1840*, University of North Carolina Press, Chapel Hill, 1996, ISBN 0-8078-4750-X
CHARPENTIER, Louis, *The Mysteries of Chartres Cathedral*, RILKO, London, 1972
GARDNER, Laurence, *Bloodline of the Holy Grail*, Element, Dorset, 1999
GILBERT, Adrian, *The Holy Kingdom*, Corgi Books, London, 1999
GOLTHER, Wolfgang, *Parzival und der Graal*, J.B. Metzlersche, Stuttgart, 1925
HANCOCK, Graham, *The Sign and the Seal*, Mandarin, London, 1996
KNIGHT, Christopher & LOMAS, Robert, *The Hiram Key*, Arrow, London, 1997
—*The Second Messiah*, Arrow, London, 1998
LANDON, H.C. Robbins, *Mozart and the Masons*, Thames & Hudson, London, 1991
NIEL, Fernand, *Les Cathares de Montsegur*, Robert Laffont, Paris, 1973
OLDENBOURG, Zoe, *Massacre at Montsegur*, Dorset Press, New York, 1990

PICKNETT, Lynn & PRINCE, Clive, *The Templar Revelation*, Corgi Books, London, 1998
ROBIN, Jean, *Operacion Orth: el increible misterio de Rennes-le-Chateau*, Heptada, Madrid, 1990
ROBINSON, John J., *Born In Blood: The Lost Secrets of Freemasonry*, M. Evans & Co., New York, 1989, ISBN 0-87131-602-1
De SEDE, Gerard, *El misterio de Rennes-le-Chateau*, Martinez Roca, Barcelona, 1993
Von SIMSON, Otto, *The Gothic Cathedral*, Harper Torchbooks, New York, 1964
STEVENSON, David, *The Origins of Freemasonry: Scotland's Century 1590-1710*, Cambridge University Press, Cambridge, 2000, ISBN 0-521-39654-9
WILSON, Ian, *The Blood and the Shroud*, Orion, London, 1998

Secret Societies, Witchcraft and the Occult

ANTON, Ted, *Eros, Magic, and the Murder of Professor Culianu*, Northwestern University Press, Evanston, 1996, ISBN 0-8101-1396-1
BARTON, Blanche, *The Secret Life of a Satanist: The Authorized Biography of Anton LaVey*, Feral House, Los Angeles, 1992, ISBN 0-922915-12-1
CARTER, John, *Sex and Rockets: The Occult World of Jack Parsons*, Feral House, Venice CA, 1999, ISBN 0-922915-56-3
CLARK, Stuart, *Thinking With Demons: The Idea of Witchcraft in Early Modern Europe*, Oxford University Press, Oxford, 1999, ISBN 0-19-820808-1
CROWLEY, Aleister, *Magick In Theory and Practice*, Dover, New York, 1976, ISBN 0-486-23295-6
DASH, Mike, *Borderlands*, Arrow, London, 1997, ISBN 0-7493-2396-5
FLINT, Valerie I.J., *The Rise of Magic in Early Medieval Europe*, Princeton University Press, Princeton, 1994, ISBN 0-691-00110-3
FLYNN, Kevin, & GERHARDT, Gary, *The Silent Brotherhood*, Signet, New York, 1995, ISBN 0-451-16786-4
GRANT, Kenneth, *The Magical Revival*, Skoob, London, 1972, ISBN 1-871438-37-3
—*Aleister Crowley and the Hidden God*, Skoob, London, 1973, ISBN 1-871438-36-5
—*Cults of the Shadow*, Skoob, London, 1975, ISBN 1-871438-67-5
—*Nightside of Eden*, Skoob, London, 1977, ISBN 1-871438-72-1
—*Outside the Circles of Time*, Frederick Muller, London, 1980, ISBN 0-584-10468-5
—*Hecate's Fountain*, Skoob, London, 1992, ISBN 1-871438-96-9
—*Outer Gateways*, Skoob, London, 1994, ISBN 1-871438-12-8
HOWARD, Michael, *The Occult Conspiracy*, Destiny, Rochester, 1989, ISBN 0-89281-251-6
HYATT, Christoper S., *Rebels & Devils: The Psychology of Liberation*, New Falcon, Tempe, 1996, ISBN 1-56184-121-8
KEEL, John A., *The Mothman Prophecies*, IllumiNet Press, Lilburn, 1991, ISBN 0-9626534-3-8
KRAMER, Heinrich & SPRENGER, James, *The Malleus Maleficarum*, Dover, New York, 1971, ISBN 0-486-22802-9
MILLEGAN, Kris (ed.), *Fleshing Out Skull & Bones: Investigations Into America's Most Powerful Secret Society*, Trine Day, Walterville, 2003, ISBN 0-9720207-2-1
OVASON, David, *The Zelator: The Secret Journals of Mark Hedsel*, Arrow, London, 1999, ISBN 0-09-925503-0
PARFREY, Adam (ed.), *Apocalypse Culture*, Feral House, San Francisco, 1990, ISBN 0-922915-

05-9
PARKER, John, *At The Heart of Darkness: Witchcraft, Black Magic and Satanism Today*, Citadel, New York, 1993, ISBN 0-8065-1428-0
PAUWELS, Louis & BERGIER, Jacques, *The Morning of the Magicians*, Mayflower, London, 1973
REGARDIE, Israel & STEPHENSEN, P.R., *The Legend of Aleister Crowley*, Falcon Press, Phoenix, 1983, ISBN 0-941404-20-X
SELIGMANN, Kurt, *The History of Magic and the Occult*, Gramercy, New York, 1997, ISBN 0-517-15032-8
SHAH, Idries, *The Secret Lore of Magic*, Citadel, Secaucus, 1972, ISBN 0-8065-0004-2
SMITH, Michelle & PAZDER, Lawrence, *Michelle Remembers*, Congdon & Lattes, New York, 1980, ISBN 0-312-92531-X
STARR, Martin P., *The Unknown God: W.T. Smith and the Thelemites*, Teitan Press, Bolingbrook, 2003, ISBN 0-933429-07-X
SUTTON, Antony C., *America's Secret Establishment:An Introduction to the Order of Skull & Bones*, Trine Day, Walterville, 2002, ISBN 0-9720207-0-5
STRIEBER, Whitley, *The Key*, Walker & Collier, San Antonio, 2001
—*The Path*, Walker & Collier, San Antonio, 2002
SYMONDS, John, *The Great Beast: The Life of Aleister Crowley*, Rider & Co., London, 1951
TEMPLE, Robert, *The Sirius Mystery*, St Martin's Press, New York, 1976, ISBN 0-312-72731-3;
—*The Sirius Mystery*, Arrow, London, 1999, ISBN 0-09-925744-0
WAITE, Arthur Edward, *The Book of Ceremonial Magic*, Barnes & Noble, New York, 1999, ISBN 0-7607-1196-8
WEBB, James, *The Occult Establishment*, Open Court, La Salle, 1991, ISBN 0-87548-434-4
WILSON, Colin, *The Occult*, Grafton, London, 1978, ISBN 0-586-05050-7
YATES, Frances A., *The Occult Philosophy in the Elizabethan Age*, Ark Paperbacks, London, 1983, ISBN 0-7448-0001-3

Interviews and Personal Contacts:

ADLER,Margot
BECK, Elizabeth
BRODSKY, Allyn
BUCKLAND, Raymond
BUCZYNSKI, Edward
CAPURO, Richard
CLAREMONT, Bonnie
JAMES, Ed
KING, Francis
KIRWAN, Larry
MARTELLO, Leo
McMURTRY, Grady
MENSCH, Martin
MILLS, Malcolm
RANDOLPH, Ellen
SLATER, Herman

SOLOMON, Jay
WASSERMAN, James

Richard Nixon and Watergate

The Presidential Transcripts, Dell, New York, 1974

The Watergate Hearings, Bantam Books, New York, 1973

COLODNY, Len and GETTLIN, Robert, *Silent Coup: The Removal of a President*, St Martin's Paperbacks, New York, 1992

HOUGAN, Jim, *Secret Agenda: Watergate, Deep Throat and the CIA*, Random House, New York, 1984

—*Spooks: The Haunting of America – The Private Use of Secret Agents*, William Morrow & Co., New York, 1978

LASKY, Victor, *It Didn't Start With Watergate*, The Dial Press, New York, 1977

LIDDY, G. Gordon, *Will: The Autobiography*, Dell, New York, 1980

LUKAS, J, Anthony, *Nightmare: The Underside of the Nixon Years*, Viking Press, New York, 1976

MAGRUDER, Jeb Stuart, *An American Life: One Man's Road to Watergate*, Pocket Books, New York, 1975

SUMMERS, Anthony, *The Arrogance of Power: The Secret World of Richard Nixon*, Penguin, New York, 2001

WOOLCOTT, Alexander and KAUFMAN, George S., *The Dark Tower: A Melodrama*, Random House, New York, 1934

SHEEHAN, Neil, et al., *The Pentagon Papers*, Bantam Books, New York, 1971

Iran-Contra

HONNEGAR, Barbara, *October Surpirse*, Tudor, 1989

HOPSICKER, Daniel, *Barry & 'the boys' – The CIA, the Mob and America's Secret History*, MadCow Press, 2000

KWITNY, Jonathan, *The Crimes of Patriots*, Simon & Schuster, New York, 1988

ROGIN, Michael, *Ronald Reagan: the Movie and Other Episodes in Political Demonology*, University of California Press, Berkeley, 1988

SICK, Gary, *October Surprise*, Times Books, New York, 1991

Vast Right-Wing Conspiracy

DIAMOND, Sara, *Spiritual Warfare: The Politics of the Christian Right*, South End Press, Boston, 1989, ISBN 0-89608-361-6

—*Not By Politics Alone: The Enduring Influence of the Christian Right*, Guilford Press, New York, 1998, ISBN 1-57230-494-4

The Nine

BROWNING, Norma Lee, *The Psychic World of Peter Hurkos*, Signet, New York, 1971

GARDNER, Erle Stanley, *Host With The Big Hat*, William Morrow, New York, 1969

GELLER, Uri & PLAYFAIR, Guy Lyon, *The Geller Effect*, Grafton Books, London, 1986

GREENBURG, Dan, *Something's There: My Adventures in the Occult*, Doubleday, New York,

1976, ISBN 0-385-03898-4
HAPGOOD, Charles H., *Mystery in Acambaro*, Adventures Unlimited Press, Kempton, 2000
HURTAK, J.J., *An Introduction to the Keys of Enoch*, The Academy for Future Science, Los Gatos, 1988
LEVY, Steven, *The Unicorn's Secret*, Prentice Hall, New York, 1988
OSTRANDER, Sheila & SCHROEDER, Lynn, *Super-Learning*, Delta, New York, 1979
— *Psychic Discoveries Behind the Iron Curtain*, Bantam, New York, 1971
PICKNETT, Lynn & PRINCE, Clive, *The Stargate Conspiracy*, Warner Books, London, 2000
PLAYFAIR, Guy Lyon, *The Indefinite Boundary*, Souvenir Press, London, 1976
—with HILL, Scott, *The Cycles of Heaven*, Pan Books, London, 1978
PUHARICH, Andrija, *URI*, Anchor Press, New York, 1974
RHINE, J.B., *New World of the Mind*, William Morrow, New York, 1953
RHINE, Louisa E., *PSI: What is It?*, Harper & Row, New York, 1975
STEARN, Jess, *Adventures Into the Psychic*, Signet, New York, 1971
—*Yoga, Youth, and Reincarnation*, Bantam, New York, 1971
SWANN, Ingo, *Penetration*, Ingo Swann Books, Rapid City, 1998
TARG, Russell, *Limitless Mind*, New World Library, Novato, 2004
—with HARARY, Keith, *The Mind Race*, New English Library, London, 1986
ULLMAN, Montague & KRIPPNER, Stanley, *Dream Telepathy*, Macmillan, New York, 1973
YOUNG, Arthur, *The Foundations of Science*, Broadside Editions, San Francisco, 1985

Quantum Consciousness

ACZEL, Amir D., *The Mystery of the Aleph: Mathematics, the Kabbalah, and the Search for Infinity*, Pocket Books, NY, 2000, ISBN 0743422996
ALBERT, David Z., *Quantum Mechanics and Experience*, Harvard University Press, Cambridge, 1993, ISBN 0-674-74112-9
DAVIES, P.C.W. & BROWN, J., *Superstrings: A Theory of Everything?*, Cambridge University Press, Cambridge, 1999, ISBN 0-521-43775-X
DOSSEY, Larry, *Space, Time & Medicine*, Shambhala, Boston, 1982, ISBN 0-87773-224-8
HONIG, William M., *The Quantum and Beyond*, Philosophical Library, NY, 1986, ISBN 8022-2517-9
HORGAN, John, *The Undiscovered Mind*, Touchstone, New York, 1999, ISBN 0-684-86578-5
JUNG, C.G., *Synchronicity: An Acausal Connecting Principle*, Princeton University Press, Princeton, 1973, ISBN 0-691-01794-8
MEIER, C.A. (ed.), *Atom And Archetype: the Pauli/Jung Letters 1932-1958*, Princeton University Press, Princeton, 2001, ISBN 0-691-01207-5
PEAT, F. David, *Synchronicity: The Bridge Between Matter and Mind*, Bantam New Age, New York, 1988, ISBN 0-553-34676-8
PENROSE, Roger, *The Emperor's New Mind*, Oxford University Press, New York, 1989, ISBN 0-19-851973-7
SMOLIN, Lee, *Three Roads to Quantum Gravity*, Weidenfeld & Nicolson, London, 2000, ISBN 0-297-64301-0

Jonestown

HOUGAN, Jim, "Jonestown, The Secret Life of Jim Jones: A Parapolitical Fugue", *Lobster 37*, Summer 1999, pp 2-20

KRAUSE, Charles A., *Guyana Massacre*, Pan Books, London, 1979

LAYTON, Deborah, *Seductive Poison*, Aurum Press, London, 2000

MEIERS, Michael, *Was Jonestown a CIA Medical Experiment?*, Edwin Meller Press, Lewiston, 1988

MILLS, Jeannie, *Six Years With God*, A&W Publishers, New York, 1979

YEE, Min S. & LAYTON, Thomas N., *In My Father's House*, Holt Rinehart Winston, New York, 1981

Evil

BLOOM, Howard, *The Lucifer Principle: A Scientific Expedition Into the Forces of History*, Atlantic Monthly Press, New York, 1997, ISBN 0-87113-664-3

CENKNER, William (ed.), *Evil and the Response of World Religion*, Paragon House, St. Paul, 1997, ISBN 1-55778-753-0

GOLDBERG, Carl, *Speaking With The Devil: Exploring Senseless Acts of Evil*, Penguin, New York, 1996, ISBN 0-14-023739-9

LING, Trevor, *Buddhism and the Mythology of Evil: A Study in Theravada Buddhism*, Oneworld, Oxford, 1997, ISBN 1-85168-132-9

O'FLAHERTY, Wendy Doniger, *The Origins of Evil in Hindu Mythology*, Motilal Banarsidass, Delhi, 1988, ISBN 81-208-0386-8

OPPENHEIMER, Paul, *Evil and the Demonic: A New Theory of Monstrous Behavior*, New York University Press, New York, 1996, ISBN 0-8147-6196-8

RUSSELL, Jeffrey Burton, *The Devil: Perceptions of Evil from Antiquity to Primitive Christianity*, Cornell University Press, Ithaca, 1987, ISBN 0-8014-9409-5

STAUB, Ervin, *The Roots of Evil: the Origins of Genocide and Other Group Violence*, Cambridge University Press, Cambridge, 1998, ISBN 0-521-42214-0

Exorcism

ALLEN, Thomas B., *Possessed: The True Story of an Exorcism*, Doubleday, New York, 1993, ISBN 0-385-42034-X

AMORTH, Gabriele, *An Exorcist Tells His Story*, Ignatius Press, San Francisco, 1999, ISBN 0-89870-710-2

CUNEO, Michael W., *American Exorcism: Expelling Demons in the Land of Plenty*, Doubleday, New York, 2001, ISBN 0-385-51076-5

LASALANDRA, Michael & MERENDA, Mark, *Satan's Harvest*, Dell, New York, 1990, ISBN 0-440-20589-1

MARTIN, Malachi, *Hostage To The Devil: The Possession and Exorcism of Five Living Americans*, Reader's Digest Press, New York, 1976, ISBN 0-8349-078-1

OESTERREICH, T.K., *Possession: Demoniacal & Other*, University Books, New York, 1966

The UFO Phenomenon

ACHENBACH, Joel, *Captured By Aliens: The Search for Life and Truth in a Very Large Universe*,

Simon & Schuster, New York, 1999, ISBN 0-684-84856-2
ADAMSKI, George, *Behind The Flying Saucer Mystery*, Warner, New York, 1974
BLUM, Howard, *Out There: The Government's Secret Quest for Extraterrestrials*, Simon & Schuster, New York, 1990, ISBN 0-671-66260-0
CONROY, Ed, *Report On Communion: An Independent Investigation of and Commentary on Whitley Strieber's* Communion, William Morrow, New York, 1989, ISBN 0-688-08864-3
CORSO, Col. Philip J., *The Day After Roswell*, Pocket Books, New York, 1998, ISBN 0-671-01756-X
FLAMMONDE, Paris, *UFO Exist!*, Ballantine, New York, 1977, ISBN 0-345-33951-7
FRIEDMAN, Stanton T., *Top Secret/Majic*, Marlowe & Co., New York, 1997, ISBN 1-56924-741-2
FULLER, John G., *Incident At Exeter*, Berkley, New York, 1967
—*The Interrupted Journey: Two Lost Hours "Aboard a Flying Saucer"*, Dial Press, New York, 1966
GOOD, Timothy, *Alien Update*, Arrow, London, 1993, ISBN 0-09-925761-0
—*Alien Base: The Evidence for Extraterrestrial Colonization of Earth*, Arrow, London, 1999, ISBN 0-09-925502-2
—*Beyond Top Secret: The Worldwide UFO Security Threat*, Pan Books, London, 1996, ISBN 0-330-34928-7
HAINES, Richard F., *CE-5: Close Encounters of the Fifth Kind*, Sourcebooks, Naperville, 1998, ISBN 1-57071-427-4
KEYHOE, Donald E., *Aliens From Space: The Real Story of Unidentified Flying Objects*, Signet, New York, 1974
KORFF, Kal K., *The Roswell UFO Crash: What They Don't Want You To Know*, Dell, New York, 2000, ISBN 0-440-23613-4
JACOBS, David M., *The Threat*, Pocket Books, New York, 1998, ISBN 0-671-02859-6
JUNG, C.G., *Flying Saucers*, Routledge, London, 1959, ISBN 0-415-27837-6
MACCABEE, Bruce, *UFO FBI Connection: The Secret History of the Government's Cover-Up*, Llewellyn, St. Paul, 2000, ISBN 1-56718-493-6
MACK, John E., *Abduction: Human Encounters With Aliens*, Ballantine, New York, 1995, ISBN 0-345-39300-7
MARRS, Jim, *Alien Agenda: Investigating the Extraterrestrial Presence Among Us*, HarperCollins, New York, 1997, ISBN 0-06-018642-9
PEEBLES, Curtis, *Watch The Skies! A Chronicle of the Flying Saucer Myth*, Berkley, New York, 1995, ISBN 0-425-15117-4
POPE, Nick, *Open Skies, Closed Minds*, Pocket Books, New York, 1997, ISBN 0-671-85530-1
RANDLE, Kevin D., *The UFO Casebook*, Warner, New York, 1989, ISBN 0-446-35715-4
— *A History of UFO Crashes*, Avon, New York, 1995, ISBN 0-380-77666-9
RANDLE, Kevin D. & SCHMITT, Donald R., , *The Truth About The UFO Crash at Roswell*, Avon, New York, 1994, ISBN 0-380-77803-3
RANDLES, Jenny & HOUGH, Peter, *The Complete Book of UFOs*, Sterling, New York, 1994, ISBN 0-8069-8132-6
REDFERN, Nicholas, *The FBI Files: The FBI's UFO Top Secrets Exposed*, Pocket Books, London, 1998, ISBN 0-671-00533-2

SHAWCROSS, Tim, *The Roswell File*, Bloomsbury, London, 1997, ISBN 0-7475-3507-8
STEIGER, Brad, *Project Bluebook*, Ballantine, New York, 1990, ISBN 0-345-34525-8
STEIGER, Brad & STEIGER, Sherry Hansen, *The Rainbow Conspiracy*, Pinnacle, New York, 1994, ISBN 0-7860-0065-1
STRIEBER, Whitley, *Communion: A True Story*, Avon, New York, 1988, ISBN 0-380-70388-2
—*Breakthrough: The Next Step*, HarperPaperbacks, New York, 1996, ISBN 0-06-100958-X
—*The Secret School*, Pocket Books, London, 1997, ISBN 0-671-00526-X
—*Confirmation: The Hard Evidence of Aliens Among Us*, St Martin's, New York, 1998, ISBN 0-312-18557-X
VALLEE, Jacques, *Passport to Magnolia: On UFOs, Folklore, and Parallel Worlds*, Contemporary Books, Chicago, 1993, ISBN 0-8092-3796-2
—*Forbidden Science*, North Atlantic Books, Berkeley, 1992, ISBN 1-55643-125-2
WARREN, Larry & ROBBINS, Peter, *Left At East Gate*, Marlowe & Co., New York, 1997, ISBN 1-56924-759-5

Psychology, Mythology and Anthropology

ADORNO, Theodor, *The Stars Down To Earth*, Routledge, London, 1994, ISBN 0-415-27100-2
BATAILLE, Georges, *Death and Sensuality: A Study of Eroticism and the Taboo*, Ballantine, New York, 1969
—*Story of the Eye*, Penguin, London, 2001, ISBN 0-14-118538-4
—*Erotism: Death & Sensuality*, City Lights Books, San Francisco, 1986, ISBN 0-87286-190-2
COOMARASWAMY, Ananda K., *The Door In The Sky*, Princeton Paperbacks, Princeton, 1997, ISBN 0-691-01747-6
COULIANO, Ioan P., *Eros and Magic in the Renaissance*, University of Chicago Press, Chicago, 1987, ISBN 0-226-12316-2
—*The Tree of Gnosis: Gnostic Mythology from Early Christianity to Modern Nihilism*, HarperSanFrancisco, San Francisco, 1990, ISBN 0-06-061615-6
ELIADE, Mircea, *Shamanism: Archaic techniques of ecstasy*, Arkana, London, 1988, ISBN 0-14-019155-0
—*The Myth of the Eternal Return*, Princeton University Press, Princeton, 1991, ISBN 0-691-01777-8
—*Images and Symbols: Studies in Religious Symbolism*, Princeton University Press, Princeton, 1991, ISBN 0-691-02068-X
—*The Sacred and the Profane: The Nature of Religion*, Harcourt, New York, 1987, ISBN 0-15-679201-X
—*Rites and Symbols of Initiation: The Mysteries of Birth and Rebirth*, Harper Torchbooks, New York, 1965
—*The Quest: History and Meaning in Religion*, University of Chicago Press, Chicago, 1975, ISBN 0-226-20397-2
JUNG, C.G., *Memories, Dreams, Reflections*, Vintage, New York, 1963
—*Psychology and Western Religion*, Princeton University Press, Princeton, 1984, ISBN 0-691-01862-6
JUNG, C.G. & KERENYI, C., *Essays On A Science Of Mythology*, Princeton University Press, Princeton, 1989, ISBN 0-691-01756-5
KEARNEY, Richard, *Strangers, Gods and Monsters*, Routledge, London, 2003, ISBN 0-415-

27258-0
LAING, R.D., *The Politics of Experience*, Pantheon, New York, 1967, ISBN 0-394-71475-X
—*The Politics of the Family and other Essays*, Vintage, New York, 1971, ISBN 0-394-71809-7
—*Self and Others*, Penguin, London, 1987, ISBN 0-14-021376-7
—*The Divided Self*, Pantheon, New York, 1969, ISBN 0-394-42226-0
LEVI-STRAUSS, Claude, *The Savage Mind*, University of Chicago Press, Chicago, 1970, ISBN 0-226-47484-4
MAUSS, Marcel, *A General Theory of Magic*, Routledge, London, 1972, ISBN 0-415-25396-9
PAZ, Octavio, *El signo y el garabato*, Biblioteca de Bolsillo, Mexico, 1991, ISBN 84-322-3083-9
—*The Labyrinth of Solitude: Life and Thought in Mexico*, Grove Press, New York, 1978, ISBN 0-394-17242-6
SONTAG, Susan, *Illness As Metaphor*, Vintage, New York, 1979, ISBN 0-394-72844-0
—*Under the Sign of Saturn*, Farrar, Straus, Giroux, New York, 1980, ISBN 0-374-28076-2
STOYANOV, Yuri, *The Other God: Dualist Religions from Antiquity to the Cathar Heresy*, Yale University Press, New Haven, 2000, ISBN 0-300-08253-3

Howard Hughes
DROSNIN, Michael, *Citizen Hughes*, Holt Rinehart and Winston, New York, 1985
FAY, Stephen, CHESTER, Lewis and LINKLATER, Magnus, *Hoax*, Viking Press, New York, 1972
IRVING, Clifford, *The Hoax*, Mandarin, London, 1981
MAHEU, Robert and HACK, Richard, *Next to Hughes*, HarperCollins, New York, 1992
PHELAN, James R. and CHESTER, Lewis, *The Money*, Orion Business Books, London, 1997

Surrealism
BRETON, Andre, *Communicating Vessels*, University of Nebraska Press, Lincoln, 1990, ISBN 0-8032-6135-7
CHOUCHA, Nadia, *Surrealism & The Occult: Shamanism, Magic, Alchemy, and the Birth of an Artistic Movement*, Destiny Books, Rochester, 1992, ISBN 0-89281-373-3
LOMAS, David, *The Haunted Self: Surrealism, Psychoanalysis, Subjectivity*, Yale University Press, New Haven, 2000, ISBN 0-300-08800-0
SECREST, Meryle, *Salvador Dali: A Biography*, Dutton, New York, 1987, ISBN 0-525-48334-9
TOMKINS, Calvin, *The Bride and the Bachelors: Five Masters of the Avant-Garde*, Viking, New York, 1974, ISBN 670-00248-8
WEYERS, Frank, *Salvador Dali: Life and Work*, Koenemann, Cologne, 2000, ISBN 3-8290-2934-9

Index

A

B

D

E

H

I

M

N

X

Y

Z

TrineDay's Featured Titles

The True Story of the Bilderberg Group

BY DANIEL ESTULIN

More than a center of influence, the Bilderberg Group is a shadow world government, hatching plans of domination at annual meetings ... and under a cone of media silence.

THE TRUE STORY OF THE BILDERBERG GROUP goes inside the secret meetings and sheds light on why a group of politicians, businessmen, bankers and other mighty individuals formed the world's most powerful society. As Benjamin Disraeli, one of England's greatest Prime Ministers, noted, "The world is governed by very different personages from what is imagined by those who are not behind the scenes."

Included are unpublished and never-before-seen photographs and other documentation of meetings, as this riveting account exposes the past, present and future plans of the Bilderberg elite.

Softcover: **$24.95** (ISBN: 9780979988622) • 432 pages • Size: 6 x 9

Dr. Mary's Monkey

How the Unsolved Murder of a Doctor, a Secret Laboratory in New Orleans and Cancer-Causing Monkey Viruses are Linked to Lee Harvey Oswald, the JFK Assassination and Emerging Global Epidemics

BY EDWARD T. HASLAM, FOREWORD BY JIM MARRS

Evidence of top-secret medical experiments and cover-ups of clinical blunders

The 1964 murder of a nationally known cancer researcher sets the stage for this gripping exposé of medical professionals enmeshed in covert government operations over the course of three decades. Following a trail of police records, FBI files, cancer statistics, and medical journals, this revealing book presents evidence of a web of medical secret-keeping that began with the handling of evidence in the JFK assassination and continued apace, sweeping doctors into cover-ups of cancer outbreaks, contaminated polio vaccine, the genesis of the AIDS virus, and biological weapon research using infected monkeys.

Softcover: **$19.95** (ISBN: 0977795306) • 320 pages • Size: 5 1/2 x 8 1/2

ShadowMasters

BY DANIEL ESTULIN

AN INTERNATIONAL NETWORK OF GOVERNMENTS AND SECRET-SERVICE AGENCIES WORKING TOGETHER WITH DRUG DEALERS AND TERRORISTS FOR MUTUAL BENEFIT AND PROFIT

THIS INVESTIGATION EXAMINES HOW behind-the-scenes collaboration between governments, intelligence services and drug traffickers has lined the pockets of big business and Western banks. Beginning with a last-minute request from ex-governor Jesse Ventura, the narrative winds between the author's own story of covering "deep politics" and the facts he has uncovered. The ongoing campaign against Victor Bout, the "Merchant of Death," is revealed as "move/countermove" in a game of geopolitics, set against the background of a crumbling Soviet Union, a nascent Russia, bizarre assassinations, wars and smuggling. DANIEL ESTULIN is an award-winning investigative journalist and author of *The True Story of the Bilderberg Group*.

Softcover: **$24.95** (ISBN: 9780979988615) • 432 pages • Size: 6 x 9

The Franklin Scandal

A Story of Powerbrokers, Child Abuse & Betrayal

BY NICK BRYANT

A chilling exposé of corporate corruption and government cover-ups, this account of a nationwide child-trafficking and pedophilia ring tells a sordid tale of corruption in high places. The scandal originally surfaced during an investigation into Omaha, Nebraska's failed Franklin Federal Credit Union and took the author beyond the Midwest and ultimately to Washington, DC. Implicating businessmen, senators, major media corporations, the CIA, and even the venerable Boys Town organization, this extensively researched report includes firsthand interviews with key witnesses and explores a controversy that has received scant media attention.

The Franklin Scandal is the story of a underground ring that pandered children to a cabal of the rich and powerful. The ring's pimps were a pair of Republican powerbrokers who used Boys Town as a pedophiliac reservoir, and had access to the highest levels of our government and connections to the CIA.

Nick Bryant is a journalist whose work largely focuses on the plight of disadvantaged children in the United States. His mainstream and investigative journalism has been featured in *Gear, Playboy, The Reader*, and on Salon.com. He is the coauthor of *America's Children: Triumph of Tragedy*. He lives in New York City.

Hardcover: **$24.95** (ISBN: 0977795357) • 676 pages • Size: 6x9

Strength of the Pack

The Personalities, Politics and Intrigues that Shaped the DEA

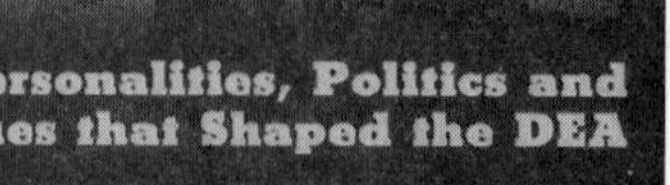

DOUGLAS VALENTINE

author of The Phoenix Program and The Strength of the Wolf

Strength of the Pack

The Personalities, Politics and Intrigues that Shaped the DEA

BY DOUG VALENTINE

Through interviews with former narcotics agents, politicians, and bureaucrats, this exposé documents previously unknown aspects of the history of federal drug law enforcement from the formation of the Bureau of Narcotics and Dangerous Drugs and the creation of the Drug Enforcement Administration (DEA) up until the present day. Written in an easily accessible style, the narrative examines how successive administrations expanded federal drug law enforcement operations at home and abroad; investigates how the CIA comprised the war on drugs; analyzes the Reagan, Bush, and Clinton administrations' failed attempts to alter the DEA's course; and traces the agency's evolution into its final and current stage of "narco-terrorism."

Douglas Valentine is a former private investigator and consultant and the author of *The Hotel Tacloban, The Phoenix Program, The Strength of the Wolf*, and *TDY*.

480 pages • Size: 6 x 9
Hardcover: **$24.95** (ISBN: 9780979988653)
Softcover **$19.95** (ISBN 9781936296095)

A Terrible Mistake

The Murder of Frank Olson and the CIA's Secret Cold War Experiments

by H.P. Albarelli Jr.

In his nearly 10 years of research into the death of Dr. Frank Olson, writer and investigative journalist H.P. Albarelli Jr. gained unique and unprecedented access to many former CIA, FBI, and Federal Narcotics Bureau officials, including several who actually oversaw the CIA's mind-control programs from the 1950s to the early 1970s.

A Terrible Mistake takes readers into a frequently bizarre and always frightening world, colored and dominated by Cold War concerns and fears. For the past 30 years the death of biochemist Frank Olson has ranked high on the nation's list of unsolved and perplexing mysteries. *A Terrible Mistake* solves the mystery and reveals in shocking detail the identities of Olson's murderers. The book also takes readers into the strange world of government mind-control programs and close collaboration with the Mafia.

H. P. Albarelli Jr. is an investigative journalist whose work has appeared in numerous publications and newspapers across the nation and is the author of the novel *The Heap*. He lives in Tampa, Florida.

Hardcover • **$34.95** ISBN 978-0977795376 • 912 pages
Softcover **$29.95** (ISBN 978-1936296088)

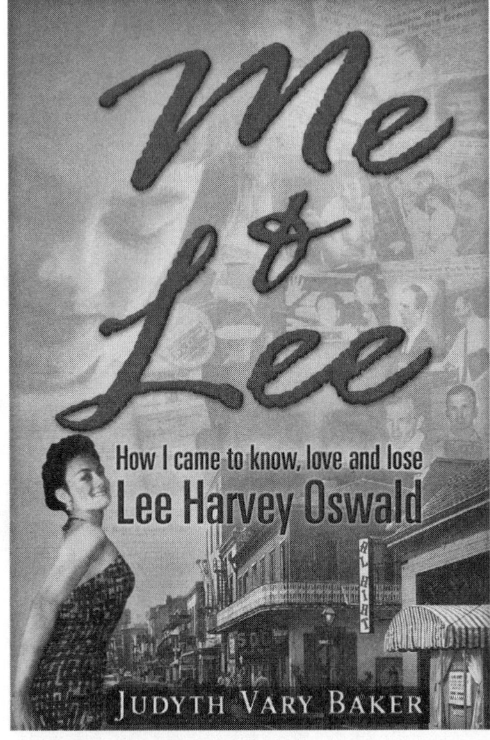

Me & Lee

How I Came to Know, Love and Lose Lee Harvey Oswald

by Judyth Vary Baker

Foreword by

Edward T. Haslam

Judyth Vary was once a promising science student who dreamed of finding a cure for cancer; this exposé is her account of how she strayed from a path of mainstream scholarship at the University of Florida to a life of espionage in New Orleans with Lee Harvey Oswald. In her narrative she offers extensive documentation on how she came to be a cancer expert at such a young age, the personalities who urged her to relocate to New Orleans, and what lead to her involvement in the development of a biological weapon that Oswald was to smuggle into Cuba to eliminate Fidel Castro. Details on what she knew of Kennedy's impending assassination, her conversations with Oswald as late as two days before the killing, and her belief that Oswald was a deep-cover intelligence agent who was framed for an assassination he was actually trying to prevent, are also revealed.

Judyth Vary Baker is a teacher, and artist. Edward T. Haslam is the author of *Dr. Mary's Monkey*. He lives in Florida.

Hardcover • **$24.95** • ISBN 9780979988677 • 480 Pages

Expendable Elite

One Soldier's Journey into Covert Warfare

BY DANIEL MARVIN , FOREWORD BY MARTHA RAYE

A special operations perspective on the Viet Nam War and the truth about a White House concerned with popular opinion

This true story of a special forces officer in Viet Nam in the mid-1960s exposes the unique nature of the elite fighting force and how covert operations are developed and often masked to permit—and even sponsor—assassination, outright purposeful killing of innocents, illegal use of force, and bizarre methods in combat operations. ***Expendable Elite*** reveals the fear that these warriors share with no other military person: not fear of the enemy they have been trained to fight in battle, but fear of the wrath of the US government should they find themselves classified as "expendable." This book centers on the CIA mission to assassinate Cambodian Crown Prince Nordum Sihanouk, the author's unilateral aborting of the mission, the CIA's dispatch of an ARVN regiment to attack and destroy the camp and kill every person in it as retribution for defying the agency, and the dramatic rescue of eight American Green Berets and hundreds of South Viet Namese.

—NEW SPECIAL VICTORY EDITION— Commemorating our Free Speech Federal Court triumph that allows you to read this book exposing the true ways of war!

—READ THE BOOK,"THEY" DON'T WANT YOU TO!—

DANIEL MARVIN is a retired Lieutenant Colonel in the US Army Special Forces and former Green Beret.

Softcover: **$19.95** (ISBN 0977795314) • 420 pages • 150+ photos & maps

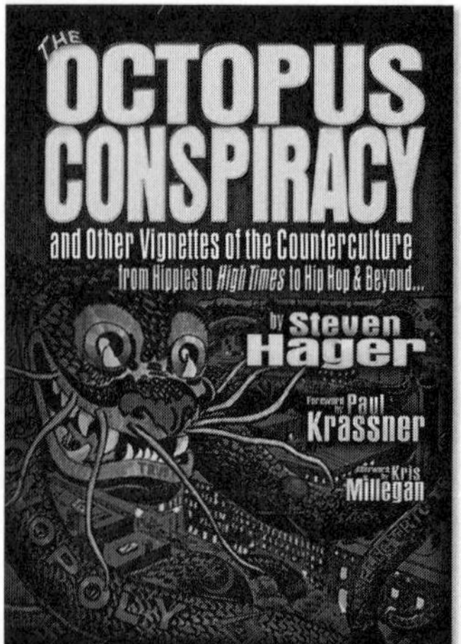

The Octopus Conspiracy

and Other Vignettes of the Counterculture from Hippies to High Times to Hip Hop and Beyond ...

BY STEVEN HAGER

Insightful essays on the genesis of subcultures from new wave and yuppies to graffiti and rap.

From the birth of hip-hop culture in the South Bronx to the influence of nightclubs in shaping the modern art world in New York, a generation of countercultural events and icons are brought to life in this personal account of the life and experiences of a former investigative reporter and editor of High Times. Evidence from cutting-edge conspiracy research including the real story behind the JFK assassination and the Franklin Savings and Loan cover-up is presented. Quirky personalities and compelling snapshots of life in the 1980s and 1990s emerge in this collection of vignettes from a landmark figure in journalism.

STEVEN HAGER is the author of ***Adventures in Counterculture, Art After Midnight,*** and ***Hip Hop.*** He is a former reporter for the New York Daily News and an editor of ***High Times.***

Hardcover: **$19.95** (ISBN 0975290614) • 320 pages • Size: 6 x 9

Fixing America

Breaking the Strangehold of Corporate Rule, Big Media, and the Religious Right

BY JOHN BUCHANAN, FOREWORD BY JOHN MCCONNELL

An explosive analysis of what ails the United States

An award-winning investigative reporter provides a clear, honest diagnosis of corporate rule, big media, and the religious right in this damning analysis. Exposing the darker side of capitalism, this critique raises alarms about the security of democracy in today's society, including the rise of the corporate state, the insidious role of professional lobbyists, the emergence of religion and theocracy as a right-wing political tactic, the failure of the mass media, and the sinister presence of an Orwellian neo-fascism.

Softcover: **$19.95**, (ISBN 0-975290681) 216 Pages, 5.5 x 8.5

The 9/11 Mystery Plane

And the Vanishing of America

By Mark Gaffney

Foreword by

Dr. David Ray Griffin

Unlike other accounts of the historic attacks on 9/11, this discussion surveys the role of the world's most advanced military command and control plane, the E-4B, in the day's events and proposes that the horrific incidents were the work of a covert operation staged within elements of the US military and the intelligence community. Presenting hard evidence, the account places the world's most advanced electronics platform circling over the White House at approximately the time of the Pentagon attack. The argument offers an analysis of the new evidence within the context of the events and shows that it is irreconcilable with the official 9/11 narrative.

Mark H. Gaffney is an environmentalist, a peace activist, a researcher, and the author of *Dimona, the Third Temple?;* and *Gnostic Secrets of the Naassenes*. He lives in Chiloquin, Oregon. Dr. David Ray Griffin is a professor emeritus at the Claremont School of Theology, and the author of *The 9/11 Commission Report: Omissions and Distortions*, and *The New Pearl Harbor*. He lives in Santa Barbara, California.

Softcover • **$19.95** • ISBN 9780979988608 • 336 Pages

Cannabis and the SOMA Solution

by Chris Bennett

from Kenef Press

"Scholarly, hip, witty, and extremely well documented . . . this book might cause a revolution in biblical studies!" —Robert Anton Wilson, author, Schrodinger's Cat Trilogy

Seeking to identify the plant origins of the early sacramental beverages Soma and Haoma, this study draws a connection between the psychoactive properties of these drinks and the widespread use of cannabis among Indo-Europeans during this time. Exploring the role of these libations as inspiration for the Indian Rig Veda and the Persian Avestan texts, this examination discusses the spread of cannabis use across Europe and Asia, the origins of the Soma and Haoma cults, and the shamanic origins of modern religion.

Chris Bennett is an expert in the use of ethnobotanicals. He has contributed articles to numerous magazines, including *Cannabis Culture* and *High Times*, and he is the author of several books, including *Green Gold the Tree of Life: Marijuana in Magic and Religion and Sex, Drugs, Violence and the Bible.*

Softcover • **$24.95** • 9780984185801 • 661 Pages

Fighting For G.O.D.

(Gold, Oil, Drugs)

by Jeremy Begin, Art by Laureen Salk

This racehorse tour of American history and current affairs scrutinizes key events transcending the commonly accepted liberal/conservative political ideologies — in a large-size comic-book format.

This analysis delves into aspects of the larger framework into which 9/11 fits and scrutinizes the ancestry of the players who transcend commonly accepted liberal/conservative political ideologies. This comic-book format analysis examines the Neo Con agenda and its relationship to "The New World Order. This book discusses key issues confronting America's citizenry and steps the populace can take to not only halt but reverse the march towards totalitarianism.

Jeremy Begin is a long-time activist/organizer currently residing in California's Bay Area. Lauren Salk is an illustrator living in Boston.

Softcover: **$9.95**, (ISBN 0977795330) 64 Pages, 8.5 x 11

Anatomyzing Divinity

Studies in Science, Esotericism and Political Theology

by James L. Kelley

Foreword by Joseph P. Farrell

This three-part analysis of modernity assesses the impact that Western thought and philosophy has had on the modern world. Pulling from the fringe of academia, the study focuses on the ancient wisdom of China, India, Egypt and the Hellenistic world. Furthermore, this treatise explores the mind of G. W. Leibniz, the man who invented calculus and laid the groundwork for binary code, which spawned nearly all digital computing. Leibniz also found his roots in the Frankish metaphysical tradition, thus thrusting forth the ideas of ancient alchemy into the modern world. Combining the study of alchemy and history, this examination forges a new window into the history of law in the West.

James L. Kelley is the author of *A Realism of Glory*. He lives in Norman, Oklahoma.

Softcover • **$14.95** • ISBN 9781936296279 • 240 Pages

Mary's Mosaic

Mary Pinchot Meyer & John F. Kennedy and their Vision for World Peace

by Peter Janney

Foreword by Dick Russell

Challenging the conventional wisdom surrounding the murder of Mary Pinchot Meyer, this exposé offers new information and evidence that individuals within the upper echelons of the CIA were not only involved in the assassination of President John F. Kennedy, but her demise as well. Written by the son of a CIA lifer and a college classmate of Mary Pinchot Meyer, this insider's story examines how Mary used events and circumstances in her personal life to become an acolyte for world peace. The most famous convert to her philosophy was reportedly President John F. Kennedy, with whom she was said to have begun a serious love relationship in January 1962. Offering an insightful look into the era and its culture, the narrative sheds light on how in the wake of the Cuban Missile Crisis, she helped the president realize that a Cold War mentality was of no use and that the province of world peace was the only worthwhile calling. Details on her experiences with LSD, its influences on her and Kennedy's thinking, his attempts to negotiate a limited nuclear test ban treaty with Soviet Premier Nikita Khrushchev, and to find lasting peace with Fidel Castro are also included.

Peter Janney is a former psychologist and naturopathic healer and a cofounder of the American Mental Health Alliance. He was one of the first graduates of the MIT Sloan School of Management's Entrepreneurship Skills Transfer Program. He lives in Beverly, Massachusetts. Dick Russell is the author of *Black Genius: And the American Experience*, *Eye of the Whale*, *The Man Who Knew Too Much*, and *Striper Wars: An American Fish Story*. He is a former staff writer for *TV Guide* magazine, a staff reporter for *Sports Illustrated*, and has contributed numerous articles to publications ranging from *Family Health* to the *Village Voice*. He lives in Boston, Massachusetts and Los Angeles.

Hardcover • **$24,95** • ISBN 978-0-9799886-3-9 • 480 Pages

America's Nazi Secret

An Uncensored History of the US Justice Department's Obstruction of Congressional Investigations into Americans Who Funded Hitler, Postwar Immigration of Eastern European War Criminals to the US, and the Evolution of the Arab Nazi Movement into Modern Middle Eastern Terrorists

by John Loftus

Fully revised and expanded, this stirring account reveals how the U.S. government permitted the illegal entry of Nazis into North America in the years following World War II. This extraordinary investigation exposes the secret section of the State Department that began, starting in 1948 and unbeknownst to Congress and the public until recently, to hire members of the puppet wartime government of Byelorussia—a region of the Soviet Union occupied by Nazi Germany. A former Justice Department investigator uncovered this stunning story in the files of several government agencies, and it is now available with a chapter previously banned from release by authorities and a foreword and afterword with recently declassified materials.

John Loftus is a former U.S. government prosecutor, a former Army intelligence officer, and the author of numerous books, including *The Belarus Secret, The Secret War Against the Jews, Unholy Trinity: How the Vatican's Nazi Networks Betrayed Western Intelligence to the Soviets*, and *Unholy Trinity: The Vatican, the Nazis, and the Swiss Banks*. He has appeared regularly as a media commentator on ABC National Radio and Fox News. He lives in St. Petersburg, Florida.

Softcover • **$24.95** • ISBN 978-1-936296-04-0 • 288 Pages

1-800-556-2012

Radical Peace

by William Hathaway

Refusing War

This symphony of voices—a loosely united network of war resisters, deserters, and peace activists in Afghanistan, Europe, Iraq, and North America—vividly recounts the actions they have personally taken to end war and create a peaceful society. Frustrated, angered, and even saddened by the juggernaut of aggression that creates more counter-violence at every turn, this assortment of contributors has moved beyond demonstrations and petitions into direct, often radical actions in defiance of the government's laws to impede its capacity to wage war. Among the stories cited are those of a European peace group that assisted a soldier in escaping from military detention and then deserting; a U.S.-educated Iraqi who now works in Iran developing cheaper and smaller heat-seeking missiles to shoot down U.S. aircraft after U.S. soldiers brutalized his family; a granny for peace who found young allies in her struggle against military recruiting; a seminary student who, having been roughed up by U.S. military at a peace demonstration, became a military chaplain and subverts from within; and a man who expresses his resistance through the destruction of government property—most often by burning military vehicles.

William T. Hathaway is a political journalist and a former Special Forces soldier turned peace activist whose articles have appeared in more than 40 publications, including *Humanist*, the *Los Angeles Times, Midstream Magazine*, and *Synthesis/Regeneration*. He is an adjunct professor of American studies at the University of Oldenburg in Germany, and the author of *A World of Hurt, CD-Ring*, and *Summer Snow*.

Softcover: **$14.95** (ISBN: 9780979988691) •240 pages • Size: 5.5 x 8.5

Perfectibilists

The 18th Century Bavarian Illuminati

BY TERRY MELANSON

The shadowy Illuminati grace many pages of fiction as the sinister all-powerful group pulling the strings behind the scenes, but very little has been printed in English about the actual Enlightenment-era secret society, its activities, its members, and its legacy ... until now.

First choosing the name Perfectibilists, their enigmatic leader Adam Weishaupt soon thought that sounded too bizarre and changed it to the Order of the Illuminati.

Presenting an authoritative perspective, this definitive study chronicles the rise and fall of the fabled Illuminati, revealing their methods of infiltrating governments and education systems, and their blueprint for a successful cabal, which echoes directly forward through groups like the Order of Skull & Bones to our own era.

Featuring biographies of more than 400 confirmed members and copiously illustrated, this book brings light to a 200-year-old mystery.

Softcover: **$19.95** (ISBN: 9780977795381) • 530 pages

Jaded Tasks

Brass Plates. Black Ops, & Big Oil - The Blood Politics of George Bush & Co.

BY WAYNE MADSEN

This investigative account details how America's economic and intelligence associations with Saudi Arabia and Pakistan led to the devastating September 11 attacks and illustrates the role that private military companies are playing in George W. Bush's "new world order." Based on personal interviews, never-before-published classified documents, and extensive research, this examination details the criminal forces thought to rule the world today—the Bush cartel, Russian-Ukranian-Israeli mafia, and Wahhabist Saudi terror financiers—revealing links between these groups and disastrous events such as 9/11.

Wayne scares the hell out of the Military-Industrial-Mendacity Complex — Greg Palast

Softcover: **$19.95**, 320 Pages, 5.5 x 8.5

Fleshing Out Skull & Bones

Investigations into America's Most Powerful Secret Society

EDITED BY KRIS MILLEGAN

An expose of Yale's supersecretive and elite Order of Skull & Bones

This chronicle of espionage, drug smuggling, and elitism in Yale University's Skull & Bones society offers rare glimpses into this secret world with previously unpublished documents, photographs, and articles that delve into issues such as racism, financial ties to the Nazi party, and illegal corporate dealings. Contributors include Antony Sutton, author of ***America's Secret Establishment***; Dr. Ralph Bunch, professor emeritus of political science at Portland State University; Webster Griffin Tarpley and Anton Chaitkin, authors and historians; and Howard Altman, editor of the ***Philadelphia City Paper***. A complete list of known members, including George Bush and George W. Bush, and reprints of rare magazine articles on the Order of Skull and Bones are included.

Softcover: **$24.95** (ISBN 0975290606) 720 pages • Size: 6x9

America's Secret Establishment

An Introduction to the Order of Skull & Bones

BY ANTONY C. SUTTON

The book that first exposed the story behind America's most powerful secret society

For 170 years they have met in secret. From out of their initiates come presidents, senators, judges, cabinet secretaries, and plenty of spooks. This intriguing behind-the-scenes look documents Yale's secretive society, the Order of the Skull and Bones, and its prominent members, numbering among them Tafts, Rockefellers, Pillsburys, and Bushes. Far from being a campus fraternity, the society is more concerned with the success of its members in the post-collegiate world.

Softcover: **$19.95** (ISBN 0972020748) 335 pages

The Oil Card

Global Economic Warfare in the 21st Century

BY JAMES NORMAN

Challenging the conventional wisdom surrounding high oil prices, this compelling argument sheds an entirely new light on free-market industry fundamentals.

By deciphering past, present, and future geopolitical events, it makes the case that oil pricing and availability have a long history of being employed as economic weapons by the United States. Despite ample world supplies and reserves, high prices are now being used to try to rein in China—a reverse of the low-price strategy used in the 1980s to deprive the Soviets of hard currency. Far from conspiracy theory, the debate notes how the US has previously used the oil majors, the Saudis, and market intervention to move markets—and shows how this is happening again.

Softcover **$14.95** (ISBN 0977795390) • 288 PAGES • Size: 5.5 x 8.5

The Hunt for Kuhn Sa

DRUG LORD OF THE GOLDEN TRIANGLE

BY RON FELDER

FOR TWO DECADES, the Burmese warlord Khun Sa controlled nearly 70 percent of the world's heroin supply, yet there has been little written about the legend the U.S. State Department branded the "most evil man in the world"—until now. Through exhaustive investigative journalism, this examination of one of the world's major drug lords from the 1970s to the 1990s goes behind the scenes into the lives of the DEA specialists assigned the seemingly impossible task of capturing or killing him. Known as Group 41, these men would fight for years in order to stop a man who, in fact, had the CIA to thank for his rise to power. Featuring interviews with DEA, CIA, Mafia, and Asian gang members, this meticulously researched and well-documented investigation reaches far beyond the expected and delves into the thrilling and shocking world of the CIA-backed heroin trade.

Ron Felber is the CEO of Chemetell, North America, and the author of eight books, including *Il Dottore: The Double Life of a Mafia Doctor*, *Presidential Lessons in Leadership*, and *Searchers: A True Story of Alien Abduction*. He lives in New Jersey.

Softover • **$19.95** • ISBN 9781936296156 • 240 Pages